HISTORY OF THE UNITED STATES

FROM THE COMPROMISE OF 1850

TO

THE FINAL RESTORATION OF HOME RULE
AT THE SOUTH IN 1877

VOL. II

HISTORY

OF THE

UNITED STATES

FROM

THE COMPROMISE OF 1850

TO

THE FINAL RESTORATION OF HOME RULE
AT THE SOUTH IN 1877

BY

JAMES FORD RHODES, LL.D., LITT.D.

MEMBER OF THE MASSACHUSETTS HISTORICAL SOCIETY

VOL. II
1854–1860

New York
THE MACMILLAN COMPANY
LONDON: MACMILLAN & CO., LTD.
1910

All rights reserved

COPYRIGHT, 1892,
BY JAMES FORD RHODES.

First published elsewhere. Reprinted December, 1900, March, 1902; September, 1904; October, 1906; November, 1907; January, 1910.

Norwood Press:
Berwick & Smith, Norwood, Mass., U.S.A.

CONTENTS

OF

THE SECOND VOLUME

CHAPTER VI

	PAGE
Diplomatic costume	1
The Gadsden treaty	7
The Reciprocity treaty with Canada	8
Bombardment of San Juan	9
The desire to obtain Cuba	10
Soulé's position at Madrid	11
Soulé's difficulty	12
Duel with Turgot	13
The *Black Warrior* affair	16
Soulé's ultimatum	19
Calderon's reply	20
War between the United States and Spain considered probable	22
Public sentiment in the United States	23
Filibusters at work	27
War with Spain imminent	28
War with Spain avoided	31
Marcy still hoping to acquire Cuba	34
Marcy and Soulé	35
The Ostend manifesto	38
Soulé resigns the Spanish mission	42
The Ostend manifesto	42

CHAPTER VII

Shall a new party be formed?	45
Action towards forming a new party	47
The Republican State convention of Michigan	48
The temperance question	49
The Know-nothing movement	50
The year one of excitement and lawlessness	56
The verdict of the Northern people on the Kansas-Nebraska act, as evidenced in the elections	58
Iowa	59
Maine; Vermont	59
Pennsylvania; Ohio; Indiana	60
Illinois	61
Douglas in the canvass	61
New York	63
Massachusetts	65
Michigan; Wisconsin	66
The elections considered	66
Seward	68
Lincoln	69
The press	71
Personal liberty laws	73
The underground railroad	74
Kansas	78
The Kansas election of March 30th, 1855	81
Indignation in the free States	83
Southern sympathy with the Missourians	84
Governor Reeder	85
The Know-nothings	87
The Republican movement gaining strength	92
The fall elections of 1855	93
Henry Wilson	96
Republican opinions	97
Kansas	98
The Wakarusa war	105

CONTENTS

The Thirty-fourth Congress	107
The contest for speaker	108
Banks elected speaker	115
The Republican National convention at Pittsburgh, February 22d, 1856	118
Relations with England	120
The President's message on Kansas	122
Reports of Douglas and Collamer	125
Description of Douglas by Mrs. Stowe	127
Speech of Douglas	129
The Republican senators on Kansas	130
Sumner's speech, "The Crime against Kansas"	131
Sumner and Butler	134
Sumner and Douglas	137
Brooks assaults Sumner	139
Character of Sumner	141
Northern sentiment	143
Southern sentiment	144
Wilson and Burlingame	145
Explanation of Brooks	146
The affair before Congress	148
Kansas	150
The destruction of Lawrence	158
John Brown	161
The massacre on the Pottawatomie	162
Civil War in Kansas	166

CHAPTER VIII

President-making	169
The Democratic National convention	171
Nomination of Buchanan	172
Seward and Chase	175
Frémont	177
McLean	179
Frémont	181
The Republican National convention	182
Nomination of Frémont	184

CONTENTS

Crampton, the English minister, dismissed 186
Kansas question in Congress 189
The Toombs bill 189
"Bleeding Kansas" 196
The Howard report 196
Oliver's report 197
Strife between the Senate and the House 201
The Presidential campaign 202
"The Union in danger" 203
Threats of Southerners 204
Letter of Rufus Choate 206
"Southern gasconade" 209
The Republicans 210
Speech of George W. Curtis 212
Fillmore's nomination endorsed by the Whigs 215
Kansas 215
Influence of Kansas in the presidential canvass 218
An educational campaign 220
The presidential campaign 221
The early State elections 226
Pennsylvania 226
Kansas 229
Pennsylvania 230
The Democrats carry Pennsylvania 233
Election of Buchanan 235

CHAPTER IX

Peace in Kansas 237
Governor Geary 239
The meaning of Buchanan's election 241
Character of Buchanan 244
Buchanan's inaugural 245
The cabinet 246
Rotation in office 248
The United States Supreme Court 249
Chief-Justice Taney 250
Justice Curtis 251

The Dred Scott case.................................... 251
The Dred Scott decision............................... 255
The dissenting opinion of Curtis..................... 257
Taney... 260
Curtis.. 262
Public opinion.. 263
Douglas on the Dred Scott decision................... 264
Lincoln on the Dred Scott decision................... 266
Seward makes the charge of conspiracy................ 268
Lincoln on the alleged conspiracy.................... 270
Robert J. Walker...................................... 271
Buchanan endorses the Calhoun doctrine............... 276
The Lecompton convention............................. 278
The panic of 1857..................................... 281
Revolt of Northern Democrats against the Lecompton scheme. 282
Douglas opposes it.................................... 282
The Kansas elections.................................. 289
Walker's filibustering expedition..................... 289
Buchanan recommends the admission of Kansas under the Lecompton constitution............................. 291
The debate in the Senate.............................. 293
Denunciation of Douglas............................... 296
Action of Congress.................................... 297
The English bill...................................... 299

CHAPTER X

Republican prospects.................................. 302
Seward on the Army bill............................... 303
Seward on popular sovereignty......................... 305
Prominence of Douglas................................. 307
Protest of Chase...................................... 307
Protest of Lincoln.................................... 308
Character of Lincoln.................................. 308
Lincoln and Douglas................................... 313
Lincoln nominated for Senator; opens the campaign.... 314
"A house divided against itself cannot stand"........ 315
Douglas's first speech of the campaign............... 318

CONTENTS

The senatorial campaign of 1858	320
The Lincoln-Douglas debates	321
The work and excitement of the campaign	337
Success of Douglas	339
Lincoln	339
Douglas	340
The October elections	343
Seward and "The Irrepressible Conflict"	344
The November elections	346
Douglas; Seward; Lincoln; Jefferson Davis	347
The President's message	349
The Cuba bill	351
Douglas	355
Jefferson Davis	357
The Fugitive Slave law	360
The Oberlin-Wellington rescue	361
The African slave-trade	367
Speech of Davis	372
Letter of Douglas	373
The *Harper's Magazine* article	373
Broderick	375
The Ohio fall election	380
John Brown's raid into Virginia	384
The attack made	393
Brown taken prisoner	396
Brown catechised	397
The Republican leaders	402
Trial of Brown	403
Letters of Brown	406
Execution of Brown	408
Public sentiment	410
Opinions of statesmen	411
Opinions of philosophers and poets	413
An estimate of John Brown and his work	414

CHAPTER XI

Assembling of the Thirty-sixth Congress.................. 417
The contest for speaker; Helper's "Impending Crisis"...... 418
Election of Pennington........................... 426
The Union in danger............................. 428
Douglas....................................... 429
Jefferson Davis................................. 430
Lincoln's Cooper Institute speech.................. 430
Seward's speech in the Senate.................... 433
The abolitionists............................... 434
Seward and Lincoln............................. 436
Lovejoy....................................... 437
Potter and Pryor............................... 439
Democratic National convention at Charleston........ 440
The Douglas platform adopted..................... 450
Secession of the delegates from the cotton States... 451
The convention of the Constitutional Union party.... 454
Debate between Davis and Douglas................. 455
The Republican National convention................ 456
The platform................................... 464
Convention work................................ 465
The balloting.................................. 469
Nomination of Lincoln........................... 470
The Baltimore convention........................ 473
Nomination of Douglas........................... 475
Nomination of Breckinridge...................... 475
The work of Congress............................ 475
The Presidential campaign....................... 477
Pennsylvania................................... 479
The African slave-trade........................ 481
Campaign work................................. 483
Douglas; threats of disunion.................... 487
Seward.. 493
New York...................................... 497
Election of Lincoln............................ 500

HISTORY OF
THE UNITED STATES

CHAPTER VI

MARCY might have pleaded the engrossing affairs of his department as a reason for not giving his attention to the domestic question which was agitating the country. In truth, he was actively employed during the year 1854; and few American Secretaries of State, in a time of peace, have had more real business to transact than fell to his lot.

Soon after assuming charge of the department, he showed that he wished to impress his plain democratic ideas upon those who represented this country abroad. Almost the first question which he took up was that of diplomatic costume. From the time of our mission to Ghent until President Jackson's day, the dress informally or officially recommended was: "A blue coat, lined with white silk; straight standing cape embroidered with gold; buttons plain, or, if they can be had, with the artillerist's eagle stamped upon them; cuffs embroidered in the manner of the cape. White cassimere breeches, gold knee-buckles; white silk stockings, and gold or gilt shoe-buckles. A three-cornered chapeau-bras; a black cockade to which an eagle has been attached. Sword, etc., corresponding." On gala-days, the uniforms should be more splendid with embroidery, and the hat decorated with a white ostrich feather.

Under the strictly democratic administration of Jackson, the President recommended some changes in the diplomatic dress in the line of cheapness and adaptation to the simplicity of our institutions. It was suggested that the blue coat be changed to black, the cape omitted, and a gold star affixed on each side of the collar of the coat; the breeches might be black or white. The chapeau-bras with the cockade and eagle and the sword were retained.

Thus the matter remained until Marcy took it up. He issued a circular on June 1st, 1853, in which he recommended to our representatives abroad that, in order to show their devotion to republican institutions, they should, whenever practicable, appear in the simple dress of an American citizen. He stated that the example of Dr. Franklin was worthy of imitation, and regretted that there ever had been a departure from that simple and unostentatious course.

Our minister at Berne was glad to inform the Secretary that the "absurd and expensive uniform" necessary to be worn at a royal court was never required in the ancient republic of Switzerland.[1] The ministers at Turin and Brussels reported that there probably would be no difficulty in carrying out the instructions of the department.[2] Our representative at Berlin received an intimation from the president minister that the king would consider an appearance before him without costume as disrespectful. He therefore did not deem it discreet to insist upon this point, but in yielding to the wishes of the monarch he was careful to procure "a very plain and simple dress."[3] The King of Sweden was perfectly willing to transact business with the American minister in citizen's clothes, but on social occasions the court

---

[1] Fay to Marcy, June 30th, 1853.
[2] Seibels to Marcy, Sept. 30th, 1853; Daniel to Marcy, Oct. 10th, 1853.
[3] Vroom to Marcy, Oct. 31st, 1853.

dress was imperatively required. The minister explained to Marcy that the king was a rigid conservative in all the antique ceremonies and exactions of his court, that the Swedish society held fast to aristocratic symbols, and his appearance at court in plain clothes would be looked upon as an endeavor to propagate republican principles.[1]

August Belmont, who was at The Hague, received permission from the king to appear at the audience in citizen's dress. Although it had been hinted that it would be more satisfactory if he wore uniform, he had replied that he must follow the wishes and instructions of his government. He went therefore to the audience in plain black clothes. In his despatch he described his appearance as singular, for the king, his aides-de-camp, and the minister of foreign affairs, the only persons who assisted at the ceremony, were in full uniform and covered with stars and decorations. Belmont was more anxious about the presentation to the queen mother, for at her court ceremony was a weightier matter than at that of the king. His brother diplomats, who had wondered at his previous temerity, were concerned about the result, for they knew that she had often resented with rudeness any infringement of etiquette. The presentation, however, took place without incident;[2] and after several months' residence in Holland, Belmont could report that he and his family had been treated by the royal family on every occasion with the utmost courtesy. Indeed, at a casino ball the queen paid him honor above any of the diplomats present by asking him to dance a quadrille; and at a court ball the king shook him most cordially by the hand and entered into an interesting and animated conversation with him of more than half an hour.[3]

Sanford, the secretary of legation, who was representing this country at Paris until the arrival of Mason, determined,

---

[1] Schroeder to Marcy, Nov. 24th, 1853.
[2] Belmont to Marcy, Nov. 8th and 25th, 1853.
[3] Ibid., Feb. 28th, 1854.

after much consideration, to act in accordance with the spirit of the instructions of the State department. Fearing that his change of dress might be misconstrued, he made known his desire to the minister of foreign affairs, who promised to make the subject understood at court. Sanford accordingly appeared at the reception to the diplomatic corps, at a dinner of the foreign minister, and at a soirée at the Tuileries in citizen's dress.[1] When Mason arrived at Paris, the first question upon which he brought his mind to bear was that of a proper costume. He had earnestly hoped that nothing would occur to cause him to deviate from the simple dress of an American citizen; but he soon perceived that it would not do to follow the example of Sanford. In the latter of two interviews with the minister of foreign affairs, the emperor's wishes were most politely conveyed to him. Nothing was specifically required, but suggestions were made to which, from a proper respect to the French government, he deemed it imperatively necessary to conform. He appeared before the emperor to present his credentials in a suit of plain black clothes, but at the first ball at the Tuileries which he attended, and on all subsequent court occasions, he wore, as he described it, "a simple uniform dress." Sanford was so disgusted with the action of his chief that he resigned the position of secretary of legation. He said that Mason adopted "a coat embroidered with gilt tinsel, a sword and cocked hat, the invention of a Dutch tailor in Paris, borrowed chiefly from the livery of a subordinate attaché of legation of one of the petty powers of the Continent. Mortified and indignant at this course," Sanford wrote, "I declined attending with him the ball at which he first figured in this toggery."[2] A letter from the Secretary of State to Sanford approving his conduct was a salve to his wounded feelings;[3] and his satisfaction was

---

[1] Sanford to Marcy, Aug. 18th, 1853.
[2] Letter of Mr. Sanford to Secretary of State Cass, Jan. 19th, 1860.
[3] Mr. Marcy to Mr. Sanford, Feb. 18th, 1854.

complete when he read a private letter from Marcy to Mason, severely animadverting upon Mason's return to a monarchical dress, when the plain black clothes "had been almost universally commended by public opinion in the United States."[1]

But nowhere did the circular of the State department create so much trouble as at the court of St. James. After considerable reflection, Buchanan had determined to wear neither gold lace nor embroidery at court, yet he desired to show a proper respect to the queen, for whom he had a most sincere regard. It had been suggested to him that he might assume the civil dress worn by General Washington. He therefore carefully examined Stuart's portrait, but came to the conclusion that fashions had so changed that such a costume would appear ridiculous. The question was still unsettled when Parliament opened in February, 1854. Two days before the meeting, he received a printed circular from the master of ceremonies, which stated, "No one can be admitted into the diplomatic tribune, or in the body of the House, but in full court dress." In consequence of this, he did not attend. Buchanan's absence from the House of Lords, at the opening of Parliament, " produced quite a sensation." "Indeed," he wrote, "I have found difficulty in preventing this incident from becoming a subject of inquiry and remark in the House of Commons."[2] When all England was excited by the prospect of war with Russia, it seems curious that this affair should have attracted so much attention; yet it was the occasion of official consideration, court gossip, and newspaper controversy. The *Times*, in describing the brilliant and imposing proceedings in the House of Lords, had stated that, amidst the blaze of stars, crosses, and ribands in the diplomatic box, the American minister, in evening dress, sate "unpleasantly conscious of

---

[1] Mr. Sanford to Mr. Cass, Jan. 19th, 1860.
[2] Buchanan to Marcy, London, Feb. 7th, 1854.

his singularity."¹ This account was speedily corrected, but the affair gave rise to a spirited discussion in the journals. One newspaper said that the exclusion of Buchanan from the ceremony would be considered in the United States "as a studied slight or determined insult."² On the other hand, an influential journal said that the absurd quarrel was entirely due to "General Pierce's republican ill-manners" and to "American puppyism," to which nothing should be conceded. "There is not the least reason," continued this journal, "why her Majesty . . . should be troubled to receive the 'gentleman in the black coat' from Yankee-land. He can say his say at the Foreign Office, dine at a chop-house in King Street, sleep at the old Hummums, and be off as he came, per liner, when his business is done."³

Three weeks after the opening of Parliament, however, Buchanan had the pleasure of writing to Marcy: "The question of court costume has been finally settled to my entire satisfaction. I appeared at the queen's levee, on Wednesday last, in the very dress which you have often seen me wear at the President's levees, with the exception of a very plain black-handled and black-hilted dress sword, and my reception was all that I could have desired. . . . I have never felt prouder, as a citizen of my country, than when I stood amidst the brilliant circle of foreign ministers and other court dignitaries in the simple dress of an American citizen."⁴ He adopted the sword, he explained to his niece, "to gratify those who have yielded so much, and to distinguish me from the upper court servants."⁵

---

[1] London *Times*, Feb. 1st, 1854.
[2] London *Examiner*, quoted in the London *Times*, Feb. 6th, 1854.
[3] London *Chronicle*, cited by New York *Evening Post*, April 8th, 1854.
[4] Buchanan to Marcy, London, Feb. 24th, 1854. The dress was black coat, white waistcoat and cravat, and black pantaloons and dress boots. Buchanan to Miss Harriet Lane, Feb. 24th, Life of Buchanan, Curtis, vol. ii. p. 114. The despatches quoted may be found in vol. ix. Senate Documents, 1st Sess. 36th Congress.
[5] Curtis, vol. ii. p. 114.

If Marcy had foreseen the number of serious questions that would come before him, he would not have taken upon himself the task of prescribing the cut of the garments for our diplomatic representatives. Buchanan expressed the opinion that Marcy had much to learn;[1] but by 1854 the steady application and diligence of the Secretary of State began to bear fruit. In the last days of 1853 a treaty was negotiated with Mexico; amendments were made to it by the Senate, and in turn agreed to by the Mexican President. It was not, however, until June 30th, 1854, that proper legislation by Congress was had to carry the provisions of the treaty into effect; and only on that day were the ratifications exchanged. This agreement is known as the Gadsden treaty. It settled the question of a disputed boundary with Mexico, the line agreed upon between the two countries being that now existing.[2] The United States gained the Mesilla valley, which was an oblong square of land containing about twenty million acres. It formed the southern part of what is now New Mexico and Arizona. The agreement also abrogated the eleventh article of the treaty of Guadalupe Hidalgo,[3] which provided that the United States should protect Mexico from the incursions of Indians. This had been found to be an onerous duty, and one almost impossible of execution. For these considerations the United States paid ten millions of dollars. This district was now much better known than in 1848. No one pretended that fertile or valuable land had been acquired, but the friends of the administration urged that this valley was a very desirable and an almost necessary route for the projected Southern Pacific railroad.[4]

---

[1] In May, 1853, Curtis, vol. ii. p. 51.   [2] In 1890.
[3] The treaty of peace of 1848 which ended the Mexican War.
[4] See Treaties and Conventions. Haswell; also debate in the House of Representatives on the appropriation necessary to carry out the treaty. The vote in the House was 103 to 62; in the Senate, on the appropriation, 34 to 6.

In June, a treaty settling the fishery question and providing for reciprocity between the United States and Canada was concluded between Marcy and Lord Elgin, Governor-General of Canada, who acted for Great Britain. It allowed United States fishermen to take sea-fish in the bays, harbors, and creeks of Canada, New Brunswick, Nova Scotia, Prince Edward Island, and of the several islands thereunto adjacent. This was a concession to our country, for by the treaty of 1818, which was then in force, United States fishermen were not allowed to take fish within three marine miles of these coasts. The advantage to Canada was in a provision that certain articles, the growth and produce of each country, should be admitted into the other free of duty.[1] The treaty was to remain in force ten years, and thereafter until either country should give notice of the wish to terminate the agreement, but it should be binding for twelve months after such notice was given.[2] This was a valuable treaty for Canada, and a desirable one for the United States; but the manner in which a majority of the Senate was obtained for its ratification, if the story told by Lord Elgin's secretary be exact, is neither creditable to Lord Elgin nor to the senators whose support he gained by wily

---

[1] Among the articles which were thus admitted were: Grain, flour, and breadstuffs of all kinds; fish of all kinds; poultry, eggs; hides, furs, skins or tails, undressed; butter, cheese, tallow; ores of metals of all kinds; coal, timber and lumber of all kinds; fish-oil, rice, broom-corn and bark; flax, hemp and tow, unmanufactured; unmanufactured tobacco. A complete list may be found in Treaties and Conventions, Haswell, p. 451; also in Blaine's Twenty Years of Congress, vol. ii. p. 621, where the treaty is discussed. In mildly criticising this treaty, the New York *Tribune*, weekly of June 17th, nevertheless declared that it was in favor of absolute free trade between British America and the United States.

[2] The ratifications were exchanged Sept. 9th, 1854. The treaty was terminated March 17th, 1866, on notice given one year previously by the United States. See Treaties and Conventions, Haswell; Blaine's Twenty Years of Congress.

In July the treaty was ratified which had been made by Commodore Perry with Japan. The principal feature of the treaty was the opening of several important Japanese ports to American vessels. See Treaties and Conventions, p. 597.

social influences; it has been known as the treaty "floated through on champagne."[1]

In July, an affair occurred in Central America which created some excitement at the North. The port of San Juan had been occupied by about three hundred adventurers, mainly negroes from Jamaica, who had caused great annoyance to an American settlement on the other side of the river. This settlement had been established by the Nicaragua Transit Company, an association of citizens of the United States, whose purpose was to open a transit-way across the Isthmus of Central America. The San Juan (or Greytown)[2] people had committed depredations on the property of the citizens of Punta Arenas, as the United States settlement was called. The trouble was still further complicated by the attempt of a body of men crossing over from Greytown to arrest the captain of one of the Transit Company's boats on a charge of murder. The American minister to Central America, Borland, happening to be there, effectually protected the captain, for he believed in the innocence of the accused, and, moreover, totally denied the jurisdiction of the intruding party. Afterwards, when Borland was in Greytown, he was subjected to insult by those presumably having authority. On receiving official accounts of these occurrences, the President sent the sloop-of-war *Cyane* to the harbor of San Juan to enforce the demands of this government. A claim for twenty-four thousand dollars for injury to property was made, an apology was demanded for the indignity offered to the United States minister, and assurances of better behavior in the future were required. No reply

---

[1] See Life of Laurence Oliphant, vol. i. p. 109 *et seq.;* Episodes in a Life of Adventure, Oliphant, p. 38 *et seq.* Oliphant's description of the Washington of 1854 is noteworthy: "Washington, 'the city of magnificent distances,' struck me as a howling wilderness of deserted streets running out into the country, and ending nowhere, its population consisting chiefly of politicians and negroes."

[2] This population gave their town the name of Greytown.

being received, the commander of the *Cyane,* after giving due notice of twenty-four hours, opened bombardment on Greytown. He ceased firing twice, in order to give an opportunity of complying with the demands which had been made; but at length, as nothing was heard from the authorities, he continued the bombardment until the town was laid in ashes. No lives were lost, and the buildings destroyed were of little value. An English war-vessel was in the harbor, and its captain protested against the attack. "This transaction," the President stated in his message to Congress, "has been the subject of complaint on the part of some foreign powers, and has been characterized with more of harshness than of justice."[1]

But all foreign affairs were unimportant compared to the diplomatic intercourse with Spain, if this be estimated by the attention it received from the Secretary of State, the excitement it caused in this country, and the interest it occasioned abroad. The desire to obtain Cuba soon began to affect Marcy, and he indulged in the dream that through his agency the island might be peaceably and honorably acquired, though in the instructions to Soulé he urged caution on his impetuous agent. At the beginning he went over the usual platitudes: it is difficult for Spain to retain Cuba, she cannot keep it long unaided, and the United States has a deep interest in its destiny after it shall cease to be a dependency of Spain. We should resist its transference to any European nation, and we should see with regret any power of Europe help Spain to keep her dominion over Cuba. Then coming to the actual matter, Soulé could understand that we would be willing to purchase the island, but he was not authorized to make any offer for it, since there is now no hope that such a proposition will be favor-

---

[1] For a full account of this affair, see the President's message of Dec. 4th, 1854, and the original documents submitted to Congress in August. The subject is discussed in Wharton's International Law Digest, sec. 224.

ably entertained. Indeed, it is believed that Spain is under obligations to England and France not to transfer Cuba to the United States. It will be of great value if the minister can ascertain at Madrid what is the exact arrangement between the three powers, and especially whether Great Britain and France are urging Spain to take steps towards the emancipation of the slaves in Cuba. The opinion was expressed that if Cuba became a republic, and there was a voluntary separation from the mother country, it would probably relieve us from further anxiety, and the United States would be willing to contribute money towards the accomplishment of such a desirable object.[1]

Buchanan was also instructed to watch the conduct of Great Britain, and to ascertain whether she was urging Spain to emancipate the negroes in Cuba and to import more Africans as free men into the island.[2]

Soulé had settled the question of his dress in literal accordance with the circular of his chief. He adopted the costume of Benjamin Franklin at the court of Louis XVI. The black-velvet clothes, richly embroidered, the black stockings, a black chapeau, and a black dress sword, set off his black eyes, black locks, and pale complexion, and gave him a striking appearance. He looked, indeed, not like the philosopher whose costume he imitated, but rather like the master of Ravenswood.[3] Contrary to general anticipation, he was received in Madrid by the queen "with marked attention and courtesy."[4] He had, however, good reason to believe that his rejection had been urged upon the Spanish cabinet by the French ambassador, by the Countess of Montijo, the mother of the Empress Eugénie of France and of the Duchess of Alba, and by the Austrian and Mexican ministers.

---

[1] Marcy to Soulé, July 23d, 1853.
[2] Marcy to Buchanan, July 2d, 1853.
[3] Memories of Many Men, Field, p. 86.
[4] Soulé to Marcy, Oct. 25th, 1853; see vol. i. pp. 394, 395.

Soon after his presentation at court, an affair occurred which gave his family an unpleasant notoriety in every capital of Europe. A ball was given by the Marquis de Turgot, the ambassador of France, in honor of the Empress Eugénie's fête-day, and to this ball all the members of the diplomatic corps were invited. Madame Soulé made a striking appearance. She had a beautiful head and expressive face, and her fine person was adorned by a rich and tasteful dress, cut low, designed by the artist of the mode at Paris. The Countess of Montijo, since her daughter had become empress, not only led society in Madrid, but mingled in state affairs with such apparent authority that she was often presumed to be the real representative of France. She needed only to make a remark to have it at once echoed. She criticised severely the toilet of Madame Soulé, and the Marquis de Turgot joined in the criticism. The Duke of Alba, brother-in-law of Napoleon III., translated the trifling words into an insulting comparison, saying as Madame Soulé was passing, "Look at Marguerite de Bourgogne." The dissolute wife of Louis X. was then in every one's mind, owing to the reappearance of Mademoiselle Georges on the Paris stage in Dumas's "La Tour de Nesle," who revived the memory of the sensation she once had made by her art and sensuous beauty in the impersonation of Marguerite. Nelville Soulé chanced to hear the remark about his mother, and, approaching the duke in a menacing manner, applied to him the epithet of *canaille*. The next morning young Soulé sent to the duke a demand for an apology. This was readily given, for the duke in his words had referred entirely to the physical likeness between Madame Soulé and Mademoiselle Georges. The lady's character was above reproach, and there was not intended the most distant comparison to the beautiful and wanton Marguerite. But this did not end the matter. The duke was taunted by the proud Castilian grandees with having been forced to eat his words by a beardless boy. Certain reports of the affair which appeared in *Galignani's Messenger* and the London journals gave the duke an opportunity to demand of Nelville Soulé that he should disavow those statements. This Soulé declined to do, maintaining that the printed accounts were correct. The duke then sent a challenge. Both were experienced swordsmen. They fought for thirty minutes, and although neither was wounded, the seconds declared that honor did not require more; the duel ended with a shaking of hands.

But the hot blood of Pierre Soulé boiled at this implied insult. He was of humble origin, and had been forced to leave France on account of advanced political opinions. Turgot, of an ancient noble family, could scarcely endure to meet on equal diplomatic footing a Frenchman of low extraction, as he considered the American minister, and, not content with secretly urging the rejection of Soulé by the court, he manifested his contempt by shrugs of the shoulders and by petty slights. Soulé now insisted on fighting Turgot, on the ground that the insult had taken place at his house, and no explanation availed to placate the fiery citizen of New Orleans. A duel was actually forced upon Turgot. Pistols were the weapons chosen. The American minister wanted the distance ten paces or under; Lord Howden, the British ambassador and second of Turgot, said that would be brutal murder, and determined that the distance should be forty paces. To this decision Soulé was obliged to submit, although he maintained that in America such a duel would be ridiculed as a farce. The first fire was without result; at the second, the ball of Soulé's pistol lodged in the thigh of his antagonist, four inches above the knee. The marquis was confined to his bed for a long time, and was lamed for life. A reconciliation between the two gentlemen never took place.[1]

---

[1] My authorities for this account are a letter of M. Gaillardet, dated Paris, Dec. 22d, 1853, to the *Courrier des États-Unis*, cited by the New York *Herald* and New York *Times* of Jan. 11th, 1854; letter from Madrid, Dec. 26th, 1853, published in the New York *Tribune* of Jan. 25th, 1854; Memories of Many Men, Field, p. 80.

This duel occurred December 17th, 1853. Six days thereafter Soulé wrote an important despatch to his chief. Spain, he said, was almost in a condition of anarchy. The ministry had no longer the confidence of the Cortes and the Senate; the queen had suspended the sessions of the legislature; the ministers wanted to resign. The most astounding rumors were in circulation about the palace. The king had been advised, when the expected royal child should be born, to protest against its legitimacy and inaugurate a movement which should expel the queen from the throne.[1] She was extremely unpopular. The most shocking stories were current regarding the "innocent Isabella," as she had been called in her youth. The best people avoided her. The lower classes only spoke of her with sneers. Anecdotes most foul were told of her orgies, and everybody believed them. Her unbridled passion, it was said, led her to debauchery in which she seemed to emulate the disorderly adventures of Catherine II. of Russia.[2]

But to return to the despatch of Soulé. He reported that in the midst of the confusion and disorder, it was difficult to transact any business. In foreign affairs, Spain did not move without consulting France or England. The influence of France was at present the more powerful of the two, and she was as much opposed to our acquisition of Cuba as was Great Britain; "and she will remain our enemy as long as she bends her neck under the yoke of the man who now holds the rod over her." Soulé spoke of the duplicity of the French minister of foreign affairs; of his own delicate position in Madrid on account of the uneasiness which his presence in Europe seemed to give the French autocrat; of the exceedingly vain and overbearing Turgot, who had charge from the emperor to cut short Soulé's course in Spain and

---

[1] Soulé to Marcy, Dec. 23d, 1853.
[2] Madrid correspondence of London *Times*, April 18th; Memories of Many Men, Field, p. 94.

nullify what influence he might gain with the court or the government.[1]

After the receipt of this despatch, it is plain that the President and Secretary of State should have decided upon the transfer of Soulé to some other diplomatic post, or, if there were none such available, that an honorable place should have been found for him at home. Soulé was an accomplished and patriotic gentleman who deserved to be treated with consideration; but, on his own showing, he could no longer be of service to this government, unless it were desired to goad Spain into a war. The sequel proves that it was most unfortunate for the reputation of our government that he was permitted to remain at Madrid. He embroiled our relations with Spain to no purpose, trying to inaugurate a system of diplomacy which, had it been adopted, would justly have incurred for us the reproach of the civilized world.

Soulé's very difficult position was made more difficult as Calderon, who held the portfolio of foreign affairs, was his personal enemy. The two had quarrelled at Washington when Calderon was the Spanish representative to this country.[2] As Soulé had apparently now no hope of accomplishing anything with the cabinet, he set to work to ingratiate himself with the queen and the queen dowager. In this he succeeded,[3] but to the last he was cordially hated by the aristocracy and the press.

The despatches of Soulé in January and February, 1854, show that he had no hope of being able to further the interests of his country by negotiation so long as Calderon should remain Secretary of State. But it was evident that a crisis in affairs was approaching, and he gloated on the difficulties which beset the cabinet. The government, not having the support of any political party, only maintained

---

[1] Soulé to Marcy, Dec. 23d, 1853.
[2] New York *Times*, May 10th, 1854.
[3] Memories of Many Men, Field, p. 79; Soulé to Marcy, Jan. 20th, 1854.

itself by a system of terror. Citizens who had run counter to the whims of the palace were sent to prison or exiled from the country. The press was closely fettered; the treasury was empty; the Bank of San Fernando peremptorily declined to make the government fresh loans, and even the usurers of Madrid were deaf to the entreaties of the court. The queen had already wasted the whole of her income for the current year. Everywhere was distress; food had doubled in price, and the poor of the capital were fed at the public charge. The queen and her secret counsellors were plotting for an absolute monarchy; the ministers, though not averse to the scheme, dared not move in it.

This condition of affairs was sure to redound to the profit of the United States, for it invited a rebellion in Cuba. It seemed unlikely that this event would be deferred later than spring, and in such a case the American minister at Madrid ought to be in a position to take an advantage of the lucky chance offered him. He begged, therefore, for specific powers and sufficient instructions.[1]

While Soulé was fretting over his lack of authority and fuming at his uncomfortable predicament, the Cuban officials played into his hands by committing an outrage on the *Black Warrior*, an American merchant steamer. She plied between Mobile and New York, stopping at Havana for passengers and mail. She had made thirty-six such voyages, almost always having a cargo for the American port, and never being permitted to bring freight to Havana. The custom of her agent was to clear her "in ballast" the day before her arrival. This practice, while contrary to the regulations of Cuban ports, had always been winked at by the authorities. It was well understood that the *Black Warrior* generally had a cargo on board, but a detailed manifest of her load had never been required. She had always been permitted to sail unmolested until, when bound from Mobile to New York, she was stopped on the 28th of February, 1854,

---

[1] Soulé to Marcy, Jan. 20th and Feb. 23d.

by order of the royal exchequer, for having violated the
regulations of the port. The agent, finding that the cause
of this proceeding was the failure to manifest the cargo in
transit, offered to amend the manifest, which under the rules
he had a right to do; but this the collector, on a flimsy pretext, refused to permit. The agent was at the same time
informed that the cargo was confiscated and the captain
fined, in pursuance of the custom-house regulations. The
cargo was cotton, valued at one hundred thousand dollars;
the captain was fined six thousand dollars. The United
States consul applied to the captain-general for redress, but
no satisfaction was obtained. A gang of men with lighters
were sent to the ship, under the charge of the *comandante*,
who ordered the captain of the *Black Warrior* to discharge
her cargo. This he refused to do. The *comandante* then
had the hatches opened, and his men began to take out the
bales of cotton. The captain hauled down his flag and
abandoned the vessel to the Spanish authorities.[1]

When the news of this affair reached Washington, it
caused excitement there; but the North was too greatly
troubled about the Kansas-Nebraska act to respond to the
feeling in official circles. The President sent a message to
the House of Representatives, stating that indemnity for the
injury to our citizens had been demanded from Spain. He
suggested that Congress should strengthen his hands by
provisional legislation adapted to the emergency, promising
that if the negotiations should fail, he would not hesitate to
use the authority and means which Congress might grant,
"to insure the observance of our just rights, to obtain redress for injuries received, and to vindicate the honor of
our flag."[2]

The day after the news was received, Marcy sent Soulé
documents which contained a history of the transaction.

---

[1] See the documents transmitted to the House of Representatives by the President, March 15th.
[2] Message of the President, March 15th.

He expressed the opinion that the outrage would cause deep indignation throughout the country, as it was the most flagrant of many unredressed wrongs of Cuba to this country.[1] Six days later the President and cabinet had considered the matter fully, and the Secretary of State was able to give authoritative instructions. Soulé was directed to present the transaction as recounted in the documents accompanying the two despatches, and to demand three hundred thousand dollars as indemnity to the owners of the *Black Warrior*.[2] The President, moreover, hoped that her Catholic Majesty would "visit with her displeasure the Cuban officials who have perpetrated the wrong." "Neither the views of this government nor the sentiments of the country," wrote the Secretary, "will brook any evasion or delay on the part of her Catholic Majesty in a case of such flagrant wrong." But lest Soulé might urge his country's demands with too great persistence, he was directed simply to present the strong features of the case and refrain from the discussion of it. He should get "as early a reply as practicable" to his demand. With this despatch was sent a special messenger, who would wait a reasonable time for the answer of the Spanish government.[3]

The journey from Washington to Madrid in 1854 took a longer time than is now required to go from Washington to Yokohama. The messenger could travel almost all of the way by rail from Paris to Bayonne; but thence he must proceed by *diligence* or by the Spanish mail. The vehicles were rickety, the roads were rough, and the traveller was seventy-six hours on the road. In the winter or early spring he suffered intensely from the cold; he was almost certain to be upset, and he might consider himself fortunate if he were not attacked and robbed by highwaymen.[4] It was the

---

[1] Marcy to Soulé, March 11th.

[2] They had abandoned the vessel; one hundred thousand dollars was for the cargo, two hundred thousand dollars for the vessel.

[3] Marcy to Soulé, March 17th.

[4] See Field's description of his journey, p. 77.

7th of April when the messenger arrived at Madrid, and put the last despatch of the Secretary of State into Soulé's hands. Three days previously had come Marcy's first communication in regard to the affair, and we may well imagine that Soulé thanked his stars for what seemed to him a lucky event. Here was a chance to extricate himself from the unpleasant position into which he had fallen after his duel with Turgot. The average American deemed the seizure of the *Black Warrior* a moderate wrong; to Soulé it appeared a gross indignity. His eagerness to obtain Cuba colored every thought and prompted every action. He believed that the man who should be instrumental in acquiring the island would be the leader of the Democratic party, and while, being foreign-born, he could not aspire to the presidency, he relished the idea of being President-maker.[1]

Soulé immediately asked Calderon for an interview; when they met on the 8th of April he gave a full history of the transaction, and left with the Spanish minister a letter which expressed the hope of the President that her Catholic Majesty would not only "make prompt reparation to the injured citizens of the United States, but also visit with her displeasure the Cuban officials."[2] Thus far Soulé confined himself to his instructions. Three days went by without a reply. The day after the interview was Sunday, which was kept with great solemnity in Spain, and Holy Week began on the Monday. Though the procrastination of Spanish officials was well known, the hot temper of the American minister would not take into account the holy season or the ingrained character of those he was dealing with. On April 11th, he sent a sharp letter to Calderon. The wrong, he said, was "of a highly grievous character," and "the United States cannot brook that the reparation due them for the insult offered to their flag and the injury done to the property of their citizens be in any way evaded or unnecessarily delayed." He demanded the sum of three hundred thousand dollars as

---

[1] See Field, p. 98.   [2] Soulé to Calderon, April 8th.

indemnity, and that all persons concerned in the perpetration of the wrong should be dismissed from her Majesty's service. He asserted that if these demands were not complied with in forty-eight hours, the government of the United States would consider that her Majesty's government had determined to uphold the conduct of its officers.[1] The secretary of legation who carried this despatch to Calderon indicated to him, by pointing to the clock, that it was now exactly twelve, and that in precisely two days at the selfsame minute an answer would be due.

Calderon had already written a reply to Soulé's first note, but did not send it until after he had received the letter of belligerent tone. It was in the usual Spanish manner, arguing for delay because authentic and complete information had not been received. The feeble Secretary of State would also have avoided a direct answer to the second note of the American minister, but his colleagues agreed on a reply, and forced him to sign it.[2] They, in turn, were undoubtedly braced in their position by the ambassadors of England and France, trained diplomats, who shrewdly surmised that Soulé had exceeded his instructions, and would not be sustained by his government. The reply sent on April 12th was couched in terms of haughty dignity that recalled the old days of Spain, when it was her custom to make imperious demands, not to hear them.

The despatch said that, considering all the circumstances of the case, the government had replied with promptness. The secretary promised that when full information was received, the affair should be carefully considered. But it was unreasonable to expect that a grave and definite determination would be arrived at when only one side of the case had been heard. The words of the American minister called

---

[1] Soulé to Calderon, April 11th.
[2] Madrid correspondence London *Times*, April 17th. This correspondent was thoroughly informed, and undoubtedly had his information from the British ambassador.

forth a reprimand. The peremptory manner of exacting satisfaction, he wrote, suggested "a suspicion that it is not so much the manifestation of a lively interest in the defence of pretended injuries as an incomprehensible pretext for exciting estrangement, if not a quarrel, between two friendly powers." But the Secretary hoped the United States government would not insist upon a decision until the expected information arrived, which would enable her Majesty's government to determine its course intelligently and justly. He added: "If, unfortunately, it should not be so, the opinion of the civilized world will decide on which side is the right." In conclusion, he wished to impress upon the mind of the American minister "that the government of her Majesty, jealous also of its decorum, is not accustomed to the harsh and imperious manner with which this matter has been expressed; which, furthermore, is not the most adequate for attaining to the amicable settlement which is wished for."[1]

The spirit of the proud Castilian spoke in this despatch. It cannot be denied that the imperious words of Soulé justified this dignified reply and severe reprimand. It has a noble ring when we consider it the answer of a weak, degenerate nation to a strong, energetic people; for the senders of this message thought that they had thrown down the gauntlet to the United States, and they expected that the next communication from the American minister would be a demand for his passports.[2] The ministry were certain of the sympathy of England and France, but, in the event of hostilities with the United States, material aid from these two countries was hardly to be hoped for, as they were now engaged in a fierce war with Russia. The Spaniards did not know that a more efficient force than England and France was working for them — public sentiment in the northern half of the Union.

---

[1] Calderon to Soulé, April 12th.
[2] Madrid correspondence London *Times*, April 20th.

In the official circles of Madrid, war with the United States was now considered as very probable, and the chances of it were seriously discussed. The most sensible men in Spain were convinced that Cuba must sooner or later belong to the United States, but no one would have dared to propose its sale.[1] Such a project would have displaced any ministry and more than likely overturned the dynasty. In the event of hostilities with the United States, none but the proud Spaniards had a shadow of doubt as to what would be the fate of Cuba, but that conquest would be a very different affair from the conquest of Mexico. The Americans would find that to win the " Queen of the Antilles " was a difficult task. The forts and the city would be obstinately defended. Nor would the Spaniards confine themselves to a defensive warfare. By the time that Havana was taken the magnificent merchant marine of the United States would be swept from the seas by privateers issuing from the ports of Spain. Nor would the fall of the capital city end the contest. The slaves would be given their freedom on condition of fighting the invaders; and when the Americans had finally obtained possession of Cuba, they might find it, as to waste and ruin and social conditions, a very St. Domingo, instead of the fair, fruitful island they had set out to conquer.[2]

On the day that the American messenger left Madrid with despatches from Soulé informing his government of the sudden check the negotiations had received, there was published the decree of the Spanish government announcing the intention of putting an effectual stop to the slave-trade and providing for a better regulation of the slaves in Cuba.[3]

---

[1] Madrid correspondence London *Times*, April 21st.

[2] The chances of such a war are well discussed in the Madrid correspondence of the London *Times*, April 21st and May 10th. Clayton said in the Senate, May 22d, that he had heard the former Spanish minister threaten that the slaves would be emancipated in Cuba rather than permit the Americans to take it by violence.

[3] Madrid correspondence London *Times*, April 17th. See discussion in the House of Commons.

This was a compliment to the influence of England, whose government had been urging Spain to this course, and was a bid for her support. Six thousand soldiers were ordered to the West Indies to reinforce the garrisons of Cuba.[1]

When the correspondence between Soulé and Calderon reached Washington, the little flurry caused by the seizure of the *Black Warrior* had subsided, except where an excitement was kept alive by the operations of filibusters. The ship and her cargo had been released. She was now plying as usual between New York and Mobile, touching at Havana, where she was treated with great consideration by the authorities.

A few days before the despatch from Madrid had arrived, Slidell, senator from Louisiana, introduced a resolution directing that the committee on foreign relations should inquire into the expediency of authorizing the President to suspend the neutrality laws. This was a move to make easy the operation of filibusters on Cuba; and if the execution of those laws were intermitted, a formidable expedition certainly would be fitted out in this country. The proposition fell flat in the Senate, aroused no interest in the border States, and when alluded to at all in the North was only mentioned with indignation. From several brief discussions in Congress, it was plainly to be seen that a proposition looking in the slightest degree to war with Spain on account of the *Black Warrior* affair would not for a moment be entertained. Not a resolution in response to the President's message had ever been introduced. Clingman and a representative from Louisiana had broached to the administration a project which should put ten million dollars at the disposal of the President, giving him authority to employ the army and navy and accept the services of fifty thousand volunteers; but Pierce, Marcy, and Davis

---

[1] Madrid correspondence London *Times*, May 10th; Soulé to Marcy, May 24th.

were earnest in their opposition to any such proposition, and the matter went no further.[1]

However, after Soulé's important despatches were received, the cabinet was reported as divided on the subject, Davis and Cushing urging that the minister should be fully sustained.[2] Soulé confidently expected that when the text of Spain's reply was read to the cabinet, he would be ordered at once to demand his passports and leave Spain, and that war would ensue.[3] But the President was not at first disposed to any such conclusion. He came to no decision, except that nothing should be positively determined until after further advices from Madrid. A Spanish ambassador to Washington was now on the way, and it might be advisable to renew with him negotiations that had come to a standstill at Madrid. Soulé was not recalled, nor was his course approved.[4]

Although the correspondence between Soulé and Calderon was kept secret in this country, the essential points of it had been communicated by the Madrid correspondent of the London *Times* to his journal. The Spanish government was proverbially leaky. What the ministers did not disclose, the queen and her secret counsellors were sure to tell. The English minister, to whom the contents of the letters had been communicated, undoubtedly assisted the representative of the *Times* in furnishing information to the British public, and was of great service in enabling him to sift the rumors which were current in Madrid. At any rate, he got

---

[1] Speeches and Writings of Thos. L. Clingman, pp. 375, 376, quoted by Von Holst.

[2] Washington correspondence of New York *Times*, May 10th. The Washington *National Intelligencer* of May 13th said: "We have reason to believe that the New York *Times* correspondent in this city possesses facilities for becoming well-informed in our diplomatic State affairs." James W. Simonton was the correspondent.

[3] Memories of Many Men, Field, p. 84.

[4] Simonton in New York *Times*, Washington, May 10th. The subsequent diplomatic correspondence confirms this.

at the gist of the correspondence. His letters were extensively copied into the American journals, so that the public were almost as well informed of the essential facts as were the cabinet. They knew that Soulé had made extraordinary demands; it was presumed he had exceeded his authority; and they knew that his demands had met with a peremptory refusal. The Northern and border States held no feeling of resentment towards Spain. Indeed, one may find expressions of amusement at the plight of Soulé, but no sentiment whatever in favor of the government gratifying his self-love by giving him its support.

Far otherwise was the sentiment of the slavery propaganda. The acquisition of Cuba was certain to increase their power in the federal Union by the addition of two or more slave States; therefore, they wanted a pretext for a war with Spain. They were convinced she would not sell Cuba,[1] and they pretended to believe that a movement was set on foot to Africanize the island. By this it was meant that the influence of Great Britain had been strong enough to induce Spain to take steps towards the emancipation of the slaves; that there was a "settled design to throw Cuba ultimately into the hands of its negro population, and to revive there . . . the scenes of San Domingo's revolution."[2] In spite of the explicit denial of this report by the Captain-General of Cuba;[3] in defiance of the assurance of the English Foreign Secretary of State that there was no foundation for the belief;[4] and although Clayton challenged Benjamin

---

[1] See the speech in the Senate, May 22d, of Mallory, of Florida.

[2] Senator Mallory's resolution introduced into the Senate, May 17th. The resolutions of the legislature of Louisiana presented to the Senate by Benjamin, May 24th, were similar in purport.

[3] Decree of the Captain-General of May 3d, published in New York *Times* of May 16th.

[4] Buchanan, in a despatch to Marcy of Nov. 1st, 1853, reported a conversation had with Lord Clarendon: "I said, 'Your lordship must be fully aware of the deep, the vital, interest which we feel in regard to the condition of the colored population of Cuba. This island is within sight

to bring as proof of the assertion an expression of belief in the story from the present Secretary of State, or from any other man who had ever held that office,[1] yet Southern sena-

---

of our shores; and should a black government like that of Hayti be established there, it would endanger the peace and domestic security of a large and important portion of our people. To come, then, to the point: it has been publicly stated and reiterated over and over again in the United States, that Spain, should she find it impossible to retain the island, will emancipate the slaves upon it; and that the British government is endeavoring to persuade her to pursue this course.' I here paused for a reply.

"He answered, 'We certainly have no wish, very far from it, to see a black government established in Cuba. We have been pressing Spain incessantly to put down the African slave-trade with Cuba; and I regret to say, without yet having produced the effect which we so much desire. . . . With the exception of urging Spain to abolish the slave-trade and endeavoring to trace out the emancipados, and do them the justice which good faith requires of us—and in this last we have had very little success—we have never had any negotiations of any kind with Spain or attempted to exercise any influence over her respecting the condition of the slaves in Cuba. We have not the most remote idea in any event of ever attempting to acquire Cuba for ourselves. We have already too many colonies, far more than are profitable to us.'"—MSS. State Department Archives.

Buchanan wrote Marcy, Nov. 12th, 1853: Lord Clarendon observed that "he was very much pained to learn there had been a violent and wholly unfounded article in the Washington *Union* charging them with an intrigue with Spain to 'Africanize' Cuba."—Ibid.

March 17th, 1854, Buchanan reported a conversation with Clarendon in which he asked: "Have Great Britain and France entered into any treaty or understanding of any kind whatever concerning Cuba, or in relation either to the present or prospective condition of that island?" He replied: "Great Britain and France have not entered into any treaty or understanding, direct or indirect, of any kind whatever concerning Cuba or in relation to the present or prospective condition of Cuba; we have never even thought of such a thing, nor have we the least intention to adopt any such course."—Ibid.

The position of England was well understood by the public. See Washington correspondence Philadelphia *Ledger*, May 28th, cited in New York *Times;* Washington correspondence New York *Courier and Enquirer*, cited in the *Independent*, June 8th.

[1] In the Senate, May 24th.

tors persistently averred that unless we interfered, the scenes of St. Domingo would be repeated within a few hours' sail of our shores. It cannot be supposed that intelligent men like Benjamin and Slidell believed this story, but they knew the credulity of the Southern people where their darling institution was concerned, and, as a similar report had created a powerful opinion in support of the annexation of Texas the spread of this tale was sure to work up a sentiment in favor of a war with Spain, and it would arouse a feeling of sympathy with the designs of the filibusters who were now actively at work.

The leader of the filibusters was Quitman, a former governor of Mississippi and a personal and political friend of Jefferson Davis. He had visited Washington in July, 1853, and, frankly disclosing his object to many distinguished men at the capital, had been delighted to hear expressions of sympathy and receive the assurance that there would not be a pretext for federal interference with his plan.[1] He had then devoted himself earnestly to the task, and in May of this year the project was almost ripe. "The great Cuban army," wrote a gentleman from Jackson, Mississippi, "will soon be ready to start, under command of our former governor, General Quitman. The men who are going from this section are of the right stripe and will 'never say die.' Mississippi rifles will tell the tale on Spanish soldiers. There is no secret

---

[1] Life and Correspondence of Gen. John A. Quitman, Claiborne, vol. ii. p. 195. Quitman is an example of a Northern man who became intensely Southern in his opinions. Born and educated in New York State, he was for a time professor at Mount Airy College, Germantown, Penn.; he studied law in Ohio, and was admitted to the bar; he went South when twenty-three years old, married a wealthy woman of Mississippi at twenty-six, and came into possession of a large estate. He served in the legislature of Mississippi, became chancellor of the State, was a brigadier-general in the Mexican war. On return from the war was elected governor, and was sent to Congress in 1854 and 1856. Throughout life Quitman was an avowed advocate of the doctrine of States-rights and a leader of the extreme Southern party.

about this movement. Every one who has been to New
Orleans says that the amount of money subscribed by the
merchants there is very heavy. Every one favors the move,
and although the New Orleans papers keep dark, yet the
subject is bar-room talk. There is no man so well qualified
as old Quitman. He has the confidence of the *sharp-shoot-
ers* of this State. . . . The plan meets with favor among the
cotton-planters, but they have not come forward with the
dimes to the amount that was anticipated." [1] A letter from
the same city a week later stated that General Quitman and
his staff were in New Orleans; that a sufficient number of
men had enlisted, but money was needed; three hundred
thousand dollars more was necessary, and Quitman and another man had almost made up their minds to mortgage
their estates to secure that amount. The state of Soulé's
negotiation was well understood; it was thought that the
filibusters were in intimate connection with him, and that
he had exceeded his instructions in the hope of bringing
about trouble between the United States and Spain, thereby
furthering the designs of those who were ready to attack
Cuba.[2]

There is no question that powerful influences were now
brought to bear upon the President with the design of having him assume a position in the *Black Warrior* affair that
would force Congress, for the honor of the country and for
the support of the executive, to authorize proceedings which
could only result in a war with Spain. The ruling spirit of
this cabal was Jefferson Davis, and as he apparently at this
moment controlled the columns of the Washington *Union*,
it was not an idle fear that he had the ascendency over the

---

[1] Private letter from Jackson, Mississippi, to a gentleman in New York
City, dated May 27th, New York *Tribune*, June 10th.

[2] Letter from Jackson, Mississippi, to the editor of the New York
Times, dated June 4th, published June 14th, the journal vouching that
it was from "an intelligent and reliable source;" see also extracts from a
"Private and Confidential" circular, issued by the Cuban conspirators in
New Orleans, published in the New York *Tribune* of June 15th.

President. "We are quite free to state," said the organ of the administration—"and in terms so emphatic and unequivocal as to admit of no misinterpretation—that if ample satisfaction is not allowed for the piratical seizure of the *Black Warrior* we shall advocate an immediate blockade of the island."[1] A few days later the organ complacently stated, as if the matter had already been decided upon, that, "in the course of the thick-coming events Cuba is bound to be admitted" into the Union.[2] The senators and representatives from the cotton States were convinced that now was a most favorable opportunity to strike for Cuba. On May 20th, news was received from Havana which seemed to indicate that the apple was ready for the plucking. Letters which reached Washington that day were full of an impending revolution in the island.[3] It was reported that the Creole proprietors were determined to stand oppression no longer; that the registration of the slaves in accordance with the decree of the Captain-General had given rise to a rumor that emancipation of the negroes would soon follow, and that this was bringing matters to a crisis.[4] The Captain-General had solemnly denounced as false and malicious the rumor that a compact had been made with Great Britain which would result in freeing the slaves. But the story continued to circulate. The authorities became alarmed, and with diligence made ready to repress an insurrection at home and repel an attack from the United States.

At the time that the important despatches from Soulé reached Washington, the attention of the administration and of the country was absorbed in the struggle over the Kansas-Nebraska bill in the House of Representatives. When the importance of these several events was realized, as tending to one certain course of action, the bill had passed the

---

[1] Washington *Union*, May 11th, cited in New York *Times*.
[2] Washington *Union*, cited by New York *Times* of May 15th.
[3] Simonton to New York *Times*, Washington, May 20th.
[4] Simonton from Washington, May 23d, New York *Times*.

House and its final enactment was a foregone conclusion. There were those who, in their enthusiasm over the parliamentary victory, not looking beyond the district of Columbia, thought that the dominant party could accomplish anything which they would undertake. Energetic and prompt action on the part of Congress or a word from the President was all that was needed to precipitate action. The cabinet were more disposed than at first to sustain Soulé, since a precedent for his demand had been found.[1] The warlike disposition of a large part of the cabinet was no secret. Five Democratic representatives from New York, who had opposed the Nebraska scheme, now issued an address to their constituents, in which they averred that there was a determination "to acquire Cuba utterly reckless of consequences." Little doubt can exist "that an effort will be made directly or indirectly at the conquest of Cuba and its incorporation into the Union as additional slave territory;" and it is a reasonable cause for fear that " we are about to be precipitated into a war " on account of the *Black Warrior* affair.[2] " We have reason to know," said the New York *Times*, in a carefully written article, "that the impression is very strong among the best-informed men at Washington that the administration has purposely arranged matters so as to render a war with Spain almost inevitable. A very distinguished gentleman, not long since a cabinet officer and likely to be well informed on the subject, has expressed the belief that we should be at war with Spain within ninety days."[3]

Yet the action was not taken by Congress, and the word was not spoken by the President. If Pierce was for a moment inclined to follow the lead of Davis in this matter, he shrank from it when confronted by the resistance of the

---

[1] Simonton, Washington, May 28th, New York *Times*.
[2] This address was to justify their action on the Kansas-Nebraska bill; was published in the New York *Times*, May 29th.
[3] June 2d.

Secretary of State and the almost certain opposition of Congress.[1] Marcy and the members of the majority averse to war were backed by the almost unanimous sentiment of the North; and their arguments, pointed as they were by constant references to the mighty force of the actual public opinion, in the end prevailed.

On the 1st of June a proclamation was issued by the President warning the filibusters who were fitting out an expedition for the invasion of Cuba that the neutrality laws would be enforced, and that they would be prosecuted. Quitman was afterwards arrested at New Orleans and obliged to give bonds that he would for nine months observe the neutrality laws of the United States. A few days after this important step was taken by the President, it became apparent that the moderate element in the administration had won and that the danger of war was past.[2]

It is highly probable that but for the strong feeling aroused at the North by the Kansas-Nebraska measure, the Southern propaganda would at this time have forced the administration and Congress into war with Spain for the conquest of Cuba. The *Black Warrior* affair would have been a contemptible cause of war between two friendly countries, but lighter pretexts than that have sufficed to bring about hostilities when the wolf nation has desired to prey upon the lamb. The conditions were supremely favorable for the United States. The only powers from which Spain could expect help were engaged in the Crimean war. Although the government of England would dislike to see the country which was disputing with her the commercial supremacy of the seas get possession of Cuba, yet Cobden represented a powerful sentiment when he declared amid cheers in the House of Commons that, "Without saying

---

[1] See Life of Davis, Alfriend, p. 97.
[2] See Simonton, Washington, June 9th and 15th, New York *Times*. I will add that the contemporaneous and subsequent events adequately confirm the reports of Simonton at the time.

one word about the expediency of giving Cuba to the United States or assisting that country to take possession of the island, he thought it would be greatly for the interests of humanity if the United States or any other power that would altogether discountenance the slave trade should possess it."[1] And Clarendon, the English foreign Secretary of State had admitted to Buchanan that Cuba was wretchedly governed. He said that he had told the Spanish minister at London "that if Spain lost Cuba it would be altogether their own fault, and they would be indebted for it to the wretched manner in which they governed the island." He further informed Buchanan "that although Spain did not deserve it at the hands of the British government, they still felt a sympathy for her arising out of their ancient alliances."[2] The Empress Eugénie would indeed have been glad to assist her native country, but France could hardly undertake another war merely for a sentiment. It was therefore unlikely that either France or England would interfere in a conflict between the United States and Spain, and this was well understood at our State department.

It is indeed true that if the difficulty could be accommodated by reasonable negotiation, a sense of justice and regard for the opinion of the civilized world should have prevented our government from pouncing upon Spain. But it was not thus that many of those in authority argued. They applied the remark of Burke to the present case. "If," the English statesman said, "my neighbor's house is in flames and the fire is likely to spread to my own, I am justified in interfering to avert a disaster which promises to be equally

---

[1] Hansard's Parl. Debates. Third Series, vol. cxxxii., April 4th, 1854; see New York *Times*, April 17th; also extract from Liverpool *Times*, quoted in the Senate by Mallory, May 22d. "In the present state of feeling in England, no great regret would be felt if the Americans were to get possession of Cuba in the scramble. In its present hands, that beautiful island is a source to us of more annoyance than any other place on the globe, Russia not excepted."

[2] Buchanan to Marcy, Nov. 1st, 1853. MSS. State Department Archives.

fatal to both." Cuba, asserted the organ of the administration, under her present rule threatens our prosperity and our honor, and there is but one single way by which the present situation can be remedied. We must take the island if needs be, in defiance of all Europe.[1] It may be affirmed with confidence that Northern public opinion excited by the Kansas-Nebraska act alone prevented this unjust war.[2] Without that power at his back, Marcy would have protested in vain. He would have been forced to resign as was Webster when he stood in the way of the annexation of Texas. And had not many Northern senators and representatives felt that they had already dared too much in the repeal of the Missouri Compromise, they could have been induced to register the decrees of the slavery propaganda in regard to Cuba.

What a foolish piece of state-craft was that of the Southern leaders in 1854! They obtained a fighting chance in

---

[1] Washington *Union*, May 11th, cited by New York *Times*, May 13th.

[2] The evidences of this statement are without number. I will cite three. Clayton said in the Senate, May 22d: "I see no reason at this time for this government's interference for the purpose of obtaining Cuba by war or violence of any kind or by the repeal of our laws of neutrality. I think it a dangerous period to make an effort of that description. There is great excitement at this time in the public mind throughout the United States in reference to the subject of slavery." The New York *Courier and Enquirer* said, June 1st: "Does the sane man live who believes that if Cuba was tendered us to-morrow with the full sanction of England and France that this people would consent to receive and annex her? . . . There was a time when the North would have consented to annex Cuba, but the Nebraska wrong has forever rendered annexation impossible." Said the New York *Times*, May 28th: "There is a growing and profound determination among the masses of the free States that slavery shall not extend itself; that the great majority for freedom must arouse and simply put the minority down—*come what may*."

None of these are radical authorities. Clayton was a Southern Whig. His position and former experience in the State department gave his utterances great weight. The New York *Courier and Enquirer* was conservative Whig. The New York *Times*, while the organ of Senator Seward, was not as radical as the *Tribune* and *Evening Post*.

II.—3

Kansas, but they threw away the pearl of the Antilles, the island which would have been a rock and a fortress for their Southern confederacy.[1]

Although the President and Secretary of State had decided against a course that would surely lead to war, they had by no means relinquished the hope of the acquisition of Cuba. Marcy was undoubtedly as anxious to get the island as was Davis, but he could not be persuaded that the end would justify any means. He was, moreover, of the opinion that money would induce Spain to part with the possession she held so dear. Before he had received the account of the *Black Warrior* negotiations, he had written to Soulé: "Should circumstances present a favorable opportunity, you are directed by the President to renew the attempt to purchase that island."[2] The secretary was so impressed with the importance of this despatch that he sent Colonel Sumner as a special messenger to deliver it. But as Soulé had practically demanded satisfaction at the point of the sword, he could not now treat for a peaceful purchase.[3] The Spanish minister of foreign affairs now notified him that the *Black Warrior* affair had been settled with her owners. The property for which the indemnity of three hundred thousand dollars was asked had been returned; the fine remitted; the *Black Warrior* had been granted the same privileges at Havana as were allowed the steamers of the English Royal Mail company, and the company to which she belonged was thoroughly satisfied with the termination of the affair. The United States government had no longer cause for complaint; the facts showed that no insult had been offered to the American flag. The Spanish minister at the close of his letter did not forbear alluding to the "peremptory demands and acrid language" of Soulé, and the "unfriendly haste" with

---

[1] See a significant article in the Richmond *Enquirer*, cited in New York *Times*, May 19th.
[2] Marcy to Soulé, April 3d.   [3] Soulé to Marcy, May 3d.

which the President of the United States had censured the action of the Captain-General of Cuba.[1]

The reply of Marcy to this communication was emphatic. "The wrong and insult to the nation," he wrote, have not been atoned; the treatment of the *Black Warrior* "was clearly an act of flagrant wrong; ... the manner in which our demand for indemnity has been met by Spain is very unsatisfactory to the President and the attempted justification of the conduct of the Cuban authorities has rather aggravated than mitigated their offence." The offence was nothing less than an attempt to plunder American citizens. Soulé was given the liberty to read this despatch to the Spanish minister of foreign affairs, but, fearing lest he might translate the emphatic words into a threat of aggressive action, his instruction was drawn up with great care. The President, wrote Marcy, "does not therefore expect you will at present take any further steps in relation to the outrage in the case of the *Black Warrior*."[2]

The correspondence between Marcy and Soulé shows the utter lack of sympathy between the two and the difference in their manner of envisaging a question. The Secretary of State had disapproved of Soulé's appointment as minister to Spain.[3] Soulé was born too late; he seemed like a knight-errant of a former century, the very opposite of a diplomat who uses language to conceal his thoughts. An insult to his nation was a grievous thing. To Soulé the course was clear —Spain should apologize or fight. Marcy, on the other hand, was a hard-headed lawyer and a representative man of business of the nineteenth century. Menacing language he thought sometimes proper, and it might be used in a Pickwickian sense. He would, indeed, have repelled the charge that he himself said more than he meant, and the result certainly justifies the language of this despatch, for

---

[1] Calderon to Soulé, May 7th. [2] Marcy to Soulé, June 22d.
[3] See New York *Evening Post*, March 7th, 1855.

in the end it was the means of bringing about a settlement of the difficulty.¹

Had not Soulé been working in a bad cause, we might admire his straightforwardness; we certainly should not fail to sympathize with him in his unpleasant position. Supposing that he would be sustained, he waited with all the patience at his command the six weeks that must necessarily elapse before he could hear from his chief. He feared that Congress would fail to take the resolve which the occasion required. In this case he would not for a moment retain a post from which he must behold the contemptuous insolence that his "discomfiture and that of the administration would be so sure to provoke."² Time went on, but not a word came from the Secretary of State. Soulé suffered "torturing anxiety;" he saw frequent intimations in the American papers that there was a disagreement between him and the cabinet. If there be the least foundation for these reports, he wrote, "pray tender at once my resignation to the President."³ Nine days later he received a despatch from Marcy, but he was "concerned not to find in it the least intimation of the light in which is viewed by the cabinet the course" he had pursued under the guidance of the Secretary of State in the *Black Warrior* affair. His private letters gave him no encouragement, and his position was becoming "so painful and delicate" that he could not think of holding it much longer. He reported that the belief was prevalent at Madrid that he had exceeded his instructions and that everything which he had done would be disavowed. Congress had certainly hurt our reputation for character by not responding promptly to the President's message of March 15th.⁴ Soulé was obviously disappointed at the

---

¹ Calderon did not see the despatch of June 22d. It was not shown to the minister of foreign affairs until Dec. 8th, and at that time a new ministry was in power.

² Soulé to Marcy, May 24th.   ³ Soulé to Marcy, June 10th.
⁴ Soulé to Marcy, June 19th.

President's proclamation against the filibusters. He saw his great desire receding from his grasp.¹ At last, fifty days after he had expected to receive a warm approbation of his course, there came cold and measured words which seemed wrung from the Secretary of State. The President, he wrote, is "satisfied with the spirited manner in which you have performed the duties of your mission," but he thinks that "weight and perhaps efficiency" will be given to the negotiation " if he should associate with you two other of our most distinguished citizens." ²

Before this despatch and the one which Soulé was instructed to read to Calderon reached him, a revolution had taken place in Spain which, starting with high anticipations of reform and hopes for liberty, really effected nothing but a change of ministry. Several engagements with the insurgents occurred. Queen Isabella ran the risk of capture by the rebels; the palace of the queen dowager was sacked and her life threatened. The chivalrous nature of Soulé here showed itself. He alone of the diplomatic body offered the queen dowager the shelter of his house and the protection of his flag.³ The change of ministry greatly improved Soulé's position, and he was able to renew the negotiations.

The news of the Spanish revolution was of considerable interest to the administration. It strengthened the hopes of Marcy that a purchase of Cuba might be effected, and it revived the desire for provisional legislation which had in March been suggested by the President. As Congress was on the point of adjourning, the Washington *Union* begged that a few millions of money should be placed at the disposal of the executive during the recess to be used in the Spanish-Cuban business.⁴ The President in a special mes-

---

¹ Soulé to Marcy, June 24th.
² Marcy to Soulé, June 24th.
³ See Memories of Many Men, Field, p. 91.
⁴ Washington *Union*, July 30th, cited by New York *Times*.

sage to the Senate hinted strongly in the same direction, but the Senate committee of foreign affairs reported that as the interval between adjournment and the next session of Congress would be short, they would not recommend any provisional measures.[1]

On the 16th of August Marcy wrote that the sending of an extraordinary commission to Spain had been abandoned, but it was suggested to Soulé that much advantage might accrue from " a full and free interchange of views " between himself, Buchanan, and Mason in regard to the acquisition of Cuba.[2] Soulé " felt much relieved by the tender of so grateful an association," and set out as soon as possible for Paris.[3] Marcy desired that the meeting should be quiet and partake of an informal character, but Soulé was fond of theatrical display and was not unwilling that the conference should attract attention by its solemn and imposing character. Ostend was selected as the place of meeting. The ministers remained there three days, then retired to Aix-la-Chapelle, where they recorded the result of their deliberations. The conference attracted attention in Europe, notwithstanding that all eyes were fixed on the siege of Sebastopol. It also gave rise to comment in the United States, although at the time the public mind was engaged by the fall elections. The paper which Buchanan, Mason, and Soulé signed is known as the Ostend manifesto. It was not published until more than four months after its transmission to the Secretary of State, and was then brought to the light by a call from the House of Representatives.

It began by stating that there had " been a full and unreserved interchange of views and sentiments," and that the committee had arrived at a cordial agreement. They were fully convinced that an earnest effort should be made im-

---

[1] This report was made Aug. 3d.   [2] Marcy to Soulé, Aug. 16th.
[3] See Soulé to Marcy, Oct. 15th.

mediately for the purchase of Cuba, and advised offering for it one hundred and twenty million dollars.[1] An argument followed to show that Cuba was necessary to the United States and that it was likewise for the manifest advantage of Spain to part with it for the price we were willing to pay. Then the three diplomats proceeded: "But if Spain, dead to the voice of her own interest, and actuated by stubborn pride and a false sense of honor, should refuse to sell Cuba to the United States, then the question will arise, what ought to be the course of the American government under such circumstances?" The answer is easy. Since "the Union can never enjoy repose nor possess reliable security, as long as Cuba is not embraced within its boundaries;" and as "self-preservation is the first law of nature with States as well as with individuals," we must apply this "great law" to the acquisition of Cuba. It is true this principle was abused in the partition of Poland, but the present is "not a parallel case;" and if we "preserve our own conscious rectitude and our own self-respect . . . we can afford to disregard the censures of the world." Therefore: "After we shall have offered Spain a price for Cuba far beyond its present value, and this shall have been refused, it will then be time to consider the question, does Cuba in the possession of Spain seriously endanger our internal peace and the existence of our cherished Union? Should this question be answered in the affirmative [it had already been so answered in the manifesto], then, by every law, human and divine, we shall be justified in wresting it from Spain if we possess the power; and this upon the very same principle that would justify an individual in tearing down the burning house of his neighbor if there were no other means of preventing the flames from destroying his own home. . . . We should be recreant to our duty, be unworthy of our gallant forefathers,

---

[1] In the publication the price was left blank, but the argument in the subsequent part of the manifesto shows plainly enough that one hundred and twenty million dollars was the sum which the diplomats had in mind.

and commit base treason against our posterity, should we permit Cuba to be Africanized and become a second St. Domingo, with all its attendant horrors to the white race, and suffer the flames to extend to our own neighboring shores, seriously to endanger or actually to consume the fair fabric of our Union. We fear that the course and current of events are rapidly tending towards such a catastrophe." To these sentiments were subscribed the names of James Buchanan, J. Y. Mason, and Pierre Soulé.

It will be plainly apparent to the reader that this manifesto expressed the sincere opinion of Soulé. That Mason, who belonged to a Virginian junto which was anxious for Cuba, should have signed it may not occasion surprise; but it remains something of a mystery why the cautious and experienced Buchanan should have agreed to a manifesto which contained notions abhorrent to justice and at war with the opinion of the civilized world. Field, who was in a position to learn the inside history of the transaction, understood that the manifesto was originally written by Soulé and then revised by Buchanan. Yet the measures recommended were so ultra that neither Buchanan nor Mason would have signed it had not Soulé cajoled them by his enthusiastic advocacy.[1] Mason was afterwards conscious that he had been overborne, for he took occasion to warn Field against the fascinations of the minister to Spain, whom he described "as a perfect bird-charmer."[2] We may presume that Soulé drew the veil and showed Buchanan the vision of the White House and persuaded him that with the next Democratic convention Cuba would be a more powerful argument than Nebraska. When we take into account the characteristics of the three men we can hardly resist the conclusion that Soulé, as he afterwards intimated, twisted his colleagues round his finger.[3]

Soulé did not propose to have any misunderstanding about the matter. He sent with the manifesto an explana-

---

[1] Memories of Many Men, p. 99. [2] Ibid., p. 76. [3] Ibid., p. 99.

tory despatch to Marcy in which he expressed his own idea without the least circumlocution. He affirmed that we must get Cuba; we must settle that matter now; never should we have a fairer opportunity. "Present indications," he wrote, "would seem to encourage the hope that we may come to that solution peaceably. But if it were otherwise," —if we must go to war for it—when could there be a better time for war than now, while the great powers of Europe "are engaged in that stupendous struggle. . . . Neither England nor France," he added, "would be likely to interfere with us."[1]

The reply of Marcy to the manifesto was chilling. He first affected to understand that the three ministers did not "recommend to the President to offer to Spain the alternative of cession or seizure" of Cuba;[2] but he proceeded to reason earnestly against such a proposition, and took direct issue with the self-preservation argument. The instructions to the minister at Madrid were completely at variance with the policy laid down in the manifesto. If Spain were disposed to entertain an offer for Cuba, the offer might be made; but there should be no attempt "to push on a negotiation" if the men in power were averse to it.[3] Field, who was acting secretary of legation at Paris, carried this despatch from Paris to Madrid and delivered it into the hands of Soulé. Soulé, elated at winning Buchanan and Mason to his views, had again indulged in glittering hopes, but these were now dashed by the measured words of the Secretary of State. After reading and pondering the despatch, he said: "My amazement is without limit. I am stunned. Of one thing only I am certain, and that is, that it is the irre-

---

[1] Soulé to Marcy, London, Oct. 20th. The manifesto is dated Aix-la-Chapelle, Oct. 18th.

[2] It has been urged that Buchanan and Mason did not understand the conclusions of the manifesto as Soulé and every one else did. See Life of Buchanan, Curtis, vol. ii. p. 136. Field, pp. 75, 100. Stripped of unnecessary verbiage, it does not seem as if the intent could have been made plainer. [3] Marcy to Soulé, Nov. 13th.

sponsible work of Mr. Marcy. The President can neither have inspired nor sanctioned it."[1]

Reflection soon convinced Soulé that personal dignity required him to throw up the Spanish mission. He and Marcy could not work together. After his resignation he gleefully reported a circumstance which demonstrated that Marcy's plan of peaceful purchase was impracticable. The minister of foreign affairs had declared in the Cortes that, in the opinion of the government, "to part with Cuba would be to part with national honor." This statement was received with unanimous and entire approbation by the representatives, and in the galleries with "frantic applause."[2] Yet Soulé did not for a moment give up the idea of the acquisition of Cuba, but under the present Secretary of State he felt that he should linger at Madrid "in languid impotence."[3] He might, however, be able to do something for the cause at Washington. The resignation of Soulé ends this inglorious chapter of our diplomatic history.[4]

The reception of the Ostend manifesto is a mark of the difference between the notions of international justice which to-day prevail and those of the decade of 1850–60.[5] Should

---

[1] Field, p. 79.   [2] Soulé to Marcy, Dec. 23d.
[3] Soulé to Marcy, Dec. 17th.
[4] Soon after Soulé's resignation, the differences between the two governments in regard to the *Black Warrior* affair were arranged in conformity to the ideas of the Secretary of State as declared in his despatch of June 22d. The pacific language of Perry, whom Soulé left in charge of affairs, aided in effecting a settlement. See statement of the Spanish minister of foreign affairs in the Cortes, May 3d, 1855. Also letter of H. J. Perry to the President, dated Madrid, April 27th, 1855, published in *National Intelligencer*, May 22d, 1855.
[5] In 1889 Secretary Blaine was supposed to be favorable to a Jingo policy. Aug. 29th, 1890, he said in a public speech: "We are not seeking annexation of territory. Certainly we do not desire it unless it should come by the volition of a people who might ask the priceless boon of a place under the flag of the Union. I feel sure that for a long time to come the people of the United States will be wisely content with our present area, and not launch upon any scheme of annexation."

any three ministers issue a similar document now, public opinion would force their recall upon any administration. The anti-slavery sentiment, however, was then well up to our present ideas. One journal said the manifesto was "weak in its reasonings and atrocious in its recommendations;"[1] another called it the "manifesto of the brigands," whose declaration meant: "If Spain will not sell us Cuba, we must steal it in order to preserve our national existence."[2] Naturally enough, the relation which the scheme bore to the maintenance of slavery affected the people who had bitterly opposed the Kansas-Nebraska bill. It seemed to them a recommendation of an offer of one hundred and twenty million dollars to Spain to give up the emancipation of slaves in Cuba and to accomplish likewise the addition of two or three slave States to the Union.[3] But if a peaceful purchase could not be effected, treasure must be wasted and lives sacrificed in order that slavery might extend its power.

European opinion of this manifesto, except that of the active revolutionists, was well expressed in a carefully written article in the London *Times*, which began: "The diplomacy of the United States is certainly a very singular profession." It was singular because the diplomats did not hatch their mischief in secret. A report of their plot was printed by order of Congress. In this Ostend manifesto a policy was avowed which, if declared by one of the great European powers, would set the whole continent in "a blaze;" or, if seriously entertained by the United States government, it would justify a declaration of war. The argument was exactly the same as that used by Russia in the last century to vindicate her interference in Poland.[4]

---

[1] New York *Evening Post*, March 6th, 1855. The document was published in the newspapers on that day.

[2] New York *Tribune*, March 8th, 1855.

[3] If Cuba had been acquired, no doubt can exist that it would have been admitted into the Union as one, two, or three slave States.

[4] London *Times*, March 24th, 1855. This journal generally leaned to the Democratic party.

It is perhaps unjust to attach to the administration of Pierce the discredit of the Ostend manifesto, for the policy therein set forth was disavowed by the Secretary of State in the name of the President. Yet as the Democratic party indirectly approved it by the nomination for President of the man who was first to sign it, it settled down in the popular mind as one of the measures of the Pierce administration. Any good in the Democratic conduct of the government from 1853 to 1857 has been almost wholly obliterated by the Kansas-Nebraska bill and the Ostend manifesto. The domestic policy was characterized by an utter disregard of plighted faith; the avowed foreign policy was marked by the lack of justice as understood by all civilized nations of the world.

CHAPTER VII

AFTER the passage of the Kansas-Nebraska act, it would seem as if the course of the opposition were plain. In the newspapers and political literature of the time, suggestions are frequent of an obvious and reasonable course to be pursued. The senators and representatives at Washington proposed no plan. They did, indeed, issue an address which was well characterized by a powerful advocate of anti-slavery at Washington. "It is unexceptionable," he wrote, "but hath not the trumpet tone."[1] That the different elements of opposition should be fused into one complete whole seemed political wisdom. That course involved the formation of a new party and was urged warmly and persistently by many newspapers, but by none with such telling influence as by the New York *Tribune*. It had likewise the countenance of Chase, Sumner, and Wade. There were three elements that must be united—the Whigs, the Free-soilers, who were of both Democratic and Whig antecedents, and the anti-Nebraska Democrats. The Whigs were the most numerous body and as those at the North, to a man, had opposed the

---

[1] G. Bailey, editor of the *National Era*, to J. S. Pike, June 6th, 1854. Pike's First Blows of the Civil War. p. 247. The address is published in the New York *Times* of June 22d. Wilson speaks of a meeting of thirty members of the House directly after the passage of the bill, which was distinct from the meeting which adopted the address. It does not appear that any particular action was taken, but it was generally conceded that a new party organization was necessary, and that an appropriate name for it would be Republican. Rise and Fall of the Slave Power, vol. ii. p. 411.

repeal of the Missouri Compromise, they thought, with some quality of reason, that the fight might well be made under their banner and with their name. For the organization of a party was not the work of a day; the machinery was complex and costly, and a new national party could not be started without pains and sacrifice.[1] Why then, it was asked, go to all this trouble, when a complete organization is at hand ready for use? This view of the situation was ably argued by the New York *Times* and was supported by Senator Seward. As the New York senator had a position of influence superior to any one who had opposed the Kansas-Nebraska bill, strenuous efforts were made to get his adhesion to a new party movement, but they were without avail. "Seward hangs fire," wrote Dr. Bailey. He agrees with Thurlow Weed; but "God help us if, as a preliminary to a union of the North, we have all to admit that the Whig party is the party of freedom!"[2] "We are not yet ready for a great national convention at Buffalo or elsewhere," wrote Seward to Theodore Parker; "it would bring together only the old veterans. The States are the places for activity, just now."[3] Undoubtedly Seward, Weed, and Raymond[4] sincerely believed that the end desired could be better accomplished if the Whig organization were kept intact. In any event their position and influence were sure. But the lesser lights of the party were of the opinion that to get and hold the national, State, and municipal offices was a function as important for a party as to spread abroad a principle; and if the Whig name and organization were maintained, length of service under the banner would have to be regarded in awarding the spoils.

---

[1] The difficulty in the way of forming a new party in the United States is well understood and explained by Prof. Bryce, American Commonwealth, vol. ii. p. 19.
[2] Bailey to J. S. Pike, May 30th. First Blows of the Civil War, p. 237.
[3] Life of Seward, vol. ii. p. 232.
[4] Raymond was editor of the New York *Times*.

Yet many Whigs who were not devoted to machine politics, and were therefore able to lay aside all personal and extraneous considerations, saw clearly that a new party must be formed under a new name, and that all the men who thus joined together must stand at the start on the same footing. They differed, however, in regard to the statement of their bond of union. Some wished to go to the country with simply *Repeal of the Kansas-Nebraska act* inscribed on their banner. As a new House of Representatives was to be elected in the fall, the aim should be to retire those members who had voted for the bill and to return those who had opposed it. Others wished to go further in the declaration of principles, and plant themselves squarely on the platform of congressional prohibition of slavery in all of the territories. Still others preferred the resolve that not another slave State should be admitted into the Union. Many suggestions, too, were made that broadened the issue. Yet, after all, the differences were only of detail, and the time seemed ripe for the formation of a political party whose cardinal principle might be summed up as opposition to the extension of slavery. The liberal Whigs felt that they could not ask the Free-soilers of Democratic antecedents and the anti-Nebraska Democrats to become Whigs. To the older partisans the name was identified with the United States bank. By all Democrats, Whig principles were understood to comprise a protective tariff and large internal improvements; to enroll themselves under that banner was to endorse principles against which they had always contended.

The first and most effective action to form a new party was taken in the West, where the political machines had not been so highly developed as in the older section of country, and where consequently a people's movement could proceed with greater spontaneity. While the Kansas-Nebraska bill was pending, a meeting of citizens of all parties was held at Ripon, Wisconsin. This differed from other meetings held throughout the North, in that the organization of a new party on the slavery issue was recommended, and the name suggested for it was "Republican."[1] Five weeks after the repeal of the Missouri Compromise had been enacted, authoritative action was taken by a body representing a wider constituency. In response to a call, signed by several thousand leading citizens of Michigan, for a State mass-meeting of all opposed to slavery extension, a large body of earnest, intelligent, and moral men came together at Jackson, Mich., on the 6th day of July. The largest hall was not sufficient to accommodate the people, and, the day being bright, the convention was held in a stately oak grove in the outskirts of the village. Enthusiasm was unbounded. The reason for a new departure was clearly shown by able men in vigorous speeches. But, in truth, the voters of Michigan fully comprehended the situation. Intelligence of a high order characterized the population of this State. Already had the educational system been established which has grown into one surpassed by none in the world, and which has become a fruitful model.[2] No people better adapted to set a-going a political movement ever gathered together than those assembled this day "under the oaks" at Jackson. The declaration of principles adopted was long, but all the resolutions, except two which referred to State affairs, were devoted to the slavery question.

It was stated that the freemen of Michigan had met in convention, " to consider upon the measures which duty demands of us, as citizens of a free State, to take in reference to the late acts of Congress on the subject of slavery, and its anticipated further extension." Slavery was declared "a great moral, social, and political evil;" the repeal of the Kansas-Nebraska act and the Fugitive Slave law was demanded; and the abolition of slavery in the District of Columbia was asked for. It was also "Resolved, that, postponing and suspending all differences with regard to political economy or administrative policy . . . we will act cordially and faith-

---

[1] Rise and Fall of the Slave Power, Henry Wilson, vol. ii. p. 410.
[2] Cooley's Michigan, p. 328.

fully in unison" to oppose the extension of slavery, and "we will co-operate and be known as 'Republicans' until the contest be terminated." It was further recommended that a general convention should be called of the free States, and of such slave-holding States as wished to be represented, "with a view to the adoption of other more extended and effectual measures in resistance to the encroachments of slavery."¹ Before the convention adjourned a full State ticket was nominated. Three of the candidates were Free-soilers, five were Whigs, and two anti-Nebraska Democrats who had voted for Pierce in 1852. The number of voters in the State opposed to the Kansas-Nebraska act was supposed to be forty thousand, of whom it was roughly estimated twenty-five thousand were Whigs, ten thousand Free-soilers, and five thousand anti-Nebraska Democrats.² On the 13th of July anti-Nebraska State conventions were held in Wisconsin, Vermont, Ohio, and Indiana. The day was chosen because it was the anniversary of the enactment of the ordinance of 1787. Resolutions similar in tenor to those of Michigan were adopted, and in Wisconsin and Vermont the name "Republican" was assumed.³

In 1854, the moral feeling of the community was stirred to its very depths. While the excitement produced by the Kansas-Nebraska legislation had let loose and intensified the agitation of the public mind, yet its whole force was by no means directed to the slavery question. The temperance question began to be a weighty influence in politics. Indeed, from the passage, three years earlier, of the Maine

---

¹ The resolutions may be found in full in Life of Z. Chandler, published by the Detroit *Post and Tribune*, p. 108. This book is my authority for the description of the convention; see also Rise and Fall of the Slave Power, vol. ii. p. 412.

² New York *Tribune*, June 21st. In November the Republican candidate for governor polled 43,652 votes.

³ See Life of Chandler, p. 113; Rise and Fall of the Slave Power, vol. ii. p. 412; Life of Chase, Schuckers, p. 165; Political Recollections, Julian, p. 144; Cleveland *Herald*.

II.—4

liquor law in the State which gave legislation of this kind its name, it had been generally discussed in New England. Prohibitory laws had been enacted in Massachusetts, Vermont, Rhode Island, Connecticut, and also in Michigan. But now the question began to exercise a powerful sway throughout the North. It was necessarily made an issue in New York, for Governor Seymour had vetoed a prohibitory law;[1] and as a governor and legislature were to be elected in the fall, the temperance men were alive and busy, determined that their doctrine should enter prominently into the canvass. All the influential advocates of a Maine law were anti-slavery men, and it is not apparent that the cause of freedom lost by union with the cause of prohibition. The pleaders for the moral law showed discretion as well as zeal. The journal which, more than all others, spoke for the religious community maintained emphatically that slavery was the first and greatest question at issue in the election.[2]

A far more important element politically was the Know-nothing movement. The Know-nothings made their power felt at the municipal elections in the spring and early summer. Their most notable success was achieved in Philadelphia, when the candidate they supported for mayor was elected by a large majority. These results opened the eyes of the politicians and of the outside public to the fact that a new force must be taken into account.

The distrust of Roman Catholicism is a string that can be artfully played upon in an Anglo-Saxon community. This feeling had been recently increased by the public mission of a papal nuncio, who came to this country to adjust a difficulty in regard to church property in the city of Buffalo. There had arisen a controversy on the matter between the bishop and a congregation, and the congregation was backed by a law of New York State. The nuncio had been received with kindness by the President, but his visit had

---

[1] March 31st.   [2] New York *Independent*, Nov. 2d.

excited tumults in Cincinnati, Baltimore, and New York.¹ Moreover, the efforts of Bishop Hughes and the Catholic clergy to exclude the Bible from the public schools struck a chord which had not ceased to vibrate.² The ignorant foreign vote had begun to have an important influence on elections, and the result in large cities was anything but pleasing to the lovers of honest and efficient government. It was averred that drunken aliens frequently had charge of the polls; that the intrigue and rowdyism which characterized recent campaigns were the work of foreigners; that the network of Jesuitism had been cunningly spread; that such was the deep corruption among politicians that availibility in a presidential candidate had come to mean the man who could secure the foreign vote. Votes were openly bought and sold, and "suckers" and "strikers" controlled the primary elections of both parties. These were the abuses. For their remedy it was argued that a new party must be formed. There were enough of good and pure men among the Democrats and Whigs to make up an organization which should be patriotic and Christian in character.³ Then war must be made against French infidelity, German scepticism and socialism, and the papacy. Of the three evils the papacy was considered the most dangerous.⁴

The principles of this new party were naturally evolved out of the ills which were deplored. An order which Washington was supposed to have given was taken as the keynote. "Put none but Americans on guard to-night," he had said when dangers and difficulties thickened around him; and the shade of the Father of his country seemed to say across the ages, "Americans should rule America." This was the fundamental doctrine of the Know-nothing party. The immediate and practical aim in view was that foreigners

---

¹ Von Holst, vol. v. p. 99; Sons of the Sires, p. 93.
² Sons of the Sires, p. 26; Sam, or the History of a Mystery, p. 524.
³ Sons of the Sires, pp. 16, 17, 46, and 87.
⁴ Ibid., pp. 50 and 52.

and Catholics should be excluded from all national, State, county, and municipal offices; that strenuous efforts should be made to change the naturalization laws, so that the immigrant could not become a citizen until after a residence of twenty-one years in this country.[1]

No one can deny that ignorant foreign suffrage had grown to be an evil of immense proportions. Had the remedies sought by the Know-nothings been just and practicable and their methods above suspicion, the movement, though ill-timed, might be justified at the bar of history. But when the historian writes that a part of their indictment was true, and that the organization attracted hosts of intelligent and good men, he has said everything creditable that can be said of the Know-nothing party. The crusade against the Catholic Church was contrary to the spirit of the Constitution, and was as unnecessary as it was unwise. The statistics showed plainly that the Catholics were not sufficiently numerous to justify alarm.[2] He who studied the spirit of the times could see this as clearly as he who compared the figures. The Catholic hierarchy can only be dangerous when human reason is repressed, and no one has ever asserted that the last half of the nineteenth century is

---

[1] All Know-nothings were agreed that the time of residence should be extended. The twenty-one years was a favorite period, as the American-born could not vote until they were twenty-one. Some, however, would be satisfied with a fifteen-year limit. Sons of the Sires, p. 71.

[2] See the figures as given in a History of the Political Campaign of 1855 by James P. Hambleton, p. 9, where Henry A. Wise states that—

The Baptists	provide accommodations for	3,247,029
" Methodists	" " "	4,343,579
" Presbyterians	" " "	2,079,690
" Congregationalists	" " "	801,835
Aggregate of four Protestant sects		10,472,133
The Catholics provide accommodations for		667,823
Majority of only four Protestant sects		9,804,310
Add the Episcopalians for		643,598
Majority of only five Protestant sects		10,447,908

an age of faith. The purposed exclusion of foreigners from office was illogical and unjust. The proposal to change essentially or repeal the naturalization laws was impracticable. Better means than these could be devised to correct the abuses of naturalization and fraudulent voting.[1]

The methods of the Know-nothings were more objectionable than their aims. The party was a vast secret society with ramifications in every State. Secret lodges were instituted everywhere, with passwords and degrees, grips and signs. The initiation was solemn. The candidate who presented himself for admission to the first degree must, with his right hand upon the Holy Bible and the cross, take a solemn oath of secrecy. Then, if he were twenty-one, if he believed in God, if he had been born in the United States, if neither he himself, nor his parents, nor his wife were Roman Catholics, and he had been reared under Protestant influence, he was considered a proper applicant. He was conducted from the ante-room to an inner chamber, where, in his official chair on the raised platform, the worthy president sate. There, with the right hand upon the Holy Bible and cross, and the left hand raised towards heaven, the candidate again took the solemn oath of secrecy, and further swore not to vote for any man unless he were a Protestant, an American-born citizen, and in favor of Americans ruling America. Then the term and degree passwords were given to the newly admitted member. The travelling password and explanation were communicated, and the sign of recognition and grip were explained. When he challenged a brother, he must ask, "What time?" The response would be, "Time for work." Then he should say, "Are you?" The answer would come, "We are." Then the two were in a position to engage in conversation in the interests of the order.

The new member was further told that notice of mass-

---

[1] See a very able argument, undoubtedly by Greeley, in the New York *Tribune*, Aug. 16th.

meetings was given by means of a triangular piece of white paper. If he should wish to know the object of the gathering, he must ask an undoubted brother, "Have you seen Sam to-day?" and the information would be imparted. But if the notice were on red paper, danger was indicated, and the member must come prepared to meet it.

The president then addressed the men who had just joined the lodge, dilating upon the perils which threatened the country from the foreign-born and the Romanists. "A sense of danger has struck the great heart of the nation," he said. "In every city, town, and hamlet, the danger has been seen and the alarm sounded. And hence true men have devised this order as a means . . . of advancing America and the American interest on the one side, and on the other of checking the stride of the foreigner or alien, of thwarting the machinations and subverting the deadly plans of the Jesuit and the Papist."

After a sufficient probation the member might be admitted to the second degree, where more oaths were taken and another password and countersign were given. But the great mystery was the name of the organization, which the president alone was entitled to communicate. At the proper time he solemnly declared: "Brothers,—You are members in full fellowship of The Supreme Order of the Star-spangled Banner."[1]

For a time the secrets were well kept, but with a membership so large, matters connected with the organization were sure to leak out, and as the theme was susceptible of humorous treatment, people made merry over the supposed revelations. A Philadelphia journal thus exposed the manner of entrance to the local lodge: You must rap at the outer door several times in quick succession, and when the sentinel peeps through the wicket, inquire, "What meets here to-night?" He will answer, "I don't know." You

---

[1] My authority for this description is A History of the Political Campaign in Virginia in 1855, J. P. Hambleton, p. 46.

must then reply, "I am one," and he will open the door. At the second door four raps and the password, "Thirteen,"[1] will obtain admission. When out in the world, when a brother gives you the grip, you must ask, "Where did you get that?" He will answer, "I don't know." You must reply, "I don't know either," and you may then enter into full fellowship with a member of the mysterious order.[2]

When the curious inquired of the members of this party what were their principles and what their object, the answer invariably was, "I know nothing;" and thus the popular name was given in derision. Yet this was not resented. The appellation expressed mystery, and mystery was aimed at. The real political and official name, however, was The American Party. A prevalent notion was that the Know-nothings always met at midnight, that they carried dark-lanterns, that they pledged themselves in the dark by the most terrible oaths,[3] and that their proceedings were inscrutable.

The number who joined these secret lodges was very large. They were made up of men who were incensed and alarmed at the power of foreign-born citizens in the elections; of those "whose daily horror and nightly spectre was the pope;"[4] and of others for whom the secret ceremonies and mysterious methods were an attraction.[5] But the most pregnant reason for the transient success of the order arose from the fact that, although the old parties at the North were rent into fragments, there was no ready-made organization to take their place. Men were disgusted and dissatisfied with their political affiliations, and yearned to enlist under a banner that should display positive and sincere aims. If the anti-Nebraska members of Congress

---

[1] Referring to the thirteen original States.
[2] Philadelphia *Register*, cited in New York *Tribune*, April 5th.
[3] See speech of Douglas in the Senate, Feb. 23d, 1855.
[4] New York *Tribune*, Nov. 28th.
[5] Life of Bowles, p. 123.

had comprehended the situation, as did the freemen of Michigan, a national Republican party would at once have been formed and the Know-nothings would have lost a large element of strength. The position of the American party on slavery was not clear. Julian, of Indiana, charged that the organization was the result of a deeply laid scheme of the slavery propaganda, whose purpose was to precipitate a new issue upon the North and distract the public mind from the question of pith and moment.[1] Douglas declared that it was simply abolitionism under a new guise.[2] Henry A. Wise, of Virginia, emphatically maintained that the object of the Know-nothing order was the destruction of slavery.[3] In general, it may be said that although at the North many anti-slavery men were in the organization, those who had the control wished to put forward their distinctive principles and keep the slavery question in abeyance. It seemed, therefore, to the Republicans that the Know-nothings, not being for them, were against them. At the South the Americans were chiefly represented by those opposed to the formation of a party on the one idea of slavery extension. Thus they incurred the displeasure of the Southerners who had made up their minds that the great issue must be settled before another could be discussed.

The Know-nothing movement, born of political unrest, augmented the ferment in the country. This was a year of excitement and lawlessness. Riots were frequent. Occasionally a band of women would make a raid on a bar-room, break the glasses, stave the whiskey casks, and pour the liquor into the streets.[4] Garrison, infatuated by his own

---

[1] Political Recollections, Julian, p. 141.
[2] Speech at Philadelphia, July 4th, 1854, Life of Douglas, Sheahan, p. 265.
[3] Speech at Alexandria, Va., Feb. 3d, 1855, History of the Political Campaign in Virginia in 1855, Hambleton, p. 93.
[4] *United States Review*, Aug., 1854, p. 103. The article entitled "Abolition and Sectarian Mobs" is a faithful exposition of the way in which the ferment of the community was regarded by old-line Democrats and rigid Conservatives.

methods and blind to the trend of events, burned the Constitution of the United States at an open-air celebration of the abolitionists in Framingham, Mass. This action drew forth a few hisses and wrathful exclamations, but these were overborne by "a tremendous shout of 'Amen.'"[1] Most of the disturbances, however, grew out of the Know-nothing crusade. A mob forced their way into the shed near the Washington monument, and broke to pieces a beautiful block of marble which came from the Temple of Concord at Rome, and had been sent by the pope as his tribute to the memory of Washington.[2] A street preacher, who styled himself the "Angel Gabriel," excited a crowd at Chelsea, Mass., to deeds of violence. They smashed the windows of the Catholic church, tore the cross from the gable, and shivered it to atoms.[3] The firemen and military were called out to aid the police in preserving order.

On one Sunday, in the City Hall Park of New York, a fight occurred between the advocates of a street preacher and those who were determined he should not speak. The latter got the worse of it, and the self-styled "missionary of the everlasting gospel," protected by a band of Know-nothings, was able to deliver his sermon.[4] On the following Sunday the street preacher held forth in Brooklyn. When his discourse was finished, he was escorted to the ferry by about five thousand Know-nothings, who, on the way, were set upon by an equally large number of Irish Catholics. An angry fight ensued, in which volleys of stones were thrown from one side and bullets fired from the other. The police were unable to suppress the riot, and the mayor sent a regiment of military to their aid.[5] During the week the excitement was intense, and on the next Sunday everything seemed ready for a violent explosion in Brook-

---

[1] Life of Garrison, vol. iii. p. 412. [2] American Almanac, 1855, p. 47.
[3] Boston *Journal*, cited by the New York *Tribune*, May 9th.
[4] New York *Times*; New York *Tribune*, May 29th.
[5] New York *Times*, June 5th.

lyn. But the authorities were prepared. The whole of the regular police force was on duty, assisted by a large number of special police and deputy sheriffs. Three regiments of military guarded the streets. The "Angel Gabriel" delivered a fierce invective against the "infernal Jesuit system" and "accursed popery." The precautions taken by the mayor to preserve the peace were so effective that only a slight outbreak took place. A detachment of the Knownothing procession was attacked by a gang of Irishmen; but the police fired at the mob, and they quickly dispersed.[1] Similar riots occurred in other cities of the country.

The public mind was so engrossed with political and moral questions that, although cholera was epidemic at the North this summer, it awakened little anxiety and caused no panic.[2]

It is now time to consider the verdict of the Northern people on the Kansas-Nebraska act as evidenced in the elections. The first election after its enactment was in Iowa.[3] Iowa had been a steadfast Democratic State. It had voted for two presidential candidates, Cass and Pierce. In the present Congress it had two Democratic senators, one Democratic and one Whig representative. Both of the senators and the Democratic representative voted for the Kansas-Nebraska bill; the Whig representative did not vote.

A governor was to be elected this year, and the Whigs

---

[1] New York *Times*, June 12th.

[2] Except perhaps in Columbia, Pa., a village of 4340 inhabitants, where the death-rate was very large. New York *Tribune*, Sept. 11th to 15th. The American Almanac gives the deaths from cholera from June 1st to Nov. 5th (although practically all of them were in June, July, and August) as follows: New York, 2425; Philadelphia, 575; Boston, 255; Pittsburgh, 600. There were deaths from cholera in nearly every Northern city. The yellow fever prevailed in Savannah and New Orleans, but with nothing like the virulence of the preceding year.

[3] It will be remembered that the elections in New Hampshire and Connecticut, whose tendency was plainly anti-Nebraska, took place while the bill was pending; see vol. i. pp. 482, 494.

had nominated James W. Grimes; a Free-soil convention had endorsed the nomination. Grimes issued a spirited manifesto, in which he declared that the extension of slavery was now the most important public question, and that Iowa, the only free child of the Missouri Compromise, should pronounce against its repeal. He made a thorough and vigorous canvass of the State, denouncing everywhere the "Nebraska infamy." The temperance issue entered slightly into the discussion, and the voters favorable to prohibition supported Grimes. The Know-nothing wave had not reached Iowa. Grimes was elected by two thousand four hundred and eighty-six majority. It was the first time the Democrats had ever been defeated in a State election, and they did not carry Iowa again for thirty-five years. Another result was the choice of a legislature which sent Harlan, an avowed Republican, to the United States Senate.[1] No doubt could exist that the meaning of this election was the condemnation of the Kansas-Nebraska bill. "You have the credit," wrote Senator Chase to Grimes, "of fighting the best battle for freedom yet fought;"[2] and two years later, when the Republican party had become a strong organization, Chase wrote the Iowa governor: "Your election was the morning star. The sun has risen now."[3]

In September, elections were held in Maine and Vermont. In Maine there were four State tickets, the Republican, the Whig, the Democratic, and that popularly termed the rum ticket. The Republican candidate for governor had a handsome plurality. Although there was no choice by the people, the Republicans had the legislature, which insured them the governor. In Vermont the canvass of the anti-Nebraska men was carried on under the name of Fusion; the result was a large majority in their favor. Vermont sent an unbroken anti-Nebraska delegation to the House of Repre-

---

[1] Life of James W. Grimes, Salter, pp. 39, 52, 63.
[2] Ibid., p. 54, Oct. 31st, 1854.
[3] Ibid., p. 58, Aug. 23d, 1856; see New York *Tribune*, Aug. 17th, 1854.

sentatives, and Maine, which had hitherto been a reliable Democratic State, only elected one Democratic congressman. The verdict of both of these States was unmistakably adverse to the Nebraska legislation. In neither of them did the temperance question have an important influence, for it had been settled. In Maine the voters of the rum ticket were a corporal's guard. Nor were the Know-nothings an appreciable element in the result.[1]

In October elections took place in Pennsylvania, Ohio, and Indiana. In Pennsylvania, the Whigs retained their organization, and the Free-soil Democrats ratified that ticket. They made opposition to the Kansas-Nebraska act the main question and elected their governor, but this was due to the assistance of the Know-nothings. The Know-nothings elected enough members to the legislature to hold the balance of power between the two parties; and the temperance question entered into the canvass, as a popular vote was taken on a prohibitory law. Yet the best test of sentiment in regard to the Missouri Compromise legislation was shown in the congressional elections. The present delegation consisted of sixteen Democrats and nine Whigs; that chosen this fall was made up of four Nebraska and five anti-Nebraska Democrats, fifteen anti-Nebraska Whigs, and one American.[2]

The anti-Nebraska People's party carried Ohio by seventy-five thousand majority and elected every representative to Congress. The anti-Nebraska party were successful in Indiana by thirteen thousand majority, and chose all the congressmen but two. In both of these States the Know-nothings co-operated with the anti-Nebraska organization. The temperance question entered into the discussion, and inured to the advantage of the successful party.[3] Yet both

---

[1] See Fessenden's remarks in the Senate, Feb. 23d, 1855.
[2] New York *Tribune*, Oct. 21st; New York *Herald*, Oct. 13th. See also New York *Times* and Tribune Almanac.
[3] New York *Tribune;* New York *Times;* Life of Chase, Schuckers, p. 165; Political Recollections, Julian, p. 144.

the temperance and Know-nothing ideas were overbalanced by the anti-slavery feeling. The verdict on that was unmistakable.[1] Lincoln, disputing with Douglas at Peoria, commended to him as a refutation of his specious reasoning "the seventy thousand answers just in from Pennsylvania, Ohio, and Indiana."[2]

The contest in Illinois, Douglas's own State, possesses an added interest. Douglas arrived at Chicago, his home, the latter part of August, and gave notice that he would address his constituents on the evening of the 1st of September. Rarely has it been the lot of a senator to speak to a more discontented crowd than he confronted that night. The anti-slavery people were embittered at his course in regard to the Missouri Compromise; the Know-nothings were incensed at his vigorous denunciation of their order in a speech made at Philadelphia, July 4th; and the commercial interest of the city was indignant because he had opposed the River and Harbor bill. During the afternoon the flags of all the shipping in the harbor were hung at half mast; at dusk the bells of the churches were tolled as if for a funeral, and above the din might be heard the mournful sound of the big city bell. A doleful air pervaded the city. A host of men assembled to hear the justification of the senator, but among them he had hardly a friend. The first few sentences of the speech were heard in silence, but when he made what was considered an offensive remark, a terrible groan rolled up from the whole assemblage, followed by the unearthly Know-nothing yell. When silence was restored, Douglas continued, but every pro-slavery sentiment was met with long-continued groans. Several statements which the audience doubted were received with derisive laughter. After an hour of interruptions, Douglas lost his temper and abused the crowd, taunting them for being afraid to give him a hearing. This was received with overpowering

---

[1] New York *Herald*, Oct. 13th; New York *Tribune*, Oct. 19th.
[2] Speech of Oct. 16th, Life of Lincoln, Howells, p. 304.

groans and hisses; and at last Douglas, convinced that further attempt would be useless, yielded to the solicitations of his friends and withdrew from the platform.[1]

In the central part of the State, however, the people heard Douglas gladly. At Springfield, the doughty champion of popular sovereignty met Lincoln in friendly discussion, but, in spite of the prestige his successful career of politician had given him, he was discomfited by the plain Illinois lawyer, the depths of whose nature had been stirred by the repeal of the Missouri Compromise. The fallacy of justifying this action by the plea that it simply instituted the great principle of self-government in the territories was shown by Lincoln in a few words that went to the hearts of the audience. "My distinguished friend," he remarked, "says it is an insult to the emigrants to Kansas and Nebraska to suppose they are not able to govern themselves. We must not slur over an argument of this kind because it happens to tickle the ear. It must be met and answered. I admit that the emigrant to Kansas and Nebraska is competent to govern himself, but I deny his right to govern any other person without that person's consent."[2]

In spite of the vigorous efforts of Douglas, Illinois did not sustain him. It is true that, owing to the popularity of their candidate for State treasurer, the Democrats carried the State ticket, and Douglas made the most of it;[3] but the anti-Nebraska people elected five out of nine congressmen, and their majority in the State on the congressional vote was more than seventeen thousand. They also controlled the legislature, and sent Lyman Trumbull, an anti-Nebraska

---

[1] Reports of Chicago *Tribune* and Chicago *Times*, cited in New York *Times*, Sept. 6th; letter from Veritas in New York *Tribune*, Sept. 7th; the *Liberator*, Sept. 8th; Life of Douglas, Sheahan, p. 271; Constitutional and Party Questions, Cutts, p. 98. The population of Chicago in 1854 was about sixty-five thousand.

[2] Life of Lincoln, Holland, p. 138.

[3] See debate in the Senate, Feb. 23d, 1855.

Democrat, to the Senate. The power of the Know-nothings was exercised in opposition to the Douglas party.

The course which the canvass took, and the result of the election in New York, exhibit a phase of the political situation different from any that prevailed in the West. An anti-Nebraska convention held in August adopted resolutions, reported by Horace Greeley, which grasped the situation fully and dealt only with the slavery question. In them every one was invited to unite "in the sacred cause of freedom, of free labor and free soil." It was a foregone conclusion that the Whigs would not give up their organization, to the maintenance of which the influence of Seward and Thurlow Weed had been directed. The Whigs, however, in their convention took pronounced ground in opposition to the extension of slavery. They nominated Clark for governor and Henry J. Raymond for lieutenant-governor. Both of these men were anti-slavery Whigs, in full sympathy with Seward. This ticket was adopted by the adjourned anti-Nebraska convention and by the Temperance party. If the fusionists had encountered no opposition save from the Democrats, the result would never have been in doubt. Both factions of this party made nominations. The Hards endorsed the Kansas-Nebraska bill; the Softs approved the policy of Pierce's administration, and nominated Horatio Seymour for governor, thus making a direct issue of prohibition.

But the Know-nothings were an unknown quantity. They had all along been feared by the Whigs, and when the grand council met at New York City in October, the anxiety knew no bounds. It was a curious political convention. Publicity is desired for ordinary gatherings of the kind; newspaper reporters are welcomed, for it is thought that a detailed account of the proceedings may awaken interest and arouse enthusiasm. But such views did not obtain in the grand council. About eight hundred delegates met at the grand-lodge room of the Independent Order of Odd Fellows. A long file of sentinels guarded the portals; newspaper reporters and outsiders were strictly excluded.

The credentials of each delegate were subjected to a rigid scrutiny before he was admitted to the hall. While no authoritative account of the transactions could be given, and profound secrecy was desired by the Know-nothings in regard to every circumstance, it leaked out that a State ticket had been nominated. Ullman, a conservative Whig, was the candidate for governor.[1] No declaration of principles was published; no public meetings were held to advocate their platform and candidates; they had not the powerful aid of a devoted press; everything was done in the dark. But every Know-nothing was bound by oath to support any candidate for political office who should be nominated by the order to which he belonged.[2]

When the November election day came the work of this mysterious organization was made manifest. The Know-nothings, said an apologist, do everything systematically and noiselessly; their votes "fall as the quietly descending dew."[3] Unseen and unknown, wrote an exponent who was elected to Congress, the order "wielded an overwhelming influence wherever it developed its power. . . . In many a district where its existence was unsuspected, it has, in an hour, like the unseen wind, swept the corruptionist from his power and placed in office the unsoliciting but honest and capable citizen."[4]

When the votes were counted, every one but the Know-nothings themselves was astounded. A current estimate of their strength as sixty thousand had seemed extravagant, but they polled more than double that number. Ullman had 122,282; Clark had 156,804; Seymour had 156,495; and Bronson, the "Hard" candidate, had 33,850. Clark's plurality was 309.

---

[1] New York *Times;* New York *Tribune.*
[2] Speech of Smith, House of Representatives, Feb. 6th, 1855; History of Political Campaign in Virginia, 1855, Hambleton, p. 51.
[3] Sons of the Sires, p. 157.
[4] A Defence of the American Policy, Whitney, p. 288.

The anti-slavery and temperance sentiment was overshadowed by the American feeling. It was conceded that the Know-nothings had drawn more from the Whigs than from the Democrats. Yet in the congressional elections the opposition to the repeal of the Missouri Compromise had full play. Twenty-seven out of a total of thirty-three representatives were chosen as anti-Nebraska men.

The election in Massachusetts took place a few days later than in New York. Here the political situation was different from that in any other State. An attempt was made to form a Republican party, and a convention was held under that name. Sumner made a powerful speech, and his influence was dominant. Henry Wilson was nominated for governor. The Whigs would not give up their organization, and the Republicans were therefore nothing but the old Free-soil party under another name.[1] The Whigs adopted strong anti-slavery resolutions, and nominated Emory Washburn for governor. The Know-nothings, by their secret methods, put Gardner in the field. Gardner had been a conservative Whig, but was now understood to be an anti-slavery man, and the bulk of his supporters were certainly opposed to slavery extension. In truth, the people of Massachusetts were all, with the exception of a few Democrats, so strongly opposed to the repeal of the Missouri Compromise that the question could not be made a political issue.[2] The contest was virtually between the Whigs and Know-nothings, and the Whig discomfiture was complete. Gardner had more than fifty thousand majority over Washburn. The Whigs had been fairly confident of success, and their amazement was unbounded. But the Know-nothings knew absolutely what they might reckon upon. Congdon relates that Brewer and he, who were the editors of the Boston *Atlas*, met Gardner in the street shortly before the election.

---

[1] See Boston *Courier, Traveller,* and *Journal;* Rise and Fall of the Slave Power, vol. ii. p. 414.

[2] See remarks of Wilson, United States Senate, Feb. 23d, 1855.

The Know-nothing candidate said to Brewer: "You had better not abuse me as you are abusing me in the *Atlas*. I shall be elected by a very large majority."[1] To Congdon, the movement seemed like "a huge joke;" and it is undeniable that the humorous side of the organization had attractions for many voters who anticipated amusement from the unlooked-for and startling effects.[2] The Congressmen elected were all Know-nothings, but all were anti-slavery. The legislature, almost wholly made up of members of the American party, sent Henry Wilson to the Senate.

Wilson's hatred of slavery was greater than his distrust of Irishmen or Catholics. Undoubtedly he would have preferred Republican to Know-nothing success; but he was ambitious for place, and he saw in the craze of the moment a convenient stepping-stone to political position. Although refused admission to one Know-nothing lodge, he persisted in his purpose, and succeeded afterwards in getting regularly initiated in another.[3]

The Republicans of Michigan and Wisconsin were eminently successful at their elections, and the results justified the steps which they had taken towards the formation of a new party.

This account of the fall elections may be tedious in its details, but it seems necessary to enter into the matter minutely in order to show whether there were important limitations to the statement that the North in the fall elections emphatically condemned the Kansas-Nebraska legislation. Douglas, with characteristic effrontery, maintained that there had been no anti-Nebraska triumph. The Democrats, he said, had been obliged to contend against a fusion which had been organized by Know-nothing councils, and their

---

[1] Reminiscences of a Journalist, Congdon, p. 145.
[2] See also Life of Bowles, vol. i. p. 124.
[3] Congdon, p. 146, see also pp. 87, 132; also Life of Bowles, p. 124; Rise and Fall of the Slave Power, chap. xxxii.; Julian's comments on the same, Political Recollections, p. 143.

mysterious way of working had taken men by surprise, and was therefore the great reason of success; but it was a Know-nothing and not an anti-Nebraska victory.[1] The groundlessness and the specious character of this explanation are shown by the detailed recital. And if we view the political revolution with regard to the fortunes of the Democratic party, the results will seem more striking than I have stated them. The Democrats had in the present House of Representatives a majority of eighty-four. In the House which was elected after the passage of the Kansas-Nebraska act, they would be in a minority of seventy-five, and on slavery questions would be obliged to form an alliance with thirty-seven Whigs and Know-nothings of pro-slavery principles.[2] Of forty-two Northern Democrats who had voted for the Kansas-Nebraska bill, only seven were re-elected.[3] The *National Intelligencer* made a comparison of the elections of 1852 and 1854, showing that without taking into account Massachusetts, the Democratic loss in the Northern States had been 347,742.[4] The most weighty reason for this revulsion of feeling was the repeal of the Missouri Compromise.[5]

Yet, considering the popular sentiment at the time of the enactment of the Nebraska bill, the declaration was not as positive and clear as might have been expected. Public indignation at the breach of plighted faith, dissatisfaction with the old parties, and the resulting political and moral agitation needed a national leader to give them proper direction. Had there been a leader, much of that magnificent moral energy which vented its force against Irishmen and Cath-

---

[1] Remarks in the Senate, Feb. 23d, 1855.

[2] I have followed the classification of the Tribune Almanac for the new Congress; for the Thirty-third Congress I followed that in the *Congressional Globe*. The members of the Thirty-fourth Congress were not all chosen by November, 1854, but nearly all from the Northern States had been elected.

[3] New York *Tribune*, Jan. 11th, 1855.   [4] Nov. 16th.

[5] See Charleston *Mercury*, Oct. 25th; New York *Herald*, Oct. 13th, Nov. 10th.

olics might have been turned into anti-slavery channels. Two men came out of the congressional contest over the Nebraska bill with apparently sufficient prestige to build up a new party. Chase, indeed, did not object to a new organization, and would have been willing to head such a movement;[1] but the chief element of the new party must come from the Northern Whigs. Chase, having entered public life under Democratic auspices, was obnoxious to the Ohio Whigs, and it would have been impossible even for a man of more tact than he to overcome the personal and political objections to his leadership.[2]

But Seward had the position, the ability, and the character necessary for the leadership of a new party. He was the idol of the anti-slavery Whigs. He was admired and trusted by most of the Free-soilers and anti-Nebraska Democrats. "The repeal of the Missouri Compromise," said the New York *Times*, "has developed a popular sentiment in the North which will probably elect Governor Seward to the Presidency in 1856 by the largest vote from the free States ever cast for any candidate."[3] "Seward is in the ascendency in this State and the North generally," said the Democratic New York *Post*.[4] "The man who should have impelled and guided the general uprising of the free States is W. H. Seward," asserted Greeley.[5]

It was the tide in Seward's affairs, but he did not take it at the flood. "Shall we have a new party?" asked the New York *Independent*. "The leaders for such a party do not appear. Seward adheres to the Whig party."[6]

Perhaps the sympathies of Seward were heartily enlisted in the movement for a new party and he was held back by Thurlow Weed. Perhaps he would have felt less trammeled had not his senatorship been at stake in the fall election. The fact is, however, that the Republican movement in the West and New England received no word of encouragement

---

[1] Life of Chase, Schuckers, p. 157.   [2] Ibid., p. 94.   [3] June 1st.
[4] May 23d.   [5] New York *Tribune*, Nov. 9th.   [6] July 27th.

from him. He did not make a speech, even in the State of New York, during the campaign. His care and attention were engrossed in seeing that members of the legislature were elected who would vote for him for senator. The Know-nothings were bitterly opposed to him, and he had no sympathy with the organization. Yet it was currently believed that his candidate for governor had endeavored to become a member of a Know-nothing lodge;[1] it was also charged that emissaries instructed by the followers of Seward had secured admission to the order.[2]

Had Seward sunk the politician in the statesman; had he made a few speeches, such as he well knew how to make, in New York, New England, and the West; had he emphatically denounced Know-nothingism as Douglas did at Philadelphia, or as he did after he had been chosen senator for another term;[3] had he vigorously asserted that every cause must be subordinate to union under the banner of opposition to the extension of slavery,—the close of the year 1854 would have seen a triumphant Republican party in every Northern State but California, and Seward its acknowledged leader. Had Douglas been in Seward's place, how quickly would he have grasped the situation, and how skilfully would he have guided public opinion! There was a greater politician and statesman in Illinois than Douglas, who was admirably fitted to head a popular movement; but beyond his own State, Lincoln was unknown: he had not a position from which he could speak with authority and which would obtain him a hearing from the whole people. No man, however, understood the situation better; and of all utterances against the Nebraska legislation, none equalled Lincoln's in making

---

[1] New York *Tribune*, Nov. 9th.

[2] Defence of American Policy, Whitney, p. 289.

[3] Douglas's speech was made July 4th, 1854. See Sheahan, p. 267; Cutts, p. 122. Seward did not criticise the principles and methods of the order until Feb. 23d, 1855, in the Senate. Even then his remarks were characterized by a certain levity which weakened their force. See *Congressional Globe*, vol. xxxi. p. 241.

plain to the people the gravity of the step which had been taken and the necessity of united action to undo the wrong. The speech which he made at Peoria in answer to Douglas tore up the sophistry, political and historical, of the Illinois senator. In it he demonstrated that the ordinance of 1787 had given freedom to their State; he told the history of the Missouri Compromise, and explained the compromise of 1850 in words which were alike clear and profound. This speech, marking justly an important epoch in the life of Lincoln, has yet little to do with the history of the country; for it was published in but one Illinois newspaper, and was not known outside of his own State.[1] It made him, indeed, the leader of his party in Illinois, and was therefore an earnest of further advancement.[2] But it is safe to say that had Lincoln been known at the North as were Seward and Chase, and had this speech been delivered in the principal States, it would have acted powerfully to fuse the jarring elements into the union which the logic of the times demanded. Douglas appreciated the force of Lincoln's arguments with the people, and admitted that they were giving him more trouble than all the speeches in the United States Senate. He begged that Lincoln would speak no more during this campaign, he himself agreeing also to desist.[3]

The history of the political campaign of this year would

---

[1] Life of Lincoln, Arnold, p. 121.

[2] See History of Lincoln, Nicolay and Hay, *Century Magazine*, vol. xxxiii. p. 863. Their remark refers to the Springfield speech. Lincoln spoke at Springfield, Oct. 4th, and at Peoria, Oct. 16th, both times in answer to Douglas. No report was made of the Springfield speech, but Lincoln wrote out the Peoria speech after its delivery, and had it published in seven consecutive issues of the *Daily Illinois Journal.* Lamon, p. 359. The two speeches were substantially the same. The Peoria speech may be found in the Campaign Life of Lincoln, by Howells. The only notice I found in Eastern newspapers of Lincoln's efforts was in a letter from Springfield to the New York *Times* of Oct. 13th, where the mention was briefly: "Lincoln made a most unanswerable speech against the repeal of the Missouri Compromise."

[3] Life of Lincoln, Herndon, p. 373; Lamon, p. 358.

not be complete without notice of the work done by the press in pushing into prominence the slavery question. The advocacy of a course of action whose ultimate end should be to give freedom to more than three million oppressed beings seemed to have an elevating influence on journalists,[1] and the anti-slavery newspapers of this year are full of the outpourings of sincere men who devoted their ability with enthusiasm to what they deemed a sacred cause. Nor will it be invidious to mention the editor who had the foremost influence in educating public sentiment.[2] Horace Greeley is the journalist most thoroughly identified with the formation of the Republican party on the platform of opposition to slavery extension. He was a man both speculative and practical,[3] and at no time did the union of these opposite qualities appear to better advantage than in the conduct of his journal during this year. He was emphatically anti-slavery, but only sought the attainable. He was strongly in favor of prohibitory legislation, and just as strongly opposed to Know-nothingism.

The 112,000 copies of the New York *Weekly Tribune* were not the measure of its peculiar influence,[4] for it was pre-eminently the journal of the rural districts, and one copy did service for many readers. To the people living in the Adirondack wilderness it was a political bible, and the well-known scarcity of Democrats there was attributed to it. Yet it was as freely read by the intelligent people living on the Western Reserve of Ohio.[5] The power which

---

[1] See Reminiscences of a Journalist, Congdon, p. 254.

[2] As an illustration, see the Kansas Crusade, Thayer, p. 40.

[3] See Congdon, p. 218.

[4] The circulation in November, 1854, was, daily, 27,360; semi-weekly, 12,120; weekly, 112,800; total, 152,280. The circulation of the weekly had nearly doubled in a year. On Feb. 10th, 1855, when the total circulation was 172,000, the *Tribune* estimated its readers at half a million.

[5] See In the Wilderness, Chas. Dudley Warner, p. 95. In the Adirondacks, if the *Weekly Tribune* "was not a Providence, it was a Bible."

this journal exerted is best appreciated in these two sections of country. Its influence in northern New York and northern Ohio is a type of what it wielded in all the agricultural districts of the North where New England and New York people predominated.[1]

It is one of the curiosities of human nature that Greeley, who exceeded in influence many of our Presidents, should have hankered so constantly for office. It is strange enough that the man who wrote as a dictator of public opinion in the *Tribune* of the 9th of November could write two days later the letter to Seward, dissolving the political firm of Seward, Weed, and Greeley. In that letter, the petulance of the office-seeker is shown, and the grievous disappointment that he did not get the nomination for lieutenant-governor, which went instead to Raymond,[2] stands out plainly.

Under the humor of the remarks about the Western Reserve is veiled a correct appreciation of the influence of this journal, see p. 96.

" Why do you look so gloomy ?" said a traveller riding along the highway in the Western Reserve, in the old anti-slavery days, to a farmer who was sitting moodily on a fence. " Because," said the farmer, " my Democratic friend next door got the best of me in an argument last night. But when I get my semi-weekly *Tribune* to-morrow, I'll knock the foundations all out from under him."—Chauncey M. Depew, at the *Tribune* celebration of its fiftieth anniversary, April 10th, 1891.

[1] The *Weekly Tribune*, in addition to being an outspoken opponent of slavery, also contained a fund of all kinds of information. Among the recollections of my school-days is that of a teacher who, amazed at the encyclopedic knowledge of passing events and current topics which one of the schoolboys displayed, went to his father to learn how he kept so thoroughly informed on politics, literature, and science, and was told: "He reads the New York *Weekly Tribune*."

[2] This letter may be found in Recollections of a Busy Life, Greeley, p. 315. It was not published until 1860; see also Memoir of Thurlow Weed.

Seward wrote Weed, Nov. 12th : " To-day I have a long letter from him [Greeley], full of sharp, pricking thorns. I judge, as we might indeed well know, from his, at the bottom, nobleness of disposition, that he has no idea of saying or doing anything wrong or unkind ; but it is sad to see him so unhappy. Will there be a vacancy in the Board of Regents this winter ? Could one be made at the close of the session ? Could he

The New York *Independent*, a weekly religious journal, had great influence in causing its readers to espouse the anti-slavery cause with devotion. From the time of the subsidence of the excitement which followed the passage of the Fugitive Slave law to the introduction of the Kansas-Nebraska bill, this newspaper had scarcely a word for politics. One would hardly have known from its columns in 1852 that a President was to be elected that year, nor did public affairs attract its attention in 1853. But with the repeal of the Missouri Compromise, the moral question entered again into politics. The *Independent* teemed with articles on the subject. Henry Ward Beecher wielded his vigorous pen in the service, and inculcated without ceasing the Christian's duty to liberty.[1] Moreover, Beecher and the *Independent* combated the principles and methods of Know-nothingism.[2]

Some of the legislatures which came into power, as a consequence of the anti-Nebraska wave, did not delay to formulate the feeling of their constituents regarding the Fugitive Slave act into laws. Personal Liberty laws, similar to the act of Vermont of 1850, were now passed by Rhode Island, Connecticut, and Michigan. Their proposed object was to prevent free colored citizens from being carried into slavery on a claim that they were fugitive slaves. In general, they provided that certain legal officers of the State should act as counsel for any one arrested as a fugitive; that negroes who were so claimed should be entitled to the benefits of the writ of habeas corpus and of trial by jury; they prohibited the use of the jails of the State for detaining fugitives; and they made the seizure of a free person with intent to reduce him to slavery a crime, the penalty for which was a heavy fine and imprisonment.[3] The practical effect of these laws

have it? Raymond's nomination and election is hard for him to bear."
—Life of Seward, vol. ii. p. 239.

[1] See biography of Henry Ward Beecher, p. 272.

[2] The extreme abolitionists represented by the *Liberator* also opposed Know-nothingism. See the *Liberator*, Nov. 10th and 17th.

[3] A succinct history and a systematic analysis of the Personal Liberty

was to surround with difficulties the apprehension of fugitive slaves, while the result hoped for was that the pursuit of them would be abandoned. These acts crystallized the public sentiment of those communities into a statute. They were dangerously near the nullification of a United States law, and, had not the provocation seemed great, would not have been adopted by people who had drunk in with approval Webster's idea of nationality. It must be noted that not until after the Fugitive Slave act had been on the statute book more than four years were the Personal Liberty laws, except that of Vermont, enacted, and it was not the unfairness of the act which caused them to be passed. While they were undeniably conceived in a spirit of bad faith towards the South, they were a retaliation for the grossly bad faith involved in the repeal of the Missouri Compromise. Nullification cannot be defended; but in a balancing of the wrongs of the South and the North, it must be averred that in this case the provocation was vastly greater than the retaliation.

Another manifestation of public sentiment may be seen in the manner that the Underground Railroad was regarded. Its aim had come to be sympathized with, and its methods were no longer unqualifiedly condemned. It was a system born of sympathy with fugitive slaves fleeing from what they considered the worst of ills. It was composed of a chain of friends and houses of refuge for the fleeing negro from Maryland through Pennsylvania and New York or New England to Canada, and from Kentucky and Virginia through Ohio to Lake Erie or the Detroit River. The arrangements were well understood by the negroes on the border, and Olmsted found that the Under-

---

laws may be found in the Fay House Monograph, Fugitive Slaves, Marion G. McDougall, p. 66; see also article of Alex. Johnston, Personal Liberty laws, Lalor's Cyclopædia. The Vermont "Act relating to the writ of habeas corpus to persons claimed as fugitive slaves and the right of trial by jury" was approved Nov. 13th, 1850. And the Vermont "Act for the defence of liberty and for the punishment of kidnapping" was approved Nov. 14th, 1854.

ground Railroad was even known in southwestern Louisiana.¹ The houses were called stations, and the sympathizing white men station-keepers or conductors.² If the fugitive successfully eluded pursuit until he reached the first station, he was reasonably sure of reaching his goal. He was given a pass to the next station, and energetic friends had means to help him along until he arrived under the protection of the British flag. William Still, a negro who styles himself chairman of the acting vigilant committee of the Philadelphia branch of the Underground Railroad, has compiled a huge volume, which is a narration of the " hardships, hair-breadth escapes, and death-struggles of the slaves in their efforts for freedom," and he also gives "sketches of some of the largest stockholders and most liberal aiders and advisers of the road."³ Men of reputation were engaged in this work. Samuel J. May glories in the fact that he was one of the conductors of the Underground Railroad.⁴ Theodore Parker was one of its managers.⁵ Thurlow Weed would sometimes turn away from his political manœuvres to give aid and comfort to a runaway slave.⁶ There was a strong undercurrent of sympathy with the fugitive, which, when it did not go to the length of breaking the law, winked at its infraction. A United States marshal at Boston, under a Democratic administration, said to James Freeman Clarke: "When I was a marshal and they tried to make me find their slaves, I would say, 'I do not know where your niggers are, but I will see if I can find out.' So I always went to Garrison's office and said, 'I want you to find such and such a negro; tell me where he is.' The next thing I knew, the fellow would be in Canada."⁷ The

---

¹ Cotton Kingdom, vol. ii. p. 37.
² Recollections of the Anti-slavery Conflict, S. J. May, p. 297.
³ The Underground Railroad, William Still, Philadelphia, 1871.
⁴ Recollections of the Anti-slavery Conflict, p. 297.
⁵ Weiss, vol. ii. p. 93   ⁶ Life of Thurlow Weed, vol. ii. p. 297.
⁷ Anti-slavery Days, Clarke, p. 87.

wife of George S. Hillard used to secrete fugitives in an upper chamber of their house in Boston; and although Hillard was a United States commissioner especially charged with the execution of the Fugitive Slave law, he affected not to know what was going on under his own roof.[1] Greeley knew politicians who would openly proclaim the duty of law-abiding citizens to assist in the recovery of fugitive slaves, yet who would secretly contribute money to be used in furthering their escape to Canada.[2] This inconsistency has been finely worked up in "Uncle Tom's Cabin," where a senator, who has been busy in his legislature, helping to make a law against giving aid and comfort to fugitive slaves who should cross the Ohio River into his own State of Ohio, is prevailed upon himself to leave a warm fireside at midnight and drive over roads deep with mud a runaway bondwoman and her child, and set them down at a station of the Underground Railroad.

The operations of this system of helping fugitives are occasionally referred to in the newspapers. One journal gleefully reports that it learns from one of the conductors that travel over his line is rapidly increasing.[3]

It must be borne in mind that the Personal Liberty laws and the Underground Railroad derive their chief historical importance not from the positive work which they accomplished, but from the circumstance that they were manifestations of popular sentiment. The number of fugitives who escaped into the free States annually did not exceed one thousand.[4] The number of arrests of fugitives, of which an account was had, from the passage of the 1850 law to the middle of 1856 was only two hundred.[5] But the ren-

---

[1] Anti-slavery Days, Clarke, p. 83.
[2] The American Conflict, Greeley, vol. i. p. 221.
[3] Detroit *Tribune*, cited by New York *Tribune*, May 17th, 1854; see also New York *Tribune*, Dec. 18th, 1854.
[4] United States Census, 1850 and 1860.
[5] Life of Parker, Weiss, vol. ii. p. 93. William Jay wrote in June,

dition of Burns drew the attention of every Northern man to three million negroes in slavery, and every fugitive who was helped on by the Underground Railroad had a number of sympathizers, and the tale of his sufferings awakened sympathy for his brothers in bondage. Some men were profoundly affected by the injustice done an inferior race; others were indignant at the growth of the political influence of the South; but, little by little, men were beginning to think that, come what may, they would no longer submit to the encroachments of slavery.

The only time that the question of slavery came up in the Senate of the second session of the Thirty-third Congress was in the debate on a bill of Toucey, of Connecticut, whose object, although disguised in generalities, was to secure the stringent execution of the Fugitive Slave act. It was called forth by the Personal Liberty laws already passed and others which were threatened, and the design was to render them nugatory. Toucey's bill went through the Senate, but was not brought up in the House. Sumner again introduced as an amendment a provision for the repeal of the Fugitive Slave law. While two and one-half years previously only three senators voted with him, he had now a following of eight; and Seward, who before had dodged the question, now not only voted with Sumner, Chase, and Wade, but delivered an invective against the whole system of fugitive slave legislation. This question was one that would not down. During the year, Maine and Massachusetts passed Personal Liberty laws. Governor Gardner vetoed the bill of the Massachusetts legislature. He was fortified by an opinion of the attorney-general of the State that the bill was "clearly repugnant to the provisions of the Constitution of the United States," and its inevitable tendency and effect would be "to bring the courts of the United States and their officers into an irreconcilable con-

---

1853, that the law had been on the statute-book two years and nine months, and not fifty slaves had been recovered under it. Autographs for Freedom, p. 39.

flict with those of the Commonwealth." The legislature, however, promptly passed the bill over the governor's veto.[1]

The Kansas question began to attract attention this year. The people in western Missouri were strongly pro-slavery, and they honestly supposed that the passage of the Kansas-Nebraska act implied that Kansas was given over to slavery. As soon as the act was signed they commenced to make settlements in the new territory, and staked out much of the best land.[2] Simultaneously, actuated by the pioneer spirit, there was a large emigration to Kansas from the Western States, especially from Iowa, Illinois, and Indiana.[3] In July, 1854, the Emigrant-Aid Company sent out its first party from New England. Eli Thayer was the soul of this enterprise. The avowed object of the company was to make Kansas a free State; and the emigrants who were at different times assisted by it went out with that end in view, as well as with the usual desire of bettering their fortunes.[4] Thayer had been successful in interesting Greeley in the movement, and had his support and the influence of the *Weekly Tribune*. Other journals kept their public informed, and appealed for encouragement of the company.[5] Nevertheless, the general opinion at this time in the North was that the plans of the western Missourians were so well laid that Kansas would

---

[1] See acts and resolves passed by the General Court of Massachusetts, in the year 1855, chap. 489, pp. 924–929. The veto message of the governor and the opinion of the attorney-general are printed in the *Liberator* of May 25th. [2] Spring's Kansas, p. 26.

[3] See speech of Douglas, Senate, April 4th, 1856; Kanzas and Nebraska, Hale, p. 233. "At this early day [July, 1854] emigrants from every Western State were pouring in. We had not yet heard of the New England Emigrant-Aid Society."—Address of Samuel N. Wood, Quarter-Centennial celebration, Publications of the Kansas Historical Society, vol. i. p. 236. Also, Kansas, by Sara T. L. Robinson, p. 27.

[4] In 1854, Thayer's company sent out five hundred emigrants; during the whole period of emigration it sent out three thousand. The Kansas Crusade, pp. 54 and 57.

[5] The Kansas Crusade, Eli Thayer, pp. 36, 69, 171.

be colonized by slave-holders and slaves.¹ But Thayer did not think so. He was as ardent a believer in popular sovereignty as Douglas himself, and in a strife between free-State and slave-State emigration he felt sure that the cause of freedom would win.² Yet his aims and those of his followers were peaceful. New England emigrants and Sharpe's rifles are closely associated in Kansas history; but during the summer and fall of 1854, the Emigrant-Aid Company did not furnish its patrons any implements of war.³ The scheme was to gain Kansas for freedom by permanently settling there more voters than the other side could send. This was in accordance with the principle of the sovereignty of the people which Douglas had invoked.

The operations of the Emigrant-Aid Company and its branches being freely reported, caused great excitement in Western Missouri. The methods of these societies were misrepresented, but their aim, openly avowed, of making Kansas a free State was in itself enough to arouse indignation, and means were devised to check this movement of New England.⁴ In October, 1854, Blue Lodges were formed in Missouri. These were secret societies, with the methods and paraphernalia of an organization, whose members are bound together by secret oaths. Their purpose was to extend slavery into Kansas. Popular sovereignty meant to them the right of Missourians to vote at the territorial elections in furtherance of the design which had given rise to the Blue Lodges.⁵

---

¹ See Seward's speech in the Senate, May 25th, 1854; also, conversation of Greeley and Thayer, The Kansas Crusade, chap. iii.; the *Liberator* of July 13th, 1855, cited in Spring's Kansas. The evidence of the statement in the text can be multiplied almost without end.

² The Kansas Crusade, pp. 22, 74, 254.

³ Spring's Kansas, p. 40; Eli Thayer's testimony, Howard Report, p. 884.

⁴ See Douglas's Report on Kansas, March, 1856; speech in the Senate, March 20th, 1856.

⁵ Report of Howard and Sherman, generally known as the Howard Report to the House of Representatives, p. 3.

Meanwhile Andrew Reeder of Pennsylvania, the governor of the territory, arrived. President Pierce appreciated that the position was an important one, and had made the selection with care. Reeder was an able lawyer and a man of energy and integrity. He had accumulated some property, had not solicited the appointment, but had been urged for the place by men of position and character.¹ He sympathized fully with Douglas in the Kansas-Nebraska legislation, was a devoted friend of the South, and, after receiving the appointment, had said in conversation that he would have no more scruples in buying a slave than a horse.² Reeder had watched the operations of the emigrant-aid societies, and before he set out for Kansas had expressed the opinion that if he had any trouble in the administration of his territory, it would come from the New England colonists.³

Governor Reeder appointed November 29th, 1854, for the election of a territorial delegate, and on that day seventeen hundred and twenty-nine Missourians came over into Kansas and swelled the pro-slavery vote.⁴ Whitfield, their candidate, would have been elected without the aid of this organized invasion, for the free-State settlers took little interest in this election, as they did not consider that the question of free institutions was in any way involved in it.⁵ Not the slightest objection was made in the House of Representatives at Washington to Whitfield's taking his seat.

The affairs in Kansas had no influence whatever on the elections of 1854. The interest they excited was slight, and they were hardly mentioned in the canvass. Lincoln, indeed, told Douglas that his popular-sovereignty doctrine

---

¹ By Judge Parker and J. W. Forney.
² Washington *Union*, cited by Nicolay and Hay, *Century Mag.* vol. xxxiii. p. 870, and by Greeley, American Conflict, vol. i. p. 237.
³ Publications of the Kansas State Historical Society, vol. i. p. 5 *et seq.;* Anecdotes of Public Men, Forney, vol. i. p. 193.
⁴ Howard Report, p. 8. ⁵ Ibid., p. 8.

was almost certain to bring the Yankees and Missourians into collision over the question of slavery in Kansas, and that it was probable that the contest would come to blows and bloodshed. With prophetic soul, he asked, "Will not the first drop of blood so shed be the real knell of the Union?"[1]

The general opinion at Washington in the winter of 1855 was that Kansas would be made slave territory. To anti-slavery men it seemed that the fight would come in Congress whether or not she should be admitted as a slave State. The acquiescence in the November election seemed to indicate that the work of the emigrant-aid companies had come to nothing and that no effective opposition to the Missourians could be expected.[2]

There was, however, an active free-State party in the territory who were looking forward to the next election to display their strength. The governor appointed March 30th, 1855, for the election of a territorial legislature. Election day was also taken note of in Missouri; and before it came, "an unkempt, sun-dried, blatant, picturesque mob of five thousand Missourians, with guns upon their shoulders, revolvers stuffing their belts, bowie-knives protruding from their boot-tops, and generous rations of whiskey in their wagons," had marched into Kansas to assist in the election of the legislature.[3] Atchison was at the head of one company, and was prominent in the direction of the movement. The invaders were distributed with military precision, and were sent into every district but one. Where the election judges were not pro-slavery men, the mob awed them into submission or drove them away by threats. Six thousand three hundred and seven votes were counted, of which more than three-quarters were cast by the Missourians.[4] Doctor

---

[1] Speech at Peoria, Oct 16th, 1854, Life of Lincoln, Howells, p. 288.
[2] See J. S. Pike's Washington letters to the New York *Tribune,* Feb. 5th, 6th, 10th, 1855, Pike's First Blows of the Civil War, p. 269 *et seq.*
[3] Spring's Kansas, p. 44; see, also, Kansas, Sara Robinson, p. 27.
[4] Howard Report, p. 30.

Robinson, who had been sent out by the Emigrant-Aid Company, and whose courage, tact, and earnestness had made him leader of the free-State party, wrote to A. A. Lawrence, of Boston :[1] " The election is awful, and will no doubt be set aside. So says the governor, although his life is threatened if he does not comply with the Missourians' demands. I, with others, shall act as his body-guard."[2] The body-guard was needed. The time for making protests was but four days, and courage was required to object to this manifestation of popular sovereignty. The Missourians threatened to kill any one who endeavored to get signers to a protest. As it was rumored that the governor was indignant at the method used to carry the election and might order a new one, they openly said that he could have fifteen minutes to decide whether he would give certificates to those who had the most votes, or be shot.[3] The scene in the executive chamber when the governor canvassed the returns was an apt illustration of the result of the Douglas doctrine, when put in force by rude people in a new country, and when a question had to be decided over which the passions of men were excited to an intense degree. The thirty-nine members who, on the face of the returns, were elected were seated on one side of the room, the governor and fourteen friends on the other. All were armed to the teeth. Reeder's pistols, cocked, lay on the table by the side of the papers relating to the elections. Protests of fraud were received from only seven districts. Although the governor did not assume to throw out members on account of force and fraud, he did set aside, on technicalities, the elections in those districts and ordered new elections. To the others he

---

[1] Amos A. Lawrence was a gentleman of wealth and social position in Boston; was treasurer of the Emigrant-Aid Company, and was personally a large contributor to it.
[2] Letter of April 4th, cited in Spring's Kansas, p. 49.
[3] Kansas, Sara Robinson, p. 29; Reeder's testimony, Howard Report, p. 936.

issued certificates, so that the pro-slavery party was largely in the ascendency in the legislature.¹

The indignation in the free States at this perversion of popular government was unbounded.² The fraud was well understood. The anti-slavery newspapers had circumstantial and truthful accounts from correspondents who were on the ground. The New England emigrants were people who could wield a facile pen. They wrote home to relations and friends letters which were read by every one in the town, and were afterwards given to the county paper for publication.³ Evidence like this from well-known people was sufficient in itself to mould the sentiment of all rural New England. There could be no dispute about the facts. Reeder came East in April, and told the story to his friends and neighbors at Easton, his Pennsylvania home. His speech through the medium of the press appealed to the whole North. He declared that the territory of Kansas in her late election was invaded by a regular organized army, armed to the teeth, who took possession of the ballot-boxes and made a legislature to suit the purpose of the pro-slavery party; and he assured his hearers that the accounts of fierce outrages and wild violences perpetrated at the election published in the Northern papers were in no wise exaggerated.⁴ Reeder's seven months' contact with aggressive advocates of slavery had revolutionized the opinions of a lifetime. This the Northern people knew, and they implicitly believed his story. The cautious, truthful, and impartial orator Edward Everett, in his Fourth-of-July oration, whose subject, "Dorchester in 1630, 1776, and 1855," seemed

---

¹ Howard Report, pp. 35 and 936; Sara Robinson's Kansas.

² See New York *Tribune, Times,* and the *Independent* for April and May.

³ See an interesting instance related by Thayer, The Kansas Crusade, p. 169.

⁴ New York *Times,* May 1st. The speech was made at Easton, Pa., April 30th.

widely remote from Kansas troubles, felt impelled to say: "It has lately been maintained, by the sharp logic of the revolver and the bowie-knife, that the people of Missouri are the people of Kansas!"[1]

At the South, popular sentiment fully justified the action of the Missourians. If the notion occurred that perhaps they had no right to vote in Kansas, their action was deemed praiseworthy as countervailing the purpose of the emigrant-aid societies. Massachusetts, which took the lead in that movement, was especially abhorred in the South. It was the hot-bed of abolitionism, and the Southern people regarded the assisted emigration as the work of the abolitionists. In this they were wrong. The Garrison abolitionists had no part whatever in the emigrant-aid companies, but discouraged their efforts in the *Liberator*, and also by speech and resolution.[2]

"We trust," said a Mobile journal, "that the Missourians will continue the good fight they have begun, and, if need be, call on their brethren in the South for help to put down by force of arms the infernal schemes hatched in Northern hot-beds of abolition for their injury."[3] "Hireling emigrants are poured in to extinguish this new hope of the South," said the Charleston *Mercury*.[4] The Democratic State convention of Georgia expressed their "sympathy with the friends of slavery in Kansas in their manly efforts to maintain the rights and interests of the Southern people over the paid adventurers and Jesuitical hordes of Northern abolitionism."[5] The South was chary of holding public meetings except during a political canvass, but the interest

---

[1] Everett's Orations and Speeches, vol. iii. p. 347.
[2] See Kansas Crusade, chap. vii.; Life of Garrison, vol. iii. p. 436 *et seq.*; Review of Kansas Crusade in *The Nation*, Nov. 7th, 1889.
[3] Mobile *Register*, cited by the New York *Tribune*, May 17th.
[4] See New York *Tribune*, June 13th.
[5] This convention was held at Milledgeville, June 6th; see New York *Tribune*, June 20th.

in Kansas prompted a departure from the usual custom, and gatherings were not infrequent to consider the demand which duty made on the supporters of slavery. Charleston, which had regarded the Kansas-Nebraska legislation with unconcern, now girded itself for the contest. At a very large and respectable meeting of its citizens it was resolved that it was their right and duty to extend to their Southern brethren in Kansas every legitimate and honorable sympathy and support.[1]

The President was sorely distressed at the turn affairs had taken in Kansas. He told Reeder that this matter " had given him more harassing anxiety than anything that had happened since the loss of his son; that it haunted him day and night, and was the great overshadowing trouble of his administration." He divulged the pressure on him for the governor's removal, and told of the bitter complaints which were made of the executive conduct of affairs in Kansas. General Atchison, he said, pressed Reeder's removal in the most excited manner, and would listen to no reasoning at all.[2] The President might have added that the persuasion he found most difficult to resist was that of Jefferson Davis, whose soul was bound up in the cause of the Missourians. Reeder saw the President almost every day for more than two weeks,[3] and made a candid exposition of the policy that ought to be pursued. " The President in our interviews," testified Reeder, " expressed himself highly pleased and satisfied with my course, and in the most unequivocal language approved and endorsed all that I had done. He expressed some regret, however, that my speech in Easton had omitted all allusion to the illegalities of the Emigrant-Aid Society, and thought it was perhaps unnecessarily strong in its denunciation of the Missouri invasion. I told him I had no knowledge of the operations of the Emigrant-Aid

---

[1] *National Intelligencer*, August 23d.
[2] Reeder's testimony, Howard Report, p. 938. [3] In May.

Company, except what was before the whole public; and that so long as they had not sent out men merely to vote and not to settle, I could not consistently denounce their course as illegal."[1]

It was plainly apparent that the President wished Reeder to resign; and at one time he offered the mission to China as an inducement, but it did not become vacant as expected. Nevertheless, he urged the matter so pertinaciously that Reeder promised to resign provided they could agree on the terms of the correspondence, and provided his successor would be sure to resist the aggressive invasions from Missouri. Draft after draft of the letter of resignation was made, and interlineations and corrections were suggested, sometimes by one, sometimes by the other, but no agreement could be reached. The President seemed to incline more and more to the Southern view. At last Reeder declared that as they could reach no agreement, he would not resign. The President replied: "Well, I shall not remove you on account of your official action; if I remove you at all, it will be on account of your speculation in lands of the territory."[2] Reeder, like every one else who went to the new territories with money, had bought lands for a rise, and it had been asserted that, considering his official position, his purchase of certain Indian lands was improper.[3] This was the last interview. Reeder soon after returned to Kansas. His removal was soon decided upon. Early in June, Jefferson Davis, in a speech at the Democratic convention of Mississippi, admitted that the choice of Reeder was a mistake, but clearly intimated that it would be speedily corrected by the appointment of his successor.[4]

---

[1] Reeder's testimony, Howard Report, p. 937.   [2] Ibid.

[3] In his testimony before the congressional committee, Reeder discusses this question fully. It does not appear that he attempted to cover up anything, but, on the contrary, he courted the fullest investigation.

[4] Letter of A. G. Brown of June 13th to the Jackson, Miss., *Mercury*, cited by the New York *Tribune*.

Thus, the Kansas question became one of great political moment. The South was practically unanimous in holding that Kansas ought to be a slave State; the predominant opinion at the North was equally decided that it should be free. This concrete shape that the issue on slavery took exerted a weighty influence in consolidating the Republican party. A practicable and attainable object was now before the people. There was also a signal illustration whither the pro-slavery policy led. It could be maintained that here was the paramount question, and the appeal could be made to those who had been affected by the Know-nothing crusade, that in this direction there were opportunity and reward for political zeal.

The Know-nothings had been highly elated at their strength, as shown in the elections of 1854; and shortly after the results were known, their National Council assembled in Cincinnati. This meeting is noteworthy from having authorized the third, or Union, degree. An imposing and impressive ceremonial was prescribed. After the candidate should take an oath, as strong as words could make it, that he would faithfully defend the Union of the States against assaults from every quarter, he would be admitted to the brotherhood of the Order of the American Union.[1] This new degree was adopted largely through the influence of Rayner, of North Carolina, an ancient Whig, from motives that did him honor. Comprehending the aim of the extreme pro-slavery party, and knowing that the secession faction was powerful enough to shape its policy, he wished to make the Know-nothing organization a sterling Union party, building it upon the ruins of the shattered Whig party of the South; and he believed that it would also draw Democrats who had supported the compromise of 1850. But the Union degree was construed to mean that the

---

[1] Rise and Fall of the Slave Power, vol. ii. p. 422. For the oath, see New York *Tribune*, June 7th, 1855.

North should keep quiet on the subject of slavery. The
Know-nothings did not see what other men saw—that the
time had now come when the political being of the North
depended on unceasing agitation.

In six months from the time that the Union degree was
instituted, it was estimated that one million and a half of
men had taken the degree; and apologists of the order did
not hesitate to assert that it controlled that number of legal
voters.[1] If their reckonings were correct, the boast that
they would elect the next President did not seem vain.

The Southern Know-nothings received a severe blow in
the Virginia election of May. There were but two tickets
in the field, the Democratic and the Know-nothing, and it
was the first important contest in the South where the opposition had enrolled itself under the Know-nothing banner.
Henry A. Wise, the Democratic candidate for governor,
made a vigorous canvass of the State; he began on the 1st
of January, and spoke regularly from the stump until obliged
from physical exhaustion to give up speaking. Wise was
an orator not unlike John Randolph. He denounced the
illiberal spirit of Know-nothingism in a cogent and effective
manner, but he was less candid in maintaining that it was
merely a new invention of the abolitionists. All the able
Democratic speakers of the State were enlisted in the canvass, and Douglas himself was pressed into the service.
Never had political excitement run so high in the Old Dominion; never had there been such a bitter contest. Wise
was elected by more than ten thousand majority, and the
result was everywhere interpreted to mean that the Know-nothings could not make a successful inroad on a Demo-

---

[1] Rise and Fall of the Slave Power, vol. ii. p. 422; A Defence of the
American Policy, Whitney, p. 285. At the time of the Philadelphia National Council, in June, 1855, the New York *Herald* estimated the Know-nothing votes at 1,375,000; and Wilson, himself a Know-nothing, had no
doubt 1,250,000 voters were enrolled in its councils. Rise and Fall of the
Slave Power, vol. ii. p. 423.

cratic State in the South.¹ Their strength could be rated at the numerical force of the Whig party. They were practically its successor, and might carry the old Whig districts and States, but beyond that it did not seem probable they would go. We hear no longer of the Whig party in the South. Most of the prominent Whigs became Know-nothings; a few joined the Democrats. Many of the Southern States had held no elections in 1854. This year they had to choose their governors and congressmen, and the contest everywhere was between the Democrats and Know-nothings. The Know-nothings did not make material gains over the Whig vote of the preceding elections.

The Know-nothings had hardly recovered from the blow of the Virginia election when their National Council met at Philadelphia.² Nearly every State sent delegates. They had come together to adopt a declaration of principles after the manner of political conventions. What they should say about slavery provoked in full meeting a hot controversy which was continued for three days in the committee on resolutions. A majority report was at last agreed to. It was the expression of the fourteen members of the committee from the Southern States, joined by those representing New York, the District of Columbia, and the territory of Minnesota. The report declared that Congress ought not to prohibit slavery in any territory or in the District of Columbia, and that it had no power to exclude any State from admission to the Union because its Constitution recognized slavery. Thirteen members of the committee from the free States and the representative of Delaware made a minority report, in which they demanded the restoration of the Mis-

---

¹ See the Political Campaign in Virginia in 1855, J. P. Hambleton. "The Virginia election has knocked the bottom out of Know-nothingism in the South," New York *Tribune*, May 29th. See also Rise and Fall of the Slave Power, vol. ii. p. 422. Forney's Anecdotes of Public Men, vol. i. p. 135.

² June 5th was the day the council began.

souri Compromise; but if efforts to that end failed, Congress should refuse to admit any State formed out of the Kansas or Nebraska territories which tolerated slavery. The contest of the committee was transferred to the whole council, where an earnest, excited, and bitter debate of three days followed. Henry Wilson led the Northern forces with address, and his speeches were so positive and to the point that he won golden opinions from those who, the year previous, had looked upon him merely as a time-server in politics. At midnight on the eighth day of the council, the Southern platform was adopted by a vote of 80 to 59. The long series of resolutions, in addition to the declaration on slavery, may be summed up as meaning "resistance to the aggressive policy and corrupting tendencies of the Roman Catholic Church," and "Americans only shall govern America."[1] The Northern delegates were in full sympathy with the platform, except the article on slavery; but their opposition to this was so unyielding that they protested against the action of the council, and issued an appeal to the people in which they stated in plain words their position.[2]

The rending in twain of the Know-nothings on the vital and obtruding question of the time was a result of great

---

[1] The platform was published in the New York *Tribune* of June 20th. From day to day there appeared in this journal a full report of the proceedings, which was sent to it by Samuel Bowles, who also reported for the Springfield *Republican* and the Boston *Atlas*. The New York *Times* had also a detailed account of the proceedings. See Rise and Fall of the Slave Power, vol. ii. p. 423 *et seq.*; Life of Samuel Bowles, vol. i. p. 137. The platform is printed in A Defence of the American Policy, Whitney, p. 294. One article of the platform deserves quotation: "A radical revision and modification of the laws regulating immigration and the settlement of immigrants. Offering to the honest immigration who, from love of liberty or hatred to oppression, seek an asylum in the United States a friendly reception and protection. But unqualifiedly comdemning the transmission to our shores of felons and paupers."

[2] New York *Tribune*, June 20th; Rise and Fall of the Slave Power, vol. ii. p. 431; Life of Samuel Bowles, vol. i. p. 138.

political importance. The Southern Know-nothings made their election contests on the national platform; the Northern Know-nothings, including even those of New York, repudiated the slavery plank when they asked for the votes of the people.[1]

Another important result of the National Council was the discovery of the fact that the Know-nothings had exhausted all the virtue of their secret machinery. The secrets had been exposed; there was no longer any mystery; the dark ways had ceased to excite terror. The Know-nothings were now holding political conventions and adopting platforms like any other political party. They appealed to the people for support, because they had certain defined principles which they wished to put into force in legislation or administration. They could no longer demand votes simply because voters had taken solemn oaths; they must justify the existence of their party by discussion and by satisfying reasons. Those who vainly supposed that the secret work of the lodges which had played such a part the preceding year could still be continued, must have been undeceived when they saw every proceeding of their National Council laid bare to the public. The wild excitement one night of the convention, when it was for a moment supposed that the correct and faithful correspondent of the New York *Tribune* had been discovered, brought to light the suspicion that a Massachusetts man was reporting for an anti-slavery journal, and the fact that a Virginia delegate was sending news to the New York *Herald*.[2] The neglect to investigate the one case or to censure the other was a tacit admission that the farce of mystery had been played for what it was worth, and that the time had come for men of sense and honor to advocate their political principles openly. From this time forward the order is better known as the American party, and it is entitled to great respect for

---

[1] See a careful editorial in the New York *Tribune* of Nov. 22d.
[2] See New York *Tribune*, June 20th.

its endeavor to work out reforms which it believed were needed. Yet the historian must aver that the Americans were not abreast of the needs of their time, for they sacrificed the greater principle to the lesser one.

Meanwhile, under the influences which had prevailed the preceding year and the stimulus of Kansas, the Republican movement was gaining strength. Chase, who expected the people's nomination for governor of Ohio,[1] had written a public letter in which he said there must be "agreement and harmony on the common platform of no slavery outside of slave States."[2] Greeley wrote home from Europe that Chase would be beaten if nominated. No better instance than this can be adduced of how ancient party prejudices still survived. Greeley, though earnestly in favor of the new movement, could not let himself forget that Chase had entered public life through an exasperating defeat of the Whigs.[3] The anti-Nebraska convention was held in Ohio, July 13th, the anniversary of the adoption of the ordinance of 1787. A majority of the delegates were Americans; and although Chase had never been a member either of the Know-nothing order or of the American organization, he was nominated for governor by a vote of nearly two to one. It seems that the anti-slavery zeal of the Ohio Americans

---

[1] See his letter to J. S. Pike, June 20th, First Blows of the Civil War, p. 295.

[2] Letter to the Republican County Committee of Portage County, June 15th, New York *Tribune*, June 28th.

[3] C. A. Dana to Pike, July 14th, Pike, p. 297. Chase wrote Pike after the election: "You will have noticed that some of our papers were not well pleased with the apparent concession of the *Tribune* that I might be defeated; or with the article since the election saying that, had another man been nominated, the result would have been a more decided anti-Nebraska victory. . . . I presume Mr. Greeley wrote the articles I refer to, and I doubt not they were written with the best intentions. But I may be allowed to doubt the policy of printing them. We want now cordial union among all the friends of the party of freedom. Nothing less will insure a victory in 1856."—Letter of Oct. 18th, Pike, p. 299.

was greater than their opposition to foreigners and Catholics.¹ The convention resolved, "That we will resist the spread of slavery, under whatever shape or color it may be attempted," and took for their party the name Republican.² In accepting the nomination Chase said: "Slavery in the territories must be prohibited by law. . . . Kansas must be saved from slavery by the voters of the free States."

It was one of the hard-fought political battles for which Ohio is famous. Chase entered the contest with spirit; he spoke in fifty-seven different places, in forty-nine counties,³ appealing to his old Democratic friends to go with him in opposing slavery extension, and arguing with the Whigs that all old differences should be sunk until the cause of freedom had prevailed. Strong efforts were made to defeat him. The pro-slavery wing of the Americans and some Conservative Whigs put up a candidate in the hope of drawing away from him enough votes to let in the Democratic nominee. But Chase was successful, his plurality reaching nearly sixteen thousand.

The Republicans carried Vermont, but were unsuccessful in Maine. The Democrats regained Pennsylvania and Wisconsin. In New York a fusion of the anti-slavery elements was made under the name Republican. The platform of the State convention, reported by Horace Greeley, called for an express prohibition by Congress of slavery in all territory of the Union, and emphatically condemned the doctrines and methods of the Know-nothings.⁴ The most important event of the New York canvass was that Seward put himself squarely at the head of the new organization. He made two speeches which indeed ought to have been made one year earlier, but they unite in so marked degree the broad views of the statesman with the practical art of the politician that they must be reckoned as one of the

---

¹ See letter of Chase, Warden, p. 346.
² Cleveland *Herald*, July 14th.   ³ Chase to Pike, Pike, p. 299.
⁴ See New York *Tribune*. The convention met Sept. 27th.

great influences of this year towards cementing divisions into one organized whole. The Albany speech was printed in the New York *Weekly Tribune*, and was undoubtedly read by more than half a million men. It described the situation in clear and homely words, and was a veritable storehouse of arguments. We may be sure that the copy of the *Tribune* which contained this speech was carefully laid away in many a country and village household; and as the discussions of the winter went on, Seward's words were referred to, quoted, and pondered. They were seed sown in fruitful ground, for every man at the North now discussed politics on all occasions. A carefully prepared speech from a man in high political position, delivered from the stump, is a more potent appeal to public opinion than a speech in Congress. The senator in the Senate may speak *at* the people, but he is to some extent confined by the limitations of the place. Ordinarily, he discusses some scheme of legislation in reply to an opponent, and when he enters into a mass of detail he loses the interest of many voters. On the other hand, the sole object of the stump speaker is to convince the people. The direct argument is enforced; the subsidiary explanation, the detailed examination, is left out, as hampering the flow of reasoning.

At Albany, Seward put forth the question to be resolved: Shall we form a new party? He explained how the slave-holders were a "privileged class," and how much national legislation there had been in their interest which affected the right and comfort of the Northern citizen; how the South got the better of the North in the appropriations, and how the slave-holder was taken care of by the tariff. "Protection is denied to your wool," he said, "while it is freely given to the slave-holder's sugar." "Slavery is not, and never can be, perpetual," he continued: "it will be overthrown either peacefully or lawfully under this Constitution, or it will work the subversion of the Constitution together with its own overthrow. Then the slave-holders will perish in the struggle. The change can now be made without violence, and by the agency of the ballot-box. The temper of the nation is just, liberal, forbearing. It will contribute any money and endure any sacrifice to effect this great and important change. . . . What, then, is wanted? Organization! Organization! Nothing but organization. . . . We have power to avert the extension of slavery in the territories of the Union, and that is enough. . . . We want a bold, outspoken, free-spoken organization—one that openly proclaims its principles, its purposes, and its objects."

He showed how the American party failed to meet the situation. Fewer words were needed to make clear how both of the Democratic factions were found wanting. He then asked: "Shall we report ourselves to the Whig party? Where is it? Gentle Shepherd, tell me where! Four years ago it was a strong, vigorous party, honorable for energy, noble achievements, and still more for noble enterprises. . . . Now there is neither Whig party nor Whig south of the Potomac. . . . The Republican organization has . . . laid a new, sound, and liberal platform broad enough" for true Democrats and true Whigs to stand upon. "Its principles are equal and exact justice; its speech open, decided, and frank. Its banner is untorn in former battles, and unsullied by past errors. That is the party for us."[1]

The Americans elected their State ticket in New York, and were also successful in Massachusetts. The result in Massachusetts, however, could not be looked upon as a reaction; for the Americans in that State were almost as strongly anti-slavery as the Republicans. It is undeniable that at the close of this year a superficial examination led many to believe that the prospect of a united anti-slavery party was not as favorable as it had been a year previous.[2]

---

[1] Seward's Works, vol. iv. p. 225. "Seward's speech at Albany on the 'privileged classes,' the oligarchy of slavery, has been the key-note of the new party."—Diary of R. H. Dana. Life by C. F. Adams, vol. i. p. 348.

[2] See New York *Tribune*, Nov. 8th; Political Recollections, Julian, p. 145; Life of Bowles, vol. i. p. 144.

But after-events have shown that the optimists were nearer right.¹ There were this year no congressmen to elect, and in but few States were governors chosen. The interest in the elections was not great. The indignation aroused by the Missouri invasion into Kansas in the spring had in part subsided, and the aim and prospects of the free-State party were not so well understood as afterwards, when the subject was ventilated in Congress. The vote was small. When all allowances are made, when the undercurrents are observed, the conclusion is irresistible that the Republican movement had made progress. Two leaders had come to the front—one a former Democrat, the other a Whig. Chase had the backing of Ohio, and few could doubt that Seward's party would in the coming year carry New York. The Republicans of Massachusetts furnished two leaders, Sumner and Wilson. Sumner's manly independence of thought prevented him from being a politician; but what in him was lacking was supplied by Wilson, who had the virtues and faults of a self-made man. He was a man of parts. "The Natick cobbler" had risen to be United States senator from the educated commonwealth of Massachusetts. Until this year his reputation had been that of a manœuvring politician and clever wire-puller, who was adroit at bargains, and whose remarkable tact had been employed in self-advancement; but the cause of anti-slavery ennobled him. It is probable that had he not become a leader of a party based on a moral idea, he would not have gone in public estimation beyond that of an intriguing politician.²

---

¹ "The events of the election show that the 'Silver Grays' have been successful in a new and attractive form, so as to divert a majority of the people in the cities and towns from the great question of the day, that is all. The country, I mean the rural districts, still remain substantially sound. A year is necessary to let the cheat wear off."—Seward to his wife, Nov. 13th, 1855, Life, vol. ii. p. 258.

² See Life of Bowles, Merriam; Reminiscences of a Journalist, Congdon; Letter of Theodore Parker to Wilson, Life of Parker, Weiss, vol. ii. p. 207; Life of R. H. Dana, C. F. Adams, vol. i. p. 247: and other

The confidence which Wilson had in the ultimate and complete triumph of the Republican party is remarkable. The cause of right, he believed, would in the end prove the cause of profit. He had now cut loose from the Know-nothings. In spite of the success of the American party in New York and Massachusetts, it had passed the zenith of its power.

The Whig party in New England died hard. It had this year a ticket in Maine, New Hampshire, Massachusetts, and Connecticut. Winthrop and Choate held aloof from the Republican party. Earnest efforts had been made to get Winthrop to take an important part in the new movement, but without success.[1] In a letter to the Whigs of his State assembled in convention, Choate denied that their party was dead. He defined their position in a felicitous phrase which at once became famous. He wrote: "We join ourselves to no party that does not carry the flag and keep step to the music of the Union."[2]

Two discernible lines of opinion actuated men to join together in the Republican party. The one was devotion to the cause of the slave, induced by sympathy for his wrongs. It was the expression of the humanitarian spirit; it was a practical corollary drawn from the teachings of Christ. This feeling had its noblest embodiment in Sumner. To him and to those he influenced, the Fugitive Slave law seemed the grossest outrage inflicted by the South upon the North.[3]

The other line of opinion was best represented by Seward, and was a protest against the increasing and encroach-

---

authorities which I cannot now name, have helped me to this estimate of Wilson.

[1] See Rise and Fall of the Slave Power, vol. ii. p. 433; Reminiscences of a Journalist, Congdon, p. 88.

[2] Letter of Oct. 1st, Life of Choate, Brown, p. 303.

[3] The address of Sumner in New York in May, published in the *Weekly Tribune* of May 19th, is an illustration of this point of view.

ing political power of the slave oligarchy.[1] The men in whom this feeling was dominant chafed at the unequal representation in Congress of the South under the Constitution. The certainty that every new slave State meant two senators devoted to slavery, and representation in the House based on three-fifths of the slaves, was their most powerful reason for the opposition to the extension of slavery. The Sumner and Seward sentiments did indeed run into each other. The influence that made men Republicans was often a mixture of the two, and perhaps no exact line of demarcation can be drawn, for the belief that slavery was an evil was at the bottom of both. Yet a careful study of the political literature of the time brings clearly to light that although with some the moral sentiment was dominant, with a much greater number the political sentiment weighed down the balance. In the main, it may be said that the former Whigs thought with Seward; that the former Free-soilers and Democrats thought with Sumner. The Garrison abolitionists held entirely aloof from the Republican movement, but there was cordial sympathy between them and Sumner. The disciples of Seward, on the other hand, had no love for the abolitionists and their methods. It was sometimes maintained that they were a drawback to the anti-slavery cause, and it was a matter of gratulation that they did not become Republicans, as they would have been a burden to carry.

Meanwhile the free-State settlers in Kansas, while working for their personal weal and what they conceived to be the best interests of the territory, were making an issue which was destined to distract Congress and excite the

---

[1] "I leave the rights and interests of the slaves in the States to their own care and that of their advocates; I simply ask whether the safety and the interests of twenty-five millions of free, non-slaveholding white men ought to be sacrificed or put in jeopardy for the convenience or safety of three hundred and fifty thousand slave-holders?"—Seward at Buffalo, Oct. 19th, 1855, Works, vol. iv. p. 249.

country. The territorial legislature assembled in July. Free-State members had been elected at the supplementary elections ordered by the governor. These were summarily unseated, and the solitary Free-soiler who was left did not long delay to retire from the body. Governor Reeder and the legislature soon quarrelled. The legislators got up a petition to the President for his removal, but the messenger who was despatched to Washington with it was met on the way with the intelligence that their object had already been accomplished.[1] The code of laws which the legislature, now in perfect unison on the slavery question, adopted, was utterly out of tune with Republican government in the nineteenth century. All the provisions relating to slaves, reported the congressional committee, were of a "character intolerant and unusual even for that class of legislation."[2] Any free person who by speaking, writing, or printing should advise or induce any slaves to rebel should suffer death. The enticement of a slave to leave his master was punishable with death or imprisonment at hard labor for not less than ten years. To declare orally or in writing that slavery did not legally exist in the territory was to incur the penalty of incarceration for not less than two years.[3] Free-State settlers interpreted this provision to mean that it was a prison offence to have the Declaration of Independence in one's house.[4] All officers of the territory, attorneys admitted to practice in the courts, and voters, if challenged, must take an oath to support the Fugitive Slave law. "In Kansas, now by usurpation a slave territory," said Senator Seward at Buffalo, "the utterance of this speech, calm and candid although I mean it to be,

---

[1] Reeder's testimony, Howard Report, p. 945.
[2] Howard Report, p. 44.
[3] The whole chapter relating to slaves is printed in Kansas, Sara Robinson, p. 80; a portion of it may be found in Greeley's American Conflict, vol. i. p. 239. The code is well characterized by Von Holst, vol. v. p. 159.
[4] Kansas, Sara Robinson, p. 116.

would be treason; the reading and circulation of it in print would be punished with death."[1] By virtue of those laws, said Clayton in the Senate, "John C. Calhoun, were he now living in Kansas, might be sent to the penitentiary."[2]

Yet in truth it might be questioned whether slavery existed in fact as well as in law. The census of February had disclosed that there were but one hundred and ninety-two slaves out of a total population of eight thousand six hundred.[3] Stringfellow, a leader of the Missourians, had endeavored to interest Southern congressmen in a scheme of negro colonization. "Two thousand slaves," he had argued, "actually lodged in Kansas will make a slave State out of it. Once fairly there, nobody will disturb them."[4] Stringfellow received promises, but they were not carried into effect. Southerners would send their young men, but not their slaves, to Kansas.[5] The failure thus to act was not because they did not appreciate the gravity of the situation, for they were disposed to believe Atchison when he wrote, "If Kansas is abolitionized, Missouri ceases to be a slave State, New Mexico becomes a free State, California remains a free State; but if we secure Kansas as a slave State, Missouri is secure; New Mexico and Southern California, if not all of it, becomes a slave State; in a word, the prosperity or ruin of the whole South depends on the Kansas struggle."[6] The Charleston *Mercury* undoubtedly represented

---

[1] Oct. 19th, Seward's Works, vol. iv. p. 250.

[2] Aug. 27th, 1856, *Congressional Globe*, 2d Sess. 34th Cong., p. 37.

[3] Howard Report, p. 44.

[4] Spring's Kansas, p. 27. See also Stringfellow's letter of Oct. 6th, 1855, to the Montgomery *Advertiser*, New York *Tribune*, Dec. 4th.

[5] "We have information from points all along the border, and we are assured that there has been no importation of slaves with the exception of a few at Shawnee Mission, while others have been sold, leaving but a very slight actual increase."—Kansas *Herald of Freedom*, cited by the *National Intelligencer*, June 14th.

[6] Atchison to gentlemen in North Carolina, Sept. 12th, 1855, cited by the New York *Tribune*, Nov. 7th.

Southern sentiment, when it spoke of the contest as one "between fanatical hirelings and noble champions of the South." That sentiment was certainly represented when it maintained that "the cause of Kansas is the cause of the South."[1]

There was an inherent difficulty in the emigration of planters with their slaves to a new territory. The owners of negroes were the owners of land. The sale of a plantation was the work of time. At the North there was an energetic and intelligent floating population which could move on short notice.[2] At the South, only the poor whites could quit their homes without long preparation. Emigrants from the North poured into Kansas while the small planters of the South were considering the project; and after the dispute broke out whether the soil should be free or slave, the most powerful of reasons prevented an emigration of slaveholders. Their property was of too precarious a nature to expose to the chances of such a contest. Hardly a slaveholder took with him to Kansas as many as five negroes.[3] One party to this struggle, therefore, was composed of poor whites of the slave-holding States and the adventurous spirits of western Missouri, assisted, to some extent, by Southern money, and led by Atchison and Stringfellow, who were playing a political game. The other party were men from the North, actual settlers, and the same kind of people that we have seen in our own day leave their homes and emigrate to Southern California and Dakota. Those who went into Kansas from Missouri as permanent settlers, or merely to vote at the elections, were, on account of their appearance and actions, called "border ruffians."

---

[1] New York *Tribune*, Nov. 7th.

[2] The difference was well stated by Thayer in a speech in the House of Representatives in 1859. See the Kansas Crusade, p. 246.

[3] Ibid. Thayer had not heard of a single slave-holder who took there as many as five negroes, but Sara Robinson speaks of Judge Elmore who had nineteen slaves, see p. 213.

They themselves finally came to glory in the opprobrious name.[1]

The leader of the free-State party, Robinson, had been in California during the troublous times which preceded the formation of a State government, and his experience was now of value. The plan of action resolved upon was to repudiate the territorial legislature as illegal; to organize at once a State government, and apply to Congress for admission into the Union. Robinson despatched a messenger to New England for Sharps rifles, which were sent to Lawrence in packages marked "books."[2] The free-State party went actively to work, and held several meetings to perfect their organization. On October 9th they elected delegates to a constitutional convention. Reeder had joined himself to this party, had been received with enthusiasm, and was on the same day elected delegate to Congress, receiving all the ballots cast.[3] The territorial legislature had ordered an election for congressional delegate, which took place October 1st. Whitfield received 2721 votes, which were all that were cast, except 17. The pro-slavery men looked upon Reeder's election as a sham; the free-State men paid no attention to the orders of the territorial legislature. Reeder was at first in favor of having his party take part in the election of October 1st, but when he attended the free-State convention at Big Springs he "was persuaded, by an examination of the territorial election law, that our voters would be excluded, and found that there was a gen-

---

[1] See letter of Atchison of Sept. 12th, published in the New York *Tribune* of Nov. 7th; also letter of same, Dec. 15th, 1855, to the editor of the Atlanta *Examiner*, *Tribune*, Jan. 19th, 1856.

[2] Spring's Kansas, pp. 59, 60. The Emigrant-Aid Company did not send any implements of war, but members of the corporation contributed money as individuals for that purpose. Lawrence was the first settlement of the Emigrant-Aid Company and the important town of the free-State party.

[3] He received 2849 votes.

eral concurrence of opinion in favor of a separate election."[1]

The constitutional convention met, October 23d, at Topeka. Nineteen of the thirty-four members were Democrats, six were Whigs, and the remaining nine were Independents, Free-soilers, and Republicans. A majority of the members were friendly to the Kansas-Nebraska act.[2] This convention formed themselves into a free and independent State, styled the State of Kansas, and framed a constitution which prohibited slavery and provided for its submission to the people.

Thus there were now two governments and two sets of people directly hostile to each other. The pro-slavery men sneered at the embryo State government, but were incensed at the action of those who had formed it. The free-State people rendered no obedience to the territorial laws, and for a while no particular effort was made to enforce them. Shannon, the new governor, sympathized with the Missourians and recognized the territorial laws as binding. A convention to organize the pro-slavery party thoroughly was held in November. Governor Shannon presided, and assured his hearers that they had the support of the President.[3] They decided to take the name of "Law-and-order party."

Until now, there had been no collision between the opposing forces. Their settlements were apart. A few outrages had been committed and broils were not uncommon, but in the main the contest was one of political expedients. The organizing temper of the free-State party had irritated the other, and the pro-slavery leaders were looking for a pretext which would bring the struggle to a head by enabling them to attack Lawrence, the town of the Emigrant-Aid Company. The inhabitants of Lawrence were devoted to freedom, and they had inspired the organized movement which was troubling their opponents. A pretext was soon

---

[1] Reeder's testimony, Howard Report, p. 946.
[2] Spring's Kansas, p. 70.
[3] Ibid., p. 84.

found. A pro-slavery squatter had a quarrel with Dow, a free-State man, in reference to a claim, and shot him in cold blood. The affair caused great excitement in the neighborhood. The murderer fled. The free-State men demanded justice. The cabins of the murderer and his friends were burned down at night. Old Jacob Branson, who was tenderly attached to Dow, was reported to have made sanguinary threats against an accomplice in the murder. A peace warrant for Branson's arrest was obtained and placed in the hands of Sheriff Jones, an energetic and sincere pro-slavery man. On November 26th, he with his posse broke into Branson's cabin at the dead of night, made the arrest, and started for Lecompton. The news spread quickly. A free-State party of fifteen was collected. They intercepted the sheriff; their squirrel guns and Sharps rifles were made ready, but Branson was surrendered without a shot. The rescuers hurried to Lawrence to counsel with Dr. Robinson. "I am afraid the affair will make mischief," Robinson said. "The other side will seize upon it as a pretext for invading the territory."[1] A meeting was called to consider the rescue, and the people of Lawrence decided that they would wash their hands of the whole matter. They were apprehensive, however, that the occasion would be used to justify an attack upon them, and they appointed a committee of safety, who immediately went to work to organize the citizens into guards and put the town in a state of defence.[2]

Sheriff Jones was in a rage at the loss of his prisoner, but he hoped that the affair, rightly used, might redound to the advantage of his party. He was a Missourian, and it naturally occurred to him that he must have recourse to his own State for help. He forthwith sent a messenger to Missouri, asking for aid. Stating publicly what he had done, he swore with a loud oath that he would have revenge. A bystander,

---

[1] Spring's Kansas, p. 90.
[2] Robinson's testimony, Howard Report, p. 1069.

holding the opinion that the sheriff of a Kansas county should report to his governor, asked, "Why not send to Governor Shannon?"[1] The propriety of this struck Jones, and he despatched a courier to Shannon with an exaggerated account of the affair, expressing the opinion that it would require three thousand men to vindicate insulted justice. The governor called out the Kansas militia and about fifty men responded.[2] The appeals of the sheriff and his friends to Missouri were more effectual. One despatch to a member of the Missouri legislature at Jefferson City read: "We want help. Communicate this to our friends."[3] The border ruffians turned out with alacrity, and in straggling companies came along towards Lawrence. By the 1st of December there were from twelve to fifteen hundred armed men encamped on the Wakarusa River in the vicinity of Lawrence. Atchison was one of their leaders. Kansas and western Missouri were all ablaze, and all eyes were fixed upon the spot where a bloody battle was expected.

Earthworks had been constructed on all sides of Lawrence, and these were defended by six hundred men, one third of whom were armed with Sharps rifles. A lot had been received just before the siege began. Dr. Robinson wrote A. A. Lawrence, of Boston, December 4th, that the Sharps rifles "will give us the victory without firing a shot."[4] Robinson was right. The marvellous stories which had spread abroad about the efficiency of these breech-loading guns caused the invaders to reflect before making an attack on the town. A howitzer sent from the North had been smuggled through the invading lines. This affair, which is known in Kansas history as the Wakarusa war, did not come to actual hostilities. The invaders breathed out threats; they fired upon the Lawrence sentries nightly; and one free-

---

[1] Testimony of L. A. Prather, Howard Report, p. 1065; see Spring's Kansas. [2] Spring's Kansas, p. 91.
[3] St. Louis *Intelligencer*, Dec. 1st, cited by New York *Tribune;* see also Kansas, Sara Robinson, p. 120. [4] Spring's Kansas, p. 93.

State man was killed under circumstances that were discreditable to his assailants.[1] The Lawrence men acted strictly on the defensive. Robinson was chosen general, and his conduct of affairs was characterized by great prudence. The Lawrence committee of safety opened communications with Governor Shannon. Shannon's first idea was to demand that the free-State men should surrender their Sharps rifles and agree to obey the territorial law. To enforce this he asked for the assistance of the United States troops at Fort Leavenworth. The President did not give them orders to interfere, and Colonel Sumner, who was in command, would take no steps without express directions. Shannon began to have suspicions that he might have been misled by his pro-slavery advisers, and when he came to Lawrence on the 7th of December, he was certain of it. He played the part of a mediator, and was successful in negotiating a treaty of peace the effect of which was to deprive the invaders of all legal countenance and standing.[2] Sheriff Jones was disgusted at the outcome, and some of the Missourians shared his indignation; but Atchison was earnest in peaceful counsels.[3] He had regard for the public sentiment of the country, and insisted that the Missourians should withdraw. "If you attack Lawrence now," he said, "you attack it as a mob; and what would be the result? You would cause the election of an abolition President and the ruin of the Democratic party."[4] The Missourians left the territory. The victory was for Lawrence. The North learned that there was a resolute party in Kansas determined to make a fight for a free State.

---

[1] Kansas, Sara Robinson, pp. 132, 145.
[2] See letters of Gov. Shannon to the President, Nov. 28th and Dec. 11th.
[3] "Gen. Stringfellow once said to me that during the struggle for Kansas, whatever severity there may have been in Atchison's plans, he always relented when the time came to put them in execution."—Leverett Spring, Magazine of Western History, vol. ix. p. 80.
[4] Spring's Kansas, p. 100.

The Topeka Constitution was voted upon by the free-State people on December 15th, and was ratified by 1731 affirmative to 46 negative votes. The question of the exclusion of free negroes had occasioned debate in the constitutional convention, and it had been agreed to have a separate vote of the people on this article. They decided by a majority of nearly three to one to exclude colored people from the State. On the 15th of January, 1856, there was an election for governor and legislature of the new commonwealth. Robinson was chosen governor. There was little interference with these elections by the pro-slavery men; they were looked upon by that party as silly performances. At only two places was there any trouble. At Leavenworth, in December, a mob seized the ballot-box and stopped further proceedings. At Easton, in January, there was an affray in which a pro-slavery man was killed. The next day his death was avenged by the Kickapoo Rangers, who cruelly assassinated a free-State leader.

Seven weeks after the election, the free-State legislature met at Topeka and prepared a memorial to Congress, asking that Kansas might be admitted into the Union as a State under the Topeka Constitution.

Thus stood affairs in Kansas when the Thirty-fourth Congress got fairly to work:

The House of Representatives, which had been elected on the issue raised on the Kansas-Nebraska act, assembled in Congress on the first Monday of December, 1855. It was a body hard to classify politically. There were Democrats, pro-slavery Whigs, pro-slavery Americans, anti-slavery Americans, and Republicans. The *Congressional Globe*, which was accustomed to indicate the partisan divisions by printing the names of the members in different type, now gave up such a classification in despair. When the next Congress met, the editor of the *Globe* returned to his usual practice. The perplexing divisions and cross-modifications which now existed had then settled down into three distinct and clearly marked parties.

The "Tribune Almanac" confessed the difficulty of a proper classification, but did not shirk the attempt. There were seventy-nine Democrats, friends of the administration, who were counted upon to support the Pierce-Douglas policy in regard to slavery. Twenty of these were from the North. One hundred and seventeen members had been elected as anti-Nebraska men, and, when chosen, it was expected that they would uphold the cause of freedom in the territories. Thirty-seven members were Whigs or Americans of pro-slavery tendencies, and all but three so classed were from the slave States. Again there was a cross-division of the one hundred and seventeen anti-Nebraska men, all of whom were from the North. Seventy-five of them had been elected as Know-nothings.[1]

The House went immediately to work to elect a speaker. An animated contest began. It was soon evident that the disorganized party conditions which had prevailed since the passage of the Kansas-Nebraska act were nearing an end, and that the slavery question and the Kansas dispute were ranging men in Congress into two political divisions. Richardson was the caucus nominee of the Democrats. He received seventy-four votes on the first trial. His supporters stuck by their candidate so persistently that they became known as "the immortal seventy-four." The opposition scattered their votes, which, on the first calling of the roll, were distributed among no less than twenty candidates. Campbell, of Ohio, received the largest number. On the 7th of December he withdrew his name, and it was then patent that Banks, of Massachusetts, who had received votes from the first, could concentrate more of the anti-Nebraska strength than any other candidate.

Banks was a self-made and largely a self-educated man. He started to work as a bobbin-boy in a cotton-factory and became a good machinist. Yet he had less genius for me-

---

[1] See speech of Smith of Tennessee, House of Representatives, April 4th, 1856; Rise and Fall of the Slave Power, vol. ii. p. 420.

chanics than for rhetoric, an art in which he gained exercise by delivering addresses on temperance. He had also tried the stage, playing the part of Claude Melnotte before a Boston audience. He had been elected to the previous Congress as a Democrat, but had opposed the Kansas-Nebraska bill. He was chosen to the present House of Representatives as a Know-nothing, but in the canvass of 1855 he had abandoned that party and had presided over the Republican convention of his State. He was sagacious in manner, impressive in speech, grave in council; but many of his political friends had a suspicion that he was not so wise as he looked.[1] Greeley, who was at Washington as the correspondent of the *Tribune*, stood up for him from the first. His fitness for the post was universally conceded, and it seemed to the veteran editor that the imputation that the anti-Nebraska movement was a "Whig trick" would be effectually refuted by taking as the candidate for speaker a former Democrat.[2]

The continued ballotings, and the discussions to which they gave rise, resulted in showing that all the members of the House could be practically classified in three parties. Their strength was well represented by the typical vote for speaker, when there came to be but the three candidates, Banks, Richardson, and Fuller of Pennsylvania. The Republicans numbered one hundred and five, the Democrats seventy-four, the National American party forty.[3] This did not take into account all the members of the House. But there were always absentees; and four anti-Nebraska men, who ought to have supported Banks, persistently threw away their votes by giving their voice for some other Republican. Banks finally reached one hundred and seven, which was his highest number. Fuller rarely had forty, but

---

[1] See Reminiscences of a Journalist, Congdon; Life of Samuel Bowles, Merriam.

[2] Greeley to the New York *Tribune*, Dec. 19th, 1855.

[3] See resolution of Smith of Alabama, and remarks of Colfax, of Indiana, *Congressional Globe*, vol. xxxi. pp. 65, 85.

it was well understood that if the Democrats would come to him, he was certain of the votes of forty Americans.

As the position of all the members on the main question was not well defined or understood, the proceedings of a certain afternoon set apart for the catechism of the candidates were important, as indicating what precise opinions had been evolved out of the chaotic political conditions which had prevailed since the passage of the Kansas-Nebraska act. The three candidates voted for the resolution which instituted the catechising. The answers of Richardson, Fuller, and Banks to questions which were propounded, and the adherence of their supporters, after they had defined their position, typified pretty nearly the division of sentiment in the country and prefigured the presidential contest.

Richardson planted himself upon the Douglas doctrine of popular sovereignty. Fuller maintained that as the territories were the common property of all the States, neither Congress nor a territorial legislature had the power to establish or prohibit slavery in the territories. When application for admission into the Union was made, the question should be decided by the State constitution. Since it was generally supposed that Fuller had been elected as an anti-Nebraska man, much surprise was occasioned when it was learned early in the session that he had veered to the South on the slavery issue. At first his votes came mostly from the North; but a month before the day of the catechism it was understood that he had satisfied the South on the Kansas question, and after that time his votes came mainly from the slave States.[1] Apparently the supporters of Richardson and Fuller might together have elected the speaker, for they agreed on Kansas; but the Democrats had resolved in caucus to support no one but a Democrat, and would not go to Fuller, who was an American. The Fuller men could not consistently vote for Richardson, as the caucus which

---

[1] Greeley to the New York *Tribune*, Dec. 11th, 1855. The day of catechism was Jan. 12th, 1856.

THE CONTEST FOR SPEAKER

nominated him had censured the Know-nothings.[1] Nor was it absolutely certain that the union of these two forces would elect a speaker. They did not constitute a majority of a full house; and if the line came to be sharply drawn between two men, one pro-slavery and the other anti-slavery, it was quite possible that the anti-slavery man would prevail.

Banks stated clearly that he was in favor of congressional prohibition of slavery in all the territories where such action was necessary to keep it out. In regard to Kansas and Nebraska, which was the question of the day, he desired that there should " be made good to the people of the United States the prohibition for which the Southern States contracted, and received a consideration. I am," he continued, "for the substantial restoration of the prohibition as it has existed since 1820." The opinion of Banks had already been generally understood, but his clear and eloquent statement gave him a commanding position before the House and the country.[2]

The hearty response from the members and from the country was an index of the concentration of the public mind on the slavery question, which had come about since the fall elections of 1854. Seventy-five men who voted for Banks had been elected as Know-nothings or through Know-nothing influence; now most of them believed that the lesser should give place to the greater issue. "The majority of the Banks men," wrote Greeley to Charles A. Dana, "are now members of Know-nothing councils, and some twenty or thirty of them actually believe in the swindle. Half the Massachusetts delegation, two thirds that of Ohio, and nearly all that of Pennsylvania are Know-nothings this day. We shall get them gradually detached."[3]

---

[1] See discussion of Dec. 20th, 1855, *Congressional Globe*, vol. xxxii. p. 62.

[2] Greeley to the New York *Tribune*, Jan. 12th, 1856.

[3] Letter of Feb. 9th, 1856. Greeley was at Washington, a close observer, and occupying a position of influence. Many of his private letters to Dana, who was managing editor of the *Tribune*, were published in the

A remark which Banks had made in a speech at Portland, Maine, during the preceding canvass, gave him trouble. He said that in certain circumstances he would be willing "to let the Union slide." The Union sentiment among Northern representatives was so strong that he now felt it necessary to declare his unalterable attachment to the Union and his willingness to fight for it, as he believed it was "the main prop of the liberties of the American people." The Union which he was willing to let slide was one whose chief object should be to maintain and propagate human slavery.[1]

The contest for the election of speaker, which lasted two months, fixed the attention of the country and excited intense interest. The most entertaining historian of the struggle is Horace Greeley, who wrote a daily account for his journal. His private letters to Dana throw light upon his public communications, and together they form a connected narrative from the point of view of an earnest Republican. The private letters show his varying hopes and fears, and reflect the passing sentiment. "I am doing what I can for Banks," Greeley writes Dana, December 1st, 1855; "but he will not be speaker. His support of the Republican against the Know-nothing ticket this fall renders it impossible. If we elect anybody, it will be Pennington or Fuller. I fear the latter. Pennington is pretty fair, considering. He will try to twist himself into the proper shape, but I would greatly prefer one who had the natural crook. . . . The news from Kansas is helping us."[2] On January 8th, 1856, Greeley writes: "We calculate to elect Banks in the course of to-morrow night. No postponement on account of the weather."[3] The Democrats in caucus had re-

---

New York *Sun*, May 19th, 1889, and are a valuable contribution to history.

[1] See discussion of Dec. 24th and 29th, 1855, *Congressional Globe*, vol. xxxii. pp. 75, 103.

[2] That is the news of the Wakarusa war. New York *Sun*, May 19th, 1889.   [3] Greeley to Dana, ibid.

solved that they would vote against any adjournment until a speaker was elected, but the project of a continuous session did not alarm the Republicans. The 9th of January was an exciting day, and the night session stormy; but no result was reached.[1] At half-past eight on the morning of the 10th, the House, through sheer weariness, adjourned. After the night session, Greeley is hopeful, and writes Dana: "We shall elect Banks yet, now you see if we do not. We made a good push towards it last night."[2] One week later Greeley is discouraged and writes to the *Tribune:* "There is no anti-Nebraska majority, . . . and that is the reason why there is no organization. The people meant to choose an anti-Nebraska House and thought they had done so; but they were deceived and betrayed."[3] The same day he writes his confidential friend: "I shall see these treacherous scoundrels through the speakership, if I am allowed to live long enough, at all events. Our plans are defeated and our hopes frustrated from day to day by perpetual treacheries on our own side."[4]

The days went by. The calling of the roll went on until one hundred and twenty-seven ballots had been taken and many propositions voted upon which had in view the organization of the House. On the morning of January 28th, Greeley wrote Dana: "We hope to elect Banks to-day." But his hopes were dashed; and in the afternoon, when the House had adjourned, he charges the failure upon "thirty double-dyed traitors, ten of them voting against us, and the other twenty cursing me because they cannot do likewise."[5]

Early in the session, Alexander Stephens had bewailed the inconsistency of his fellow-representatives. "If men were reliable creatures," he wrote his brother, "I should say" Banks never can be elected. "But my observation

---

[1] Greeley to New York *Tribune*, Jan. 9th.
[2] Greeley to Dana, Jan. 10th, 1856, New York *Sun*, May 19th, 1889.
[3] Jan. 17th, 1856.
[4] Greeley to Dana, Jan. 17th, 1856.   [5] Idem, Jan. 28th, 1856.

has taught me that very little confidence is to be placed on what they say as to what they will do."[1]

Richardson withdrew his name, and the Democrats transferred their strength to Orr, of South Carolina. But he was no more successful than Richardson in attracting votes from the Southern Americans, so he also retired from the contest. On the 1st of February a resolution was offered declaring that Aiken, of South Carolina, should be elected speaker. This received 103 affirmative to 110 negative votes. Aiken was a man of sterling character, personally very popular, and, although he had the name of owning more slaves than any one in the country and was a devout disciple of Calhoun, he was more acceptable to the Southern Know-nothings than Orr and Richardson. When the House adjourned on this afternoon, the Democrats were elated and some of the Republicans depressed. It was certain that the resolution—already many times offered and always voted down—providing that a plurality should elect, would on the morrow prevail. This would, it was supposed, insure the election of Aiken. At the levee that evening, the President warmly congratulated him on his probable success. A dozen anti-Nebraska caucuses were held, where the weak-hearted offered timorous counsels, but where the majority felt confident. It was determined to stand by Banks at all hazards.

Soon after the reading of the journal on February 2d, Smith, a Democrat of Tennessee, offered a resolution which provided that the House should proceed immediately to vote for a speaker; if, after three votes had been taken, no candidate had received a majority, then on the fourth calling of the roll the member receiving the largest number of votes should be declared elected speaker. Smith expected that the adoption of this rule would result in the choice of Aiken. The resolution was carried by 113 yeas to 104 nays. All the Republicans voted for it, as

---

[1] Dec. 11th, 1855, Life of Stephens, Johnston and Browne, p. 300.

they had persistently favored the plan of having a plurality elect. Twelve Democrats joined them. The end of the protracted contest was now in sight, and the interest was overmastering. The three votes were taken without result. The House then proceeded to vote the one hundred and thirty-third time, the fourth and last under the plurality rule. As the roll was called, the anxiety was without bounds. The Americans who clung to Fuller were besought to save the Union by voting for Aiken. The votes were recorded; there remained the announcement of the result. The confusion was great. All the members were standing, and trying vainly to be heard in expostulation or appeal. One member shouted out a motion to adjourn, which was quickly declared out of order by the presiding officer. John W. Forney, the clerk of the former House, a strong Democrat, until recently one of the editors of the Washington *Union*, had presided over the House during the trying situation of the past two months with impartiality and admirable skill. The time had come for a prompt decision and emphatic statement. The precedent was to have a resolution adopted stating that the member who had the largest number of votes should be declared speaker. But Forney was afraid that another vote, in the wild excitement prevailing, might overturn the result reached. He and the tellers, who represented both parties, quickly consulted together, and they decided to declare Banks elected. The Republican teller gained the attention of the House and said: "Gentlemen, the following is the result of the one hundred and thirty-third vote: Banks, 103; Aiken, 100; Fuller, 6; Campbell, 4; Wells, 1; therefore, according to the resolution which was adopted this day, Nathaniel P. Banks is declared speaker of the House of Representatives for the Thirty-fourth Congress." The pent-up emotion of many weeks broke forth in wild tumult. The hall resounded with cheers, which the vanquished tried to overpower with hisses. When order was partially restored, an American from Kentucky protested that, as the precedent of 1849 had not been followed, Banks had not been chosen speaker. This protest occasioned an exhibition of feeling which showed that Southern chivalry was not all a sham. Clingman, Aiken, and other Southern Democrats rebuked the cavillers and maintained that Banks had been fairly and legally chosen. A resolution to that effect was adopted by an overwhelming vote, and Banks was escorted to the chair.[1]

The day after the election, Greeley wrote Dana: "Of course you understand that the election of Banks was 'fixed' before the House met yesterday morning. He would have had three votes more if necessary, perhaps five. There has been a great deal of science displayed in the premises, and all manner of negotiations. A *genuine* history of this election would beat any novel in interest."[2] Two weeks later, Greeley is still full of the transaction, and writes Dana that if he sees a certain man in New York soon, "make him give you a private account of the Banks election—inside view. He may be as great a rascal as he is represented; if so, I begin to see the utility of rascals in the general economy of things. Banks would never have been elected without him. He can tell you a story as interesting as 'The Arabian Nights,' and a great deal truer. He has done more, and incurred more odium, to elect Banks than would have been involved in beating ten speakers."[3]

The latent influences, whatever they may have been, had only to do with a few floating votes. Most of the members

---

[1] In this account, besides the *Congressional Globe*, I have consulted Greeley's letters to the New York *Tribune;* his private letters to Dana; Simonton's letters to the New York *Times;* Forney's Anecdotes of Public Men, vol. i.; Life of A. H. Stephens, Johnston and Browne; see also speech of J. A. Smith, of Tennessee, House of Representatives, April 4th.

[2] Washington, Feb. 3d, 1856, New York *Sun*, May 19th, 1889.

[3] Washington, Feb. 16th, ibid. In H. H. Bancroft, vol. xviii. p. 702, bribery in the election of Banks as speaker is alluded to.

who voted for Banks did so for the reason that John Sherman, of Ohio, gave. I understand Banks to take this position, Sherman said before the day of the catechism, "that the repeal of the Missouri Compromise was an act of great dishonor, and that under no circumstances whatever will he —if he have the power—allow the institution of human slavery to derive benefit from that repeal."[1] For the members of whom Sherman was a type, and for the Republicans of the Northern States, the election of Banks was a victory of freedom over slavery. It was even asserted that it was the first victory which had been gained within the memory of men living.[2] It was, moreover, a triumph of the young Republican party. Friend and foe had repeatedly on the floor of the House denominated all the supporters of Banks as Republicans. The Democrats chafed at the adoption of that name. The Republican party of which Jefferson was the father had been the forerunner of their own, and to use that designation seemed like stealing their thunder. To distinguish, therefore, the modern party from the ancient, they called it the Black Republican; and they maintained that the adjective was appropriate, as the Banks men were devoted to the cause of the negro. Yet if the Democrats were fond of appealing to the name of Jefferson, the Republicans were fonder still of referring to his declared principles.

The discussion that was held at intervals between the votes for speaker turned almost entirely on some phase of the slavery question. Even the American movement was treated in its relation to the absorbing issue. Humphrey Marshall, a Kentucky Know-nothing, said that he found no American party in Washington; that the engrossing subject was the negro.[3] The long contest was marked by the absence of bitterness; good temper prevailed, and the struggle was conducted with dignity and forbearance. This was not due so much to the shadow of the serious situation which hung

---

[1] Jan. 9th.   [2] New York *Tribune*, Feb. 6th.
[3] Greeley to the New York *Tribune*, Dec. 5th, 1855.

over the House as it was to the good-humor of the members. The dissolution of the Union was freely talked of, but the Southern threats were not considered serious. The declaration of a Virginia Hotspur, that "if you restore the Missouri Compromise or repeal the Fugitive Slave law, this Union will be dissolved," was received with "laughter and cries of 'Oh, no!'" The night session, though exciting, was characterized by no violence of speech or action. The only outrageous act of the whole contest was the assault upon Horace Greeley in the streets of Washington by Rust, a member of Congress from Arkansas, on account of a severe stricture in the *Tribune* for a resolution he had introduced.

The election of Banks was an important event for a party whose organization dated back but one and a half years. It was the triumph of a section; all his supporters came from the North. It gave additional point to the Republican National convention which had been called by the chairmen of the Republican State committees of Maine, Vermont, Massachusetts, New York, Pennsylvania, Ohio, Michigan, Indiana, and Wisconsin. Delegates from twenty-three States assembled at Pittsburgh on the 22d of February. No men were more prominent in the deliberations than the editors of the two leading Republican journals. Greeley counselled extreme caution. "Not only our acts but our words," he said, "should indicate an absence of ill-will towards the South." The American question must be treated "with prudence and forbearance. There are hundreds of whole-hearted Republicans in the American ranks. But the American as a *National* organization is not friendly to us."[1] Henry J. Raymond wrote the address which was unanimously adopted by the convention.[2] The author related the his-

---

[1] Speech at the convention.

[2] One gets a glimpse of the rivalry between these journalists in Greeley's letter to Dana of March 2d. "Have we got to surrender a page of next *Weekly* to Raymond's bore of an address? The man who could inflict six columns on a long-suffering public, on such an occasion, cannot possibly know enough to write an address. Alas for Wilson's glorious

rifles to Kansas . . . *and on the other side are the constituted authorities of the United States.*"[1]

The Democratic majority[2] in the Senate did not take hold of the matter at once; they waited for Douglas, their leader, to give expression to their views, but he was detained from Washington by illness. As soon, however, as he arrived, he set himself diligently to work. That part of the annual message which related to Kansas, and also the special message, had been referred to the committee on territories. On the 12th of March, Douglas made a report in which he discussed the question thoroughly. The Emigrant-Aid Company was the scape-goat, and its operations were made to do great service in his argument. In his view the territorial legislature was a legal body, and its acts were lawful; the Topeka movement repudiated the laws of the territorial government, and was in defiance of the authority of Congress. Three senators joined with Douglas in the majority report; one only, Senator Collamer, of Vermont, dissented. The Topeka movement, Collamer averred, had been entered into because the free-State people saw no other source of relief; "thus far this effort for redress is peaceful, constitutional, and right." The true remedy is the entire repeal of the Kansas-Nebraska act. "But," he continued, "if Congress insist on proceeding with the experiment, then declare all the action by this spurious foreign legislative assembly utterly inoperative and void, and direct a reorganization, providing proper safeguard for legal voting and against foreign force." Yet there was another way to end the trouble, and that was to admit Kansas as a free State under the Topeka Constitution.

The two reports were read to the Senate by their

---

[1] Boston *Post*, Feb. 15th. The New York *Journal of Commerce*, the Albany *Argus*, and Philadelphia *Pennsylvanian* take similar ground.

[2] The Senate was composed of thirty-four administration Democrats, thirteen Republicans, twelve Whigs or Americans, all but one of whom were from the slave States.

authors. When Collamer had finished, Sumner rose and said: "In the report of the majority the true issue is smothered; in that of the minority, the true issue stands forth as a pillar of fire to guide the country. . . . I have no desire to precipitate the debate on this important question, under which the country already shakes from side to side, and which threatens to scatter from its folds civil war." . . . But I must repel "at once, distinctly and unequivocally, the assault which has been made upon the Emigrant-Aid Company of Massachusetts. That company has done nothing for which it can be condemned under the laws and Constitution of the land. These it has not offended in letter or spirit; not in the slightest letter or in the remotest spirit. It is true, it has sent men to Kansas; and had it not a right to send them? It is true, I trust, that its agents love freedom and hate slavery. And have they not a right to do so? Their offence has this extent, and nothing more."

In the calmer light of historical disquisition, we may approve every word of this indignant burst of Sumner.

Meanwhile the House had resolved by 101 yeas to 100 nays that the Missouri Compromise ought to be restored.[1] Whitfield had taken his seat as delegate from Kansas without objection; but a memorial from Reeder had been presented, in which he claimed the place. By the middle of February, Greeley was convinced that the session would be barren of legislative results. He wrote Dana: "We cannot (I fear) admit Reeder; we cannot admit Kansas as a State; we can only make issues on which to go to the people at the Presidential election."[2] When the matter seemed coming to a head in the Senate, Greeley thought it wise to moderate the zeal of his associates, and wrote Dana: "Do not let your folks write more savagely on the Kansas question than I do. I am fiery enough."[3]

---

[1] On Jan. 26th, before the election of the speaker.
[2] Feb. 16th, New York *Sun*, May 19th, 1889.   [3] In March, ibid.

On the 19th of March, the House took a step which, of the whole session, turned out to be its most valuable action relating to Kansas affairs. It resolved that the speaker should appoint a committee of three to inquire into the trouble in Kansas generally, and particularly into the frauds attempted or practised at any of the elections. Ample powers were furnished, and protection, if necessary, was requested from the President. It is, wrote Greeley to the *Tribune*, "the best day's work of the session except that of electing Banks."[1] William A. Howard of Michigan, John Sherman of Ohio, Republicans, and Mordecai Oliver, Democrat, of Missouri, were appointed the committee.

On the next day, Douglas addressed the Senate in support of the bill which he had drawn to embody the views that he had laid down in his report. It provided that when Kansas "shall contain 93,420 inhabitants (that being the present ratio for a member of Congress) a convention may be called by the legislature of the territory to form a constitution and State government;" six months' residence in the territory was a necessary qualification for voters.

The graphic pen of Harriet Beecher Stowe has given a description of Douglas as he appeared this winter, and she has vividly characterized his manner of argument. She did not hear the speech of March 20th, but she listened to a subsequent debate on the memorial of the self-styled free-State legislature of Kansas, which served as the text for this remarkable characterization. The author of "Uncle Tom's Cabin," and the society in which she moved, scorned Douglas. Her soul was bound up in the anti-slavery cause, and one might have expected from her a diatribe, only differing in force from those which fellow New England writers were publishing on every opportunity. But she was almost as much artist as abolitionist; and from the Senate gallery she looked upon the scene with the eye of an observer and student of character. In her description

---

[1] Letter of March 19th.

there is much of penetration. Severe as it is, one detects the striking impression made on the sensitive woman of genius by the man who was an intellectual giant.

"This Douglas," Mrs. Stowe writes, "is the very ideal of vitality. Short, broad, and thick-set, every inch of him has its own alertness and motion. He has a good head and face, thick black hair, heavy black brows and a keen eye. His figure would be an unfortunate one were it not for the animation which constantly pervades it; as it is, it rather gives poignancy to his peculiar appearance; he has a small, handsome hand, moreover, and a graceful as well as forcible mode of using it—a point speakers do not always understand. . . . He has two requisites of a debater—a melodious voice and a clear, sharply defined enunciation. . . . His forte in debating is his power of mystifying the point. With the most off-hand assured airs in the world, and a certain appearance of honest superiority, like one who has a regard for you and wishes to set you right on one or two little matters, he proceeds to set up some point which is *not* that in question, but only a family connection of it, and this point he attacks with the very best of logic and language; he charges upon it horse and foot, runs it down, tramples it in the dust, and then turns upon you with—'Sir, there is your argument! Did not I tell you so? You see it is all stuff;' and if you have allowed yourself to be so dazzled by his quickness as to forget that the routed point is not, after all, the one in question, you suppose all is over with it. Moreover, he contrives to mingle up so many stinging allusions to so many piquant personalities that by the time he has done his mystification a dozen others are ready and burning to spring on their feet to repel some direct or indirect attack, all equally wide of the point. His speeches, instead of being like an arrow sent at a mark, resemble rather a bomb which hits nothing in particular, but bursts and sends red-hot nails in every direction. . . . Douglas moves about the house," she continues, as the recognized leader of the Southern men. "It is a merciful providence that with all his alertness and adroitness, all his quick-sighted keenness, Douglas is not witty—that might have made him too irresistible a demagogue for the liberties of our laughter-loving people, to whose weaknesses he is altogether too well adapted now." [1]

Much of Douglas's speech of March 20th has the peculiarity of reasoning which Mrs. Stowe describes. It was, however, the strong legal argument which the position of the President and the Democrats required. The contrast between the legal territorial legislature and the "revolutionary, rebellious, and insurrectionary" Topeka movement was stated with overmastering force. Under the senator's magic power, one seemed to see the border ruffians, whose implements of civilization were the revolver, the bowie-knife, and the bottle of whiskey, in the character of champions of law and order; while the New England emigrants, who went with Bibles, books containing the masterpieces of our literature, the implements of husbandry, and steam-engines and boilers,[2] were "daring and defiant revolutionists. The whole responsibility of all the disturbances in Kansas," Douglas declared, in a culminating stroke of inconsequence, "rests upon the Massachusetts Emigrant-Aid Company and its affiliated societies."

Greeley appreciated the force of Douglas's argument. It was "a fluent and practised lawyer's plea at bar; . . . its delivery was set off by an impressive, emphatic manner," he wrote. He used more than two columns of his journal to refute the speech, but he could not forbear from paying the senator's manner a high compliment. "Douglas," he wrote, "has one point of superiority as a speaker over most of his contemporaries in Congress—he never hurries through or slurs over his sentences, but wisely assumes that what he thinks it worth his while to say, he may justifiably take time to say well; and that if it be fit that

---

[1] Letter from Washington, New York *Independent*, May 1st.
[2] See Kansas Crusade, Thayer, p. 187.

he should speak, it is fit also that his peers should hear and understand."[1]

The Kansas question afforded the Republican senators a great opportunity to define their position and put in concrete shape their principles before the country. All the troubles, every outrage in Kansas, pointed the argument in favor of congressional prohibition of slavery in the territories. Hale, of New Hampshire, made, in Greeley's opinion, the best speech of his life.[2] The new Republican senators from Illinois and Iowa, Trumbull and Harlan, made their mark. Wade's effort was called by Simonton "a magnificent invective."[3] Wilson made a stirring and effective speech, which found favor generally with the Republicans; ten thousand copies were subscribed for by members of the House before he had finished speaking.[4] It was gall and wormwood to the Southerners, and many threats of personal violence were made against him.[5] Collamer made a fine legal argument, and Greeley, who, since dissolving the firm of Seward, Weed, and Greeley, could not treat the New York senator fairly, wrote privately to Dana: "Collamer's speech is better than Seward's, in my humble judgment."[6] The truth is not always told in confidential correspondence. The personal feeling of Greeley found vent in communing with his friend, but he expressed the opinion of the country and the judgment of the historian when he wrote to his journal that Seward's speech was "the great argument," and stood "unsurpassed in its political philosophy."[7] Simonton had heard every speech which Seward had ever made in the Senate, but he was sure that this overtopped

---

[1] Greeley to New York *Tribune*, March 20th.
[2] Ibid., Feb. 28th.
[3] Simonton to New York *Times*, April 19th.
[4] Greeley to New York *Tribune*, Feb. 19th.
[5] Simonton to New York *Times*, Feb. 20th.
[6] Letter of April 7th.
[7] Greeley to New York *Tribune*, April 9th.

them all.[1] The praise was merited. The words were those of a great statesman. The thoughtful and reading men of the North could not despair of the republic when their views found such masterly expression in the Senate.

The Republicans, and those inclined in that direction, of every part of the country, were great readers. Men who were wavering needed conviction; men, firm in the faith, needed strong arguments with which they might convince the wavering. Young men who were going to cast their first vote wanted to have the issue set plainly before them. Boys who would soon become voters were deeply interested in the political literature; those who had read "Uncle Tom's Cabin" in 1852 were now reading Republican speeches and newspapers. Never in the world had political thinkers and speakers a more attentive and intelligent public than in the North between 1856 and 1860; and the literature was worthy of the public. As people thought more deeply on the slavery question, the New York *Weekly Tribune* increased its circulation. On the day that it published Seward's speech, one hundred and sixty-two thousand copies were sent out.[2] The Republican Association at Washington printed and sold at a low price a large number of Republican documents. Among them were "Governor Seward's Great Speech on the Immediate Admission of Kansas," Seward's Albany and Buffalo speeches, the speeches on Kansas in the Senate, of Wilson, Hale, Collamer, and Harlan. The supply of this sort of literature makes it evident that the Republican Association knew the people whom it must persuade were those who could be reached only by cogent reasoning; the demand shows the desire for correct political education.

The most startling speech made during the debate, the one which, from the events succeeding, became the most celebrated, was that of Charles Sumner. It was delivered on

---

[1] Simonton to New York *Times*, April 9th.
[2] Edition of April 2d.

the 19th and 20th days of May and was published under the title of "The Crime against Kansas." Two days previously he wrote Theodore Parker: "I shall pronounce the most thorough philippic ever uttered in a legislative body."[1] He thought he had girded himself with the spirit of the Athenian, and in one glorious passage his imitation went to the letter of the greatest of orations.[2] Sumner stated the question as one involving "liberty in a broad territory;" a territory which had "advantages of situation," "a soil of unsurpassed richness and a fascinating, undulating beauty of surface, with a health-giving climate," and which was "calculated to nurture a powerful and generous people, worthy to be a central pivot of American institutions. . . . Against this territory," he continued, "a crime has been committed which is without example in the records of the Past." It is greater than the crime of Verres in Sicily. Popular institutions have been desecrated; the ballot-box has been plundered. "Not in any common lust for power did this uncommon tragedy have its origin. It is the rape of a virgin territory, compelling it to the hateful embrace of slavery; and it may be clearly traced to a depraved longing for a new slave State, the hideous offspring of such a crime, in the hope of adding to the power of slavery in the national government. Yes, sir, when the whole world, alike Christian and Turk, is rising up to condemn this wrong, and to make it a hissing to the nations, here in our republic *force*—ay, sir, FORCE—has been openly employed in compelling Kansas to this pollution, and all for the sake of political power. . . . Such is the crime." The criminal is the slave power, and

---

[1] Life of Parker, Weiss, vol. ii. p. 179.

[2] It is curious that, in the excitement prevailing after the assault on Sumner, Butler should bethink himself of his pride in scholarship: "The best part of his [Sumner's] late speech is a periphrasis of Demosthenes. . . . I do not say it is a plagiarism; but it is a remarkable imitation, as far as one man incapable of comprehending the true spirit of Demosthenes could imitate him."—Butler, June 13th.

has "an audacity beyond that of Verres, a subtlety beyond that of Machiavel, a meanness beyond that of Bacon, and an ability beyond that of Hastings." Fresh, probably, from reading the entrancing tale of "The Rise of the Dutch Republic" which his friend Motley had just published, Sumner declared that the tyranny now employed to force slavery upon Kansas was kindred to that of Alva, who sought to force the Inquisition upon the Netherlands.

The crime against Kansas is "*the crime of crimes;*" it is "*the crime against nature*, from which the soul recoils, and which language refuses to describe." David R. Atchison, like Catiline, "stalked into this chamber, reeking with conspiracy; and then, like Catiline, he skulked away to join and provoke the conspirators, who at a distance awaited their congenial chief." His followers were "murderous robbers from Missouri;" they were "hirelings picked from the drunken spew and vomit of an uneasy civilization, lashed together by secret signs and lodges," and they "have renewed the incredible atrocities of the assassins and of the Thugs."

The reader may be reminded that although the date of Sumner's speech is later than the time to which I have brought down the history of events in Kansas territory, nothing further of importance occurred until May of this year, and his philippic was based only on those transactions which have already been related in this work. These citations, therefore, will give an idea of his extravagant statements as well as of his turgid rhetoric; and they show the license which he allowed himself in the use of words when wrought up on the subject of slavery.[1] It is the speech of a

---

[1] The *Quarterly Review* of London said: "That speech is an example and a proof of the deterioration of American taste. Sumner is well known in England, indeed in Europe, as a man of good sense and good taste almost to the edge of fastidiousness." The writer then cites three passages, one of which is the last quotation in the text, and another will be cited later on, and proceeds: "Sumner is too able and practised a speaker not to adapt himself to his audience. This must be the imagery that

sincere man who saw but one side of the question, whose thought worked in a single groove, and worked intensely. "There is no other side," he vehemently declared to a friend.[1]

Sumner's speech added nothing of legal or political strength to the controversy. The temperate arguments of the senators who preceded him were of greater weight. But the speech produced a powerful sensation. The bravery with which he hurled defiance towards the South and her institutions challenged admiration. Before this session, on one occasion when he was delivering a fierce invective, Douglas said to a friend: "Do you hear that man? He may be a fool, but I tell you that man has pluck. Nobody can deny that, and I wonder whether he knows himself what he is doing. I am not sure whether I should have courage to say those things to the men who are scowling around him."[2] But Sumner knew not fear; and his sincerity was absolute. His speech was prepared with care. To write out such a philippic in the cool seclusion of the study, and deliver it without flinching, was emphasizing to the Southerners that in Sumner they had a persistent antagonist whom the fury of their threats could not frighten.

If there had been no more in Sumner's speech than the invective against the slave power, he would not have been assaulted by Preston Brooks. Nor is it probable that the bitter attack which the senator made on South Carolina would have provoked the violence, had it not been coupled with personal allusions to Senator Butler, who was a kinsman of Brooks.[3] In order that the whole extent of the provocation may be understood, it is necessary to quote

---

delights the gravest and the most intelligent body that America possesses; and as such Sumner, much as he may have been ashamed of it, was perhaps justified in using it."

[1] Article of George W. Curtis, Appletons' Cyclopædia of Biography.

[2] Eulogy on Sumner, Carl Schurz, Lester, p. 637; also Reminiscences, Ben: Perley Poore, vol. i. p. 461.

[3] See remarks of Brooks in the House, July 14th, 1856.

Sumner's most exasperating reflections. "The senator from South Carolina [Butler]," he said, "and the senator from Illinois [Douglas], who, though unlike as Don Quixote and Sancho Panza, yet, like this couple, sally forth together . . . in championship of human wrongs." "The senator from South Carolina has read many books of chivalry, and believes himself a chivalrous knight, with sentiments of honor and courage. Of course he has chosen a mistress to whom he has made his vows, and who, though ugly to others, is always lovely to him; though polluted in the sight of the world, is chaste in his sight—I mean the harlot slavery. For her his tongue is always profuse in words. Let her be impeached in character, or any proposition made to shut her out from the extension of her wantonness, and no extravagance of manner or hardihood of assertion is then too great for this senator. The frenzy of Don Quixote, in behalf of his wench, Dulcinea del Toboso, is all surpassed." On the second day of his speech Sumner said: "With regret I come again upon the senator from South Carolina [Butler], who, omnipresent in this debate, overflowed with rage at the simple suggestion that Kansas had applied for admission as a State; and with incoherent phrases, discharged the loose expectoration of his speech, now upon her representative, and then upon her people. There was no extravagance of the ancient parliamentary debate which he did not repeat; nor was there any possible deviation from truth which he did not make. . . . The senator touches nothing which he does not disfigure—with error, sometimes of principle, sometimes of fact. He shows an incapacity of accuracy, whether in stating the Constitution or in stating the law, whether in the details of statistics or the diversions of scholarship. He cannot open his mouth but out there flies a blunder."[1]

---

[1] The attack on South Carolina, which, for want of space, I have not ventured to quote, may be found in Appendix to *Congressional Globe*, vol. xxxiii., 1st column of page 543.

A careful perusal of Butler's remarks, as published in the *Congressional Globe*, fails to disclose the reason of this bitter personal attack. His remarks were moderate. He made no reference to Sumner.[1] His reply to Hale, though spirited, was dignified and did not transcend the bounds of a fastidious parliamentary taste. Yet it must be said that his defence of Atchison, which to-day reads as a tribute to a generous, though rough and misguided, man, was very galling to an ardent friend of the free-State party of Kansas, such as Sumner. Butler was a man of fine family, older in looks than his sixty years, courteous, a lover of learning, and a jurist of reputation. He was honored with the position of chairman of the Senate judiciary committee. When Sumner first came to the Senate, although he was an avowed Free-soiler, the relations between him and Butler were friendly; they were drawn together by a common love of history and literature. When he made his speech on the Kansas-Nebraska bill, Butler paid him a well-chosen compliment at which he expressed his gratification. In June, 1854, however, the two had a very warm discussion in the Senate on the Fugitive Slave law, growing out of the rendition of Burns, in which Butler replied to Sumner's forcible remarks with indignation. Afterwards Butler sent him word that their personal intercourse must be entirely cut off. The only reason which the South Carolina senator could assign for the present personal attack was that Sumner's vanity had been mortified from thinking that he did not come out of the controversy of 1854 with as much credit as he ought, and this was his opportunity for retaliation.[2]

But no one understanding Sumner's character can accept

---

[1] I refer to his remarks at several different times on Kansas in this session of the Thirty-fourth Congress. Several times in the Thirty-third Congress he indulged in personalities towards Sumner. These were collected by Wilson, and stated in his speech of June 13th, 1856.

[2] See Butler's speech in the Senate, June 12th, 1856.

this as an explanation. There was nothing vindictive or revengeful in his nature. Besides, he was too much wrapped up in his own self-esteem to give more than a passing thought to a social slight from a slave-holding senator, even though he were a leader in the refined and cultivated society of Washington. Sumner's speech seems excessively florid to the more cultivated taste of the present; he might have made a more effective argument, and one stronger in literary quality without giving offence. The speech occasioned resentment not so much on account of severe political denunciation, as on account of the line of personally insulting metaphor. Yet he did not transgress the bounds of parliamentary decorum, for he was not called to order by the President or by any other senator. The vituperation was unworthy of him and his cause, and the allusion to Butler's condition[1] while speaking, ungenerous and pharisaical. The attack was especially unfair, as Butler was not in Washington, and Sumner made note of his absence. It was said that Seward, who read the speech before delivery, advised Sumner to tone down its offensive remarks, and he and Wade regretted the personal attack.[2] But Sumner was not fully "conscious of the stinging force of his language."[3] To that, and because he was terribly in earnest, must be attributed the imperfections of the speech. He would annihilate the slave power, and he selected South Carolina and her senator as vulnerable points of attack.

The whole story of Sumner's philippic, and its results, cannot be told without reference to his sharp criticism of Douglas. "The senator from Illinois," he said, "is the squire of slavery, its very Sancho Panza, ready to do all its humiliating offices. This senator, in his labored address, vindicating his labored report—piling one mass of elaborate

---

[1] The habits of the South Carolina senator were notoriously intemperate.
[2] Reminiscences, Perley Poore, vol. i. p. 462; Life of Wade, Riddle, p. 242.
[3] Eulogy of Schurz, Lester, p. 667.

error upon another mass—constrained himself to unfamiliar decencies of speech. . . . Standing on this floor, the senator issued his rescript, requiring submission to the usurped power of Kansas; and this was accompanied by a manner —all his own—such as befits the tyrannical threat. Very well. Let the senator try. I tell him now that he cannot enforce any such submission. The senator, with the slave power at his back, is strong; but he is not strong enough for this purpose. He is bold. He shrinks from nothing. Like Danton, he may cry: '*L'audace! l'audace! toujours l'audace!*' but even his audacity cannot compass this work. The senator copies the British officer who, with boastful swagger, said that with the hilt of his sword he would cram the 'stamps' down the throats of the American people, and he will meet a similar failure."

When Sumner sat down, Cass, the Nestor of the Senate, rose and said: "I have listened with equal regret and surprise to the speech of the honorable senator from Massachusetts. Such a speech—the most un-American and unpatriotic that ever grated on the ears of the members of this high body—I hope never to hear again here or elsewhere."

When Cass had finished, Douglas spoke of the "depth of malignity that issued from every sentence" of Sumner's speech. "Is it his object," Douglas asked, "to provoke some of us to kick him as we would a dog in the street, that he may get sympathy upon the just chastisement?" If the senator, Douglas continued, had said harsh things on the spur of the moment, and "then apologized for them in his cooler hours, I could respect him much more than if he had never made such a departure from the rules of the Senate. . . . But it has been the subject of conversation for weeks that the senator from Massachusetts had his speech written, printed,[1] committed to memory. . . . The libels, the gross

---

[1] The speech was not printed until after delivery, but it was in the printer's hands and mainly in type before spoken in the Senate; see Wilson's speech, June 13th.

insults, which we have heard to-day have been conned over, written with a cool, deliberate malignity, repeated from night to night in order to catch the appropriate grace; and then he came here to spit forth that malignity upon men who differ from him—for that is their offence." Douglas furthermore charged Sumner with being a perjurer, for he had sworn to support the Constitution and yet publicly denied that he would render obedience to the fugitive law. Sumner's reply was exasperating. "Let the senator remember," he said, "that the bowie-knife and the bludgeon are not the proper emblems of senatorial debate. Let him remember that the swagger of Bob Acres and the ferocity of the Malay cannot add dignity to this body; . . . that no person with the upright form of man can be allowed, without violation of all decency, to switch out from his tongue the perpetual stench of offensive personality," taking for a model "the noisome squat and nameless animal." Douglas made an insulting retort, and Sumner rejoined: "Mr. President, again the senator has switched his tongue, and again he fills the Senate with its offensive odor." Douglas ended the angry colloquy by declaring that a man whom he had branded in the Senate with falsehood was not worthy of a reply.

Two days after this exciting debate (May 22d), when the Senate at the close of a short session adjourned, Sumner remained in the Chamber, occupied in writing letters. Becoming deeply engaged, he drew his arm-chair close to his desk, bent over his writing, and while in this position was approached by Brooks, a representative from South Carolina and a kinsman of Senator Butler. Brooks, standing before and directly over him, said: "I have read your speech twice over carefully. It is a libel on South Carolina and Mr. Butler, who is a relative of mine." As he pronounced the last word, he hit Sumner on the head with his cane with the force that a dragoon would give to a sabre-blow.[1] Sumner

---

[1] The cane was gutta-percha, one inch in diameter at the larger and

was more than six feet in height and of powerful frame, but penned under the desk[1] he could offer no resistance, and Brooks continued the blows on his defenceless head. The cane broke, but the South Carolinian went on beating his victim with the butt. The first blows stunned and blinded Sumner, but instinctively and with powerful effort he wrenched the desk from its fastenings, stood up, and with spasmodic and wildly directed efforts attempted unavailingly to protect himself. Brooks took hold of him, and, while he was reeling and staggering about, struck him again and again. The assailant did not desist until his arm was seized by one who rushed to the spot to stop the assault. At that moment Sumner, reeling, staggering backwards and sideways, fell to the floor bleeding profusely and covered with his blood.[2]

The injury received by Sumner was much more severe than was at first thought by his physicians and friends. Four days after the assault, he was able to give at his lodgings his relation of the affair to the committee of the House of Representatives. But, in truth, the blows would have killed most men.[3] Sumner's iron constitution and perfect health warded off a fatal result; but it soon appeared that the injury had affected the spinal column. The next three years and a half was a search for cure by a man who, with the exception of a severe fever when he was thirty-three, had rarely known what it was to be ill. He submitted himself to medical treatment at Washington, Boston, and London.

---

five-eighths of an inch in diameter at the smaller end. Brooks served in the cavalry during the Mexican war.

[1] See Pierce's Sumner, vol. iii. p. 470.

[2] See the evidence taken by the committee of the House of Representatives, *Congressional Globe*, vol. xxxii. part 2.

[3] Seward wrote his wife, July 5th, 1856: "Sumner is much changed for the worse. His elasticity and vigor are gone. He walks, and in every way moves, like a man who has not altogether recovered from a paralysis, or like a man whose sight is dimmed, and his limbs stiffened with age. . . . His vivacity of spirit and his impatience for study are gone."—Life of Seward, vol. ii. p. 282.

He was re-elected to the Senate by an almost unanimous vote of the Massachusetts legislature,[1] and tried twice to resume his duties. But Sumner, who was accustomed to ten hours of intellectual work out of the twenty-four, could not now bear the ordinary routine of the day. At last he went to Paris and put himself under the care of Dr. Brown-Séquard, whose treatment of actual cauterization of the back eventually restored him to a fair degree of health; but he never regained his former physical vigor. He was not able to enter regularly again on his senatorial career until December, 1859. He did not speak again until June, 1860, when he described in burning words the "Barbarism of Slavery."

To take a man unawares, in a position where he could not defend himself, and injure the seat of his intellect was truly a dreadful deed.

He who was thus struck down in the strength of a splendid manhood was a man of rare physique, vigorous brain, and pure heart; a senator devoted to his work, punctilious in attentiveness to routine, eager for self-improvement. He so loved intellectual labor that he never lost a day.[3] The feeling of revenge was foreign to his nature. Stretched on a bed of pain, compelled by shattered nerves to give up the study and the work that were his life, he felt no resentment towards Brooks.[4]

Full of manly independence, he would submit to no leader, bow to no party, nor solicit any member of the legislature for a vote. His very presence, said a warm political and personal friend, "made you forget the vulgarities of political life."[5] He was the soul of honor; and his abso-

---

[1] He had every vote in the Senate, and 333 out of 345 in the House. Recollections of Charles Sumner, Johnson, *Scribner's Magazine*, vol. x. p. 298.

[2] He was a good example of Spencer's "healthy man of high powers." —Data of Ethics, p. 190. [3] George W. Curtis.

[4] Johnson, *Scribner's Monthly*, vol. viii. p. 483.

[5] Schurz, see Lester, p. 668.

lute integrity extended even to the most trivial affairs of life. Duty was to him sacred, the moral law a daily influence; his thoughts, his deeds, were pure. His faults were venial, and such as we might look for in a spoiled child of a city of culture. He was vain, conceited, fond of flattery, overbearing in manner, and he wore a constant air of superiority.[1]

He was a profound student of words, but he studied them too much in the lifeless pages of dictionaries, and too little in the living discourse of his fellow-men, so that he failed to get an exact impression of their force and color.[2] Consequently, he gave offence at times where none was intended,[3] a fault for which he grievously answered.

Preston Brooks, the man who did Sumner this lasting

---

[1] See J. D. Long, Webster Centennial, vol. i. p. 164. "Sumner requires adulation."—Francis Lieber. See the whole letter, Life of Lieber, p. 296.

Longfellow, making an entry Aug. 29th, 1856, in his diary of a dinner with Prescott, where all the guests were Republicans, writes: "When I came away they were enumerating Sumner's defects, or what they imagined to be such."—Life of Longfellow, vol. ii. p. 282; see also Life of R. H. Dana, C. F. Adams, vol. i. pp. 214, 234.

"Charles Sumner was a handsome, unpleasing man, and an athlete whose physique proclaimed his physical strength. His conversation was studied but brilliant, his manner deferential only as a matter of social policy; consequently he never inspired the women to whom he was attentive with the pleasant consciousness of possessing his regard or esteem."—Life of Jefferson Davis, by his wife, vol. i. p. 557.

[2] Sumner "was curious in dictionaries. He had five of the English language among his tools. His Webster and Worcester were presentation copies from the authors. Walker, Pickering, and Johnson were often brought down from the congressional library. It was no unusual thing for the senator, when in full tide of work, to call to his secretary to look up a word in Worcester, and to read the secondary meanings and quotations. Then to refer to Webster, then to Walker, then to Johnson, then to Pickering, and finally the word was used or thrown out, according to the weight of authority."—Johnson, *Scribner's Magazine*, vol. viii. p. 477.

[3] Johnson, *Scribner's Magazine*, vol. viii. p. 479. "Sumner's silly way of saying the bitterest things without apparent consciousness of saying anything harmful."—Francis Lieber, Life of Lieber, p. 297.

injury, was not a ruffian; he came from one of the good South Carolina families. He was well educated, and had been a member of the House of Representatives for three years, where his conduct had been that of a gentleman. He has been called "courteous, accomplished, warm-hearted, and hot-blooded, dear as a friend and fearful as an enemy."[1]

The different manner in which the North and the South regarded this deed is one of the many evidences of the deep gulf between these two people caused by slavery. The North was struck with horror and indignation. The legislature of Massachusetts immediately took action, and characterized the assault by resolution in fitting terms. Indignation meetings were held all over the North. Edward Everett, who was a type of Northern conservatism, prefaced the delivery of his oration on Washington at Taunton, Mass., by saying: "The civil war, with its horrid train of fire and slaughter, carried on without the slightest provocation against the infant settlements of our brethren on the frontier of the Union—the worse than civil war which, after raging for months unrebuked at the capital of the Union, has at length, with a lawless violence of which I know no example in the annals of constitutional government, stained the floor of the Senate chamber with the blood of a defenceless man, and he a senator from Massachusetts. . . . O my good friends! these are events which, for the good name, the peace, the safety of the country, it were well worth all the gold of California to blot from the record of the past week."[2] The tendency at the North was to forget entirely the personal provocation, and to regard the assault on Sumner as an outrage by the slave power, because he had so vehemently denounced the

---

[1] Frederic Law Olmsted, Introduction to The Englishman in Kansas, written in 1857, after the death of Brooks.

[2] It is necessary to give the whole quotation, that the meaning of the orator may be preserved. The reference to Kansas is to the destruction of printing-offices and the hotel at Lawrence, and the sack of the town which will be later related.

South and her institution. Attendant circumstances gave color to this opinion. Keitt, a representative from South Carolina, stood by, during the assault, brandishing his cane in a menacing manner, and threatening Simonton and others who rushed in to interfere. Edmundson, a representative from Virginia, was at hand to render assistance if necessary.

Ever since the excitement growing out of the Burns case, in May and June, 1854, when Sumner had denounced the Fugitive Slave law in vigorous terms, he had been very obnoxious to the South, and at that time he was warned that he stood in personal danger. He was hated by the South much more intensely than any other Republican. The Southern congressmen stood by Brooks, but they justified his action on account of the supposed insult to his kinsman and State, and they endeavored to make out that Sumner's injuries were slight. The inevitable disagreement of physicians occurred, and there was show of reason, when the excitement ran the highest, for thinking that his hurt would be temporary.[1]

At Washington, congressional propriety, senatorial courtesy, and the conviction that the Senate chamber had been desecrated, modified the public expression of Southern sentiment. But in the slave States themselves the feeling was given full rein, and it was plainly apparent that the assault was approved of by the press and the people.[2] The com-

---

[1] It was at this time that the Washington *Union* said: "According to the code of political morals which seems to prevail in Massachusetts, it is not only no offence, but praiseworthy, for a senator in Congress to avail himself of his position to indulge day after day in the grossest vituperation and calumny; but, on the other hand, if some opponent thus abused and slandered seeks for satisfaction by applying his gutta-percha to the head of the senator, the crime is so shocking that all Black Republicandom is filled with indignation meetings." Cited by New York *Evening Post*, May 29th. Forney was no longer editor of the Washington *Union*.

[2] See citations from Southern journals in Von Holst, vol. v. p. 328 *et seq.*; also New York *Independent*, June 12th; New York *Tribune*, June 24th. A few Southern journals, which were, with one exception, formerly Whig in politics, condemned the assault. They were the Baltimore *Amer-*

ments of the newspapers and the resolutions of public meetings show that the satisfaction felt at the resentment of a personal insult was merged in the delight that a notorious and hateful abolitionist had been punished. When Brooks returned to South Carolina, he received an enthusiastic welcome. He was honored as a glorious son of the Palmetto State, and making him the present of a cane was a favorite testimonial.[1] South Carolina was as jubilant as Massachusetts was sorrowful and incensed. The strife between the North and the South had long been personified by the antagonism between these States, and now, by common consent, they bodied forth the principles of slavery and freedom.

Senator Wilson said in the Senate: "Sumner was stricken down on this floor by a brutal, murderous, and cowardly assault." Butler impulsively cried, "You are a liar!"[2] Brooks challenged Wilson to a duel. The Massachusetts senator declined the challenge in a brave and consistent letter, repeating the words he had employed.[3] Representative Burlingame, of Massachusetts, in the House of Representatives, denounced the assault "in the name of that fair play which bullies and prize-fighters respect. What!" he said, "strike

---

ican and the *Patriot*, the Louisville *Journal*, the Augusta *Chronicle*, the Wilmington (N. C.) *Herald*, the Petersburg *Express*, the St. Louis *Intelligencer*, Clarksville (Tenn.) *Jeffersonian*, the Memphis *Bulletin*.

[1] A cane presented him by gentlemen of Charleston bore the inscription, "Hit him again." Columbia (S. C.) *Banner*, cited by New York *Independent*, June 12th. One presented him by a portion of his constituents was inscribed, "Use knock-down arguments." New York *Tribune*, June 6th. "The students of the University of Virginia have voted a splendid cane to the Hon. Mr. Brooks for his attack on Mr. Sumner. The cane is to have a heavy gold head, which will be suitably inscribed, and also bear upon it a device of a human head, badly cracked and broken."
—Philadelphia *Pennsylvanian*, May 31st.

[2] Rise and Fall of the Slave Power, vol. ii. p. 486. Butler immediately apologized to the Senate, and the words are not reported in the *Congressional Globe*. This was May 27th. [3] Ibid.

a man when he is pinioned—when he cannot respond to a blow! Call you that chivalry?"[1] Although the remarks of Burlingame were at first explained away, they eventually resulted in a challenge from Brooks. This was promptly accepted, and the arrangement of details was referred by Burlingame to Lewis D. Campbell. Campbell selected for the meeting a place near the Clifton House, Niagara Falls, but Brooks declined to fight the duel there, on the ground that in the excited state of feeling at the North he would not be permitted to reach Canada in safety.[2]

The explanation of Brooks in the House of Representatives did not make his assault on Sumner appear any less infamous to Northern men who were unfamiliar with "the code of honor." He said: "I went to work very deliberately, as I am charged—and this is admitted—and speculated somewhat whether I should employ a horse-whip or a cowhide; but knowing that the senator was my superior in strength,[3] it occurred to me that he might wrest it from my hand and then—for I never attempt anything I do not perform—I might have been compelled to do that which I would have regretted the balance of my natural life. The question has been asked why did I not invite the senator to personal combat in the mode usually adopted. . . . My answer is that I knew the senator would not accept a message; and having formed the unalterable determination to punish him, I believed that the offence of sending a hostile message, superadded to the indictment for assault and battery, would subject me to legal penalties

---

[1] These remarks were made June 21st.

[2] For the full details of this transaction see Rise and Fall of the Slave Power, vol. ii. p. 491. I could not reach Canada, Brooks wrote, "without running the gantlet of mobs and assassins, prisons and penitentiaries, bailiffs and constables."—New York *Times*, July 25th. Brooks had been tried for assault in a District of Columbia court, and fined three hundred dollars. New York *Tribune*, July 10th.

[3] Brooks was six feet one inch tall.

more severe than would be imposed for a simple assault and battery."[1]

At the North the assault of Brooks was considered brutal and cowardly; at the South, his name was never mentioned without calling him gallant or courageous, spirited or noble. This difference in the standards of conduct of people of the same country, race, and religion shows how slavery had demoralized its supporters. It was noted and explained by Olmsted. "Southerners," he wrote, "do not feel magnanimity and the fair-play impulse to be a necessary part of the quality of spirit, courage, and nobleness. By spirit they apparently mean only passionate vindictiveness of character, and by gallantry mere intrepidity."[2] The South rallied to Brooks as the champion of their cause.

The North was stirred to the depths. Doctor Holmes expressed the feeling in his toast: "To the surgeons of the city of Washington—God grant them wisdom! for they are dressing the wounds of a mighty empire and of uncounted generations."[3] Seward said in the Senate:[4] "The blows that fell on the head of the senator from Massachusetts have done more for the cause of human freedom in Kansas and in the territories of the United States than all the eloquence—I do not call it agitation—which has resounded in these halls from the days when Rufus King asserted that cause in this chamber, and when John Quincy Adams defended it in the other house, until the present hour." Sumner's speech was a powerful factor in influencing public sentiment. Under the title of "The Crime against Kansas," half a million copies of it were circulated.

The day after the assault many members of Congress

---

[1] This speech was made July 14th.
[2] F. L. Olmsted's Introduction to The Englishman in Kansas, written in 1857, p. xix.
[3] Life of Sumner, Nason, p. 227.   [4] June 24th.
[5] So Sumner, when in Paris, told De Tocqueville. George F. Hoar in the *North American Review*, vol. cxxvi. p. 1.

went to their seats armed.¹ An exciting time was anticipated in the Senate, but the proceedings were tame. Wilson gave a temperate relation of the facts, and Seward offered a resolution for the appointment of a committee to consider the affair. This was agreed to, but not a Republican was given a place on the committee. In due time they reported that the "assault was a breach of the privileges of the Senate," but that it was not within its jurisdiction, and could only be punished by the House of Representatives. This report received the approbation of the Senate almost unanimously, there being but one vote against it. A committee was appointed by the House which took a large amount of evidence, and the majority reported a resolution in favor of the expulsion of Brooks. On this resolution, the vote was 121 to 95; but as it required two thirds, it was not carried. Only three Southern representatives publicly condemned the assault; only one voted to expel Brooks.² After the decision by the House, Brooks made a speech, which he ended by resigning his place as representative. His district re-elected him almost unanimously: there were only six votes against him.³

The evidence of Sumner taken on his sick-bed mentioned that when he returned to consciousness after the assault, he was lying on the floor with his bleeding head supported on the knee of a friend, and that at a distance, looking on but offering no assistance, were Douglas and Toombs. When he was assisted to the lobby of the Senate, he recognized Slidell, of Louisiana. These gentlemen felt that it was incumbent on them to make an explanation. Slidell stated that he was in the antechamber engaged in conversation with Douglas and others. A messenger of the Senate in great trepidation entered and said some one was beating

---

[1] Pike to the New York *Tribune*, May 23d, Pike's First Blows of the Civil War, p. 339.
[2] Von Holst, vol. v. p. 326.   [3] Ibid., p. 328.

Sumner. "We heard this remark," Slidell said, "without any particular emotion; for my own part, I confess I felt none. . . . I remained very quietly in my seat; the other gentlemen did the same; we did not move." Douglas stated that on hearing the remark of the messenger, "I rose involuntarily to my feet. My first impression was to come into the Senate chamber and help to put an end to the affray, if I could; but it occurred to my mind in an instant that my relations to Mr. Sumner were such that if I came into the Hall, my motives would be misconstrued, perhaps, and I sat down again." A moment afterwards hearing that Brooks had beaten Sumner badly, he went into the Senate chamber. Toombs saw part of the assault; he did not render Sumner any assistance. Hearing some gentlemen condemn the action, he stated to Brooks or to some of his own friends that he approved it.[1]

Before leaving this subject, fairness requires that allusion should be made to the speech of Butler,[2] which is a plaintive regret for what had taken place. Yet he magnified the offence of Sumner; he assumed that the hurt was not serious, and defended the attack of Brooks. The blood of Sumner's friends must have boiled as they heard or read the speech at the time; but, in the cool atmosphere of the present, the mournful words of Butler almost elicit sympathy for him in the part which the interests of his family and his order compelled him to play. His statement how he should have acted had he been present in the Senate when Sumner made his speech is necessary to the history of the transaction. "My impression now is," he said, "that I should have asked the senator, before he finished some of the paragraphs personally applicable to myself, to pause; and if he had gone on, I would have demanded of him, the next morning, that he should review that speech, and retract or modify it, so as to bring it within the sphere

---

[1] These explanations were made May 27th.
[2] June 12th and 13th.

of parliamentary propriety. If he had refused this, what I would have done I cannot say; yet I can say that I would not have submitted to it. But what mode of redress I should have resorted to, I cannot tell."

Brooks died the following January, but not before he had confessed to his friend, Orr, that he was sick of being regarded as the representative of bullies, and disgusted at receiving testimonials of their esteem.[1] Butler lived but a few days over a year from the time that the assault was made in satisfaction of what was deemed his injured honor.

During the first months of 1856, the interest in Kansas territory divided the attention of the country with the proceedings in Congress. There was note of preparation for the spring campaign at the North and at the South. Atchison made an appeal to the slave States. "Let your young men come forth to Missouri and Kansas!" he wrote; "let them come well armed!"[2] Well-attended public meetings were held all over the cotton States, at which gentlemen of property and standing presided. The object was to get men to enlist, and to raise money for their support in the expected Kansas war. The communities were roused by violent speeches in which the danger to the Southern institution was effectively portrayed.[3] It was proposed in the Georgia legislature to appropriate fifty thousand dollars to aid emigration to Kansas; and it was understood that the money would be used to arm and equip military companies. Milder counsels, however, prevailed when the project came to a vote, and it was not carried.[4] A bill to assist emigrants to Kansas was introduced into the Alabama legislature, and, with

---

[1] Rise and Fall of the Slave Power, vol. ii. p. 495.

[2] D. R. Atchison to the editor of the Atlanta (Ga.) *Examiner*, New York *Tribune*, Jan. 19th.

[3] See *National Intelligencer*, Feb. 17th, March 18th, April 1st; The Englishman in Kansas, Gladstone, p. 6; letter from Montgomery, Jan. 22d, New York *Tribune*, Feb. 2d.

[4] *National Intelligencer*, Feb. 23d.

much reason, it was proposed to get the means by a separate tax upon the slave property of the State. The results at the South were not commensurate with the efforts, mainly for the reason that ready money was hard to be obtained, while the men who were willing to go would be dependent for their support on the contributions of the wealthier citizens. If fiery newspaper articles could have created men and money, there would have been no lack.

Yet one notable company was raised through the energy and sacrifice of Colonel Buford, of Alabama. He issued an appeal for three hundred industrious and sober men, capable of bearing arms and willing to fight for the cause of the South. He would himself contribute twenty thousand dollars, and he agreed to give each man who enlisted forty acres of good Kansas land and support him for a year.[1] He sold his slaves to provide the money he had promised.[2] Owing to the fervent appeals of the press, contributions from many quarters were obtained, and the enthusiasm was not confined to the men. A daughter of South Carolina sent to the editor of a newspaper a gold chain which would realize enough to furnish one man, and she begged him to let the ladies of her neighborhood know when more money was needed, for then, she wrote, "we will give up our personal embellishments and expose them for sale."[3]

Buford raised two hundred and eighty men[4] from South Carolina, Georgia, and Alabama. Many of them were the poor relations and dependants of the wealthy slave-holders; others were poor whites. Some were intelligent, and afterwards proved worthy citizens; but the majority were ignorant and brutal, and made fit companions for the Missouri border ruffians, by whom they were received with open

---

[1] This appeal is printed in the *Liberator* of Feb. 1st.
[2] Montgomery (Ala.) *Mail*, Montgomery *Advertizer*, Mobile *News*, cited in the *Liberator* of Feb. 22d.
[3] Edgefield (S. C.) *Advertiser*, cited by New York *Times*, March 7th.
[4] New Orleans *Picayune*, cited by the *Independent*, May 1st.

arms.¹ The day that Buford's battalion started from Montgomery, they marched to the Baptist church. The Methodist minister solemnly invoked the divine blessing on their enterprise; the Baptist pastor gave Buford a finely bound Bible, and said that a subscription had been raised to present each emigrant with a copy of the Holy Scriptures. Three or four thousand citizens gathered on the river bank to bid them farewell, and there were not lacking "the bright smiles and happy faces" of the ladies to cheer them on. A distinguished citizen made them an address, saying that "on them rested the future welfare of the South; they were armed with the Bible, *a weapon more potent than Sharpe's rifles;* and, in the language of Lord Nelson, 'every man was expected to do his duty.'"² The South Carolina contingent had not, on leaving home, been provided with Bibles; it had there been proclaimed that all the equipment needed was a good common country rifle.³

At the North, the importance of the conflict in Kansas was appreciated. The feeling may have been no deeper than at the South, but the manifestations of it were more numerous. The *Tribune* declared that "the duty of the people of the free States is to send more true men, more Sharpe's rifles, and more field-pieces and howitzers to Kansas!"⁴ The New York *Times* said: "The question of slavery domination must and will be fought out on the plains of Kansas."⁵ These sentiments were everywhere echoed. Public meetings in aid of Kansas were held all

---

¹ Kansas correspondence New York *Tribune*, April 26th and May 3d; Geary and Kansas, Gihon, p. 73; Sara Robinson's Kansas, pp. 241, 271.

² Montgomery *Journal*, cited by the *Independent*, April 17th.

³ Charleston (S. C.) *News*, March 27th, cited by the *National Intelligencer*. Senator Iverson, of Georgia, said that Buford's men went to Kansas unarmed. Wilson said that was true, but when they got to the territory Governor Shannon armed them and called them out as part of his military force. *Congressional Globe*, vol. xxxiii. pp. 844, 855.

⁴ New York *Weekly Tribune*, Feb. 2d. ⁵ Feb. 15th.

over the free States; committees to collect money and use it properly were appointed; emigration was in every way encouraged. Bryant wrote to his brother: " The whole city (New York) is alive with the excitement of the Kansas news, and people are subscribing liberally to the Emigrants' Aid Society. The companies of emigrants will be sent forward as soon as the rivers and lakes are opened, and by the 1st of May there will be several thousand more free-State settlers in Kansas than there now are. Of course they will go well armed."[1]

The most warlike demonstration, and one which excited the greatest attention, was at New Haven. Charles B. Lines, a deacon of a New Haven congregation, had enlisted a company of seventy-nine emigrants. A meeting was held in the church shortly before their departure for the purpose of raising funds. Many clergymen and many of the Yale College faculty were present. The leader of the party said that Sharps rifles were lacking, and they were needed for self-defence. After an earnest address from Henry Ward Beecher, the subscription began. Professor Silliman started it with one Sharps rifle; the pastor of the church gave the second; other gentlemen and some ladies followed the example. As fifty was the number wanted, Beecher said that if twenty-five were pledged on the spot, Plymouth Church would furnish the rest.[2] Previous to this meeting, he had declared that for the slave-holders of Kansas the Sharps rifle was a greater moral agency than the Bible; and from that time the favorite arms of the Northern emigrants became known as " Beecher's Bibles."[3]

---

[1] Letter dated Feb. 15th, Life of Bryant, Godwin, **vol. ii. p. 88.**

[2] New York *Independent*, March 23th. The number of rifles wanted was subscribed.

[3] Ibid., Feb. 7th. Remark of Senator Butler, *Congressional Globe*, vol. xxxii. p. 1094. A somewhat different explanation is given in the Biography of Henry Ward Beecher, p. 283; see also correspondence between Beecher and Lines, New York *Times*, April 4th.

The Democratic journal of Boston charged the college professors of New Haven with being guilty of overt treason; and the Democratic newspapers of New York classed together the border ruffians of Missouri and the abolition ruffians of New England.[1]

The winter in Kansas was unusually severe. The ground was covered with snow. For weeks the thermometer ranged from ten to thirty degrees below zero, and once the mercury froze within and burst the bulb.[2] The sufferings of the settlers were intense. Their hastily built houses and cabins lacked comfort; it was impossible to keep them warm. Mrs. Robinson relates that water would freeze in the tumblers on the table while the family were at breakfast; that the bread could be cut only as it was thawed before the fire, and the apples and potatoes were as hard as rocks.[3] The tale told by this faithful diarist of the sufferings of the men and women in the territory makes one feel that their lot was indeed hard; for the contest with nature followed fast upon the civil strife. "To face a Missouri mob," she wrote, "is nothing to facing these winds which sweep over the prairies."[4] Yet a Siberian winter might be regarded as nature's protest against the adaptability of Kansas to negro slavery. The few slaves in the territory fared badly. Judge Elmore, probably the largest slave-holder in Kansas, and his wife had to exert themselves to the utmost to keep their nineteen negroes alive. He was himself obliged to haul wood and cut it to keep them warm; nevertheless, one old man froze to death in his bed, and another was so severely frost-bitten that he was injured for life.[5]

---

[1] Boston *Post*, March 28th; New York *Journal of Commerce*, cited by the *Liberator*, Feb. 29th.
[2] Letter to New York *Times*, Feb. 14th. See Sara Robinson's Kansas.
[3] See Sara Robinson's Kansas, p. 166.
[4] Ibid., p. 165; see also Six Months in Kansas, by a Lady, p. 153 *et seq.*
[5] Sara Robinson's Kansas, p. 213; Reeder's Diary, Kansas Hist. Soc., vol. i. p. 13.

The destruction of Lawrence was threatened during the winter, but the severity of the weather prevented any operations. The tone of the letters received in February at Washington from the free-State settlers gave reason to believe that a bloody conflict was imminent.¹ March, however, passed without a demonstration, and for the first part of April quiet reigned; "a quiet," Mrs. Robinson wrote, "which seemed almost fearful from the very stillness."² In April the congressional investigating committee, Buford and his men, and the New Haven colony, arrived. The committee went immediately to work taking the testimony, which proved an invaluable document for the Republican party of 1856. It is likewise excellent evidence for the historian of the period.³ The New Haven colony settled at a place on the Kansas River sixty-five miles above Lawrence. They at once set to work ploughing and planting; they surrounded themselves with all obtainable appliances of civilization, and it was their hope that in a few years they would have in their Kansas home the comforts to which they had been used in Connecticut.⁴ It was soon apparent that Buford's men knew not how to plough or to sow, but it seemed likely that they might be put to other service. In April, emigrants from the North began to arrive in large numbers; but besides Buford's battalion, it does not appear that there were accessions of consequence from the Southern States.⁵

On the 19th of April, Sheriff Jones came to Lawrence and attempted to arrest one of Branson's rescuers, who resisted and struck the sheriff. Four days later, Jones reappeared

---

¹ Greeley to New York *Tribune.* March 1st.
² Sara Robinson's Kansas, p. 191.
³ This report comprises 1188 pages. Much of the testimony was published in the Republican newspapers at the time that it was taken. Three hundred and twenty-three witnesses were examined. Spring's Kansas, p. 108. ⁴ New York *Independent*, June 19th.
⁵ Sara Robinson's Kansas, p. 196; New York *Independent*, May 1st; Spring's Kansas, pp. 105, 165.

in the town with a detachment of United States soldiers which had been furnished him by Governor Shannon. He arrested six men on the charge of contempt of court. In the evening, while sitting in the tent of Lieutenant McIntosh, who was in command of the soldiers, Jones was shot in the back. A public meeting of Lawrence citizens promptly disavowed any connection with the affair, and pledged themselves to do their best to bring the guilty party or parties to justice. The wound was not fatal, but it was for some time reported that Jones was dead. As he was a hero among the border ruffians, they breathed forth vengeance against Lawrence, and demanded, in their forcible language, that the abolition town should be wiped out.

At this time Judge Lecompte, the chief justice of the territory, came to the aid of the pro-slavery party. He charged the grand jury, in session at Lecompton, that the laws passed by the pro-slavery territorial legislature were of United States authority and making;[1] that all who "resist these laws resist the power and authority of the United States, and are therefore guilty of high treason. . . . If you find that no such resistance has been made, but that combinations have been formed for the purpose of resisting them, and that individuals of influence and notoriety have been aiding and abetting in such combinations, then must you find bills for constructive treason." The grand jury, without taking any evidence, indicted Reeder, Robinson, Lane, and others for treason; they also recommended the abatement, as a nuisance, of the newspapers *The Herald of Freedom* and *The Kansas Free State*, published at Lawrence; and as the Free-State hotel in Lawrence had been constructed with a view to military occupation and defence, they recommended that it be demolished. An attempt was made to arrest Reeder at Lawrence while he was examining a witness before the congressional investigating committee, but he put himself upon his privilege, claimed the protection of the committee,

---

[1] For an account of these laws, see p. 99.

told the United States deputy marshal that he would defend himself, and that the attempt to arrest him would be attended with peril. The officer deemed it prudent to relinquish his purpose. Reeder afterwards escaped from the territory in disguise.

Robinson started for the East on a mission for the cause in which he was engaged, but he was stopped at Lexington, Missouri. This arrest was arbitrary, but he was detained there under guard until the proper legal papers came from Kansas; he was then taken to Lecompton, where he was held a prisoner for four months.

On the 11th of May, the United States marshal for Kansas territory, Donaldson, issued a proclamation to the people stating that he had certain writs to execute in Lawrence; his deputy had been resisted on a similar errand and he had every reason to believe that the attempt to execute the writs would be resisted by a large body of armed men; therefore he commanded all the law-abiding citizens of the territory to appear at Lecompton as soon as possible in sufficient force to execute the law. No call could have better pleased the border ruffians. Now had come the long-wished-for opportunity to wipe out the odious town of Lawrence, and send its inhabitants north to Nebraska, where they belonged. Through all the threats and fulminations of the pro-slavery party, it plainly appears that they sincerely thought that the intent of the Kansas-Nebraska act was to give one territory to slavery, the other to freedom; therefore the settlement of Northern people in Kansas was a cheat and an encroachment on their rights. There were probably, however, not more than fifty slave-holders in Kansas, and all that kept the pro-slavery cause alive was the powerful backing it had from western Missouri.

The publication of the marshal's proclamation increased the commotion in eastern Kansas and western Missouri and the alarm of the Lawrence people. Their trusted leader, Robinson, was a prisoner, and there was no one to take his place; but they decided to temporize, which was undoubtedly the best policy. They had already requested Governor Shannon to send them United States troops for protection, but this he refused to do. Now, as they heard of the gathering of the clans on the Missouri border, they held a public meeting and solemnly averred that the statement and inference in Donaldson's proclamation were false. They also endeavored to placate the marshal, but without avail.

The marshal's posse began to collect in the neighborhood of Lawrence. On the 19th of May a young man, returning from Lawrence, was shot by two of the pro-slavery horde, apparently for no other reason than that he was an abolitionist. Three adventurous spirits of Lawrence rode out to avenge his murder, and one of them was killed.

On the 21st of May, the marshal's posse gathered on the bluffs west of the town. It was composed of the Douglas County (Kansas) Militia, the Kickapoo Rangers, other companies from eastern Kansas led by Stringfellow, the Missouri Platte County Rifles with two pieces of artillery commanded by Atchison, three other companies of border ruffians, and Buford and his men. It was a swearing, whiskey-drinking, ruffianly horde, seven hundred and fifty in number. The irony of fate had made them the upholders of the law, while the industrious, frugal community of Lawrence were the law-breakers. The deputy-marshal, attended with a small escort, walked into the town and made some arrests. Not the slightest resistance was offered. The business of the United States official was soon completed; but the sheriff of Douglas county had work to do, and Donaldson turned over the posse to Sheriff Jones, saying: "He is a law-and-order man, and acts under the same authority as the marshal." Jones, the idol of the pro-slavery party, was received with wild demonstrations of delight. Under his lead the posse marched into the town, dragging their five pieces of artillery and with banners flying. No company, however, carried the flag of the Union. One banner had a single white star and bore the inscriptions, "Southern Rights" and "South Carolina;" another had in blue letters on a white ground—

"Let Yankees tremble, abolitionists fall;
Our motto is, Give Southern rights to all."

The offices of the obnoxious newspapers were quickly destroyed; the types and presses were broken, and, with the books and papers, thrown into the street or carried to the river. The writ against the splendid stone hotel just completed remained to be executed. At this point Atchison counselled moderation; Buford also disliked to aid in the destruction of property. But Jones was implacable. His wound still rankled and he was bent on revenge. He demanded of Pomeroy, the representative of the Emigrant-Aid Company, all the Sharps rifles and artillery in the town. The rifles were refused on the ground that they were private property, but a cannon was given up. Four cannon were then pointed at the hotel and thirty-two shots were fired, but little damage was done. The attempt was then made to blow it up with kegs of powder, but without success. At last the torch was applied and the hotel destroyed. The liquors and wines found in the Yankee hotel were not disdained, and the glee felt at the outcome of the movement was increased by frequent potations. The ruffians were ripe for mischief; and when Sheriff Jones said his work was done and the posse dismissed, they sacked the town and set fire to Governor Robinson's house.[1]

The revelry was kept up as those who composed the posse journeyed to their homes. Jubilant border ruffians were everywhere met on the routes of travel, drinking to

---

[1] My authorities for this relation are Spring's Kansas; Sara Robinson's Kansas; Reeder's Diary, Kansas Historical Society's Publications; Geary and Kansas, Gihon; The Englishman in Kansas, Gladstone; the Conquest of Kansas, Phillips; Message and Documents, 1856–57, part i.; article of Amos Townsend, sergeant-at-arms of the congressional committee, Magazine of Western History, March, 1888; The Kansas Conflict, Charles Robinson. The author is the Dr. Robinson and Governor Robinson referred to in the text.

the victory which had crowned their efforts. But it was a victory worse than a defeat. The attack on Lawrence took place the day before the assault on Sumner; the news of it came to the people of the North a little later. These were two startling events; their coincidence in time was used with great impression by the Republican press. Freedom's representative had been struck down in the Senate chamber; the city dedicated to freedom on the plains of Kansas had been destroyed. Such were the texts on which the liberty-loving journalists wrote, and their masterly pens did full justice to the theme. The first reports were exaggerated. They were to the effect that Lawrence was in ruins, that many persons were killed, and that Pomeroy had been hanged by a mob.[1] Nevertheless, after all misstatements had been corrected and the true history of the affair arrived at, it still remained a most pregnant Republican argument. When President Pierce heard of the motley crowd assembled by the marshal as a posse, he feared the business would be managed badly, and telegraphed Governor Shannon and Colonel Sumner that the United States troops were sufficient to enforce the laws, and that they only should be used. But before this despatch was sent, the mischief had been done.

At no time had the enthusiasm for free Kansas in the North been so great as when the news of this attack on Lawrence became disseminated. Meetings for the aid of Kansas were everywhere held. The burden of the speeches was the attempt to crush out Freedom's stronghold in Kansas and the effort to silence Sumner in the Senate. Men enlisted in the cause, and money was freely subscribed.[2]

---

[1] See New York *Weekly Tribune*, May 31st. But one man was killed, and he was a pro-slavery man. A brick from the Free-State hotel fell upon him with a fatal result. Conquest of Kansas, Phillips.

[2] "The raid upon Lawrence, and the blockade of the Missouri river, added to the false imprisonment of our leading men, aroused the indignation of the North to such an extent that the freedom of Kansas was secure. From this time no further effort was required to raise colonies. They raised themselves."—Kansas Crusade, Thayer, p. 211.

In the territory itself, most of the free-State party were at first dismayed; but there were others in whom a spirit of bitter revenge was aroused. John Brown now appeared prominently on the scene. He had come to Kansas the previous October to join his sons, who had settled at Osawatomie, but the motive which led him was his powerful desire to strike a blow at slavery.

John Brown was ascetic in habits, inflexible in temper, upright in intention. In business he was fertile in plans, but their execution brought failure, for he was what people called a visionary man. He raised sheep, cultivated the grape, made wine, and for some years was extensively engaged in partnership with a gentleman of capital in buying and selling, as well as growing, wool. He had good opportunities, but missed them, while his ventures were unprofitable. Being constantly harassed with debts, he could not pay his creditors, and died insolvent.[1]

John Brown was born out of due time. A stern Calvinist and a Puritan, he would have found the religious wars of Europe or the early days of the Massachusetts colonies an atmosphere suited to his bent. He read the Bible diligently, and he drew his inspiration from the Old Testament. His intimate letters, a curious mixture of pious ejaculations and worldly details, of Scripture quotations and the price of farm products, call to mind the puritanical jargon of Cromwell's time. Indeed, the great Protector was his hero: he early imbibed a hatred of slavery, and was eager to earn money not as the price of comforts and luxuries, for his life

---

[1] Brown's plan of grading wool, which engaged the support of Perkins, his wealthy partner in the wool commission business, was, however, based on correct principles, and only failed because it was in advance of his time. When disaster came and the firm was loaded with debts, these were saddled upon Perkins as the responsible partner; and while his loss was heavy, he never had the feeling that Brown's conduct had been other than strictly honest. I am indebted for this information to my friend Mr. Simon Perkins, a son of the gentleman who was in partnership with Brown.

II.—11

was of a Spartan frugality, but as the means of freeing the slaves.

Brown, who admired Nat Turner as much as he did George Washington, was tender to the negro, and had brooded for years over the wrongs of the slaves. With this feeling dominant in his mind he had come to Kansas and enlisted in the Wakarusa war, but denounced the treaty of peace which terminated it: the action of the free-State party seemed to him pusillanimous. Narrow-minded and of moderate intellectual ability, Brown despised the ordinary means of educating public sentiment, and had no comprehension of government by discussion. In his opinion, Kansas could only be made free by the shedding of blood, and that work ought at once to begin.[1]

When the attack on Lawrence was threatened, the Brown family and their followers were called upon to aid in the defence; but, on the way, they heard of the destruction which had taken place, and turned back. The news made a profound impression on Brown. He felt that the acts of the pro-slavery horde must be atoned for. He reckoned up that since and including the murder of Dow,[2] five free-State men had been killed. Their blood must be expiated by an equal number of victims. "Without the shedding of blood, there is no remission of sins," was one of his favorite texts. A direction was given to his fanatical thoughts by remembering that threats had been made against his family by some pro-slavery settlers at Dutch Henry's crossing of the Pottawatomie. He called for volunteers to go on a secret expedition. Four sons, a son-in-law, and two other men accompanied him. John Brown's word was law to his family. He had the power of communicating to them his enthusiasm for the cause of freedom; but when he declared

---

[1] The facts on which I have based this characterization I have drawn from Life and Letters of John Brown, F. B. Sanborn; Life of Captain John Brown, by James Redpath; Essay on John Brown, by Von Holst.

[2] See p. 104.

that the object of his mission was to sweep off all the pro-slavery men living on the creek, Townsley, one of the men, demurred. Brown said: "I have no choice. It has been decreed by Almighty God, ordained from eternity, that I should make an example of these men."[1] Yet it took a day to persuade Townsley to continue with the expedition. On Saturday night, May 24th, the blow was struck. Brown and his band went first to the house of Doyle, and compelled a father and two sons to go with them. A surviving son afterwards testified under oath that the next morning "I found my father and one brother, William, lying dead in the road, about two hundred yards from the house. I saw my other brother lying dead on the ground, about one hundred and fifty yards from the house, in the grass, near a ravine; his fingers were cut off and his arms were cut off; his head was cut open; there was a hole in his breast. William's head was cut open, and a hole was in his jaw, as though it was made by a knife; and a hole was also in his side. My father was shot in the forehead and stabbed in the breast."[2] The band then went to Wilkinson's house, reaching there past midnight. They forced him to open the door, and demanded that he should go with them. His wife was sick and helpless, and begged that they should not take her husband away. The prayer was of no avail. The next day Wilkinson was found dead, "a gash in his head and in his side."[3] A little later in the night the band killed William Sherman in like manner. In the morning his body was found. His skull was split open in two places, and some of his brains was washed out by the water. A large hole was cut in his breast, and his left hand was cut off, except a little piece of skin on one side."[4] The execution was done with short cutlasses which had been brought from Ohio by John Brown. He gave the signal; his devoted followers struck the blows. Townsley, twenty-

---

[1] Spring's Kansas, p. 144.
[3] Ibid., p. 1180.
[2] Oliver Report, p. 1177.
[4] Ibid., p. 1179.

three years afterwards, stated that Brown shot the elder Doyle, but he himself denied that he had had a hand in the actual killing.[1] The deed was so atrocious that for years his friends and admirers refused to believe that he had been at all concerned in it.[2] They shut their eyes to patent facts, for at the time it was easy to get at the truth. The affidavits in regard to the affair, which Oliver, the Democratic member of the congressional committee, caused to be taken, his speech in the House, explaining and confirming the evidence, the universal belief of free-State and pro-slavery men in the territory, established beyond any reasonable doubt that John Brown and his party were guilty of these assassinations. Considering the general character of the border settlers, those who were killed were not exceptionally bad men.[3] They had made threats against the Browns and maltreated a store-keeper who had sold lead to free-State men. But the Browns had also made threats; and in Kansas, in 1856, threats were common, and frequently unmeaning. If every word spoken by the border ruffians were taken at its proper value, Robinson and Reeder had long stood in jeopardy. It was reported that even John Sherman had been threatened.[4] There was absolutely no justification for these midnight executions.[5]

A tender-hearted son of John Brown, who did not accompany this expedition, said to his father a day or two after the massacre: "Father, did you have anything to do

---

[1] See Reminiscences of Old John Brown, G. W. Brown, pp. 17 and 72; Sanborn, p. 273; Redpath, p. 119; The Kansas Conflict, Charles Robinson, p. 265.

[2] In Redpath's Life of Captain John Brown, published in 1860, this view is prominent. Sanborn's book, however, published in 1885, gives the facts freely and fairly, and the author attempts to justify the deed.

[3] That is the conclusion of Professor Spring, p. 147; see, also, The Kansas Conflict, Charles Robinson, p. 484. Sanborn has a different view, see p. 257.

[4] Correspondence New York *Tribune*, May 25th; Sara Robinson's Kansas, p. 272.

[5] See The Kansas Conflict, Charles Robinson, chap. xi.

with that bloody affair on the Pottawatomie?" Brown replied: "I approved of it." The son answered: "Whoever did it, the act was uncalled for and wicked." Brown then said: "God is my judge. The people of Kansas will yet justify my course."[1]

In passing judgment at this day, we must emphasize the reproach of the son; yet we should hesitate before measuring the same condemnation to the doer and to the deed. John Brown's God was the God of Joshua and Gideon. To him, as to them, seemed to come the word to go out and slay the enemies of his cause. He had no remorse. It was said that on the next morning when the old man raised his hands to Heaven to ask a blessing, they were still stained with the dried blood of his victims.[2] What the world called murder was for him the execution of a decree of God. But of the sincerity of the man there can be no question.

Of the historical significance of this deed and Brown's subsequent actions we may speak with great positiveness. He has been called the liberator of Kansas, but it may be safely affirmed that Kansas would have become a free State in much the same manner and about the same time that it actually did, had John Brown never appeared on the scene of action. The massacre on the Pottawatomie undoubtedly made the contest more bitter and sanguinary, but there is no reason for thinking that its net results were of advantage to the free-State cause.[3]

As tidings of these executions became known a cry of horror went up throughout the territory. The squatters on Pottawatomie Creek, without distinction of party, met together and denounced the outrage and its perpetrators.[4] The free-State men everywhere took pains to disavow any connection with such a mode of operation. The border ruf-

---

[1] Sanborn, p. 250.   [2] Ibid., note, p. 270.
[3] Professor Spring's judgment is: "John Brown is a parenthesis in the history of Kansas."—Kansas, p. 137; see also pp. 140, 149, 162; also The Kansas Conflict, Charles Robinson. p. 276 *et seq.*
[4] Spring's Kansas, p. 147; The Kansas Conflict, Charles Robinson, p. 275.

fians were wild with fury. While Governor Robinson was at Leavenworth a prisoner, on the way to Lecompton, an excited mob threatened to take him from his guard and lynch him.[1] Threats were also made to hang the free-State prisoners who were at Lecompton.[2]

Governor Shannon promptly sent a military force to the Pottawatomie region to discover, if possible, those who had been engaged in the massacre and arrest them. The border ruffians also took the field, eager to avenge the murder of their friends. Pate, who commanded the sharpshooters of Westport, Missouri, feeling confident that Brown was the author of the outrage, went in search of him. Brown, hearing that he was sought, put himself in the way of the Missourian, gave battle, and captured the border-ruffian company. "I went to take Old Brown," wrote Pate, "and Old Brown took me."[3]

All the military organizations of the free-State party made ready for war. Among the Northern emigrants there were adventurers who were attracted by the prevailing disorder. These, for the most part, came into the territory in the spring of 1856; and there were others who, under ordinary conditions, might have been made steady colonists, but whose natural pugnacity was incited by the attack on Lawrence.

The pro-slavery leaders, alarmed at the flood of Northern emigration that poured into the territory, laid an embargo on the Missouri River, which was the great highway from the East to Kansas. Sharps rifles and other suspicious freight were seized. Travellers bound for Kansas, unable, according to the Missouri standard, to give a good account of themselves, were sent back down the river.[4]

Kansas was now in a state of civil war, a struggle of Guelphs and Ghibellines. Governor Shannon issued a proc-

---

[1] Kansas, Sara Robinson, p. 271; The Englishman in Kansas, Gladstone, p. 65; The Kansas Conflict, Charles Robinson, p. 282.

[2] Reminiscences of Old John Brown, G. W. Brown, p. 13.

[3] Spring's Kansas, p. 156. [4] Ibid., p. 166.

lamation commanding all armed companies to disperse, and Colonel Sumner set out with fifty United States dragoons to execute the governor's order. He forced Brown to release the prisoners, but, although a deputy marshal was with him, no arrests were made. Colonel Sumner then met two hundred and fifty Missourians, under the command of Whitfield, the pro-slavery delegate to Congress, and ordered them back. They went home, but on the way they pillaged the hated town of Osawatomie, and left behind them the dead bodies of two or three Free-soilers.[1]

Guerrilla bands of both parties wandered over the country, and whenever they met they fought.[2] In a great part of the territory husbandry was neglected. Redpath, who was a newspaper correspondent and free-State warrior, relates that in the district between Osawatomie and Lawrence, men went out to till the soil in companies of five or ten, armed to the teeth.[3] Phillips saw delicately reared New England women working in the fields.[4] "Whenever two men approached each other," Redpath wrote, "they came up pistol in hand, and the first salutation invariably was: 'Free-State or pro-slave?' . . . It not unfrequently happened that the next sound was the report of a pistol."[5]

The Topeka party kept up their organization; their legislature assembled July 4th. Colonel Sumner, under the requisition of the secretary of the territory, Woodson, who, in the absence of Shannon, was acting governor, went to Topeka with an effective force of dragoons and artillery, and ordered the legislators to disperse. To the administration at Washington this move was distasteful. The President

---

[1] Spring's Kansas, p. 162.
[2] Phillips's Conquest of Kansas, p. 313.
[3] Life of John Brown, p. 108.
[4] Conquest of Kansas, p. 359.
[5] Life of John Brown, p. 108; see also private letter cited by Wilson, Senate debate, July 9th.

and cabinet looked upon the assemblage as a "town-meeting," and did not relish the idea of its dispersion, under their authority, at the point of the bayonet.[1]

---

[1] Spring's Kansas, p. 135; also the endorsement, Aug. 27th, of Jefferson Davis, Secretary of War, on Sumner's letter of Aug. 11th, Senate Documents, 3d Sess. 34th Cong. vol. iii.

CHAPTER VIII

THE attention of the country was at this period divided between the doings at Washington and in Kansas and President-making. Astute Democratic politicians felt that success depended largely upon the man whom their convention should nominate. Kansas was the question before the country, and a logical adherence to Democratic ideas would seem to demand the nomination of Douglas or Pierce. The one had inaugurated the new policy, the other had enforced it. They were both popular in the South, and it could not now be gainsaid that Southern principles and Southern interests were the dominant force in the Democratic party. Pierce was the first choice of the South, and Douglas the second. Either would have been eminently satisfactory; and had the President or senator concentrated the whole Southern strength, it would have made him the nominee.

But there were Southern politicians who saw what the majority of Northern Democrats saw—viz., that while the South would be almost solid for any possible nominee of the party, the important consideration was to nominate the man who could secure the greatest number of electoral votes from the North. All except two slave States, Maryland and Kentucky, which Fillmore might dispute, were certain to vote for the Democratic nominee; but Northern votes were needed to elect, and the probable Democratic States were Pennsylvania, New Jersey, Indiana, Illinois, and California. Of these, Pennsylvania was the most important, her vote being considered absolutely necessary.

James Buchanan was a Pennsylvanian; he had been out of the country when the Kansas-Nebraska act was passed, therefore he now loomed as a candidate. Two adroit Southern politicians—Wise of Virginia and Slidell of Louisiana—early espoused his candidacy.[1] This question, however, had to be answered to the South: was he sound on the Kansas-Nebraska policy, as were the battle-scarred veterans Douglas and Pierce? A private letter, written the previous December from London, by Buchanan to Slidell was published, in which he said that the Missouri Compromise was gone forever, and the settlement made by the Kansas-Nebraska act should be inflexibly maintained.[2]

In May, Buchanan more precisely defined his position in a speech made to a committee from the Pennsylvania State convention, which had unanimously recommended him for the presidency.[3] It is clear that it was the aim of the friends of Buchanan to show before the convention that he was in harmony with Democratic principles as understood in the South.

Yet Pierce and Douglas were regarded as the Southern candidates, while Buchanan was supported by substantially all those Democrats who deprecated the repeal of the Missouri Compromise or who had consented to it only after

---

[1] See letters of Wise, Letters and Times of the Tylers, vol. ii. p. 521 *et seq*. "I have no idea," Wise writes, Sept. 23d, 1855, "that any slave-holding Democrat can get the next or any nomination for the presidency." Nov. 18th, 1855, he writes: "Our policy is to go in for Buchanan with all our might;" see also letter from Wise, March 5th, 1856, published in New York *Evening Post*, April 21st. As to Slidell, see Life of Buchanan, Curtis, vol. ii. p. 173.

[2] Buchanan to Slidell, London, Dec. 28th, 1855, New York *Tribune*, April 5th, 1856; New York *Times*, April 8th, copied from the Washington *Union*.

[3] The resolutions of the Pennsylvania Democratic State convention and Buchanan's remarks are printed in the *Congressional Globe*, vol. xxxii. p. 1195. The speech of Jones, of Pennsylvania, who had them read in the House, impresses one with the efforts made by the friends of Buchanan to curry Southern favor.

long hesitation.¹ The outside pressure from the North in favor of the nomination of Buchanan was very strong. But in the preliminary work it became apparent to his supporters that if the friends of Pierce and Douglas combined, they could name the candidate, while to secure the necessary two-thirds for the Pennsylvania statesman seemed a difficult undertaking. But as the delegates were on the way to the convention, the news of the assault on Sumner came to them,² and before the convention got to work they heard of the destruction of Lawrence. One of these events was the natural result of the Kansas policy of Pierce and Douglas, the other seemed its logical concomitant. The responsibility of these two for the unhappy state of affairs in Kansas was intensified, and, if the question of availability should exercise paramount influence, the nomination of either was rendered impossible.

The convention met at Cincinnati the 2d day of June, and adopted its declaration of principles without opposition. The platform condemned the aims of the Know-nothings; declared that "the Democratic party will resist all attempts at renewing, in Congress or out of it, the agitation of the slavery question;" and resolved that "the American Democracy recognize and adopt the principles contained in the organic laws establishing the territories of Nebraska and Kansas as embodying the only sound and safe solution of the slavery question." ³

On the first ballot Buchanan had 135 votes, Pierce 122, Douglas 33, and Cass 5. Buchanan received 103 votes from the North and 32 from the slave States. He had all the delegates from Virginia and Louisiana. This proved a nucleus for Southern support, and was of importance, as the Buchanan movement was engineered by Wise and Slidell.

---

¹ There was an important exception; the Hards of New York were for Buchanan; the Softs for Pierce and Douglas.
² Forney's Anecdotes of Public Men, vol. ii. p. 254.
³ See History of Presidential Elections, Stanwood, p. 200.

Pierce received 72 and Douglas 14 votes from the slave States. Fourteen ballots were taken, both Buchanan and Douglas gaining at the expense of Pierce. On the tenth, Buchanan received a majority of the votes cast. After the fourteenth trial Pierce was withdrawn. The fifteenth stood: Buchanan, 168; Douglas, 118. The Southern votes of Pierce, with the exception of those from Tennessee and three from Georgia, had gone to Douglas; his New England friends had divided.[1] The sixteenth ballot showed practically no change. After it was taken Richardson obtained the floor and read a despatch from Douglas, which stated that Buchanan, having obtained a majority of the convention, ought to be nominated, and he hoped his friends would "give effect to the voice of the majority."[2] Buchanan then received the nomination by a unanimous vote. John C. Breckinridge, of Kentucky, was chosen as the candidate for Vice-President, Kentucky being considered one of the doubtful slave States.

Buchanan's nomination was the triumph of availability and a concession to Northern public sentiment. He had engaged himself to give fair play in Kansas, and it was supposed that he desired to see that territory come into the Union as a free State.[3] Until the assault on Sumner, the chances of the three candidates were apparently equal. Preston Brooks in Washington and the border ruffians in Lawrence turned the tide in favor of Buchanan.[4] The party was afraid to go to the country with Douglas or Pierce as standard-bearer on account of the connection of each with the existing troubles in Kansas.

---

[1] *National Intelligencer;* Boston *Post;* History of Presidential Elections, Stanwood, p. 199.

[2] New York *Tribune.*

[3] Forney's Anecdotes of Public Men, vol. i. p. 325; vol. ii. p. 254.

[4] Forney's Anecdotes of Public Men; *National Era,* June 12th. The account of S. M. L. Barlow, cited by Curtis, vol. ii. p. 170, ignores the preponderance of Northern sentiment for Buchanan, but gives an interesting history of the work done for him at Cincinnati.

The nomination of Buchanan was eminently satisfactory to Northern Democrats. The conservative and high-minded men of the party were pleased, believing that the Union would be safe in his hands. He was expected to attract the support of conservative Whigs, who thought Fillmore had no chance, and who were alarmed at the sectional character of the Republican party. The politicians not holding office were well satisfied, for the nomination of Buchanan seemed to insure victory. He could carry Pennsylvania, which Douglas or Pierce would probably have failed to do. The Key-stone State was necessary to success; for if it did not go Democratic at the October election, little reliance could be placed on the other Northern Democratic States. Pennsylvania, said a Democratic editor who, having been ardently in favor of Pierce, greeted the rising sun, has long been the key-stone of the Democratic arch, and will now be the key-stone of the Union.[1] A careful reading of the Democratic journals impresses one that the convention had made the strongest nomination possible.[2] The disappointed candidates early pledged their support, and this was honestly given.

The arguments freely used to gain adherents for Buchanan at the North at first threatened to hurt his cause at the South. That a man was acceptable to the few Free-soil Democrats who still encumbered the old party was no recommendation to Southerners; but when they looked into his record, they became assured that he might serve their section as well as Pierce had served it. The Richmond *Enquirer*, a most ardent pro-slavery journal, examined the congressional career of Buchanan and found that "he never gave a vote against the interests of slavery, and never ut-

---

[1] Boston *Post*, June 7th.

[2] This was also the opinion of Republicans. Seward wrote his wife, June 10th: "The temper of the politicians [meaning Republican politicians], I see, is subdued by Buchanan's nomination, and indicates retreat, confusion, rout in the election."—Life of Seward, vol. ii. p. 277.

tered a word which could pain the most sensitive Southern heart."

The declaration of principles adopted at Cincinnati was sometimes called a "Douglas platform"[1] and sometimes a "Southern platform."[2] The platform might be represented as looking one way and the candidate the other. But when the committee notified Buchanan of his nomination, his speech in reply satisfied the South. He fully endorsed the Cincinnati platform. He said that the slavery question was paramount, and the endeavor of his administration would be to settle it in a manner to give peace and safety to the Union and security to the South. He believed that the Kansas-Nebraska bill was necessary as a fit supplement to the compromise measures of 1850. When Buchanan had finished his formal speech, he said: "If I can be instrumental in settling the slavery question upon the terms I have named, and then add Cuba to the Union, I shall, if President, be willing to give up the ghost and let Breckinridge take the government."[3] Senator Brown, of Mississippi, one of the committee, heard this remark, and it so aroused his enthusiasm that he wrote to a friend: "The great Pennsylvanian is as worthy of Southern confidence and Southern votes as Calhoun ever was."

The nomination of Frémont[4] was virtually decided upon before the Republican convention met. It was a selection reached by a full comparison of views in the press, in private correspondence, and confidential conversations, and an honest and open canvass of the merits and strength of prominent Republicans. If merit alone were considered, everything pointed to Seward as the proper nominee, for no man in the country so fully represented Republican principles and aims. But if his unpopularity with the anti-slavery

---

[1] See speech of Douglas, New York, June 11th; Boston *Post,* June 13th.
[2] *National Era,* June 12th.
[3] Letter of Senator Brown to S. R. Adams, June 18th, published in *National Era,* Aug. 21st.   [4] Infra, p. 181.

Know-nothings made it seem unwise to put him up, and if the Whigs, though numerically the largest portion of the Republican party, were willing to sacrifice their desire of having an ancient Whig for their standard-bearer, then consistency demanded the nomination of Chase. The more radical members of the party were clearly of this conviction. Dr. Bailey, of the *National Era*, was at first for Chase and later for Seward. For the sake of sharply defining their principles he was content to wait, if need be, until 1860 for the election of a President. Theodore Parker wrote to Sumner that his first choice was Seward, and his second Chase;[2] and the historian feels no hesitancy in affirming that as the Republican party of 1856 had more disinterested and sincere men in its ranks than any party in this country before or since, as its members were honestly devoted to a noble principle, it was not true to its constitution and aims when it passed over Seward and Chase and descended upon Frémont.

Had the party with one accord looked to Seward as its leader; had the majority of its prominent and influential men, after canvassing all the points and weighing all the arguments, settled down to the conviction that the logic of the situation and the character of the party demanded his nomination, he would have accepted it gladly and entered into the contest with spirit. It was personal enmities, his too Whiggish views, and the question of availability that forbade. Yet had he decided to make a fight for the nomination, his friends would have urged it with pertinacity and zeal; care would have been taken to send delegates to Philadelphia favorable to him; and after a contest with Frémont, he

---

[1] Dr. Bailey "is eaten up with the idea of making Chase President," Greeley wrote Dana, Dec. 1st, 1855, New York *Sun*, May 19th, 1889. "Seward wants to be the candidate, and Dr. Bailey, of the *National Era*, is for him, content to wait till 1860 for a victory."—Samuel Bowles to H. L. Dawes, April 12th, 1856, Life of Bowles, Merriam, vol. i. p. 172.

[2] Life of Parker, Weiss, vol. ii. p. 130.

would undoubtedly have been nominated.¹ Seward was bold in words, timorous in action; he hesitated to claim the place which was rightfully his. It is possible that his own mind was warped by the reasoning of Thurlow Weed, his political mentor, who, regarding the situation with the narrow eye of a practical politician, would not have Seward run the race when there was so little probability of his election.² After it had been decided that he should not contest the nomination, he expressed a plaintive regret that he had taken the course marked out for him.³ Yet it is hardly supposable that even his optimism was proof against the prevailing opinion that his election was impossible; and his confident expression in the Senate was not the judgment of cooler moments.⁴ By the 18th of April it was known that

---

¹ John A. King, in his speech at the Republican convention, said: "I had hoped that circumstances would have permitted us to present to this convention the name of W. H. Seward. I believe, if that state of things could have existed, that name would have received the universal approbation of this convention." Robert Emmet, the temporary chairman of the convention, said at a ratification meeting in New York city: "Had it not been for the refusal of Mr. Seward himself, who charged his friends not to permit his nomination, he would have been nominated;" see also Life of Thurlow Weed, vol. ii. p. 245. I may add that in the contemporaneous political literature the indications are numerous that Seward would have received the nomination had a well-directed effort been made in his behalf. See also Blaine's Twenty Years of Congress, vol. i. p. 126.

² See Seward's letter to Weed, April 4th; to his wife, June 6th, 13th, 14th, 17th, Life of Seward, vol. ii. pp. 269, 276, 277, 278.

³ See his letter of May 4th to Thurlow Weed, Life of Thurlow Weed, vol. ii. p. 244.

⁴ Seward said in the Senate, March 12th: "I give those honorable gentlemen [Douglas and Toucey] notice that they have but about three hundred and fifty days left in which they will have the power of wielding the military and naval arms of this nation." In a confidential letter to Baker in 1855, Seward shows great doubts of Republican success in 1856, and adds, "I do not want that you and I should bear the responsibility of such a disaster," and "I am by no means ready to accept the command, if tendered."—Life of Seward, vol. ii. p. 252.

Seward was not a candidate for the nomination.[1] The disappointment of the Democrats and conservative Americans at this virtual announcement seemed to confirm the wisdom of the decision.[2]

There was a common objection to Seward and Chase; they were too pronounced on the slavery question. Both were on record in favor of the abolition of slavery in the District of Columbia, and of the repeal of the Fugitive Slave law, points on which it was deemed unadvisable to make an issue at the coming election. Moreover, the Chase movement never acquired popular strength outside of Ohio, and by the middle of April he was no longer seriously considered a candidate.

Some time during the winter the Republicans, who were casting about for an available candidate, lighted upon Frémont. His fitness had been urged by the German press;[3] he was early nominated for President by Banks, who said, at a dinner in Boston, that Frémont would soon write a letter defining plainly his position on the Kansas question.[4] Early in April this letter appeared.[5] It had the earmarks of shrewd politicians. Addressed to Governor Robinson of Kansas, an old California friend, it was nothing but a warm expression of sympathy with the free-State cause in Kansas. It gave notice to the public that he was a formal candidate for the Republican nomination, and the comments to which it gave rise made the fact apparent that he had powerful backing. Francis P. Blair, John Wentworth, Banks, Thurlow Weed, and Greeley were for him.[6] Dan Mace, a prom-

---

[1] See editorial in New York *Times* of that date.
[2] See New York *Times*, April 23d and 25th.
[3] The New York *Abend-Zeitung* maintained that the first suggestion of his name came from the German press.
[4] Reminiscences of a Journalist, Congdon, p. 152.
[5] It is printed in the campaign Life of Frémont, by John Bigelow, p. 447.
[6] See Life of Thurlow Weed, vol. ii. p. 245. See the strong argument for an available candidate, New York *Tribune*, April 30th.

inent and influential congressman from Indiana, a former Democrat, spoke for a large number when he wrote: "It will never do to go into the contest and be called upon to defend the acts and speeches of old stagers. We must have a position that will enable us to be the charging party. Frémont is the man for the operation."[1]

As an available candidate, Frémont had strong recommendations. He had been a Democrat, and the feeling among those who were formerly Democrats was that one of their number ought to be the standard-bearer.[2] The Germans, among whom were not a few educated and liberty-loving men, exiles from the fatherland after the failure of the revolution of 1848, were enthusiastically in his favor.[3] Yet he was not obnoxious to the Know-nothings; and, as was said by Emmet, the temporary chairman of the convention which nominated him, Frémont "had no political antecedents."[4]

Two days after the letter of Frémont to Robinson was published, Pike wrote to the New York *Tribune* from Washington: "Among the Republicans there is a strong apparent current for Frémont. Some say it is all set running by the politicians and will not do."[5]

After the virtual withdrawal of Seward, the preponderance of opinion was that availability should determine the candi-

---

[1] This was a private letter, written April 20th, but the Indiana *Courier* published it, and it was copied by the New York *Evening Post*.

[2] See, for example, the letter of Dan Mace already cited; also article in John Wentworth's Chicago *Democrat*, quoted by New York *Evening Post*; also New York *Abend-Zeitung*, June 14th.

[3] New York *Abend-Zeitung*, June 6th and 13th; *Die Freie Presse*, Philadelphia, cited by *Evening Post*, June 18th; New York *Staats-Demokrat*, June 13th; see quotations from several German papers, New York *Evening Post*, June 16th. A majority of the hundred German papers in the country were for Frémont, statement made by Schneider, of the Illinois *Staats-Zeitung* at the convention.

[4] At the ratification meeting, New York city.

[5] Pike's First Blows of the Civil War, p. 322.

date; but every one did not admit that the most available candidate was Frémont. Frequent mention began to be made of Judge McLean, of the United States Supreme Court.[1] He had long been in public life. A cabinet officer under Monroe and John Quincy Adams, he had been appointed to the Supreme bench by Jackson, and this position he had filled twenty-six years. He was a man of talents and of spotless integrity; and there can be no question that he was much better fitted for the presidency than Frémont. When the presidential nomination now became a possibility, he began to define his opinions. To correct a misapprehension regarding his position, he wrote a letter stating that he had never doubted that Congress had power under the Constitution to prohibit slavery in a territory, but it was equally clear Congress could not constitutionally institute it.[2] A few days before the Republican convention met, a second letter from Judge McLean was published. The troubles in Kansas were, in his opinion, "the fruits of that ill-advised and mischievous measure—the repeal of the Missouri Compromise;" and the remedy was "the immediate admission of Kansas as a State into the Union under the constitution already formed."[3]

Conservative Republicans advocated McLean; also antislavery Americans and those who distrusted Frémont. Pike, one of the editorial staff of the New York *Tribune*, and more radical than his chief, was from the first opposed to Frémont. As soon as his candidacy was avowed, Pike wrote from Washington to the New York *Tribune:* "Of the prominent candidates, Colonel Frémont is the most questionable by his antecedents, and the one upon whom strong doubts centre. Let there be no haste, and no dropping of the substance in the pursuit of the shadow. The opposition to Ne-

---

[1] McLean was from Ohio.
[2] McLean to Cass, Washington, May 13th.
[3] McLean to Chief Justice Hornblower, of New Jersey, dated June 6th, published in the New York *Evening Post*, June 14th.

braskaism stands on a principle. In the selection of a candidate this must be recognized first of all. Availability is good in its place; but let all look sharp that we do not abandon what we know to be good for that which, though promising, may prove deceptive."[1]

When the choice was narrowed down to McLean and Frémont, Pike much preferred McLean. The rebukes that he received from his associates in New York accurately represent the drift of opinion. "We do not consider Judge McLean quite S. O. G. here,"[2] wrote Greeley; "but if you know any facts making in favor of his orthodoxy, please send them on.... Considering how forcibly you have written in favor of having a candidate of whose zeal and fidelity there could be no dispute, we feel that there is something that needs explaining in your recent zeal for McLean. Friend Pike, do you know that is a Delilah of a town in which you chance just now to be lodged? Have you heard that it is unfavorable to the rigidity and perpendicularity of backbone? Do you know that men have gone there honest and come away rascals? Have you heard that a virtue less savage than mine would hardly have been proof against its manifold and persistent seductions? Beware, O friend and compatriot!"[3]

Charles A. Dana wrote to Pike in the same strain: "Do not growl about an old fogy like McLean. One of the first of duties is to get rubbish out of the way. He belongs decidedly to that category. With you, I do not care who is the candidate so it is not a marrowless old lawyer whose mind has illustrated itself by so many perverse and perverting decisions. Why do you not stick to your original idea in going to Washington—that of getting some straight-out man nominated? For a fellow who started with that virtu-

---

[1] April 12th, Pike's First Blows of the Civil War, p. 322.
[2] Sound on the goose—political slang of the day.
[3] Private letter from Greeley to Pike, May 21st, Pike's First Blows of the Civil War, p. 337.

ous purpose, it seems to me you have deteriorated. You ought to rejoice at the interment of such a candidate rather than shed tears by the quart when he is done for."[1]

Frémont could lay claim to no experience in civil life. He had, indeed, been for a short term senator from California, but his exertions were wholly confined to matters of local interest. At that time (1849–51) he said he was a Democrat by principle and education; but as he belonged to the anti-slavery portion of the party in California, he was defeated when seeking a re-election.[2] What brought him before the public mind were his daring and energetic explorations in the West; a halo of romance clung around his expeditions. A glamour was cast over his affairs of love. The story of his attachment to the daughter of Senator Benton, her devotion, and their romantic marriage crowned his heroic exploits. He was now but forty-three years old; active and adventurous, he seemed a fit leader for a young and aggressive party, and it was expected that the qualities which had made him a determined explorer would make him an executive officer of decision. The movement in his favor, initiated by the politicians, took the popular heart; in the West, wrote Bowles, it "is going like prairie fire."[3]

It may be safely said that the larger portion of prominent Republicans who thus yielded to the argument of availability were not actuated by the desire for office, or the wish to have a hand in the disposition of the patronage; but they feared that, unless they got the executive and the command of the army, Kansas might be made a slave State. The mass of Republicans sincerely felt that the cause of freedom was bound up in the success of their party. They were therefore gratified when, on the 29th of April, Fré-

---

[1] Private letter of Dana to Pike, May 21st, Pike's First Blows of the Civil War, p. 338.

[2] See Life of Frémont, Bigelow, pp. 390, 428.

[3] Samuel Bowles to H. L. Dawes, April 19th, Life of Bowles, Merriam, vol. i. p. 172.

mont planted himself squarely in favor of the Republican idea. He wrote a letter to a New York meeting, saying that he was inflexibly opposed to the extension of slavery.[1]

Yet from one point of anti-slavery sentiment came the anxious inquiry of Theodore Parker to Sumner, "Do tell me how far is Frémont reliable?"[2] and from another point, Lincoln wrote E. B. Washburne, urging him and his Republican associates in Congress to go to Philadelphia and use their exertions and influence in favor of McLean.[3]

The delegates who met at Philadelphia the 17th of June were not chosen by means of complicated party machinery. In their selection, there had been no strife. No animated contests between those favoring different candidates had occurred. Other conventions have had more prominent and abler men, but no national political convention of a great party was ever composed to so large an extent of sincere, unselfish, and patriotic citizens as that which began its deliberations on this anniversary day of Bunker Hill. The Republican movement was in that state where it attracted only men of earnest convictions. In some localities, aspiring souls made sacrifices when they took part in it. The high social and trade influences of New York City and Philadelphia were arrayed against it, and even in Boston many old Whig families of aristocratic pretensions held aloof from the new party. Where success was problematical, the prospect did not allure hangers-on and office-seekers. It is one of the curiosities of politics that this convention of honest and competent men made a nomination that Republicans have not ceased to apologize for. Yet they did but register the popular will.[4]

---

[1] Life of Frémont, Bigelow, p. 449.
[2] May 21st, Life of Parker, Weiss, vol. ii. p. 180.
[3] Note of E. B. Washburne in The Edwards Papers, p. 246.
[4] As my view of the convention and its result differs from that of E. B. Washburne, justice to my readers demands that I should quote what he says: "I was present not as a member, but as an interested spectator. The nomination of Frémont was a set-up job from the beginning, and all

When the convention were ready to ballot, the name of Chase was formally withdrawn. Every one understood from the first day that Seward was not a candidate. The New York delegation, influenced greatly by Thurlow Weed, were enthusiastically in favor of Frémont. Judge Spalding, of Ohio, by authority withdrew the name of McLean, and Frémont would then have been nominated with but few dissenting voices, had not the indomitable Thaddeus Stevens begged for delay. He said that the only man who could carry Pennsylvania, McLean, had been withdrawn, and he asked that the convention adjourn in order that the Pennsylvania delegation might have time to consult in view of the changed conditions. His wish was acceded to. He then made an impassioned appeal to his fellow-delegates from Pennsylvania, many of whom were for Frémont, to support McLean unanimously. "I never heard a man speak with more feeling or in more persuasive accents," wrote Washburne. "He closed his speech with the assertion that the nomination of Frémont would not only lose the State of Pennsylvania to the Republicans, but that the party would be defeated in the Presidential election."[1]

---

the opposition which was offered to that nomination by many of the most influential, judicious, and patriotic men of the party could avail nothing. . . . All chances for the election of a Republican President in 1856 were deliberately thrown away by the Philadelphia convention, and, it might be said, in the face of light and knowledge. In the state of feeling then existing in the country, Judge McLean, or any Republican statesman of national reputation, could have easily been elected. The first time I saw Dayton after the defeat of the Frémont and Dayton ticket, I told him what I believed then, and what I believe now, that if the ticket had been reversed he would have been elected President of the United States."—Note to The Edwards Papers, p. 246, written in 1884. I should have been glad to adopt this view, but, with all deference to the advantages and long political experience of Washburne, I do not believe the contemporary evidence warrants it; yet as the candid expression of a spectator, and of one who knew what little inside history there was of the convention, it should not be overlooked.

[1] E. B. Washburne, The Edwards Papers, p. 246. See also article of

The delegates reassembled. At the request of Pennsylvania, New Jersey, and Ohio, the name of Judge McLean was again placed before the convention and an informal ballot taken. It resulted in 359 votes for Frémont and 196 for McLean. From the Republican point of view, the doubtful States were Pennsylvania, New Jersey, Indiana, Illinois, and California. Since the nomination of Buchanan, the hope of winning Pennsylvania from the Democrats seemed almost vain. A majority of the delegates from all of these States except California voted for McLean.[1]

A formal ballot was now taken, Frémont receiving all but 38 votes. William L. Dayton, of New Jersey, was nominated for Vice-President. On the informal ballot which preceded this nomination, Abraham Lincoln received 110 votes.[2]

Before the nominations were made, the platform was unanimously adopted amidst great enthusiasm. The convention resolved that "it is both the right and the duty of Congress to prohibit in the territories those twin relics of barbarism, polygamy and slavery." It severely arraigned the administration for the conduct of affairs in Kansas, and demanded that Kansas should be immediately admitted as a State with her present free constitution. It "Resolved, That the highwayman's plea, that 'might makes right,'

Russel Errett on the Convention of 1856, Magazine of Western History, vol. x. p. 257. He was present at the convention, and writes: "I do not think Stevens thought success probable (however possible it might be) with McLean; but with any one else it was impossible, in his view." He "thought the fate of the party was bound up in his candidate."

[1] From Pennsylvania, 71 delegates voted for McLean, 10 for Frémont; New Jersey, 14 for McLean, 7 for Frémont; Indiana, 21 for McLean, 18 for Frémont; Illinois, 19 for McLean, 14 for Frémont. Ohio gave McLean 39 votes out of 69, and Maine 11 out of 24. Each State had a representation in the convention equal to three times its electoral vote.

[2] In this account of the convention I have consulted the New York *Evening Post*, New York *Times*, New York *Tribune*, Life of Frémont by Bigelow.

embodied in the Ostend circular, was in every respect unworthy of American diplomacy, and would bring shame and dishonor upon any government or people that gave it their sanction."[1]

Since by common consent availability was to determine the candidate, it seemed at the time as if the convention had acted wisely in nominating Frémont instead of McLean. The nomination of McLean would have been looked upon as a bid for the Know-nothing vote; it would probably have lost more Germans than it attracted Americans, and would have hampered the party in its future course.[2] The discussion on a resolution that touched upon the Know-nothing question, its adoption, and the firm and enthusiastic determination to nominate Frémont were evidence that the Republicans wished to cut loose from their Know-nothing affiliations and make the fight on one cardinal principle. In Pennsylvania the anti-slavery and American ideas had been so closely intertwined that it seemed to Stevens and his sympathizers that all was lost if the Americans were not placated. The convention listened to their arguments with attention, but were not convinced.

There was another objection to the nomination of McLean. He was on the Supreme bench, and a feeling prevailed that judges of the highest court lowered themselves and their court when they entered into a contest for the presidency.[3]

---

[1] The platform, with all but one resolution, may be found in History of Presidential Elections, Stanwood, p. 205.

[2] The New York *Abend-Zeitung* of June 13th said that hardly one-tenth of the Germans would vote for McLean. See also Von Holst, vol. v. p. 363. After the election (Dec. 23d), Dana wrote Pike: " In my judgment, we are a great deal better off as we are than we should have been with McLean elected; but as for his coming within a gunshot of Frémont's vote, it is all gammon. He could not have carried the Northwest, and would not have got over 170,000 in this State."—First Blows of the Civil War, p. 354. Frémont received in New York State 276,007 votes.

[3] This view is ably argued in a leading editorial of the New York

The North Americans, as those were called who seceded from the American convention that nominated Fillmore, held a convention shortly before the Republicans and nominated Banks for President. He declined. When the delegates, who had adjourned pending the action of the Philadelphia convention, reassembled, they nominated Frémont.[1]

The country was too much excited over the assault on Sumner and the destruction of Lawrence, and too much interested in the outcome of the political conventions, to pay much attention to an important diplomatic transaction which came to a head on the 29th of May. On that day Congress was informed that the President had ceased to hold intercourse with the British minister, Crampton, had sent him his passport, and had revoked the exequaturs of the British consuls at New York, Philadelphia, and Cincinnati. The offence was that they had conducted in this country an extensive system of recruiting for the British foreign legion, in violation of the laws and sovereign rights of the United States. The acts complained of had been performed the previous year while England was in the midst of the Crimean war.[2] The withdrawal of Crampton and

---

Tribune, June 5th. The confidential expression of a brother justice is of interest: "Judge McLean hopes, I think, to be a candidate for the office. He would be a good President, but I am not willing to have a judge in that most trying position of being a candidate for this great office."—Letter of B. R. Curtis to Geo. Ticknor, April 8th, 1856, Memoir of B. R. Curtis, vol. i. p. 180.

[1] But they did not endorse the nomination of Dayton; they named Johnston, of Pennsylvania, for Vice-President. As an intimation of the different shades of opinion, it may be noted that the conservatives seceded from the North American convention and nominated Commodore Stockton for President. The abolitionists who believed in political action had already nominated Gerrit Smith for President and Frederick Douglass for Vice-President; but it was well understood at this time that there were practically only three tickets in the field. Any one who wished to vote could find a representative of his principles in Buchanan, Frémont, or Fillmore. See New York *Herald*, June 21st.

[2] See Marcy to Dallas, May 27th.

the three consuls had been asked for, but the request was refused by the British government.¹

Before the President had promulgated his decision, the action was in English official circles deemed probable; and Dallas, our minister at London, felt certain that when the news of Crampton's dismissal came, he would in turn receive his passports from the British government.² In one of his anxious moments he had a talk with the experienced Russian ambassador, who assured him that there was no cause for worry; that if Crampton were dismissed, the English government would make light of it, or their indignation would be "mildly expressed and of very short duration." "No ministry," the Russian added, "would last a month, in the present condition of England, that should quarrel with the United States."³ By the last of May, however, "the public pulse was at fever heat" in England. Dallas wrote: "If the *Times* and the *Post*⁴ are reliable organs, I shall probably quit England soon, *never* to return; an indiscriminating retaliation amounts to an original insult, and will require many years to be forgotten. It will not surprise me if I should turn out to be the last minister from the United States to the British Court."⁵

---

¹ "The President's whole cabinet felt so kindly to Crampton that they examined narrowly the evidence against him, and would gladly have believed that he had been innocent of violating the neutrality of America towards the contending nations, but were at last unwillingly convinced of the fact."—Life of Jefferson Davis, by his Wife, vol. i. p. 569.

² Private letter of Geo. M. Dallas to Marcy, April 20th, Letters from London, p. 22.   ³ Dallas to Marcy, May 6th, ibid., p. 33.

⁴ The *Post* was the official organ of the ministry.

⁵ Dallas to Mr. D., June 6th, Letters from London, pp. 43, 45. "Those who endeavor to persuade themselves that we shall learn the dismissal of Mr. Crampton without enforcing the retirement of Mr. Dallas are calculating upon an amount of endurance totally inconsistent with the character of Englishmen."—London *Times*, June 5th, cited in the New York *Times*, June 24th.

"The dismissal of Mr. Crampton must be followed by the dismissal of Mr. Dallas."—London *Post*, June 13th, cited in New York *Times*, July 1st.

But when the news came that Crampton had been dismissed, it was found that no one was in favor of war except a few officials and some of the newspapers. The manufacturing and mercantile classes made themselves felt as being unconditionally opposed to war with the United States.[1] The Liverpool Reform Association protested against it.[2] Immense placards were posted all over England by order of the Manchester peace conference, protesting in the most emphatic terms against war with America.[3] The country was much relieved when Lord Palmerston in the House of Commons "announced formally the determination of the cabinet 'not to terminate their present amicable relations with Mr. Dallas.'"[4] The sentiment of the Northern States was decidedly averse to war with England. It was felt that nothing should be permitted to divert the attention of the country from the serious domestic question which agitated it from one end to the other. During this whole controversy Northern people reposed entire confidence in Marcy; they thought the honor of the country safe in his hands, and were certain that they would not be forced into war with England unless it were unavoidable.[5]

The party conventions had formulated their principles

---

[1] Letters from London, p. 47.   [2] New York *Times*, July 1st.
[3] New York *Herald*, June 23d.
[4] Dallas to Marcy, June 17th, Letters from London, p. 50.
[5] See, for example, the New York *Independent*, March 20th; Pike to the New York *Tribune*, April 28th; see also Washington correspondence *Journal of Commerce*, July 8th; and Dallas to Marcy, June 17th, Letters from London, p. 51.

"Probably no greener Secretary of State ever entered upon the duties of that post; yet few or none ever filled it more effectively. Several of his State papers will long be treasured and admired, and he may be said to have reflected honor even on the administration of General Pierce—an achievement to which few men would have proved equal. That he was its good genius was very generally realized. That he never approved nor countenanced the violation of the Missouri Compromise is beyond doubt."—New York *Tribune*, July 11th, 1857, on the occasion of Marcy's death.

and put up their candidates. The vital question, from whatever side it was approached, turned on Kansas; yet Congress had passed no act and determined on no policy in regard to the territory. Senator Crittenden proposed that a request be preferred to the President that he send Lieutenant-General Scott to Kansas—"a man," said Crittenden, "who in such a contest carries the sword in his left hand, and in his right, peace, gentle peace"—but the proposition did not meet the approval of the Democratic majority.[1] Yet the Democrats could plainly see that if they expected to carry the doubtful Northern States at the presidential election, it was necessary that they should make an effort to allay the existing troubles in Kansas. Five days after the adjournment of the Republican convention, on the 24th of June, Senator Toombs introduced a bill which, in fairness to the free-State settlers, went far beyond the measure that earlier in the session had been drawn by Douglas to carry into effect the recommendations of his report and the message of the President.

The bill provided that a census should be taken in Kansas; that all white males twenty-one years old, who were *bona-fide* inhabitants on the day of the census, should be registered as voters; that the voters should proceed to elect on the Tuesday after the 1st day of November next delegates to a constitutional convention. Irregularities and fraud at the election, and intimidation of voters, were guarded against. There were to be five competent persons, appointed by the President and confirmed by the Senate, to carry into effect the provisions of the act. Under their direction the census was to be taken and the registration of

---

[1] This proposition was made at the suggestion of R. C. Winthrop, of Boston, to whom Crittenden writes: "When it was first offered it appeared to be received with general favor; but the reflections and, I suppose, the *consultations* of the night brought forth next day a strong opposition. The source of this was no doubt in the White House and its appurtenances."—Life of Crittenden, Coleman, vol. ii. p. 129.

voters made. The delegates were to meet on the first Monday of December, when, if deemed expedient, they should proceed to form a constitution and State government for admission into the Union as a State.

Toombs said that his object was "to preserve and protect the integrity of the ballot-box," and to have "a fair and honest expression of the opinion of the present inhabitants" of Kansas. If other means more proper and effectual could be devised by the Senate, he was willing to adopt them. He had provided for the election in November in order that there might be sufficient time to determine those who were justly entitled to vote; he chose the presidential-election day, as voters in adjoining States would be occupied at their own homes and unable to interfere with a fair expression of the popular will in Kansas.

When Toombs said that he was willing to take the will of the people in a proper and just manner and abide by the result, he was sincere. An old Whig, he had the Whig love of the Union. Believing that its existence depended on the defeat of Frémont, he was willing to make concessions to Northern public sentiment for the sake of averting Republican success. In January he had delivered a lecture on slavery in Boston, where he was listened to with attention. The conservative Whigs turned out to hear a moderate exposition of Southern views from one whom they deemed a liberal-minded and whole-souled Southern gentleman.[1] A month after his return from Boston, he expressed the opinion in the Senate that Kansas would probably be a free State.[2] A few days before he introduced his bill, however, he saw Stringfellow at Washington, whom Stephens regarded as "our main man in Kansas." Stringfellow had come direct from the territory and had given Toombs reason to believe that there was a fair prospect of making Kansas a

---

[1] See extracts from the Boston *Traveller and Journal*, cited by the *Liberator*, Feb. 1st and 15th.

[2] Feb. 28th, *Congressional Globe*, vol. xxxiii. p. 116.

slave State.¹ Toombs was an able lawyer and an honest man; though harsh and intolerant in expression, he was frank in purpose.² He undoubtedly thought that by the operation of his bill there was an even chance, but no more, of Kansas becoming a slave State.

On the 30th of June, Douglas introduced from the committee on territories what was substantially the Toombs bill. He remarked that as thirty-seven of the ninety-one days of the session of the Senate since the House was organized had been devoted to the Kansas question, he should insist that an early vote be taken on the measure proposed. An animated and able debate followed. Hale confessed that the bill was nearly unexceptionable in its terms;³ Trumbull admitted that "a liberal spirit seems to be manifested on the part of some senators of the majority to have a fair bill," and in many of its features it met his approbation;⁴ Seward regarded the measure as a concession, if not a compromise;⁵ and Simonton wrote to his journal that "upon its face it seems to be one of the fairest measures ever proposed to an American Congress."⁶

So long as the discussion was confined to the details of the bill the Democrats had the better of the argument, and they occupied a fairer position, apparently, than the Republicans. Wilson objected that it was unfair to register as voters only those who were now residing in the territory, when the free-State men had been plundered, outraged, and driven out of the territory, and when their leaders had been

---

¹ Letter of A. H. Stephens to his brother, June 14th, Life of Stephens, Johnston and Browne, p. 309.

² See Greeley's opinion, Letter from Washington to the *Tribune,* Feb. 28th.

³ July 1st, *Congressional Globe,* vol. xxxii. p. 1520.

⁴ July 2d, ibid., vol. xxxiii. pp. 778, 781.

⁵ Ibid., p. 789; but in a letter to his wife, Seward called it "the new sham evasive Kansas bill," Life of Seward, vol. ii. p. 280.

⁶ Letter to New York *Times,* July 2d; but he prefaced that remark by saying that the bill was "an ingenious fraud."

imprisoned, or had escaped to avoid arrest. To this the reply was made that Buford's men had been expelled by Colonel Sumner, but it was easily shown that at this game the free-State party had suffered more than the other.[1] This objection was, however, fully obviated by an amendment offered by Douglas and agreed to.[2]

The territorial laws were inveighed against by the Republicans. It was understood by some senators that the bill abrogated the obnoxious laws, but as doubt remained, an amendment was adopted that did render them null and void in unequivocal terms.[3] The operation of the bill would undoubtedly liberate the free-State prisoners.

Another objection was that the appointment of the commissioners rested with the President, who, Wade had no doubt, would appoint Atchison and Stringfellow or men of like principles.[4] This was met by the statement of Cass, in whom every one had confidence, that he felt authorized to say that the President would impartially select the commissioners from the "different shades of party in the country," and would, moreover, appoint the best men that could be got.[5]

Yet if this objection, as also another that no provision was made to submit the Constitution to a vote of the people of Kansas, still remained, the Republican senators could not overlook the fact that they had been asked to amend the bill and perfect it.[6] There would probably have been no difficulty in incorporating a section requiring ratification by the popular vote before the measure left the Senate. The Republican House might have proposed to name the commission in the bill,[7] and it is not certain that the Senate

---

[1] See *Congressional Globe*, vol. xxxiii. pp. 773, 774. [2] Ibid., p. 795.
[3] See Seward's remarks, ibid., p. 791, and the Geyer amendment, p. 799.
[4] Ibid., p. 756; see also Seward's remarks, p. 792.
[5] Ibid., vol. xxxii. p. 1519; see the reiteration of Douglas and Pugh, vol. xxxiii. pp. 295, 866.
[6] So stated by Trumbull, ibid., p. 781.
[7] See New York *Times*, July 7th.

would have objected, for in the closing days of the session a spirit of compromise between the two Houses prevailed; or the persons the President intended to appoint might have been submitted to the leaders of both parties. It is unlikely that he would have refused to do his part towards an adjustment of the differences,[1] for the manifestations of Northern sentiment were having a potent effect at the White House.

The difference between the Douglas bill introduced in March and the present measure was great. It showed the effect of Northern sentiment which had been stirred up by the assault on Sumner and the destruction of Lawrence. The enthusiasm at the Republican convention alarmed the Democrats, and the election of Frémont seemed not improbable.[2] Under these influences, they were disposed to meet the Republicans more than half-way; and had the Toombs bill been introduced before the startling events occurred which had so profoundly affected the country, the conservative Republicans would have determined the course of the party, and a successful effort would probably have been made to arrive at a compromise on the basis proposed.[3] But now, if the Democrats had receded, the Republicans had advanced. Their convention had declared for congressional prohibition of slavery in the territories. While it was probable that the Toombs bill would make Kansas a free State,[4] it was not certain, and the Republicans would now only accept a certainty.

When the Republicans in the senatorial debate passed from the criticism of details to the general principle, their

---

[1] See letter of A. H. Stephens, Johnston and Browne, p. 315.

[2] "The Democrats are profoundly alarmed. Hence their change from denunciation to compromise, concerning Kansas."—Seward to his wife, July 5th, Life of Seward, vol. ii. p. 282.

[3] See a very careful editorial in the New York *Times* of March 8th.

[4] See New York *Tribune*, July 9th; Kansas Crusade, Thayer, p. 245; Spring's Kansas, p. 210.

position, in the light of history, was invulnerable. Seward rose to the height that the occasion demanded. He objected to the bill because " it treated the subject of slavery and freedom as if they were equal, to be submitted to a trial by the people," and he plainly intimated that no amendment would satisfy him unless it prohibited slavery in Kansas.[1]

Toombs and his Southern friends thought that when they offered freedom an equal chance with slavery, the measure of justice was full. Douglas and his followers pretended to think so. Seward, on the other hand, with the approval of the Republican party, maintained that the one principle was more sacred than the other and demanded especial protection from the general government. This position was fraught with weightier consequences than they dreamed. Reid, of North Carolina, saw the future more clearly than did the Republicans, and told the Senate solemnly that if a majority of the Northern people became prepared to endorse the doctrine avowed by Seward, the Union could not last an hour longer.[2]

The Toombs bill came to a vote the 2d of July, and was passed by 33 to 12. The nays were practically a measure of Republican strength in the Senate,[3] and in that slow-changing body the time seemed indeed far distant when a majority could be secured to vote for giving freedom a better chance in the territories than slavery.

The proposition of the Republicans was to admit Kansas as a State under the Topeka Constitution. A bill providing for this had been introduced early in the session by Seward, and the Republicans came gradually to take that position.[4] When the national convention was held, no opposition was made to the resolution declaring that policy. It was con-

---

[1] *Congressional Globe*, vol. xxxiii. p. 794.   [2] Idem, p. 792.

[3] Dodge, a Democrat from Wisconsin, voted against the bill on account of instructions from his legislature; but Fish and Sumner were absent.

[4] See letter of Pike to New York *Tribune*, April 24th, Pike's First Blows of the Civil War, p. 322.

sistent, therefore, that Seward should maintain that his bill was a sure and just way of settling the difficulty, for it would immediately admit Kansas as a free State. On the day after the Senate passed the Toombs measure, the Republican House gave answer by voting a bill to admit Kansas under the Topeka Constitution.[1]

The alternative offered by the Republicans does not deserve the commendation that may be freely awarded to their opposition to the Toombs bill. The Topeka Constitution had been adopted by a self-styled convention which had not the authority of law, was irregular, and only represented a faction.[2] To admit Kansas as a State with a Constitution thus framed and a government so established would have been a monstrous precedent. It is doubtful whether the trained legislators among the Republicans would have advocated such a policy, had they not known that by no possibility could such a measure pass the Senate.[3] But defective as the proposal was before Congress, it was strong before the country. It had the merit of simplicity, and a noble end in view. It must be looked upon as an election cry rather than as a serious effort by the Republicans to settle the difficulty by a legislative expedient.

The House did not consider the Toombs bill. Nor did it endeavor to compose the differences between it and the Senate, for the Dunn proposition could not be called such an attempt. One section of that bill restored the Missouri restriction, which of course could not pass the Senate; while other provisions were not satisfactory to many Republicans, although they voted for the measure. It was put through under operation of the previous question, and without any debate whatever.[4]

---

[1] The vote was 99 to 97.   [2] See p. 103.
[3] When the House bill was considered in the Senate, the Toombs bill was substituted for it, and passed a second time.
[4] The bill is printed in the *Congressional Globe*, vol. xxxii. p. 1815. The vote was 89 to 77. Dunn was a Fillmore man; he acted sometimes with the Republicans, but could not always be depended upon.

The Democrats charged that the Republicans did not desire to settle the trouble; that "bleeding Kansas" was a thrilling party catchword which they had use for until November. "An angel from heaven," declared Douglas in the Senate, "could not write a bill to restore peace in Kansas that would be acceptable to the abolition Republican party previous to the presidential election."[1] It is true the lower motive was mixed with the higher. The Republicans were but men. Of these former Whigs and Democrats, politics had been the trade of many who were keenly alive to the potent effect of an expressive cry in a political campaign. They were backed by the free-State settlers of Kansas, who opposed the Toombs bill, while the pro-slavery party favored it.[2] The Democrats were well satisfied with the advances they had made, and they adopted a resolution in the Senate to print twenty thousand copies of the Toombs bill, which they purposed to circulate as an electioneering document.

The majority of the House committee which had been sent to Kansas to investigate affairs made their report July 1st, and the facts elicited contributed much to the congressional discussion of this question. The committee had examined three hundred and twenty-three witnesses,[3] and the evidence was annexed to the report. The statement of the majority was signed by Howard and Sherman, and is an able and fair paper. Its conclusions are indisputable, and established that—The territorial elections were carried by fraud; that the territorial legislature was an illegally con-

---

[1] July 9th, *Congressional Globe*, vol. xxxiii. p. 844. Three years later Douglas had the same notion. He said to Cutts: "It was evident during all the proceedings that the Republicans were as anxious to keep the Kansas question open as the Democrats were to close it, in view of the approaching presidential election."—Constitutional and Party Questions, p. 108.

[2] See protest of Lieut.-Gov. Roberts, New York *Times*, July 15th; Lawrence (Kansas) correspondence of the New York *Times*, July 11th and 21st; Sara Robinson's Kansas, pp. 319, 323.

[3] Spring's Kansas, p. 108; see p. 155.

stituted body, and its enactments were null and void; that neither Whitfield nor Reeder was legally elected delegate; that "in the present condition of the territory a fair election cannot be held without a new census, a stringent and well-guarded election law, the selection of impartial judges, and the presence of United States troops at every place of election; . . . the various elections held by the people of the territory preliminary to the formation of the State government [*i. e.* under the Topeka Constitution] have been as regular as the disturbed condition of the territory would allow; and the Constitution passed by the convention held in pursuance of said elections embodies the will of a majority of the people."

On the 11th of July, Oliver made a minority report which has historical interest: in it was submitted the testimony telling the story of the Pottawatomie massacre by John Brown and his party. In the speech which Oliver made elucidating his report, he stated that, although the committee heard of these assassinations while on the Missouri border, Howard and Sherman refused to take evidence concerning them, on the ground that under the resolution of the House the committee had no power to examine into transactions which had taken place since their appointment.[1]

However, the report of Oliver, the testimony submitted, and the explanation of it in his speech, put the matter before the country, and it is amazing that the horrible story did not do appreciable injury to the cause of the free-State party by bringing about a reaction in public sentiment at the North. The outrages on the Northern settlers were a never-failing argument of Republican journals and speakers. Their record showed that in a year and a half seven free-State men had been killed by the border ruffians,[2] while on the Pottawatomie in a single night five pro-slavery men had been deliberately and foully murdered. The evidence was

---

[1] See amplification of this statement, and colloquy between Oliver and Sherman, *Congressional Globe*, vol. xxxiii. p. 1012; also Spring's Kansas, p. 145.   [2] New York *Tribune*, June 14th.

brought before Congress and the country in a shape that told a clear and convincing tale; it is the material that historians and biographers now mainly use when they construct the story. Yet the Democratic press, senators, and representatives, excepting Oliver, made almost no use of it. Their accounts are meagre, their allusions fragmentary and rare. The first news of the massacre was published equally by journals of both parties; but soon there appeared a free-State version which admitted the killing, but averred that a pro-slavery gang was caught in the act of hanging a free-State settler, and, in effecting the rescue, his friends shot five of their enemies. This explanation was widely circulated by the Republican journals and believed by their readers; but it was given an emphatic denial by Oliver in his report and speech; and although the report was published by the Democratic newspapers, it was not made the subject of earnest comment, nor was attention called to the speech.[1]

---

[1] In carefully looking over the debates on Kansas, I found, with the exception of the speech of Oliver, made July 31st, but one reference to the massacre on the Pottawatomie, that of Toombs, *Congressional Globe*, vol. xxxiii. p. 869; but he was apparently prevented from enlarging upon it by the sharp inquiry of Fessenden: " Have you any proof of it ?"

I have examined or have had examined the files of the New York *Journal of Commerce*, the New York *Herald*, the Philadelphia *Pennsylvanian* (Forney's paper), the Washington *Union*, and the Cleveland *Plain Dealer*, and I am struck with the fact that substantially no use was made of this occurrence, which offered a good occasion for the *tu quoque* argument. All of these were Democratic journals, with the exception of the New York *Herald*, which occupied a peculiar position. It believed that Kansas ought to be a slave State, and yet it supported Frémont. For its reason for supporting Frémont, see extract from it in the *Liberator* of Aug. 15th. There is not an editorial comment in the *Herald*. The *Journal of Commerce* had a short editorial mention when it published the testimony (June 19th). By the *Pennsylvanian*, Brown is not referred to, the massacre is mentioned simply as a report, Oliver is spoken of twice, but no allusion is made to his speech. The Cleveland *Plain Dealer* published part of the testimony without comment. The Republican papers generally did not publish the Oliver report, says the *Journal of Commerce*, July 23d.

Contrasting this treatment with the stirring articles in the Republican papers, suggested by the Howard report, one is led to the conviction that the Democrats failed to make good use of their opportunities; for they continued to rehearse their threadbare charges against the emigrant-aid companies and the New England men who went out bearing Sharps rifles. The truth is that the Pottawatomie massacre was so at variance with the whole course and policy of the free-State party in Kansas up to that time that its horrible details were not credited in the East. The Kansas outrages were regarded as the stock-in-trade of the Republicans, and, until this affair took place, they were anxious to have full light cast on occurrences in the territory. The testimony of impartial observers was that the pro-slavery men were lawless and aggressive, and the free-State settlers submissive, industrious, and anxious for liberty and order.[1]

G. W. Brown, the editor of the *Herald of Freedom*, of Lawrence, in 1856, writes in 1879-80: "The opposition press, both North and South, took up the damning tale ... of that midnight butchery on the Pottawatomie.... Whole columns of leaders from week to week, with startling head-lines, liberally distributed capitals, and frightful exclamation-points, filled all the newspapers." He further states that he believes had it not been for that massacre Frémont would have been elected. See Reminiscences of Old John Brown, p. 26. If G. W. Brown were writing from recollection, he probably had in mind the six border-ruffian papers, published in Kansas and on the Missouri border. The Missouri *Republican*, published in St. Louis, was also full of the matter; but it had a correspondent who commanded a border-ruffian company in Kansas, Captain Pate. The Burlington (Iowa) *Gazette* had a fierce editorial on the subject, June 25th. But the papers I have previously named are fairly representative of the tone of the Eastern Democratic press. That the Pottawatomie massacre had a marked influence on Kansas affairs in the summer of 1856 there is abundant reason to believe (see p. 165); but I have not been able to discover that it had any influence detrimental to the Republicans in the presidential canvass.

[1] See letter from Lawrence, Kansas, July 1st, of a conservative Whig who went there with the idea that the stories of Kansas outrages were got up for political effect. Boston *Bee*, cited by the *Liberator*, July 18th. T. H. Gladstone who, according to Olmsted, was a very impartial ob-

Their previous good character prevented the country from believing that the killing done in their name by one of their number was an unprovoked massacre.[1]

Distrust in the border-ruffian accounts now caused the line of Democratic argument to be drawn differently from what might have been supposed. They maintained that the stories of the Kansas outrages were exaggerated;[2] that many of them were manufactured in the Republican newspaper offices;[3] that at election riots in Eastern cities more men were killed in twelve months than in the same length of time in Kansas.[4] The stately Democratic organ of New York city announced with satisfaction that "Kansas outrages are becoming scarce."[5] Everywhere may be observed Democratic anxiety to keep Kansas affairs out of sight, while the Republican journals and speakers insist all the more strongly on making them a subject of continual agitation.

---

server, writes: "Whatever testimony I gathered in Kansas was, for the most part, obtained from pro-slavery men." "Among all the scenes of violence I witnessed, it is remarkable that the offending parties were invariably on the pro-slavery side."—The Englishman in Kansas, T. H. Gladstone, pp. 12, 64. The whole book is an elaboration of these two statements.

See also extract from letter of Dr. Smith, a conservative and ex-mayor of Boston, cited by Wilson, July 9th, *Congressional Globe*, vol. xxxiii. p. 856; also a private letter quoted ibid., p. 853. When Seward (June 11th), Wilson (July 2d, 9th), and Wade (July 9th) described and denounced in emphatic terms the Kansas outrages, it is surprising that the Democrats did not retort with the story of the Pottawatomie massacre. See *Congressional Globe*, vol. xxxii. p. 1394; vol. xxxiii. pp. 755, 773, 854.

[1] See, for example, speech of Barclay, a Democrat, July 1st, *Congressional Globe*, vol. xxxii. p. 1523.
[2] Stephens, June 28th, ibid., vol. xxxiii. pp. 725, 727; Brown, ibid., vol. xxxii. p. 1387; Weller, ibid., vol. xxxiii. p. 842; Pugh, ibid., p. 867.
[3] See the *Daily Pennsylvanian*, June 18th and 23d, July 1st; also Washington *Union*.
[4] Stephens, *Congressional Globe*, vol. xxxiii. p. 725; Geyer, ibid., p. 787; Albany *Argus*, July 1st.
[5] *Journal of Commerce*, June 24th.

The committee on elections of the House had reported against the admission of Whitfield as a delegate and in favor of that of Reeder; but the House took a different view. It decided that neither was entitled to the seat, the vote against Whitfield standing 110 to 92, and against Reeder 113 to 88.

The Republicans had on all occasions criticised the executive administration of Kansas affairs. In the closing days of the session this took shape by the House attaching to two appropriation bills riders which dictated to the President a limited policy in the interest of the free-State settlers of Kansas. After a committee of conference the House receded from its amendments to one of the bills, but on the army appropriation it made a stubborn fight. This amendment had been offered by John Sherman, and virtually prohibited the employment of United States soldiers by the President to enforce the laws of the Kansas territorial legislature. The Senate struck it out. Three conferences failed to bring the two Houses to any agreement. On the 18th of August, while the representatives were considering the matter, the hour arrived which had, by joint resolution the preceding month, been fixed upon as the time of adjournment, and the speaker declared the House adjourned without day. The army appropriation bill had thus failed to become a law. Despite the excitement attendant upon this disagreement on a question that already shook the country from side to side, the closing scenes in the Senate and House were orderly and dignified. Banks had made an efficient speaker. By his prompt decisions and impartial bearing, serious difficulties were tided over.

The President immediately called an extraordinary session of Congress, and the two Houses convened August 21st. The congressional game of battledore and shuttlecock between the House and the Senate went on for a while; but August 30th the House receded from its position, and passed the army appropriation bill without the Kansas amendment by a vote of 101 to 98. The result was not reached by some of the Republicans backing down, for all the supporters of Frémont voted to adhere, but the Buchanan and Fillmore men acting together were sufficient to control the House.[1] Although this House has for convenience been spoken of as Republican, since it chose Banks as speaker and adopted some Republican measures, the majority was always uncertain.[2] Indeed, it was only because the Democrats and Americans did not act unitedly, or were more irregular in their attendance, that the Republicans were able to carry any points whatever.[3]

With the adjournment of Congress the contest was transferred to the country,[4] and the issue was clearly marked. Frémont represented the people who emphatically condemned the repeal of the Missouri Compromise; who demanded that Congress should prohibit slavery in all the territories, and that Kansas should be admitted as a free State. Buchanan accepted unreservedly the Cincinnati platform, and in his letter he elaborated one resolution sufficiently to show to any doubting ones at the South that he was sound on the policy inaugurated by the Kansas-Nebraska act. At the same time, he was well aware that to win the doubtful Northern States some issue other than the Douglas and Pierce Kansas policy must be thrust forward into the canvass. His letter gave the key-note of the Northern campaign, and was adroitly worded so as to rouse the enthusiasm of the moderate Democrats who had been his especial support in the convention, and also to attract conservative

---

[1] All Fillmore men present but Dunn voted with the Democrats.

[2] "This House of Representatives is like the moon. It shines brightest and smoothest at a distance. More than half the majority are Americans engaged in demoralizing the Congress and the country."—Seward to Weed, April 21st; see also letter to his wife, July 5th, Life of Seward, vol. ii. pp. 270, 282.

[3] See article in New York *Tribune*, Sept. 3d. On the irregularity of the attendance of Southern men, see letters of A. H. Stephens, Johnston and Browne, p. 315.

[4] The extraordinary session of Congress came to an end Aug. 30th.

Whigs who could not fully approve the formal declarations of any one of the parties. Taking for a text an allusion in the platform, he averred that the Democratic party was strictly national; he hoped that its mission was to overthrow all sectional parties; he made reference to the warning of the Father of his country against forming parties on geographical lines, and maintained that the Democrats were devoted to the cause of the Constitution and the Union.[1]

In taking this ground, Buchanan operated on a powerful sentiment. It could not be denied that not only were the Republicans unable to carry a slave State, but that south of Mason and Dixon's line and the Ohio River their ticket would not practically receive a vote. It had long been the custom in nominating candidates for President and Vice-President to take one from the North and the other from the South. While there had been exceptions to this rule, they had occurred in a condition of country very different from the present.[2] Frémont, born in Savannah, and educated in Charleston, South Carolina, was a citizen of California, and Dayton was from New Jersey. The strength of Buchanan's dignified allusion lay in the fact that the sectional character of Republican principles forced upon them, by the very nature of the case, sectional candidates. The free States had 176 electoral votes, while the slave States had but 120, and on account of the enthusiasm following the Republican convention it was not deemed improbable

---

[1] The letter may be found in the Campaign Life of Buchanan, by Horton, p. 414. It is dated June 13th. Only the first portion of the letter is given by Curtis. While the letter was written before the Republican Convention, there was no question whatever that both the candidates nominated would be from the North. In a public letter, July 2d, to the Tammany Society, of New York city, he made his meaning specific, and spoke of the National Democratic party "rallying to defend the Constitution and the Union against the sectional party who would outlaw fifteen of our sister States from the confederacy."

[2] In 1828, Adams and Rush, who made one ticket, were from the North, and Jackson and Calhoun, who made the other, were from the South.

at the South that Frémont might carry every non-slaveholding State.¹ The idea caused great irritation. This feeling was immediately typified in the action of the citizens of a Virginia county, who banished from their midst a resident because he had been a delegate to the Philadelphia convention.²

In a speech at Albany, Fillmore gave plain expression to the sentiment which Buchanan, in his carefully prepared formal paper, had only hinted at. "We see," Fillmore said, " a political party presenting candidates for the presidency and the vice-presidency selected for the first time from the free States alone, with the avowed purpose of electing these candidates by suffrages of one part of the Union only to rule over the whole United States. Can it be possible that those who are engaged in such a measure can have seriously reflected upon the consequences which must inevitably follow in case of success? Can they have the madness or folly to believe that our Southern brethren would submit to be governed by such a chief magistrate? . . . I speak warmly on this subject, for I feel that we are in danger. . . . We are treading upon the brink of a volcano that is liable at any moment to burst forth and overwhelm the nation."³

The Southerners did not delay to point Buchanan's allusion and Fillmore's statements. "The election of Frémont," wrote Senator Toombs, " would be the end of the Union, and ought to be. The object of Frémont's friends is the conquest of the South. I am content that they shall own us

---

¹ See in Georgia *Telegraph* a letter from New York, July 10th, cited by New York *Tribune*.

² See letter of Underwood of July 7th to New York *Evening Post*, cited by the *Liberator*, Aug. 15th.

³ This speech was made June 27th. It is printed in the New York *Tribune*, July 2d. The important part of it may be found in the *Congressional Globe*, vol. xxxiii. p. 716, where is also printed Fillmore's letter accepting the American party nomination.

when they conquer us, but not before."[1] Governor Wise, who had supported Buchanan at Cincinnati, wrote: Frémont's "election would bring about a dissolution of the American confederacy of States, inevitably."[2] The Richmond *Enquirer* declared that "the election of Frémont would be certain and immediate disunion."[3] Senator Slidell, a trusted friend of Buchanan, wrote: "I do not hesitate to declare that if Frémont be elected, the Union cannot and ought not to be preserved."[4] Senator Mason averred that in the event of Republican success "but one course remains for the South—immediate, absolute, eternal separation."[5] Quotations of like tenor from Southern public men and newspapers may be multiplied; they came for the most part from the supporters of Buchanan.[6] John Minor Botts, who was on the Fillmore electoral ticket in Virginia, took occasion to say that if Frémont were elected the South would not break up the Union; and the Richmond *Enquirer*

---

[1] To a Virginia friend, dated Washington, July 8th, printed in the New York *Tribune* of Aug. 13th.

[2] Richmond, Sept. 6th, to a friend in Pennsylvania, published by the *Pennsylvanian*. It must be remembered that the *Pennsylvanian* was Forney's paper, and that he was the trusted friend of Buchanan.

[3] Aug. 29th.

[4] To the Louisiana Central Committee, New York *Evening Post*, Sept. 11th.

[5] Sept. 29th, letter declining to be present at the Brooks dinner, New York *Times*, Oct. 14th.

[6] See *Congressional Globe*, vol. xxxiii. pp. 775, 792, 1206; Georgia *Constitutionalist*, Sept. 22d; citations in *National Intelligencer*, Sept. 30th, *Liberator*, Oct. 10th, and *Evening Post*, Oct. 6th and 7th. The South Carolina utterances were radical. Keitt at Lynchburg, *Evening Post*, Sept. 22d; Charleston *Mercury*, cited by the *Post*, Sept. 29th; Boyce and Orr, ibid., Oct. 17th; Brooks and Butler, the *Liberator*, Oct. 24th. "The Southern press, of every political shade of opinion, with hardly an exception, threatens disunion in the event of defeat in the present contest for the presidency."—New York *Times*, Aug. 29th. The New Orleans *Picayune* and *Daily Bee*, however, repudiated the disunion talk, and so did Senators Houston, Bell, and Clayton. See New York *Times*, Sept. 19th.

demanded that he should at once quit Virginia, advising him not to "wait for honors of ostracism nor provoke the disgrace of lynching."[1]

The feeling of many Northern Whigs found its aptest expression in a letter of Rufus Choate. Of this great lawyer we have a confidential opinion from a true friend, and one who was often pitted against him in forensic contest. Richard H. Dana wrote: Choate "has shown himself the brilliant, rich, philosophical orator, the scholar, and the kindly, adroit, and interesting man. He has not commanded respect as a man of deep convictions, earnest purpose, and reliable judgment."[2] Although this characterization was written three years previous to 1856, it shows that Choate from his very nature could have little sympathy with the aggressive anti-slavery movement; but, before he declared himself for Buchanan, he meditated long and earnestly, and weighed the arguments of all sides with care. Had he been less conscientious, he would naturally have drifted into the support of Fillmore, as did his intimate friends Everett and Hillard and as did Winthrop, whose manner of envisaging a subject was much the same.[3] But as the contest was between Frémont and Buchanan, it seemed to Choate that the patriot must decide between the two. Having decided, "silence," said he, "in such a sad state of things as environs us now is profoundly ignominious."[4] There were more friends and pleasanter associations among the Republicans, but duty seemed to point the other way, and his declaration for Buchanan was disinterested and sincere. He made for the Democrats a beautiful and forcible argument; and an element of power in the campaign was the decision to support Buchanan of men whom he fitly represented.

---

[1] Sept. 22d.

[2] This was written in 1853, Life of R. H. Dana, by C. F. Adams, vol. i. p. 246.

[3] George Ticknor was also for Fillmore, Life and Letters, vol. ii. p. 333.

[4] Reminiscences of Rufus Choate, Parker, p. 292.

"The first duty of Whigs," wrote Choate to the Maine Whig State Central Committee, " is to unite with some organization of our countrymen to defeat and dissolve the new geographical party, calling itself Republican. . . . The question for each and every one of us is . . . by what vote can I do most to prevent the madness of the times from working its maddest act—the very ecstasy of its madness—the permanent formation and the actual present triumph of a party which knows one half of America only to hate and dread it; from whose unconsecrated and revolutionary banner fifteen stars are erased or have fallen; in whose national anthem the old and endeared airs of the Eutaw Springs and the King's Mountain and Yorktown, and those later of New Orleans and Buena Vista and Chapultepec, breathe no more. . . . The triumph of such a party puts the Union in danger. . . . And yet some men would have us go on laughing and singing at a present peril, the mere apprehension of which, as a distant and bare possibility, could sadden the heart of the Father of his country, and dictate the grave and grand warning of the Farewell Address." If the Republican party, Choate continued, "accomplishes its objects and gives the government to the North, I turn my eyes from the consequences. To the fifteen States of the South that government will appear an alien government. It will appear worse. It will appear a hostile government. It will represent to their eye a vast region of States organized upon anti-slavery, flushed by triumph, cheered onward by the voices of the pulpit, tribune, and press; its mission to inaugurate freedom and put down the oligarchy; its constitution the glittering and sounding generalities of natural right which make up the Declaration of Independence. . . . Practically the contest, in my judgment, is between Mr. Buchanan and Colonel Frémont. In these circumstances, I vote for Mr. Buchanan." [1]

---

[1] The whole letter is well worth reading. It is printed in Brown's Life of Choate, p. 321.

In this letter there was powerful reasoning. While Choate maintained that Frémont's election was certain danger, the success of Buchanan would by no means extinguish the hope of having Kansas a free State. If there were a just administration of affairs in the territory, which there was good reason to expect from Buchanan, and if it were delivered " over to the natural law of peaceful and spontaneous immigration," when the proper time came it would "choose freedom for itself," and it would "have forever what it chooses." It is indeed impossible to assign to Choate's letter a weighty influence, for he was not widely known out of New England and New York, States which went overwhelmingly for Frémont; yet the considerations urged were those that in various shapes determined the votes of enough Northern men to elect Buchanan. For it was a transition period in politics, and, since the two great parties had clearly defined their position, there were many citizens still uncertain which way to go.[1] It was to these floating voters, who were Americans or Whigs and devoted to the Union, that arguments like that of Choate appealed with irresistible force.[2]

But on those who were already Republicans the reasoning had no effect whatever, for, from their point of view, the assumption that Frémont's election would cause disunion was unwarranted. They did not believe that the Southern threats were sincere. Their opinion was represented by the remark of Senator Wilson. "Threats have been thrown out," said he, "that if the 'Black Republicans' triumph in 1856, the Union will be dissolved. ... Sir, you cannot kick out of the Union the men who utter these impotent threats."[3] The whole tone of the Republican

---

[1] See on this point remarks of Seward at Auburn, Oct. 21st, Works, vol. iv. p. 278.

[2] The letter of Choate drew out many replies; perhaps the most celebrated was that of George W. Curtis, published in the New York *Times*, Sept. 11th. [3] In the Senate, April 14th, cited by Von Holst.

canvass, the speeches on the stump, the able discussion of the situation by the press, show that these menaces were regarded as Southern gasconade. The Frémont newspapers made haste to copy the most violent speeches and articles, for it was their opinion that a wide circulation of these threats would help their cause.[1]

After-events demonstrated that, in this respect, Fillmore and Choate understood the situation better. The private and confidential correspondence of the time shows that these expressions were not bluster. "Should Frémont be elected," wrote Buchanan, August 27th, to a friend in Boston, "he must receive 149 Northern electoral votes at the least, and the outlawry proclaimed by the Republican convention at Philadelphia against fifteen Southern States will be ratified by the people of the North. The consequences will be *immediate* and inevitable."[2] Two weeks later he wrote confidentially to Professor Read: "I am in the daily receipt of letters from the South which are truly alarming, and these from gentlemen who formerly opposed both nullification and disunion. They say explicitly that the election of Frémont involves the dissolution of the Union, and this immediately."[3] In a private letter, Governor Wise said: "The Southern States are going strong and unanimous. . . . They *will not* submit to a *sectional election* of a *Free-soiler* or Black Republican. . . . If Frémont is elected . . . this Union will not last one year from November next. . . . The country was never in such danger."[4] "It is quite sensibly felt by all," wrote ex-President Tyler, "that the success of the Black Republicans would be the knell of the Union."[5]

---

[1] There is hardly a number of the New York *Times* or *Tribune* that does not support this statement. Where the matter is specifically discussed, see for example New York *Times*, Sept. 26th, Oct. 3d, and Oct. 14th; New York *Tribune*, Aug. 13th. See also the opinion of the Springfield *Republican*, Life of Bowles, Merriam, vol. i. p. 155. [2] Curtis, vol. ii. p. 180.
[3] Ibid., p. 182.
[4] Aug. 15th, Letters and Times of the Tylers, vol. ii. p. 531.
[5] July 21st, ibid., p. 532.

It was fortunate, indeed, that the Republicans could not lift the veil and peer into the future. Had that power been given them, their party would only have developed slowly and through painful effort, for, while the sentiment of freedom was now strong at the North, that of the Union was stronger. The potent reason of the grand Republican expansion of 1856 was that the statesmen and politicians had marked out a way in which the moral and intelligent feeling of the country could assert itself without bating a jot of love for the Union or reverence for the Constitution.

Never in our history, and probably never in the history of the world, had a more pure, more disinterested, and more intelligent body of men banded together for a noble political object than those who now enrolled themselves under the Republican banner. The clergymen, the professors in the colleges, the men devoted to literature and science, the teachers in the schools, were for the most part Republicans. The zeal of many preachers broke out in the pulpit, and sermons were frequently delivered on the evils of slavery, the wrong of extending it, and the noble struggle freedom was making on the plains of Kansas. The Northern people of 1856 were a church-going people, and it must be reckoned an element of weight in the campaign that so large a proportion of the clergy exerted their influence directly or indirectly in favor of Frémont. On the Sunday before election, most of the ministers of New England preached and prayed from their pulpits against the success of Buchanan.[1] From the partisans of Buchanan and Fillmore came constant deprecation that ministers should so forget their holy calling as to introduce politics into the pulpit.[2]

---

[1] Letter of Buchanan to Joshua Bates of London, Nov. 6th, Life of Buchanan, Curtis, vol. ii. p. 183. Choate would not have found this letter pleasant reading. Buchanan calls New England "that land of isms," and Boston "a sad place."

[2] See the New York *Tribune*, July 12th, 19th, Aug. 13th, 16th, Oct. 11th; New York *Herald*, Sept. 13th, and the file of the *Independent, passim;* also New York *Times*, Sept. 30th.

In number, influence, and circulation, the religious press was overwhelmingly on the side of the party opposed to slavery-extension.[1] The religious journal was generally published to reach the bulk of its readers on Saturday, that the subjects it discussed might be read and pondered in the quiet hours of the Sabbath. Its arguments received, therefore, the most careful attention, and the work of making voters for Frémont continued even on the day when the secular newspapers did not appear. Some of the expressions call to mind the puritanical fervor of an earlier time. The *Independent*, the ablest religious journal of the day, recognized in the nomination of Frémont "the good hand of God;" and as election day drew near it said: "Fellow-Christians! Remember it is for Christ, for the nation, and for the world that you vote at this election! Vote as you pray! Pray as you vote!"[2]

Professors Silliman of Yale and Felton of Harvard had spoken out for Frémont in a manner which betokened that they represented the preponderant opinion of their college faculties; and the feeling in these older colleges was a type of that prevailing in most of the institutions of learning at the North.[3]

Impressed by the importance of the issue, literary men forsook their quiet retreats to help the cause they deemed sacred. Emerson addressed a town meeting; Longfellow took part in a political gathering; Bryant entered into the canvass with ardor, and advocated the election of Frémont by speech as well as by pen; and George William Curtis frequently spoke to his fellow-citizens urging them to vote for the Republican candidates.[4] Washington Irving declared

---

[1] See New York *Herald*, Sept. 13th and 15th; the *Independent*, Sept. 18th.   [2] June 26th and Oct. 16th.
[3] See New York *Tribune*, July 19th; Life of Silliman, Fisher, vol. ii. p. 251.
[4] New York *Tribune*, July 19th; also Life of Bryant, Godwin, vol. ii. p. 91.

his purpose of voting for Frémont.[1] Longfellow wrote to Sumner that one reason why he did not want to go to Europe was on account of losing his vote in the autumn. "I have great respect for that now," he continued, "though I never cared about it before."[2] He notes in his journal that all the guests with whom he dined one day at Prescott's were Frémont men.[3] N. P. Willis, one of the best-known *littérateurs* of his day, relates how he drove five miles one night to hear Curtis deliver a stump-speech. He at first thought the author of the Howadji "too handsome and well-dressed" for a political orator, but, as he listened, his mistake was apparent. He heard a logical and rational address, and now and then the speaker burst "into the full tide of eloquence unrestrained." Willis declared that although fifty years old he should this year cast his "virgin vote," and it would be for Frémont.[4] Harriet Beecher Stowe published another anti-slavery novel, which, though far inferior to her masterpiece, found many readers.[5] Whittier in passionate verse begged votes for Frémont.

The history of this phase of the campaign would not be complete without extended reference to the oration of George William Curtis, delivered to the students of the Wesleyan University at Middletown, Connecticut, on the subject, "The Duty of the American Scholar to Politics and the Times."[6]

"I would gladly speak to you," said he, "of the charms of pure scholarship; of the dignity and worth of the scholar; of the abstract relation of the scholar to the State. . . . But

---

[1] Philadelphia *Times*, cited by the New York *Times*, Nov. 1st.

[2] June 24th, Life of Longfellow, S. Longfellow, vol. ii. p. 282.

[3] Ibid., p. 287.

[4] Private letter, published in the New York *Evening Post*, cited by New York *Times*, Oct. 8th.

[5] Dred, A Tale of the Dismal Swamp. The publishers stated that sixty thousand copies were sold in twelve days, New York *Tribune*, Oct. 18th; see also the *Liberator*, Oct. 3d.

[6] Delivered Aug. 5th.

would you have counted him a friend of Greece who quietly discussed the abstract nature of patriotism on that Greek summer day through whose hopeless and immortal hours Leonidas and his three hundred stood at Thermopylæ for liberty?" And the American scholar of to-day must know " that freedom always has its Thermopylæ, and that his Thermopylæ is called Kansas. . . . Because we are scholars, shall we cease to be citizens?" In the Senate, a "scholar pleads the cause dear to every gentleman in history, and a bully strikes him down. In a republic of freemen, this scholar speaks for freedom, and his blood stains the Senate floor. There it will blush through all our history. That damned spot will never out from memory, from tradition, or from noble hearts. . . . Of what use are your books? Of what use is your scholarship? Without freedom of thought, there is no civilization or human progress; and without freedom of speech, liberty of thought is a mockery." The orator continued: "There is a constant tendency in material prosperity, when it is the prosperity of a class and not of the mass, to relax the severity of principle;" but every state has a class "which by its very character is dedicated to eternal and not to temporary interests; whose members are priests of the mind, not of the body, and who are necessarily the conservative party of intellectual and moral freedom. . . . The scholar is the representative of thought among men, and his duty to society is the effort to introduce thought and the sense of justice into human affairs. He was not made a scholar to satisfy the newspapers or the parish beadles, but to serve God and man. While other men pursue what is expedient, and watch with alarm the flickering of the funds, he is to pursue the truth and watch the eternal law of justice." The duty of the American scholar " in this crisis of our national affairs" is to fight the battle of liberty by resisting the extension of slavery. "The advocacy of the area of its extension is not a whim of the slave power, but is based upon the absolute necessities of the system." But now "twenty millions of a moral people, politically dedicated to Liberty, are asking themselves whether their government shall be administered solely in the interest of three hundred and fifty thousand slave-holders. . . . Young scholars, young Americans, young men, we are all called upon to do a great duty. Nobody is released from it. It is a work to be done by hard strokes and everywhere. I see a rising enthusiasm, but enthusiasm is not an election; and I hear cheers from the heart, but cheers are not voters. Every man must labor with his neighbor—in the street, at the plough, at the bench, early and late, at home and abroad. Generally, we are concerned in elections with the measures of government. This time it is with the essential principle of government itself."

This finished oration suffers much by detached quotation. Read as a whole, one sees the argument unfolding, and is led on step by step to the point where the scholar is made to see that he would be recreant to his high calling if he did not vote and work for Frémont. It had a wide circulation,[1] and to college men, and men who read much, it spoke with mighty accents. The sincere and thoughtful orator had an earnest purpose; he looked upon politics from a lofty plane. Certainly no candidate for President has ever had his election urged in words that breathe forth purer aspirations, and more sublime and cogent reasons have never been given for political work. The voter who was influenced by that argument must have felt that he had been borne into a political atmosphere which was freed from foul exhalations.

To the conservative, practical man of 1856, the formal, measured words of James Buchanan must have seemed the essence of practical wisdom; the ardent phrases of Curtis, while fit perhaps for professors and students, quite inadequate as a guide of political action. Yet only a few years were needed to show that the inferences drawn by Buchanan

---

[1] It was published in the New York *Weekly Tribune* of Aug. 16th. The circulation of the paper that day was 173,000. The oration was afterwards published in pamphlet form by a New York house.

became for him a stumbling-block and a foolishness. A few years more demonstrated that the speculative truth proclaimed by Curtis was the highest practical wisdom.

It was appreciated that the first voters and the young men would be an important element on the Republican side in the campaign. Sumner, who, in the words of Seward, was "contending with death in the mountains of Pennsylvania,"[1] wrote: "It is the young who give a spontaneous welcome to Truth when she first appears as an unattended stranger. . . . The young men of Massachusetts act under natural impulses when they step forward as the body-guard of the Republican party. When the great discoverer Harvey first announced the circulation of the blood, he was astonished to find that no person *upwards of forty* received this important truth. It was the young only who embraced it."[2]

Fillmore received an accession of strength by the endorsement of the national Whig convention held at Baltimore September 17th. It was remembered that the day was the anniversary of Washington's Farewell Address. One of the resolutions alluded to his warning against geographical parties; another condemned the Democrats equally with the Republicans. The position of the Fillmoreans may be described as oscillating between the other two parties. In the same speech in which Fillmore had expressed his alarm at the sectional character of the Republican party, he had severely condemned the repeal of the Missouri Compromise. Although he was first nominated by the Americans, the peculiar tenets of that organization made no figure in the canvass.[3]

Side by side with the political canvass in the States went on the contest in Kansas. It had now degenerated into a

---

[1] Letter of Seward to his wife, Aug. 17th, Life, vol. ii. p. 287.
[2] Letter from Cresson, Pa., Aug. 5th, New York *Weekly Tribune*, Aug. 30th.
[3] See Seward's speech at Auburn, Oct. 21st, Works, vol. iv. p. 279.

guerrilla warfare. The adventurous spirits among the free-State men had been worked up to violence by the destruction of Lawrence, and the pro-slavery party were inflamed by the massacre on the Pottawatomie. Missouri and Kansas border ruffians robbed, plundered, and murdered their antagonists. A new route from the North by the way of Iowa and Nebraska had been opened by which parties of Northern adventurers came into the territory. In their violent deeds these imitated the ruffians. Occasionally the factions would meet, and a skirmish, dignified in Kansas history with the name of a battle, would result. Free-State marauders robbed frugal pro-slavery residents, and the border ruffians pillaged the industrious free-State settlers. The historian of Kansas confesses it difficult to determine "which faction surpassed the other in misdeeds."[1] In the populous districts civil war raged. Women and children fled from the territory. Men slept on their arms. The country was given over to highway robbery and rapine; "the smoke of burning dwellings darkened the atmosphere."[2] The Kansas of 1856 "weltered in havoc and anarchy."[3] Yet the loss of life was not so great as might be supposed. Competent authority, after systematic and thorough investigation, estimated the loss of life from November 1st, 1855, to December 1st, 1856, at about two hundred. The destruction of property in the same period was considered to be not less than two million dollars, of which one-half was directly sustained by the bona-fide settlers of Kansas.[4]

Reeder was advocating free Kansas in the Eastern States; Robinson was in prison. The direction of the free-State cause fell to James H. Lane, an erratic person, a man without character, who sought by any means political advancement. John Brown also figures as a leader in this guerrilla

---

[1] Spring, p. 176.
[2] Geary's farewell address.   [3] Spring, p. 190.
[4] Report of commissioners of Kansas territory, July, 1857. Reports of Committees, 2d Sess. 36th Cong., vol. iii. part i. p. 92.

warfare. Urged on by a gloomy fanaticism, he thought there was no way of destroying slavery except by killing slave-holders. Although the name of Lane became a terror to the pro-slavery party, and John Brown was truly called "the old terrifier," it does not appear that their misdirected energy accomplished aught towards making Kansas free territory. Although their martial operations were directed with skill and bravery, they were in the end borne down by superior numbers with the result of "a total military collapse of the free-State cause."[1]

If we confine our attention simply to the local transactions in the territory, it cannot be maintained that any advantage accrued to freedom in Kansas from the time of the destruction of Lawrence to September 9th, the day of the arrival at Fort Leavenworth of Governor Geary, who took the place of Shannon. The check given to Northern emigration by the unsettled state of affairs was but a superficial gain for the pro-slavery party, for the tale of "bleeding Kansas" was being told in eloquent accents and with profound results at every Republican meeting east of the Missouri river.

Although Lane and Brown were this summer the prominent representatives of the free-State cause, yet the Northern settlers were not united in approving of their predatory and guerrilla warfare. While it is true that one of the Kansas factions did violent deeds in the name of law and order, and the other committed crimes in the name of liberty, it is also true that, in a balancing of acts and character, the free-State adherents of 1856 stand immeasurably superior to the pro-slavery partisans in everything that goes to make up industrious, law-abiding, and intelligent citizens. The free-State men lost by far the larger amount of property, and the destruction caused by the pro-slavery faction was much the greater.[2]

---

[1] Spring, p. 190.
[2] The destruction of property owned by pro-slavery men from Nov.

Although the influence upon the national political campaign exerted by the conflict in Kansas can hardly be overestimated, the details of the conflict are comparatively insignificant and need not detain us. But the story of Kansas, which in our day Professor Spring has told impartially and without "a blur of theory," is not the story that the truth-seeking voter of 1856 heard at Republican meetings and read in Republican newspapers. The correspondents of the New York *Tribune* and New York *Times* furnished, for the most part, the facts on which a judgment was based. While they were diligent, able, and interesting newspaper writers, they were strong partisans, ready to believe the most atrocious outrages related of the border ruffians, and apt to suppress facts that told against their own party.[1]

The Republican newspapers were full of Kansas news, arranged under startling head-lines and commented upon in emphatic editorials. That their efforts in forming public sentiment were effective is evident when the truth-seeking Emerson could publicly declare: " There is this peculiarity

---

1st, 1855, to Dec. 1st, 1856, was $77,198.99; that owned by free-State men, $335,779.04. Property taken or destroyed by pro-slavery men, $318,718.63; that by free-State men, $94,529.40. Awards made by Kansas Territory Commissioners, 1859, Reports of Committees, 2d Sess. 36th Cong., vol. iii. part i. p. 90. My authorities for this brief sketch of Kansas history during the summer of 1856 are Spring's Kansas; Geary and Kansas, by Gihon; Sara Robinson's Kansas; The Englishman in Kansas, Gladstone; Publications of the Kansas Historical Society; Conquest of Kansas, Phillips; Six Months in Kansas; Letter from Lawrence, Sept. 7th, to the New York *Times;* Life of John Brown, Sanborn; Life of John Brown, Redpath.

[1] "That the excitement in the Eastern and Southern States in 1856 was instigated and kept up by garbled and exaggerated accounts of Kansas affairs, published in the Eastern and Southern papers, is true, most true; but the half of what was done by either party was never chronicled!"—Report of Commissioners of Kansas Territory. See also an impartial article in the New York *Times,* Sept. 9th; also Reminiscences of John Brown, G. W. Brown, p. 48.

about the case of Kansas, that all the right is on one side."[1] The Democratic journals and speakers had little to say about the marauding operations of free-State adventurers. There are, indeed, occasional references to the Northern army under the lead of "the notorious Jim Lane;" but in the main, when forced to meet the stories of Kansas outrages, they have, as Emerson said, "but one word in reply—namely, that it is all exaggeration, 'tis an abolition lie."[2]

Meetings for the relief of Kansas were continually held. Reeder had everywhere crowded audiences when he discoursed on the theme nearest his heart. A convention of Kansas aid committees assembled at Buffalo to discuss the past work and arrange for future operations. Since it was the unanimous opinion that the efforts for raising men and money should be redoubled, Gerrit Smith immediately subscribed fifteen hundred dollars per month during the war.[3] The *Tribune* asked for a special subscription from their readers for the aid of freedom in Kansas, and from time to time published the names of the donors.[4] At a Kansas relief meeting held in Detroit, Zachariah Chandler, a candidate for United States Senator from Michigan, put down his name for ten thousand dollars.[5] Emerson, with quaint sincerity, said that, in order "to give largely, lavishly," to the Kansas people, "We must learn to do with less, live in a smaller tenement, sell our apple-trees, our acres, our pleasant homes. I know people who are making haste to reduce their expenses and pay their debts, not with a view to new accumulations, but in preparation to save and earn for the benefit of the Kansas emigrants."[6] Indeed, one of the

---

[1] Remarks at a Kansas relief meeting in Cambridge, Sept. 10th, the *Liberator*, Sept. 19th; Miscellanies, p. 241.   [2] Ibid.

[3] *Tribune*, July 19th. He had previously given $10,000 to the cause, Life of Smith, Frothingham, p. 233.

[4] July 24th. The amount subscribed up to Nov. 15th, as published in the *Weekly Tribune* of that date, was $15,523.19.

[5] June 2d, Life of Chandler, Detroit *Post and Tribune*, p. 120.

[6] *Liberator*, Sept. 19th; Miscellanies, p. 243.

potent arguments for the Republican cause was summed up in the expression "Bleeding Kansas." The Democrats taunted the Republicans by saying that they were trying to elect their candidate by "shrieks for freedom." This was immediately taken up as a watchword, and when the summer elections went their way, they were glad to announce that "Iowa, Maine, and Vermont, shriek for freedom."

Yet on the part of the Republicans it was an educational campaign of high value. Their newspapers in zeal and ability were superior to those of the other side. New York city, then as now, took the lead in journalism, and it is an indication of how the press stood everywhere at the North, except in Pennsylvania, when we note that the four great organs of public opinion, the *Tribune*, *Times*, *Herald*, and *Post*, supported Frémont. The publication of campaign documents was immense, and great care was taken to circulate them freely. Never before had such serious reading-matter been put into the hands of so many voters, and never before had so many men been willing to take time and pains to arrive at a comprehension of the principles involved in a presidential canvass. An indication of Republican willingness to repose on the wisdom of the fathers is shown by the publication of the Declaration of Independence and the Constitution as a part of a campaign document. The widespread interest is betokened by the appeal of Henry Ward Beecher in the *Independent* for money to print tracts which were to be sent "up and down the hills and valleys of Pennsylvania, carrying truth, by the silent page, to hundreds and thousands of men who have never been reached by the living speaker."[1]

The influence of women was a factor of inestimable value. The moral side of the political question they were well fitted to grasp. That slavery was wrong, that it ought not to be extended, seemed to them primal truths; and the unobtrusive sway of mothers, wives, and sisters was exerted

---

[1] Oct. 2d.

with greater effect than ever before in public affairs. Certainly government by the people has shown few more inspiring spectacles than the campaign of 1856 at the North.

The conduct of the Republicans during the canvass was almost faultless. The private characters of Buchanan and Fillmore were above reproach; but even had they not been so, their personal affairs would have attracted little attention, for the overpowering sway of the principles at issue was everywhere manifest. Perhaps the only charges that can be made against the Republican press are, exaggeration regarding Kansas affairs and giving currency to a supposed statement of Toombs without sufficient foundation. He was falsely reported to have said that he would yet "call the roll of his slaves under the shadow of Bunker Hill monument."[1] Buchanan's share in the Ostend manifesto was properly used against him, but the Cuban question was so entirely swallowed up in the territorial that this line of attack attracted little attention.

The Democrats, wishing to turn away Northern consideration from the real issue, were free with personal imputations against Frémont. The assertion that he was or had been a Roman Catholic gave the most trouble, for the Republicans desired to gain the Know-nothing vote. The most authoritative denials did not prevent the reiteration of the charge.[2] Charges were also made against the integrity of Frémont on account of certain operations in California.[3]

---

[1] See the *Liberator*, Feb. 15th; Pike's First Blows of the Civil War, p. 344; Life of Theodore Parker, Weiss, vol. ii. p. 223.

[2] Reminiscences of a Journalist, Congdon, p. 154; New York *Weekly Tribune*, Aug. 9th and Oct. 18th.

[3] See remarks of Toombs, *Congressional Globe*, vol. xxxiii. p. 771; Life of Frémont, Bigelow, chap. xiv.; New York *Tribune*, Sept. 3d. The charges were believed in California, and there he was not at all popular. H. H. Bancroft, vol. xviii. p. 702. In his own State he received less than one-half of the vote of Buchanan, and a much smaller vote than Fillmore.

In the light of his subsequent career, it can not be said that these were disproved to the satisfaction of a judicial mind; but they were not for a moment credited by his supporters, and did not have an appreciable influence on the result. Nor did the apparently admitted story that he was involved in California speculations, and that his notes would not sell in the New York market at even two per cent. a month, affect his popularity.[1]

The contest at the South between Buchanan and Fillmore was sluggish and uninteresting. There were practically but two doubtful States, and the August State election in Kentucky demonstrated that Fillmore could only hope to carry Maryland.

The sagacious politicians of each side stated the problem thus: Of the 149 electoral votes necessary to elect, Buchanan was sure of 112 from the South. He must get, then, the twenty-seven votes of Pennsylvania and ten more. Either Indiana or Illinois would give the required number, or New Jersey and California together. These five were the only doubtful Northern States. Frémont was reasonably certain of 114 electoral votes. To be elected he must also get Pennsylvania and eight more, or else carry all the doubtful States except Pennsylvania; but the chance of securing Pennsylvania was much better than that of getting all of the others. Thus the contest practically settled down to the Keystone State, and it was doubly important because a State election preceded the presidential election of November.

The issue had been made. On both sides the conditions for success were understood. It needed only to persuade and get out the arbiters. A campaign ensued which, for enthusiasm and excitement, surpassed any the country had seen except that of 1840. The old voters were constantly reminded of that memorable year. There was no difficulty in getting up Republican meetings. Processions number-

---

[1] New York *Tribune*, Aug. 27th.

ing thousands were common; good music and inspiring campaign songs were constantly heard, and there were few gatherings not graced with the presence of intelligent and devoted women. The meetings were immense. At Pittsburgh, the number assembled was estimated at one hundred thousand freemen. It was said to be a greater gathering than either the Dayton or Tippecanoe meeting of 1840.

"The truth is that the people are much more for us than we have supposed," wrote Dana. "I have been speaking around a good deal in clubs, and am everywhere astonished at the depth and ardor of the popular sentiment. Where we least expect it, large and enthusiastic crowds throng to the meeting and stay for hours with the thermometer at one hundred degrees. It is a great canvass; for genuine inspiration, 1840 could not hold a candle. I am more than ever convinced that Frémont was the man for us."[1] The prominent men of the country could be frequently heard. It is an indication of the varied talent enlisted in the cause that on one evening Hale and Beecher, and on the next Wilson and Raymond, addressed a large crowd of New York city Republicans. Seward did not speak until October 2d. The reason he assigned was that his health was so impaired that he needed rest.[2] Dana wrote confidentially that "Seward was awful grouty."[3] The reflection must have come to him that he, instead of one who only began to labor in the vineyard at the eleventh hour, might have been the embodiment of this magnificent enthusiasm.

In reply to an invitation to attend a meeting in Ohio, Sumner wrote from Philadelphia: "I could not reach Ohio except by slow stages; and were I there, I should not have the sanction of my physician in exposing myself to the ex-

---

[1] C. A. Dana to Pike, July 24th, First Blows of the Civil War, p. 346.
[2] Letter to Howard at Detroit, Sept. 12th, published in the New York Tribune.
[3] Aug. 9th, to Pike, First Blows of the Civil War, p. 347.

citements of a public meeting, even if I said nothing. This is hard—very hard for me to bear, for I long to do something at this critical moment for the cause."¹ A few days after this letter was published, Republicans had the opportunity of reading an account of a numerously attended banquet in South Carolina given to Preston S. Brooks by the constituents of his district, where, amid vehement cheering, he was presented with a cane on which was inscribed, "Use knock-down arguments."²

Banks one afternoon delivered a speech in Wall Street from the balcony of the Merchants' Exchange, and was listened to by twenty thousand men.³ You ask me "as to Banks's speech," wrote Greeley to an intimate friend. "I think St. Paul on Mars Hill made a better—I mean better for Mars Hill; I am not sure that Banks's is not better adapted to Wall Street. I trust Banks himself does not deem it suited to the latitude of Bunker Hill or Tippecanoe."⁴

Besides reading documents and listening to speeches, the enthusiasm manifested itself in street parades and torchlight processions. Pioneers with glittering axes marched ahead, Rocky-Mountain glee-clubs sang campaign songs, and the air rang with shouts of "Free speech, free soil, and Frémont," the lusty bands dwelling upon "Frémont" with the staccato cheer.⁵ Although in liveliness and enthusiasm

---

¹ Sumner to Lewis D. Campbell, published in the New York *Times*, Oct. 3d.

² See New York *Times*, Oct. 8th, where is published a full account of the proceedings and speeches. This affair attracted much attention from the Republican press. ³ New York *Times*, Sept. 26th.

⁴ Greeley to Pike, Oct. 6th, First Blows of the Civil War, p. 350.

⁵ A letter to the *Nation* of Sept. 18th, 1890, states that the staccato cheer was invented during this campaign; but the writer is mistaken in the statement that the torchlight companies were called "Wide-awakes." I have not seen that name used in any of the campaign literature. The "Wide-awakes" were a Republican invention of 1860 (see History of Lincoln, Nicolay and Hay, vol. ii. p. 284); but the term "wide-awake" was used by the Know-nothings (see the "Wide-awake Gift, a Know-nothing Token for 1855").

this resembled the 1840 campaign, there was a marked difference. The Whigs had then gone to the country without a platform, and the canvass was a frolic; now the Republicans advocated a platform which was so positive in its utterances that no mistake could be made about its meaning. There was, therefore, now a serious devotion to principle, and an earnest determination that the Harrison campaign lacked. The jollity of 1840 is the delight of the humorist; the gravity of 1856 is the study of the political philosopher.

It is difficult to apportion the enthusiasm between a cause and a candidate; but after drinking deep of the campaign literature, one is forced to the conviction that much was for the cause and little for the man; that Republican principles added lustre to the name of Frémont, while Frémont himself gave little strength to the party other than by the romantic interest that was associated with his record as an explorer.[1] His nomination was indeed received with enthusiasm. Several campaign biographies were published which familiarized the public with the stirring events in his life; but while his "disastrous chances," his "moving accidents by flood and field," and his "hair-breadth 'scapes" made him a hero in the eyes of youth who fed on Cooper and Gilmore Simms, the fuller knowledge of his career was unsatisfactory to many earnest and thoughtful Republicans. The most was made of his being "the brave Pathfinder." The planting of the American flag on the highest peak of the Rocky Mountains was deemed an heroic feat. Yet practical people could not fail to inquire why the qualities of a daring explorer fitted a man to be chief magistrate of the republic at a critical juncture. Little by little, it began to be understood that Frémont was a vulnerable candidate, and, while the charges of corruption were not believed, it was admitted they needed explanation. He did

---

[1] His romantic marriage added to this interest, and "Frémont and Jessie" was a favorite campaign cry. Jessie Benton was the name of his wife.

not, therefore, stand before the country with the same character of absolute integrity as did Buchanan and Fillmore.[1]

The Iowa congressional election in August was favorable to the Republicans. In September, Maine and Vermont gave unmistakable evidence of the direction in which the tide was setting in New England. Maine was an old Democratic State; the Republican candidate for governor was Hannibal Hamlin, who, though voting against the Kansas-Nebraska bill, had not formally severed his connection with the Democratic party until June of this year. Then from his place in the Senate he had declared that, as he considered the repeal of the Missouri Compromise the cause of all the present ills, and as the Cincinnati convention had endorsed that repeal, he could no longer act with the Democrats, but must oppose them with all his power. He was now elected governor of Maine by a handsome majority. In Vermont three quarters of the votes were cast for the Republican ticket.

The Republicans were highly elated at these results. All eyes were now turned to the "October States"—Pennsylvania, Ohio, and Indiana. No concern was felt about Ohio, and much less depended upon Indiana than on the Keystone State. The election of October 14th in Pennsylvania was for minor State officers, that of canal commissioner being the most important. There were two tickets in the field—one the regular Democratic, the other the Union, which was supported by Republicans, Americans, Whigs, and anti-Nebraska Democrats;[2] or, stated differently, one ticket had the support of the "Buchaniers," the other that of the "Frémonters," and ostensibly of the "Fillmoreans." The con-

---

[1] My authorities on the campaign of 1856 are New York *Tribune*, *Times*, *Herald*, and *Post*, the *Independent*, the *Liberator*, Boston *Post*, Boston *Atlas;* Life of Samuel Bowles, Merriam; Political Recollections, Julian; Reminiscences of a Journalist, Congdon.

[2] There were three State officers to be elected on a general ticket. One of the candidates was an old-line Whig, another was a Republican, and the third an anti-Nebraska Democrat.

test was vigorous and excited. The Republicans were aggressive. They pointed to "bleeding Kansas;" they charged that the civil war in that territory was a result of the repeal of the Missouri Compromise, and they demanded a policy which should incontestably make Kansas a free State.

Their best speakers traversed Pennsylvania, making eloquent and able appeals, and the State was flooded with campaign documents. It was clearly discerned where the danger lay. West of the Alleghany Mountains, the enthusiasm for Frémont was like that in New England, New York, and Ohio; but as one travelled eastward a different political atmosphere could easily be felt, and when one reached Philadelphia, which was bound to the South by a lucrative trade, the chill was depressing.[1] The business and social influences of conservative Philadelphia were arrayed against the Frémont movement. The Pennsylvania Dutch, by whom the eastern counties were largely peopled, were set in their way of political thinking; they distrusted change. They were told that Frémont was an abolitionist; they believed that abolitionism was dangerous to the Union; they were attached to the Union, for its existence implied order and security; they were thrifty and prosperous, and much preferred order to the liberty of the black man. Campaign work such as had stirred to the depths New England, New York, Ohio, and the Northwest was carried on by the Republicans to a greater extent in Pennsylvania. They hoped that, while this was a community slower to educate, it would yield to persistent and overflowing effort.

The Democrats dodged the issue. Instead of defending the Douglas and Pierce policy, they averred that the Union was in danger. "I consider," wrote Buchanan, privately, "that all incidental questions are comparatively of little importance in the presidential question, when compared with

---

[1] See article by Russel Errett, *Magazine of Western History*, July, 1889. "There is no Republican organization or life in eastern Pennsylvania and New Jersey."—Seward to his wife, Aug. 3d, Life of Seward, vol. ii. p. 284.

the grand and appalling issue of union or disunion. . . . In this region the battle is fought mainly on this issue. We have so often cried 'wolf' that now, when the wolf is at the door, it is difficult to make the people believe it; but yet the sense of danger is slowly and surely making its way in this region."[1]

The appeal for the Union was a legitimate party cry, and it answered well in Philadelphia and the Pennsylvania Dutch counties, but there were parts of the State where an additional argument was needed. The manner in which this necessity was met reflects, in the light of subsequent history, discredit on Buchanan or his managers. Howell Cobb, of Georgia, who had the reputation of a straightforward man, and who in 1851 had distinguished himself by a vigorous canvass in his State against the disunion faction, and John Hickman, a congressman from Pennsylvania who had voted for the admission of Kansas under the Topeka Constitution, spoke from the stump all over the Chester valley, advocating Buchanan's election, and promising fair play in Kansas.[2] At many Democratic mass-meetings in different parts of the State, banners were borne on which was inscribed "Buchanan, Breckinridge, and Free Kansas," the orators maintaining that Kansas was certain to be free if Buchanan were elected.[3] Forney, who was chairman of the Democratic State central committee, and at that time an intimate personal and political friend of Buchanan, avers that this line of argument was based on a positive promise from him that there "should be no interference against the people of Kansas."[4] The advo-

---

[1] Life of Buchanan, Curtis, vol. ii. p. 180. Buchanan lived near Lancaster, in the southeastern part of Pennsylvania.

[2] Forney's Anecdotes of Public Men, vol. ii. p. 239.

[3] See Wade's speech in the Senate, Dec. 4th; New York *Times*, Oct. 7th, Nov. 19th. "All over the country the Democratic party put upon their flags, transparencies, and banners 'Buchanan, Breckinridge, and Free Kansas.' "—John Sherman, House of Representatives, Dec. 8th.

[4] See Forney's Anecdotes, vol. i. pp. 15 and 361; vol. ii. pp. 240, 421. In a speech at Tarrytown, N. Y., Sept. 2d, 1858, Forney declared that

cacy of the Democratic candidates by Reverdy Johnson, an old-line Whig, and by Barclay, a Democratic congressman from western Pennsylvania, who had voted for the admission of Kansas under the Topeka Constitution, was an added influence in this direction.

The Democrats had in their campaign the cordial assistance of the President. Shannon's administration of Kansas affairs had become a scandal. Unsteady in habits and purposes, he was execrated by the free-State men; his continuance in office gave additional force to every story of "bleeding Kansas." In August he was removed, and John W. Geary, of Pennsylvania, a man of good standing, was appointed in his place. The report went that Geary had said that peace must be restored or Buchanan could not carry Pennsylvania.[1] The difficulty of his mission was emphasized when, on the way to Kansas, he met Shannon fleeing in abject fear, because at the last the pro-slavery leaders had taken offence as their former tool would not do their entire bidding.[2] But the new governor set himself energetically

---

during the canvass of 1856 Buchanan said to him a thousand times: "The South must vote for me, and the North must be secured; and the only way to secure the North is to convince those gentlemen that when I get in the presidential chair I will do right with the people in Kansas. I am now sixty-six years of age. I have reached that time of life when I cannot have any ambition for re-election, and if I have, the only way to secure it is to be strong with my own people at home. I watched this struggle from my retirement in London; I have seen what I conceive to be the mistakes of others. I am not responsible for the administration of President Pierce; therefore I will inaugurate a new system." Forney further said: "I sowed the State with private letters and private pledges upon this question. There is not a county in Pennsylvania in which my letters may not be found, almost by hundreds, pledging Mr. Buchanan, in his name and by his authority, to the full, complete, and practical recognition of the rights of the people of Kansas to decide upon their own affairs."—New York *Tribune*, Sept. 3d, 1858.

[1] Sara Robinson's Kansas, p. 339; The Kansas Conflict, Charles Robinson, p. 323.

[2] Spring, p. 187; Geary and Kansas, Gihon, p. 104.

to work to bring back order. He took an impartial view of the situation; in his effort at pacification, he leaned neither to one side nor to the other, but pursued the course he had marked out with judgment, decision, and success. On the 30th of September he sent the Secretary of State a despatch which was a splendid Democratic argument in the impending contest. "Peace now reigns in Kansas," Geary wrote. "Confidence is gradually being restored. Citizens are returning to their claims. Men are resuming their ordinary pursuits, and a general gladness pervades the entire community. When I arrived here, everything was at the lowest point of depression. Opposing parties saw no hope of peace, save in mutual extermination, and they were taking the most effectual means to produce that terrible result."[1]

The Democratic organization in Pennsylvania was perfect. Unlike other Northern States, Buchanan was there upheld by the most influential newspapers, which were subsidized by "a system of general and liberal advertising."[2] There were many wealthy Democrats in Philadelphia and eastern Pennsylvania, and money flowed in freely from other States. Douglas, while loyally striving to keep Illinois Democratic, was also able to contribute money liberally to aid in carrying the Keystone State.[3] The governor of North Carolina, with other gentlemen, issued a "private and confidential" circular begging for money. "Pennsylvania must be saved at every hazard," they said. "We appeal to you, therefore, as a Democrat and a patriot, to contribute forthwith whatever amount of money you can, and raise what you can from others."[4] The Republican journals charged—probably with truth—that the clerks in the departments at Washington, the officers in the New York

---

[1] Message and Documents, 1856-57, part i. p. 154.

[2] Forney's Anecdotes of Public Men, vol. ii. pp. 239, 240; also article by Russel Errett, *Western Magazine of History*, July, 1889.

[3] Life of Douglas, Sheahan, p. 443.

[4] The circular was dated Raleigh, Sept. 20th, was published in the Raleigh *Register* of Oct. 22d, and copied in the New York *Times*, Oct. 24th.

City Custom-house, and the laborers in the Brooklyn Navy-yard were assessed for the Pennsylvania campaign fund.¹ It was credibly reported that one hundred and fifty thousand dollars was sent into Pennsylvania from the slave-holding States; that August Belmont contributed fifty thousand dollars; and that other Wall-street bankers and brokers, alarmed at Southern threats and fearing serious financial loss in the event of disunion, put into Forney's hands one hundred thousand dollars more.² The allegations of the defeated party regarding the outlay by the other must always be taken with a grain of allowance, yet a fair consideration of all the circumstances makes it reasonable to suppose that the Democrats had much the larger supply of the sinews of war.³

It certainly seemed to the Republicans that the Democrats were better provided with means. "We Frémonters of this town," wrote Greeley from New York to an intimate friend, "have not one dollar where the Fillmoreans and Buchaniers have ten each, and we have Pennsylvania and New Jersey both on our shoulders. Each State is utterly miserable, as far as money is concerned; we must supply them with documents, canvass them with our best speakers, and pay for their rooms to speak in and our bills to invite them."⁴

---

¹ See New York *Tribune*, Oct. 2d; *Evening Post*, Oct. 21st; Boston *Atlas*, Oct. 18th.

² New York *Times*, Oct. 24th; *Evening Post*, Oct. 21st; Boston *Atlas*, Oct. 23d.

³ For charges of Republican expenditure, see Life of Stephens, Johnston and Browne, p. 316. Stephens writes Aug. 31st: "I understand that the Republicans have spent $500,000 on Pennsylvania. These merchants of the North, who have grown rich out of us, are shelling out their money like corn now to oppress us." See also North Carolina circular before referred to. The report that Stephens heard was an exaggeration. The New York *Times* estimate of the expenditure by the Democrats for the State election was "very nearly $500,000," and I feel confident that the Democrats spent more than the Republicans.

⁴ Greeley to Pike, Aug. 6th, First Blows of the Civil War, p. 346. The Republicans of Massachusetts sent money to Pennsylvania. Reminiscences of a Journalist, Congdon, p. 153.

The Democrats were successful in manufacturing enthusiasm for their candidate in his native State, and the abbreviation "Buck and Breck" readily lent itself to a resounding campaign cry. On the eve of election they had a serene confidence of probable success in October and certain victory in November.

Greeley advised his confidant that the fight was "hot and heavy in Pennsylvania. . . . There is everything to do there, with just the meanest set of politicians to do it that you ever heard of."[1] Dana was hopeful. Nine days before the election he wrote: "The election in Pennsylvania week after next will go by from thirty thousand to forty thousand majority against Buchanan, and so on. The tide is rising with a rush, as it does in the Bay of Fundy; and you will hear an awful squealing among the hogs and jackasses when they come to drown. . . . I suppose there are about two hundred orators, great and small, now stumping Pennsylvania for Frémont."[2]

Reeder, who had been a personal and political friend of Buchanan, came out for the Republican candidates, and this was thought good for over three thousand votes in his district. Dana wrote: "The Democrats are terrified and demoralized. . . . My impression now is that every free State will vote for Frémont."[3] Bryant wrote his brother from New York city: "We expect a favorable report from Pennsylvania. The Buchanan men here are desponding, and it seems to be thought that if the State election goes against them, then the presidential election will go against them also. I do not think that certain, however, though it is probable."[4]

The day which terminated this heated contest came, and the result of the voting was awaited with breathless anxiety. Passion had been so wrought up that the timid feared

---

[1] Greeley to Pike, Sept. 21st.
[2] Dana to Pike, Oct. 5th.
[3] Ibid.
[4] Letter of Oct. 14th, Life of Bryant, Godwin, vol. ii. p. 92.

lest the contest of words should be followed by blows. They thanked God that the weather in Philadelphia, which was raw, cold, drizzling, and uncomfortable, kept the turbulent spirits within doors. All felt relief when it passed without bloodshed. Perhaps the tension was increased by the report of the anticipated meeting of fifteen Southern governors at Raleigh to consider what steps should be taken in the event of the election of Frémont.

The excitement in the evening was greatest in Philadelphia. The City of Brotherly Love was in an uproar. No one went to bed. The halls where returns were received were crowded; in the streets there was an anxious, excited throng.[2] Several days elapsed before it was certain how the State had gone, but at last it became known that the Buchanan State ticket had been successful by a majority of less than 3000 in a vote of 423,000.

The Republicans charged that the Democrats had carried the State by fraud and bribery. Years afterwards Forney wrote: "We spent a great deal of money, but not one cent selfishly or corruptly."[3] It is indeed difficult to believe that money was not used to purchase voters by some of Forney's henchmen, although he may not have been privy to the transactions, for the astute party manager does not always care to inquire closely into the means by which results are reached. But there is no need of the stale cry, invariably repeated by the defeated party, to account for the later success of the Democrats in the presidential election.[4]

---

[1] New York *Times*, Oct. 14th. The meeting had been proposed by Governor Wise for Oct. 13th. Only three governors actually met.

[2] Ibid., Oct. 14th and 15th.

[3] Anecdotes of Public Men, vol. ii. p. 240. Governor Robinson, who was a member of the Republican National Committee, writes: "The October vote of Pennsylvania was offered to the Republican National Executive Committee for a consideration; but the money was not forthcoming, and the transfer was made to the other party."—The Kansas Conflict, p. 338.

[4] I will transcribe two references to fraud which were honest expressions. Letcher, who was for Fillmore, wrote Crittenden, Oct. 2d: "When

If the State went Democratic, Buchanan's election was certain; if the Union ticket were successful, while a great impetus would be given to the Frémont movement, his election would not be assured. Yet fearing the influence, many conservative Fillmoreans, urged by the sentiments to which Choate had given expression, voted with the Democrats. It is not important whether this was brought about by collusion between the chairman of the American State committee and Forney; but it is certain that, by official direction or tacit consent, many Americans and Whigs bolted their own State ticket.

If the Fusionists had been successful by a small majority, would Frémont have carried Pennsylvania in November and been elected President? Probably not. There was no possibility of getting the bulk of Fillmore's supporters to vote the fusion Frémont-Fillmore electoral ticket which was proposed and actually adopted;[1] and the minute the opposition to Buchanan was divided, he was certain to carry the State by a handsome plurality.[2] Buchanan himself seemed to think that in any event he would receive the electoral vote of Pennsylvania,[3] a confidence based on substantial reasons.[4]

in Philadelphia I saw the game fully, and told our friends that money and fraud would beat us in the State elections."—Life of Crittenden, Coleman, vol. ii. p. 133. The other refers more particularly to the November election, and was written by Silliman in his diary, Nov. 19th: "There has been much fraudulent voting on the side of Buchanan. Many thousands Irish and not a few Germans have been at the command of the slave party. But a still more important cause of defeat has been that the late President Fillmore has been in the field by his own consent."—Life of Silliman, by Fisher, vol. ii. p. 251.

[1] See New York *Times*, Oct. 20th.
[2] The vote in November was: Buchanan, 230,710; Frémont, 147,510; Fillmore, 82,175. Buchanan's majority over Frémont, 83,200; over both, 1025. The vote of Philadelphia may be of interest as illustrating some statements in the text: Buchanan, 38,222; Fillmore, 24,084; Frémont, 7993.
[3] See letter, Curtis, vol. ii. p. 181.
[4] See articles of Russel Errett, *Magazine of Western History*, July and

On the 14th of October, State elections were also held in Ohio and Indiana. Ohio went Republican, but Indiana went Democratic, thus making the assurance of Buchanan's election doubly sure.

The November election registered what the October elections had virtually decided. Buchanan carried Pennsylvania, New Jersey, Indiana, Illinois, and California, and all the slave States but Maryland, receiving 174 electoral votes. Frémont had 114 electors, and Fillmore the 8 votes of Maryland.[1] From the congressional elections it was apparent that the Democrats would also have a majority in the next House of Representatives.

After the disappointment at failing to elect their candidates was over, the Republicans felt that they had reason for self-congratulation. In spite of the complaints of the lack of organization and money in Pennsylvania, the Republicans of a later day could not have wished the campaign different. For it was conducted on the inspiration of a principle, and any manipulation of Pennsylvania voters would have been a blot upon this virgin purity. The immense Frémont vote could be traced along the lines of latitude, springing from New England influence where good and widely extended common-school systems prevailed.[2] The problem now was simply to educate and inspire the

---

Aug., 1889. Errett was a member of the Republican State Executive Committee. See the files of the New York *Evening Post*, the *Times, Herald*, and *Tribune*, from Oct. 14th to the November election.

[1] The popular vote was: Buchanan, 1,838,169; Frémont, 1,341,264; Fillmore, 874,534. Buchanan received in the free States, 1,226,290; in the slave States, 611,879. Fillmore received in the free States, 394,642; in the slave States, 479,892. The vote of South Carolina is not comprised in any of these totals. Those electors were chosen by the legislature. The only votes Frémont received in the slave States were: Delaware, 308; Maryland, 281; Virginia, 291; Kentucky, 314. These figures are based on those given in Stanwood's History of Presidential Elections.

[2] See New York *Independent*, Nov. 13th; Springfield *Republican*, cited in Life of Bowles, Merriam, vol. i. p. 160; Olmsted's Texas Journey, p. xxvi.

people of the Northern States that had voted for Buchanan. Whittier expressed the general feeling when he sang:

"If months have well-nigh won the field,
What may not four years do?"

Considering the weakness of Frémont's character, which later years brought to light, it was fortunate he was not elected President. One shudders to think how he would have met the question of secession, which assuredly would have confronted him at the beginning of his administration.

The cause being much stronger than the candidate, it is probable that Seward or Chase would have carried the same States and received substantially the same votes that went to Frémont. This is an interesting supposition, in view of Seward's ambition for the next presidential nomination; for had he made the run of 1856, he would undoubtedly have been the Republican candidate four years later. Before the smoke of the battle had cleared away, many journals, struck with the astonishing vote Frémont had received, nominated him for the standard-bearer of 1860.[1]

---

[1] "Nobody knew better than Seward that if he had been the candidate for the presidency in 1856, he would have received the same vote that Frémont did, and that his nomination in 1860 would have inevitably followed and he would have entered the White House instead of Lincoln. Seward more than hinted to confidential friends that Weed betrayed him for Frémont.

"Weed himself told the following story: He and Mr. Seward were riding up Broadway, and when passing the bronze statue of Lincoln, in Union Square, Seward said, 'Weed, if you had been faithful to me, I should have been there instead of Lincoln.' 'Seward,' replied Weed, 'is it not better to be alive in a carriage with me than to be dead and set up in bronze?'"—Random Recollections by H. B. Stanton, p. 96.

The explanation of Weed's course given in his Life (vol. ii. p. 245) is more rational.

CHAPTER IX

"PEACE has been restored to Kansas," said Buchanan in a jubilant speech after the October victory. "As a Pennsylvanian, I rejoice that this good work has been accomplished by two sons of our good old mother State, God bless her! We have reason to be proud of Colonel Geary and General Smith.¹ We shall hear no more of bleeding Kansas. There will be no more shrieks for her unhappy destiny."² Quiet continued, and on November 7th Geary telegraphed that he had made "an extended tour of observation through a large portion of this territory." He was glad to report that "the general peace of the territory remains unimpaired, confidence is being gradually restored, business is resuming its ordinary channels, citizens are preparing for winter, and there is a readiness among the good people of all parties to sustain my administration."³

At first the free-State people did not look upon Geary with favor; they were disposed to regard him as worse than Shannon.⁴ But when it appeared that his intention was to do justice, the influential portion of the free-State party gave him a cordial support. Lane and John Brown had left the territory, and the leadership fell again to Robin-

---

¹ General Smith was put in command of the United States troops in Kansas, in the place of Colonel Sumner transferred. He was a pro-slavery man, but his prejudices did not interfere with a faithful and ready discharge of duty. See Geary and Kansas, Gihon, pp. 92, 298.
² Curtis, vol. ii. p. 176.
³ Message and Documents, 1856–57, part i. p. 172.
⁴ Topeka correspondence of the New York *Tribune,* Sept. 25th.

son, who had been released from prison. At the time that the President sent his annual message to Congress, Geary still retained the good will of the administration. Pierce, in announcing "the peaceful condition of things in Kansas," commended the "wisdom and energy of the present executive" of the territory.

The Republican journals began to record brighter news from Kansas.[1] From Washington came the welcome report of the removal of Lecompte, between whom and that cruel and unjust judge whose career had been made familiar to American readers by the glowing pen of Macaulay a likeness was frequently drawn.[2] Encouraged and incited by letters from Kansas, a large number of emigrants were preparing to move in the spring;[3] and the general belief throughout the North found expression in the public statement of Granger, a Republican congressman from New York: "Kansas is to come in as a free State—*easy*."[4] Profoundly influenced by the large Republican vote, moderate Southern men, of whom Aiken was a type, were willing to give up the contest and let Kansas enter the Union with a free constitution.[5]

But the Kansas conspirators had no such intention. They were contending for political preferment and power. While they were, for the most part, adventurers without property or slaves, yet by espousing the pro-slavery cause they secured the powerful backing of the slave interest of the whole

---

[1] See New York *Tribune*, Nov. 27th.

[2] The comparison between Jeffreys and Lecompte is often made in Kansas literature. It was impressed upon the mind of John Sherman. He said in the House of Representatives, July 31st: "Let us stop the hounds of Judge Lecompte, lest our country be disgraced by another 'Campaign in the West,' so infamous in English history; and beware lest a repetition of that historical crime shall bring again the fate of James II. and of Jeffreys." The removal of Lecompte was several times reported, and the President was on the point of making it, but it was not actually made. [3] New York *Tribune*, Dec. 27th and 30th.

[4] Washington correspondence, Dec. 31st, and New York *Tribune*, Jan. 7th, 1857. [5] Pike's First Blows of the Civil War, p. 363.

country. At an election in October, 1856, a delegate to Congress and a new territorial House of Representatives were chosen. The free-State people declined to vote, and the representatives elected were ignorant, besotted, and rabid, easily influenced by the little clique of pro-slavery agitators at Lecompton. The legislature was determined to force slavery on the territory; and as Geary sought "to do equal and exact justice to all men,"[1] they came into violent collision. The pro-slavery faction denounced the governor's impartial policy; he was even threatened with assassination. All the federal officers of the territory hampered him by every means in their power. In February, 1857, a deputation with the surveyor-general of the territory, John Calhoun, at their head, went to Washington, and by various influences succeeded in prejudicing the administration against the governor. When they returned to Lecompton, their newspaper announced that Geary was certain to be removed. Meanwhile his despatches to Washington, giving a correct account of affairs, were not answered, and it became apparent to him that a policy of justice to Kansas was not what the party in power at Washington wanted. On the 4th of March he resigned his position.[2]

Geary had exhibited executive talents of a high order. Combining courage, firmness, and discretion, he was an ideal governor of the territory whose agitations he had calmed.[3] Had he been supported by the outgoing and incoming administrations, he could have settled the Kansas question with justice and success. It was a potent argument that Reeder and Geary, who had gone out to Kansas firm and consistent Democrats, should have ended their official career by leaning to the free-State side. It was one of many indications that the free-State party, in spite of its failings, deserved full sympathy from the North.

---

[1] Gov. Geary's Farewell Address.
[2] See Geary and Kansas, Gihon; Spring's Kansas.
[3] See The Kansas Conflict, Charles Robinson, pp. 332, 337, 341.

A keen observer at Washington reported that the prospects of Kansas were "bedimmed;"[1] for the deputation from the territory had found abundant sympathy at the capital.[2] Their cause was that of the pro-slavery cabal of which Jefferson Davis, by his ability and position, was the chief. As Secretary of War, having control of the troops in Kansas, his public despatches manifest that his feelings were heartily enlisted on the side of the border ruffians. Impartiality, such as would have befitted his office, was lacking. His one-sided view is apparent when contrasted with the instructions of Marcy to Geary. There is even a glimmer of fairness in the orders of the President when compared with the communications emanating from the War Department.

But what Pierce thought was now a matter of small importance. Assuming the presidential office with the best of intentions, he came to serve the slave power with faithfulness and zeal. Two Northern Presidents before him had been said to lean towards Southern interests, but Pierce went immeasurably beyond them. With him it was not a leaning; it was devotion.

Under his administration began that complete subserviency of the Democratic party to the South which, during the six years before the war, was its distinctive feature. It may be observed that Northern Democrats then began to hold the tenet that slavery was the proper and blessed condition of the negro.

The tendency of the Democratic party had for years been towards a better friendship to the South than that of the Whigs. Pierce, as a Democratic President, could not have resisted this tendency, while social influence and sympathy went also for much in bearing him swiftly with the tide. The open manner in which Southerners dispensed hospitality charmed his generous heart; his convivial habits, offen-

---

[1] Letter of Feb. 23d, Pike's First Blows of the Civil War, p. 363.
[2] See The Kansas Conflict, Charles Robinson, p. 340.

sive to New England people were a recommendation to the free-hearted gentlemen of the South; while his grosser breaches of propriety, exceeding the calls of conviviality, were by them condoned.

All eyes were directed to the incoming chief. Two distinct lines of argument had been advocated to secure the election of Buchanan. One was that of the Southern extremists. Their opinion now found expression in the statement of the Richmond *Enquirer* that the result was "a striking evidence of the growing popularity of negro slavery;"[1] in the message of the governor of South Carolina, recommending the reopening of the African slave-trade;[2] and also in the advocacy of this policy by a portion of the Southern press and by the delegates of three States at the Southern Commercial convention.[3] It is true that a majority of Southern Democrats did not approve this advanced position. The Southern convention, by a vote of 67 to 18, laid on the table a resolution requesting their representatives in Congress "to use their best efforts to procure a repeal of all laws interdicting the African slave-trade."[4] In the national House of Representatives, moreover, only eight voted against a resolution declaring utter opposition to the reopening of the slave-trade.[5] Yet for all this, it began to be apparent that the South was going with startling rapidity the whole length demanded by the principle, Slavery is right, and ought to be extended.[6]

---

[1] Cited by Von Holst, vol. v. p. 465.

[2] Message of Nov. 21st, 1856, New York *Tribune*, Dec. 6th, 1856.

[3] *De Bow's Review*, vol. xxii. p. 91. It was held at Savannah, Dec. 8th, 1856.   [4] Ibid.   [5] This was Dec. 15th, 1856.

[6] See the discussion at the commercial convention, *De Bow's Review*, vol. xxii. p. 216. The editor remarks: "The reopening of the African slave-trade has only been proposed as a subject of discussion among the Southern people, in order that its merits and demerits may be freely canvassed, and not as a subject upon which the existing facts and information would warrant at present a decided opinion."—Ibid., p. 663. See letter of Lieber to Allibone, Life of Lieber, p. 292. Lieber spent twenty-two years in Columbia.

"The victory of Buchanan," wrote Francis Lieber from Columbia, S. C., "the victory of Southern bullyism, the acknowledgment of Northern men that, right or wrong, they yield because the South threatens to secede, will inflame and inflate pro-slavery to such enormity and tyranny over the free States, and madden it in its ungodly course of extending slavery within the United States and into neighboring countries where it had been extinguished. . . . Such a course will be pursued that civilization herself will avert her face and weep."[1] An evidence of Lieber's statement was the undisguised Southern sympathy with William Walker, who had gone on a filibustering expedition to Nicaragua, made himself president of that republic, and issued a decree which repealed all laws against slavery, thus legally establishing it on soil that had been free thirty-two years. He was impelled to this action by the belief that the peculiar institution of the South needed extension for its security, and he likewise thought that such a policy would raise up for his scheme of dominion a powerful support in the slave States.[2]

The line of argument which secured the doubtful Northern States for Buchanan was that which, as has been said before, found its aptest expression in the letter of Rufus Choate. Buchanan, he had asserted, "has large experience in public affairs; his commanding capacity is universally acknowledged; his life is without a stain. . . . He seems at this moment, by the concurrence of circumstances, more completely than any other, to represent that sentiment of nationality, tolerant, warm, and comprehensive, without which—without increase of which—America is no longer America."[3] Choate argued, moreover, that a policy "easy, simple, and

---

[1] Letter of Oct. 23d to Hillard, Life of Lieber, p. 290.

[2] See Von Holst, vol. v. chap. x.; The Story of the Filibusters, Roche; The War in Nicaragua, written by Gen. William Walker; Walker's Expedition to Nicaragua, by W. V. Wells.

[3] Letter of Choate to Maine Whig Committee, Life of Choate, Brown, p. 327.

just" would make Kansas a free State. In December, Edward Everett wrote Buchanan, telling him frankly, "I did not vote for you," but congratulating him on his election, and sincerely wishing him success. "The policy of the present administration," Everett continued, "has greatly impaired (as you are well aware) the conservative feeling of the North, has annihilated the Whig party, and seriously weakened the Democratic party in all the free States. . . . You may, even in advance of the 4th of March, do much to bring about a better state of things in Kansas, and prevent the enemies of the Constitution from continuing to make capital out of it."[1] The hope of Everett was undoubtedly the hope of most of the men who had voted for Fillmore; and the belief of Choate was practically that of all intelligent and disinterested Northern Democrats.

Would the new President incline to the Southern extremists, or would his course meet the expectations of Northern conservatives, of whom Everett and Choate were types? It was to a certain extent an arithmetical problem. The slave States had given Buchanan 112 electoral votes, and the free States 62. The Southern press did not cease to emphasize the fact that the South had elected him, and we may be sure that this argument was persistently urged by all the Southern statesmen who visited Wheatland[2] between the election and the coming of Buchanan to Washington.

While the hopes of the Everett and Choate conservatives ran high, the Republicans expected nothing from the new President. They had not given up the cause of free Kansas, but they saw no reason for believing that his policy would be favorable to it. They felt that the problem must be worked out by the free-State party in the territory, and by the Republicans in the Northern States.[3]

---

[1] Letter of Dec. 8th, 1856, Life of Buchanan, Curtis, vol. ii. p. 185.

[2] The name of Buchanan's home, near Lancaster, Pa.

[3] See the files of the New York *Tribune* and the *Independent* from Nov., 1856, to Feb., 1857, inclusive.

Just before the new year, Buchanan wrote John Y. Mason at Paris: "The great object of my administration will be to arrest, if possible, the agitation of the slavery question at the North, and to destroy sectional parties."[1] Had the contents of that private letter been disclosed to Everett and Choate, they would have said, It means free Kansas; for to them it was patent that only by the "easy, simple, and just" policy of making Kansas free could the slavery agitation at the North be arrested. If that were the notion of Buchanan when he penned those words, he changed his mind before the inauguration day. The "bedimmed prospects" of Kansas in February arose from the treatment of Geary by the Pierce administration; but it then became apparent that Buchanan would use no influence on the side of freedom before he took the reins of office. Moreover, the leaders of the South, who shaped the policy of the Democrats, were still determined to have Kansas a slave State; and it seemed plain to Republican observers that unless Buchanan were an uncommon man, he would be a tool in their hands, as had been his predecessor.[2]

Choate and Everett overrated his capacity and firmness. The idea one gets of the Buchanan of 1857 from the faithful story of his life by Curtis is that of a man of fair talents working in a groove, filling many public positions respectably, but none brilliantly. Politically, he was always ready to serve his party and willing to follow other leaders. He never desired to branch off independently. While in Congress he did not show ability as a parliamentary leader, and his nature unfitted him to be a vehement advocate. He was an ordinary Secretary of State; he filled the position of minister to England honorably and discreetly, as have many gentlemen before and since.[3] Cold, measured, and

---

[1] Letter, Dec. 29th, 1856, Curtis, vol. ii. p. 185.
[2] See New York *Tribune*, Dec. 10th, 1856, Jan. 7th, 1857; Pike to *Tribune*, Feb. 23d, First Blows of the Civil War, p. 363.
[3] His great indiscretion was signing the Ostend Manifesto. See Bry-

reticent, he acquired a reputation for sagacity because he never committed himself until pushed for an answer.

Yet he was a voluminous letter-writer, and filled pages with platitudes and wearisome repetitions. Decorous in manner, he may fitly be called a gentleman of the old school; but he was not a man of culture. Not a gleam of learning appears in his familiar letters. Spending much time in Europe, enjoying the society of distinguished and educated men, the scientific development of his century and the noble literature of his language were to him sealed books. He was inferior in intelligence and power of reasoning to Jefferson Davis, in statesmanship and parliamentary talent to Douglas, in correctness and vigor of judgment to Marcy, while in decision and force of character he was inferior to them all.[1]

When Buchanan wrote his inaugural at Wheatland, he was probably wavering between the policy represented by Jefferson Davis and that represented by Everett and Choate, with an inclination towards the latter. When, after coming to Washington, he inserted a clause in his address referring to the expected decision of the Supreme Court in the Dred Scott case,[2] he may have been still wavering, but the leaning was in the direction of the Southern idea.[3]

He spoke to the sixty-two electoral votes of the doubtful Northern States when he said that he was convinced that he owed his "election to the inherent love for the Constitution and the Union which still animates the hearts of the American people;" and also when he declared that, "having determined not to become a candidate for re-election, I

---

ant's estimate of Buchanan, letter of Jan. 22d, 1858, Life of Bryant, Godwin, vol. ii. p. 105.

[1] See Foote's Casket of Reminiscences, and Forney's Anecdotes of Public Men.

[2] Life of Buchanan, Curtis, vol. ii. p. 187.

[3] New York *Tribune* and *Times*, March 5th, 1857; Pike's First Blows of the Civil War, p. 365.

shall have no motive to influence my conduct in administering the government except the desire ably and faithfully to serve my country, and to live in the grateful memory of my countrymen."

He spoke to the one hundred and twelve electoral votes of the South when he said: "A difference of opinion has arisen in regard to the point of time when the people of a territory shall decide this question [of slavery] for themselves. This is happily a matter of but little practical importance. Besides, it is a judicial question, which legitimately belongs to the Supreme Court of the United States, before whom it is now pending, and will, it is understood, be speedily and finally settled. To their decision, in common with all good citizens, I shall cheerfully submit, whatever this may be, though it has ever been my individual opinion that, under the Kansas-Nebraska act, the appropriate period will be when the number of actual residents in the territory shall justify the formation of a constitution with a view to its admission as a State into the Union."

Buchanan showed astounding complacency when he said: "The whole territorial question being thus settled upon the principle of popular sovereignty—a principle as ancient as free government itself—everything of a practical nature has been decided. . . . May we not, then, hope that the long agitation on this subject [of slavery] is approaching its end, and that the geographical parties to which it has given birth, so much dreaded by the Father of his country, will speedily become extinct?"

Two days after the inauguration the nominations for the cabinet were sent to the Senate. Cass was Secretary of State; Howell Cobb, of Georgia, had the Treasury department; Floyd, whose chief recommendation seemed to be that he belonged to the first families of Virginia, was Secretary of War; Toucey, of Connecticut, whose senatorial term had just expired and whose strong Southern sympathies had debarred him from any further political preferment which was dependent on the popular voice, was made

Secretary of the Navy; Thompson, a Mississippi states-rights man, had the Interior department; Brown, of Tennessee, was Postmaster-General; and Jeremiah S. Black, one of the judges of the Pennsylvania Supreme Court, a jurist of uncommon talent and a man of vigorous mind, was appointed Attorney-General. The new cabinet was far inferior in capacity to the retiring one.

In point of political ability, Howell Cobb dominated his associates, and it was at once prophesied that he would be the master-spirit of the administration. He was a Unionist in 1850, and deemed by the Northern Whigs "sagacious and conservative."[1] He was frank and genial; but it remained a question whether he would like the drudgery of the Treasury department, and it was on all sides admitted that it would be difficult for him to equal the brilliant administration of his predecessor, who had been a master of finance.

Only one member of the cabinet could be said to reflect in any way the Northern conservative feeling typified by Everett and Choate, and that was Cass; but he was nearly seventy-five, and was believed to be an indolent man. Moreover, his speeches in the Senate did not promise a safe and judicious conduct of foreign affairs; still, there seems to have been no alarm on this point, for it was understood that Buchanan would be his own Secretary of State, and Cass merely a first assistant. Cass, like Toucey, was a senator repudiated by his own State. The place he had held for two terms was now filled by a Republican, Zachariah Chandler.

Three members of the cabinet were from the free States, and four from the slave States. The Republicans expected nothing for the cause of freedom from such a cabinet, or from a President whose proclivities were shown in their appointment.

Considering that one Democratic President had succeeded

---

[1] Letter of B. R. Curtis to Geo. Ticknor, Feb. 27th, 1857, Life of B. R. Curtis, vol. i. p. 192.

another, the scramble for office was surprising. In less than two months after the election, the conviction was forced upon Buchanan that the pressure would be nearly as great as if he had succeeded a Whig. Rotation in office was advocated as a true Democratic principle. "I cannot mistake," wrote Buchanan in a private letter, "the strong current of public opinion in favor of changing public functionaries, both abroad and at home, who have served a reasonable time. They say, and that too with considerable force, that if the officers under a preceding Democratic administration shall be continued by a succeeding administration of the same political character, this must necessarily destroy the party."[1]

Soon after the inauguration it was evident that Buchanan had committed himself to the principle of rotation in office, and the report went: "The ins look blue, the outs hopeful."[2] When an officer was reappointed it was considered an exception, and reasons were given in the press why a change was not made. Marcy was said to have dryly remarked: "They have it that I am the author of the office-seeker's doctrine that 'to the victors belong the spoils,' but I certainly should never recommend the policy of pillaging my own camp."[3] Northern Democratic senators were active in urging a distribution of the patronage where it would do them the most good, for the current of Northern opinion admonished them that much management was needed to retain their places.

When the great American question of the century had to be grappled with, Buchanan and his cabinet were devoting their time, strength, and ability to investigating the merits of candidates for postmasters, collectors, and tide-waiters.

---

[1] Buchanan to John Y. Mason, Dec. 29th, 1856, Curtis, vol. ii. p. 185.
[2] Simonton from Washington to New York *Times*, March 9th. See also the *Times*, March 13th; the New York *Herald* of March 9th, 11th, 19th, 23d, and the *Tribune* of March 28th and April 18th.
[3] New York *Herald*, March 23d.

It would not have been so pitiable had the search been simply to find men of business ability and integrity for the positions; but that was not the problem. How could the interest of the Democratic party in this State or that district best be promoted? What could be done with the patronage in the way of preserving the political life of this Northern senator or that Northern representative? These were the questions put to the President for solution. In a short time, Buchanan, who was the very picture of health when he left Wheatland, looked haggard and worn out, largely on account of the pressure from the hungry horde of office-seekers.[1]

We have seen in the course of this work many attempts of the national legislature and the executive to settle the slavery question. We have now to consider a grave attempt in the same line by the United States Supreme Court. The reverence for this unique and most powerful judicial tribunal of the world was profound. It is possible that from the time of the decision of the Dartmouth College case to the death of Chief Justice Marshall, the court held a loftier place in public opinion than in 1857; for Marshall was one of the world's great judges, and he had forcibly impressed his wonderful legal mind upon the country's jurisprudence. At that time De Tocqueville had written: In the hands of the Supreme Court "repose unceasingly the peace, the prosperity, the existence even, of the Union."[2] But in 1857 the reverence for the Supreme Court was greater than now.[3] In much of the political literature of

---

[1] Buchanan had what was known as the National-Hotel disease, which was the beginning of his physical disability. "The National-Hotel disease, a disorder which, from no cause that we could then discover, had attacked nearly every guest at the house, and from the dire effects of which many never wholly recovered."—Curtis, vol. ii. p. 188, account of J. B. Henry.

[2] De la Démocratie en Amérique, vol. i. p. 252. See also Lectures on the English People, Freeman, p. 191, and American Commonwealth, Bryce, chap. xxiv. [3] 1892.

the day it is regarded almost as a fetich; it was looked upon as something beyond the pale of ordinary human institutions. When men became Supreme Court judges, they were believed to be no longer actuated by the prejudices and passions of common humanity. During the slavery agitation there had been propositions of various kinds to refer disputed questions to this court, on the theory that there a wholly impartial and severely just decision might be had. The Democrats who disagreed about the construction of the Kansas-Nebraska act concurred in the proposal to leave the question to the highest judicial tribunal.

In 1857, the Supreme Court was composed of Chief Justice Taney, Justices Wayne, Daniel, Catron, Campbell, Democrats from the slave States; Grier and Nelson, Democrats, and McLean, a Republican, and Curtis, a Whig, from the free States. From the importance of their personality, two of these judges deserve special notice.

Chief Justice Taney belonged to one of the old Roman Catholic families of Maryland, and was himself a devout adherent of that religion. A good student of law, he devoted much time to history and letters; and the thoughts, words, and style of great writers had for him a powerful charm. He especially loved Shakespeare and Macaulay. He rose to eminence at the Maryland bar; he was an untiring worker, and allowed nothing to distract him from his professional duties and domestic life. Of a passionate nature, he had very decided political opinions. President Jackson appointed him Attorney-General, and he soon became the President's trusted and confidential adviser. When Duane, the Secretary of the Treasury, refused to withdraw the government deposits from the United States Bank, Jackson removed him and put Taney in his place. Taney understood banking and finance, and, being a man after Jackson's own heart, supported the President unreservedly in his war against the bank. The Senate refused to confirm Taney as Secretary of the Treasury, and Jackson appointed him Justice of the Supreme Court. Chief Justice Marshall, though disliking the President and his policy, had a good opinion of Taney's legal ability, and made an effort to secure his confirmation; but action on his nomination was indefinitely postponed. In July, 1835, Marshall died, and Jackson appointed Taney Chief Justice. As the political complexion of the Senate had changed, he did not fail of confirmation, although he had for opponents Webster and Clay.

To fill the place of Chief Justice Marshall was a difficult task, and Taney suffered continually by comparison with his great predecessor; yet as the years went on, he gained solid reputation by accurate knowledge of law, clearness of thought, and absolute purity of life. His written opinions are characterized by vigor of style, reflecting the hours he passed with the masters of our literature.[1]

Curtis had the rich New England culture. By nature a lawyer, he had received at the Harvard law school, sitting at the feet of Judge Story, the training which those who thirsted for legal knowledge could acquire from the instructions of such a teacher. He was thoroughly read in English history. He owed his appointment as justice to Webster, who, when Secretary of State, recommended him most highly to President Fillmore.[2] Curtis was an absolutely impartial judge. His reasoning was clear to laymen and a delight to lawyers. Though his style was a model of compression, he never forgot a point nor failed to be perspicuous. His course on the bench was a fine testimonial to the choice of Webster, whom New England lawyers regarded as the master of their profession.[3]

In the Dred Scott case the opposing principles of slavery and freedom came sharply into conflict in the judicial opin-

---

[1] See Memoir of R. B. Taney, Tyler; Sumner's Jackson.

[2] Fillmore had also formed a very high opinion of Curtis, see correspondence between Fillmore and Webster, Life of Webster, Curtis, vol. ii. p. 531.

[3] See Life and Writings of B. R. Curtis; Life of R. H. Dana, by C. F. Adams, vol. ii.

ions of Taney and Curtis. The negro Dred Scott had several years previously sued for the freedom of himself and family, and the case came up to the Supreme Court in a regular way. The detailed history of the affair has for our purpose no importance; it went through various stages, and many collateral points were involved. While the freedom or slavery of four negroes was at stake, the interest in their fate is completely overshadowed by the importance of the questions to which the suit gave rise. As a matter of fact, Dred Scott, after being remanded to slavery by the Supreme Court, was emancipated by his master;[1] but he had served as a text for weighty constitutional and political arguments.

Standing out beyond the merits of the case and all other points involved, two questions of vast importance were suggested by the facts. Could a negro whose ancestors had been sold as slaves become a citizen of one of the States of the Union? For if Dred Scott were not a citizen of Missouri, where he had mostly lived, he had no standing in the United States Court.

The second question, Was the Missouri Compromise constitutional? came up in this manner. Dred Scott had been taken by his master, an army surgeon, to Fort Snelling, which was in the northern part of the Louisiana territory, now Minnesota, and had remained there for a period of about two years. In this territory slavery was forever prohibited by the Missouri Compromise, and the counsel for Dred Scott maintained that by virtue of the restriction, residence there conferred freedom on the slave. Thus might arise the question, Was the Missouri Compromise constitutional? and this carried with it the more practical question, Had Congress the power to prohibit slavery in the territories? On the basis of the assertion of this power, the

---

[1] See Seward's speech, United States Senate, March 3d, 1858. By inheritance Dred Scott became the slave of the family of a Massachusetts congressman, who emancipated him, his wife, and daughters. See History of Lincoln. Nicolay and Hay, vol. ii. p. 81, note.

Republican party was builded; and if this power did not inhere in Congress, the Republican party had constitutionally no reason for existence.

The case was first argued in the spring of 1856. Justice Curtis wrote Ticknor, April 8th, the result of the conferences of the judges: "The court will not decide the question of the Missouri-Compromise line — a majority of the judges being of opinion that it is not necessary to do so. (This is confidential.) The one engrossing subject in both houses of Congress, and with all the members, is the presidency; and upon this everything done and omitted, except the most ordinary necessities of the country, depends."[1]

At the term of court, December, 1856, the case was reargued, and the counsel discussed all the questions involved. Still, the judges decided to view the matter only in its narrow aspect, and in its particular bearing on the status of Dred Scott and his family. To Justice Nelson, of New York, was assigned the duty of writing the opinion of the court. He astutely evaded the determination whether the Missouri Compromise act was constitutional; nor did he consider it necessary to pass upon the citizenship of the negro, but in arguing the case on its merits the decision was reached that Dred Scott was still a slave. Had this been the conclusion of the matter, the Dred Scott case would have excited little interest at the time, and would hardly have demanded more than the briefest notice from the historian.

But there now began a pressure on the Southern judges, who constituted a majority of the court, to decide the weighty constitutional question involved in the case. The unceasing inculcation of Calhoun's doctrine regarding slavery in the territories had now brought Southern Democrats, and among them the five Southern judges, round to that notion. Of course the pressure was adroit and considerate, for the judges were honest men impressed with the dignity of their position. The aim was simply to induce

---

[1] Memoir of B. R. Curtis, vol. i. p. 180.

them to promulgate officially what they privately thought. It is a tradition that Justice Campbell held back. This is to a certain degree confirmed by a letter of his written long after the event;[1] but if three Southern judges were decidedly in favor of pronouncing a judgment on the constitutional question, it needed only to gain the chief justice to carry along with them Campbell, and perhaps the two Democratic judges from the North. Before the Dred Scott decision was pronounced, Taney, both in character and ability, stood much higher than any other member of the court.

The chief justice was gained. The bait held out to his patriotic soul was that the court had the power and opportunity of settling the slavery question. He had now nearly reached the age of eighty, and, had he been younger, he might have detected the flaws in the reasoning which led him to so decided a position. "Our aged chief justice," wrote Curtis, February 27th, 1857, in a private letter, "grows more feeble in body, but retains his alacrity and force of mind wonderfully," though he "is not able to write much."[2] Certainly the Dred Scott opinion of Taney shows no weakness of memory or abated power of reasoning; but it may have been that age had enfeebled the will and made him more susceptible to influences that were brought to bear upon him.

Before Justice Nelson read his opinion in conference, Justice Wayne, of Georgia, at a meeting of the judges, stated that the case had excited public interest, and that it was expected that the points discussed by counsel would be considered by the court. He therefore moved that the chief justice should "write an opinion on all of the questions as the opinion of the court."[3] This was agreed to, but some of the judges reserved the privilege of qualifying their as-

---

[1] See Memoir of Taney, Tyler, p. 382.
[2] Curtis to Ticknor, Memoir, vol. i. p. 192.
[3] Letter of Justice Campbell, Memoir of Taney, Tyler, p. 382.

sent. Justice Wayne had worked industriously to bring this about, and his efforts had an important influence in persuading the chief justice, and Judges Grier, of Pennsylvania, and Catron, of Tennessee, of the expediency of such a course.[1] This determination, though shrouded in the secrecy of Supreme Court consultations, leaked out. Reverdy Johnson, whose constitutional argument had a profound influence on Taney, made his plea December 18th, 1856, and on New Year's Day of 1857, Alexander Stephens wrote to his brother: "The decision [of the Dred Scott case] will be a marked epoch in our history. I feel a deep solicitude as to how it will be. From what I hear, *sub rosa*, it will be according to my own opinion on every point, as abstract political questions. The restriction of 1820 will be held to be unconstitutional. The judges are all writing out their opinions, I believe, seriatim. The chief justice will give an elaborate one."[2] On the 5th of January, Pike wrote the New York *Tribune* that the rumor was current in Washington that the Supreme Court had decided that Congress had no constitutional power to prohibit slavery in the territories.[3]

Two days after the inauguration of Buchanan, Chief Justice Taney delivered the opinion of the court. He stated that one of the questions to be decided was: "Can a negro whose ancestors were imported into this country and sold as slaves become a member of the political community formed and brought into existence by the Constitution of the United States, and as such become entitled to all the rights and privileges and immunities guaranteed by that instrument to the citizen?" The answer is no. Negroes "were not intended to be included under the word 'citizens'

---

[1] Memoir of B. R. Curtis, vol. i. p. 206; see also letter of Campbell just cited, and opinion of Justice Wayne; also Pike's First Blows of the Civil War, p. 352.

[2] Life of Stephens, Johnston and Browne, p. 318; Stephens was a disciple of Calhoun.

[3] Pike's First Blows of the Civil War, p. 355.

in the Constitution, and therefore can claim none of the rights and privileges which that instrument provides for and secures to the citizens of the United States." Moreover, " In the opinion of the court, the legislation and histories of the times, and the language used in the Declaration of Independence, show that neither the class of persons who had been imported as slaves, nor their descendants, whether they had become free or not, were then acknowledged as a part of the people, nor intended to be included in the general words used in that memorable instrument.

"It is difficult, at this day, to realize the state of public opinion in relation to that unfortunate race which prevailed in the civilized and enlightened portions of the world at the time of the Declaration of Independence, and when the Constitution was framed and adopted. But the public history of every European nation displays it in a manner too plain to be mistaken.

"They had for more than a century before been regarded as beings of an inferior order, and altogether unfit to associate with the white race, either in social or political relations; and so far inferior that they had no rights which the white man was bound to respect, and that the negro might justly and lawfully be reduced to slavery for his benefit. He was bought and sold, and treated as an ordinary article of merchandise and traffic, whenever a profit could be made by it. The opinion was at that time fixed and universal in the civilized portion of the white race. It was regarded as an axiom in morals as well as in politics, which no one thought of disputing, or supposed to be open to dispute; and men in every grade and position in society daily and habitually acted upon it in their private pursuits, as well as in matters of public concern, without doubting for a moment the correctness of this opinion."

Citing the famous clause of the Declaration of Independence which asserted " that all men are created equal," the chief justice said: " The general words above quoted would seem to embrace the whole human family, and if they were used in a similar instrument at this day would be so understood. But it is too clear for dispute that the enslaved African race were not intended to be included, and formed no part of the people who framed and adopted this declaration."

The chief justice put the other constitutional question plainly: Was Congress authorized to pass the Missouri Compromise act "under any of the powers granted to it by the Constitution?" The Louisiana territory "was acquired by the general government, as the representative and trustee of the people of the United States, and it must therefore be held in that character for their common and equal benefit. . . . It seems, however, to be supposed that there is a difference between property in a slave and other property, and that different rules may be applied to it in expounding the Constitution of the United States." But "the right of property in a slave is distinctly and expressly affirmed in the Constitution. . . . And no word can be found in the Constitution which gives Congress a greater power over slave property, or which entitles property of that kind to less protection than property of any other description." It is the opinion of the court, therefore, that the Missouri Compromise act " is not warranted by the Constitution, and is therefore void."

All of the judges read opinions. The four Southern judges and Grier distinctly agreed with the chief justice that the Missouri Compromise was unconstitutional; and they concurred sufficiently in the other points to constitute his conclusions the opinion of the court, as it was officially called. It thus received the assent of two-thirds of the judges. Justice Nelson read the opinion he had prepared when it was decided to confine the judgment of the court to the merits of the case, while Justices McLean and Curtis dissented from the determination of the court. As Curtis covered more fully and cogently the ground, we have now to consider his opinion.

"I dissent," he began, "from the opinion pronounced by

II.—17

the chief justice. . . . The question is, whether any person of African descent whose ancestors were sold as slaves in the United States can be a citizen of the United States. . . . One mode of approaching this question is to inquire who were citizens of the United States at the time of the adoption of the Constitution.

"Citizens of the United States at the time of the adoption of the Constitution can have been no other than citizens of the United States under the confederation. . . . It may safely be said that the citizens of the several States were citizens of the United States under the confederation. . . . To determine whether any free persons descended from Africans held in slavery were citizens of the United States under the confederation, and consequently at the time of the adoption of the Constitution of the United States, it is only necessary to know whether any such persons were citizens of either of the States under the confederation at the time of the adoption of the Constitution.

"Of this there can be no doubt. At the time of the ratification of the Articles of Confederation, all free native-born inhabitants of the States of New Hampshire, Massachusetts, New York, New Jersey, and North Carolina, though descended from African slaves, were not only citizens of those States, but such of them as had the other necessary qualifications possessed the franchise of electors, on equal terms with other citizens. . . . I shall not enter into an examination of the existing opinions of that period respecting the African race, nor into any discussion concerning the meaning of those who asserted in the Declaration of Independence that all men are created equal; that they are endowed by their Creator with certain inalienable rights ; that among these are life, liberty, and the pursuit of happiness. My own opinion is that a calm comparison of these assertions of universal abstract truths, and of their own individual opinions and acts, would not leave these men under any reproach of inconsistency ; that the great truths they asserted on that solemn occasion they were ready and anxious to make effectual wherever a necessary regard to circumstances, which no statesman can disregard without producing more evil than good, would allow; and that it would not be just to them, nor true in itself, to allege that they intended to say that the Creator of all men had endowed the white race exclusively with the great natural rights which the Declaration of Independence asserts. But this is not the place to vindicate their memory. As I conceive, we should deal here . . . with those substantial facts evinced by the written constitutions of States, and by notorious practice under them. And they show, in a manner which no argument can obscure, that in some of the original thirteen States free colored persons, before and at the time of the formation of the Constitution, were citizens of those States." Therefore, " my opinion is that under the Constitution of the United States every free person born on the soil of a State, who is a citizen of that State by force of its constitution or laws, is also a citizen of the United States."

In considering the power of Congress to prohibit slavery in the territories, Justice Curtis cited "eight distinct instances, beginning with the first Congress, and coming down to the year 1848, in which Congress has excluded slavery from the territory of the United States; and six distinct instances in which Congress organized governments of territories by which slavery was recognized and continued, beginning also with the first Congress and coming down to the year 1822. These acts were severally signed by seven Presidents of the United States, beginning with General Washington and coming regularly down as far as John Quincy Adams, thus including all who were in public life when the Constitution was adopted.

" If the practical construction of the Constitution, contemporaneously with its going into effect, by men intimately acquainted with its history from their personal participation in framing and adopting it, and continued by them through a long series of acts of the gravest importance, be entitled to weight in the judicial mind on a question of construction, it would seem to be difficult to resist the force of the acts above adverted to."

Furthermore, " Slavery, being contrary to natural right, is created only by municipal law." Then, " Is it conceivable that the Constitution has conferred the right on every citizen to become a resident on the territory of the United States with his slaves, and there to hold them as such, but has neither made nor provided for any municipal regulations which are essential to the existence of slavery? . . . Whatever theoretical importance may be now supposed to belong to the maintenance of such a right, I feel a perfect conviction that it would, if ever tried, prove to be as impracticable in fact as it is, in my judgment, monstrous in theory."

Every possible phase of this question was considered by Justice Curtis, and the conclusion arrived at was that the acts of Congress which had prohibited slavery in the territories, including of course the Missouri Compromise, " were constitutional and valid laws."

That a man of the years of Taney could construct so vigorous and so plausible an argument was less remarkable than that a humane Christian man could assert publicly such a monstrous theory. Yet such work was demanded by slavery of her votaries. The opinion of Taney was but the doctrine of Calhoun, announced for the first time in 1847,[1] and now embodied in a judicial decision. As the North grew faster than the South, as freedom was stronger than slavery, it was the only tenable theory on which slavery could be extended. It is a striking historical fact that in but thirteen years of our history, from 1847 to 1860, could such an opinion have been delivered from the Supreme bench. Only by the conviction that slavery was being pushed to the wall, in conjunction with subtle reasoning like that of Calhoun, who tried to obstruct the onward

---

[1] See Vol. I. p. 94.

march of the century by a fine-spun theory, could a sentiment have been created which found expression in this opinion of Taney, outraging as it did precedent, history, and justice.

That Taney committed a grievous fault is certain. He is not to be blamed for embracing the political notions of John C. Calhoun; his environment gave that shape to his thoughts; but he does deserve censure because he allowed himself to make a political argument, when only a judicial decision was called for. The history of the case shows that there was no necessity for passing upon the two questions we have considered at length. Nothing but an imperative need should have led judges, by their training and position presumably conservative, to unsettle a question that had so long been acquiesced in. The strength of a constitutional government lies in the respect paid to settled questions. For the judiciary to weaken that respect undermines the very foundations of the State. As Douglas sinned as a statesman, so Taney sinned as judge; and while patriotism and not self-seeking impelled him, the better motive does not excuse the chief justice; for much is demanded from the man who holds that high office. Posterity must condemn Taney as unqualifiedly as Douglas.[1]

---

[1] The whole argument of Taney and Curtis on the two points I have made prominent are really a part of constitutional history. All the opinions were in 1857 printed by Howard in convenient pamphlet form, taken verbatim from his reports. The Memoir of Taney by Tyler, and the Memoir of B. R. Curtis by G. T. Curtis, are simply invaluable in a study of this subject. That of G. T. Curtis has an added interest, as he was the counsel for Dred Scott who made the constitutional argument. He is, moreover, able to consider the subject from the point of view of the historian as well as the lawyer. Interest in this decision has been recently revived by a discussion of it in the New York *Nation* for April 7th and April 21st, 1892. It called attention to Governor Andrew's analysis of the decision, and in the issue of April 21st gave an extract from his speech. This speech, which was delivered in the Massachusetts House of Representatives, March 5th, 1858, may be found in full in *The Liberator*, March 26th, 1858.

It is probable that Taney in his inmost heart regretted the part he had been made to play, when he saw that his opinion, instead of allaying the slavery agitation, gave it renewed force. The acerbity displayed in his subsequent correspondence with Justice Curtis grates the heart: they are extraordinary letters from a gentleman of high breeding to one with whom he had held friendly and official relations; and it is reasonable to suppose that while Taney bated not a jot of his convictions, he was vexed that he had descended from his high place to no good purpose, and annoyed that so many eminent lawyers thought his argument had been crushed by the rejoinder of Curtis.[1]

If Taney spoke for Calhoun, Curtis spoke for Webster. He had on his side common-sense and justice, even as had his master when disputing with Calhoun. If Taney furnished arguments for the Democrats, Curtis showed that the aim of the Republicans was constitutional. It was a profound remark of Dana on the death of Webster that "he had done more than any living statesman to establish the true Free-soil doctrines."[2]

Pike wrote to the New York *Tribune* that the Supreme Court of the United States "has abdicated its just functions and descended into the political arena. It has sullied its ermine; it has draggled and polluted its garments in the filth of pro-slavery politics." The opinion of the chief justice deserves "no more respect than any pro-slavery stump-speech made during the late presidential canvass."[3] Rhetoric of this sort made a stirring newspaper letter, and appealed to the radical spirits of the Republican party; but the leaders knew that this opinion of the court was a fact of

---

[1] See Memoir of B. R. Curtis, vol. i. p. 211 *et seq.* Compare the letter of Taney to Curtis, Nov. 3d, 1855, Tyler's Taney, p. 327, with the cavalier manner in which he receives the letter announcing Curtis's resignation, Sept. 7th, 1857, Memoir of B. R. Curtis, vol. i. p. 254.

[2] Life of R. H. Dana, C. F. Adams, vol. i. p. 223.

[3] Pike's First Blows of the Civil War, pp. 368, 370.

tremendous import, and must be met by argument and not by declamation. If the opinion of the court were binding on the country, the Republican party must dissolve or give up its fundamental principle, for it was laboring in an unconstitutional manner. How, then, could the reverence of the Northern people for the highest judicial tribunal be reconciled with a disregard of this opinion? Fortunately, Justice Curtis rose to the height of the situation, and in his opinion gave the key-note to the constitutional argument against the opinion of the court being in any way binding on the political consciences of the people. After mentioning the technical steps by which the court reached the question of the power of Congress to pass the Missouri Compromise act, Curtis said: "On so grave a subject as this, I feel obliged to say that, in my opinion, such an exertion of judicial power transcends the limits of the authority of the court, as described by its repeated decisions, and, as I understand, acknowledged in this opinion of the majority of the court. . . . I do not consider it to be within the scope of the judicial power of the majority of the court to pass upon any question respecting the plaintiff's citizenship in Missouri, save that raised by the plea to the jurisdiction; and I do not hold any opinion of this court or any court binding when expressed on a question not legitimately before it. The judgment of this court is that the case is to be dismissed for want of jurisdiction, because the plaintiff was not a citizen of Missouri, as he alleged in his declaration. Into that judgment, according to the settled course of this court, nothing appearing after a plea to the merits can enter. A great question of constitutional law, deeply affecting the peace and welfare of the country, is not, in my opinion, a fit subject to be thus reached."

Not Republicans alone saw the matter in this light under the guidance of so earnest and able a jurist. Fillmore wrote Curtis that his arguments were unanswerable;[1] and un-

---

[1] Memoir of B. R. Curtis, vol. i. p. 251.

doubtedly nearly every Northern man who had voted for Fillmore agreed with his chief.

The Southern Democrats were in high glee at the decision. "What are you going to do about it?" they tauntingly asked of the Republicans;[1] and they went to work circulating the opinion of the court as a campaign document. Twenty thousand copies of the opinions of the judges were printed by order of the Democratic Senate. When the Republicans saw clearly their proper course, they vied with the Democrats in giving wide currency to the action of the court. One of their important campaign documents contained the full opinions of Taney and Curtis, and abstracts of the others.[2] People always desire to summarize a long political paper, and Taney's opinion was soon condensed into the aphorism that "negroes had no rights which the white man was bound to respect." This was not fair to Taney, but the dissemination of the saying as the dictum of the court was a most effective weapon in the North against slavery, and had much to do with deepening Northern sentiment in opposition to it.

Douglas soon spoke for the Northern Democrats.[3] He emphatically endorsed the decision of the court, lauded the characters of Taney and the associate judges, and maintained that "whoever resists the final decision of the highest judicial tribunal aims a deadly blow to our whole republican system of government."

It was perfectly plain to Southern Democrats and Republicans that this decision shattered the doctrine of popular sovereignty; for if Congress could not prohibit slavery in a territory, how could it be done by a territorial legislature, which was but a creature of Congress? And as, according

---

[1] See Pike's First Blows of the Civil War.
[2] This was published by the New York *Tribune*.
[3] At Springfield, Ill., at the request of the United States Grand Jury, June 12th. This speech was published in the New York *Times* of June 23d, but is not inserted in any of the three biographies of Douglas.

to the decision, slaves were property the same as horses and mules, the Southern emigrant to Kansas had the same right to take his negroes there that the Northern emigrant had to take his live-stock. Both alike claimed the protection of the general government; and if emigration went on under these conditions, the territory was liable to be slave territory before the people could in any manner be called upon to determine the question. A less adroit man than Douglas would have been daunted, but he boldly asserted that the Dred Scott decision and his popular-sovereignty doctrine were entirely consistent. While the master's right to his slave in a territory, he said, "continues in full force under the guarantees of the Constitution, and cannot be divested or alienated by an act of Congress, it necessarily remains a barren and a worthless right, unless sustained, protected, and enforced by appropriate police regulations and local legislation, prescribing adequate remedies for its violation. These regulations and remedies must necessarily depend entirely upon the will and wishes of the people of the territory, as they can only be prescribed by the local legislatures. Hence the great principle of popular sovereignty and self-government is sustained and firmly established by the authority of this decision."

This attempted reconciliation of two irreconcilable principles must have provoked a smile from Southern Democrats and Republicans. But at the North, Douglas had been steadily gaining in popularity since January 1st, 1856; and as he was a consummate party leader, he was nearing the point where he only had to make a daring assertion to have it echoed by his many satellites and believed in by his followers, who were practically the Democratic party of the North. While he was ordinarily verbose, he cared not to dwell on this point; he passed at once to other points of the decision which he could sincerely advocate. He could not resist referring in a triumphant tone to the fact that the repeal of the Missouri Compromise, for which he had been so much abused, had now turned out to be simply the abrogation of a statute constitutionally null and void.

The reasoning of Taney in regard to the citizenship of the negro was amplified by Douglas in the manner that gave the key-note to his followers. Read at this day, Taney's argument impresses one with its power. It is inhuman. It was effectually refuted. But it was a great piece of specious reasoning, and, translated by Douglas into the language of the stump, it made the staple argument of Northern Democrats from this time to the war. We have seen the course of opinion at the South—how slavery, from having been regarded an abstract evil, came to be looked upon as a positive good. Opinion among the Northern Democrats went through a similar evolution, for the evil was first endured, then pitied, and now embraced. With the approval of the principles of the Dred Scott decision, the last step was taken. Because the negro was inferior to the white man, the Northern Democrats now argued, slavery was his fit condition. This sentiment shows itself in the press, in the friendly discussion at the village store and by the fireside. The Northern Democrats of 1840 to 1850 thought slavery an evil in the abstract; there were even devoted partisans who had conscientious scruples about supporting Polk because he was a slave-holder. Many of these same men were now gravitating to the point of thinking that a favor was done the negro when he was reduced to slavery. This argument, while not unknown in Northern Democratic literature before 1857, becomes prominent after the publication of the Dred Scott decision. Taney's opinion was swallowed by the followers of Douglas, and everywhere reproduced and paraphrased. It was the Kansas-Nebraska act and the Dred Scott opinion which made the national Democrats a pro-slavery party.

Douglas was not left unanswered. Two weeks later Abraham Lincoln, his Illinois rival, then much less widely known, an inferior orator, yet with a greater gift of expression, made a reply. This speech, which was published in the

East,[1] states the Republican position in a manner to carry conviction to those who could only be influenced by homely arguments, and at the same time its reasoning strikes the historical student with great force. It therefore deserves more than a passing notice. Who resists the decision? Lincoln asked. "Who has, in spite of the decision, declared Dred Scott free, and resisted the authority of his master over him? . . . But we think the Dred Scott decision is erroneous. We know the court that made it has often overruled its own decisions, and we shall do what we can to have it overrule this. We offer no resistance to it." The condition of the black man, Lincoln asserted, is worse now than at the time of the Declaration of Independence and the adoption of the Constitution. "In those days our Declaration of Independence was held sacred by all, and thought to include all; but now, to aid in making the bondage of the negro universal and eternal, it is assailed and sneered at, and construed and hawked at and torn, till, if its framers could rise from their graves, they could not at all recognize it. All the powers of the earth seem rapidly combining against him [the negro]. Mammon is after him, ambition follows, philosophy follows, and the theology of the day is fast joining the cry. . . . There is a natural disgust in the minds of nearly all white people to the idea of an indiscriminate amalgamation of the white and black races; and Judge Douglas . . . makes an occasion for lugging it in from the opposition to the Dred Scott decision. He finds the Republicans insisting that the Declaration of Independence includes all men, black as well as white, and forthwith he boldly denies that it includes negroes at all, and proceeds to argue gravely that all who contend it does, do so only because they want to vote, and eat, and sleep, and marry with the negroes! . . . Now, I protest against the counterfeit logic which concludes that, because I do not want a black woman for a slave, I must necessarily

---

[1] In the New York *Times*, July 7th. It was delivered June 26th. It is printed in the Life of Lincoln by W. D. Howells, p. 170.

want her for a wife. I need not have her for either; I can just leave her alone. In some respects she is certainly not my equal; but in her natural right to eat the bread she earns with her own hands, without asking leave of any one else, she is my equal, and the equal of all others."[1]

One widespread charge in reference to the Dred Scott decision must be spoken of. In 1858, it was given the stamp of approval by Seward and Lincoln, who had then become the two leaders of the Republican party. Seward said in the Senate, March 3d: "Before coming into office, Buchanan approached, or was approached by, the Supreme Court of the United States. . . . The court did not hesitate to please the incoming President by . . . pronouncing an opinion that the Missouri prohibition was void. . . . The day of inauguration came—the first one among all the celebrations of that great national pageant that was to be desecrated by a coalition between the executive and judicial departments, to undermine the national legislature and the liberties of the people." The people were "unaware of the import of the whisperings carried on between the President and the chief justice." The President "announced (vaguely indeed, but with self-satisfaction) the forthcoming extra-judicial exposition of the Constitution, and pledged his submission to it as authoritative and final. The chief justice and his associates remained silent."[2] The only evidence for the charge of Seward lay in the statement of the President in his inaugural, that the question as to the time when people of a territory might exclude slavery therefrom was pending before the Supreme Court, and would be speedily settled.[3] Undoubtedly Buchanan then knew what would be substantially the decision of the court on the territorial question, but so did a thousand other men. The clause in the inaugural which gave rise to this charge was not in-

---

[1] Much more copious extracts from this able speech may be found in Nicolay and Hay's History, vol. ii. chap. v.
[2] Seward's Works, vol. iv. p. 585 *et seq.*   [3] See p. 245.

serted until he arrived at Washington.¹ He reached Washington March 2d, and on that day might have read in the New York *Tribune:* "We learn from trustworthy sources that the Supreme Court of the United States, in the Dred Scott case, will, by a large majority, sustain the extreme Southern ground, denying the constitutionality of the Missouri Compromise. Probably Judges Curtis and McLean will alone dissent."

An editorial article, however carefully written, is of course not absolute historical evidence, but in this case it confirms the notion we might get from the history of the decision as previously related. Other Supreme Court decisions have leaked out. Judges have confidential friends; and the truth is sometimes told by the pronouncing of some doubtful phrase or by an ambiguous giving-out. But however Buchanan got his intelligence, his character and that of Taney are proof that the chief justice did not communicate the import of the decision to the President-elect. That either would stoop from the etiquette of his high office is an idea that may not be entertained for a moment; and we may be sure that with Taney's lofty notions of what belonged to an independent judiciary, he would have no intercourse with the executive that could not brook the light of day.²

If any one used personal influence with Taney, it was Reverdy Johnson, who had argued the constitutional question on the pro-slavery side. His argument undoubtedly had great weight; and his social relations with Taney were such that his views could be enforced in private conversation.³ If persuasion of that kind were used, it was probably

---

¹ See Life of Buchanan, Curtis, vol. **ii. p. 187.**

² For Buchanan's remarks as to this charge see Curtis, vol. ii. p. 207, note.

³ See remarks of George T. Curtis on the death of Reverdy Johnson, Proceedings of the Bench and Bar *in memoriam*, p. 12. Pike wrote to the *Tribune,* speaking of Reverdy Johnson: "No man is so intimate with, and

in the way of urging the chief justice to give to the country, in the form of a Supreme Court decision, political views cordially agreed on by Taney and Johnson; and it must be admitted as unlikely that such arguments would have prevailed had not the Democrats been successful at the presidential election.

Taney was so incensed at the speech of Seward that he told Tyler, who was afterwards his biographer, that had Seward been nominated and elected President in 1860 instead of Lincoln, he would have refused to administer to him the oath of office.[1]

The contrast between Seward and Lincoln may be seen in their different treatment of this matter. The tact of Lincoln is shown in making the charge by intimation and by trenchant questions; then, with humor and exquisite skill, giving a homely illustration which struck the popular mind so forcibly that the notion conveyed by it undoubtedly became the belief of the Republican masses as long as the Dred Scott decision remained a question of politics.

"When we see a lot of framed timbers," said he, "different portions of which we know have been gotten out at different times and places and by different workmen—Stephen, Franklin, Roger, and James, for instance[2]—and when we see these timbers joined together and see they exactly make the frame of a house or a mill, all the tenons and mortices exactly fitting, and all the lengths and proportions of the different pieces exactly adapted to their respective places, and not a piece too many or too few, not omitting even scaffolding—or if a single piece be lacking, we see the place in the frame exactly fitted and prepared yet to bring such

---

no man possesses so much influence over, the chief justice as he." Ex-Senator Bradbury told me that the current idea among Northern Democrats in 1857 was that it was Johnson who induced Taney to give the political decision. [1] Tyler's Taney, p. 391.

[2] Stephen A. Douglas, Franklin Pierce, Roger B. Taney, James Buchanan.

piece in—in such a case, we find it impossible not to believe that Stephen and Franklin and Roger and James all understood one another from the beginning, and all worked upon a common plan or draft drawn up before the first blow was struck."[1]

As politics go, the argument of Lincoln was perhaps allowable. Submission to the decision of the Supreme Court, that august body reverenced by all, the department of the government which is the balance-wheel, was urged by Douglas and all Democratic orators with great force. The escape suggested by Justice Curtis was sufficient for the most intelligent voters; but the line drawn was technical, and something that could better be laid hold of seemed needed to influence the mass of the party. For all the Republicans of 1857 and 1858 required satisfying reasons, and the charge of conspiracy between the governmental departments seemed well adapted for the purpose.

While the Dred Scott decision gave a theoretical basis to slavery in the territories, it did not settle the Kansas question. But a movement of the pro-slavery party was in progress to form a State government. Instructed by the vote of those who took part in the election of October, 1856, the territorial legislature had fixed upon the third Monday of June, 1857, as the day for the election of delegates to a constitutional convention. Impressed with the importance of Kansas affairs, Buchanan asked Robert J. Walker to take the position of governor. Walker in talent and reputation was far above the ordinary level of the territorial governor. He had been senator, and as Secretary of the Treasury had practically framed the tariff act of 1846; he had, moreover, been urged upon

---

[1] Speech at Springfield, June 16th, 1858, Lincoln and Douglas Debates, p. 3. Douglas was not present when this speech was made, but afterwards during the Lincoln-Douglas debates he several times emphatically denied the charge of conspiracy between Taney, Pierce, Buchanan, and himself. This charge was indeed unsupported by evidence, and was only suggested by a striking coincidence of events.

Buchanan for the Treasury department.[1] He was born in Pennsylvania, but had long been a resident of Mississippi.

"It was long before I would agree to go to Kansas," Walker afterwards said. "I refused two or three times verbally and once in writing."[2] But the President insisted, and brought every possible influence to bear upon him to change his determination. Douglas earnestly and excitedly urged him to go to Kansas. At last he said he would go, provided his wife would withdraw her objections. To secure her consent, the President called upon her, argued that peculiar reasons pointed to Walker as the best fitted man in the country to pacify Kansas, and succeeded in convincing her that patriotic duty demanded that he should accept the mission. He furthermore made the condition that there should be a perfect concurrence between the President and himself in regard to the policy to be adopted in Kansas; and, without doubt for the purpose of knowing what would satisfy the Republicans, he had, before he left Washington, a private conference with Seward.[3] In Walker's judgment, the true construction of the Kansas-Nebraska act required the submission to the people of any constitution that might be framed, and in this opinion the agreement of Buchanan was unequivocal.[4] Another condition made was that General Harney should be sent there to take command of the troops.[5]

Walker had a fit coadjutor. The President appointed as secretary of the territory, Frederick P. Stanton, of Tennessee, a man of character, ability, and decision, " of persuasive

---

[1] See Life of Dix, vol. i. p. 322.

[2] Testimony before the Covode committee, see their Report, p. 105.

[3] Seward to his son, Life, vol. ii. p. 299. He also wrote: "Walker sees his way through the governorship of Kansas to the Senate, and through the Senate to the presidency."

[4] Testimony before the Covode Committee, Report, pp. 105, 106; see also letter of Walker to Cass, Dec. 15th, 1857, Senate Docs. 1st Sess. 35th Cong., vol. i. p. 122; Speech of Douglas, Milwaukee, Oct. 13th, 1860.

[5] Walker to Cass, July 15th.

address but honest ambition."[1] He had had ten years' experience of public life, having been for that time a representative in Congress.

Stanton was able to reach Kansas before his chief, and he found awaiting him the important duty of making the apportionment of delegates to the constitutional convention. The census and registration had been unfair and defective; in more than half of the counties there was no registration. This perplexed him, but after carefully considering the matter, in the brief time the law allowed him, he came to the conclusion that he had no choice but to apportion the delegates to the several counties on the returns which had been made.[2] This action irritated the free-State party.

Walker arrived in Kansas May 26th, and published his inaugural the next day. It was the address of a fair-minded but partisan Democrat. It had been submitted to Buchanan and Douglas, and was approved by both.[3] Walker would have been glad to see Kansas a slave State; but, on looking over the ground, he saw that this end could not be attained by fair means. As a result of all the effort, there were now but two or three hundred slaves in the territory. Since its certain destiny seemed to be that of a free State, he was anxious that it should be Democratic, and towards that end he bent his energies.[4] The emigration from the free States had been large this spring;[5] he estimated that there were in the territory nine thousand free-State Democrats, eight thousand Republicans, six thousand five hundred pro-slavery Democrats, five hundred pro-slavery

---

[1] Seward, Senate speech, March 3d, 1858.

[2] See address of Stanton, Publications of Kansas Hist. Soc., vol. i. p. 149; Spring's Kansas, p. 212.

[3] Walker's testimony. Covode Committee Report, p. 106; Constitutional and Party Questions, Cutts, p. 121; Speech of Douglas, Milwaukee, Oct. 13th, 1860.

[4] Walker to Cass, July 15th, Senate Docs. 1st Sess. 35th Cong., vol. i. p. 26; Covode Committee Report, p. 107.

[5] New York *Tribune*, March 28th and April 18th.

Know-nothings;[1] and his aim was to bring about a concert of action between the two Democratic factions, but this could only be done on the basis of making Kansas a free State. In his inaugural, he had urged all citizens to take part in the coming election, and at Topeka, when making a manly speech, he replied to the question what he would do should the forthcoming convention refuse to submit the constitution to the people. "I will join you, fellow-citizens," he said, "in opposition to their course. And I doubt not that one much higher than I, the chief magistrate of the Union, will join you."[2]

But the free-State party were not reassured. They declined to participate in the election of June 15th for delegates to the constitutional convention. Out of nine thousand two hundred and fifty-one registered voters, which was less than one-half of the actual number, only two thousand two hundred persons took part in choosing delegates to the notorious Lecompton convention.[3]

By July, Walker found that a Kansas governor had to tread a thorny path. While making an impression on free-State Democrats, and leading some moderate Republicans to see that he desired to measure out justice, the radicals under the lead of Lane threatened mischief at Lawrence. Trouble, however, was avoided by the promptness with which the governor collected troops in the neighborhood of the city, and at the close of his official career he had the satisfaction of writing that not a drop of blood had been shed by the federal troops during his administration.[4]

The proclamation which he issued to the people of Lawrence increased the already prevailing tendency towards a

---

[1] Private letter of Walker to Buchanan, Covode Committee Report, p. 115.

[2] This speech was made June 6th, Spring's Kansas, p. 213; Walker to Cass, July 15th, 1857.   [3] See Stanton's message of Dec. 8th.

[4] Walker to Cass, Dec. 15th.

division in the Republican ranks. Senator Wilson had visited Kansas and urged the policy of voting at the October election for members of the territorial legislature, and the larger faction of Republicans under the lead of Robinson were beginning to see the wisdom of such a course.[1]

At the same time, Walker's policy of equal and exact justice brought upon him the extreme displeasure of the active politicians of the Southern States. While professing that he was not disturbed by these assaults, his frequent mention of them in his despatches shows that they greatly annoyed him, especially because they threatened to prevent the union between the two Democratic factions he was so anxious to bring about.[2] One newspaper said he had "delivered Kansas into the hands of the abolitionists."[3] Another emphatically demanded his removal in the name of the South.[4] Leading politicians of South Carolina, Georgia, and Mississippi, among whom Jefferson Davis and Senator Brown were prominent, denounced him in unmeasured terms, and some of them went so far as to censure the President for having appointed him;[5] and the Democratic State conventions of Georgia and Mississippi criticised his course in strong resolutions.[6]

Still, Buchanan stood by Walker. On the 12th of July he wrote privately to the governor: "On the question of submitting the Constitution to the *bona-fide* resident settlers of Kansas, I am willing to stand or fall. In sustaining such a principle we cannot fall. It is the principle of the Kansas-Nebraska bill, the principle of popular sovereignty, and the principle at the foundation of all popular government. The more it is discussed, the stronger it will become. Should the

---

[1] Senate Docs., 1st Sess. 35th Cong., vol. i. pp. 43, 46; Wilson's Rise and Fall of the Slave Power, vol. ii. p. 537; Stanton's Address, Pub. Kansas Hist. Soc., vol. i. p. 164; Spring's Kansas, p. 215.
[2] See his despatches to Cass of July 15th, 20th, and Aug. 3d.
[3] Richmond *South*, cited by New York *Times*, July 14th.
[4] Vicksburg *Sentinel*, cited by New York *Times*, July 14th.
[5] Casket of Reminiscences, Foote, p. 114; New York *Tribune*, July 30th.
[6] Von Holst, vol. vi. p. 70.

convention of Kansas adopt this principle, all will be settled harmoniously."[1]

We cannot clearly trace the workings of the President's mind to determine the time when he began to recede from this position. In August, however, he took occasion publicly to endorse the Calhoun doctrine in the strongest terms. In a letter to citizens of Connecticut he said that at the time of the passage of the Kansas-Nebraska act slavery existed, "and still exists, in Kansas, under the Constitution of the United States. This point has at last been finally decided by the highest tribunal known to our laws. How it could ever have been seriously doubted is a mystery. If a confederation of sovereign States acquire new territory at the expense of their common blood and treasure, surely one set of the partners can have no right to exclude the other from its enjoyment by prohibiting them from taking into it whatever is recognized to be property by the common constitution."[2]

This showed the startling progress of an idea destined to work great mischief. When, in 1847, Calhoun first announced the doctrine in the Senate, it was received with general disfavor, and he never called for a vote on the resolutions embodying this principle: it was afterwards scouted by Webster. Now the judicial and executive departments of the government had given it their entire adhesion. It must have occurred to wily Southern leaders that a President who thought it a mystery that the Calhoun doctrine could ever have been seriously doubted was a fit instrument to carry out their designs in Kansas.

As late as July, or after the delegates to the constitutional convention had been elected, Walker was still popular with the pro-slavery Democrats in the territory. His course was endorsed by them, and it was universally understood that the constitution, when framed, would be submitted to a pop-

---

[1] Covode Committee Report, p. 112.
[2] Senate Docs. 1st Sess. 35th Cong., vol. i. p. 74.

ular vote.¹ But as soon as it became known in the South that the delegates to the constitutional convention were of the pro-slavery party, a systematic agitation began which demanded that the convention adopt a pro-slavery constitution and ask for admission into the Union.² The leaders of this agitation were the Southern extremists, of whom Jefferson Davis was a type. They soon gained a foothold in Washington with the administration or with others high in authority.³ It was generally believed that Cobb, the Secretary of the Treasury, and Thompson, the Secretary of the Interior, were the official promoters of this movement. It is undeniable that the public sentiment of Georgia and Mississippi, their States, was powerfully exercised in this direction. The testimony of Thompson bears out this view as far as he himself is concerned; for the hint he gave to the emissary he sent to Kansas was quite sufficient to give credence to the later prevailing opinion in the territory, that the Lecompton policy was approved, if not engineered, by the administration.⁴

But the supposed connection at this time of Cobb with the conspiracy cannot be reconciled with the story he told the Covode committee, that as late as October he urged by letter to a member of the convention the out-and-out submission of the Constitution to the people.⁵

The convention met at Lecompton in September. After a session of five days, it temporarily adjourned to await the result of the October election. Walker had urged the abandonment of the Topeka movement, and had succeeded in convincing the free-State men who followed Robinson that it was their duty to take part in the regular election for the territorial legislature. It was the most general and peace-

---

¹ Walker's testimony, Covode Committee Report, p. 108.
² See Martin's and Thompson's testimony, Covode Committee Report, pp. 158, 315; also Walker to Cass, Dec. 15th.
³ See Walker's testimony, p. 111.
⁴ See Thompson's testimony, p. 314. ⁵ Cobb's testimony, p. 318.

ful election that had occurred in the territory, and in but two places were there glaring frauds. From Oxford there was a forged return of 1628 votes; the town had but fifty voters. In McGee county, where there were certainly not twenty voters, 1266 pro-slavery ballots were alleged to have been cast.[1] If the Oxford and McGee returns were allowed, the legislature would be pro-slavery; if they were thrown out, it would be free-State. Governor Walker and Secretary Stanton visited these places, and when they saw beyond doubt that the fraud was glaring, they honorably carried out the pledges they had given the Kansas people. Having found certain technical defects, they were not obliged to go behind the returns, and they soon issued proclamations throwing out the returns from Oxford and McGee, where the astounding frauds had been perpetrated.[2] This gave the free-State party nine of the thirteen councilmen and twenty-four of the thirty-nine representatives.[3]

The constitutional convention reassembled the 19th of October, but three days went by before a quorum was secured. The body was a rump. Pro-slavery delegates were going to speak for a community which was overwhelmingly in favor of a free State; but the small Kansas clique represented the aim of the slavery propaganda, and were obedient to the instructions which had been brought to them from Washington. Had the convention not been protected by United States troops, it would never have been permitted to finish its work; an outraged people would have driven the members from the territory.[4] It was easy to see that if the constitution were submitted to the people, it would be voted down by a large majority. After much discussion, a plan was resolved upon, which showed ingenuity but entire lack of fairness. The crucial section of the constitution which the convention adopted was: "The right of

---

[1] Walker's testimony, p. 109; Spring's Kansas, p. 218.
[2] Stanton's Address, Kansas Hist. Soc. Pub., vol. i. p. 153.
[3] Spring's Kansas, p. 220.   [4] Kansas Hist. Soc. Pub., vol. i. p. 252.

property is before and higher than any constitutional sanction, and the right of the owner of a slave to such slave and its increase is the same and as inviolable as the right of the owner of any property whatever." Another provision of the constitution was that it could not be amended until after the year 1864, and even then no alteration should " be made to affect the rights of property in the ownership of slaves."

An election was appointed for the 21st of December, when the people might vote for the constitution with slavery or for the same constitution with no slavery. They were to have no opportunity to vote against the constitution; and even the submission of the slavery question was a delusion. If the " constitution with slavery " carried, the section above cited and others supporting it were parts of the organic act. But if " constitution with no slavery " carried, then slavery should " no longer exist in the State of Kansas, except that the right of property in slaves now in this territory shall in no measure be interfered with." " The alternative presented was like submitting to the ancient test of witchcraft. . . . If the accused, upon being thrown into deep water, floated, he was adjudged guilty, taken out and hanged; but if he sank and was drowned, he was adjudged not guilty—the choice between the verdicts being quite immaterial." [1]

It was a shallow and wicked performance, worthy perhaps of a border-ruffian convention, representing only twenty-two hundred voters; but it is astounding when we know there is reason to believe that the plan emanated from Southern politicians of high position at Washington. Before the vote on it was finally taken, John Calhoun, the surveyor-general of the territory, and president of the convention, called on Walker, outlined the project and asked his concurrence, assuring him that it was the programme of the administration, and, if he would give it his support, the presidency of the United States lay open to him. Walker

---

[1] Spring's Kansas, p. 223.

inquired of Calhoun if he had a letter from the President. "He said he had not, but that the assurance came to him in such a manner as to be entirely reliable; that this particular programme [which was finally adopted in Kansas] was the programme of the administration." Walker promptly replied that he would never assent to it. "I consider," said he, "such a submission of the question a vile fraud, a base counterfeit, and a wretched device to prevent the people voting even" on the slavery question. "I will not support it," he continued, "but I will denounce it, no matter whether the administration sustains it or not."[1]

Buchanan was not privy to this project. His confidential letter to Walker of October 22d[2] shows that at that time he knew nothing of the plot which was hatched under his very eyes; and his "solemn, grave, and serious" assurances to the same effect in November convinced Walker and must satisfy the historian.[3] But after the constitution had been adopted by the convention, the President became its persistent advocate. Cobb was easily won, if he needed winning, and he had more influence over Buchanan than any member of the cabinet.[4] He was undoubtedly the mouthpiece of the Southern junto, and knew how to play upon the feelings of his venerable chief. Buchanan had great admiration for the Southern politicians, and with it there was mingled a sentiment of fear.[5] Ambition had no part in determining his action, for in his inaugural he had pledged himself not to be a candidate for re-election; but he was timid, and in his intercourse with the Southerners, the feebleness of his will is plainly apparent. He told Forney that he "changed his course because certain Southern States had threatened that if he did not abandon Walker and Stanton they would

---

[1] Walker's testimony, Covode Committee Report, p. 110.
[2] Printed in Nicolay and Hay's History, vol. ii. p. 110.
[3] Walker's testimony, p. 114.
[4] See Memorial volume of Howell Cobb, p. 29; Casket of Reminiscences, Foote, p. 113.
[5] Casket of Reminiscences, Foote, p. 113.

be compelled either to secede from the Union, or take up arms against him." [1]

The public interest at the North in Kansas had largely died out. " Bleeding Kansas," which had been the topic of discussion everywhere in 1856, was no longer heard of. Kansas, indeed, had ceased to bleed. The firm and just rule of Governor Walker, supported by the presence of the United States troops, maintained the peace which had been restored by Geary. Little occurred during the spring and summer on which an agitation might be based, and by the time the conspiracy of making Kansas a slave State began to be suspected, the country was in the distress of a financial panic. The failure of the Ohio Life Insurance and Trust Company, August 24th, was a symptom of overtrading, and a precursor of the ruin that followed. While bankers were concerned about their honor, merchants and manufacturers straining their credit, and clerks and laborers losing their places, the trouble in Kansas seemed far distant. But the trouble at home was an actual affair that weighed on every moment. "The revulsion in the business of the country," wrote Buchanan to Walker, "seems to have driven all thoughts of 'bleeding Kansas' from the public mind." [2]

The Kansas plot of 1857 was that of a junto, and indeed it only came to light shortly before the assembling of Congress. It was a conspiracy under constitutional guise, and the only place where this battle could be fought was on the floor of Congress. The fall elections were favorable to the Democrats, and before the Lecompton policy was sprung upon the people they seemed to have regained the popular ascendency that had been trembling in the balance since the Kansas-Nebraska policy was inaugurated.

---

[1] Forney's testimony, Covode Committee Report, p. 296. The States were Georgia, Alabama, and Mississippi; see Forney's Vindication, Philadelphia *Press*, Sept. 30th, 1858.

[2] Oct. 22d, Nicolay and Hay, vol. ii. p. 111. See also Philadelphia *Press*, Oct. 10th. In a future volume, I purpose to consider the panic of 1857 more fully.

Many Northern Democrats, however, were excited when they learned of the Lecompton scheme. Forney opposed it in his Philadelphia newspaper,[1] and the Democratic press of Illinois immediately denounced the action of the convention. The sentiment among the Democrats of Ohio and the Northwest was in general the same, but the opposition would have protested vainly against the scheme had not the ablest leader of the Democratic party, Douglas, put himself at its head. On receipt of the news at Chicago, he immediately made it known that he should strenuously oppose the pro-slavery plan. On arriving at Washington to attend the session of Congress, he called on the President to discuss the matter. The radical difference between the two became apparent. When Buchanan said he must recommend the policy of the slave power, Douglas said he should denounce it in open Senate. The President became excited, rose and said: "Mr. Douglas, I desire you to remember that no Democrat ever yet differed from an administration of his own choice without being crushed. Beware of the fate of Tallmadge and Rives." Douglas also rose, and in an emphatic manner replied: "Mr. President, I wish you to remember that General Jackson is dead."[2] The Senate, which met December 7th, was composed of thirty-seven Democrats, twenty Republicans, and five Americans. In two years the Republicans had increased their number by five. To name all the Republican senators will convey a good idea of the growth of the party since its organization; for while the changes in the Senate are slow, it is a body in which may be traced the progress of a movement that is steady and sure.

Fessenden and Hamlin represented Maine; Hale and Clark, New Hampshire; Collamer and Foot, Vermont; Sumner and Wilson, Massachusetts; Foster and Dixon, Connect-

---

[1] Forney's testimony, p. 296.
[2] Speech of Douglas, Milwaukee, Oct. 13th, 1860, cited by Nicolay and Hay; see Washington *National Intelligencer*.

icut; Simmons, Rhode Island; Seward and Preston King, New York; Simon Cameron, Pennsylvania; Wade, Ohio; Trumbull, Illinois; Zachariah Chandler, Michigan; Durkee and Doolittle, Wisconsin; and Harlan, Iowa.

When Congress assembled, it was well understood that the President had espoused the cause of the Southern junto; but when he delivered his annual message, the time had not arrived to state clearly his position.[1] He dilated, however, on Kansas affairs, and said that while he had expected that the convention would submit the constitution to the people, it really had decided to give them a chance to express their opinion on slavery, which was the only important question at issue.

On December 9th, Douglas spoke boldly and resolutely against the Lecompton scheme. At the time the delegates to the constitutional convention were chosen, he said, it was understood by the national government, by the territorial government, and by the people of the territory that they were to be elected only to frame a constitution and to submit it to the people for their ratification or rejection. "Men high in authority, and in the confidence of the territorial and national government, canvassed every part of Kansas during the election of delegates, and each one pledged himself to the people that no snap judgment was to be taken. . . Up to the time of meeting of the convention, in October last, the pretence was kept up, the profession was openly made, and believed by me, and I thought believed by them, that the convention intended to submit a constitution to the people, and not to attempt to put a government in operation without such a submission." But instead of that, "All men must vote for the constitution, whether they like it or not,

---

[1] Alexander Stephens writes, Nov. 29th: "The administration have staked their all upon sustaining the Kansas Constitution as it may be ratified;" and Dec. 1st: "The administration is for the Kansas Constitution;" and Dec. 4th: Douglas "is against us—decidedly but not extravagantly."—Johnston and Browne, p. 326.

in order to be permitted to vote for or against slavery. . . . That would be as fair an election as some of the enemies of Napoleon attributed to him when he was elected First Consul. He is said to have called out his troops and had them reviewed by his officers with a speech, patriotic and fair in its professions, in which he said to them: 'Now, my soldiers, you are to go to the election and vote freely just as you please. If you vote for Napoleon, all is well; vote against him, and you are to be instantly shot.' *That was a fair election.* This election is to be *equally fair*," exclaimed the senator, in a tone of exquisite irony.[1] "All men in favor of the constitution may vote for it—all men against it shall not vote at all. Why not let them vote against it ? . . . I have asked a very large number of the gentlemen who framed the constitution, quite a number of delegates, and a still larger number of persons who are their friends, and I have received the same answer from every one of them. . . . They say if they allowed a negative vote, the constitution would have been voted down by an overwhelming majority, and hence the fellows shall not be allowed to vote at all."

It was a manly speech. His language was courteous, but his manner was bold, haughty, and defiant. "Henceforth," wrote Seward to his wife, "Douglas is to tread the thorny path I have pursued. The administration and slave power are broken. The triumph of freedom is not only assured, but near."[2] "He never seemed to have so much heart in any of his public discussions as now," wrote Simonton to the New York *Times;* "never was he more resolute and scornfully defiant of all assaults or opposition."[3] "He met the issue fairly and manfully," wrote the correspondent of the *Independent,* "and acquitted himself triumphantly. It was the forensic effort of his lifetime, and will live long after himself and his opponents in his party have passed from the

---

[1] See Washington correspondence New York *Independent*, Dec. 12th.
[2] Letter of Dec. 10th, Life of Seward, vol. ii. p. 330.
[3] Dec. 12th.

stage of political action."[1] This speech will "mark an important era in our political history." "The struggle of Douglas with the slave power will be a magnificent spectacle to witness," wrote the correspondent of the *Tribune*.[2] It seemed curious to read his praises in the *Tribune* and *Independent*, yet he was far from coming on to Republican ground. For he declared: "If Kansas wants a slave-State constitution, she has a right to it; if she wants a free-State constitution, she has a right to it. It is none of my business which way the slavery clause is decided. I care not whether it is voted down or voted up."

The usual explanation of the course of Douglas is that as his senatorial term would soon expire, and as a legislature would be chosen in 1858 to elect his successor, he saw clearly that if he espoused the Lecompton cause, he would surely be defeated. To insure his political life, therefore, it was necessary to oppose the scheme.[3] This explanation is true as far as it goes, but it does not compass the whole subject nor the whole man. The course of Douglas had been such that men had lost faith in his political consistency and honesty; so it is not surprising that when he came to do a noble act, it was generally supposed he did it from purely interested motives. But apart from politics, Douglas was a man of honor; his word was as good as his bond, and he was true to his friends.[4] He loved fair dealing, and this sentiment was outraged by the proceedings in Kansas; the honesty of his nature could not brook such a course. Had he acted entirely from the interested motive, he might have waited until the President formally recommended the Lecompton Constitution before he took it upon himself to make a breach in his party, hoping meanwhile that the dif-

---

[1] Dec. 12th.   [2] Dec. 9th and 10th.
[3] See New York *Tribune*, Dec. 19th; Simonton to New York *Times*, Dec. 12th; Nicolay and Hay, vol. ii. p. 123; Life of Jefferson Davis, Alfriend, p. 103; Three Decades, Cox, p. 58; Twenty years of Congress, Blaine, vol. i. p. 140; speech of Schurz, Sept., 1860, Speeches, p. 168.
[4] See Herndon's Life of Lincoln, p. 404.

ferences might be compromised. It was intimated by his Democratic opponents that he had acted rashly and thrust this question upon Congress. The immediate decision, the prompt burst of indignation, the speech delivered rapidly and without preparation,[1] seem the actions of an honest man. In the bitter debates he had with Democratic senators, he appears at times inspired by noble thoughts; as he went over the platitudes of his popular-sovereignty principle, there was a sound of sincerity and fair dealing. Popular sovereignty in 1854 was indeed a sham; yet the doctrine had a vital meaning when applied to the present state of affairs in Kansas. He spoke with candor, and exhibited a true appreciation of the correct principles of government.

He was too good a partisan not to know what he had undertaken when he set himself against the South and the Democratic machine of the North. He had served one and had had a hand in engineering the other long enough to know that it was not the primrose path he had begun to tread. At the close of the speech of December 9th, as he spoke of the possibility of his party relations being severed by the course he had marked out for himself, he grew deeply affected;[2] but he asserted emphatically that, come what may, he should follow the principle of popular sovereignty. For a statesman to head a revolt against his party required moral courage; and as this action of Douglas was a severe blow to the slave power, and probably insured Republican success in 1860, it would be gratifying to believe that he was prompted by noble as well as by interested motives.[3]

The Democratic party of 1857 was a powerful machine, strongly intrenched in all three departments of the government. No Democrat but one of rare courage and indomitable energy would have set himself in opposition to it. In

---

[1] See remarks of Douglas, Dec. 16th.

[2] See the *Liberator*, Dec. 18th.

[3] See a thoughtful article in the New York *Tribune* of July 12th, 1858, where the course and probable motives of Douglas are fairly discussed.

the North, before the Lecompton scheme was broached, no Democrat stood higher than Cass; he apparently represented the moderate element of the party. Foote says that Cass "confessed frankly his entire condemnation of Buchanan's conduct in the Lecompton matter."[1] But he did not publicly protest; and though he was rich and not dependent on his place, he held his portfolio, and registered the decrees of the slave power in the most pitiable despatches.

It is only by comparison with Buchanan and Cass that the conduct of Douglas can be seen in its true light. Four years before he had committed a grievous fault; he was now beginning the atonement.

After the speech of December 9th, the breach between Douglas and the administration was complete. Threats were given out that the patronage would be remorselessly used against those who followed the Illinois senator. The Southerners denounced him without stint, the hot-headed menacing him with personal violence.[2] The press controlled by the administration was bitter against him. Every pensioned letter-writer, said Douglas, intimates that I have "deserted the Democratic party and gone over to the Black Republicans;" and the report is circulated everywhere "that the President intends to put the knife to the throat of every man who dares to think for himself on this question and carry out his principles in good faith."[3] Different senators were set upon Douglas. Bigler, of Pennsylvania, made a personal defence of the President; Green, of Missouri, a labored technical argument; and Fitch, of Indiana, a bitter personal attack. The debate between Douglas and Fitch was spirited, and excited great interest. Douglas struck the key-note of the opposition to the Lecompton scheme when he said he regarded it "as a trick, a fraud upon the rights of the people."[4]

[1] Casket of Reminiscences, p. 117.
[2] Washington correspondence New York *Tribune*, Dec. 11th.
[3] See remarks of Douglas, Dec. 21st.
[4] This debate took place Dec. 22d.

The independent Democratic press sustained Douglas, and some public meetings were held to express approval. It was apparent before the new year that the Western Democracy would stand by him.[1]

In November, Governor Walker came to Washington on a leave of absence. He found that his action in throwing out the fraudulent returns, made under the auspices of the pro-slavery party, had lost him the favor of the administration. He was persistently opposed to the Lecompton policy, and nothing was left for him but to resign. His letter of resignation re-enforced powerfully the argument of Douglas. "I state it as a fact," he wrote, "based on a long and intimate association with the people of Kansas, that an overwhelming majority of that people are opposed" to the Lecompton Constitution, "and my letters state that but one out of twenty of the press of Kansas sustains it. . . . Any attempt by Congress to force this constitution upon the people of Kansas will be an effort to substitute the will of a small minority for that of an overwhelming majority of the people." Before concluding he made a passing allusion to "the peculiar circumstances and unexpected events which have modified the opinions of the President upon a point so vital as the submission of the constitution."[2]

Meanwhile, Stanton, who in the absence of Walker was acting governor, did effectual work for the free-State cause. The excitement at the result of the Lecompton convention was great. Threats were freely made by the people that they would not submit to such an outrage. There was one loud call on the governor to convene at once in extra session the territorial legislature, in which the free-State men had a majority. After some hesitation, Stanton yielded to the popular will. The free-State party considered the proposed election of the 21st of December as a sham, and would take

---

[1] See New York *Times*, Dec. 16th; Remarks of Douglas, Dec. 21st.

[2] This letter is dated Dec. 15th, Senate Docs., 1st Sess. 35th Cong., vol i. p. 122.

no part in it. The legislature, therefore, provided for an election to be held January 4th, 1858, at which a fair and proper vote might be taken on the constitution. When the news of Stanton's action reached Washington, he was at once removed and Denver appointed in his place.

The election decreed by the Lecompton convention took place. The vote stood: For the constitution with slavery, 6226; for the constitution without slavery, 569. Later investigation showed that 2720 of these votes were fraudulent.

On January 4th, 1858, the other election took place. The vote stood: For the constitution with slavery, 138; for the constitution without slavery, 24; against the constitution, 10,226.

A comparison of the two elections established a fact known to those best informed, that a handsome majority of the people in Kansas were in favor of a free State.

The territorial legislature was now master of the situation. When it began to investigate the election frauds, John Calhoun and his associates, who had been concerned in them, fled from the territory.[1]

Despite the anxious endeavors of the President to serve his masters, all was not harmony between him and the Southern men. There were lengths to which even he would not go. The propaganda wanted not only Kansas, but they cast longing eyes on Central America. William Walker, having failed in his first attempt to hold possession of Nicaragua, had gone on another filibustering expedition; but as soon as he began operations he and his party were arrested by Paulding, an American naval commander, and brought to the United States. Buchanan thought that Paulding, while acting from pure and patriotic motives, had committed a grave error. Yet although disapproving his action,

---

[1] See Reports of Committees, 1st Sess. 35th Cong., vol. iii.; Stanton's Address, Kansas Hist. Soc. Pub.; Spring's Kansas.

the President was none the less determined to execute the neutrality laws of the United States.[1]

"The Walker and Paulding imbroglio just now embarrasses us," wrote Alexander Stephens, who was the leader of the Lecomptonites in the House. "Our sympathies are all with the filibusters. We do not now agree with the administration on this Central-American question; but if we denounced it as we feel it deserves to be, we endanger their support of our views of the Kansas question." A little later he wrote: "The Walker-Paulding affair I look upon as a great outrage." The reason of the administration "line of policy and opposition to Walker was their hostility to his enterprise, because, if successful, he would introduce African slavery there."[2]

But Buchanan was loyal to the South in the Kansas affair. He was so obtuse that he could not see what one of his earliest and warmest Southern supporters plainly saw. Governor Wise, of Virginia, wrote a public letter December 30th, 1857, in which he took substantially the ground of Douglas and Walker. Three weeks later he wrote privately: "If Congress adopts that Lecompton schedule, Democracy is dead; and the administration can save it *now;* it cannot after that act. . . . The game of the disunionists is to drive off every Northern Democrat from Buchanan on the Kansas question. . . . and they will succeed unless the President alters his conclusions very soon. Walker, Douglas, and Forney are all nothing to me. I wish to serve and save the administration."[3]

The contest was wearing out Buchanan. Simonton wrote of him as "perplexed, harassed, and wearied," and subject to "eccentric outbursts of choler" when discussing Kansas affairs; that he abused the Illinois senator for having got the country into a predicament by his Kansas-Nebraska bill

---

[1] See special message of Jan. 7th, 1858.
[2] Letters of Jan. 3d and 20th, Johnston and Browne, p. 328.
[3] Wise to Robert Tyler, Letters and Times of the Tylers, vol. ii. p. 543.

and for now refusing to face its legitimate consequences.[1] Stephens went to see the President the 2d of February, and wrote: "He is run down and worn out with office-seekers and the cares which the consideration of public affairs has brought upon him. He is now quite feeble and wan. I was struck with his physical appearance; he appears to me to be failing in bodily health."[2]

On the 2d of February, Buchanan took the final step. He sent to Congress a copy of the Lecompton Constitution which he had received from John Calhoun, and a message recommending the admission of Kansas under that organic act. He argued that "the Lecompton convention, according to every principle of constitutional law, was legally constituted, and was invested with power to frame a constitution. . . . They did not think proper to submit the whole of this constitution to a popular vote, but they did submit the question whether Kansas should be a free or slave State to the people." This was "the all-important question." "Domestic peace will be the happy consequence of its admission." "It has been solemnly adjudged by the highest judicial tribunal known to our laws that slavery exists in Kansas by virtue of the Constitution of the United States. Kansas is therefore at this moment as much a slave State as Georgia or South Carolina. Without this the equality of the sovereign States composing the Union would be violated, and the use and enjoyment of a territory acquired by the common treasure of all the States would be closed against the people and the property of nearly half the members of the Confederacy."

What must Rufus Choate have thought as he read this message and remembered the glowing periods in which he had advocated the election of Buchanan! In the previous November, when the public began to see that the President

---

[1] Simonton to New York *Times*, Jan. 30th.
[2] Letter of Feb. 3d, Johnston and Browne, p. 329.

was about to throw himself into the arms of the South, Choate had begged Everett to write a series of papers that "would bless mankind and rescue Buchanan. I entreat you to give him and all conservative men an idea of a patriot administration. Kansas must be free, and the nation kept quiet and honest." [1]

Judge Elmore, a prominent pro-slavery man of Kansas and a member of the Lecompton convention, went to Washington, at the instance of Governor Denver, to urge the President not to send the Lecompton Constitution to Congress; he was furnished with a letter from the governor arguing strenuously against the proposed policy. Buchanan was sorry he had not had this information earlier, but he had already prepared his message and shown it to several senators; it must therefore go to Congress.[2]

It was a pitiable message to come from a Northern man. Pierce had served the South well, but it could now be truthfully said that Buchanan was serving her still better. When the web of subterfuge was brushed away, the position of the President amounted to this: It is determined by the slavery propaganda that Kansas shall be a slave State. There is now one more free than slave State in the Union, and Kansas is needed to restore the equilibrium. To make it a slave State by fair means is impossible. We have now a chance to make it one under the color of law, and this opportunity we are going to use to the best of our ability.

The President would have shrunk from such a statement of his reasoning. He was probably deluded by his own argument, but he did not deceive many. "I confess," Senator Hammond afterwards said, "my opinion was that the South herself should kick that constitution out of Congress."[3] "Scarcely a Democrat can be found who will attempt to

---

[1] Letter of Nov. 17th, Life of Choate, Brown, p. 344.
[2] Denver's address, Kansas Hist. Soc. Pub., vol. i. p. 170.
[3] Speech at Barnwell Court-house, S. C., Oct. 29th, 1858, Hammond's Speeches and Letters, p. 327.

vindicate the Lecompton movement *per se*," wrote Raymond from Washington.[1] " Every intelligent man with whom I have conversed," wrote Letcher from Kentucky to Crittenden, " thinks Douglas has the right on his side."[2]

The message of the President went to the committee on territories, and gave rise to three reports. That of the majority, presented by Green, was a lawyer's technical argument for an injustice. Collamer presented the Republican view, and his report was signed by Wade; while Douglas offered an unanswerable argument. " The Lecompton Constitution," he averred, " is not the act of the people of Kansas, and does not embody their will." By a " system of trickery in the mode of submission, a large majority, probably amounting to four-fifths of all the legal voters of Kansas, were disfranchised and excluded from the polls on the 21st of December;" and at the election of the 4th of January, a lawful and valid one, " a majority of more than ten thousand of the legal voters of Kansas repudiated and rejected the Lecompton Constitution."

The debate on the bill for the admission of Kansas under the Lecompton Constitution elicited little that has not been touched upon. The argument on one side was bare technicality, and on the other justice. Many of the Republican senators spoke; and Crittenden, of Kentucky, opposed the bill in a speech of power. The arguments of Southern senators were notable for the use they made of the Dred Scott decision. Benjamin, one of the ablest lawyers of the South, asserted: " It is obvious that since the decision of the Supreme Court of the United States in the Dred Scott case, it is decided that from the origin, all this agitation of the slavery question has been directed against the constitutional rights of the South ; and that both Wilmot provisos and Missouri-Compromise lines were unconstitutional."[3]

---

[1] To the New York *Times*, March 24th.
[2] Life of Crittenden, Coleman, p. 141.   [3] Speech of Feb. 8th.

Brown, of Mississippi, maintained that if Douglas had stood by the President, there would have been no agitation. " There would not have been a ripple on the surface," he said; " or if there had been, it would have subsided and died away in the great ocean of oblivion where other ripples have gone, and we should almost without an effort introduce Kansas into the Union. Sir, the senator from Illinois gives life, he gives vitality, he gives energy, he lends the aid of his mighty genius and his powerful will, to the opposition on this question." [1]

The remarks of Jefferson Davis deserve more than a passing allusion, as he was the ablest senator from the South, and was one of the triumvirate of Davis, Toombs, and Hunter, who assumed the direction of Southern affairs. Moreover, we see by means of his speech whither the South was drifting. Sick in body, he dragged his weak and attenuated frame to the Capitol in order to give vent to the extremest sentiments of his section. " A man not knowing into what presence he was introduced," said he, " coming into this Chamber, might, for a large part of this session, have supposed that here stood the representatives of belligerent States, and that instead of men assembled here to confer together for the common welfare, for the general good, he saw here ministers from States preparing to make war upon each other. . . . Sir, we are arraigned day after day as the aggressive power. What Southern senator during this whole session has attacked any portion or any interest of the North? In what have we now or ever, back to the earliest period of our history, sought to deprive the North of any advantage it possessed? The whole charge is, and has been, that we seek to extend our own institutions into the common territory of the United States. Well and wisely has the President of the United States pointed to that common territory as the joint possession of the country." . . . The Southern States " present a new problem,

---

[1] Speech of Feb. 4th.

one not stated by those who wrote on it in the earlier period of our history. It is the problem of a semi-tropical climate, the problem of malarial districts, of staple products. This produces a result different from that which would be found in the farming districts and cooler climates. A race suited to our labor exists there. Why should we care whether they go into other territories or not? Simply because of the war that is made against our institutions; simply because of the want of security which results from the action of our opponents in the Northern States. Had you made no political war upon us, had you observed the principles of our Confederacy as States, that the people of each State were to take care of their domestic affairs, or, in the language of the Kansas bill, to be left perfectly free to form and regulate their institutions in their own way, then, I say, within the limits of each State the population there would have gone on to attend to their own affairs, and have had little regard to whether this species of property or any other was held in any other portion of the Union. You have made it a political war. We are on the defensive. How far are you to push us?"[1]

The irreconcilable nature of the difference between the Southerners and Republicans was shown by a colloquy between Toombs and Wade. "The Wilmot-proviso man," said Toombs, "holds that you can prohibit slavery forever in the territories. That means that you can cram freedom, whether the people want it or not; but take care how you cram slavery." "That is it," promptly replied Wade.

The executive patronage was used to push the bill through Congress. The political guillotine was set in motion, and office-holders who sympathized with Douglas were removed without ceremony. The whole business of the Post-office department was said to be the turning-out of the apostates

---

[1] Remarks of Feb. 8th.

and supplying their places with the faithful.[1] There was, said Forney, "a series of proscriptions such as no civilized country has ever seen exercised upon independent men."[2]

As the contest thickened, the denunciation of Douglas grew more bitter at the South. "Traitor" was the favorite term applied to him. The Southern Democrats, wrote Raymond from Washington, "have transferred their hatred of the Republicans to him. . . . I have very little doubt that if compelled to choose between Douglas and Seward for President, the whole band of pro-slavery fire-eaters, with Toombs at their head, would vote for the latter."[3] The Washington *Union* called him "traitor," "renegade," and "deserter;"[4] but the *Liberator* praised him.[5]

The entire West was enthusiastic in the support of Douglas. In the Middle and Eastern States executive patronage and dictation were powerful enough to divide the sentiment of the party.[6] The Republicans were at first disposed to regard the fight as a factional contest, and they did not feel implicit confidence in Douglas; but as it went on, they confessed his boldness and consistency, and saw that, although his principles were different from theirs, both were battling in unison for freedom in Kansas. He was now the central figure of the country, and was compared to a lion holding his opponents at bay. In every debate he held his own, for he was more than a match for any of his opponents.

While the excitement in Washington was very great—perhaps greater than when the Missouri Compromise was repealed[7]—the agitation in the country did not approach the feeling aroused at the time the Kansas-Nebraska act

---

[1] New York *Times*, Feb. 5th, 16th, 23d; the *Independent*, March 18th; Life of Douglas, Sheahan, p. 387.

[2] Forney's testimony, Covode Committee Report, p. 296; Forney's Vindication, Philadelphia *Press*, Sept. 30th, 1858.

[3] New York *Times*, March 26th.

[4] See *Congressional Globe*, vol. xxxvii. p. 199. [5] See issue of Feb. 26th.

[6] See Pike's First Blows of the Civil War, p. 383.

[7] New York *Times*, Feb. 23d.

was pending. Sumner had resumed his seat in the Senate; he could not debate, but at important junctures he was able to vote. He wrote to Parker: "What is doing in Massachusetts? Is everybody asleep? No resolutions *vs.* Lecompton."[1] The reason of this comparative apathy was partly that the contest seemed to be one between Democratic factions, and partly that the public had grown weary of the Kansas question. Moreover, the public mind was not engrossed with politics. The hard times which followed the financial panic were the every-day consideration. A widespread religious revival also absorbed the attention and energy which would otherwise have been devoted to politics.[2]

The day before the vote was taken, Douglas rose from a sick-bed to make another bold and manly protest against the action proposed. He resented executive dictation, averring that he should vote according to his sense of duty, according to the will of his State, and according to the interests of his constituents.

March 23d, the bill for the admission of Kansas under the Lecompton Constitution passed the Senate by 33 yeas to 25 nays. Broderick of California, Pugh of Ohio, and Stuart of Michigan, Democrats, and Bell and Crittenden, Southern Americans, voted with Douglas and the Republicans in the negative. It was strange enough to see Douglas voting on a political question with Hale, Seward, Sumner, and Wade.

It now remains to consider the action of the House. The House was composed of one hundred and twenty-eight Democrats, ninety-two Republicans, and fourteen Americans, Orr, of South Carolina, being speaker. It was moved to refer the President's Lecompton message to a special committee of fifteen. This gave rise to a heated session, lasting all night. A violent altercation occurred between Keitt, of South Carolina, and Grow, of Pennsylvania. Keitt was the aggressor, and it was commonly reported that Grow knocked

---

[1] March 5th, Life of Parker, Weiss, vol. ii. p. 219.
[2] In a future volume I shall give an account of this revival.

him down; but the South Carolinian, in making an apology afterwards, said he was utterly unconscious of having received any blow.[1] Stephens wrote: "Last night we had a battle-royal in the House. Thirty men at least were engaged in the fisticuff. Fortunately no weapons were used. Nobody was hurt or even scratched, I believe; but bad feeling was produced by it. It was the first sectional fight ever had on the floor, I think; and if any weapons had been on hand it would probably have been a bloody one. All things here are tending to bring my mind to the conclusion that the Union cannot or will not last long."[2]

The political atmosphere of Washington was highly charged. Shortly after this affray in the House, Cameron, of Pennsylvania, and Green, of Missouri, had a controversy in the Senate, and each gave the other the lie. The Vice-President interfered with decision, and a personal encounter was prevented, but Green threatened to settle the affair five minutes after the Senate should adjourn.[3] But no challenge was sent, and the following day both gentlemen made the usual personal explanations. Out of this affair, however, grew an agreement between Cameron, Wade, and Chandler, in which they asserted that in the event of any Republican senator receiving gross personal abuse, they would make his cause their own and "carry the quarrel into a coffin."[4]

The President's message was afterwards referred to a select committee of fifteen in the House, and three reports were made representing the different shades of opinion. Stephens wrote the majority report, and averred that a large number of States would look upon the rejection of Kansas "with extreme sensitiveness, if not alarm." The

---

[1] See New York *Times* correspondence, Feb. 26th; *Congressional Globe*, vol. xxxvi. p. 623; Recollections of Mississippi, R. Davis, p. 371.

[2] Letter of Feb. 5th, Johnston and Browne, p. 329.

[3] *Congressional Globe*, vol. xxxvii. p. 110.

[4] See Life of Chandler, p. 144; Life of Wade, Riddle, p. 250.

Senate bill being under consideration, Montgomery, a Democrat of Pennsylvania, on the 1st of April, offered an amendment which was substantially the same as one which had been proposed by Crittenden in the Senate and which had been rejected by that body. It provided that the Lecompton Constitution should be submitted to a vote of the people of Kansas; if assented to, Kansas should become a State on the proclamation of the President; if rejected, the inhabitants of the territory were authorized and empowered to form a constitution and State government.

This amendment was carried in the House by a vote of 120 to 112. Every member but one was in his seat when the vote was taken:[1] ninety-two Republicans, twenty-two Democrats, and six Americans voted for the amendment; one hundred and four Democrats and eight Americans voted against it.[2]

The Senate would not accept this amendment; it asked for a committee of conference. The House voted to adhere, but agreed to the conference. In this committee, English, a representative from Indiana, who had voted for the Crittenden-Montgomery amendment, proposed a compromise which was agreed to, accepted by both Houses and became a law. This measure offered Kansas a large grant of government lands, and provided that the proposition should be voted on by the people of Kansas. If a majority voted for acceptance, Kansas should be admitted into the Union under the Lecompton Constitution by proclamation of the President. If the people rejected the offer, then the territory could not be admitted as a State until its population reached the number required for a representative. It was in effect a bribe of land to induce the people of Kansas to accept the Lecompton Constitution. The bill was acceptable to the Lecomptonites; Green, Hunter, and Stephens having, with English, signed the conference-committee report, while Seward and Howard dissented. When this measure was pre-

---

[1] New York *Independent*, April 8th.   [2] New York *Times*, April 2d.

sented, Douglas, according to Wilson, wavered.[1] In his speech he said he had hoped to find in it such provisions as would enable him to give it his support; but he did not consider it "a fair submission to the people under such circumstances as to insure an unbiassed election and fair returns."[2]

Douglas voted against the English bill, and so did Broderick, Stuart, and Crittenden, while Pugh sided with the majority. There were 31 yeas and 22 nays. Broderick gained laurels in the controversy. The adroit use of the patronage of the administration diminished gradually the number of Northern Democrats who had set out to oppose the Lecompton policy, but he remained steadfast and earnest. Forney regarded him as the soul of the little party; Wilson speaks of him as "ever brave and true;" and Seward wrote that the moral influence of Stuart and Broderick, especially Broderick, was prodigious.[3]

The English bill passed the House by a vote of 120 to 112; of the twenty-two anti-Lecompton Democrats twelve voted against it, while nine gave their votes in its favor, and one failed to record his vote. The administration and its agents had been busy in drumming up supporters. The Secretary of the Treasury was especially active.[4] The patronage of the government was used in an unblushing manner; large contracts for supplies for the military expedition to Utah were distributed to influence votes of representatives; and money was directly employed to aid in the passage of the measure.[5] Haskin, of New York, was tempted with the grant of a township of land, but he spurned the

---

[1] Rise and Fall of the Slave Power, vol. ii. p. 563; see also speech of Carl Schurz, Sept., 1860, Speeches, p. 169.   [2] Speech of April 29th.

[3] Forney's Anecdotes of Public Men, vol. i. p. 25; Rise and Fall of the Slave Power, vol. ii. p. 563; Seward to Pike, April 15, First Blows of the Civil War, p. 417.   [4] Casket of Reminiscences, Foote, p. 118.

[5] See Covode Committee Report and testimony of Wendell, Bean, and Walker; *Atlantic Monthly*, vol. iii. p. 478; Forney's Vindication, Philadelphia *Press*, Sept. 30th, 1858.

offer.[1] It would not be just to infer that all the anti-Lecompton Democrats who changed did so from interested motives, for Governor Walker gave an honest opinion in favor of the English bill;[2] and there were, undoubtedly, congressmen who regarded the matter from the same point of view. Nor were the patronage and money all used to secure the passage of the English measure, for from the time that the Lecompton Constitution was sent to Congress these agencies were at work on the members of the House to procure the adoption of the administration policy.

We may anticipate the chronological order of events and relate that on August 2d a vote was taken in Kansas in accordance with the act that had passed Congress; 13,088 votes were cast, and 11,300 of them were against the English proposition.[3] This disposed of the Lecompton Constitution, and effectually determined that slavery should not exist in Kansas. But the question left an irreconcilable breach in the Democratic party which was big with consequences for the Republicans and for the country.

---

[1] See letter of Haskin to Wilson, Rise and Fall of the Slave Power, vol. ii. p. 565.

[2] See letter to Congressmen Cox and Lawrence, April 27th, New York *Times*, May 4th.

[3] Spring's Kansas, p. 236.

CHAPTER X

IN the summer and fall of 1857, the prospects of the Republican party did not seem bright. There was a natural reaction from the high enthusiasm which characterized the campaign of the preceding year. The *Tribune* argued elaborately to prove that the Republican party was not dead, but admitted that the failure to achieve success in 1856 had caused a dropping-off of those who had gone into the movement, thinking it would carry the country and give them a chance at the offices.[1] In the Northwest, the outlook for the new party was especially gloomy.[2] The result of the fall elections all over the North was discouraging. A large falling-off of the Republican vote, due to apathy and the engrossing attention caused by the financial stringency, was nearly everywhere noted. It is undeniable that, until it became known that Douglas intended to oppose the policy of the administration, the future looked very unpromising for the Republicans. But after the contest was fairly entered upon, a general cheerfulness might be observed in Republican circles. Senator Wade wrote to Pike: "My opinion is that the end of the old Locofoco party is at hand. It gives 'signs of woe that all is lost.' They are hopelessly broken and must die. The party is in the same fix that the old Whig party was in on the repeal of the compromise—divided in the middle, North and South. I hope to be able, during the session, to preach its funeral sermon."[3] No mat-

---

[1] See New York *Weekly Tribune*, Aug. 6th.
[2] Life of Douglas, Sheahan, p. 383.
[3] Jan. 10th, 1858, First Blows of the Civil War, p. 378.

ter what might be the result, the fight could only inure to the benefit of the Republicans. The Republican party, said a New Orleans journal, "seemed on the brink of dissolution, but has recently been galvanized into renewed symptoms of vitality and vigor" by the apostasy of Stephen A. Douglas. And another said, "Only the other day the hopes of the Black Republicans were down to zero; now they are apparently up to vernal heat."[1]

When Republicans gathered together, president-making became a favorite topic of discussion. The names in every one's mouth, as possible candidates in 1860, were Seward, Frémont, Banks, Chase, or Bissell.[2] It was quite apparent that Seward thought the Republican nomination worth striving for; yet his course during the winter leaves one in doubt as to the theory upon which he was working. Indeed his career is full of inconsistencies. In 1850 he was the radical of radicals, and in the higher-law doctrine reached a more extreme position than he ever afterwards took; in 1854 he held back from the formation of the Republican party; with the advance in 1855 and 1856, he now veered round to the conservative side.

His course on the army bill was a surprise. On account of difficulties with the Mormons in Utah, that seemed to require an additional military force, it was proposed to increase the army. Seward, separating himself from all of his Republican friends except Cameron, supported the bill for this purpose. The main objection of the Republicans arose from the fear that the army would be improperly employed in Kansas. Seward's remarks in favor of the bill drew an indignant rebuke from Hale. "I have listened," Hale said, "with extreme pain and disappointment and mortification

---

[1] The New Orleans *Bee* and the New Orleans *Delta*, cited by Von Holst, vol. vi. p. 177.

[2] New York *Courier and Enquirer*, cited by the New York *Times*, Jan. 1st, 1858. Bissell had been elected governor of Illinois over Richardson in 1856.

to the speech which he has made—a pain equal to that with which I heard the great statesman of New England, Daniel Webster, some eight years ago, with the ripe honors of nearly threescore and ten years, bring himself and his fame and his reputation, and lay them down as an offering at the footstool of the slave power. . . . Is it a time for my friends, is it a time for the distinguished senator from New York, upon whom the eyes and the hearts of the friends of liberty have centred and clustered, when such dangerous and fatal and damnable doctrines are proclaimed and practised upon by the Executive of the United States, to vote seven thousand extra men to him?"

Seward said in reply: "I know nothing, I care nothing—I never did, I never shall—for party;" and then his optimism, ever a prominent feature of his character, broke forth. "I am very sorry," he exclaimed, "that the faith of the honorable senator from New Hampshire is less than my own. He apprehends continual disaster. He wants this battle continued and fought by skirmishes, and to deprive the enemy of every kind of supplies. Sir, I regard this battle as already fought; it is over. All the mistake is that the honorable senator and others do not know it. We are fighting for a majority of free States. They are already sixteen to fifteen; and whatever the administration may do—whatever anybody may do—before one year from this time we shall be nineteen to fifteen."[1]

Fessenden was disgusted, and on the day of this debate wrote confidentially: "Seward, I understand, is to make a speech for the bill. He is perfectly bedeviled. He will vote alone, so far as the Republicans are concerned; but he thinks himself wiser than all of us."[2]

---

[1] Seward reckoned on the admission of Minnesota, Oregon, and Kansas. This debate took place Feb. 2d.

[2] Fessenden to Pike, First Blows of the Civil War, p. 379. Seward wrote his son, Feb. 5th: "The onslaught upon me was a breaking-out of discontent among my associates. I treated it with kindness and without

Whether the course of Seward was dictated by a noble independence of party trammels, or whether he was trimming to catch the moderate element among the Republicans and Democrats at the North, it seems impossible to decide. In his speech on the Lecompton question, he gave his adhesion to the doctrine of popular sovereignty, and said that he would cheerfully co-operate with Douglas, Stuart, and Broderick, "these new defenders of the sacred cause in Kansas."[1]

This speech drew from Chase a mild protest. "I regretted," he wrote, "the apparent countenance you gave to the idea that the Douglas doctrine of popular sovereignty will do for us to stand upon for the present."[2] The expressions of Seward indicated a harmony of feeling between Douglas and the Republicans that at one time promised an important combination and perhaps a new party. Greeley was willing to go a great way in that direction, and possibly among the mixed motives for his course was the desire to head off Seward from the presidency. The letter of Greeley dissolving the firm of Seward, Weed, and Greeley had been written and delivered, but it had not been made public; yet one might see in the columns of the *Tribune* a studied distrust of the New York senator.[3] An inside rumor at Washington was current that the *Tribune* was for Douglas for President.[4] Those who knew Greeley's despair of electing a candidate on the straight Republican issue, and his intense predilection for an available man,[5] were quite ready to

---

feeling in my private conversation and bearing, and, on the whole, it has done no harm and much good. It needed this to avert the tendency of our party to make a false issue on this Mormon question."—Life of Seward, vol. ii. p. 335.

[1] March 3d, Seward's Works, vol. iv. p. 596.

[2] Letter of March 11th, Life of Chase, Warden, p. 343.

[3] See editorial in the New York *Times*, Feb. 9th.

[4] Letter of Israel Washburn to Pike, March 16th, First Blows of the Civil War, p. 403.

[5] Illustrating this, see letter of Greeley to George E. Baker, Life of Thurlow Weed, vol. ii. p. 255.

believe the report. Many Southerners were of the opinion that Douglas was willing to be the candidate of the Republicans.[1]

But Douglas was practical. A legislature was to be elected in Illinois this fall to choose a senator in his place, while the presidential contest was two years off. The friendly relations that existed during the winter between him and the Republicans, and their frequent conferences, had for a result that all the leading Eastern Republicans, nearly every senator, and many representatives were anxious that their party should make no opposition to Douglas in Illinois. Wilson, Burlingame, and Colfax were especially active in urging this policy.[2] Israel Washburn, a congressman from Maine, wrote confidentially that he was willing Douglas should be anything else but President.[3] Greeley and Bowles, with their powerful journals, warmly favored his return to the Senate, unopposed by the Republicans.[4]

The *Times*, which had been the New York city organ of Seward, thought the formation of a new party probable. It would be composed of Douglas Democrats and Republicans, who were not abolitionists, and Douglas would be its leader. This journal approved the purpose of Seward to act cordially with Douglas, and maintained that the recognition of the principle of popular sovereignty was all that was needed to allay the slavery agitation.[5]

---

[1] Speeches and writings of Clingman, p. 450.

[2] Rise and Fall of the Slave Power, vol. ii. p. 567; Life of Bowles, Merriam, vol. i. pp. 229 and 232; Life of Lincoln, Herndon, p. 394; Life of Colfax, Hollister, p. 119. See also speech of Kellogg, of Illinois, in the House, March 13th, 1860, Appendix to *Congressional Globe*, 1st Sess. 36th Cong., cited by Von Holst.

[3] Washburn to Pike, March 16th, First Blows of the Civil War, p. 403.

[4] Life of Bowles, Merriam, vol. i. p. 229; Recollections of a Busy Life, Greeley, p. 358; New York *Tribune*, June 24th; see also Life of J. R. Giddings, Julian, p. 351.

[5] See New York *Times*, March 5th, Feb. 9th, and April 27th.

Seward, however, had no mind to stand aside for Douglas; but the notion then prevalent, that success could not be achieved on the radical platform of 1856, had probably lodged in his brain. Moreover, no lawyer could have the same confidence in the principle of congressional prohibition of slavery in the territories, after the Dred Scott decision, that he had before. It may be that Seward thought he could use Douglas for his own benefit and that of the country. He told Herndon there was no danger of the Republicans taking up Douglas, for they could not "place any reliance on a man so slippery;"[1] and his personal friend, James Watson Webb, denied in June that Seward was in favor of the return of Douglas to the Senate.[2]

It is nevertheless true that in the spring of 1858, Douglas was the best-known and most popular man at the North, where his popular-sovereignty doctrine was deemed a wonderful political invention that was certain to settle the slavery question in the interest of freedom.[3]

Chase, who had the preceding year been elected a second time governor of Ohio, protested, in an emphatic letter, against the tendency of the prominent Eastern Republicans. "That Douglas acted boldly, decidedly, effectively, I agree," he wrote; "that he has acted in consistency with his own principle of majority-sovereignty, I also freely admit. For his resistance to the Lecompton bill as a gross violation of his principle, and to the English bill for the same reason, he has my earnest thanks. I cannot forget, however, that he has steadily avowed his equal readiness to vote for the admission of Kansas as a slave or a free State, . . . and that he has constantly declared his acquiescence in the Dred Scott decision."[4]

---

[1] This was probably some time in March. See Life of Lincoln, Herndon, p. 394.
[2] History of Lincoln, Nicolay and Hay, vol. ii. p. 139.
[3] As illustrating this, see Political Recollections, Julian, p. 166.
[4] Chase to Pike, May 12th, First Blows of the Civil War, p. 419.

But more important still, the Republicans of Illinois, under the lead of Abraham Lincoln, their candidate for senator, protested.

We have already had glimpses of Lincoln; it is now time to describe him more fully. His mother, a daughter of a Virginia and Kentucky planter, was a woman of strong intellect. Herndon reports a conversation, in which Lincoln said that she was a natural child and he had inherited from her his mental power; but there is good reason for believing that she was born in wedlock.[1] His father was a shiftless, poor white of Kentucky, who was taught by his wife to read painfully and write clumsily. Abraham Lincoln's family moved to Indiana when he was seven; when he had just passed his twenty-first birthday, they forsook Indiana and settled in Illinois.

When he was nominated for President, a Chicago journalist, desiring to write a campaign biography, asked him for facts concerning his early life. "It can all be condensed," he replied, "into a single sentence, and that sentence you will find in Gray's 'Elegy':

"'The short and simple annals of the poor.'"[2]

His school education was meagre, his business ventures unprofitable. He neglected his shop to read Shakespeare and Burns, and preferred discussing politics with his customers to selling them goods; but he had a fine sense of honor in money matters, and was scrupulous in discharging debts which the mismanagement and misfortune of others threw upon him. He studied law, and at the age of twenty-eight began practice; but he loved politics better than law. In his study of the one and his devotion to the other may be seen the efforts at self-education that made up in some degree his lack of scholastic training.

Lincoln was not a reader of wide range, but he studied thoroughly the Bible and Shakespeare. The moral, philosophic, and literary quality of these works so permeated his

---

[1] Nancy Hanks, Hitchcock.   [2] Herndon, p. 2.

soul and gave such vigor to his speech that it might be said of him, "Beware of the man of one book." Learning the surveyor's art as a means of livelihood, he nurtured at the same time his innate love of mathematics, and later, in private study, he mastered the six books of Euclid. The Bible, Shakespeare, and Euclid furnished strong mental discipline, and were perhaps the best of all books for self-education. Lincoln's emotional nature was touched by the poems of Burns, and by others written in his own day. He delighted in the physical sciences, and liked fiction, but cared little for history, and thought biographies were lies.

"The life of the streets" taught Lincoln, as it did Socrates.[1] He loved and believed in the common people, but the common people whom he amused with his anecdotes were American-born and country and village residents. Thinking that the finest humor could be found among the lower orders of the country people, he garnered up their jokes for use on a larger stage. The stories he told to the admiring and gaping crowd of the tavern were of the bar-room order; if witty, it mattered not to him that they were broad. Loving leisure, he might have been called in those days (1830–1835) a loafer; but his personal morals remained unscathed. He used neither liquor nor tobacco, although he took pleasure in a horse-race and a cock-fight.

Lincoln, like Socrates, was odd in his personal appearance, though with a different grotesqueness of exterior. And to Lincoln, as to Socrates, were denied the felicity of domestic life and the pleasures of a quiet home. He loved the practice of law on the circuit, where he had the constant and congenial society of brother attorneys; and when Sunday came, instead of going home as did his companions, he lingered to pursue his Socratic studies among the loungers of the tavern. But after beginning the study of law and interesting himself in politics, he found that while he had

---

[1] This comparison is suggested by a thoughtful review in the *Nation* of the Life of Lincoln by Herndon, vol. xlix. p. 173.

ideas, it was necessary to grope about for words to express them. He therefore took time from his beloved mathematics to give to the study of grammar.

Devotion to politics made him a member of the Illinois legislature; and in 1837, with one associate only, he made a protest against certain resolutions which had passed maintaining "that the right of property in slaves is sacred to the slave-holding States." These two caused to be spread upon the journal their opinion that slavery was "founded on both injustice and bad policy." Six years before, Lincoln made his second visit to New Orleans, and while the remarks put into his mouth, that the iron of slavery had run into him then and there, and when he got a chance he would hit it hard, are apocryphal, he was without doubt profoundly moved by his glimpses of chattel slavery.[1]

Keenly appreciating humor, he was yet subject to deep fits of melancholy. The humorist afterwards known as Petroleum V. Nasby saw him for the first time in 1858, and thought his the saddest face he had ever looked upon. In spite of his life passing, as it were, open to public gaze, Lincoln was reticent about the deepest feelings of his nature, and had hardly a friend to whom he opened his whole soul. His searching self-examination calls to mind Marcus Aurelius. He was simple, candid, kind, but rarely praised another. Deemed physically lazy, he was intellectually energetic, and had great power of application. Reading few books, he thought long and carefully on what he read; his opinions were wrought out by severe study and patient reflection.

In 1846 he was elected to Congress, and gratified his hatred of slavery, during the single term he served, by voting for the Wilmot proviso forty-two times. His two years at Washington made him realize the power which a knowledge of literature gives a man in public life. Afterwards, in travelling on the circuit, he carried, besides his constant com-

---

[1] Miss Tarbell's *Early Life of Lincoln*, p. 112; Lincoln, *Complete Works*, Vol. I., p. 641.

panion Euclid, a copy of Shakespeare, to the study of which he again assiduously devoted himself.

He reached eminent rank in his profession, being esteemed the strongest jury-lawyer in the State; but he was a bad advocate in an unjust cause. His clearness of statement was remarkable, and his undoubted sincerity carried conviction.

The repeal of the Missouri Compromise diverted Lincoln's attention from law to politics. Prominent in the Illinois canvass of 1854, he became, on the election of an anti-Nebraska legislature, a candidate for United States senator. But there were five anti-Nebraska Democrats whose choice was Lyman Trumbull. These would not, under any circumstances, vote for Lincoln or another Whig. Although he could control forty-seven votes, which was within four of the necessary number to elect, yet, rather than risk the election of a Democrat, he, with rare judgment and magnanimity, advised his friends to go for Trumbull, who accordingly was chosen on the tenth ballot.

Lincoln felt deep disappointment at failing to secure the coveted place, for his ambition was great. When a young man, in a fit of profound depression, he said to the most intimate friend he ever had: "I have done nothing to make any human being remember that I have lived. To connect my name with events of my day and generation, and so impress myself upon them as to link my name with something that will redound to the interest of my fellow-men, is all that I desire to live for."[1] From that time on he had thirsted for fame. He would gladly feed on popularity, and had confidence in his ability to do mighty things, should the opportunity offer. Yet his speech was modest. In the debates of 1858 with Douglas, when seemingly overtopped by the greatness of his rival, his expressions of self-depreciation were so marked as now to strike one painfully, even as with a dim suggestion of the humbleness of Uriah Heep.

How keenly he felt his failure to obtain a hearing is illus-

---

[1] Herndon, p. 217.

trated by an occurrence in 1857. Associated with Edwin M. Stanton and George Harding in a case of great importance that was to be tried in the United States Circuit Court before Judge McLean at Cincinnati, it lay between Lincoln and Stanton as to who should make the second argument. It was finally decided in favor of the Pennsylvanian. Lincoln thought Stanton purposely ignored him and treated him with rudeness; while Stanton was little impressed with the ability of the other, whose appearance, manner, and garb, suited perhaps to the prairie, were but ill adapted for intercourse with the serious attorneys and grave judges of the East.[1]

Ungainly as Lincoln appeared, he had the instincts of a gentleman. In a speech at Springfield this year he said: I shall never be a gentleman "in the outside polish, but that which constitutes the inside of a gentleman I hope I understand, and am not less inclined to practise than others."[2]

When Lincoln entered upon political life he became reticent regarding his religious opinions, for at the age of twenty-five, influenced by Thomas Paine and Volney, he had written an extended essay against Christianity with a view to its publication. A far-seeing friend, however, took the manuscript from him and consigned it to the flames. At the period that our story covers, Lincoln did not believe in the inspiration of the Scriptures or the divinity of Christ, and in moments of gloom, or when wrestling with deep reflection, he doubted the existence of a personal God and a future life. The religious writer whom he chiefly read, and whose influence he felt most, was Theodore Parker. The argument in Chambers's "Vestiges of the Creation" struck him with force; his scientific mind laid fast hold of the doctrine of evolution hinted at in that famous work.

Standing out beyond all other characteristics of Lincoln, manifesting itself in private life, in business, during legal

---

[1] See Herndon, p. 353. The case involved the McCormick Reaper patent, and it had been understood by Lincoln that Harding, a very eminent patent lawyer of Philadelphia, was to make the "mechanical argument."

[2] Speech at Springfield, July 17th, 1858.

consultation, in forensic contest, and illuminating his strife for political place and power, is his love of truth and justice. When twenty-four years old he was called "honest Abe." At no time, and in no circumstances of his life, did he do aught that threw the faintest taint of suspicion upon this title spontaneously given in a rude village of Illinois.

Such was Lincoln at the age of forty-nine, when he stood forth to contest the senatorship with the most redoubtable debater of the country. He and Douglas had first met in 1834, and the rivalry between them, begun early, did not end until 1860. Both aspired to the hand of the same woman, and Lincoln's manly and rugged qualities proved more attractive than the fascinations of the eloquent and dashing Douglas. Yet in the race for political preferment, Douglas far outstripped the other. Though four years younger, he went to Congress four years earlier; and when Lincoln was a representative, he was a senator, with apparently many years of political honors before him. This greater success was largely due to the fact that Douglas belonged to the dominant party in Illinois. In 1858, Douglas had a great national reputation, while Lincoln's name had only begun to reach beyond the confines of his own State.[1] Douglas, however, knew his rival better than did the people of the East. On hearing that Lincoln would be his opponent, he said to Forney: "I shall have my hands full. He is the strong man of his party—full of wit, facts, dates—and the best stump-speaker, with his droll ways and dry jokes, in

---

[1] My authorities for this characterization of Lincoln are the Life by Herndon; the History by Nicolay and Hay; the biographies of Lamon, Arnold, Holland, Raymond, and Stoddard; and the Reminiscences published by the *North American Review*. On his religious views especially, see Herndon, p. 435 *et seq.*; Lamon, pp. 486, 496, 499; and for a different view from that taken in the text, though relating to a later period of Lincoln's career, see Holland, p. 236; Nicolay and Hay, vol. vi. p. 339; Arnold, p. 179; Recollections of President Lincoln, by L. E. Chittenden, pp. 219, 223, 382, 428, and chapter xlvi.; see also *The Nation*, June 4th, 1891.

the West. He is as honest as he is shrewd; and if I beat him, my victory will be hardly won."[1] Douglas, in his first speech of the campaign, paid to Lincoln a generous compliment. "I have known," said he, "personally and intimately, for about a quarter of a century, the worthy gentleman who has been nominated for my place, and I will say that I regard him as a kind, amiable, and intelligent gentleman, a good citizen, and an honorable opponent."[2]

The Republican State Convention, meeting at Springfield, June 16th, unanimously nominated Lincoln as the senatorial candidate of the party. He addressed the delegates in the most carefully prepared speech he had ever made.[3] Fully aware for some time previous what the action of the convention would be, he had thought earnestly on the principles he should lay down as the key-note of the campaign. As ideas occurred to him, he wrote them down on scraps of paper, and when the convention drew near, after weighing every thought, scrutinizing each sentence, and pondering every word, he fused them together into a connected whole. Esteeming that this would be for him a pregnant opportunity, he paid great attention to the art as well as the matter of his discourse. Drawing inspiration from a careful reading of the greatest of American orations, he modelled the beginning of his speech after Webster's exordium.[4]

Lincoln began: "If we could first know where we are and whither we are tending, we could better judge what to do and how to do it. We are now far into the fifth year since a policy was initiated with the avowed object, and confident promise, of putting an end to slavery agitation. Under the operation of that policy, that agitation has not only not ceased, but has constantly augmented. In my opinion, it will not cease until a crisis shall have been reached and

---

[1] Forney's Anecdotes of Public Men, vol. ii. p. 179.
[2] Douglas at Chicago, July 9th, Lincoln and Douglas Debates, p. 9.
[3] Nicolay and Hay, vol. ii. p. 136.
[4] Herndon, pp. 397 and 400.

passed. 'A house divided against itself cannot stand.' I believe this government cannot endure permanently half slave and half free. I do not expect the Union to be dissolved—I do not expect the house to fall—but I do expect it will cease to be divided. It will become all one thing or all the other. Either the opponents of slavery will arrest the further spread of it, and place it where the public mind shall rest in the belief that it is in the course of ultimate extinction; or its advocates will push it forward till it shall become alike lawful in all the States, old as well as new—North as well as South." [1]

No Republican of prominence and ability had advanced so radical a doctrine. Lincoln knew that to commit the party of his State to that belief was an important step, and ought not to be taken without consultation and careful reflection. He first submitted the speech to his friend and partner, Herndon. Stopping at the end of each paragraph for comments, when he had read, "A house divided against itself cannot stand," Herndon said: "It is true, but is it wise or politic to say so?" Lincoln replied: "That expression is a truth of all human experience, 'A house divided against itself cannot stand.' . . . I want to use some universally known figure expressed in simple language as universally well known, that may strike home to the minds of men in order to raise them up to the peril of the times; I do not believe I would be right in changing or omitting it. I would rather be defeated with this expression in the speech, and uphold and discuss it before the people, than be victorious without it."

When we consider Lincoln's restless ambition, his yearning for the senatorship, and his knowledge that he was starting on an untrodden path, there is nobility in this response. Two years before he had incorporated a similar avowal in a speech, and had struck it out in obedience to the remonstrance of a political friend. Now, however, actuated by

---

[1] Lincoln-Douglas Debates, p. 1.

devotion to principle, and perhaps feeling that the startling doctrine of 1858 would ere long become the accepted view of the Republican party, he was determined to speak in accordance with his own judgment. Yet as he wanted to hear all that could be said against it, he read the speech to a dozen of his Springfield friends, and invited criticism. None of them approved it. Several severely condemned it. One said it was "a fool utterance," another that the doctrine was "ahead of its time," while a third argued that "it would drive away a good many voters fresh from the Democratic ranks." Herndon, who was an abolitionist, alone approved it, and exclaimed: "Lincoln, deliver that speech as read, and it will make you President."

After listening patiently to the criticisms of his friends, who ardently desired his political advancement, he told them that he had carefully studied the subject and thought on it deeply. "Friends," said he, "this thing has been retarded long enough. The time has come when these sentiments should be uttered; and if it is decreed that I should go down because of this speech, then let me go down linked to the truth—let me die in the advocacy of what is just and right."[1]

After his startling exordium, Lincoln described the advance made by the cause of slavery in virtue of the Dred Scott decision, related how different events led up to the announcement of the opinion of this court, and intimated by his well-known allegory that there was a conspiracy among high parties in the State.[2] He then addressed himself to the argument now frequently maintained, that the slave power could be best opposed by Republicans enrolling themselves under the leadership of Senator Douglas. "There are those who denounce us openly to their own friends," said he, "and yet whisper us softly that Senator Douglas is the aptest instrument there is" to overthrow "the power of the present political dynasty.... They wish us to *infer* all

---

[1] See Herndon, pp. 398, 400.   [2] See p. 270.

from the fact that he now has a little quarrel with the present head of the dynasty; and that he has regularly voted with us on a single point upon which he and we have never differed. They remind us that he is a great man, and that the largest of us are very small ones. Let this be granted. But 'a living dog is better than a dead lion.' Judge Douglas, if not a dead lion for this work, is at least a caged and toothless one. How can he oppose the advance of slavery? He does not care anything about it. His avowed mission is impressing the public heart *to care nothing about it.* . . . He has done all in his power to reduce the whole question of slavery to one of a mere right of property. . . . Clearly he is not now with us—he does not pretend to be, he does not promise ever to be.

"Our cause, then, must be intrusted to, and conducted by, its own undoubted friends — those whose hands are free, whose hearts are in the work—who *do care* for the result. Two years ago the Republicans of the nation mustered over thirteen hundred thousand strong. We did this under the single impulse of resistance to a common danger, with every external circumstance against us. Of strange, discordant, even hostile elements, we gathered from the four winds, and formed and fought the battle through, under the constant hot fire of a disciplined, proud, and pampered enemy. Did we brave all then to falter now?—now when that same enemy is wavering, dissevered, and belligerent? The result is not doubtful. We shall not fail—if we stand firm, *we shall not fail.* Wise counsels may accelerate or mistakes delay it, but, sooner or later, the victory is sure to come."[1]

On the 9th of July, Douglas reached his Chicago home. He had a magnificent and enthusiastic reception, in striking contrast to the one of four years previous. It was a worthy tribute on account of the determined fight he had made against the administration; nor was the friendly feel-

---

[1] Lincoln-Douglas Debates, pp. 4, 5.

ing towards him confined to the Democrats. Besides his present political popularity, his hold on Chicago people was strong, for he was an eminent citizen of this city of enterprise, devoted to its prosperity, and giving gages of his faith by large investments in its real estate. He was generous, too, and had made a gift of ten acres of valuable land to be used as the site for the University of Chicago. Chicago on this day delighted to do honor to its distinguished citizen, and Douglas was proud of his "magnificent welcome."

His speech was in his best manner. He exulted that the Lecompton battle had been won, and that the Republicans had come around to the doctrine of popular sovereignty. In arguments that are familiar to my readers, he vindicated this principle, and pointed to his record from 1854 as displaying consistency and fidelity. He complimented Lincoln personally[1] and then seized upon his "house-divided-against-itself" doctrine to show the issue that lay between them. With much ingenuity he construed this declaration to mean a desire for uniformity of local institutions all over the country, and as an attack upon State sovereignty and personal liberty. In truth, Douglas averred, "Variety in all our local and domestic institutions is the great safeguard of our liberties." The direct and unequivocal issue between Lincoln and himself was: "He goes for uniformity in our domestic institutions, for a war of sections until one or the other shall be subdued; I go for the great principle of the Kansas-Nebraska bill, the right of the people to decide for themselves."

In regard to Lincoln's criticism of the Dred Scott decision, Douglas said: "I have no idea of appealing from the decision of the Supreme Court upon a constitutional question to the decisions of a tumultuous town meeting;" and "I am free to say to you that, in my opinion, this government of ours is founded on the white basis. It was made by the white man, for the benefit of the white man, to be

---

[1] See p. 314.

administered by white men in such manner as they should determine."[1]

Lincoln heard this speech, and the next evening replied to it. But his argument was much inferior in force and in diction to that of his speech at Springfield; it showed a want of careful preparation, without which he was never at his best. Douglas replied to him at Bloomington, July 16th, and had much to say about the doctrine of the "house divided against itself." It invited, he maintained, a warfare of the States. Lincoln "has taken his position," he continued, "in favor of sectional agitation and sectional warfare. I have taken mine in favor of securing peace, harmony, and good-will among all the States."[2] In this speech, Douglas praised the New York *Tribune* and the Republicans for the course they had taken during the last session of Congress.

At Springfield, the next day, Lincoln rejoined. He declared that the doctrine of popular sovereignty, as expounded by Douglas, was "the most arrant humbug that had ever been attempted on an intelligent community." He denied the charge that he invited a war of sections. He had only expressed his expectation as to the logical result of the existence of slavery in the country, and not his wish for such an outcome. Moreover, he had again and again expressly disclaimed the intention of interference with slavery in the States. He then charged Douglas himself with being the cause of the present agitation. "Although I have ever been opposed to slavery," said he. "up to the introduction of the Nebraska bill I rested in the hope and belief that it was in the course of ultimate extinction. For that reason it had been a minor question with me. I might have been mistaken; but I had believed, and now believe, that the whole public mind—that is, the mind of the great majority —had rested in that belief up to the repeal of the Missouri Compromise." He again criticised the Dred Scott decision and exclaimed: "I adhere to the Declaration of Indepen-

---

[1] Lincoln-Douglas Debates, pp. 10, 11, 12.   [2] Ibid., p. 31.

dence. If Judge Douglas and his friends are not willing to stand by it, let them come up and amend it. Let them make it read that all men are created equal except negroes."[1]

The opening notes of the campaign were favorable to Douglas. Coming to his home with well-won prestige, the hearty and sincere reception of Chicago seemed to foreshadow that the people of Illinois would say by their votes in November, "Well done, good and faithful servant." The usual means to rouse campaign enthusiasm were not lacking, and at every place he had an ovation. Cannon thundered out a welcome, bands of music greeted him, every evening meeting ended with a display of fireworks. Special trains were at his disposal, and committees of escort attended his every movement. In the decorations of the locomotive that hauled his train and the car on which he rode, on every triumphal arch under which he passed in the cities that welcomed him, and on the banners borne in the processions that turned out to do him honor, was emblazoned the motto "Popular Sovereignty." Money was not lacking to produce the blare and flare of the campaign; for, lavish himself, and mortgaging his Chicago real-estate for means to meet his large expenses, Douglas felt free to accept the contributions of liberal friends.[2]

Lincoln's "house-divided-against-itself" declaration was received with joy by the Democrats. By the Republican party workers it was deemed a great mistake. To them, at best, the contest seemed unequal. Their candidate had no right to handicap himself by the assertion of a principle far in advance of his party and of what the occasion demanded. It was apparent to Lincoln and his advisers that the current was setting against him; nevertheless, he had not the slight-

---

[1] Lincoln-Douglas Debates, pp. 57, 59, 60, 63.
[2] See Life of Douglas, Sheahan; Life of Douglas, by H. M. Flint; Lincoln-Douglas Debates, p. 55.

est regret for the positive manifesto he had put forth. Thinking that the adroit and plausible Douglas could be better answered if they spoke from the same platform, it was determined that Lincoln should challenge him to a series of joint debates. The challenge was accepted and the arrangement made for seven meetings—one in each congressional district, except those districts containing Chicago and Springfield, where both had already spoken.

The places selected were Ottawa and Freeport, which were in strong Republican districts, whose congressmen were Lovejoy and Washburne; Galesburg, representing a locality of moderate Republican strength; Quincy and Charleston, situated in districts that gave fair Democratic majorities; and Alton and Jonesboro, strong Democratic localities. Jonesboro was in what was known as "Egypt;" it gave that year to John A. Logan, the Democratic candidate for congressman, more than 13,000 majority.

In 1856 the vote in Illinois was: For Buchanan, 105,348; for Frémont, 96,189; and for Fillmore, 37,444. The Republican hope of success lay in securing a large proportion of the vote that had been cast for Fillmore. Northern Illinois, in conformity with the general trend of Western settlement, had been peopled from New England, New York, and northern Ohio, and was strongly Republican; while southern Illinois, receiving its population mainly from Virginia and Kentucky, was as strongly Democratic. The central part of this State was the battle-ground. Douglas had an advantage in that eight of the twelve State senators holding over were Democrats; moreover, the legislative apportionment was based on the census of 1850, but the State census of 1855 had shown a much larger proportional increase in the northern part of the State than in the southern.

Lincoln must win the favor of the abolitionists of whom Lovejoy was a type, of the moderate Republicans, and of the old-line Whigs and Americans. He must contend against the opposition of many Eastern Republicans, of whom Greeley was the most outspoken, and against the lukewarmness of others.¹ But as the canvass proceeded and the issue became clearly defined, the New York *Tribune* could not consistently do aught but give Lincoln a hearty support.²

Appreciating the importance of the old Whig vote, and hoping that his former devotion to that party and its principles would prove a potent influence to attract support, Lincoln was grieved when he learned that Senator Crittenden, of Kentucky, whom he highly esteemed, was favorable to the election of Douglas, and would not remain silent when asked for sympathy.³ Douglas also tried to win the favor of the old-line Whigs, and he gladly referred to his efforts when he "acted side by side with the immortal Clay and the godlike Webster" in favor of the compromise measures of 1850.⁴

It seemed at first as if it would be a desperate struggle to keep intact the Democratic vote; for while Douglas had the machinery of the party and practically all of the Democratic press, the patronage of the administration was powerfully used against him. The proscription of Douglas Democrats holding office was relentless. The organ of the administration saw little choice between Lincoln and Douglas, and thought that true Democrats stood in the position of the woman who looked on at the fight between her husband and the bear.⁵ The rancor of Buchanan against Douglas had by no means abated with the adjournment of Congress, and it was whispered that the bitter abuse of the Little Giant in the editorial columns of the *Union* was directly inspired by the President from his summer retreat. The administration party had legislative tickets in nearly every

---

¹ See Nicolay and Hay, vol. ii. p. 140; Herndon, pp. 391 and 413; and the file of the New York *Times* during the contest.
² See editorial in New York *Tribune*, July 12th, and the file of that paper to the end of the campaign.
³ Life of Crittenden, Coleman, vol. ii. p. 162.
⁴ Lincoln-Douglas Debates, p. 39.
⁵ Washington *Union*, Aug. 28th.

district, and while they avowed that their object and hope were to elect enough members to hold the balance of power and secure an administration Democrat for senator, every one knew that the only appreciable result of their action was to divide the Democratic party and help the Republicans.[1]

Douglas several times spoke bitterly of the war that was made upon him within his party. "The Washington *Union*," he said on one occasion, "is advocating Mr. Lincoln's claim to the Senate. . . . There is an alliance between Lincoln and his supporters, and the federal office-holders of this State and presidential aspirants out of it, to break me down at home."[2] In the last debate, referring to the trouble between Douglas and the administration, Lincoln declared: "All I can say now is to recommend to him and to them to prosecute the war against one another in the most vigorous manner. I say to them, 'Go it, husband! Go it, bear!'"[3]

The two leaders met first at Ottawa, August 21st. That Lincoln was willing to pit himself against Douglas in joint debate showed an abiding confidence in his cause and in his ability to present it. For he had to contend with the ablest debater of the country, the man who in senatorial discussion had overmastered Seward, Chase, and Sumner, and who more recently had discomfited the champions of Lecompton. Lincoln had less of the oratorical gift than Douglas, and he lacked the magnetism that gave the Little Giant such a personal following. Tall, lean, gaunt, and awkward, his appearance as he rose to speak was little fitted to win the sympathy of his hearers. "When he began speaking," writes Herndon, "his voice was shrill, piping, and unpleasant. His manner, attitude, his dark, yellow face, wrinkled and dry, his oddity of pose, his diffident movements"[4] — all seemed

---

[1] Life of Douglas, Sheahan, p. 431.
[2] At Freeport, Lincoln-Douglas Debates, p. 105.
[3] At Alton, ibid., p. 223. [4] Life of Lincoln, p. 406.

against him. But when he got into the heart of his subject, he forgot his ungainly appearance; his soul, exalted by dwelling upon his cause, illumined his face with earnestness, making it lose "the sad, pained look due to habitual melancholy;"[1] and his voice and gestures became effective. From every speech of Lincoln breathed forth sincerity and devotion to right. Whatever other impressions were received by the crowds who gathered to hear him in the summer and fall of 1858, they were at one in the opinion that they had listened to an honest man.

The conditions of the Ottawa debate were that Douglas should open with an hour's speech, Lincoln to follow for one hour and a half, and Douglas to have thirty minutes to close. In the succeeding debates, the time occupied was the same, but the privilege of opening and closing alternated between the two speakers.

In the speech beginning the discussion, Douglas again sneered at the "house-divided-against-itself" doctrine, charged Lincoln with being an abolitionist because he had opposed the Dred Scott decision and had construed the "all-men-are-created-equal" clause of the Declaration of Independence to include the negro. "I do not believe," declared Douglas, "that the Almighty ever intended the negro to be the equal of the white man. . . . He belongs to an inferior race, and must always occupy an inferior position."[2]

In calling Lincoln an abolitionist at Ottawa, it was not wholly for the effect it would have on the immediate audience—for the district that sent Lovejoy to Congress, and the people who cheered the doctrine of the "divided house" when Douglas repeated it to condemn it,[3] were not to be affected by that name—but it was rather for the wider audience who would read the speeches in print. If Douglas could fasten on Lincoln the name abolitionist, it would have

---

[1] Ibid., p. 405.
[2] Lincoln-Douglas Debates, p. 71.   [3] Ibid., p. 70.

an influence in the central part of the State, where the old-line Whigs might turn the scale either way. The Illinois abolitionist differed from those who acknowledged Garrison and Phillips as their leaders, in that he believed in political action, and was not a disunionist; yet political definitions are frequently confused, and if a man were deemed an abolitionist, it would not be unnatural to think that he subscribed to Garrison's dogmas — "The United States Constitution is a covenant with death and an agreement with hell," and "No Union with slave-holders." In Illinois as a whole, and, for that matter, generally throughout the North, it was a bar to political preferment to be known as an abolitionist.

Lincoln was not, however, in any sense of the word an abolitionist. He quoted from his Peoria speech of 1854 to show exactly his position, then added: "I have no purpose to introduce political and social equality between the white and the black races. There is a physical difference between the two which, in my judgment, will probably forever forbid their living together upon the footing of perfect equality; and inasmuch as it becomes a necessity that there must be a difference, I, as well as Judge Douglas, am in favor of the race to which I belong having the superior position. I have never said anything to the contrary; but I hold that, notwithstanding all this, there is no reason in the world why the negro is not entitled to all the natural rights enumerated in the Declaration of Independence—the right to life, liberty, and the pursuit of happiness. I hold that he is as much entitled to these as the white man."[1] He continued in the strain, and in almost the words, of his Springfield speech of 1857.[2]

Lincoln replied to the criticism on his "house-divided-against-itself" doctrine. "The great variety of the local institutions in the States," said he, "springing from differences in the soil, differences in the face of the country and in the climate, are bonds of union. They do not make 'a

---

[1] Lincoln-Douglas Debates, p. 75.   [2] See p. 266.

house divided against itself,' but they make a house united. If they produce in one section of the country what is called for by the wants of another section, and this other section can supply the wants of the first, they are not matters of discord, but bonds of union—true bonds of union. But can this question of slavery be considered as among these varieties in the institutions of the country? I leave it to you to say whether, in the history of our government, this institution of slavery has not always failed to be a bond of union, and, on the contrary, been an apple of discord, and an element of division in the house."[1]

It was in the Ottawa speech, when alluding to the vast influence of Douglas, that Lincoln made an oft-quoted remark—the assertion, indeed, of an old political truth, yet a truth not always comprehended, and at this time an important lesson for Republicans to learn. The forcible expression of it by their Illinois leader shows how profoundly he had grasped the situation. "In this and like communities," said he, "public sentiment is everything. With public sentiment nothing can fail; without it, nothing can succeed. Consequently, he who moulds public sentiment goes deeper than he who enacts statutes or pronounces decisions. He makes statutes and decisions possible or impossible to be executed."[2]

The importance of the Freeport debate, which occurred six days after that at Ottawa, arises from the catechising of each candidate by the other. Lincoln answered frankly the seven questions put to him by Douglas. The four important statements were: he was not in favor of the unconditional repeal of the Fugitive Slave law; was not pledged to the abolition of slavery in the District of Columbia, nor to the prohibition of the slave-trade between the different States; but he did believe it was the right and duty of Congress to prohibit slavery in all of the territories.[3] The crowd of people that listened to the debate at Freeport

---

[1] Lincoln-Douglas Debates, p. 76. [2] Ibid., p. 82. [3] Ibid., p. 88.

inclined as strongly to abolitionism as any audience that could be gathered in Illinois, and Lincoln's answers regarding his position on the Fugitive Slave law and the abolition of slavery in the District of Columbia must have been unpalatable to many who heard him. It was ground much less radical than Seward, Chase, and Sumner had taken at different times; for the unconditional repeal of the Fugitive Slave law, and the abolition of slavery in the District of Columbia, were, after 1850, the demands of Free-soilers and conscience Whigs. But Lincoln had never been through the Free-soil stage. As a Whig, following Clay and influenced by Webster, he had acquiesced in the compromise of 1850,[1] and his belief in making political action turn on the slavery question was born of the repeal of the Missouri Compromise. His never-varying principle, to which at all times and in all places he adhered, was the prohibition by Congress of slavery in the territories.

Lincoln likewise asked Douglas four questions. In the answer to one, Douglas enunciated what is known as the Freeport doctrine. The question of Lincoln was: "Can the people of a United States territory, in any lawful way, against the wish of any citizen of the United States, exclude slavery from its limits prior to the formation of a State constitution?"[2] It was necessary for Douglas, in his reply, to reconcile his principle of popular sovereignty with the Dred Scott decision. "It matters not," he said, "what way the Supreme Court may hereafter decide as to the abstract question whether slavery may or may not go into a territory under the Constitution; the people have the lawful means to introduce it or exclude it, as they please, for the reason that slavery cannot exist a day or an hour anywhere unless it is supported by local police regulations. Those police regulations can only be established by the local legislature; and if the people are opposed to slavery, they will elect representatives to that body who will by unfriendly

---

[1] Lincoln-Douglas Debates, p. 130.   [2] Ibid., p. 90.

legislation effectually prevent the introduction of it into their midst. If, on the contrary, they are for it, their legislation will favor its extension. Hence, no matter what the decision of the Supreme Court may be on that abstract question, still the right of the people to make a slave territory or a free territory is perfect and complete under the Nebraska bill."[1]

This answer attracted more attention throughout the country than any statement of Douglas during the campaign; and, while he could not have been elected senator without taking that position, the enunciation of the doctrine was an insuperable obstacle to cementing the division in the Democratic party. The influence of this meeting at Freeport is an example of the greater interest incited by a joint debate than by an ordinary canvass, and illustrates the effectiveness of the Socratic method of reasoning. During this same campaign, Douglas had twice before declared the same doctrine in expressions fully as plain and forcible,[2] but without creating any particular remark; while now the country resounded with discussions of the Freeport theory of "unfriendly legislation."

During this debate, Douglas lost the jaunty air that had characterized his previous efforts. Brought to bay by the remorseless logic of Lincoln, he was nettled to the point of interlarding his argument with misrepresentation; and, as the audience was lacking in sympathy with him, his abuse of the "Black Republican party," and of Lincoln and Trumbull, provoked running comments from the crowd, until, at last, apparently losing his temper, he was drawn into an undignified colloquy with some of his hearers.

A passage from Lincoln's concluding speech at Freeport

---

[1] Lincoln-Douglas Debates, p. 95.
[2] At Bloomington, July 16th, where he spoke of legislation being "unfriendly;" and at Springfield, July 17th, when he said, "Slavery cannot exist a day in the midst of an unfriendly people with unfriendly laws."
—Ibid., pp. 35, 49.

must be cited, as it shows a prevalent opinion about Douglas in Illinois, and was, moreover, not controverted by him during these debates; it likewise confirms what has been previously stated. Judge Douglas, affirmed Lincoln, at the last session of Congress, "had an eye farther North than he has to-day. He was then fighting against people who called *him* a Black Republican and an abolitionist. . . . But the judge's eye is farther South now. Then it was very peculiarly and decidedly North. His hope rested on the idea of visiting the great 'Black Republican' party, and making it the tail of his new kite. He knows he was then expecting from day to day to turn Republican and place himself at the head of our organization."[1]

It is interesting to follow these debates in their chronological order as the country in 1858 followed them. It was an intellectual duel between him who represented the best element of the Democratic party and the man who was building up principles, facts, and arguments into a well-defined and harmonious political system. "It was no ordinary contest, in which political opponents skirmished for the amusement of an indifferent audience," said McClernand, who had taken part in the campaign on the side of Douglas; "but it was a great uprising of the people, in which the masses were politically, and to a considerable extent socially, divided and arrayed against each other. In fact, it was a fierce and angry struggle, approximating the character of a revolution."[2]

It is not, however, necessary for our purpose to consider every meeting in detail. There was in the debates much of an ephemeral and personal character. In the personal controversy, Lincoln displayed more acerbity than his opponent. This was not surprising, since Douglas did not show entire fairness. When a charge was refuted, he had a way of making it in another shape, so that it was impossible to

---

[1] Lincoln-Douglas Debates, pp. 108, 109.
[2] House of Representatives, March 13th, 1860.

get him to admit that he was mistaken. Although frequently exhibiting a hasty temper, he was usually brimming over with good feeling, and this circumstance, together with his effective manner of reiterating a charge, gave him an evident superiority over Lincoln in this feature of the discussion. There was a great desire, on the part of the debaters, to get the better of one another in the immediate judgment of the actual audience; and this gave rise to personal repartees. Here Lincoln did not appear to advantage, on account of his ungainly way of putting things; nor was Douglas altogether happy, because of his great desire to gain immediate points by employing the debater's tricks.

Douglas, better practised in the amenities of debate, paid Lincoln more than one graceful compliment, but Lincoln had no words of unmeaning praise for his opponent. In his hits at Douglas there are touches of sullen envy mixed with self-depreciation, and laments that fortune should have showered gifts on the Little Giant, while bestowing but meagre favors on himself. He had long envied Douglas, and it galled him that his early rival had succeeded so well in winning fame, while he, conscious of equal intellectual power and of higher moral purpose, should be little known beyond his own State.[1]

But when the discussion turned on principles, the advantage of Lincoln is manifest. As the contest proceeded it grew hotter; and his bursts of eloquence, under the influence of noble passion, are still read with delight by the lovers of humanity and constitutional government. The positions that Douglas had advanced required a cool head to maintain everywhere an appearance of consistency between them. In the increasing heat of the controversy, he sometimes overlooked this, and was influenced too much by his immediate audience, forgetting for the moment that the whole country was looking on, and would read in tranquil hours his every word.

---

[1] See, besides the Debates, Lamon, p. 341; Holland, p. 155.

In all the debates, Douglas had little to say on the Lecompton question, although, when he did touch upon it, he spoke well; but, in the main, he seemed again the Douglas of 1854. The radical difference between him and the Republicans appears in every debate; they could agree on anti-Lecompton, but on nothing else; and now that the Lecompton question was settled, it left the former contention in full vigor.

Divested of oratorical flourish, there is little variety in the speeches of Douglas. He scouted continually the idea that the "all-men-are-created-equal" clause of the Declaration of Independence referred to the negro. He charged the Republicans with having formed a sectional party, and in every debate condemned his opponent's doctrine of the "house divided against itself." His most forcible expression on this subject was at Charleston.[1] "Why should this government," he asked, "be divided by a geographical line—arraying all men North in one great hostile party against all men South? Mr. Lincoln tells you that 'a house divided against itself cannot stand.' . . . Why cannot this government endure divided into free and slave States, as our fathers made it? When this government was established by Washington, Jefferson, Madison, Jay, Hamilton, Franklin, and the other sages and patriots of that day, it was composed of free States and slave States, bound together by one common Constitution. We have existed and prospered from that day to this, thus divided. . . . Why can we not thus continue to prosper?"[2]

Lincoln's reply was forcible: "There is no way," he said, "of putting an end to the slavery agitation amongst us but to put it back upon the basis where our fathers placed it; no way but to keep it out of our new territories—to restrict it forever to the old States where it now exists. Then the public mind *will* rest in the belief that it is in the course of ultimate extinction. That is one way of putting an end to

---

[1] Sept. 18th.   [2] Lincoln-Douglas Debates, p. 155.

the slavery agitation. The other way is for us to surrender, and let Judge Douglas and his friends have their way and plant slavery over all the States; cease speaking of it as in any way a wrong; regard slavery as one of the common matters of property, and speak of negroes as we do of our horses and cattle. But while it drives on in its state of progress as it is now driving, and as it has driven for the last five years, I have ventured the opinion, and I say to-day, that we will have no end to the slavery agitation until it takes one turn or the other. I do not mean that when it takes a turn towards ultimate extinction, it will be in a day, nor in a year, nor in two years. I do not suppose that in the most peaceful way ultimate extinction would occur in less than a hundred years at least; but that it will occur in the best way for both races, in God's own good time, I have no doubt."[1]

In the Jonesboro debate, Lincoln had made clear the fallacy of the Freeport doctrine. But in the rejoinder, Douglas showed what a powerful argument the Dred Scott decision was against the cardinal Republican principle of prohibition by Congress of slavery in the territories.[2]

The great historical importance of these debates lies in the prominence they gave Lincoln. The distinction was well deserved. In the Peoria speech of 1854, the Springfield address of 1857, and his published speeches of the 1858 campaign, we have a body of Republican doctrine which in consistency, cogency, and fitness can nowhere be equalled. Lincoln appealed alike to scholars, men of business, and the common people, for such clearness of statement and irrefragable proofs had not been known since the death of Webster. The simple, plain, natural unfolding of ideas is common to both Lincoln and Webster; and their points are made so clear that, while under the spell, the wonder grows how doubts ever could have arisen about the matter. But while it is the sort of reasoning that seems easy for the

---

[1] Lincoln-Douglas Debates, p. 157.   [2] Ibid., pp. 127, 135.

hearer or reader, it is the result of hard work on the part of the author. A distinguished thinker has said that mathematical studies are of immense benefit to the student "by habituating him to precision. It is one of the peculiar excellencies of mathematical discipline that the mathematician is never satisfied with *à peu près*. He requires the *exact* truth;" and the practice of mathematical reasoning "gives wariness of mind; it accustoms us to demand a sure footing."[1] Undoubtedly the days and nights given by Lincoln to Euclid had much to do with fitting him so well for this contest.

His simple and forcible vocabulary was due to the study of the Bible and Shakespeare. In the habitual use of words that were more common before the eighteenth century than since, Webster and Lincoln are alike. With Webster this was a deliberate choice, but Lincoln had found the Elizabethan language a fit vehicle for his thoughts, and his studies had gone no further.

Some further extracts from Lincoln's speeches are necessary in order fully to understand the historical importance of these debates. He said at Galesburg:[2] "The real difference between Judge Douglas and the Republicans . . . is that the judge is not in favor of making any difference between slavery and liberty—that he is in favor of eradicating, of pressing out of view, the questions of preference in this country for free or slave institutions; and consequently every sentiment he utters discards the idea that there is anything wrong in slavery. Everything that emanates from him or his coadjutors in their course of policy carefully excludes the thought that there is anything wrong in slavery. If you will take the judge's speeches, and select the short and pointed sentences expressed by him—as his declaration that he 'don't care whether slavery is voted up or down'—you will see at once that this is perfectly logical, if you do

---

[1] Examination of Sir William Hamilton's Philosophy, by John Stuart Mill, vol. ii. pp. 310, 311. [2] Oct. 7th.

not admit that slavery is wrong. If you do admit that it is wrong, Judge Douglas cannot logically say he don't care whether a wrong is voted up or voted down. Judge Douglas declares that if any community want slavery, they have a right to have it. He can say that logically if he says that there is no wrong in slavery; but if you admit that there is a wrong in it, he cannot logically say that anybody has a right to do wrong. He insists that, upon the score of equality, the owners of slaves and owners of property—of horses and every other sort of property—should be alike and hold them alike in a new territory. That is perfectly logical if the two species of property are alike, and are equally founded in right. But if you admit that one of them is wrong, you cannot institute any equality between right and wrong."[1]

Lincoln had no patience with the new construction of the Declaration of Independence. "Three years ago," he declared, "there had never lived a man who had ventured to assail it in the sneaking way of pretending to believe it, and then asserting it did not include the negro. I believe the first man who ever said it was Chief Justice Taney, in the Dred Scott case, and the next to him was our friend Stephen A. Douglas. And now it has become the catchword of the entire party."[2]

This remark was made during the last debate at Alton.[3] In this city, which looked across the river upon the State of Missouri, where Southern sympathy was strong, and which was famous in abolition annals as the place where Lovejoy had been murdered by a pro-slavery mob, Lincoln reached a greater height of moral power and eloquence than he had attained since his opening Springfield speech.

"When that Nebraska bill was brought forward, four years ago last January, was it not," he asked, "for the avowed object of putting an end to the slavery agitation? ... We were for a little while *quiet* on the troublesome

---

[1] Lincoln-Douglas Debates, p. 181.
[2] Ibid., p. 225.
[3] Oct. 15th.

thing, and that very allaying plaster of Judge Douglas's stirred it up again. . . . When was there ever a greater agitation in Congress than last winter? When was it as great in the country as to-day? There was a collateral object in the introduction of that Nebraska policy, which was to clothe the people of the territories with a superior degree of self-government beyond what they had ever had before. . . . But have you ever heard or known of a people anywhere on earth who had as little to do as, in the first instance of its use, the people of Kansas had with this same right of self-government? In its main policy and in its collateral object, *it has been nothing but a living, creeping lie from the time of its introduction till to-day.*" [1]

Lincoln made a good argument drawn from the letter of the Constitution. "The institution of slavery," he said, "is only mentioned in the Constitution of the United States two or three times, and in neither of these cases does the word 'slavery' or 'negro race' occur; but covert language is used each time, and for a purpose full of significance; . . . and that purpose was that in our Constitution, which it was hoped and is still hoped will endure forever—when it should be read by intelligent and patriotic men, after the institution of slavery had passed from among us, there should be nothing on the face of the great charter of liberty suggesting that such a thing as negro slavery had ever existed among us. This is part of the evidence that the fathers of the government expected and intended the institution of slavery to come to an end. They expected and intended that it should be in the course of ultimate extinction. And when I say that I desire to see the further spread of it arrested, I only say I desire to see that done which the fathers have first done. When I say I desire to see it placed where the public mind will rest in the belief that it is in the course of ultimate extinction, I only say I desire to see it placed where they placed it. It is not true that our fathers, as

---

[1] Lincoln-Douglas Debates, p. 228.

Judge Douglas assumes, made this government part slave and part free. . . . The exact truth is, they found the institution existing among us, and they left it as they found it. But in making the government they left this institution with many clear marks of disapprobation upon it. They found slavery among them, and they left it among them because of the difficulty, the absolute impossibility, of its immediate removal. And when Judge Douglas asks me why we cannot let it remain part slave and part free, as the fathers of the government made it, he asks a question based upon an assumption which is itself a falsehood; and I turn upon him and ask him the question, when the policy that the fathers of the government had adopted in relation to this element among us was the best policy in the world —the only wise policy—the only policy that we can ever safely continue upon—that will ever give us peace, unless this dangerous element masters us all and becomes a national institution—*I turn upon him and ask him why he could not leave it alone.*" [1]

The stock complaint about the agitation of slavery was effectively answered. "Judge Douglas has intimated," said Lincoln, "that all this difficulty in regard to the institution of slavery is the mere agitation of office-seekers and ambitious Northern politicians. . . . Is that the truth? How many times have we had danger from this question? . . . Is it not this same mighty, deep-seated power that somehow operates on the minds of men, exciting and stirring them up in every avenue of society—in politics, in religion, in literature, in morals, in all the manifold relations of life? Is this the work of politicians? Is that irresistible power which for fifty years has shaken the government and agitated the people to be stilled and subdued by pretending that it is an exceedingly simple thing, and we ought not to talk about it? If you will get everybody else to stop talking about it, I assure you I will quit before they have half done so. But

---

[1] Lincoln-Douglas Debates, p. 229.

where is the philosophy or statesmanship which assumes that you can quiet that disturbing element in our society which has disturbed us for more than half a century, which has been the only serious danger that has threatened our institutions? I say, where is the philosophy or statesmanship based on the assumption that we are to quit talking about it, and that the public mind is all at once to cease being agitated by it? Yet this is the policy here in the North that Douglas is advocating—that we are to care nothing about it! I ask you if it is not a false philosophy? Is it not a false statesmanship that undertakes to build up a system of policy upon the basis of caring nothing about *the very thing that everybody does care the most about?*—a thing which all experience has shown we care a very great deal about?" [1]

The real issue, Lincoln affirmed, is whether slavery is right or wrong. "That is the issue that will continue in this country when these poor tongues of Judge Douglas and myself shall be silent. It is the eternal struggle between these two principles — right and wrong — throughout the world. They are the two principles which have stood face to face from the beginning of time, and will ever continue to struggle. The one is the common right of humanity, and the other the divine right of kings. It is the same principle, in whatever shape it develops itself. It is the same spirit that says, 'You work and toil and earn bread, and I'll eat it.' No matter in what shape it comes, whether from the mouth of a king who seeks to bestride the people of his own nation and live by the fruit of their labor, or from one race of men as an apology for enslaving another race, it is the same tyrannical principle." [2]

The excitement in Illinois mounted up to fever heat. Never had there been such a campaign. That of 1856 was calm by comparison. The debates did not take place in halls, for no halls were large enough. These meetings were held in the afternoon, in groves or on the prairie, and the

---

[1] Lincoln-Douglas Debates, pp. 230, 231.   [2] Ibid., p. 234.

audiences were from five thousand to ten thousand. At the Charleston meeting it was estimated twenty thousand were present.[1] Everywhere women vied with men in their interest in the contest.

The joint meetings and the speeches of which mention has been made by no means measure the work of the two candidates. Lincoln spoke incessantly. In the hundred days of the campaign, Douglas made one hundred and thirty speeches.[2] As the Little Giant had the Republicans and the influence of the administration to fight, his efforts seemed heroic; and during the campaign the opinion was universal that, if successful, it would be because his personal prowess had overcome great odds, while defeat might mean his political death.

A host of lesser Illinois aspirants were constantly engaged in campaign work. Members of Congress were to be chosen at the same election, and the candidates stumped thoroughly their districts. Candidates for the legislature occupied a more conspicuous place than usual, for on the successful party would fall the duty and honor of naming for senator one of the two men who were making Illinois famous. Corwin and Chase came from Ohio, and Colfax from Indiana, to assist Lincoln in this memorable struggle. Money was used on both sides more freely than common in a senatorial campaign, but it was employed only for legitimate purposes.[3] Listening to the arguments of Lincoln and Douglas, the meanest voter of Illinois must have felt that he was one of

---

[1] Arnold, p. 147.   [2] Nicolay and Hay, vol. ii. p. 146.

[3] Greeley wrote in 1868: "While Lincoln had spent less than a thousand dollars in all, Douglas in the canvass had borrowed and dispensed no less than eighty thousand dollars, incurring a debt which weighed him down to the grave. I presume no dime of this was used to buy up his competitor's voters, but all to organize and draw out his own; still, the debt so improvidently, if not culpably, incurred remained to harass him out of this mortal life."— *Century Magazine*, July, 1891, p. 375, when this paper of Greeley was first published. I believe this to be a correct statement.

the jury in a case of transcendent importance, and that, inasmuch as the ablest advocates of the country were appealing to him, he would have deemed it base to traffic in his vote. The party managers knew that success lay only in convincing the minds of men.

The contemplation of such a campaign is inspiriting to those who have faith in the people; for, although Lincoln did not succeed, the Republicans made a material gain over 1856, and paved the way for a triumph in 1860.

Personal popularity saved Douglas from defeat; he had a majority of eight in the legislature. But the Republican State ticket was elected, the head of it receiving 125,430 votes, while the Douglas Democrat polled 121,609, and the Buchanan Democrat 5071. The total vote had increased over that of the presidential election — an unusual occurrence. This was due to the great interest awakened by the battle of the giants. The Republicans gained more of the increased vote than the Democrats;[1] but many sincere friends of Lincoln thought that the announcement of the "house-divided-against-itself" doctrine had caused his defeat.[2]

The exultation of Douglas at his triumph was loud and deep. Lincoln ardently desired a seat in the United States Senate, but, accustomed to defeat, he gave way to no expressions of bitter disappointment. Indeed, he had hardly expected a better result, but he was glad he had made the race. He wrote: "It gave me a hearing on the great and durable question of the age which I could have had in no other way; and though I now sink out of view and shall be forgotten, I believe I have made some marks which will tell for the cause of civil liberty long after I am gone."[3]

Lincoln had no regrets about his first Springfield speech. Sumner asked him a few days before his death if at the time he had any doubt about that declaration. He replied: "Not

---

[1] Democratic gain measured by the vote for the Douglas ticket, 16,261; Republican gain, 29,241.
[2] See Lamon, p. 407.   [3] Nicolay and Hay, vol. ii. p. 169.

in the least. It was clearly true."[1] Although he had failed to win the senatorship, his speeches had impressed his Illinois friends with the notion that he was a possible candidate for the presidency, and they broached the subject to him. Lincoln's reply was modest and sincere: "What," said he, "is the use of talking of me whilst we have such men as Seward and Chase, and everybody knows them, and scarcely anybody outside of Illinois knows me. Besides, as a matter of justice, is it not due to them? . . . I admit that I am ambitious and would like to be President . . . but there is no such good luck in store for me as the presidency of these United States."[2] But there was no question in the mind of Douglas regarding the fitness of Lincoln. Being asked his opinion of his late antagonist by Senator Wilson on the first opportunity after the election, Douglas said: "Lincoln is an able and honest man, one of the ablest men of the nation. I have been in Congress sixteen years, and there is not a man in the Senate I would not rather encounter in debate."[3]

Important in its bearing on the future was the impression made by these debates beyond the State of Illinois. The speeches were published in full in the Chicago journals; many of them found a place in the St. Louis, Cincinnati, and New York newspapers,[4] and beyond all else, a Western Republican looked for the verdict of New York and New England. Illinois, in 1858, was politically and socially as far from New York city and Boston as Nebraska is to-day.[5] The readers of the New York journals were, however, kept well informed as to the progress of the campaign, and enough speeches on each side were published to convey a correct idea of the issue between the debaters.

Yet public attention centred in Douglas. He had now

---

[1] Sumner's Eulogy on Lincoln, Sumner's Works, vol. ix. p. 380.
[2] Arnold, p. 155; The Lincoln Memorial, pp. 473-476.
[3] Rise and Fall of the Slave Power, vol. ii. p. 577.
[4] See Arnold, p. 142; New York *Tribune, Times,* and *Post.*
[5] In 1892.

with him nine-tenths of the Northern Democrats, and they followed his progress with intense interest. "On the occasion of our recent visit to New York," wrote the editor of the Philadelphia *Press*, "we had an opportunity of commingling freely with citizens from all parts of the Union, especially during the Cable Carnival,[1] and almost the first questions propounded were: 'What is your news from Illinois? When have you heard from Senator Douglas? God speed him! May he be successful!' And this was the language of all parties, almost without exception. The interest of the American people in the extraordinary contest in which Judge Douglas is engaged increases with every day."[2]

Even among Republicans of the East the contest seemed noteworthy only because Douglas was engaged in it. Before making the Springfield speech that opened the campaign, Lincoln was generally regarded as a backwoods lawyer who had more temerity than discretion in offering to contest the senatorship with Douglas, against the advice of the wisest Republicans of the East.

But with the publication of the "house-divided-against-itself" speech in the *Tribune*, the eyes of Eastern observers began to be opened to the fact that a new champion had appeared; and when Lincoln challenged Douglas to a joint debate, the public realized that a worthy foeman had entered the lists. The *Tribune*, in spite of Greeley's deprecating the contest, and the *Post* gave Lincoln a loyal support. The *Times*, on the contrary, obviously sympathized with Douglas; while the Springfield *Republican* only came reluctantly to the support of Lincoln.[3]

Lincoln had attentive readers in New England.[4] Twenty-

---

[1] The celebration over the completion of the Atlantic cable.
[2] Issue of Sept. 7th. Forney was editor of the *Press*, and probably wrote this article. "Upon Illinois the eyes of the whole Union are now fixed with intense interest."—Forney's Vindication, Philadelphia *Press*, Sept. 30th.   [3] See Life of Bowles, Merriam, vol. i. p. 234.
[4] See the Boston *Atlas* during the campaign.

three years afterwards, Longfellow wrote that he well remembered the impression made upon him by Lincoln's speeches in "this famous canvass."[1] Parker wrote in August, 1858: "I look with great interest on the contest in your State, and read the speeches, the noble speeches, of Mr. Lincoln with enthusiasm."[2] A few days later, however, Parker showed that he did not comprehend the need of sinking unimportant issues, in order that the immediate and practical question should stand clearly forth. "In the Ottawa meeting," he wrote, "to judge from the *Tribune* report, I thought Douglas had the best of it. He questioned Mr. Lincoln on the great matters of slavery, and put the most radical questions . . . before the people. Mr. Lincoln did not meet the issue. He made a technical evasion. . . . Daniel Webster stood on higher anti-slavery ground than Abraham Lincoln now. Greeley's conduct I think is *base*. . . . He has no talent for a leader. If the Republicans sacrifice their principle for success, then they will not be lifted up, but blown up. I trust Lincoln will conquer. It is admirable education for the masses, this fight!"[3]

The contest was watched with respect and admiration by every one at the North except by the administration party. A thorough discussion of the issues before the country, which was certain in a debate between two representative men, was by no means desired by the President and his friends. His organ thought the debates a "novel and vicious procedure," the campaign disgraced by "indecencies" and "disreputable vituperation." There was little choice between Lincoln and Douglas. Douglas was a renegade, Lincoln "a shallow empiric, an ignorant pretender, or a political knave," and the two "a pair of depraved, blustering, mischievous, low-down demagogues."[4]

---

[1] Arnold, p. 142.   [2] To Herndon, Aug. 28th, Weiss, vol. ii. p. 240.
[3] To Herndon, Sept. 9th, Weiss, vol. ii. p. 241.
[4] Washington *Union*, Sept. 2d, 3d, 8th, 16th, 22d.

After the election the tone of the Eastern Republican press was that of pæans to the victor because his success was a severe blow to the administration. Yet sympathy did not lack for the vanquished, who had made for himself, so one heard on all sides, a national reputation.[1] As Douglas had won this hard-fought field, he was now the most glorious son of his country. No one came near him in popular estimation; it was generally conceded that he would be the Democratic candidate for President in 1860, and would probably be elected.

Since "nothing succeeds like success," it was for the most part supposed in the East that as Douglas had won the prize, he had overpowered his antagonist in debate. This remained the prevalent opinion until, in 1860, the debates were published in book form. Since then the matured judgment is that in the dialectic contest, Lincoln got the better of Douglas. No one would now undertake to affirm the contrary; but Lincoln had an immense advantage in having the just cause, and the one to which public sentiment was tending. Douglas showed great power, and, had chance or disposition put him on the anti-slavery side, it is certain he would have been an effective champion. This we know in view of the speeches he made in the Lecompton debate when he pleaded for justice and fairness. But we cannot in imagination transpose the two contestants. It is impossible for the mind to conceive Lincoln battling for any cause but that of justice.

The October elections in Pennsylvania, Ohio, Indiana, and Iowa were decidedly adverse to the administration. That in Pennsylvania attracted especial notice. It was a strong condemnation when the President's own State, usually counted on for a good Democratic majority, emphatically censured his policy. The Republicans, Americans, and anti-Lecompton Democrats united, and won a complete victory. Of twenty-five members of Congress, the administra-

---

[1] See the New York *Tribune, Times, Post,* and *Independent.*

tion party elected but three, while in the previous House the Democrats had fifteen. "We have met the enemy in Pennsylvania, and we are theirs," wrote Buchanan to his niece. To her this cold reticent man came nearer to opening his mind than to any other person. He proceeded to relate that a number of congenial friends had dined with him, and " we had a merry time of it, laughing, among other things, over our crushing defeat. It is so great that it is almost absurd." In this letter he reflects on the causes of the change. " Poor bleeding Kansas is quiet," he continued, " and is behaving herself in an orderly manner; but her wrongs have melted the hearts of the sympathetic Pennsylvanians, or rather Philadelphians. In the interior of the State the tariff was the damaging question." [1]

Between the October and November elections occurred an event of prime importance. Seward delivered at Rochester his celebrated irrepressible-conflict speech; it was a philippic against the Democratic party and its devotion to slavery. As the slave-holders, he said, contributed " in an overwhelming proportion to the capital strength of the Democratic party, they necessarily dictate and prescribe its policy." He exposed the injustice of the slave system, and contrasted the good of freedom with the evil of slavery. He averred that between the two there was a collision. " It is an irrepressible conflict between opposing and enduring forces, and it means that the United States must and will, sooner or later, become either entirely a slave-holding nation or entirely a free-labor nation." [2]

Few speeches from the stump have attracted so great attention or exerted so great an influence. The eminence of the man combined with the startling character of the doctrine to make it engross the public mind.[3] The Democrats

---

[1] Buchanan to Miss Lane, Oct. 15th, Curtis, vol. ii. p. 241.

[2] This speech was delivered Oct. 25th. Seward's Works, vol. iv. p. 289.

[3] The same notion may be found in previous speeches of Seward (Life,

looked upon Seward as the representative Republican. When, in the Illinois canvass, Douglas referred to a suppositional Republican President, it was to Seward by name.[1] Jefferson Davis called him "the master mind" of the Republican party.[2]

The Republicans looked upon the doctrine announced in the Rochester speech as the well-weighed conclusion of a profound thinker and of a man of wide experience, who united the political philosopher with the practical politician. It is true that four months previously the same idea had been expressed by Lincoln, but the promulgation of a principle by the Illinois lawyer was a far different affair from the giving of the key-note by the New York senator. It is not probable that Lincoln's "house-divided-against-itself" speech had any influence in bringing Seward to this position.[3] He would at this time have certainly scorned the notion of borrowing ideas from Lincoln; and had he studied the progress of the Illinois canvass, he must have seen that the declaration did not meet with general favor. It must also be borne in mind that in anti-slavery sentiment the people of New York were far in advance of the people of Illinois, and Seward spoke to a sympathetic audience. "The unmistakable outbreaks of zeal which occur all around me," he began, "show that you are earnest men."

In February of this year there had been bodied forth in Seward the politician who sought to discern in which way the tide of opinion was setting. Now, a far-seeing statesman spoke. It would, indeed, be difficult to harmonize the speech of February in the Senate with the declaration at Rochester in October; one was compared to Webster's 7th-of-March speech, and the other commended by the

---

vol. ii. p. 352); but it is in the shape rather of a suggestion than a forcible and precise declaration.

[1] Lincoln-Douglas Debates, p. 48.
[2] Speech at Jackson, Miss., Nov. 11th, the *Liberator*, Dec. 3d.
[3] See Lincoln's remarks on this subject at Columbus, Sept., 1859, Lincoln-Douglas Debates, p. 244.

abolitionists. The most that can be said is that the earlier expression was a burst of inconsiderate optimism, while the later speech was the earnest conviction of many years, which Seward deemed opportune to proclaim after the signal strength the Republicans had displayed in the October elections. In conclusion, the speaker replied to the charge of scoffers that the Republican party was a party of one idea. "But that idea," he exclaimed, "is a noble one—an idea that fills and expands all generous souls. . . . I know, and you know, that a revolution has begun. I know, and all the world knows, that revolutions never go backwards."[1]

The November elections emphasized what was foreshadowed in October. The North condemned unmistakably the administration, and, except in Pennsylvania, there was but one question before the public mind. There the prostration of the iron industry, a result of the panic of 1857, was charged by the Republicans to the tariff bill enacted in March of that year, and the responsibility of the reduction of duties was cast upon the Democrats.[2] Such an argument, presented to laborers who neither had work nor the prospect of any, undoubtedly aided the opposition in carrying the State.[3] In New England, New York, and the Northwest, where the defeat of the administration party was overwhelming, the tariff question was regarded with indifference. There was but one explanation of the result. The people intended to censure the Lecompton policy of the President and to show their disapproval of his evident Southern leaning.[4]

To trace the decomposition of political parties which has been going on since 1852, and the formation of new com-

---

[1] Seward's Works, vol. iv. p. 302.

[2] In a future volume I purpose to discuss the tariff of 1846, and the tariff of 1857, in connection with the material prosperity of the decade of 1850–60.

[3] See New York *Tribune*, Oct. 16th; Washington *Union*, cited by New York *Times*, Oct. 26th. [4] See New York *Times*, Nov. 5th.

binations which began in 1854, has been a complicated matter, for there have been many streams, seemingly running in independent channels. From the close of 1853 to the beginning of the war, however, the political history is easier to grasp, for the reason that leaders have arisen under whom the people have arrayed themselves, looking to them for guidance. Four leaders represented substantially the political sentiment of the country. Douglas, Seward, Lincoln, and Jefferson Davis were the exponents; and all but former old-line Whigs, Americans, and abolitionists recognized in one of them a leader whom they looked to for education on the issues of the day.

Jefferson Davis, now the leader of the Southern Democrats, was regarded by them with somewhat of the veneration that had been accorded to Calhoun. Like Calhoun, he could depend on a following beyond the Democratic ranks, on account of being the special representative of Southern interests. It was not a vain boast of Senator Hammond when he said that the South "is almost thoroughly united." As he explained, "The abolitionists have at length forced upon us a knowledge of our true position, and compelled us into union—a union not for aggression, but for defence."[1] If the peculiar institutions of the South were threatened, Davis might reckon practically on the support of that whole section; and that being the case, it is of little importance that a party organization in opposition to the regular Democrats was kept up.

Davis had passed the summer at the North, and his speeches in several of the cities had made a profound and favorable impression. He had sought the bracing climate of New England for the improvement of his health, although an unfriendly Southern biographer states that he had

---

[1] Speech at Barnwell Court-house, S. C., Oct. 29th. Speeches and Letters of J. H. Hammond, pp. 352, 356. The Southerners rarely made a distinction between Republicans and abolitionists; but the difference was clear, and always recognized at the North.

caught the presidential fever, and his journey through the North was intended to work up sentiment in his favor.[1] His speech at Portland, Maine, called out by a serenade, was a graceful response to people who had shown him "gentle kindness," who had given him a "cordial welcome" and a "hearty grasp." He spoke in eloquent terms of the common possession by the North and the South of the Revolutionary history, praised the Constitution, appealed for the Union, and complimented in felicitous terms Yankee skill and enterprise.[2] He addressed the Democrats of Boston and New York, both of which cities received him with enthusiasm. If he had indulged in dreams of the presidency, they were ruthlessly dispelled by the result of the fall elections, which demonstrated that no Southern Democrat could be elected President. It was also said that his Mississippi constituents found fault with the fervent union sentiments he had uttered at the North, and he therefore made a speech at Jackson, Mississippi, to define his position.[3] He then asserted that if an abolitionist were elected President—and, in his view, Seward, Lincoln, and Chase were abolitionists—it would be the duty of Mississippi to secede from the Union.[4]

The Republicans of New York State and New England were by no means unanimous in endorsing Seward's Rochester speech. The New York *Times*, once his organ, called the assertion that all the States must ultimately become free or slave a glittering generality. It further maintained that, although the Frémont campaign had been fought out on the platform of demanding congressional prohibition of slavery in the territories, and although it was true that most Republicans thought it the correct principle, yet the Supreme Court in the Dred Scott opinion had denied that right,

---

[1] Life of Jefferson Davis, Pollard, p. 51.

[2] This speech, not at all partisan in its nature, is printed in the Life of Davis, Alfriend, p. 122.

[3] Boston *Atlas*, cited by the *Liberator*, Dec. 3d.

[4] The *Liberator*, Dec. 3d.

and the point must be considered settled. The only way now that slavery could be constitutionally prohibited in the territories was through the operation of the Douglas doctrine of popular sovereignty. Yet there was comfort in the fact that Kansas was certain to be free, and that no dispute now existed regarding the establishment of slavery in any territory. It even appeared that the agitation of slavery was subsiding, and it was quite probable that the campaign of 1860 would be made on other issues.[1] The Springfield *Republican* thought Seward's irrepressible-conflict declaration impolitic, and liable to do him and his party damage.[2]

The President sent his message to Congress at the usual time. He showed great satisfaction that the Kansas question no longer troubled the country, and said that we had much reason for gratitude to Almighty Providence that our political condition was calmer than one year ago, for then "the sectional strife between the North and the South on the dangerous subject of slavery had again become so intense as to threaten the peace and perpetuity of the Confederacy." In his discussion of the Kansas question, not the faintest intimation appears that he and the pro-slavery party had made a mistake in their endeavor to force slavery upon Kansas. On the contrary, his action was viewed with complacency, and he maintained that had his advice been followed, the agitation would have been sooner allayed and Kansas would now be a free State instead of a free territory. Referring to his Lecompton policy, the President said: "In the course of my long public life, I have never performed any official act which, in the retrospect, has afforded me more heartfelt satisfaction." The lesson of the elections was lost upon him; he had learned nothing. His discussion of the Kansas matter was a tissue of misrepresentations, although it is probable they imposed on few but himself and his office-holding satellites. It is impossible to

---

[1] See the *Times* of Nov. 9th, 16th, 19th, 26th, and Dec. 3d.
[2] Life of Bowles, vol. i. p. 243.

deny to Buchanan a certain measure of sincerity in his extraordinary utterances; but if he were sincere, he was strangely dull and perverse.

The President referred to the business condition of the country. The hard times, a sequel of the panic of 1857, still continued, but he thought the effects of the revulsion were slowly but surely passing away. The revenue of the government, however, had fallen short of the expenditure, and he recommended an increase of the duties on imports. In dilating upon internal affairs beyond the domain of politics, the President neglected to allude to the yellow-fever epidemic that had visited Mobile and New Orleans. In this he did not follow the example of his predecessor, who had made a sympathetic mention of the ravages caused in 1853 by the dread disease. But there was abundant reason for the difference. The mortality this year was less than in 1853; for while the fever was of the malignant type, it had not so many fresh subjects to prey upon, and was apparently more skilfully treated.[1] In any event, therefore, it would not have produced the impression on the public mind that was discernible five years before; and it failed even in the effect its importance warranted, on account of the minds of men being engrossed with political and financial affairs.

The President showed that he was anxious to acquire Cuba, and, with fatuity rather than disingenuousness, he assigned for a reason that as Cuba was "the only spot in the civilized world where the African slave-trade is tolerated," its cession to this country would put an end to that blot upon civilization. Buchanan can now only be looked upon as the tool of Southern Democrats. Every one, except apparently the President, knew that their restless longing for Cuba was prompted by the desire to extend their political power and offset the new free States that were coming into the Union; that, far from wishing the African slave-trade

---

[1] American Almanac of 1860, p. 386; The Diary of a Samaritan, p. 322.

suppressed, they were now chafing against the United States statutes which forbade it and made it piracy.

While the President said plainly that our national character would not permit us to acquire Cuba in any way except by honorable negotiation, yet he suggested that circumstances might arise where the law of self-preservation would compel us to depart from this course, thereby faintly reaffirming the doctrine of the Ostend Manifesto. As he purposed negotiating for the purchase of the island, he asked Congress for an appropriation of money to be used as an advance payment immediately on the signature of the treaty with Spain, so that he might nail the bargain without waiting the ratification of the Senate.

The response of the Southern Democrats was prompt. Slidell reported a bill from the committee on foreign relations to appropriate thirty million dollars for the purpose requested by the President. On the same day the news came from Spain of the sensation caused by the President's message. It had been made the subject of an interpellation in the Cortes, to which the Minister of State had responded, amidst the enthusiastic cheers of the delegates, that a proposition to dispossess Spain of the least part of her territory would be considered an insult. The Cortes voted unanimously that it would support the government in preserving the integrity of the Spanish dominions.[1] Seward called the attention of the Senate to the reception of the President's message in Spain. Had the project been one of honorable negotiation for a peaceful purchase, it would of course have gone no further; but there was an ulterior intention, and the bill was consequently made a special order for the first day of the following week. The subject gave rise to considerable discussion, in which the aims of the annexation party were clearly disclosed. It had been a favorite theory that Spanish officials could be bribed to do what they would emphatically disclaim in the open Cortes; and

---

[1] See New York *Tribune*, Jan. 24th, 1859.

Doolittle, of Wisconsin, charged that this thirty million dollars was intended to be used in this manner as secret-service money.[1]

It came out in the debate that the Southerners were willing to give from one hundred and twenty-five to two hundred millions for the island; but if they could not buy it, they were prepared, as Mallory, of Florida, disclosed, to take Cuba and talk about it afterwards, as Frederic the Great did when he marched into Silesia.[2]

The Cuban question was the occasion of one of those bitter controversies between Northern and Southern senators that were now characteristic of every session.[3] The Homestead bill had passed the House, and the Republicans were eager to have it considered in the Senate; the 25th of February had come; the short session was drawing to a close, and the Cuban bill, which could by no possibility pass the House, had the precedence. Seward urged that it should be laid aside, arguing that the Homestead bill "is a question of homes, of lands for the landless freemen," while "the Cuba bill is the question of slaves for the slave-holders." This irritated Toombs, who, as soon as he could get

---

[1] *Congressional Globe*, vol. xxxviii. p. 907.

[2] Von Holst, *Congressional Globe*, vol. xxxviii. p. 1332. I have not discussed foreign relations under the Buchanan administration. Curtis, in his Life of Buchanan, has devoted chapter x. vol. ii., to that subject. For the very important controversy on the right of search, asserted in 1858 by Great Britain in reference to merchantmen suspected of being engaged in the slave-trade, see, also, International Law Digest, Wharton, vol. iii. sect. 327; Letters from London, Dallas, vol. ii. p. 28.

[3] "In 1859, there was an unspoken feeling of avoidance between the political men of the two sections, and even to some extent between such of their families as had previously associated together. Unconsciously, all tentative subjects were avoided by the well-bred of both sections; it was only when some 'bull in a china shop' galloped over the barriers good-breeding had established that there was anything but the kindest manner apparent. Still, the restraint was unpleasant to both sides, and induced a rather ceremonious intercourse."—Life of Jefferson Davis, by his wife, vol. i. p. 574.

the floor, exclaimed: "Mr. President, there is one class of people whom I despise as American senators, and that is, demagogues; but there is another class that I despise a great deal more, and that is the people who are driven by demagogues. . . . When you have a great question of national policy which appeals to the patriotism of the whole American people, a plain and naked question, then we hear of 'land to the landless.' If you do not wish to give thirty millions for the acquisition of Cuba, say so by your vote, aye or no; and then I will take up your 'land for the landless.' . . . But we do not want to be diverted from a great question of public policy by pretences or by pretexts, or by the shivering in the wind of men in particular localities."

Wade, who knew no fear, and was ever ready to take up the gauntlet thrown down by a fiery Southerner, sprang to his feet, excited by worthy passion,[1] and exclaimed: "I am very glad that this question has at length come up. I am glad, too, that it has antagonized with this nigger question. We are 'shivering in the wind,' are we, sir, over your Cuba question? You may have occasion to shiver on that question before you are through with it. . . . The question will be, shall we give niggers to the niggerless, or land to the landless? . . . When you come to niggers for the niggerless, all other questions sink into perfect insignificance. But, sir, we will antagonize these measures. I appeal to the country upon them. I ask the people, do you choose that we should go through the earth hunting for niggers, for really that is the whole purpose of the Democratic party. They can no more run their party without niggers than you could run a steam-engine without fuel. That is all there is of Democracy; and when you cannot raise niggers enough for the market, then you must go abroad fishing for niggers through the whole world. Are you going to buy Cuba for land for the landless? What is there? You will find three quarters of a million of nig-

---

[1] Life of Wade, Riddle, p. 262.

gers, but you will not find any land—not one foot, not an inch."[1]

At the close of the debate this day, for the purpose of testing the sense of the Senate, a motion was made by a friend of the measure to lay the bill on the table. This was negatived by a vote of 30 to 18. The next day Slidell withdrew the bill, as he was satisfied it could not be pressed to a vote without a sacrifice of the appropriation bills, thereby involving an extra session. He asserted, however, that the Senate on the preceding day had as clearly expressed its opinion on the subject as if there had been a final vote.

The Lincoln-Douglas debates had put an end to the project of a union between Douglas and the Republicans. While Eastern men and Republican journals might regret that such a combination had not been effected, it was apparent that after the positions Douglas had been forced to take by the inexorable logic of Lincoln, there remained but little common ground between them. Now, however, as the Lecompton question was out of the way, and the Kansas question no longer before the country, it was a matter of moment whether the breach in the Democratic party could be healed. Shortly after the close of the Illinois canvass, Douglas made a trip through the South and was received with enthusiasm at Memphis and New Orleans, where he made formal speeches. His journey was not so much a bid for support from the South in his presidential aspirations as it was an endeavor to make converts to his doctrine. His line of argument was the same in Tennessee and Louisiana as it had been in Illinois, and there was entire consistency between his speeches.[2] It was stated, however, that only a coterie of public men welcomed him at New

---

[1] *Congressional Globe*, vol. xxxviii. p. 1354.

[2] The New York *Times*, which still inclined to Douglas, published the Memphis and New Orleans speeches. See the *Times* of Dec. 17th, 1858, and the *Tribune*, Dec. 6th, 1858.

Orleans, and that the prominent members of the party, being devoted to the administration, held aloof. From the tone of the Southern press, it is evident that in many sections of the South, Douglas would have been coldly received, for he was looked upon as a traitor to Southern interests.[1] The pro-slavery faction at Washington was likewise bitterly opposed to him. The President was represented as implacable; he justly laid at the door of Douglas his mortifying defeat in the attempt to force the Lecompton Constitution upon Kansas, and the repudiation of his policy by the Northern people. The Freeport doctrine of the Illinois senator seemed heresy to those who implicitly believed in the Calhoun principle, especially as they were now preparing to give that principle a further extension. These two forces working together, resentment and a sincere difference in views, resulted in the Democratic caucus deposing Douglas from the chairmanship of the committee on territories, a position he had held ever since he had been in the Senate. This action was taken while Douglas was on his Southern tour. When he returned to the North, he received ovations at New York, Philadelphia, and Baltimore, and was cordially welcomed at Washington. He apparently seemed disposed to submit to his removal in silence. It began to be said that his presidential aspirations were so potent that he was willing to yield some of the points in dispute; and his support of the thirty-million Cuba bill gave color to this belief.[2]

But those who thought or hoped that the division in the Democratic party might be cemented were undeceived by the fierce debate of February 23d in the Senate, when it became apparent that the difference was irreconcilable. An amendment by Senator Hale, of New Hampshire, to an appropriation bill, offered probably for the purpose of

---

[1] See extracts from Southern journals. The *Liberator*, Jan. 7th, 1859.
[2] New York *Times*, Feb. 22d; see also letter of Letcher to Crittenden, Life of Crittenden, Coleman, vol. ii. p. 170.

bringing to the surface the slumbering disagreement, furnished the text for the discussion. The Vice-President, Breckinridge, who more than once had contributed his efforts in the direction of harmony, tried to have a vote taken promptly on the amendment, hoping that as only nine days of the session remained, they might pass without making more pronounced the schism in the party; but Brown, of Mississippi, demanded a hearing, and his sincere expressions were the beginning of a hot debate between the Democratic factions.

"I neither want to cheat nor to be cheated in the great contest that is to come off in 1860," he said. He therefore proposed to give his opinion on a question that would have a most important bearing on the presidential election. "We have," he averred, "a right of protection for our slave property in the territories. The Constitution, as expounded by the Supreme Court, awards it. We demand it, and we mean to have it." If the territorial legislature will not protect us, "the obligation is upon Congress. . . . If I cannot," he continued, "obtain the rights guaranteed to me and my people under the Constitution, as expounded by the Supreme Court, my mind will be forced irresistibly to the conclusion that the Constitution is a failure, and the Union a despotism, and then, sir, I am prepared to retire from the concern." Brown wished, moreover, to say that he utterly repudiated the whole doctrine of squatter sovereignty.[1] He understood the position of Douglas, since the statement at Freeport of the theory of "unfriendly legislation," but he wanted to know how the other Northern Democratic senators stood on this question.[2]

Perhaps if Douglas had been ruled only by his wish to be President, he would have remained silent; but it was not

---

[1] By opponents the principle Douglas advocated was often called squatter sovereignty. He himself made a distinction between "squatter" and "popular" sovereignty. See Cutts, p. 123.

[2] *Congressional Globe*, vol. xxxviii. p. 1241.

his nature to allow such an avowal to pass unnoticed. As soon as Brown sat down, Douglas leaped to the floor, demanded recognition, and defended his doctrine of popular sovereignty in earnest arguments, familiar to the readers of this work. He made the emphatic declaration: "I tell you, gentlemen of the South, in all candor, I do not believe a Democratic candidate can ever carry any one Democratic State of the North on the platform that it is the duty of the federal government to force the people of a territory to have slavery when they do not want it."[1]

Jefferson Davis replied to Douglas: "The senator asks," said he, "will you make a discrimination in the territories?" that is, will you give slave property a greater measure of protection than you would dry-goods, liquors, horses, or cattle? Davis boldly answered: "I say yes. I would discriminate in the territories wherever it is needful to assert the right of a citizen. . . . I have heard many a siren's song on this doctrine of non-intervention; a thing shadowy, fleeting, changing its color as often as the chameleon." If the Democratic party, he continued, "is to be wrecked by petty controversies in relation to African labor; if a few Africans brought into the United States, where they have been advanced in comfort and civilization and knowledge, are to constitute the element which will divide the Democratic party and peril the vast hopes, not only of our own country but of all mankind, I trust it will be remembered that a few of us, at least, have stood by the old landmarks of those who framed the Constitution and gave us our liberty; that we claim nothing more now from the government than the men who formed it were willing to concede. When this shall become an unpopular doctrine, when men are to lose the great States of the North by announcing it, I wish it to be understood that my vote can be got for no candidate who will not be so defeated. I agree with my colleague that we are not, with our eyes open, to be cheated."

---

[1] *Congressional Globe*, vol. xxxviii. p. 1247.

After several senators had spoken, Douglas got an opportunity to rejoin: "The senator from Mississippi," he exclaimed, "says if I am not willing to stand in the party on his platform, I can go out. Allow me to inform him that I stand on the platform, and those that jump off must go out of the party."

An acrimonious colloquy between Douglas and Davis ensued. Davis spoke of men who sought "to build up a political reputation by catering to the prejudice of a majority to exclude the property of a minority;" and Douglas retorted by saying he hated "to see men from other sections of the Union pandering to a public sentiment against what I conceive to be common rights under the Constitution. . . . I hold," he continued, "that Congress ought not to force slavery on the people of the territories against their will." " I wish to say," Davis replied, "that what the government owes to person and property is adequate protection, and the amount of protection which must be given will necessarily vary with the character of the property and the place where it is held; that any attempt, therefore, to create a prejudice by talking about discrimination between different kinds of property is delusive." I tell you, Davis said, addressing himself to Douglas, you, with your opinions, would have no chance to get the vote of Mississippi to-day. "I should have been glad," he continued, "if the senator, when he had appeared in the Senate, had answered the expectation of many of his friends, and by a speech here have removed the doubt which his reported speeches in the last canvass of Illinois created. . . . He has confirmed me, however, in the belief that he is now as full of heresy as he once was of adherence to the doctrine of popular sovereignty, correctly construed."[1]

Pugh, Broderick, and Stuart, senators from Ohio, California, and Michigan, agreed with Douglas, and the Southern senators agreed with Davis. This new doctrine of the slave

---

[1] For this debate see *Congressional Globe*, vol. xxxviii. p. 1255 *et seq.*

power had been broached in the press before the assembling of Congress;[1] now it was given the seal of approval by the party leaders. In the view of the Southern Democrats, it was simply the logical extension of the Calhoun doctrine and the Dred Scott opinion, yet to the Northern mind it was a startling advance. Calhoun and Taney had maintained that Congress had no right or power to prohibit slavery in the territories, while Davis now held that Congress was bound to protect it. One was the denial of a power, the other the assertion of a positive duty. If we recall the steady encroachment of the slave power, no detailed argument will be necessary to show that Douglas and his adherents were nearer to the Democratic faith of 1848–1850 than Davis and his followers. The assertion of this novel doctrine was one more arrogant pretension; it was one step farther towards the nationalization of slavery, and it made permanent the division in the Democratic party. Davis and his followers broke up the Democratic party as a prelude to breaking up the Union.

The country fully appreciated the importance of this debate of February 23d, and the general opinion of the public was that it had made the schism irreconcilable. The formation of an independent Northern Democratic party, which would either carry the country or give the victory to the Republicans, was presaged, and a split in the next Democratic national convention, appointed at Charleston, was prophesied.[2]

Besides what has been mentioned, other events of the session demonstrated a lack of affinity between Northern and Southern Democrats. The Pacific Railroad scheme, dear to the North, was killed in the Senate by indirection. The Homestead bill passed the House, with, however, only three

---

[1] Richmond *Enquirer*, cited by New York *Times*, Nov. 16th, 1858; Rise and Fall of the Slave Power, Wilson, vol. ii. p. 656.
[2] See Pike in the New York *Tribune*, Feb. 28th; the New York *Times*, Feb. 25th and March 1st; New York *Herald*, Feb. 25th.

members from the slave States voting in favor of it; but in the Senate it was overslaughed by the appropriation bills and the Cuba thirty-million measure, and, although persistent efforts were made, it was impossible to get it considered. The Southern Democratic senators were successful in preventing an increase of the tariff, which had been recommended by the President. Although it was represented to them with great force that unless the duties on iron manufactures were raised, Pennsylvania, which the Democrats had lost at the last election, could not be recovered, the argument was unavailing.[1]

The Fugitive Slave law was this year brought prominently before the public mind. The difficulty in capturing fugitives, the doubt about a decision, the expense and risk of conveying the adjudged slave from communities whose sympathy was aroused in his behalf, had the effect of making rare the pursuit of a runaway negro. The South held it a grievous wrong that fugitives could seldom be regained save at a greater cost than the negro's worth, but the opinion was now settling down that no remedy existed for the evil. Attempts were made in New York and Pennsylvania to crystallize the public sentiment into personal-liberty laws; and although the proposed measures failed of enactment, they had strong supporters. In Massachusetts, a bill which went far beyond the existing personal-liberty law, and specifically forbade the rendition of fugitive slaves, was only defeated in the House of Representatives by a majority of three.[2]

Great excitement was caused in Philadelphia regarding an alleged fugitive who had been arrested. A tumult was raised in the street near the court-house, and an immense crowd assisted at every stage of the proceedings. Never had that community been so stirred up over a runaway ne-

---

[1] See New York *Herald*, Jan. 30th, Feb. 1st, 3d, 4th, and 7th; Pike to the New York *Tribune*, Feb. 2d. See Debate on Bigler's Resolutions.
[2] The *Liberator*, April 2d, 8th, 15th; New York *Times*, April 15th.

gro. It is possible that an attempt at rescue would have been made, had not the commissioner found a technical defect in the proof and discharged the prisoner.[1]

One of the most notable prosecutions under the Fugitive Slave act took place in Cleveland, Ohio, in the months of April and May. Cleveland was the business and political centre of the Western Reserve, and nowhere in the country outside of Massachusetts was the anti-slavery sentiment so strong as in this district. The population was made up of Connecticut and Massachusetts people, and the puritanical love of liberty, law, and order existed in a marked degree, while the narrowness of spirit common to provincial communities of New England had been broadened by the necessity of adopting larger methods in the freer atmosphere of the West.

Oberlin was a conspicuous place in this district, and an important station on the Underground Railroad.[2] Oberlin College had fame abroad, not for deep learning and wide culture, but for its radical methods. The feature of co-education of boys and girls was adopted without reserve. Of the twelve hundred students who yearly resorted there, five hundred were, as the catalogue called them, ladies.[3] If the college did not make profound scholars, it sent forth into the world earnest men and women.

In 1859, Oberlin College was especially known as a centre of strong anti-slavery opinions and deep religious convic-

---

[1] New York *Tribune* and Philadelphia *Evening Bulletin*, cited by the *Liberator*, April 15th; New York *Times*, April 8th.

[2] Oberlin, by Fairchild, p. 114. The authorities of a neighboring township, sneering at the anti-slavery zeal which distinguished Oberlin, showed this feeling in an unmistakable manner. The guide-board on the Middle Ridge Road, six miles from Oberlin, indicated its direction, "not by the ordinary index finger, but by the full-length figure of a fugitive running with all his might to reach the place."—Ibid., p. 117.

[3] In the catalogue for 1858–59, for which I am indebted to Mr. Root, the librarian, the number is set down as 736 "gentlemen" and 513 "ladies."

tions. Actuated by those sentiments, the reception given to the higher-law doctrine as a rule of action towards the Fugitive Slave act was zealous and complete. By its friends, Oberlin was called a highly moral and severely religious town, "an asylum for the oppressed of all God's creation, without distinction of color." [1] By its enemies it was stigmatized as a hot-bed of abolitionism, and as "that old buzzards' nest where the negroes who arrive over the Underground Railroad are regarded as dear children." [2]

In September, 1858, a slave-catcher whose manner and appearance called to mind Haley in "Uncle Tom's Cabin," [3] while at Oberlin seeking some of his own escaped slaves, lighted upon a negro by the name of John, who had, more than two years previously, fled from a Kentucky neighbor. After having procured the necessary papers and the assistance of the proper officers, fearing that there might be trouble if the arrest were attempted in the village, Jennings, the slave-catcher, had the negro decoyed a short distance from Oberlin, where he was seized and taken to Wellington, a village nine miles distant and a station on the railroad to Columbus. Here it was proposed to take the fugitive for examination before a United States commissioner.

The long stay of Jennings in Oberlin had already excited suspicion as to the nature of his visit. The news of this capture quickly spread, and the people of Oberlin were ready to act in the manner that, according to their view, the occasion demanded. A large crowd of men, many of whom were armed, proceeded rapidly to Wellington, and took the negro from his captors without firing a shot or harming a person. The negro was promptly driven off in a wagon and escaped effectually from the clutches of his claimant.

Thirty-seven men were indicted under the provisions of the

---

[1] Remark of Spalding, attorney for defence, Oberlin-Wellington rescuers' trial, Oberlin-Wellington Rescue, p. 77.
[2] Remark of Bliss, attorney for prosecution, ibid., p. 166.
[3] Cleveland *Herald*, April 7th, 1859.

act of 1850 for the rescue of the fugitive. Among them was a superintendent of a sabbath-school, a professor, and several students of Oberlin College. Never had a more respectable body of prisoners appeared at the bar than the gentlemen who were now arraigned in the United States District Court at Cleveland; nor did they lack defenders. Four eminent attorneys of Cleveland volunteered for the defence. Sympathy and interest combined to induce them to give their services without a fee. All of them had political aspirations, and three were eager for the next Republican nomination to Congress in this district, where that nomination was equivalent to election. The sympathy of the community was so completely with the prisoners that the path to political preferment lay through efforts on their behalf. On the other hand, there was no lack of energy on the part of the prosecution, who had the sympathy of the judge, and the active countenance of the administration at Washington. The district attorney associated with himself an able lawyer, and professional pride actuated them to extraordinary efforts.

The first person tried was Simeon Bushnell. A struck jury was demanded. Twelve worthy citizens from different parts of the judicial district were the panel: all were Democrats. Some of them, indeed, were representative men of their communities, who reverenced the Constitution of the United States, and believed that all laws made in pursuance thereof should be rigidly executed; yet they had warm feelings, and were willing to give the benefit of the doubt to the accused.

The scene in the court-room was worthy of memory. A judge who had a high idea of the dignity of his office; attorneys who were fighting for reputation; the prisoner, a man of unsullied character; a remarkable jury composed of men whom only a sense of duty could have induced to leave their homes and business; the court-room crowded with intelligent people, whose sympathy was warm for the prisoner—all combined to make this trial an important episode in the anti-slavery struggle of the decade before the war.

The law was plain, the evidence clear, and the verdict of the jury, as might have been expected, was "guilty." The interesting pleas of the attorneys were heard by a crowd of men and women who filled the court-room to overflowing. The attorney for the prosecution sneered at the fact that when the Oberlin people went to Wellington for the rescue of the negro, they proclaimed that they were acting under the higher law. Riddle, who spoke first for the defence, and who, the forthcoming year, was elected to Congress from the Cleveland district, boldly declared: "I am a votary of that higher law;" and when he said, "If a fugitive comes to me in his flight from slavery and is in need of . . . rest and comfort and protection, and means of further flight, so help me the great God in my extremest need, he shall have them all," the court-room resounded with the most enthusiastic applause.[1]

Spalding, who also spoke for the defence, and was elected to Congress from the Cleveland district in 1862, maintained that Bushnell was in danger of losing his liberty for nothing else than "obeying the injunction of Jesus Christ, 'Whatsoever ye would men should do to you, do ye even so to them.'"[2] It was with some reason that the district attorney grimly asked: "Are we in a court of justice, or are we in a political hustings?" And when, yielding to passion, he abused the Republican press of Cleveland and the audience of the court-room, he had further evidence of the prevailing sentiment in unmistakable hisses.[3]

Until the end of the Bushnell trial, each man under indictment had been released on his own recognizance; but now, as the result of an outrageous decision of the judge and consequent wrangling between the attorneys, the Oberlin people determined not to enter recognizance or give their word of honor to the marshal that they would appear in the court-room when wanted, and they were therefore taken

---

[1] Oberlin-Wellington Rescue, p. 56.   [2] Ibid., p. 63.
[3] Ibid., pp. 82, 83.

to jail. It was a self-imposed martyrdom; but the fact could not be ignored that these respectable people were in prison, and the preaching on Sunday of Professor Peck from the jail-yard produced a remarkable sensation.

The court proceedings were called political trials, but when contrasted with state-cases in Europe, except in England, and when compared with English political trials before this century, it is impossible for the historian to draw a stern picture of governmental tyranny. The men in jail were regarded by the community as heroes; the judge and district attorney, whose impolitic course had led them to accept imprisonment, were objects of execration.

The second person tried was Charles Langston, whose color and race naturally evoked sympathy. The technical points in his favor were made the most of by his attorneys, but the jury, a fresh panel, found him guilty.

Bushnell was sentenced to pay a fine of six hundred dollars and costs, and to be imprisoned in the county jail for sixty days. Before Langston was sentenced, availing himself of the usual privilege, he made an eloquent speech. It was a pathetic description of the disabilities under which the negro labored, of the prejudices against himself on account of his color shared by judge, prosecutors, and jury, and from which even his able and honest counsel were not free. It was indisputable, he maintained, that he had not been tried by his peers. The audience that filled the court-room listened to these remarks which by turns produced sensation and gained applause. When Langston finished, the room rang with loud and prolonged demonstrations of approval. Langston's sentence was a fine of one hundred dollars and costs, and imprisonment for twenty days.

The impression produced by these trials deepened. Meetings of sympathy were held all over the Western Reserve, and on May 24th an immense mass-convention assembled at Cleveland, and heartily cheered the orators of the day as they denounced slavery and the fugitive law. Governor

Chase made a discreet speech. While he was strongly anti-slavery in feeling, he urged upon his audience that the great remedy for the evils they felt lay in the people themselves, at the ballot-box.[1] The Oberlin and Wellington delegations, headed by their bands, marched to the jail, and were addressed from the jail-yard by Langston, Professor Peck, and other prisoners.[2]

In the meantime, the grand jury of Lorain county—the county in which Oberlin and Wellington are situated—had indicted, under a statute passed in 1857,[3] the men who had captured the fugitive, for kidnapping and attempting to carry out of the State in an unlawful manner the negro John, and they were arrested. After lengthy negotiations, a compromise was made by which the Lorain county authorities agreed to dismiss the suits against the alleged kidnappers. The United States were to enter a *nolle prosequi* in the remaining rescue cases. The Oberlin prisoners were released; a hundred guns were fired in Cleveland in their honor, and Oberlin gave them an enthusiastic reception. A few days later Bushnell, having served out his sentence, was given, on his return home, the welcome of a conquering hero.[4]

The sentiment excited by these events is worthy of study, for they made a profound impression on the people of the Western Reserve, and had a material influence on the Republican party of the State. At their convention, held in June, they demanded the repeal of the Fugitive Slave act.[5] Nor was the influence confined to Ohio, for in all the Western States the proceedings were watched with great interest; and New England was, of course, concerned in the result of action that might fitly be ascribed to her influence.[6] These manifestations were not from sympathy with the negro

---

[1] New York *Times*, May 31st.
[2] Oberlin-Wellington Rescue, p. 257.
[3] Laws of Ohio, vol. liv. p. 186.
[4] See Oberlin-Wellington Rescue.
[5] Cleveland *Herald*, June 3d.
[6] See the *Liberator* of 1859, pp. 66, 73, 84, 88, 90.

John, who was known to be a stupid and worthless fellow. A humane feeling for the oppressed race was, indeed, aroused by the manly bearing of Langston, but the overshadowing cause of these outbursts of sentiment arose from the fact that the execution of the fugitive law was a badge of the dominion of the slave power over the North; and the majority of the people of Ohio were ready to resolve that they would no longer be the servants of the Southern oligarchy. This feeling found fit expression in the words of Governor Chase, who, better than any other Republican, represented the sentiment of Ohio.[1] While the compromise that put a stop to the further prosecution of the prisoners was properly regarded a victory for the Oberlin people, yet the conviction and imprisonment of Bushnell and Langston demonstrated that the federal law most obnoxious to the inhabitants of the Western Reserve could be executed among them, and proved the law-abiding character of the people.

A far different course of events may be noted at the South. In August, 1858, the slaver *Echo*, bound for Cuba, with more than three hundred African negroes on board, was captured by a United States vessel and taken to Charleston, South Carolina. An arrangement was made by the President with the Colonization Society for the transportation of the negroes to Africa. The federal authorities made an endeavor to prosecute the crew of the *Echo*. At first the grand jury found no bill against them; but on a later consideration they were indicted for piracy under the United States statute of 1820. They were tried in the United States Circuit Court at Charleston, and the jury brought in a verdict of not guilty. Senator Hammond, of South Carolina, admitted in the Senate that the sentiment of his State was against the execution of the laws referring to the slave-trade, and the Charleston *Mercury* thought the action of the jury reasonable, because it would have been "inconsistent, cruel, and hypocritical in them to condemn men to death for

---

[1] See his speech, New York *Times*, May 31st.

bringing slaves into a community where they are bought and sold every day."¹

A more flagrant violation of United States law is seen in the case of the yacht *Wanderer*. She landed over three hundred negroes, direct from Africa, at Brunswick, Georgia. They were sent up the river and sold, being distributed throughout the State, and some of them were taken as far as Memphis. Measures were instituted by the attorney-general and the federal authorities in Georgia to punish the offenders; the owner and the captain of the yacht and others were indicted, but a jury could not be found to convict them.² It is undeniable that many negroes were smuggled into the South and sold as slaves, in spite of the United States statutes, which were as stringent as words could make them. There are men in every community whose cupidity will tempt them to evade the law, and the temptation was now very great. A succession of good crops, with a large demand for cotton at a high price, had made the South very prosperous. Labor was scarce, and the only source open for a supply was Africa. Slaves in the United States were selling at exorbitant prices, for their value had risen one hundred per cent. in fifteen years. "The very negro," said Senator Hammond, "who, as a prime laborer, would have brought four hundred dollars in 1828, would now, with thirty more years upon him, sell for eight hundred dol-

---

¹ *De Bow's Review*, vol. xxvii. p. 362; Remarks of Senator Hammond, May 23d, 1860. See the *Liberator*, Dec. 24th and 31st, 1858, and the New York *Times*, April 19th, 1859; the President's Message, Dec., 1858.

² J. S. Black to the President, Senate Docs. 2d Sess. 35th Cong., vol. vii.; the President's Message, Dec. 19th, 1859; the debate in the Senate, May 21st and 23d, 1860; the Savannah *Republican*, cited by New York *Tribune*, Dec. 17th and 24th, 1858; the *Tribune*, March 14th, 1859; the Washington *Union*, cited by New York *Times*, Dec. 24th, 1858; the New York *Times*, April 19th and May 6th, 1859; the *Liberator*, Jan. 14th, 1859; Annual Report of the American Anti-Slavery Society for the year ending May 1st, 1860, p. 22.

lars."[1] In Africa, negroes were ridiculously cheap, and, could the slave-trader escape the clutches of the law, the profit was enormous.[2] Public sentiment winked at the infraction of the law; Southern officials, though clothed with federal authority, were lax in its enforcement, and a United States judge of South Carolina came to the support of the offenders by a preposterous decision.[3]

The governmental investigation of this illicit traffic was perfunctory. When a large number of slavers for the Cuban slave-trade were fitted out in New York city, and suffered to depart unmolested,[4] it is easy to believe that Southern officials closed their eyes to the smuggling of negroes into their districts. The assurance of the President that no Africans, except those on the *Wanderer*, had been imported into the South cannot be accepted as historic truth.[5] A reported statement of Douglas in a private conversation, although the conversation is only vouched by anonymous authority, is so fully characteristic, and the discussion was one so naturally suggested by attendant circumstances, that we may believe it is in substance correctly related; and, while the facts may not be accepted as absolute, the impression conveyed is fully warranted. Douglas stated that no doubt could exist that the African slave-trade had been carried on for some time; he confidently believed that fifteen thousand Africans were brought into the country last year, which was a greater number than had been imported in any year when the traffic

---

[1] Speeches and Letters, p. 345.

[2] *De Bow's Review*, vol. xxv. pp. 166, 392, 493; vol. xxvi. p. 649.

[3] New York *Courier and Enquirer* and Boston *Atlas*, cited by the *Liberator*, Jan. 14th; Debate between Senators Wilson and Hammond, May 23d, 1860; Annual Report of the American Anti-Slavery Society, May 1st, 1860, p. 28.

[4] Von Holst, vol. vi. p. 325; Rise and Fall of the Slave Power, vol. ii. p. 618; Report of the American Anti-Slavery Society, May 1st, 1860, p. 24; *De Bow's Review*, vol. xxii. p. 430; vol. xxiii. p. 53.

[5] See President's Message, Dec. 19th, 1859; also *Harper's Monthly*, Oct., 1859, p. 695.

was legal. He had seen "with his own eyes three hundred of those recently imported miserable beings in a slave-pen at Vicksburg, Mississippi, and also large numbers at Memphis, Tennessee."[1] That Douglas considered it a vital question is evident from a statement he made in a letter replying to an inquiry whether his name would be presented to the Charleston convention as a candidate for the presidential nomination. "I could not accept the nomination," he wrote, "if the revival of the African slave-trade is to become a principle of the Democratic party."[2]

Thinking that this declaration was not sufficiently emphatic, he later wrote a letter devoted almost exclusively to this question. Believing that the perpetual prohibition of the African slave-trade after 1808 was an obligation growing out of an essential compromise of the Constitution, he wrote: "I am irreconcilably opposed to the revival of the African slave-trade in any form and under any circumstances."[3]

These expressions were called forth by the growing sentiment of the South. The subject is freely discussed in *De*

---

[1] "A Native Southerner" to the New York *Tribune*, writing from Washington, Aug. 20th. The *Tribune*, Aug. 26th, editorially remarks of the statement of Douglas: "We presume that this is perfectly true; at any rate, we must believe that Mr. Douglas has ample means of knowing whereof he affirms." "A Native Southerner," alluding to the conversation he had reported, writes to the *Tribune*, Aug. 24th: "I owe an apology to the gentleman who gave me the details of that conversation for making it public, as I have since been informed it was strictly a private and confidential conversation, and was imparted to me with no idea that it would go any further; and it certainly should not, had secrecy been enjoined on me." For a number of instances of importation of Africans, see Report of the American Anti-Slavery Society, May 1st, 1860, p. 21 *et seq.* As to the dereliction of duty of the United States government regarding the suppression of the slave-trade, and the reported action of England remonstrating against the reopening of the slave-trade between the United States and Africa, see New York *Tribune*, Aug. 26th.

[2] Letter to J. S. Dorr, June 22d, Life of Douglas, Flint, p. 168.
[3] Letter to Peyton, Aug. 2d, New York *Times*, Aug. 16th.

Bow's Review of 1857 and 1858. In August, 1858, it was the opinion of the editor that a very large party in the cotton States, large enough in some of them to control sentiment and policy, believed that a limited revival of the African slave-trade was indispensable to the South in order to maintain her political position.[1] In January, 1859, the editor could complacently say: "No cause has ever grown with greater rapidity than has that of the advocates of the slave-trade."[2] The Southern convention which met at Vicksburg in May demonstrated that De Bow had not failed to read aright the signs of the times. It was a fine body of men, morally and intellectually, who came together to deliberate on the interests of their section.[3] After a thorough discussion of the question, they resolved that "all laws, State or federal, prohibiting the African slave-trade, ought to be repealed." The vote was 40 to 19, each State casting its electoral vote. Georgia, Arkansas, Alabama, Mississippi, Louisiana, and Texas voted for the resolution, while Tennessee and Florida voted against it, and South Carolina was divided.[4]

The contrast between the way in which obnoxious federal laws were enforced in the Western Reserve of Ohio and, on the other hand, in South Carolina and Georgia, is significant. Although, under Pierce and Buchanan, the execution of a law that bore hard upon the anti-slavery sentiment of a community was more rigorous than the execution of a law offensive to pro-slavery feeling, yet had the administration been so disposed it could not have enforced its will against the dominant sentiment of the South, for its own officers were faithful to their own States rather than to the nation they represented. While mobs in the South did not attend the attempted execution of the laws against

---

[1] *De Bow's Review*, vol. xxv. p. 166.

[2] Ibid., vol. xxvi. p. 51. For Southern sentiment see also Wilson's remarks in Senate, May 23d, 1860; and the Annual Report of the American Anti-Slavery Society, May 30th, 1860, p. 15.

[3] *De Bow's Review*, vol. xxvi. p. 713.   [4] Ibid., vol. xxvii. p. 99.

the slave-trade, as had happened at the North in certain Fugitive-Slave-law cases, the Southern people had a quiet and determined way of asserting their demands. Opposition would have been dangerous; and opposition was not made. When it came to action on the slavery question, a Southern community moved as one man; the dissenters were terrified into silence. At the North opinion was always divided.

The Republican convention of Ohio and the Vicksburg Southern convention may be regarded as representing the extreme political sentiments of the North and the South. Their official declarations are characteristic of the emotions inspired by freedom and by slavery. One demanded the repeal of a federal law repugnant to justice and mercy; the other demanded the abrogation of United States statutes that were an expression of the sublime humanity of the century.

Jefferson Davis spoke, July 6th, to the Democratic State convention of Mississippi. We certainly should strive, he said, for the repeal of the 1820 act, which makes the slave-trade a piracy; but he considered it impracticable to attempt the abrogation of the law of 1818 [1] that prohibited the traffic. Yet, as a matter of right, legislation regarding the importation of Africans ought to be left to the States. Assuming that to be the case, he did not believe it the interest of Mississippi to have more negroes; but the conclusion for Mississippi is not applicable to Texas, New Mexico, or to future acquisitions to be made south of the Rio Grande. Ten years ago, men might have been found at the South who asserted that slavery was wrong, but such has been the progress of "truth and sound philosophy" that now "there is not probably an intelligent mind among our own citizens who doubts either the moral or the legal right of the institution of African slavery, as it exists in our country." He affirmed and elaborated his ideas of Southern rights in the territories. The umpire, the Supreme Court, he averred, "has decided the issue in our favor; and though

---

[1] Supplementary to the Act of 1807. See vol. i. p. 29; Du Bois, Suppression of the Slave Trade, p. 118.

placemen may evade, and fanatics rail, the judgment stands the rule of right, and claims the respect and obedience of every citizen of the United States." He thought the acquisition of Cuba eminently desirable, and in addition to the usual reasons for it he urged another—"the importance of the island of Cuba to the Southern States if formed into a separate confederacy." This was not a mere theoretical consideration, for, he declared, "in the contingency of the election of a President on the platform of Mr. Seward's Rochester speech, let the Union be dissolved."[1]

In the letter of June, Douglas not only made clear his position regarding the African slave-trade, but he averred that if the doctrine that ascribed to Congress the power of establishing slavery in the territories should be foisted into the Democratic creed, he could not accept the nomination for President from the Charleston convention.[2] It is worth while calling attention to the fact that whatever ambiguity and inconsistency there may have been in the utterances of Douglas previous to the Lecompton dispute, his expressions after his revolt against the President were unequivocal. He did not resort to silence, a not uncommon refuge of politicians when divisions in their own party are manifest, but he made occasions to enunciate his principles, for he deemed their acceptance necessary to the welfare of the country. In this portion of his career, history must concede that Douglas was actuated by a bold and sincere patriotism. Southern politicians like Clingman, anxious to see the breach in the party repaired, were amazed that after the adjournment of Congress, Douglas would not let the question rest, but must appear as a controversialist in the columns of *Harper's Magazine*.[3] His article entitled "Popular Sovereignty in the Territories" appeared in the September number. It was a heavy and labored essay, far different from the

---

[1] This speech was published in the New York *Tribune* of Aug. 31st.
[2] Letter to Dorr, Life of Douglas, Flint, p. 168.
[3] Speeches and Writings of Clingman, p. 450.

quality of his speeches, which were commonly bright and pungent.

While, from his point of view, the doctrine that Congress could prohibit slavery in the territories was as false as the one that Congress must protect it, his argument in the main was directed against the position the Southern Democrats had taken under the lead of Davis. Opening with an allusion to the irrepressible-conflict declaration of Seward and the "house divided against itself" of Lincoln, he maintained, in the course of the article, that if the Southern proposition were true, the idea of the irrepressible conflict would be realized, and it would not be an idle dream that the United States might become "entirely a slave-holding nation." He went into a long historical argument to show that his principle of popular sovereignty was as ancient as Jefferson, and believed in by the fathers of the Constitution; and he defended the compromise measures and the Kansas-Nebraska act with the main purpose of showing that the present doctrine of the Southern Democrats was an innovation in the Democratic creed.

The appearance of an article in the most popular magazine on the vital question agitating the public mind, by the foremost man of the country, was a political event; and the more remarkable as it was then a thing almost unknown for distinguished public men to write in the magazines. Attorney-General Black undertook to answer Douglas in an article published in the organ of the administration at Washington.[1] Douglas replied and a pamphlet controversy followed. The discussion excited attention; but events now moved with such rapidity that the issues discussed were soon neglected, and the controversy left no lasting impression.

Between the administration and the Douglas Democrats at the East it was a war of pamphlets; in California it was war to the death. In Senator Broderick, the leader of the

---

[1] This article appeared anonymously in the Washington *Constitution* of Sept. 10th.

anti-Lecomptonites, we see a man whose rise to a conspicuous position was only made possible by the peculiar conditions of American life. He was of obscure origin, and the year of his birth was doubtful.[1] His father had been a stone-cutter at Washington. When Broderick, in the Senate, replied to Hammond's sneer at the manual laborers of the North, he pointed to the capitals which crowned the pilasters of the Senate chamber as his father's handiwork. The son of an artisan, he had himself been a mechanic, and he felt no shame in replying thus to the aristocrat of South Carolina, who could see nothing but degradation in work by the hands. His youth was passed in New York city. When he became a man, his business was keeping a grog-shop. He was a Tammany leader of the roughs, and foreman of a fire-engine company in the days before steam fire-engines, when volunteer firemen in New York were a potent political force. Notwithstanding such antecedents, his habits were correct, his morals good, his integrity unquestioned. Better than the society of firemen and Tammany braves did he love the quiet of his room, where, among his books, he sought to remedy the defects of early training. Political disappointment drove him in 1849 to California. He was a member of the convention that framed the constitution of that State, and he afterwards served in the legislature.

The Democratic party in California, owing principally to the strife for patronage and influence, was divided into two factions. Gwin was already the leader of one; Broderick became the leader of the other. When the Lecompton dispute occurred, Gwin, Southern in birth and feeling, and his followers, who were called the chivalry, naturally gravitated to the side of the administration. Broderick, the son of an Irishman, hating aristocracy, marshalled his adherents, who were for the most part Irish and German laborers, called mudsills, under the anti-Lecompton banner. The struggle was intensified by a quarrel regarding the disposition of

---

[1] Variously given as 1818 and 1819.

the federal patronage under President Buchanan. Gwin, in return for Broderick's assistance in his second election as senator, sold to his former opponent the patronage of the State; but this, even before the Lecompton dispute, Buchanan would not deliver.

In Washington, Broderick stood high. The purity of his life and his scrupulous honesty, associated with pride, energy, and ambition, commanded respect from men of both sections and of all parties. Fearless and frank, the serious and reflective cast of mind of this man, alone in the world, without relatives or family, was an added charm for those who knew best his early circumstances. One cannot but wonder whether, had fortune bestowed upon him opportunities for education in an environment of refining influences, his career might not have been an unalloyed benefaction to his country.

In California, his reputation was that of a managing politician who knew how to put to use the lessons he had learned from the Tammany organization. Yet, though surrounded by corruption and willing to bribe others, he would not himself touch the spoils. Believing that if he entered into the game of politics in California, he must employ the tricks in vogue, he played one opponent against another in a discreditable way; yet he remained faithful to his word, and was always better than the men who surrounded him. In a society reeking with foulness, his personal morals were unscathed.

The fiercest conflict between the two factions in California was at hand. Broderick was advised to go to Europe to avoid an apparently hopeless contest with malignant enemies. But, although his senatorship was not at stake, he would not shirk from the responsibility that leadership thrust upon him. On leaving the East he was much depressed. Shortly before sailing for San Francisco he said to Forney: "I feel, my dear friend, that we shall never meet again. I go home to die. I shall be challenged, I shall fight, and I shall be killed."

The campaign in California was unsurpassed for bitterness. Men in that State were not accustomed to mince their words; to them, common courtesy in a political conflict seemed strangely out of place. The most violent abuse, the most insolent vituperation, were the best of arguments. On such a canvass Broderick entered, trying at first to be decent and to demean himself according to the fashion of the East. It soon appeared that the Lecompton men would give no quarter and were determined to crush their most powerful enemy. Judge Terry, of the California Supreme Court, had referred to Broderick in an insulting manner, and this Broderick had resented in an expression of like tenor. An insignificant person, hearing Broderick's words, challenged the senator to fight. He replied June 29th, that until the canvass was over he would neither notice an insult nor fight a duel. Although suffering from a prostrating disease, Broderick engaged in the campaign with ardor. Knowing that his enemies were hounding him to death, he no longer spared them. His denunciation of Gwin was bitter in the extreme. He said his colleague was "dripping with corruption." Though no orator, Broderick had a blunt and effective way of putting things, and it was a stinging blow to the chivalry and their leader when he told the whole story of the senatorial bargain, and described Gwin as cringing to him for support.

The election took place September 7th. The defeat of Broderick's party was overwhelming. On the day after election, Terry resigned his position as judge and sent a challenge to Broderick on account of the mildly offensive words used in June. The senator hesitated, but finally accepted the challenge. The duel took place September 13th, ten miles from San Francisco. By Terry's winning the toss, his duelling pistols were used. Terry was a Texan, a dead shot, accustomed to affairs of honor; his pistols were set with hair triggers. By intention or accident, Broderick got the one more delicate on the trigger. He was ill, weak, and consequently nervous, but stood his ground with the courage of a martyr. The duel was at ten paces. After the combatants should say they were ready, the word would be given, "Fire—one—two." The pistols were not to be raised until the word "fire." When that was pronounced, Broderick raised his pistol, but, owing to the delicacy of the trigger, it went off prematurely, and the ball entered the ground about four paces in advance of him. A second later Terry, taking deliberate aim, shot him through the breast.

In two days Broderick was dead and California in mourning. His funeral at San Francisco was imposing. Ten thousand people were mourners. Colonel Baker, the most eloquent orator of the State, with the dead body coffined before him, delivered the funeral oration, paying a noble tribute to the man who was his friend.

"Fellow-citizens," Baker said, "the man that lies before you was your senator. From the moment of his election his character has been maligned, his motives attacked, his courage impeached, his patriotism assailed. It has been a system tending to one end. And the end is here. What was his crime? Review his history—consider his public acts—weigh his private character—and before the grave encloses him forever, judge between him and his enemies. As a man to be judged in his private relations, who was his superior? It was his boast—and, amidst the general license of a new country, it was a proud one—that his most scrutinizing enemy could fix no single act of immorality upon him. Temperate, decorous, self-restrained, he had passed through all the excitements of California unstained. No man could charge him with broken faith or violated trust. Of habits simple and inexpensive, he had no lust of gain. He overreached no man's weakness in a bargain, and withheld no man his just dues. Never in the history of the State has there been a citizen who has borne public relations more stainless in all respects than he. But it is not by this standard that he is to be judged. He was a public man, and his memory demands a public judgment. What was his public crime? The answer is in his own words: 'They have killed me because I was opposed to the extension of slavery and a corrupt administration.'" The orator made a manly protest against the duello. "The code of honor," said he, "is a delusion and a snare; it palters with the hope of a true courage, and binds it at the feet of crafty and cruel skill. . . . It substitutes cold and deliberate preparation for courageous and manly impulse; . . . it makes the mere 'trick of the weapon' superior to the noblest cause and the truest courage."

The funeral oration was pathetic and caused profound emotion; at its close orator and people wept in sympathy. It was calculated to stir up men's hearts, and it impressed in glowing words the conviction that Broderick had been hunted to the death by his antagonists. Baker, in 1861, met an heroic end at the battle of Ball's Bluff; but before he fell, the martyrdom of Broderick had borne fruit. It produced a mighty revolution in public opinion. The "chivalry," the Southern party, lost forever their power in the State. In the legislature elected the next year, the Douglas Democrats and Republicans together had a large majority, and when the Southern States began to secede, they passed a resolution pledging that California would remain faithful to the Union. Although Terry's life was prolonged thirty years, he never lived down what people called the deliberate murder of Broderick. At length, having grossly assaulted Justice Field, of the United States Supreme Court, he met his death from the shot of the marshal who, on account of threats uttered by Terry, had been assigned to the protection of the judge.

The death of Broderick created a profound sensation in the East. All knew that he was a victim to the wrath of the slavery propaganda. A journalist at Washington, who both reflected and guided public opinion, looked upon his loss as a public calamity. In New York city he was mourned as a citizen, and appropriate obsequies were held to pay him the last tribute of respect and affection.[1]

---

[1] My authorities for this account are the San Francisco journals of the

The most noticeable political campaign of the year east of the Mississippi River was in Ohio. That State, unlike most of the others, had an exciting election every year, for the governor and congressmen were elected in alternate years. Moreover, the State and congressional elections came in October, anticipating by one month most of the contests, so that, next to Pennsylvania, Ohio was the most important State of the Union as indicating the direction of popular sentiment. Though generally Republican, hard struggles for mastery were frequent.

The Republican candidate for governor was William Dennison, of Columbus. The Democrats nominated Judge Ranney, of Cleveland. Ranney wielded a good and powerful influence in his community; but as he lived in districts at first strongly Whig and afterwards Republican, he was rarely elected to office, although frequently a candidate, and the only national reputation he gained was that of a great lawyer. But in his own State he was known to be more than an able advocate; he was a profound jurist. The bent of his mind was legal, and, surmounting the obstacles of poverty and lack of opportunities, he acquired a partial education in school and college. When, in course of time, he came to the lawyer's office and the law library, he there mastered the principles which were the basis of his science. As a member of the Ohio constitutional convention, he had a great share in making the organic law; as judge of the Ohio Supreme Court, he interpreted it in a series of decisions which for sound doctrine, clearness of thought and expression, are probably not surpassed in the court records

---

day, copious extracts from which are copied into the New York *Tribune* and *Herald;* the editorial articles in each journal; a tribute by Broderick's friend, George Wilkes, cited by the *Tribune* of Oct. 19th; H. H. Bancroft, vol. xviii. chaps. xxiii. and xxiv., and vol. xxiv. pp. 251 and 272; Royce's California, p. 495; Forney's Anecdotes of Public Men, vol. i. p. 27; Pike's First Blows of the Civil War, p. 446. "Editor's Easy Chair," *Harper's Magazine,* Jan., 1860. In the account of the duel, I follow mainly the sworn testimony before the coroner's jury.

of any State. In his own community, he was esteemed for his honesty and purity of life. He loved to settle disputes outside of the courts. He was the champion of the poor and of those who lacked social distinction, yet he comprehended the rights of property as well as the rights of man.[1]

This canvass was different from most of the other exciting campaigns of Ohio in that the candidates for the governorship met one another several times in joint debate. As a speaker and reasoner, Ranney was much superior to Dennison; but Dennison had the better cause, and the one to which Ohio opinion was strongly tending. The Democrats of Ohio, with the exception of the office-holders, were followers of Douglas, whose principles Ranney expounded with vigor. But Ranney hated slavery worse than did his leader. He maintained that under the operation of popular sovereignty, all the territories were certain to come into the Union as free States. The shadow of the Oberlin persecution being over the canvass, the exact measure of obedience to the Fugitive Slave law entered into the discussion. Dennison was apparently affected by the speeches of Lincoln the previous year, and took a position calculated to attract the Fillmoreans of 1856.[2]

Lincoln and Douglas were also brought into the canvass. Though not meeting in joint discussion, their speeches were to a certain extent a continuation of the debates of 1858. Lincoln came out as a party leader more prominently than in the preceding year.[3] He asserted at Columbus that the most imminent danger threatening the purpose of the Republican organization was the "insidious Douglas popular sovereignty."[4] In this speech he utterly demolished as a

---

[1] See *Western Magazine of History*, vol. ii. p. 205.
[2] See debate at Cleveland, Sept. 15th, Cleveland *Plain Dealer* and *Herald*.
[3] See also Lincoln's letter to Colfax, Nicolay and Hay vol. ii. p. 178.
[4] Lincoln-Douglas Debates, p. 242.

logical and constitutional argument the doctrine which Douglas so earnestly advocated. But that doctrine, like many other political principles, was stronger in practical working than in theory. When Ranney stated at Cleveland that Nebraska, Utah, and New Mexico would undoubtedly be free, he stated the well-matured conviction of people best informed. It was true that the legislature of New Mexico had passed an act to provide for the protection of slaves, but no slaves were in the territory, and none were expected; the enactment was simply for political effect and to further the fortunes of a few adventurers.[1] Nor did the South expect to derive any benefit from this action.[2] It was idle to talk of sending slaves to the barren wastes and rocky regions of New Mexico, when not enough negroes could be had to cultivate the cotton fields and rice and sugar plantations of the South. It is clear that under the operation of natural forces, if the executive administration were fair and inclined to freedom, every territory would remain free and become a free State. A great many people held this opinion in 1859. There were, indeed, Republicans who thought they had no issue left.[3] If the Southern States had remained in the Union, congressional prohibition of slavery in the territories after the election of Lincoln would at first have been impossible, for the Republicans would have been in a minority in Congress.

The action of the New Mexico legislature was, however, a good argument for Republicans to use with anti-slavery men against the proposition that popular sovereignty would effectually prevent the extension of slavery. But Lincoln used a better one in his Cincinnati speech when he intimated that

---

[1] Arizona and New Mexico, H. H. Bancroft, p. 683. In spite of the efforts of the slave-holders, said Seward at Lawrence, Kan., Sept. 26th, 1860, they have got "freedom in Kansas, and practically in New Mexico, in Utah, and California."—Seward's Works, vol. iv. p. 392.

[2] See *De Bow's Review*, vol. xxvi. p. 601.

[3] See New York *Times*, July 29th; Pike's First Blows of the Civil War, p. 445.

it would be preposterous for those wishing to prevent the spread of slavery to enlist under the Douglas banner, for Douglas had never said that slavery was wrong, but asserted rather that he did not care whether it was "voted up or voted down."[1] In truth, Douglas, both at Columbus and Cincinnati, had rejoiced as much at the action of New Mexico in establishing slavery on paper as at the action of Kansas in repealing the slave code foisted upon her by the first legislature.[2] The strong partisan arguments of Lincoln in his two Ohio speeches were justifiable from his point of view, and in the light of after-events may probably be so regarded. He showed greater self-confidence than he had displayed in his Illinois speeches. He was obviously complimented to have his name linked with Seward's as an expounder of Republican doctrine, and he impressed upon his hearers the absolute need of a national party that should oppose the extension of slavery by action of Congress. In the Columbus speech he addressed himself to the *Harper's Magazine* article, finding little difficulty in pointing out material facts of history which Douglas had overlooked or suppressed. But in the Cincinnati speech Lincoln himself twisted our constitutional history, though we may be sure it was from lack of correct information and not with the intention to deceive.

Dennison was elected governor of Ohio by thirteen thousand majority; the Democrats were defeated in Pennsylvania, and the Republicans carried Iowa.

While the Republicans of the October States were rejoicing at their success, and those of the November States were preparing for the last electoral contest of the year, John Brown startled the country by making a violent attack on

---

[1] Lincoln-Douglas Debates, p. 257.
[2] These speeches of Douglas were published in the New York *Times*, Sept. 9th and 13th. The one at Columbus was telegraphed entire, an unusual thing in those days, and it was considered a remarkable newspaper feat.

slavery in Virginia. On Monday, October 17th, the news came that a large body of abolitionists and negroes had captured the United States arsenal at Harper's Ferry, had taken possession of the bridge which crosses the Potomac, fortifying it with cannon, had cut telegraph wires, stopped trains, killed several men, and had seized many prominent citizens who were held as hostages. It was also reported that the slaves in the neighborhood had risen and that the surrounding country was in a high state of alarm, expecting all the horrors of a servile revolt. Later in the day more correct information was obtained. It became known that Captain Brown was the leader and that his force did not exceed twenty-two men. On the following morning the welcome intelligence came that the Virginia militia and the United States troops had suppressed the insurrection, and that most of the insurgents had been killed or taken prisoners.

This event, which struck the country with amazement and distracted public attention from all other concerns, was not the result of a sudden impulse, but had been long in preparation. More than twenty years before, John Brown had told his family that the purpose of his life was to make war on slavery by force and arms. He asked his children if they were willing to join him and do all in their power to "break the jaws of the wicked and pluck the spoil out of his teeth;" and when they signified assent, he administered to them a solemn oath of secrecy and devotion.[1] Brown's family was large; their unquestioned obedience and the consecration of their lives to his service call to mind the story of the patriarchs. He had long been satisfied that the "milk-and-

---

[1] Sanborn, p. 39. Letter of Sanborn to the *Nation*, Dec. 20th, 1890, communicating a letter of John Brown, Jr. This letter was drawn out by an article in the *Andover Review* for Dec., 1890, by Wendell P. Garrison, which questioned whether the Harper's Ferry scheme or one similar to it had long been entertained. See also Garrison in the *Andover Review* for Jan., 1891, p. 59.

water principles" of the abolitionists, as he called their belief in moral suasion, would effect nothing. Happening to be in Boston in May, 1859, he became an attentive listener to the speeches made at the New England anti-slavery convention. At its close he passed judgment on their method by saying: "These men are all talk; what is needed is action—action!" Nor, in his opinion, could anything be expected from the Republicans, for they were opposed to meddling with slavery in the States where it existed.[1]

The Kansas experience of Brown had convinced him that he could get followers in any undertaking, no matter how desperate. It had also brought him into contact with men of means and influence, who were willing to back him in his peculiar crusade against slavery. Not the least astonishing thing in this strange history is the manner of men whom he induced to aid him in the conspiracy against the laws of their common country. Gerrit Smith, the rich philanthropist; Theodore Parker, the noted preacher; Dr. S. G. Howe, an enthusiast in the cause of suffering humanity; Thomas W. Higginson, the pastor of a free church at Worcester; Stearns, a successful business man of Boston; Sanborn, fresh from college, ready to give his income and sacrifice his small property for the cause—these were Brown's trusted friends. That he could attach to himself men of such differing aims, holding such positions in society, and make out of them fellow-conspirators, is proof of the strong personal magnetism he exerted on sympathetic natures. John A. Andrew, a man of parts who afterwards distinguished himself as the war governor of Massachusetts, once casually met Brown, and, though seeing him but a few minutes, "was very much impressed by him," and thought him "a very magnetic person."[2]

---

[1] Life of Frederick Douglass, p. 279; Testimony of William F. M. Arny before the Mason Committee; Sanborn, p. 421; Life of Garrison, vol. iii. p. 488.

[2] Testimony of John A. Andrew before the Mason Committee, p. 192.

Brown's occupation in Kansas seemingly gone, he deemed the time had come to strike a blow in another quarter. Leaving a little company of followers in Iowa, to whom little by little he had imparted his plans, and who were devoting the leisure of the winter to military drill, he came East in January, 1858, seeking the sinews of war. Wishing a full and complete conference with his friends, he asked Parker, Higginson, Stearns, and Sanborn to meet him at Peterboro', New York, the home of Gerrit Smith. Sanborn only could make the journey; he reached the house of the philanthropist on the evening of February 22d. After dinner Brown disclosed his plan. With a small body of trusty men he proposed to occupy a place in the mountains of Virginia, whence he would make incursions down into the cultivated districts to liberate slaves. As they were freed he would arm them. He would subsist on the enemy, fortify himself against attack, and by his mode of operation make slavery insecure in the country in which he should first raise the standard of revolt, so that masters would sell their remaining slaves and send them away. Then operations might be indefinitely extended until his name should become a terror all through the South, and the tenure of property in man precarious. At the same time, his success would attract from the North and from Canada recruits, eager to take part in this movement for the destruction of slavery. As his adherents might increase to a great number, he had prepared a scheme of provisional government which he submitted to his friends. At the worst, he would have a retreat open to the North. Arms were already provided for his enterprise, and with eight hundred dollars in money he could begin operations in May.[1]

As Brown unfolded his plan to the little council, amazement sat on every brow. To attempt so great an enterprise with means so small seemed unspeakable folly. His friends

---

[1] Sanborn, p. 439; Life of Frederick Douglass, pp. 279, 420; Mason Report.

discussed the project and criticised it in detail, but every obstacle had been foreseen by Brown, and to each objection he had a ready answer and a plausible argument. When the hopelessness of defying the slave power and making war upon the State of Virginia with so small a band was urged, he replied: "If God be for us, who can be against us?"[1] The council sat until after midnight. The discussion was renewed the next day. The enthusiasm and confidence of Brown almost persuaded his friends; at any rate, they saw it would be vain to oppose him, and it seemed equally clear he must be renounced or assisted. At last, when apart from the rest of the company, Gerrit Smith said to Sanborn: "You see how it is; our dear old friend has made up his mind to this cause, and cannot be turned from it. We cannot give him up to die alone; we must support him. I will raise so many hundred dollars for him; you must lay the case before your friends in Massachusetts, and perhaps they will do the same. I see no other way." This was in accordance with Sanborn's own view, and he returned at once to Boston to perform his part in the undertaking. A letter from Brown to Sanborn, shortly after, gives us a glimpse of his inmost thoughts. The words are such as could only come from "a regular old Cromwellian dug up from two centuries."[2] "I have only had this one opportunity in a life of nearly sixty years," Brown wrote; "and could I be continued ten times as long again, I might not again have another equal opportunity. God has honored but comparatively a very small part of mankind with any possible chance of such mighty and soul-satisfying rewards. . . . I expect nothing but to 'endure hardness;' but I expect to effect a mighty conquest, even though it be like the last victory of Samson."[3]

When Sanborn apprised Theodore Parker of the project,

---

[1] Sanborn, p. 439.
[2] Wendell Phillips at Plymouth Church, Brooklyn, Nov. 1st, 1859.
[3] Sanborn, p. 444.

the latter became anxious to see Brown, who, on that suggestion, made a visit secretly to Boston. There, in a room of the American House, the Massachusetts friends and the old Puritan plotted together. Brown deserved that name as well by lineage as by character. He was a direct descendant of Peter Brown, one of the Pilgrims who had come over in the *Mayflower*, and both of his grandfathers had fought in the Revolutionary War.

He wrote from Boston to his son, giving the result of his visit: "My call here has met with a most hearty response, so that I feel assured of at least tolerable success. I ought to be thankful for this. All has been effected by a quiet meeting of a few choice friends, it being scarcely known that I have been in the city." [1]

A fund of one thousand dollars was raised. In many of their communications, the conspirators used a cipher. Brown assumed the name of Hawkins. When begging his daughter to consent that her husband should accompany him, he called his followers scholars and their work would be going to school.[2] The enterprise was also spoken of as the wool business, and Sanborn wrote that Hawkins "has found in Canada several good men for shepherds, and, if not embarrassed by want of means, expects to turn his flock loose about the 15th of May."[3] After Parker's failing health had driven him to Europe, he asked in a letter from Rome: "Tell me how our little speculation in wool goes on, and what dividend accrues therefrom."[4]

But the immediate execution of the plan was checked by an untoward circumstance. Brown had previously made the acquaintance of Forbes, a European adventurer, had engaged him as drill-master on account of his military experience, and had injudiciously confided to him his purpose of attacking slavery in one of the border States. Being unable to draw money from the friends of Brown, Forbes

---

[1] Sanborn, p. 440.   [2] Ibid., p. 441.
[3] Ibid., p. 457; see also p. 447.   [4] Life of Parker, Frothingham, p. 462.

divulged to Senators Seward and Wilson at Washington that Brown had an unlawful object in view, for which he was going to use rifles belonging to the Massachusetts State Kansas committee. Wilson immediately wrote to Dr. Howe, protesting against any such employment to be made of the arms, and advising that they be taken from the custody of Brown. Stearns, the chairman of the Massachusetts State Kansas committee, then warned Brown that no use must be made of the arms other than for the defence of Kansas. A few days later Smith, Parker, Howe, Stearns, and Sanborn held a meeting at the Revere House, Boston, and decided that the attack on slavery in Virginia must be postponed. They also determined that Brown ought to go at once to Kansas.[1]

He appeared in the territory in June. Having heretofore been smooth-shaven, his long white beard now served as a disguise to many who had known him in other days.[2] Although peace had been nominally restored in Kansas, the most terrible deed of blood the territory had known was perpetrated in the spring of 1858. Hamilton, a Georgian leader of a pro-slavery band, soured at the triumph of the free-State party, had made a black-list of persons whom he deemed deserving of death on account of their exertions for the free-State cause. Near Marais des Cygnes, he had in a raid taken a number of prisoners. Selecting eleven, he had them drawn up in a line, and, without trial or ceremony, shot in cold blood. Five fell dead and five were wounded.[3] When Brown reached Kansas, the country resounded with the horror of this massacre, but opportunity for retaliation did not occur until late in the year. Hearing that a negro, his wife, two children, and another negro were to be sold and sent away from a Missouri plantation, Brown, with a

---

[1] Sanborn, p. 456 et seq.; testimony of Seward, Wilson, and Howe before the Mason committee.
[2] Life of Captain John Brown, Redpath, p. 199.
[3] Spring's Kansas, p. 246; Sanborn, p. 481; Redpath, p. 200.

small company, crossed the Missouri line, liberated the five slaves to whose aid he went, and also set six others free. In the accomplishment of this work, one of the slave-holding party was killed. The governor of Missouri put a price of three thousand dollars on Brown's head and he was pursued; but he defeated one party of pursuers in a fight, eluded others, and, bringing his party of freedmen safely through Kansas, Nebraska, Iowa, Illinois, and Michigan, he saw them on the 12th of March, 1859, ferried across from Detroit to Windsor in Canada.[1]

The Kansas exploit delighted the friends of Brown, with the exception of Dr. Howe, who disapproved of his taking property from the slave-holders, which he had done to give the fugitives an outfit. During the winter, Howe had accompanied Theodore Parker to Cuba, and on his return had made a stay in South Carolina, where he accepted the hospitality of Wade Hampton and other rich planters. It was some time before he was willing to render Brown any aid. The idea of a slave insurrection, in which such noble mansions as he had visited should be given to the torch and their inmates to the knife, struck him with horror. Parker was away, and Higginson, since the postponement of the plan had not met his approval, thereafter took less interest in it; thus the burden of the financial part of the undertaking fell upon Smith, Stearns, and Sanborn. They, however, made up in zeal what they lacked in number.[2]

More than four thousand dollars was contributed in aid of the Virginia enterprise. Most of this sum passed through the hands of the secret committee, and nearly all the donors knew for what purpose the money would be used. Of this amount, Smith contributed seven hundred and fifty dollars, and Stearns one thousand dollars. But although it was known that a foray would be made in Virginia, no one of the committee, except Sanborn, had an intimation that the blow

---

[1] Sanborn, p. 482 *et seq.*; Spring's Kansas, p. 252.
[2] Sanborn, pp. 491, 493.

might be struck at Harper's Ferry.[1] Brown was secretive, and men like Smith and Stearns did not, for obvious reasons, desire to be apprised of the full details of the project. That Brown was going to make a raid into Virginia was probably not known to more than fifty persons besides his family and armed followers, though a thousand may have had good reason to suspect that he intended to attack slavery by force in some part of the South.[2] It must be borne in mind that at this time the steadfast friends of Brown refused to credit the charge that he had been concerned in the Pottawatomie executions.[3]

For arms he had two hundred Sharps rifles, two hundred revolvers, and nine hundred and fifty pikes.[4] The pikes were to arm the slaves who should fly to his standard. "Give a slave a pike and you make him a man" was one of his maxims.[5] The Republican members of the Senate committee that investigated the Harper's Ferry invasion reported that Brown perverted the fire-arms from the purpose for which he had received them.[6] While this is a warrantable inference from the testimony before the committee, later disclosures show that the rifles and revolvers had become the individual property of Stearns; that he was in full sympathy with the Virginia scheme as the Massachusetts friends understood it, and had willingly given the arms to Brown.[7]

Brown, having decided that he would strike the blow at Harper's Ferry, rented in July two houses on the Kennedy farm, on the Maryland side of the Potomac, four miles from

---

[1] See Sanborn, p. 450. Sanborn says: Whether Smith 'knew that Harper's Ferry was to be attacked is uncertain; for this was communicated only to a few persons except those actually under arms" (p. 545). Smith wrote in 1867: "I had not myself the slightest knowledge nor intimation of Brown's intended invasion of Harper's Ferry."—Life of Smith, Frothingham, p. 254; see also p. 259 et seq.

[2] Sanborn, pp. 418, 496.   [3] See p. 164.
[4] Blair's testimony, Mason Report.   [5] Redpath, p. 206.
[6] See Report, p. 23.   [7] Sanborn, p. 464.

the United States armory in the Virginia village. He collected his munitions of war at Chambersburg, Pennsylvania. The fire-arms were sent by his son from Ohio, and the pikes by the manufacturer from Connecticut, both being shipped to I. Smith & Sons, and so delivered by the railroad company. It was also a place of meeting for the volunteers, and thence the men and materials were quietly conveyed to the Kennedy farm. A notable circumstance in these days of preparation was the conference between Brown and Frederick Douglass in an old stone quarry near Chambersburg. They had long been intimately acquainted, and met at Brown's request to consider the work in hand, of which Douglass had an inkling. Now the old Puritan declared that it was his settled purpose to take Harper's Ferry, for the capture of a place so well known " would serve as notice to the slaves that their friends had come and as a trumpet to rally them to his standard." Douglass combated the design with the strongest of arguments. You not only attack Virginia, he urged, but you attack the federal government, and you will array the whole country against you; furthermore, you are going into a perfect steel-trap; once in, you will never get out alive; you will be surrounded and escape will be impossible. But the cogent reasoning and earnest manner of Douglass failed to shake the purpose of Brown. After he had flatly refused to join the expedition, the old Puritan, giving him a fraternal embrace, said: " Come with me, Douglass; I will defend you with my life. I want you for a special purpose. When I strike, the bees will begin to swarm, and I shall want you to help hive them."[1] Many of Brown's followers remonstrated with him when the Harper's Ferry plan was disclosed. One of his sons said: "You know how it resulted with Napoleon when he rejected advice in regard to marching with his army to Moscow." But in the end, by persuasion and by

---

[1] Life of Frederick Douglass, p. 325 *et ante;* Sanborn, p. 538 *et seq.*

threatening resignation as their leader, he silenced all objections.¹

The Kennedy farm was in an unsuspecting neighborhood. The gathering of the forces, the load of very heavy boxes, excited no suspicion; the presence of so many strangers whose ostensible occupations were but a thin disguise, aroused little curiosity. In August, the Secretary of War received an anonymous letter from Cincinnati, in which the plot was disclosed, the leader's name given, and the proposed point of attack correctly stated; but Floyd only gave it a passing notice and set afoot no investigation.²

The moment for which Brown had waited twenty years had now come. Everything was ready for the blow. On the cold, dark Sunday night of October 16th, he mustered eighteen followers, five of whom were negroes. After giving them his orders, he said: "Now, gentlemen, let me press this one thing on your minds. You all know how dear life is to you, and how dear your lives are to your friends; and in remembering that, consider that the lives of others are as dear to them as yours are to you. Do not, therefore, take the life of any one if you can possibly avoid it; but if it is necessary to take life in order to save your own, then make sure work of it." ³ With the command, "Men, get on your arms; we will proceed to the Ferry," they started from the Kennedy farm. Each man was armed with a rifle and revolvers. Men were sent ahead to tear down the telegraph wires on the Maryland side. Soon the whole party arrived at the covered bridge across the Potomac which connected Maryland and Virginia, and was jointly used by the Baltimore and Ohio Railroad and the citizens. This was taken possession of, the watchman made a prisoner, and the bridge left guarded. Reaching the Virginia side, Brown and two followers broke into the United

---

¹ Sanborn, p. 541.
² See testimony before the Mason committee.
³ Cook's confession, New York *Tribune*, Nov. 26th, 1859.

States armory, and, seizing the watchmen, remained there on guard. Other men took the arsenal near by, where the public arms were deposited, and the rifle-works half a mile away on the Shenandoah River. These buildings were all national property, but not under military guard; the men in charge were civic police engaged by the War Department.[1]

By midnight Brown was master of Harper's Ferry. The lights in the town were put out and the telegraph wires cut. To secure hostages and to make a beginning of conferring freedom on the slaves, he sent out a party to bring in some prominent citizens of the surrounding country with their negroes. To give dramatic force to the exploit, the house of Colonel Lewis Washington, the great-grandson of a brother of George Washington, was visited, and the owner arrested. That which was supposed to be the sword of Frederick the Great, presented by him to the Father of his country, was taken. Brown, in his war of liberation, wanted to bear the sword of him who had gained the country's independence, and to set free, first of all, the slaves of a Washington. The result of this midnight incursion was the arrest of two proprietors, and the bringing into the armory of several slaves.[2]

At half-past one in the morning, the mail train from Wheeling to Baltimore arrived and was stopped by the guard on the bridge. The negro porter employed at the station, a freeman, went out to look for the watchman, and, not heeding an order to halt, turned to run back, was shot and mortally wounded. Before sunrise the train was allowed to go forward, but the conductor first assured himself that the bridge was safe by walking across it with Brown. As the train proceeded towards Baltimore, the news of the foray spread far and wide.[3]

---

[1] Mason Report, and testimony; Sanborn, p. 552.
[2] Washington's testimony before the Mason committee; Sanborn, p. 552.
[3] Mason Report; New York *Herald* and *Tribune;* Sanborn, p. 555.

When the people of Harper's Ferry aroused themselves in the morning, they found a hostile force in possession of the strongholds of their town and holding most of the available fire-arms. Men on their way to work, citizens passing through the streets, were taken prisoners. The church bells were rung; the citizens gathered together; such as had squirrel-rifles and shot-guns organized themselves into companies; the alarm spread, and militia companies from neighboring towns hastened to the scene. Fighting began. Men fell on both sides, among them the mayor of Harper's Ferry and a landed proprietor, a neighbor and friend of Washington, who had gone to the village to attempt his liberation.

For four or five hours after daybreak, Brown might have retreated to the mountains. This he was urged to do by his trustworthy men, but before noon his retreat into Maryland was cut off, and by the middle of the afternoon all the men except those in the armory under Brown's immediate command were killed, captured, or dispersed. At midday Brown withdrew the remnant of his force, with his principal hostages, into the engine-house in the armory yard. The doors and windows were barred, and port-holes were cut through the brick wall. The firing from the outside now became terrible. When the assailants could be seen, their shots were returned by the besieged. One of Brown's sons had been mortally wounded, and the other was instantly killed in the fight of the afternoon.[1] Colonel Washington, who was a prisoner in the engine-house, afterwards said: "Brown was the coolest and firmest man I ever saw in defying danger and death. With one son dead by his side, and another shot through, he felt the pulse of his dying son with one hand and held his rifle with the other, and commanded his men with the utmost composure, encouraging them to be firm and to sell their lives as dearly as they

---

[1] Three of Brown's sons were engaged in the raid; one escaped.

could."[1] Yet the remorseless spirit which governed the stern Puritan that terrible night on the Pottawatomie had departed. He was humane to his prisoners. Instead of wreaking vengeance on them because his sons were dead and dying by his side, he urged them to seek sheltered corners out of the reach of the flying bullets. Not one of them was harmed. Nor would he allow his men to fire on noncombatants outside. "Don't shoot," he would say; "that man is unarmed."[2]

On Monday evening, when Colonel Robert E. Lee, a man who later was destined to win imperishable fame, arrived with a company of United States marines, the force in the engine-house was reduced to Brown himself and his six men, two of whom were wounded. Not wishing to put the lives of the prisoners in jeopardy in the confusion of a midnight assault, Lee delayed operations until daylight Tuesday. Then his summons to surrender having been met with a refusal, his men, using a heavy ladder as a battering-ram, forced an entrance into the engine-house. Brown was cut down by the sword, receiving several wounds on the head, and also bayonet thrusts in the body. He and his followers who remained were quickly taken into custody. Of the nineteen men who had left the Kennedy farm, ten were killed, five taken prisoners, and four had escaped. Two of these were afterwards arrested in Pennsylvania. Of the inhabitants and attacking parties, five were killed and nine wounded.[3]

Virginia was in an uproar. While the baser sort would gladly have lynched Brown and treated him like a dog, gentlemen of education and position could not repress the instinct to admire his courage. It had long been a jeer at

---

[1] Statement to Governor Wise, Speech of Wise at Richmond, Redpath, p. 273.

[2] The article of Dangerfield, one of the prisoners, in the *Century Magazine*, cited by Sanborn, p. 556; Speech of Governor Wise, Redpath, p. 273; John Brown, Von Holst, p. 134.

[3] Lee's Report; Sanborn.

the abolitionists that they did not dare to preach their doctrine at the South; now men had come into their midst to bear testimony with the sword against the wrong of slavery. But any regard for Brown's personal qualities was merged into wonder and alarm at the possible extent of the conspiracy, and the desire was great to know who had been his backers in this expedition. Senator Mason arrived at Harper's Ferry the afternoon of Tuesday, October 18th, and put many questions to the old Puritan, who was lying on the floor of the armory office, his hair matted, and his face, hands, and clothes stained with blood. Brown was asked who had sent him here? Who had furnished the money? How many were engaged with him in the movement? When did he begin the organization? and where did he get the arms? To these questions of Mason and Vallandigham, a congressman from Ohio who assisted in this examination, Brown had but one reply: "I will answer freely and faithfully about what concerns myself — I will answer anything I can with honor, but not about others."

This conversation was set down word for word by a New York *Herald* reporter, and immediately given to the world. It revealed an heroic spirit with an ideal passing comprehension. Such a spirit seemed strangely out of place in a country devoted to material aims and in a century of positive scepticism.

Our object in coming, he said, was "to free the slaves, and only that." When asked by Mason, "How do you justify your acts?" he replied: "I think, my friend, you are guilty of a great wrong against God and humanity—I say it without wishing to be offensive—and it would be perfectly right for any one to interfere with you so far as to free those you wilfully and wickedly hold in bondage. . . . I think I did right," the old Puritan continued, "and that others will do right who interfere with you at any time and all times. I hold that the golden rule, 'Do unto others as ye would that others should do unto you,' applies to all who would help others to gain their liberty." He considered his enterprise "a religious movement" and "the greatest service man can render to God;" he regarded himself "an instrument in the hands of Providence." "I want you to understand, gentlemen," he explained, "that I respect the rights of the poorest and weakest of colored people oppressed by the slave system just as much as I do those of the most wealthy and powerful. That is the idea that has moved me, and that alone. We expected no reward except the satisfaction of endeavoring to do for those in distress and greatly oppressed as we would be done by. The cry of distress of the oppressed is my reason and the only thing that prompted me to come here. . . . I wish to say, furthermore," he afterwards said, "that you had better—all you people at the South—prepare yourselves for a settlement of this question, that must come up for settlement sooner than you are prepared for it. . . . You may dispose of me very easily. I am nearly disposed of now; but this question is still to be settled—this negro question, I mean; the end of that is not yet." [1]

Governor Wise, who came to Harper's Ferry the day of this conversation, was impressed with the bearing of Brown. In a public speech at Richmond, he said: "They are mistaken who take Brown to be a madman. He is a bundle of the best nerves I ever saw, cut and thrust, and bleeding and in bonds. He is a man of clear head, of courage, fortitude . . . and he inspired me with great trust in his integrity, as a man of truth. He is a fanatic, vain and garrulous, but firm and truthful and intelligent." [2] Emerson, struck with the intercourse between Wise and Brown, said: "Governor Wise, in the record of his first interviews with his prisoner, appeared to great advantage. If Governor Wise is a superior man, or inasmuch as he is a superior man, he distinguishes John Brown. As they confer, they understand each other swiftly; each respects the other. If

---

[1] New York *Herald*, Oct. 21st; Sanborn, p. 562.
[2] Redpath, p. 273.

opportunity allowed, they would prefer each other's society and desert their former companions." [1]

John Brown's dream of many years had been shattered. The result was what any man of judgment would have foreseen. In the light of common-sense, the plan was folly; from a military point of view it was absurd. The natural configuration of the ground, the accessibility of Harper's Ferry to Washington and Baltimore, doomed him in any event to destruction. To attack with eighteen men a village of fourteen hundred people, the State of Virginia, and the United States government seems the work of a madman. Only by taking into account his unquestioning faith in the literal truth of the Bible can any explanation of his actions be suggested, for Brown was in ordinary affairs as sane a man as ever lived, and of no mean ability as a leader in a guerrilla war.

To Emerson he seemed " transparent," a " pure idealist." [2] Gerrit Smith thought of all men in the world, John Brown was "most truly a Christian," and that he did not doubt "the truth of one line of the Bible." [3] Like the Puritans of two centuries before, he drew his most impressive lessons from the Old Testament; he loved to dwell upon the wonders God had wrought for Joshua and for Gideon. His plan seemed no greater folly than was the attempt of Joshua to take a walled city by the blowing of trumpets and by shouts of the people; nor was he more foolish than Gideon, who went out to encounter a great army with three hundred men bearing only trumpets and lamps and pitchers. Yet the walls of Jericho had fallen flat at the noise, and Gideon had put to flight, amidst great confusion, Midianites and Amalekites, who were like the grasshoppers for multitude. And as the old Puritan was doing God's work, he felt that God

---

[1] Lecture on " Courage," Nov. 8th, 1859.
[2] Remarks at a meeting for the relief of John Brown's family, Boston, Nov. 18th, 1859.
[3] Life of Gerrit Smith, Frothingham, pp. 237, 258.

would not forsake him.¹ The evasive replies he gave when pressed to account for his military folly make plain that he held something back which he deemed too sacred to put into categorical answers to an unfriendly examination. To this was likewise due a lack of coherence in his apology.

He did not expect "a general rising of the slaves;" he expected "to gather them up from time to time and set them free." The Southerners could not comprehend that Brown was sincere when he discoursed in this wise. In their view he had "whetted knives of butchery for our mothers, sisters, daughters, and babes."² To Northern statesmen it was clear that he could attain success only by inciting a servile war and letting passions loose such as had made the tale of San Domingo one over which civilization weeps. Nor is it surprising that practical men could have no other idea when Gerrit Smith, the trusted friend and helper of John Brown, had in the August previous publicly written: "Is it entirely certain that these [slave] insurrections will be put down promptly, and before they can have spread far? . . . Remember that telegraphs and railroads can be rendered useless in an hour. Remember, too, that many who would be glad to face the insurgents would be busy in transporting their wives and daughters to places where they would be safe from that worst fate which husbands and fathers can imagine for their wives and daughters."³

Brown knew the history of San Domingo, and in the career of Toussaint he took delight. When he should strike a signal blow such as the capture of Harper's Ferry, he expected the slaves of Virginia and the free negroes of the North to flock to his standard.⁴ He brought with him arms for thirteen hundred men, and the stored equipments of the

---

¹ See letter to Sanborn, p. 457.
² Governor Wise to Mrs. Child, Oct. 29th, New York *Tribune*, Nov. 8th. ³ Frothingham, p. 241.
⁴ Testimony of Realf, Mason committee.

arsenal were sufficient for an army. His provisional constitution shows that he was anxious to avoid the horrors of San Domingo. One article granted to every prisoner a fair and impartial trial, and another provided that "persons convicted of the forcible violation of any female prisoner shall be put to death."[1] But the negroes would not rise. The captured slaves, into whose hands he put the pikes, held them listlessly, making common cause with their masters, and were glad when the fight was over to return to their bondage.[2]

The feeling of the South towards John Brown may be imagined; it need not be described. Consider how men of property would now feel at a violent attack of anarchists on their houses and goods, and one will have a partial conception of the horror and indignation that in 1859 prevailed at the South. The sensation at the North was profound. The conspirators were alarmed, for their complicity was suspected and they immediately destroyed all questionable correspondence.[3] It was reported that Governor Wise had made a requisition on the governor of New York for Gerrit Smith. His house was guarded, and his friends said that nothing less than a regiment of soldiers would suffice to take him from his home.[4] The nervous tension on the philanthropist was so great that his mind gave way, and he was taken to a mad-house.[5] Dr. Howe, Stearns, Sanborn, and Frederick Douglass went to Canada; Higginson pursued the even tenor of his way.[6]

Yet, in truth, the Southern leaders cared little for the apprehension of these amiable conspirators, who were rightly

---

[1] Article XLI. See Mason Report, p. 57.
[2] Testimony of Washington and Allstadt, Mason committee.
[3] Sanborn, p. 514. From this statement Higginson must be excepted.
[4] See letter of a New York *Herald* correspondent from Peterboro, Oct. 31st; Frothingham, p. 243.   [5] Frothingham, p. 245.
[6] Frothingham, p. 243; Wilson's Rise and Fall of the Slave Power, vol. ii. p. 605; Sanborn, p 514.

judged to have no political influence. But if they could fasten active support of the enterprise on prominent Republican leaders, an important point would be gained. As the November elections were pending, Northern Democrats were alive to the injury their opponents would sustain could it be shown that Seward, Chase, Sumner, and Hale had in any way been engaged in the conspiracy. There was not the slightest evidence to that effect; but the charge was not effectually silenced until the following year, when the thorough investigation by a Senate committee of the subject showed that these Republican leaders knew no more of John Brown's plan than the rankest Democrats of the South. In the excitement of the moment, however, the charge was made with impudent assertion, and the story invented that Seward and other prominent Republicans had met John Brown at Gerrit Smith's house in the spring of 1859.[1]

By way of varying the charge of direct knowledge, it was maintained that Brown had only practically applied Seward's doctrine of the irrepressible conflict. As a significant argument, the New York *Herald*, on the Wednesday after the Harper's Ferry raid, when the excitement was at the highest, printed Seward's "irrepressible-conflict" speech by the side of the startling news from Virginia.[2] The next day the editor averred that "Seward is the arch-agitator who is responsible for this insurrection,"[3] and a few days later argued that he should be prosecuted as a traitor.[4] This line of discourse, though for the most part intended to influence the coming elections, was by some men taken seriously.[5]

Seward, being in Europe, made no reply to these Democratic arguments. The Republican press and speakers met them in a dignified way, taking occasion to reiterate that their party had no intention of interfering with slavery in the States, and condemning the raid at Harper's Ferry,

---

[1] New York *Herald*, Nov. 2d and 4th.   [2] Ibid., Oct. 19th.
[3] Ibid., Oct. 20th.   [4] Nov. 1st.
[5] See, for example, letter from 29 Wall Street to the *Herald* of Nov. 2d.

yet at the same time heaping no abuse upon the head of Brown. During the excitement of the first news, when it was supposed that Brown himself had been killed, Greeley best expressed the feeling of sympathetic Republicans.

"There will be enough," he wrote, "to heap execration on the memory of these mistaken men. We leave this work to the fit hands and tongues of those who regard the fundamental axioms of the Declaration of Independence as 'glittering generalities,' believing that the way to universal emancipation lies not through insurrection, war, and bloodshed, but through peace, discussion, and the quiet diffusion of sentiments of humanity and justice. We deeply regret this outbreak; but remembering if their fault was grievous, grievously have they answered for it, we will not by one reproachful word disturb the bloody shrouds wherein John Brown and his compatriots are sleeping. They dared and died for what they felt to be right, though in a manner which seems to us fatally wrong. Let their epitaphs remain unwritten until the not distant day when no slave shall clank his chains in the shades of Monticello or by the graves of Mount Vernon." [1]

The elections were favorable to the Republicans. The John Brown raid undoubtedly had some influence in diminishing their vote, but the effect was not great. "Do not be downhearted about the Old Brown business," Greeley wrote Colfax before the election. "Its present effect is bad, and throws a heavy load on us in this State . . . but the ultimate effect is to be good. . . . It will drive on the slave power to new outrages. . . . It presses on the 'irrepressible conflict;' and I think the end of slavery in Virginia and the Union is ten years nearer than it seemed a few weeks ago." [2]

Brown was taken prisoner October 18th; the preliminary examination was had the 25th. He was immediately indicted by the grand jury, and on Wednesday, the 26th, arraigned

---

[1] New York *Tribune*, Oct. 19th.   [2] Life of Colfax, Hollister, p. 150.

for trial before the circuit court of Jefferson county, Virginia, which was sitting at Charlestown, ten miles from Harper's Ferry. The reason afterwards given to Brown, by the attorney for the prosecution, for the unusual haste was that the regular term of the court began immediately after the capture of the prisoners; if not tried then, they could not be tried until the spring term.[1] But the public sentiment of the community called for a speedy trial, and, with newspapers and people demanding summary vengeance by lynch-law, the authorities were right in any event to take prompt action.[2] Yet it seemed cruel to sympathizers with the old Puritan that the process must go on before he had recovered from his wounds, and while he was obliged from weakness to lie upon a pallet in the court-room.

Wednesday was consumed in getting a jury, and on Thursday the examination of witnesses began. Counsel for Brown were at first assigned by the court; later, lawyers came from Boston and Cleveland and volunteered their services for his defence, while, on the fourth day of the trial, Chilton, an attorney of eminent ability from Washington, appeared. Chilton had been retained by John A. Andrew, of Boston, and Montgomery Blair, of Maryland; he was a native of Virginia, had represented his State in Congress, and now made an able plea for the prisoner on technical grounds.[3] The counsel for Brown assigned by the State desired at the commencement to make the defence on the ground of insanity. Brown, raising himself from his pallet, said: "I am perfectly unconscious of insanity, and I reject, so far as I am capable, any attempts to interfere in my behalf on that

---

[1] See paper on the Trial and Execution of John Brown, by General Marcus J. Wright, Papers of the American Historical Association, vol. iv. p. 121.

[2] See citations from the Southern press by the *Liberator*, Nov. 11th; Wright, p. 115.

[3] Testimony of John A. Andrew before the Mason committee; Wright, p. 117; see plea of Chilton as published in New York *Herald* of Nov. 1st.

score." [1] On Monday, October 31st, the fifth day of the trial, the jury, after a deliberation of three quarters of an hour, brought in a verdict of "Guilty of treason, and conspiring and advising with slaves and others to rebel, and murder in the first degree." The trial was fair;[2] no other result was possible. Two days afterwards, Brown was brought into court to receive his sentence.[3] When asked whether he had anything to say why sentence should not be pronounced upon him, he arose and in a distinct voice said: "I deny everything but what I have all along admitted, of a design on my part to free slaves. . . . I never did intend murder or treason or the destruction of property, or to excite or incite slaves to rebellion, or to make insurrection. . . . Now, if it is deemed necessary that I should forfeit my life for the furtherance of the ends of justice, and mingle my blood further with the blood of my children and with the blood of millions in this slave country, whose rights are disregarded by wicked, cruel, and unjust exactments, I say, let it be done. . . . I feel entirely satisfied with the treatment I have received on my trial. Considering all the circumstances, it has been more generous than I expected; but I feel no consciousness of guilt." [4] The judge then sentenced him to be hanged in public on Friday, the 2d of December. The case was taken to the Court of Appeals by Chilton and a Richmond attorney, but a writ of error to the judgment rendered by the Circuit Court was refused.[5]

From the end of the trial until the execution took place, Charlestown, though under martial law, was in a state of excitement bordering on frenzy. All Virginia was in alarm,

---

[1] New York *Herald*, Oct. 28th.
[2] The paper of General Wright was written to establish that fact; see also Greeley's American Conflict, vol. i. p. 294; and John Brown, by Von Holst, p. 154.
[3] New York *Herald*, Nov. 1st.   [4] Ibid., Nov. 3d.
[5] New York *Tribune*, Nov. 21st; testimony of J. A. Andrew, Mason committee.

and Richmond at one time in a panic of fear. The wide belief that an attempt to rescue Brown would be made, the burning of several barns at night in the vicinity of Charlestown, which was construed to be the prelude to an extended slave insurrection, made the people nervous and apprehensive.[1] There was no ground for the fear of a rescue,[2] or of a rising of the slaves; though Governor Wise kept a large body of troops constantly on the ground, it is improbable that he shared the fears of the citizens.[3]

The replies of Brown in the conversation with Mason, his bearing, and the sincere and pregnant expressions of his letters between the verdict and the execution, showed him a hero, and won him that admiration of choice spirits that is granted only to those who dare much and sacrifice much in the cause of humanity. Most of his letters were published in the *Tribune*, *Liberator*, and other newspapers of the North, and their utterances set people to pondering on the cause that this man was willing to die for. "Everything that is said of John Brown," remarked Emerson, "leaves people a little dissatisfied; but as soon as they read his own speeches and letters they are heartily contented—such is the singleness of purpose which justifies him to the head and heart of all."[4]

To his brother Brown wrote: "I am quite cheerful in view of my approaching end, being fully persuaded that I am worth inconceivably more to hang than for any other purpose.[5] . . . I count it all joy. 'I have fought the good fight,' and have, as I trust, 'finished my course.'"[6] To his

---

[1] See the files of the New York *Herald* and *Tribune*.
[2] See Report of Collamer and Doolittle, p. 23.
[3] See remarks of Senator Wilson, Senate, Dec. 8th.
[4] Speech at Salem, Jan. 6th, 1860.
[5] "The saying of this true hero, after his capture, that he was worth more for hanging than for any other purpose, reminds one, by its combination of wit, wisdom, and self-devotion, of Sir Thomas More."—Autobiography of John Stuart Mill, p. 268.
[6] Nov. 12th, Sanborn, p. 588.

old teacher he wrote: "As I believe most firmly that God reigns, I cannot believe that anything I have done, suffered, or may yet suffer will be lost to the cause of God or humanity. And before I began my work at Harper's Ferry, I felt assured that in the worst event it would certainly pay. . . . I have been a good deal disappointed as it regards myself in not keeping up to my own plans; but I now feel entirely reconciled to that even—for God's plan was infinitely better, no doubt, or I should have kept to my own. Had Samson kept to his determination of not telling Delilah wherein his great strength lay, he would probably have never overturned the house. I did not tell Delilah, but I was induced to act very contrary to my better judgment." [1] Making suggestions to his wife regarding the education of their daughters, he said at the close of a letter to her: "My mind is very tranquil, I may say joyous." [2]

To his cousin he expressed himself as content with his fate. "When I think how easily I might be left to spoil all I have done or suffered in the cause of freedom, I hardly dare wish another voyage, even if I had the opportunity." To his younger children, to take from them the thought that the manner of his death would be ignominious, he wrote: "I feel just as content to die for God's eternal truth on the scaffold as in any other way;" [3] and on the same day he assured his older children that "a calm peace seems to fill my mind by day and by night." With prophetic soul he added: "As I trust my life has not been thrown away, so I also humbly trust that my death will not be in vain. God can make it to be a thousand times more valuable to his own cause than all the miserable service (at best) that I have rendered it during my life." [4] To a clergyman who had sent him sympathizing words he wrote: "I think I feel as happy as Paul did when he lay in prison. He knew if they killed him, it would greatly advance the

---

[1] Nov. 15th, Sanborn, p. 590.
[3] Nov. 22d, ibid., p. 596.
[2] Nov. 16th, ibid., p. 593.
[4] Ibid., p. 597.

cause of Christ; that was the reason he rejoiced so. On that same ground 'I do rejoice.' . . . Let them hang me; I forgive them, and may God forgive them, for they know not what they do. I have no regret for the transaction for which I am condemned. I went against the laws of men, it is true, but 'whether it be right to obey God or men, judge ye.'"[1] In his letter to Judge Tilden, of Cleveland, he said: "It is a great comfort to feel assured that I am permitted to die for a cause;"[2] and among the last words to his family, was: "John Brown writes to his children to abhor with undying hatred that sum of all villanies—slavery."[3]

The sun rose bright and clear on the morning that the old Puritan was to die. Fears of a rescue still prevailed; cannon were in position before the jail, and several companies of infantry guarded the place. It was nearly eleven o'clock when Brown was taken from his prison. He had handed to one of the guards a paper on which was written: "I, John Brown, am now quite certain that the crimes of this guilty land will never be purged away but with blood. I had, as I now think vainly, flattered myself that without very much bloodshed it might be done."[4] Soldiers marched ahead of the wagon in which the old Puritan, seated on his coffin, rode. As his glance went from the sky to the graceful outlines of the blue mountains, he said: "This is a beautiful country." To those who were with him, he declared that he did not dread death, nor had he ever in his life known what it was to experience physical fear. As he got out of the wagon at the gallows, his manner was composed, and he mounted the steps of the platform with a steady tread. Around the scaffold fifteen hundred Virginia troops were drawn up in battle array. Howitzers were placed to command the field, a force of cavalry was posted as sentinels, while scouts and rangers were on duty outside of the enclosure. Citizens were not allowed to approach the scene of execution, and

---

[1] Nov. 23d, Sanborn, p. 598.
[3] Nov. 30th, ibid., p. 615.
[2] Nov. 28th, ibid., p. 609.
[4] Ibid., p. 620.

strangers had been warned to keep away from Charlestown. Brown made no speech. When he had occasion to say anything to the sheriff, his voice was strangely natural. He stood blindfolded on the platform, the noose was adjusted about his neck. Everything was ready, still the sheriff did not receive the signal. The colonel in command was waiting until the escort of the prisoner had taken its proper place. It was a trying ten minutes, but Brown stood, so wrote Colonel Preston, an officer on duty, "upright as a soldier in position, and motionless. I was close to him and watched him narrowly, to see if I could detect any signs of shrinking or trembling in his person, but there was none." At last the sheriff received the signal, the rope that held up the trap-door was cut, and John Brown was sent into eternity. Solemnity and decorum ruled. Colonel Preston broke the awful silence around him: "So perish all such enemies of Virginia! All such enemies of the Union! All such foes of the human race!" It was the undoubted sentiment of every man present.

"Brown died like a man," wrote Francis Lieber, "and Virginia fretted like an old woman. . . . The deed was irrational, but it will be historical. Virginia has come out of it damaged, I think. She has forced upon mankind the idea that slavery must be, in her own opinion, but a rickety thing."[2] As reflecting the sentiment of Concord, Louisa Alcott set down in her diary that, "The execution of Saint John the Just took place December second;"[3] and Longfellow con-

---

[1] In this account of the execution I have in the main followed the letter of Colonel Preston, an officer of the corps of cadets, written from Charlestown, Dec. 2d, 1859, the day of the execution. This letter was made part of General Wright's paper before the American Historical Association. I have drawn some facts from Sanborn and have carefully consulted Redpath and the correspondents of the New York *Herald* and *Tribune*. Six companions of Brown, who had been taken prisoners, were afterwards hanged.

[2] Private letter, The Life and Letters of Francis Lieber, p. 307.

[3] Life and Letters of Louisa M. Alcott, p. 105.

fided to his journal: "This will be a great day in our history; the date of a new revolution, quite as much needed as the old one. Even now, as I write, they are leading old John Brown to execution in Virginia for attempting to rescue slaves! This is sowing the wind to reap the whirlwind, which will come soon."[1]

Much sympathy was expressed with the old Puritan in many parts of the North. Churches held services of humiliation and prayer at the hour the execution was to take place; in some cities funeral bells were tolled and minute-guns were fired; large meetings were held to lament the martyr, glorify his cause, and aid his family. In both houses of the Massachusetts legislature a motion was made to adjourn on account of the execution.[2] For the most part, these public manifestations were under the auspices of the abolitionists, and of those who inclined to their views. It was recognized by the Garrison abolitionists that inconsistency lay between their homilies against the use of force and their admiration for John Brown; but the touch of nature was too strong for fine-spun theories, and the followers of Garrison were active and earnest in all of these demonstrations. The *Liberator* had columns of eulogy to a paragraph of deprecation. The American Anti-slavery Society designated a period of its calendar "The John Brown Year," and in its report pages were devoted to the glorification of the old Puritan, while three sentences sufficed for the disapproval of his method.[3]

The deed of John Brown, which engrossed public attention to such an extent that the death of the most celebrated writer

---

[1] Life of Longfellow, Samuel Longfellow, vol. ii. p. 347.

[2] The motions were, of course, defeated. In the Senate the vote stood 11 to 8, and in the House 141 to 6. For an account of the various demonstrations, see especially the New York *Tribune* and the *Liberator*.

[3] See especially the *Liberator* of Nov. 25th. The twenty-seventh annual report of the American Anti-slavery Society was called "The Anti-slavery History of the John Brown Year;" see particularly p. 130.

of America, Washington Irving, passed comparatively unheeded,[1] gave rise to comments and opinions out of which may be evolved a judgment of what place he will fill in history. The four representative men of the country spoke positively. Jefferson Davis called it " the invasion of a State by a murderous gang of abolitionists," who came " to incite slaves to murder helpless women and children . . . and for which the leader has suffered a felon's death." He asserted that Seward's " irrepressible-conflict " speech contained the germ that may have borne this bloody fruit.[2] Douglas intimated that Brown was a horse-thief,[3] and spoke of him as " a notorious man who has recently suffered death for his crimes upon the gallows." It was his " firm and deliberate conviction that the Harper's Ferry crime was the natural, logical, inevitable result of the doctrines and teachings of the Republican party;" and he asserted that the " house-divided-against-itself " doctrine of Lincoln and the " irrepressible-conflict " principle of Seward tended to produce such acts as the raid of John Brown.[4]

Before Seward and Lincoln expressed their views, the Harper's Ferry invasion had been the subject of several days' debate in the Senate. The debate arose on the resolution to appoint a committee to investigate the affair, and continued on the resolution of Douglas, which had in view legislation to prevent such attempts in the future. There had been a free interchange of opinions. The Southerners were aggressive; the Republicans judicious but firm; they regretted and disapproved of the act, yet sympathized with

---

[1] Thoreau, Last Days of John Brown, North Elba, July 4th, 1860; see also New York *Herald* and *Tribune*.

[2] Senate, Dec. 8th, 1859.

[3] The basis of this charge was the fact that Brown, in his Missouri exploit, captured men who pursued him on horseback, and that, though he released the men, he kept the horses and afterwards sold them in Ohio.

[4] Senate, Jan. 23d, 1860. See *Congressional Globe*, 1st Sess. 36th Cong., pp. 553, 554.

the man. The mass of Republicans were nevertheless perplexed, and looked to their leaders for guidance.[1] Lincoln spoke at the Cooper Institute, February 27th, 1860, and referred to John Brown in cold, measured, and judicial words: "John Brown's effort was peculiar," said he. "It was not a slave insurrection, it was an attempt by white men to get up a revolt among slaves, in which the slaves refused to participate. In fact, it was so absurd that the slaves, with all their ignorance, saw plainly enough it could not succeed. That affair in its philosophy corresponds with the many attempts related in history at the assassination of kings and emperors. An enthusiast broods over the oppression of a people, until he fancies himself commissioned by Heaven to liberate them. He ventures the attempt, which ends in little else than in his own execution."[2]

Two days later, Seward spoke in the Senate more sympathetically, and in words better calculated to meet with favor from those whose feeling for the man balanced their condemnation of the violent breach of the law. "The gloom of the late tragedy in Virginia," said he, "rested on the Capitol from the day when Congress assembled." Brown "attempted to subvert slavery in Virginia by conspiracy, ambush, invasion, and force. The method we have adopted, of appealing to the reason and judgment of the people, to be pronounced by suffrage, is the only one by which free government can be maintained anywhere, and the only one as yet devised which is in marked harmony with the spirit of the Christian religion. While generous and charitable natures will probably concede that John Brown and his associates acted on earnest, though fatally erroneous, convictions, yet all good citizens will nevertheless agree that this attempt to execute an unlawful purpose in Virginia by invasion, in-

---

[1] An admirable statement of public opinion may be found in the *Atlantic Monthly* for March, 1860, p. 378, in a criticism by C. E. Norton of Redpath's Life of John Brown.

[2] Life of Lincoln, Howells, p. 206.

volving servile war, was an act of sedition and treason, and criminal in just the extent that it affected the public peace and was destructive of human happiness and life." We lament, the senator continued, "the deaths of so many citizens, slain from an ambush and by surprise." We may regret "the deaths even of the offenders themselves, pitiable, although necessary and just, because they acted under delirium, which blinded their judgments to the real nature of their criminal enterprise."[1] That Lincoln and Seward both represented and shaped the dominant opinion of their party is evident from the declaration of the National Republican convention, meeting in the May following, that the Harper's Ferry invasion was "among the gravest of crimes."

Had philosophers and poets remained dumb, these expressions from men of affairs would have ended the chapter, and it might have been left for after-years to question the prosaic judgment of statesmen, rendered in the piping times of peace. But men who lived in the spirit, on whom rested no responsibility for the march of government, who, as Thoreau expressed it, were not obliged to count "the votes of Pennsylvania & Co.," had already spoken. They put into words the feeling of many abolitionists and of many men who regularly voted the Republican ticket. "I wish we might have health enough," said Emerson, "to know virtue when we see it, and not cry with the fools 'madman' when a hero passes;" and this was greeted with prolonged applause by the Boston audience who had gathered to hear his lecture on "Courage."[2] The same evening he further spoke of Brown as "that new saint, than whom none purer or more brave was ever led by love of men into conflict and death— the new saint awaiting his martyrdom, and who, if he shall suffer, will make the gallows glorious like the cross;" and this sentiment was responded to with enthusiasm by the immense audience of Tremont Temple.[3]

---

[1] Works, vol. iv. p. 636.   [2] The *Liberator*, Nov. 18th.
[3] Memoir of Emerson, Cabot, p. 597; the *Liberator*, Nov. 11th. This

"Some eighteen hundred years ago," said Thoreau, "Christ was crucified; this morning, perchance, Captain Brown was hung. These are the two ends of a chain which is not without its links. He is not old Brown any longer; he is an angel of light. . . . I foresee the time when the painter will paint that scene [the interview of Brown and Senator Mason], no longer going to Rome for a subject; the poet will sing it, the historian record it; and, with the Landing of the Pilgrims and the Declaration of Independence, it will be the ornament of some future national gallery, when at least the present form of slavery shall be no more here. We shall then be at liberty to weep for Captain Brown."[1]

Victor Hugo, the greatest genius living, an exile for the cause of liberty, thus wrote of the event upon which England and France were looking with wonder: "In killing Brown, the Southern States have committed a crime which will take its place among the calamities of history. The rupture of the Union will fatally follow the assassination of Brown. As to John Brown, he was an apostle and a hero. The gibbet has only increased his glory and made him a martyr."[2] The poet who compassed all history wrote for the old Puritan this epitaph: *Pro Christo sicut Christus.*[3]

A century may, perchance, pass before an historical estimate acceptable to all lovers of liberty and justice can be made of John Brown. What infinite variety of opinions may exist of a man who on the one hand is compared to Socrates and Christ, and on the other hand to Orsini and

---

lecture was delivered Nov. 8th. Emerson also delivered two set speeches on John Brown, published in vol. xi. of his Works.

[1] A plea for Captain John Brown, read at Concord, Oct. 30th.

[2] Cited in the twenty-seventh annual report of the American Antislavery Society, p. 161.

[3] Actes et Paroles pendant l'Exil, in which may be found two eloquent tributes to John Brown. "Pour nous, qui préférons le martyre au succès, John Brown est plus grand que Washington."—Jean Valjean, vol. v. Les Misérables.

Wilkes Booth! The likeness drawn between the old Puritan and these men who did the work of assassination revolts the muse of history; yet the comparison to Socrates and Christ strikes a discordant note. The apostle of truth and the apostle of peace are immeasurably remote from the man whose work of reform consisted in shedding blood; the teacher who gave the injunction "Render unto Cæsar the things that are Cæsar's," and the philosopher whose long life was one of strict obedience to the laws, are a silent rebuke to the man whose renown was gained by the breach of laws deemed sacred by his country. As time went on, Emerson modified his first exuberant judgment, and, when printing ten years later his lecture on "Courage," omitted the expressions here cited as his opinion of the old Puritan.[1]

Of the influence of the Harper's Ferry invasion something remains to be said. It does not appear that it gained votes for Lincoln in the presidential contest of 1860; nor did it, as was at first feared, injure the Republican cause. It is a notable circumstance that John A. Andrew, who presided at a John Brown meeting and said that whether the enterprise was wise or foolish, "John Brown himself is right,"[2] was elected governor of Massachusetts by the Republicans in 1860 by a very large majority, his vote falling but two thousand behind that of Lincoln. On the other hand, it is certain that if John Brown had never lived, Lincoln would have been elected President, and secession would have ensued; although the Harper's Ferry raid did indeed furnish a count in the indictment of the Southern States against the North,[3] and may have been one of the influences impelling Virginia to join the Southern Confederacy.

After the war began, the words full of meaning and the

---

[1] Life of Emerson, Cabot, p. 597.   [2] The *Liberator*, Nov. 25th.
[3] For example, see letter of A. H. Stephens to Lincoln, Dec. 30th, 1860, Letters and speeches, Cleveland, p. 153. Also *De Bow's Review*, Jan. and March, 1860.

stirring music of the John Brown song inspired Northern soldiers as they marched to the front; and it was a dramatic incident, and one that excited many emotions, when the Webster regiment, of Massachusetts, whose quartet had composed the words and adapted them to the music of a Methodist hymn, burst out at Charlestown, March 1st, 1862, on the spot where the old Puritan was hanged, with

"John Brown's body lies a-mouldering in the grave,
But his soul goes marching on." [1]

And who can say that the proclamation of emancipation would have met as hearty a response, that Northern patriots would have fought with as much zeal, and the people sustained Lincoln in the war for the abolition of slavery as faithfully, had not John Brown suffered martyrdom in the same cause on Virginia soil? [2]

---

[1] The John Brown song originated in the spring of 1861. For an account of its origin and development, see A Famous War Song: A Paper read before the United Service Club, Philadelphia, by James Beale, late of Twelfth Mass. Vol. Regiment, the Webster Regiment (Philadelphia, 1890). "I said to a great gathering in the South in 1881 that I expected to live to see Confederate soldiers or their children erect a monument to John Brown at Harper's Ferry, in token of the liberty which he brought to the white men of the South."—Edward Atkinson, in the Boston *Herald* of Nov. 1st, 1891.

[2] For a consideration of John Brown from another point of view, see Nicolay and Hay, vol. ii. chap. xi. For a reply, see John Brown, edited by F. P. Stearns, which includes the essay of Von Holst. On the subject generally see Whittier's poem "Brown of Ossawatomie;" Blaine, vol. i. pp. 155, 156; Garrison, vol. iii. p. 493; Thurlow Weed, vol. ii. p. 258; W. P. Garrison, *Andover Review*, Dec., 1890, and Jan., 1891; Life of Bowles, vol. i. p. 251; Political Recollections, Julian, p. 169; S. S. Cox, p. 50.

CHAPTER XI

John Brown was hanged Friday, December 2d. The excitement was still intense when, on the following Monday, the Thirty-sixth Congress assembled. "Virginia is arming to the teeth," wrote ex-President Tyler from his plantation. "More than fifty thousand stand of arms already distributed, and the demand for more daily increasing. Party is silent and has no voice. But one sentiment pervades the country: security *in the Union*, or separation. An indiscreet move in any direction may produce results deeply to be deplored. I fear the debates in Congress, and, above all, the speaker's election. If excitement prevails in Congress, it will add fuel to the flame which already burns so terrifically."[1]

The Senate was composed of thirty-eight Democrats, twenty-five Republicans, and two Americans.[2] Since the meeting of the previous Congress, the Republicans had gained five senators. Two new States had been admitted by the last Congress. Minnesota, with a constitution prohibiting slavery, had come into the Union without objection from the Southerners, although she made one more weight in the balance of free against slave States. But her first senators and representatives were Democrats. Oregon, too, was admitted with a free constitution. The main opposition to her admission came from the Republicans, for the reason that her population was not equal to the number required for

---

[1] John Tyler to his son, Dec. 6th, 1859, Letters and Times of the Tylers, vol. ii. p. 555.   [2] There was one vacancy.

a representative, and as Kansas was held to this rule, it was deemed unjust to admit Oregon unless Kansas should also be made a State; moreover, the constitution of Oregon was criticised in that it forbade the entrance of free negroes or mulattoes into the State. Another objection, not so clearly expressed, was that Oregon being strongly Democratic, it was expected that she would furnish the coming year three electoral votes for the Democrats, besides at once notably increasing their strength in the Senate. In the House the admission of Oregon only commanded the votes of fifteen Republicans, none of them but Colfax being prominent in the councils of his party.[1] Although regarded as a Democratic victory, it was really an anti-slavery gain. There were now eighteen free to fifteen slave states, and Oregon as well as Minnesota cast her vote in 1860 for Lincoln. Nowhere in the existing territory of the country was there a possibility of carving out another slave State.

The House was composed of one hundred and nine Republicans, eighty-eight administration Democrats, thirteen anti-Lecompton Democrats, and twenty-seven Americans; all but four of the Americans were from the South.[2] No one party having a majority, a contest for speaker was inevitable. On the first ballot the Republicans divided their votes between John Sherman, of Ohio, and Grow, of Pennsylvania; but immediately after the ballot was announced, Grow withdrew his name. Clark, of Missouri, soon obtained the floor and offered a resolution that no representative who had endorsed and recommended the insurrectionary book, Helper's "Impending Crisis," was fit to be speaker of this House.

---

[1] The vote for admission was: 92 Lecompton Democrats, 7 Anti-Lecompton Democrats, 15 Republicans—total, 114: against admission, Republicans, 73; Southern Democrats, 18; South Americans, 10; anti-Lecompton Democrats, 2—total, 103. See analysis of vote by New York *Tribune*, Feb. 14th, 1859.

[2] This classification is corrected from those in the *Congressional Globe* and Tribune Almanac.

"The Impending Crisis of the South: How to Meet It," was the title of a book written by a poor white of North Carolina, to show that slavery was fatal to the interests of the non-slaveholding whites of the South. Although the writer's manner was highly emotional, sincerity flowed from his unpractised pen. The facts were in the main correct; the arguments based on them, in spite of being disfigured by abuse of the slave-holders and weakened by threats of violent action in a certain contingency, were unanswerable. The book was an arraignment of slavery from the standpoint of the poor white, and in his interest. "Uncle Tom's Cabin" was full of burning indignation at the wrong done the slave, and John Brown sacrificed his life willingly for him; while Helper, though he had the prejudices of his class against the black, made a powerful protest against the institution in the name of the non-slaveholding white. "Oligarchal despotism must be overthrown; slavery must be abolished," he declared; but "we long to see the day arrive" when the negroes shall be removed from the United States, and their places filled by white men.[1]

This book, published in 1857, had not at first a large circulation, but in 1859 it began to attract attention from those earnestly in favor of the Republican cause. A compend of its contents was published in cheap form for gratuitous distribution, and this enterprise received the written approval of many members of Congress, among whom were Sherman and Grow. The burden of Helper's argument was that the abolition of slavery would improve the material interests of the South by fostering manufactures and commerce, thus increasing greatly the value of land, the only property of the poor whites, and giving them a larger market for their products. The country and the cities would grow; there would be schools, as at the North, for the education of their children, and their rise in the social scale would be marked. The reasoning, supported as it was

---

[1] Helper, pp. 345, 381.

by a mass of figures, could not be gainsaid. Had the poor white been able to read and comprehend such an argument, slavery would have been doomed to destruction, for certainly seven voters out of ten in the slave States were non-slaveholding whites. It was this consideration that made Southern congressmen so furious, for to retain their power they must continue to hoodwink their poorer neighbors.

The second day of the session was exciting. Clark spoke on his resolution, and had extracts from the Helper compend read to show that it was an incendiary publication. Millson, of Virginia, declared that "one who consciously, deliberately, and of purpose lent his name and influence to the propagation of such writings is not only not fit to be speaker, but is not fit to live." These remarks were aimed at Sherman, now the sole Republican candidate for speaker, and he deemed it proper to make a reply. He had read neither book nor compend, and did not recollect signing the recommendation; to a pointed question he made the frank answer: "I am opposed to any interference whatever by the people of the free States with the relations of master and slave in the slave States." Keitt, of South Carolina, charged upon the Republicans the responsibility of Helper's book and John Brown's foray, exclaiming: "The South here asks nothing but its rights. . . . I would have no more; but, as God is my judge, as one of its representatives, I would shatter this republic from turret to foundation-stone before I would take one tittle less." Thaddeus Stevens, with grim humor, replied: "I do not blame gentlemen of the South for the language of intimidation, for using this threat of rending God's creation from the turret to the foundation. All this is right in them, for they have tried it fifty times, and fifty times they have found weak and recreant tremblers in the North who have been affected by it, and who have acted from those intimidations." An angry colloquy between Crawford, of Georgia, and Stevens ensued; the House was in an uproar; the clerk was power-

THE CONTEST FOR SPEAKER

less to preserve order; members from the benches on both sides crowded down into the area, and it was feared that a physical collision between Northern and Southern representatives would take place.[1] Morris, of Illinois, who exerted himself to allay the tumult, said the next day: "A few more such scenes . . . and we shall hear the crack of the revolver and see the gleam of the brandished blade." Yet the dignity of the place and their position restrained men from violence, and quiet was at length restored. It was not, however, until near the close of the proceedings of the following day that the House took the second ballot. Sherman then received 107, nine votes short of an election; Bocock, a Democrat of Virginia, had 88; Gilmer, an American of North Carolina, 22; while 14 votes were scattering.

The House, proceeding without rules, unrestricted by the formalities of legislation, and lacking the guidance of chairmen of committees, with the clerk in the chair who had neither the authority nor the dignity of a speaker, became a great debating society in which the questions for debate were: Is slavery right or wrong? Ought it to be extended or restricted? The greater part of the talking was done by Southern men, and their feelings were wrought up to the highest pitch. Lamar, of Mississippi, declared that the Republicans were not "guiltless of the blood of John Brown and his co-conspirators, and the innocent men, the victims of his ruthless vengeance." Helper's book, said Pryor, of Virginia, riots "in rebellion, treason, and insurrection," and is "precisely in the spirit of the act which startled us a few weeks since at Harper's Ferry." The leader of the Republican party, Seward, was an especial object of attack, and his declaration of the irrepressible conflict received hot censure. Lamar suspected that he was implicated in the John Brown invasion.[2] Reuben Davis, of Mississippi, called him a

---

[1] *Congressional Globe;* New York *Tribune.*

[2] Remarks of Dec. 7th. This suspicion in regard to Seward was common at the South. When part of Brown's party took possession of the

traitor.[1] From such expressions there followed naturally the threat to dissolve the Union in case the Republicans elected a President. "We will never submit to the inauguration of a Black Republican President," declared Crawford, of Georgia, amidst applause from Southern Democrats, and he averred, "I speak the sentiment of every Democrat on this floor from the State of Georgia." This sentiment was reiterated in many forms and at every stage of the proceedings. "The Capitol resounds with the cry of dissolution, and the cry is echoed throughout the city," wrote Senator Grimes.[2] The speeches of Southern members may be summed up in abuse of John Brown, Helper, Seward, Greeley, and John Sherman, and in threats of disunion. The choice of Sherman for speaker, said Pryor, will be a presage of "the ultimate catastrophe, the election of William H. Seward" for President. The Republicans, for the most part, held aloof from the discussion; they were always ready for a ballot, but it was impossible to get a vote every day. Corwin, an orator who never failed to command attention, made a moderate and witty speech, which for the time being put the House in good humor; but the political atmosphere was sultry, and in the arena of the representatives' hall, men swayed by powerful emotions had a chance to vent them, unhampered by the most intricate of parliamentary rules. Applause and hisses on the floor, echoed almost unchecked by the crowded galleries, added fuel to the flame.

The arrangement of the hall had a tendency to increase the excitement. By resolution adopted at the previous session, the desks were ordered to be removed from the floor of the House, and such a rearrangement of the seats of members made as would bring them together into the smallest convenient space. The committee who had reported

---

schoolhouse near Harper's Ferry, the schoolmaster asked if Seward were concerned in the raid. Testimony Mason committee.

[1] Remarks of Dec. 8th.
[2] To his wife, Life of Grimes, Salter, p. 121.

this resolution thought the change expedient and desirable, and an important step towards many legislative reforms. The chief argument for retaining the desks, the committee said, "is the strongest reason for their abolition—namely, the convenient facility which they afford members for writing letters and franking documents. It would certainly seem as if the very first duty of a representative in Congress was not simply to attend bodily in his place, but to listen to, and understand, and, when occasion requires it, to participate in the discussions and proceedings of the body of which he is a member." The immense size of the hall, the committee continued, made it difficult to hear a member when speaking; and if members came into nearer contact, greater attention could be paid to the discussions. The British House of Commons, of six hundred and fifty-four members, it was stated, held its sessions in a much smaller hall than our House of Representatives, which had to accommodate only two hundred and thirty-six. Under this order, benches were arranged so that the House was brought into the smallest possible compass consistent with convenient and comfortable seats, and about one third of the space of the hall was left vacant. The new arrangement, however, did not suit the majority of the members. Three weeks after the election of a speaker, they ordered the benches taken out and the desks and chairs restored; but this was not actually done until after the close of this Congress. It is a matter of regret that the experiment was not given a longer trial. The desks were not, however, brought back on account of the heated debates of this session, but because the members missed their convenience.

The closer physical contact, the enforced attention to every remark, undoubtedly added to the excitement of the daily meetings. The participants in an angry colloquy could easily meet. One day Kellogg and Logan, both of Illinois, had an altercation growing out of a charge made against Senator Douglas; on another, a hot personal dispute on the floor of the House between Branch, of North

Carolina, and Grow, of Pennsylvania, led to a virtual challenge to a duel from Branch, which met a dignified refusal from Grow. Both were afterwards arrested and placed under heavy bonds to keep the peace.[1] Another day, when Haskin, an anti-Lecompton Democrat from New York, was making excited and bitter personal remarks about a colleague, a pistol accidentally fell to the floor from the breast-pocket of his coat. Some members, believing that he had drawn the weapon with the intention of using it, were wild with passion. Many Democrats rushed towards the centre area near which Haskin stood. The loud cries for order, the nervous demands for the sergeant-at-arms, and the clamor of excitement, made a scene of pandemonium.[2] A bloody contest that day was imminent. "The members on both sides," wrote Senator Grimes, of Iowa, "are mostly armed with deadly weapons, and it is said that the friends of each are armed in the galleries."[3] Senator Hammond told the same story. "I believe," he wrote to Lieber, "every man in both houses is armed with a revolver—some with two—and a bowie-knife."[4]

The practice among Southerners of carrying concealed weapons was not uncommon. Among Northern men it was rarer, though they were led to it by the domineering tone and menacing words they were every day obliged to hear. They were determined not to fight duels; the moral sense of every Northern community was opposed to that manner of settling disputes. With the shadow of Broderick's death resting over the Capitol, it was seen that they were invited to an unequal contest; for in the code of honor and the art of duelling the slave-holders were adept, and had the advantages of skill over inexperience. Nevertheless, Republican

---

[1] New York *Tribune*, Jan. 2d and 4th, 1860.
[2] See *Congressional Globe* and New York *Tribune*, Jan. 13th, 1860.
[3] Grimes to his wife, Salter, p. 121.
[4] Life of Lieber, p. 310; see also New York *Tribune*, Jan. 13th, 1860; Recollections of Mississippi, Reuben Davis, p. 383.

members were resolved to defend themselves if attacked, and carried weapons in order to be ready for an emergency. The gravity of the situation was felt. Men were aware of the consequences that might flow from a bloody affray on the floor of the House, and counsels of forbearance from both sides were frequent. The Republicans showed great moderation; it was rare that one of them spoke; they were anxious to organize the House; and rather than lose time they let extravagant assertions pass uncontradicted, and bore in silence taunts and gibes from those who displayed plantation manners in the assembly of the nation.

The House remained in session the week between Christmas and New-Year's Day. During the intervals of debate, ballots were taken. On the twenty-fifth ballot, January 4th, 1860, Sherman came within three votes of election, and he came no nearer in any subsequent trials. The plurality rule was proposed but not pressed to a vote, as the Republicans knew the Southern members would filibuster against its adoption. Nor were any night sessions held, although Greeley thought the Republicans should have insisted on a vote on the plurality rule, and held night sessions if necessary to accomplish the purpose.[1] Such procedure, however, would have increased the friction between the parties and sections.

In spite of the bitter personal attacks made upon him, Sherman maintained during the contest a dignified composure. Corwin had taken pains to explain the difference between Republicans and abolitionists; but Sherman was frequently called an abolitionist, perhaps with the design of vilifying him at the South as Seward was vilified. General Sherman, then at the head of a military academy in Louisiana, relates how he was looked upon with suspicion on account of being the brother of the "abolition candidate" for speaker.[2] On January 20th, John Sherman was able to explain how his

---

[1] See Greeley to Colfax, Life of Colfax, Hollister, p. 153.
[2] Sherman's Memoirs, vol. i. p. 148.

name had come to be signed to the recommendation of the compend of Helper's book. It was done by proxy.[1] He that day declared: "I am for the Union and the Constitution, with all the compromises under which it was formed and all the obligations which it imposes." When I came here, he continued, "I did not believe that the slavery question would come up; and but for the unfortunate affair of Brown at Harper's Ferry I did not believe that there would be any feeling on the subject. Northern men came here with kindly feelings, no man approving the foray of John Brown, and every man willing to say so; every man willing to admit it as an act of lawless violence; . . . but this question of slavery was raised by the introduction of the resolution of the gentleman from Missouri. It has had the effect of exciting the public mind with an irritating controversy."

A combination of Democrats and Southern Americans would have been able to name the speaker, but this seemed impossible to effect. Still, Smith, an American of North Carolina, received, January 27th, 112 votes, within three of an election, and Sherman's vote on the same ballot fell to 106. The House then adjourned from Friday to Monday, January 30th. When it met, Sherman withdrew his name, and Pennington, of New Jersey, was placed in nomination by the Republicans. Five ballots were taken on three successive days. February 1st, on the forty-fourth trial, Pennington received 117 votes, exactly the number necessary to elect. Three representatives, who would not vote for Sherman, had come to his support to end the contest.[2] Penning-

---

[1] For full explanation, see *Congressional Globe*, 1st Sess. 36th Cong., p. 547; also his letter to Gen. Sherman, Dec. 24th, 1859, where he writes: "It was a thoughtless, foolish, unfortunate act."—*Century Magazine*, November, 1892, p. 90.

[2] They were Adrian, anti-Lecompton Democrat from New Jersey; Briggs, American, New York; Henry Winter Davis, American, from Maryland. Three anti-Lecompton Democrats—Hickman and Schwartz, from Pennsylvania, and Haskin, from New York—voted most of the time for Sherman; and Reynolds, anti-Lecompton Democrat from New York, was ready to join them if his vote would elect. All four voted for Pennington.

ton was sent to Congress by the People's party, but was regarded as a conservative Republican, and had constantly voted for Sherman while Sherman was a candidate. The contest lacked three days of being as long as that which terminated in the election of Banks; but then one hundred and thirty-three ballots were taken, while now there had been only forty-four. Good-humor and courtesy had marked the previous contest, where now were acrimony and defiance. There was then a suspicion that bribery had brought about the result; now passions more intense than avarice ruled supremely. Both times the discussion turned on the slavery question, but it was now a more strongly marked feature of the contest, and characterized by greater bitterness. Threats of disunion were then received with laughter; now they were too frequent and earnest to be treated lightly, even by those Republicans who believed they were uttered for mere effect. In the four years the divergence of the North and the South had grown into strong antagonism.

The excitement in the House extended throughout the country. Congressmen received a significant and hearty support in their threats of disunion from the Southern press.[1] Senator Bigler, of Pennsylvania, wrote: "The excitement seems to abate slightly in Congress, but it is on the rise in nearly every Southern State. . . . Nothing has made so much bad blood as the endorsement of the Helper book, and the attempt now making to promote a man who did this to the responsible station of speaker of the House. The next most offensive thing is the sympathy manifested for old Brown."[2] The speakership contest had made Help-

---

[1] See Richmond *Enquirer*, Jan. 1st, 6th, 20th, 1860; Washington *Constitution* (the administration organ), Jan. 5th, 13th; Raleigh *Standard*, cited by *Constitution*, Jan. 14th; see the Mobile *Tribune*, Demopolis (Ala.) *Gazette*, New Orleans *Courier*, and Richmond *Whig*, cited by the *Liberator*, Jan. 6th.

[2] To Robert Tyler, Dec. 16th, 1859, Letters and Times of the Tylers, vol. ii. p. 255.

er's book famous, and given it an astounding circulation. Although the book could not openly be sold at the South, and a Methodist minister, a native of North Carolina, was imprisoned for circulating the book, yet many copies found their way by stealth to that region.[1] But the ignorance of the poor white was too dense to be penetrated by Helper's arguments, which had little, if any, appreciable influence on the South. At the North great piles of "The Impending Crisis" might be seen on the counter of every book-store, news-depot, and newspaper-stand. It proved a potent Republican document, especially in the doubtful States of New Jersey, Pennsylvania, Indiana, and Illinois, where it was easier to arouse sympathy for the degraded white than for the oppressed negro.[2]

General Scott wrote Senator Crittenden confidentially: "The state of the country almost deprives me of sleep."[3] Union-saving meetings were held in the Eastern cities to deplore the widening breach between the two sections, and to condemn equally the abolitionists and the fire-eaters of the South, as the advocates of secession began to be called. Wendell Phillips, with a certain degree of justice, thus characterized these gatherings: "The saddest thing in the Union meetings was the constant presence, in all of them, of the clink of coin—the whir of spindles—the dust of trade. You would have imagined it was an insurrection of peddlers against honest men."[4] The Union-savers, wrote Bryant, "include a pretty large body of commercial men."[5] The Southern trade, always of importance to the Eastern cities, was now of especial consequence, for the South had scarcely felt the effects of the panic of 1857, while the West still labored under great business depression. "The Southern

---

[1] Helper's Impending Crisis, p. 395; New York *Tribune*, April 12th.
[2] Pike's First Blows of the Civil War, p. 469.
[3] Life of Crittenden, Coleman, vol. ii. p. 182.
[4] Speeches and Lectures, p. 316.
[5] Life of Bryant, Godwin, vol. ii. p. 128.

trade is good just now," wrote Bryant to John Bigelow, "and the Western rather unprofitable. Appleton says there is not a dollar in anybody's pocket west of Buffalo."[1] A black list of New York merchants, called abolition houses, and a white list, called constitutional houses, were published in the South, and Southern buyers were advised, and even warned, to place their orders with the proper parties.[2] Northern business men and agents of Eastern houses received warning at Savannah that they had better return home, as it would be useless for them to solicit orders on account of the sentiment now prevailing. Gratified at the success of this move, Southerners argued that "non-intercourse is the one prescription for Northern fanaticism and political villany."[3] Health-seekers accustomed to go South, to avoid the rigor of the Northern winter, were counselled to change their plans and visit the West Indies or Europe, as the mere fact of hailing from the North might subject them to annoyance or insult from the Southern populace.[4]

The gravity of the situation demanded an expression from the four representative men of the country, especially as three of them were avowed candidates for the presidency. The differences between Douglas and the Southern senators coming up in the Senate, he declared to them: "I am not seeking a nomination. I am willing to take one, provided I can assume it [the nomination] on principles that I believe to be sound; but in the event of your making a platform that I could not conscientiously execute in good faith if I were elected, I will not stand upon it and be a candidate. . . . I have no grievances, but I have no concessions. I have no

---

[1] Life of Bryant, Godwin. vol. ii. p. 128.
[2] New York *Tribune*, Jan. 23d.
[3] Savannah *Republican;* see also Memphis *Avalanche*, cited by New Orleans *Picayune*, Jan. 26th; also *Picayune*, Feb. 15th, and Charleston *Courier*, Jan. 6th and March 17th.
[4] New York *Tribune*, Jan. 21st.

abandonment of position or principle; no recantation to make to any man or body of men on earth." [1]

The responsibility of leadership imposed upon Jefferson Davis a comparatively guarded expression of his views. But he gave the Senate to understand that the Union would be dissolved in the event of the election of a radical Republican like Seward on the platform of the " irrepressible-conflict" speech.[2] On the 2d of February Davis introduced a series of resolutions to define the position of Southern Democrats. The fourth was the crucial one; it declared that neither Congress nor a territorial legislature, by direct or indirect and unfriendly legislation, had the power to annul the constitutional right of citizens to take slaves into the common territories; but it was the duty of the federal government to afford for slaves, as for other species of property, the needful protection.[3]

These declarations of Douglas and Davis had more than usual significance in view of the approaching national Democratic convention, and seemed to show that the breach in the party was irreconcilable. Davis said, in effect, to Douglas, You must come on to our platform or you will get no Southern support in your candidature for President; while Douglas had declared that he would not yield a jot, and that he was backed by two-thirds of the Democratic party.[4]

Lincoln, on invitation of the Young Men's Central Republican Union of New York city, obtained, to his great delight, a hearing in the East, delivering a speech, February 27th, in the Cooper Institute to a brilliant audience.[5] " Since the days of Clay and Webster," said the *Tribune* the next morning, " no man has spoken to a larger assemblage of the intellect and mental culture of our city." Lincoln had a

---

[1] Remarks of Jan. 12th.

[2] *Congressional Globe*, 1st Sess. 36th Cong., pp. 574, 577.

[3] These resolutions may be found in the *Congressional Globe*, 1st Sess. 36th Cong., p. 658.   [4] Ibid., p. 424.

[5] Nicolay and Hay, vol. ii. p. 216.

long time to prepare his address, and to no previous effort of his life had he devoted so much study and thought. But on appearing before the New York city audience, he was at first a little dazzled, and, moreover, disconcerted at his personal appearance. The new suit of clothes that had seemed so fine in his Springfield home was in awkward contrast with the neatly fitting dress worn by William Cullen Bryant, the chairman of the meeting, and other New York gentlemen who graced the platform.[1] But the earnest manner and power of expression overcame the effect produced by his ungainly appearance. The speech was a success. "No man," said the *Tribune*, "ever before made such an impression on his first appeal to a New York audience." The speech is worthy of great praise, and ought to be read entire by him who would fully understand the history of the year 1860.[2] "I do not hesitate to pronounce it," wrote Greeley some years later, "the very best political address to which I ever listened—and I have heard some of Webster's grandest."[3]

Lincoln showed conclusively that the fathers held and acted upon the opinion that Congress had the power to prohibit slavery in the territories; that the Republican party, therefore, was not revolutionary but conservative, for it maintained the doctrine of the men who had made the Constitution. Addressing himself to the Southern people, he said: "Some of you are for reviving the foreign slave-trade; some for Congress forbidding the territories to prohibit slavery within their limits; some for maintaining slavery in the territories through the judiciary; some for the 'great principle' that 'if one man would enslave another, no third man should object,' fantastically called popular sovereignty; but never a man among you in favor of federal prohi-

---

[1] Herndon, p. 454.
[2] It is given in full in the Life of Lincoln by Howells, and in the Life by Raymond. Liberal extracts are made by Nicolay and Hay.
[3] *Century Magazine*, July, 1891, p. 373. An address of Greeley, written about 1868, and first published in 1891.

bition of slavery in federal territories, according to the practice of our fathers who framed the government under which we live. Not one of all your various plans can show a precedent or an advocate in the century within which our government originated. . . . You say we have made the slavery question more prominent than it formerly was. We deny it. We admit that it is more prominent, but we deny that we made it so. It was not we, but you, who discarded the old policy of the fathers." Alluding to the Southern threats of disunion, he said: "Your purpose, then, plainly stated, is that you will destroy the government unless you be allowed to construe and enforce the Constitution as you please, on all points in dispute between you and us. You will rule or ruin in all events."

Addressing himself to the Republicans, he referred to the encroaching demands of the slave power and asked, What will satisfy the South? "This, and this only," he answered: "cease to call slavery *wrong* and join them in calling it *right*. And this must be done thoroughly—done in *acts* as well as in *words*." The South thinking slavery right and " our thinking it wrong is the precise fact upon which depends the whole controversy. Thinking it right, as they do, they are not to blame for desiring its full recognition as being right; but thinking it wrong as we do, can we yield to them? Can we cast our votes with their view and against our own? In view of our moral, social, and political responsibilities, can we do this? Wrong as we think slavery is, we can yet afford to let it alone where it is, because that much is due to the necessity arising from its actual presence in the nation; but can we, while our votes will prevent it, allow it to spread into the national territories, and to overrun us here in these free States? . . . Let us not be slandered," Lincoln continued, "from our duty by false accusations against us, nor frightened from it by menaces of destruction to the government. . . . Let us have faith that right makes might; and in that faith let us, to the end, dare to do our duty as we understand it."

Two days later, Seward spoke in the Senate. Of an unimposing physical figure, with a husky voice, angular gestures, and a dry didactic manner, he held spell-bound for two hours the Senate chamber and galleries, crowded with the distinguished and intellectual men and the graceful women of the nation's capital. It was the pregnant matter of the discourse and the commanding position of the speaker that attracted this profound attention.

Almost at the outset Seward said: "It will be an overflowing source of shame as well as of sorrow if we, thirty millions, . . . cannot so combine prudence with humanity, in our conduct concerning the one disturbing subject of slavery, as not only to preserve our unequalled institutions of freedom, but also to enjoy their benefits with contentment and harmony."[1] "Men, States and nations," he continued, "divide upon the slavery question, not perversely, but because, owing to differences of constitution, condition, or circumstances, they cannot agree." He alluded to the encroachments of the slave power, mentioning the governor's veto of the act of the Nebraska legislature dedicating that territory to freedom, the legal establishment of slavery in New Mexico, and he referred to the fact that "savage Africans have been once more landed on our shores." He asked, "Did ever the annals of any government show a more rapid or more complete departure from the wisdom and virtue of its founders? . . . There is not," he declared, "over the face of the whole world to be found one representative of our country who is not an apologist for the extension of slav-

---

[1] In connection with this remark and the general drift of Seward's speech, the opinion of Professor Bryce is interesting. "It is possible that a higher statesmanship might have averted" the civil war.—*American Commonwealth*, vol. ii. p. 201. Bryce also expresses the conjecture that cabinet government might have solved the slavery question without war. "But it was the function of no one authority in particular to discover a remedy, as it would have been the function of a cabinet in Europe."—Ibid., p. 317. See abstract of Von Holst's criticism of this statement, *The Nation*, April 24th, 1890.

II.—28

ery." Now, "we hear menaces of disunion, louder, more distinct, more emphatic than ever," so that, while hitherto the question for the Republican party has been, "How many votes can it cast?" it is now, "Has it determination to cast them?" Nevertheless, we should "consider these extraordinary declamations [for disunion] seriously and with a just moderation." The motto inscribed on the banner of the Republican party will be "Union and Liberty;" but "if indeed the time has come when the Democratic party must rule by terror, instead of ruling through conceded public confidence, then it is quite certain it cannot be dismissed from power too soon." Yet, "I remain now in the opinion ... that these hasty threats of disunion are so unnatural that they will find no hand to execute them."[1]

This speech, the calm, temperate discussion of an exciting question by a statesman, was one of great power. Seward, of all leading Republicans the most obnoxious to the South, and thought to be assured of the Republican nomination, owed it to his party to allay if possible, without abating a jot of principle, the unnecessary fears of what would happen should he become President; and for that purpose this speech was calculated. It was likewise a frank exposition of his ideas for the benefit of the Republican national convention soon to assemble at Chicago, and an outline of the spirit and principles in which he would administer the government should he be nominated and elected President.

The speech was severely criticised by the abolitionists, because it was not a vigorous enforcement of the "irrepressible-conflict" doctrine. They appealed from Seward in the Capitol to Seward on the stump. "The temptation which proved too powerful for Webster," wrote Garrison, "is seducing Seward to take the same downward course."[2] "Seward makes a speech in Washington on the tactics of the Republican party," said Wendell Phillips, "but he phrases

---

[1] Seward's Works, vol. iv. p. 619 *et seq.*
[2] The *Liberator*, March 9th.

it so as to suit Wall Street." ¹ This was the captious criticism of men who, far in the vanguard of public opinion, were impatient because political leaders did not keep pace with them. They failed to recognize that Seward and Lincoln, in their opposition to slavery, were going just as far and as fast as the people would follow. The influence of the abolitionists in the decade between 1850-60 was by no means commensurate with their ability and zeal. Their meetings were frequent, their conventions well attended, their resolutions wordy and emphatic. Yet they rejected the most feasible and regular means of checking the slave power, for the reason that the Republicans did not go far enough. These only proposed to prohibit slavery in the territories, while the abolitionists were for its abolition in the States. To take no part in elections was a tenet of Garrison and Phillips; and they were apt to criticise Republicans as severely as they did Democrats. An earnest writer and organizer like Garrison and an orator like Phillips could hardly devote themselves to a work for ten years without making themselves felt. Yet the only practical result of their labor lay in the fact that, having convinced men that slavery was wrong, they made Republican voters, while they were urging their followers not to vote. The work of Garrison and his disciples between 1831-40, in arousing the conscience of the nation, had borne good fruit; but that work was done. The public mind had now to grapple with the question, How could the sentiment that slavery was wrong accomplish results and stop the spread of the evil? The abolitionists said, By disunion; while the Republicans, intending to preserve union and liberty, proposed constitutional and regular methods. Yet it was better for the cause that Garrison and Phillips wrought outside of the Republican party. Their radical notions could not be held within platforms, nor could they follow a political leader. It was a frequent charge of Southerners that Garrison and Phillips

---

[1] New York *Tribune*, March 22d.

were apostles whom the Republicans delighted to honor, while in the Republican literature we see long explanations and emphatic denials that Republicans are abolitionists, or have anything in common with them.

The party that had for representatives two such men as Seward and Lincoln was indeed fortunate. That their speeches of 1858 and 1860, made absolutely without consultation, so closely resembled each other is evidence that two great political minds ran in the same channel; and, as both interpreted acutely popular sentiment, it is evidence, too, of the length to which Republican voters were willing to go. Both men realized that an effort should be made to attract the Fillmore voters of 1856; and although neither reaffirmed his declaration of 1858, nothing in these speeches indicated the smallest change of opinion. Lincoln's speech received far less attention than Seward's. Every sentence of the senator was dissected and every word weighed. " I hear of ultra old Whigs in Boston," wrote Bowles to Thurlow Weed, "who say they are ready to take up Seward upon his recent speech." [1]

When we consider that Seward and Lincoln were prominent candidates for the presidential nomination, and that the convention would assemble in two months and a half, such able and bold discussion by them of the issue before the country commands our admiration. Understanding the character of Lincoln as we do now, the combination of moral feeling and political sagacity which marks the Cooper Institute address seems entirely in keeping with the man. The veering course of Seward makes students of history doubt whether he had strong convictions. But his public speeches guided opinion, and were conceived in a higher moral atmosphere than he breathed when engaged in political manipulation.

For some time after the election of the speaker, peace had reigned in the House of Representatives, but on the 5th of

---

[1] Life of Weed, vol. ii. p. 260.

April a violent scene took place. In committee of the whole, Lovejoy had the floor and proceeded to make an anti-slavery speech. "Slave-holding," he asserted, "is worse than robbing, than piracy, than polygamy. . . . The principle of enslaving human beings because they are inferior . . . is the doctrine of Democrats, and the doctrine of devils as well; and there is no place in the universe outside the five points of hell and the Democratic party where the practice and prevalence of such doctrines would not be a disgrace." As Lovejoy spoke, his manner as boisterous as his words were vehement, he advanced into the area and occupied the space fronting the Democratic benches. Pryor, of Virginia, left his seat, moved quickly towards Lovejoy, and, with gesture full of menace, exclaimed, in a voice of anger: "The gentleman from Illinois shall not approach this side of the House, shaking his fists and talking in the way he has talked. It is bad enough to be compelled to sit here and hear him utter his treasonable and insulting language; but he *shall not*, sir, come upon this side of the House shaking his fist in our faces."

Potter, of Wisconsin, stepped towards Pryor and shouted: "We listened to gentlemen on the other side for eight weeks, when they denounced the members upon this side with violent and offensive language. We listened to them quietly and heard them through. And now, sir, this side *shall* be heard, let the consequences be what they may."

The point of order I make, replied Pryor, is that the gentleman shall speak from his seat; "but, sir, he *shall not* come upon this side shaking his fist in our faces and talking in the style he has talked."

"You are doing the same thing," cried Potter.

"You shall not come upon this side of the House," said Barksdale, of Mississippi, menacingly to the face of Lovejoy. "Nobody can intimidate me," uttered Lovejoy, with a loud voice.

And now thirty or forty members had gathered in the area around Lovejoy and Pryor, shouting and gesticulating.

The confusion was great; men trembled with excitement and passion; rage distorted many faces; it seemed as if the long-dreaded moment of a bloody encounter on the floor of the House had come. Above the din might be heard the voice of Potter, saying, "I do not believe that side of the House can say *where* a member shall speak, and they shall not say it;" also the cries of a member from Mississippi and a member from Kentucky insisting that Lovejoy could not speak on their side," let the consequences be what they will."

"My colleague shall speak," said Kellogg. The chairman of the committee, having in vain tried to preserve order, called the speaker to the chair and reported the disorder to the House. The speaker begged gentlemen to respect the authority of the House and take their seats. "Order that black-hearted scoundrel and nigger-stealing thief to take his seat, and this side of the House will do it," shouted Barksdale. The efforts of the speaker were at last successful; order was restored, the chairman of the committee resumed the chair, and Lovejoy went on. The speech was interspersed with remarks from Barksdale, calling Lovejoy "an infamous, perjured villain," "a perjured negro-thief," and from another Mississippi member terming him a "mean, despicable wretch." Nothing daunted Lovejoy. "You shed the blood of my brother on the banks of the Mississippi twenty years ago," he cried to the Southerners, "and what then? I am here to-day, thank God, to vindicate the principles baptized in his blood. . . . But I cannot go into a slave State," he continued, "and open my lips in regard to the question of slavery—" "No," interrupted a Virginia member, "we would hang you higher than Haman."

"The meanest slave in the South is your superior," cried Barksdale. Lovejoy was, however, permitted to finish his speech, and for a few days the story of his bearding the slave-holders in the representatives' hall of the nation filled the North.[1]

---

[1] My account is taken from the *Congressional Globe* and the New York *Tribune*.

Out of the proceedings of this day a quarrel grew between Pryor and Potter. Pryor demanded "the satisfaction usual among gentlemen for the personal affront you offered me in debate." Potter accepted the challenge, and, using his privilege, named bowie-knives as the weapons. The second of Pryor, without consulting him, refused to allow his principal to engage in combat by "this vulgar, barbarous, and inhuman mode."

This incident produced a greater sensation at the North than its intrinsic importance warranted. The reason is not far to seek. In Washington, Northern congressmen were taunted as cowards because they would not practise the code of honor, and in the Southern States the boast that one Southron could thrash four Yankees frequently accompanied the threats of disunion. Neither Lovejoy nor Potter had quailed before the menaces of the fire-eaters. Such action awakened the feeling in the breasts of many Northern men that they were as ready to fight for their own proper rights as were the vaunting Southerners; that on equal terms they were equally brave. Potter's choice of the bowie-knife had a grim fitness, for it was a popular implement of the South, and might be considered slavery's contribution to the practice of single combat, although not recognized by the code.

Potter was the hero of but a day. Public attention, taken for the moment from the approaching Charleston convention, returned to it with renewed force. We all know the absorbing interest taken beforehand in the convention of a great party whose platform or candidates are matters of uncertainty; but never before nor since has there been such an intensity of curiosity, interest, and concern as now prevailed regarding the action that would be taken by the national Democratic convention.

A Southern view of the situation from a conservative standpoint is best given in a confidential letter of Senator

---

[1] The correspondence was published in the New York *Tribune* of April 17th.

Hammond to Francis Lieber. "The Lovejoy explosion," he wrote, April 19th, "and all its sequences which were so threatening last week, has been for the present providentially cast in the shade by the intensified and utterly absorbing interest in the Charleston convention. . . . I assure you . . . that unless the slavery question can be wholly eliminated from politics, this government is not worth two years', perhaps not two months', purchase. . . . Unless the aggression on the slave-holder is arrested, no power short of God's can prevent a bloody fight here, and a disruption of the Union. . . . While regarding this Union as cramping the South, I will nevertheless sustain it as long as I can. . . . I firmly believe that the slave-holding South is now the controlling *power* of the world—that no other power would face us in hostility. Cotton, rice, tobacco, and naval stores command the world; and we have sense to know it, and are sufficiently Teutonic to carry it out successfully. The North without us would be a motherless calf, bleating about, and die of mange and starvation."[1]

It was unfortunate both for the Northern Democrats and the Union that at this critical juncture the national convention should meet at Charleston, the hot-bed of disunion. The place had been selected four years previously,[2] when harmony prevailed in the party and Douglas was a favorite of the South. Although having a population of but forty thousand, Charleston was marked by wealth and refinement, and tinctured with more of the aristocratic spirit than any other city of the country. Its citizens were generous and hospitable, but their entertainment was for people of their own way of thinking; it does not appear that they opened their houses to Northern delegates who came to advocate the cause of Douglas. The appearance and conduct of the Tammany delegation excited disgust in the minds of

---

[1] Life and Letters of Francis Lieber, p. 310.
[2] Greeley's American Conflict, vol. i. p. 309; Cleveland *Plain Dealer*, April 26th.

the elegant residents, who had only known by hearsay their Northern allies; while to Northern Democrats the haughty bearing they encountered seemed little in keeping with the character of their party, which they regarded essentially as the party of the people. The appearance of wealth and luxury shown in the mansions, in gay equipages, and in the rich dress of the ladies was a novel sight to all Northern visitors except to those living in a few of the Eastern cities; the forced economy of the West for the last three years was in painful contrast with the lavish display that might be seen any pleasant afternoon on the fashionable drive of Charleston.[1]

At this time Southern travel was exclusively confined to health-seekers and Eastern business men, so that most of the Northern delegates saw, for the first time in their lives, slavery face to face. Many of them, curious to look into the workings of the institution, availed themselves of several opportunities to visit the slave mart, and were present at a slave auction. A delegate who has given a graphic account of his investigations, expressed surprise at the manifestation of so little feeling by negroes about to be sold. He saw none of the indecent and outrageous scenes described in abolition prints, yet the strange spectacle of human beings sold like horses was one of the most revolting sights he had ever seen.[2] The exuberant prosperity of the South did not seem an object of envy to the Northern visitors, because it was attended with slavery, and they were shocked to hear men rated wealthy on account of the high price of negroes.

The delegates were a strong body of men. The politicians who came were of the better class; lawyers, men of

---

[1] New York *Tribune*, April 23d. My mother, who accompanied my father to Charleston, he being a delegate, has given me a lively description of her impressions of the city and people.

[2] J. W. Gray to the Cleveland *Plain Dealer*, April 20th and 30th; see also National Political Conventions of 1860, Halstead, p. 61.

business, and planters of large influence and high character in their respective communities, though little known beyond their own States, were glad to have the honor of assisting in the deliberations of their party's national council. The selections had for the most part been made with care, and, except in New York and Pennsylvania, the action of the minor conventions that met to choose delegates was little disturbed by the operations of machine politics. But few senators or congressmen had seats in the convention. It actually seemed as if one of the conditions the constitutional fathers had hoped to secure in providing for the choice of a President by electors was fulfilled in this nominating assemblage of the great party. "It was desirable," wrote Hamilton, in defending the mode of appointment of the chief magistrate, "that the sense of the people should operate in the choice of the person to whom so important a trust was to be confided. This end will be answered by committing the right of making it, not to any pre-established body, but to men chosen by the people for the special purpose, and at the particular conjuncture. It was equally desirable that the immediate election should be made by men most capable of analyzing the qualities adapted to the station. . . . A small number of persons, selected by their fellow-citizens from the general mass, will be most likely to possess the information and discernment requisite to such complicated investigations."[1] The convention was composed of about six hundred delegates; but three hundred and three, the exact number of electors, was the total vote, each State casting its electoral vote.

Another condition, however, that the constitutional fathers had deemed of vital importance was completely set at naught by the convention system. "It was also peculiarly desirable," Hamilton argued, "to afford as little opportunity as possible to tumult and disorder. . . . And as the electors chosen in each State are to assemble and vote in the State

---

[1] The *Federalist*, No. lxviii.

in which they are chosen, this detached and divided situation will expose them much less to heats and ferments, which might be communicated from them to the people, than if they were all to be convened at one time, in one place." Yet many evils now attendant upon the national political conventions did not accompany the one at Charleston. As the city was small, the local outside pressure was not heavy; and, not being easy of access, only a small number of strangers came from different parts of the country to shout for their particular candidate and increase the difficulty of careful procedure. The hall in which the sessions were held could only accommodate two thousand people. Deliberative action was more feasible there than in the monstrous buildings where now the delegates play their parts to an audience of many thousands.

The antagonism between the delegates from the cotton States and those from the West was the main feature of the situation.[1] It proclaimed in an emphatic manner the schism in the party. The sections divided on a man, Douglas being the pivot on which the convention turned. As he stood for a principle, the minute the making of a platform began, the radical difference was obvious. The West, from personal loyalty and enthusiasm, determined to have Douglas, and they carried nearly the whole North with them, for it was patent that he could poll more votes in the free States than any other candidate. His nomination implied a certain platform, and meant resistance to the domination of Southern extremists in the party. On the other hand, the delegates from the slave States thought Douglas as bad as Seward, and popular sovereignty as hateful as Sewardism, and in their demand for a plain statement of principles and not one facing both ways, they asked for a platform on which Douglas could not possibly stand, and which would render his nomination impossible. These differences came to the surface before the convention met, and were promi-

---

[1] The cotton States had fifty-one votes, the West sixty-six.

nent in the first day's proceedings. The agitation of the whole country centred at Charleston. Men asked, Would there be wisdom enough in the convention to do something towards allaying the agitation, or would it only be increased, as had been the result of the actual session of Congress? The difficulty seemed insurmountable. It was evident that unless the delegates from the cotton States could frame the platform or name the candidate, they would secede from the convention, and it was just as apparent to the North that the Douglas men could concede neither. But this the Southerners did not see. They generally had the privilege of dictating the declaration of principles and controlling the nomination; and although the Western opposition was fiercer than any they had previously met, they could not doubt that it would eventually give way. You deny us our rights in the territories, complained the South. We will stand by you in all of your just claims, replied those whom the slogan of Douglas had called to the contest, but the demands of the fire-eaters we will not concede.[1]

The gravity of the situation was appreciated by all. Union meant probable success, disagreement implied certain defeat. It was noted that intemperate drinking, so frequent where a mass of men gathered on a political errand, was absent. Boisterous merriment would have seemed a discordant note while the shadow of dissolution hung over the convention. The delegates felt the weight of responsibility resting upon them; their faces were serious, even sad. "In this convention," said the Charleston *Mercury*, "where there should be confidence and harmony, it is plain that men feel as if they were going into a battle."[2] Charleston being a religious community, the old Episcopal Church of St. Michael was open daily, and specially ordered prayers

---

[1] "Dinna hear the slogan? 'Tis Douglas and his men," was a favorite expression of the Douglasites.
[2] April 21st, cited by Cleveland *Plain Dealer*.

for the success of the Southern cause were offered up. The supplications of the priest were responded to by a goodly number of women. On the day of the most exciting debate, when the critical period had arrived, the clergyman who opened the session prayed for a happy and harmonious conclusion of the present deliberations.[1] At the same time, fervent abolition preachers at the North were praying for a disruption of the Charleston convention.[2]

The convention met Monday, April 23d. The Douglas men had a majority in number of the delegates, but as California and Oregon acted with the South, the anti-Douglas men had seventeen States out of thirty-three. Thus, having a majority on the committees, they were able to name the president of the convention. Caleb Cushing was chosen for the position. Both factions were anxious to have the platform settled before balloting for a candidate, a course decided upon the second day. The committee on resolutions, composed as usual of one member from each State, went industriously to work. They were anxious to agree; their sessions were protracted and earnest. It seemed as if the fate of the party lay in the hands of those thirty-three men, but they were really only representatives of Douglas and Jefferson Davis. The Southern delegates had in caucus determined to stand by the Davis Senate resolutions; the Northern delegates were committed to the position of Douglas. The irrepressible conflict had invaded the Democratic party, and its convention was a house divided against itself. On the fifth day the committee on resolutions made known their disagreement, and presented a majority and minority report.

The platform of the majority of the committee declared that the territorial legislature has no power to abolish slavery in a territory, to prohibit the introduction of slaves

---

[1] Charleston *Daily Courier*, April 27th.
[2] See Cleveland *Plain Dealer*, June 2d.

therein, or destroy the right of property in slaves by any legislation whatever; and that it is the duty of the federal government to protect, when necessary, slavery in the territories. The platform of the minority in committee reaffirmed the Cincinnati platform. In substance, it asserted that the Democratic party was pledged to abide by the Dred Scott decision, or any future decision of the Supreme Court on the rights of property in the States or territories. Henry B. Payne, of Ohio, submitted the minority report, and defended it in an earnest speech. He was a lawyer of culture and a gentleman of refinement who loved the Union and his party and reverenced the Constitution. Always an impressive speaker, his mien was especially solemn as he made a conciliatory appeal to the South. Every gentleman who had signed the minority report, he said, "had felt in his conscience and in his heart that upon the result of our deliberations and the action of this convention, in all human probability, depended the fate of the Democratic party and the destiny of the Union." This was not the usual clap-trap exaggeration of convention oratory, but it was the expression of the sincere feeling of thoughtful Northern men. We should have been no patriots, Payne continued, if we had brought into our deliberative conference any but an earnest and honest desire to adjust the differences that exist in our party. Citing the opinion of many Southerners to show that once the Southern idea of popular sovereignty was the same as that of the North, he declared, "The Northern mind is thoroughly imbued with the principle of popular sovereignty. . . . We ask nothing for the people of the territories but what the Constitution allows them, for we say we abide by the decision of the courts, who are the final interpreters of the Constitution. The Dred Scott decision, having been rendered since the Cincinnati platform was adopted, renders this proper. We will take that decision and abide by it like loyal, steadfast, true-hearted men. . . . I would appeal to the South to put no weights on the North —to let them run this race unfettered and unhampered. If the appeal is answered, the North will do her duty in the struggle."[1]

Payne's speech was received with loud demonstrations of approval from the Northern delegates and with respect by those of the South. But the eloquence of a Demosthenes could not have persuaded them to take the platform advocated by Payne, unless coupled with the condition that they might name the candidate. At the afternoon session, Yancey, of Alabama, the champion of the fire-eaters and the most eloquent orator of the South, took the floor amid deafening and prolonged cheers. The Southern gentlemen rose to their feet, and the ladies in the galleries waved their handkerchiefs as he advanced to the platform.[2] He was tall and slender, with long black hair, a mild and gentlemanly manner, and an habitual expression of good humor; dressed in pronounced Southern style, his appearance was picturesque. As he opened his mouth, his words of passion, uttered in a soft, musical voice, gave him the rapt attention of the audience. "We came here," he said, "with one great purpose. First, to save our constitutional rights, if it lay in our power to do so. . . . We are in the minority, as we have been taunted here to-day. In the progress of civilization, the Northwest has grown up from an infant in swaddling-clothes into the free proportions of a giant people. We therefore, as the minority, take the rights, the mission, and the position of the minority. What is it we claim? We claim the benefit of the Constitution that was made for the protection of minorities; that Constitution which our fathers made that they and their children should always observe—that a majority should not rely upon their numbers and strength, but should loyally look into the written compact and see where the minority was to be respected and protected. The proposition you make [those favoring

---

[1] These citations are taken from the speech as published in the Charleston *Courier* and compared with the report of the Charleston *Mercury*.
[2] Charleston *Courier*.

the minority report] will bankrupt us of the South. Ours is the property invaded—ours the interests at stake. The honor of our children, the honor of our females, the lives of our men, all rest upon you. You would make a great seething caldron of passion and crime if you were able to consummate your measures. . . . You acknowledged that slavery did not exist by the law of nature or by the law of God—that it only existed by State law; that it was wrong, but that you were not to blame. That was your position, and it was wrong. If you had taken the position directly that slavery was right and therefore ought to be . . . you would have triumphed, and anti-slavery would now have been dead in your midst. But you have gone down before the enemy so that they have put their foot upon your neck; you will go lower and lower still, unless you change front and change your tactics. When I was a schoolboy in the Northern States, abolitionists were pelted with rotten eggs. But now this band of abolitionists has spread and grown into three bands—the Black Republican, the Freesoilers, and squatter-sovereignty men—all representing the common sentiment that slavery is wrong. I say it in no disrespect, but it is a logical argument that your admission that slavery is wrong has been the cause of all this discord." [1]

The extreme demands of the South had been formulated, and as soon as Yancey closed, Senator Pugh, of Ohio, who was very near to Douglas, and now his only follower in the Senate, sprang to his feet. He thanked God that a bold and honest man from the South had at last spoken and told the whole truth of the demands of the South. The exaction was made of Northern Democrats that they should say slavery is right and ought to be extended. "Gentlemen of the South," declared Pugh, "you mistake us—you mistake us: we will not do it." [2] Excitement and fatigue compelled

---

[1] These extracts are taken from the Charleston *Courier;* see also Politics and Pen Pictures, Henry W. Hilliard, p. 286 *et ante.*

[2] National Political Conventions of 1860, Halstead, p. 49.

THE CHARLESTON CONVENTION

the convention to adjourn before he had concluded; but he returned to the charge in the evening, and spoke with animation and energy. A demand by a Connecticut delegate for the previous question, so that a vote might be taken on the platform, set the convention in an uproar. The tumult was not checked until the chair recognized a motion of adjournment, which, on a vote by States, was carried by a small majority.[1] The debate had demonstrated that agreement was impossible; but on Saturday, the following day, and the sixth day of the convention, Senator Bigler, a friend of Buchanan, made an attempt to pour oil upon the troubled waters, and moved that both platforms be recommitted. This was carried, and at four o'clock in the afternoon the committee reported again two platforms, slightly changed in phraseology, but in essence unaltered. A dreary debate followed. Then the Douglas men tried hard to get a vote. The Southerners filibustered, and confusion prevailed to the extent that the president threatened to leave the chair unless his authority were respected. In the end, the convention decided to adjourn.

And now Sunday intervened. The most gloomy anticipations had been realized. The delegates were brought face to face with a condition of things which indicated that one side or the other must yield or the convention would break up. It was idle to attempt to carry a Northern State on the Yancey platform, but why could not the South accept the Douglas declaration of principles? It was more favorable to the slave States than any platform ever adopted by a Democratic national convention. Unquestionably if a Southern man, sound according to the ideas of the slavery propaganda, or another Pierce or Buchanan, could have been nominated, the Southern delegates would have ceased their ado about the platform. But this was precisely what the Douglas men could not concede. No ultra pro-slavery man, no Northern man with Southern principles, could carry

---

[1] National Political Conventions of 1860, Halstead, pp. 50, 51.

a Northern State, no matter what was the platform. After all discussion and innumerable suggestions, the delegates were back where they started from. Douglas was the only man who could make a strong contest at the North, and his strength lay in the fact that he represented opposition to the slave power. The followers of Douglas were justified in adhering strictly to their platform and candidate, for the two were inseparable. Having temperately explained their reasons, they were bound to pursue the course marked out and use the power that a majority of the convention gave them. They did indeed resent being called abolitionists, a favorite taunt of the Southerners; but from the Southern standpoint, any one who opposed the programme of the extension of slavery deserved that name.

On Monday, after the day of rest and reflection, the delegates met. They no longer ventured to hope that an agreement might be reached. The two factions could now only logically carry out that which their previous action had determined. The Douglas platform was adopted by a vote of 165 to 138. The division was practically on Mason and Dixon's line, only twelve from the slave States voting for it and thirty from the free States voting against it. Buchanan's malice against Douglas knew no bounds, and his power had been directed to securing anti-Douglas delegates from the North. Administrative patronage had dictated their choice in California and Oregon, and had obtained a portion of the delegations of Massachusetts, New Jersey, and Pennsylvania. But although they were accompanied by a large body of office-holders,[1] their influence was not great, and served little more than to deceive some Southerners regarding the practical unanimity of Democratic sentiment at the North.

After the adoption of the platform, the chairman of the Alabama delegation rose, and, protesting against the action

---

[1] "Five hundred and seven office-holders at Charleston."—J. W. Gray, a delegate, to the Cleveland *Plain Dealer*, April 30th.

of the convention, announced that Alabama would formally withdraw. Mississippi, Louisiana, South Carolina, Florida, Texas, and Arkansas protested in the same strain, and declared their purpose of secession. Before each delegation left their seats, one of their number made a short speech to justify their course; the remarks of Glenn, of Mississippi, were especially thrilling. Pale with emotion, his eyes glaring with excitement, he averred that the solemn act of the Mississippi delegation was not conceived in passion or carried out from mere caprice or disappointment. It was the firm resolve of the great body they represented. The people of Mississippi ask, What is the construction of the platform of 1856? You of the North say it means one thing; we of the South another. They ask which is right and which is wrong? The North have maintained their position, but, while doing so, they have not acknowledged the rights of the South. We say, go your way and we will go ours. But the South leaves not like Hagar, driven into the wilderness friendless and alone, for in sixty days you will find a united South standing shoulder to shoulder.[1]

The cheers and prolonged applause greeting the speaker as he finished his speech, and the demonstrations of approval that came from the ladies, who had turned out in numbers to see the first act in the drama of secession played, were evidence that disunion was popular. Yet to all but the most enthusiastic fire-eaters and a few Northern men disposed to levity, the moment was supremely solemn. Men looked alarmed as they thought to what this action might lead. Their eyes were suffused with tears, feeling that they were witnessing the disruption of the great party of Jefferson and Jackson. They trembled when asking themselves, was this the prelude to the dissolution of the Union?—that Union, strong and great; for they felt that

---

[1] National Political Conventions of 1860, Halstead, p. 66; Richmond *Enquirer*.

> "Humanity with all its fears,
> With all the hopes of future years,
> Is hanging breathless on thy fate!"

On the next day the convention decided that two-thirds of the whole electoral vote was necessary to nominate, and then proceeded to ballot. Georgia in the meantime having withdrawn, only 253 votes were cast, and 202 were necessary to a choice. On the first ballot, Douglas received $145\frac{1}{2}$; Hunter, of Virginia, 42; Guthrie, of Kentucky, $35\frac{1}{2}$; scattering, 30. In two days the convention cast fifty-seven ballots, Douglas several times receiving $152\frac{1}{2}$ votes, a majority of the whole electoral vote, and under a majority rule he would have been nominated. On May 3d, the tenth day of the convention, the delegates, seeing that it was impossible to reach any result, adjourned to meet at Baltimore the 18th of June. The seceders meanwhile had formed themselves into a convention and adopted a platform. Now they terminated their proceedings by a resolution to meet again at Richmond on the second Monday of the same month.[1]

Gloomy thoughts were the portion of Northern and border-State men as they wended their way homeward. They had assisted in the disruption of the party to which they were devotedly attached, and in whose fortune, it seemed to them, was bound up the fate of the country. They saw the immense patronage and power of the administration of the government, which they had held so long, receding from their grasp. They could not now ignore the strong probability that the Republican convention at Chicago would name the next President, and in that event they could have little doubt, after what had taken place at Charleston, that the Southern extremists would lead their States into secession. The followers of Yancey were so bitter against Doug-

---

[1] In this account of the convention, besides the authorities already quoted, I have consulted the files of the *Liberator*, the Philadelphia *Press*, the Washington *Constitution*, and the New Orleans *Picayune*.

las that they must have felt exultation at preventing for the moment his nomination. But all prominent men at the South did not share their sentiments. Alexander Stephens understood the motives underlying their action and expressed himself frankly in a private letter to his friend. "The seceders intended from the beginning to rule or ruin," he wrote; "and when they find they cannot rule, they will then ruin. They have about enough power for this purpose; not much more; and I doubt not but they will use it. Envy, hate, jealousy, spite—these made war in heaven, which made devils of angels, and the same passions will make devils of men. The secession movement was instigated by nothing but bad passions. Patriotism, in my opinion, had no more to do with it than love of God had with the other revolt."[1]

Yet Stephens was not blind to what the secession at Charleston tended. In conversation with his friend Johnston shortly after the adjournment of the convention, he said: "Men will be cutting one another's throats in a little while. In less than twelve months we shall be in a war, and that the bloodiest in history. Men seem to be utterly blinded to the future."

"Do you not think that matters may yet be adjusted at Baltimore?" asked his friend. "Not the slightest chance of it," was the reply. "The party is split forever. Douglas will not retire from the stand he has taken. . . . The only hope was at Charleston. If the party could have agreed there, we might carry the election. . . . If the party would be satisfied with the Cincinnati platform and would cordially nominate Douglas, we should carry the election; but I repeat to you that is impossible."

"But why must we have civil war, even if the Republican candidate should be elected?" Johnston inquired. "Because," answered Stephens, "there are not virtue and pa-

---

[1] Letter to R. M. Johnston, June 19th, Life by Johnston and Browne, p. 365.

triotism and sense enough left in the country to avoid it. Mark me, when I repeat that in less than twelve months we shall be in the midst of a bloody war. What is to become of us then God only knows. The Union will certainly be disrupted."[1]

On the 9th of May, the remnant of old-line Whigs and Americans calling themselves the Constitutional Union party met in convention at Baltimore. It was a highly respectable body, and not to be despised in point of ability. An absence of the younger men was noticeable. The delegates were, for the most part, venerable men who had come down from a former generation of politicians, and who, alarmed at the growth and bitterness of the sectional controversy, had met together to see if their efforts might avail something to save the endangered Union. A patriotic spirit animated the assemblage. Fully recognizing the impending peril of the country, their action, from their point of view, was calculated to allay the trouble. But their remedy for the sore was a plaster, when it rather needed cauterization. Their platform was: "The Constitution of the country, the union of the States, and the enforcement of the laws;" and they nominated—For President, Bell, of Tennessee; and for Vice-President, Everett, of Massachusetts; men of honesty and experience, who were a fit expression of the patriotic and conservative sentiments animating a large number of citizens that looked to this convention for guidance.[2]

The contest at Charleston was now transferred to the floor of the Senate, where the principals could speak in person. Jefferson Davis, with an arrogant manner[3] all his

---

[1] This remarkable conversation is given by Johnston and Browne, p. 355.

[2] See National Political Conventions of 1860, Halstead; the New York *Tribune*. One gets a good idea of the spirit animating this party from the confidential correspondence of Crittenden, see Life, by Coleman, vol. ii. pp. 182 to 212.

[3] "Public sentiment proclaims that the most arrogant man in the

own, asserted: "We claim protection [for slavery in the territories], first, because it is our right; secondly, because it is the duty of the general government;" and he demanded, What right has Congress to abdicate any power conferred upon it as trustee of the States? But we make you no threat, he said; we only give you a warning.[1] Douglas, in replying to Davis several days later, took occasion to explain his position in reference to the Democratic convention. "My name never would have been presented at Charleston," said he, "except for the attempt to proscribe me as a heretic, too unsound to be the chairman of a committee in this body, where I have held a seat for so many years without a suspicion resting on my political fidelity. I was forced to allow my name to go there in self-defence; and I will now say that had any gentleman, friend or foe, received a majority of that convention over me, the lightning would have carried a message withdrawing my name." Douglas intimated that Yancey and his followers had begun in 1858 to plan disunion, and that the secession movement at Charleston was their first overt act. The Davis resolutions in the Senate were substantially the Yancey platform of Charleston, and while senators who advocated them might not mean disunion, those principles insisted upon "will lead directly and inevitably to a dissolution of the Union."[2]

On the 17th of May a heated debate between Douglas and Davis took place, which at the end was attended with personalities. "I have a declining respect for platforms," Davis said. "I would sooner have an honest man on any sort of a rickety platform you could construct than to have a man I did not trust on the best platform which could be

---

United States Senate is Jefferson Davis. Nor does there seem to be much doubt that in debate he is the most insolent and insufferable. The offence consists not so much in the words used as in the air and mien which he assumes towards opponents."—Editorial, New York *Tribune*, April 14th.

[1] Davis made an elaborate speech May 7th.
[2] Speech of Douglas, May 16th.

made." "If the platform is not a matter of much consequence," demanded Douglas, "why press that question to the disruption of the party? Why did you not tell us in the beginning of this debate that the whole fight was against the man and not upon the platform?" After several days a vote on the Davis resolution was reached, and though the phraseology of the crucial proposition had been changed, its essence was the same as when originally introduced.[1] Every Democratic senator but Pugh[2] voted for it; but the appearance of harmony was illusory, for the position of Douglas and Pugh had more Democratic adherents among the people than the Davis resolution could muster.

While Douglas and Davis were wrangling in the Senate, the Republicans were holding their convention at Chicago. It was fitting that the party, that had its origin in the Northwest, should now meet in the typical city, which, with a population of little more than one hundred thousand, had already made the word Chicago synonymous with that of progress. Five slave States—Delaware, Maryland, Virginia, Kentucky, and Missouri—were represented, and four hundred and sixty-six delegates made up the convention. They met in a "wigwam"[3] built for the occasion, which, it was said, would hold ten thousand people. By the second day of the convention thirty thousand to forty thousand strangers, mostly from the Northwest, had flocked to the city, eager to be associated with the great historic event that was promised, and thinking perhaps to affect the result by their presence and their shouts.[4] For since the disruption of the Charleston convention the Republicans had felt that if they took advantage of the situation, they would

---

[1] See p. 430. [2] Douglas was not present.
[3] The building called a wigwam was a temporary frame structure, and the name is still applied in Western cities by Republicans to buildings used for party purposes.
[4] Nicolay and Hay, vol. ii. p. 264; National Political Conventions, Halstead, p. 140.

surely elect their candidate for the presidency. Victory was in the air, and office-seekers, who, since 1858, had formed a noticeable part of the Republican organization,[1] were now on hand in number, for the purpose of making prominent their devotion to the party and its principles. The contrast between this and the national convention of 1856 is worthy of remark. Then a hall accommodating two thousand was quite sufficient, now a wigwam holding ten thousand was jammed, and twenty thousand people outside clamored for admittance; then the wire-pullers looked askance at a movement whose success was problematical, now they hastened to identify themselves with a party that apparently had the game in its own hand; then the delegates were liberty-loving enthusiasts and largely volunteers, now the delegates had been chosen by means of the organization peculiar to a powerful party, and in political wisdom were the pick of the Republicans; then the contest to follow seemed but a tentative effort and the leading men would not accept the nomination, while now triumph appeared so sure that every one of the master spirits of the party was eager to be the candidate. And the most potent cause of this change was the split in the Democratic party, which began with the refusal of Douglas to submit to Southern dictation.

"The convention is very like the old Democratic article," wrote an observer; and he has also told the tale of the bibulous propensities of the outsiders who had come to exert a pressure in favor of Seward or Lincoln. Though a Republican himself, he was forced to confess that greater sobriety had characterized the assemblage at Charleston.[2] No convention had ever attracted such a crowd of lookers-on. Never before had there been such systematic efforts to create an opinion that the people demanded this or that candidate. Organized bodies of men were sent out day and

---

[1] See Lincoln-Douglas Debates, p. 230.
[2] Halstead, pp. 121, 122, 132.

night to make street demonstrations for their favorite, or were collected to pack the audience-room in the convention hall, so that vociferous cheers might greet each mention of his name. These procedures were very different from those of similar Whig gatherings heretofore, which had been marked by respectability and decorum.

Before Lincoln made his Cooper Institute speech, the mention of his name as a possible nominee for President by the Chicago convention would have been considered a joke anywhere except in Illinois, Indiana, Ohio, and Iowa. That New York address, however, had gained him many friends, among whom was William Cullen Bryant.[1] His speeches in New England that followed made it patent at the East that he might become a formidable opponent of Seward. The reception he had in New York and New England convinced Lincoln himself that the Chicago nomination was attainable, and, ceasing to take interest in his law practice, he set himself at work to secure the prize. An acute observer of the drift of opinion, a good judge of men in the face of large events, Lincoln was clumsy in the attempt to manipulate a delegation and awkward in the use of money to promote his candidacy.[2] The movement in Illinois, which had been growing since the debates of 1858, culminated in giving him a most enthusiastic endorsement at the State convention held at Decatur the 9th of May. Lincoln himself was present, and John Hanks marched in among the crowd in the wigwam, bearing on his shoulder the two historic rails, on which was inscribed: "From a lot made by Abraham Lincoln and John Hanks in the Sangamon bottom in the year 1830."[3] Loud and prolonged cheers bore testimony to the effect of this manoeuvre. The following week at Chicago the continued hurrahs for "honest old Abe, the rail-splitter," told the Seward men of unlooked-for strength in one of the competitors for the nomination.

---

[1] Life by Godwin, vol. ii. p. 123.   [2] Herndon, p. 457.
[3] Lamon, p. 445; Herndon, p. 460.

Before the delegates assembled at Chicago, the condition of the contest was expressed in sporting parlance as "Seward against the field." But by the first day of the convention it became evident that the struggle would be between Seward and Lincoln. Chase had been unable to secure the united delegation of his own State, and his candidacy did not assume the prominence that was due to his ability and position.¹ A month and a half before the convention met he had little hope of securing the nomination,² and was prepared to acquiesce in that of Seward. "There seems to be at present," he wrote, "a considerable set towards Seward. Should the nomination fall to him, I shall not at all repine."³ Edward Bates, of Missouri, had the powerful support of Greeley and the New York *Tribune*, and also of Francis P. Blair and his sons. Knowing him to be eminently sound on the slavery question, they thought his nomination would please better than any other the conservative Republicans. Moreover, it would deprive of force the charge that their party was sectional, and give them a chance of carrying Missouri, a slave State. Pennsylvania was nearly united in support of Cameron, but the vote she would give him on the first ballot would be well understood as only the usual compliment to a favorite son. A few Ohio, Pennsylvania, and Indiana men wanted McLean,⁴ while Senator Wade had friends who hoped that the time might come when he could be sprung upon the convention as a dark horse.

---

¹ The year before the convention, Chase had been looked upon as a possibly successful contestant against Seward. "My impression is," wrote Dana to Pike, June 23d, 1859, "that we had better concentrate on Chase, and that he is the only man we can beat Seward with."—Pike's First Blows of the Civil War, p. 441.

² See letter of April 2d to Pike, Pike's First Blows of the Civil War, p. 505. ³ Letter of March 19th, ibid., p. 503.

⁴ Regarding preferences of Thaddeus Stevens and other Pennsylvania delegates for McLean, see account of A. K. McClure, Boston *Herald*, Sept. 6th, 1891.

Seward's claim for the nomination was strong. He was the representative man of the party, and well fitted both by ability and experience for the position to which he aspired. Intensely anxious for the nomination, and confidently expecting it, he was alike the choice of the politicians and the people.[1] Could a popular vote on the subject have been taken, the majority in the Republican States would have been overwhelmingly in his favor. One day at Chicago sufficed to demonstrate that he had the support of the machine politicians. What was urged as the most serious objection to Seward was his weakness in the doubtful States of Pennsylvania, New Jersey, Indiana, and Illinois. Pennsylvania and one of the others must be carried to insure the election of a Republican President. These States, situated on the border, were strongly tinctured with conservatism. In all four of them Seward was weak, for the reason that he was regarded as the exponent of the radical element of the party. His "irrepressible-conflict" speech had done much to lessen his availability. Why Lincoln's "house-divided-against-itself" declaration should not also have precluded his nomination is one of the curiosities of politics, although it is easily explicable. Seward paid the penalty of the greater fame, for a hundred men had read his speech where one had looked at Lincoln's. Yet it is true that the notion of Seward's greater radicalism had a basis in the fact that he had averred the higher-law doctrine—a position from which Lincoln especially held himself aloof. Seward stood in so marked a degree for the radical element of the party that eight of the Illinois delegates, who had been chosen from the northern part of the State, and represented advanced anti-slavery communities, were at heart for him, though they loyally carried out their instructions and voted for Lincoln.[2]

---

[1] Pike, Washington, May 20th, p. 517.

[2] Letter of Leonard Swett to J. H. Drummond, May 27th, 1860, published in the Portland (Me.) *Express*, and copied into the New York *Sun* of July 26th, 1891.

Moreover, Seward was especially objectionable in Pennsylvania, from having been outspoken against the Know-nothing movement, which had been strong in that State. The former American element, deemed an important part of the People's party, had to be placated, for it had not been deemed wise even to assume the name Republican in the Keystone State. Besides there were men more radical than Seward—men who sympathized with him in his opposition to Know-nothingism—who were nevertheless averse to his nomination, because they did not like his political associations. A man of unquestioned integrity himself, Seward had intimate connections with men who were full of schemes requiring public grants. For these his vote and influence were frequently used. "He is a believer in the adage," said Pike, "that it is money makes the mare go."[1] "I was not without apprehensions," wrote Bryant, when congratulating Lincoln, "that the nomination might fall upon some person encumbered with bad associates,"[2] and it was Seward he had in mind. "There were reasons," wrote Charles A. Dana in the *Tribune*, a month after the convention, "against Seward's nomination connected with the peculiar state of things at Albany, and the possibility of its transference to Washington."[3] In March, Dana, in a private letter to Pike, had hinted at the connection between "Seward stock" and "New York city street railroad" schemes in Albany.[4] Bryant had, in the December previous, mentioned to Bigelow why Seward's prospects were not brightening. "This iteration," he wrote, "of the misconstruction put on his phrase of 'the irrepressible conflict between freedom and slavery' has, I think, damaged him a good deal; and in this city there is one thing which has damaged him still more. I mean the project of Thurlow Weed to give charters for a set of city

---

[1] First Blows of the Civil War, p. 518.
[2] Letter of June 16th, Life by Godwin, vol. ii. p. 142.
[3] New York *Tribune*, June 18th.
[4] First Blows of the Civil War, p. 501.

railways, for which those who receive them are to furnish a fund of from four to six hundred thousand dollars, to be expended for the Republican cause in the next presidential election." [1] These expressions represented a widespread sentiment,[2] to which many allusions may be found in the political literature of 1850–60. The objection based on that feeling was little mentioned in the newspaper discussions previous to the convention, for, the general presumption being that Seward would secure the nomination, the Republicans wished to avoid furnishing arguments to the enemy.

While much of the outside volunteer attendance from New York and Michigan favoring Seward was weighty in character as well as imposing in number, the organized body of rough fellows from New York city, under the lead of Tom Hyer, a noted bruiser, made a great deal of noise without helping his cause. Their appearance, as they marched through the streets headed by a gaily uniformed band, was in a certain way striking, but their arguments when not on parade were little fitted to win support from New England and the West. "If you do not nominate Seward, where will you get your money?"[3] they considered an unanswerable question; and the assurance that Seward's friends would put up money enough to carry Pennsylvania, in their opinion, settled the doubt that existed about the Keystone State.[4] All the outside pressure was for Seward or Lincoln, there being practically none for the other candidates. While many of Seward's followers were disinterested and sincere, others betrayed unmistakably the influence of the machine. Lincoln's adherents were men from Illinois, Indiana, and Iowa, who had come to Chicago bent on having a good time and seeing the rail-splitter nominated, and while traces of

---

[1] Letter of Dec. 14th, 1859, Life, by Godwin, vol. ii. p. 127.
[2] See also Recollections of a Busy Life, Greeley, p. 312; and Lincoln and Seward, Gideon Welles, p. 27.
[3] Horace Greeley, New York *Tribune*, May 22d.
[4] Halstead, p. 142.

organization might be detected among them, it was such organization as may be seen in a mob.

Thus stood affairs when the convention organized on Wednesday morning, May 16th. David Wilmot, of Pennsylvania, the author of the Wilmot proviso, was the temporary chairman; George Ashmun, of Massachusetts, the friend of Webster, who had labored hard for his nomination in 1852, was chosen for the permanent presiding officer. When the platform was reported on the second day of the proceedings, Giddings offered as an amendment to the first resolution the oft-quoted assertion of the Declaration of Independence. Giddings represented the abolitionist element of the party; and, lest the convention should go too far in that direction, it was attempted to choke him off. However, respect for fair play conquered, and he was allowed to present his amendment, but it was voted down. Giddings then left the convention in sorrow and anger. A little later, George William Curtis obtained the floor and offered as an amendment to the second resolution the clause of the Declaration beginning "all men are created equal"—substantially the same that Giddings had proposed—advocating it in earnest words. "I have to ask this convention," he said, " whether they are prepared to go upon the record and before the country as voting down the words of the Declaration of Independence? I ask gentlemen gravely to consider that in the amendment which I have proposed I have done nothing that the soundest and safest man in all the land might not do; . . . and I ask gentlemen to think well before, upon the free prairies of the West, in the summer of 1860, they dare to wince and quail before the men of Philadelphia of 1776—before they dare to shrink from repeating the words that these great men enunciated."[1] The effect of this speech was electric; it was greeted with deafening applause, and no further objection was made to reasserting the principles of the Declaration of Independence. This

---

[1] Halstead, p. 137.

action conciliated Giddings and, through him, the radical element of the party.

The platform was prepared with care. The aim of the committee had been to allow the greatest liberty of sentiment consistent with an emphatic assertion of the cardinal Republican doctrine. In this they succeeded admirably.[1] The platform paid a tribute to the Union; asserted that the rights of the States should be maintained inviolate; denounced the John Brown invasion "as among the gravest of crimes;" censured the attempt of the Buchanan administration to force the Lecompton constitution upon Kansas; denounced the new dogma that the Constitution of its own force carries slavery into the territories; declared the Democratic doctrine of popular sovereignty a "deception and fraud;" denied "the authority of Congress, of a territorial legislature, or of any individual to give legal existence to slavery in any territory;" branded "the recent reopening of the African slave-trade . . . as a crime against humanity and a burning shame to our country and age;" demanded the admission of Kansas; asserted that sound policy requires the adjustment of duties upon imports so as "to encourage the development of the industrial interests of the whole country;" demanded a homestead bill; and opposed any change in the naturalization laws. The authors of the platform, by steering clear of disputed questions, gave it throughout an aggressive tone. There is but one plank, said the New York *Tribune*, editorially, "that on the tariff —which will be likely to give rise to objections in any quarter;"[2] and when that resolution was read, Pennsylvania, the pre-eminently doubtful State, went wild with joy.[3] The silence on the Fugitive Slave law, on personal liberty bills, and on the abolition of slavery in the District of Columbia, also the avoidance of mentioning the Dred Scott decision,

---

[1] See Horace Greeley, New York *Tribune*, May 22d. Greeley was one of the committee on resolutions.

[2] May 18th.   [3] Halstead, p. 135.

were significant. The platform received the enthusiastic support of the followers of Seward, Lincoln, and the other candidates. After the vote had been taken on its adoption, the great hall rang with applause and with cheers from ten thousand lusty throats.

It was now six o'clock of Thursday, the second day, and the convention adjourned without taking a ballot. Everything seemed to point to the nomination of Seward on the morrow. Just before midnight, Greeley, who sat as a delegate from Oregon, persistently advocated Bates, and yet was earnestly in favor of almost anything to beat Seward, telegraphed the *Tribune:* "My conclusion, from all that I can gather to-night, is that the opposition to Governor Seward cannot concentrate on any candidate, and that he will be nominated."[1] Halstead sent the same word to his journal.[2] The Seward canvass had been made with vigor and, on the whole, with discretion. Thurlow Weed, Seward's trusted friend and counsellor, was the leader of the forces. No man of the opposition equalled him in adroitness and political management. On the floor of the convention, the cause was intrusted to William M. Evarts, of New York, Austin Blair, of Michigan, and Carl Schurz, of Wisconsin, who were backed by their respective delegations. The episode of which Curtis had been the hero redounded to the credit of Seward.[3] The New-Yorkers were exultant. At their headquarters, the Richmond House, champagne flowed freely in celebration of the expected victory, and Seward bands of music went the rounds, serenading the different delegations from whom support was expected.[4]

But during this night, made hideous by bacchanalian shouts, the blare of brass instruments and the noise of the drum, earnest men, believing that success depended on the

---

[1] Date of despatch, Thursday, May 17th, 11:40 P.M., published in Friday morning's New York *Tribune.*
[2] Cincinnati *Commercial.* See Halstead, p. 142.   [3] Ibid., p. 141.
[4] Ibid.

nomination of some other man than Seward, were indefatigably at work. Prominent among them were Andrew Curtin, the nominee of the People's party for Governor of Pennsylvania, and Henry S. Lane, the Indiana Republican candidate for governor, who urged, in accents of undoubted sincerity, that if Seward were the standard-bearer they could not carry their respective States at the State elections in October, which would determine the national contest. Nothing could be done with Ohio, another October State; she would not unite on any candidate, on either the first or second ballot.[1] An impression was made on Virginia; and New England, really for Seward, was influenced by the argument of availability especially and strongly urged by Greeley, whose political influence was never greater than now.

All this opposition effort pointed either to Lincoln or Bates. Could it be concentrated on one or the other? Although Bates had earnest supporters in Indiana,[2] that State naturally inclined to Lincoln, and it was eminently desirable that her entire vote should be cast for him on the first ballot. Any wavering or hanging back was this night overcome by the promise of David Davis, the manager for Lincoln, of a cabinet position to Caleb Smith, one of the Indiana delegates at large, in case of Lincoln's election.[3] All but a few of the Pennsylvania delegates would vote for Cameron on the first ballot. The question was, to whom would her vote go on the second? Cameron himself, although not at Chicago, was for Seward,[4] and it had been expected before the meeting of the convention that his influence would bring most of the delegates over to the support of the New York

---

[1] Greeley, New York *Tribune*, May 22d.
[2] Letter of Swett, May 26th, 1860, Life of Colfax, Hollister, p. 142.
[3] Herndon, p. 471; Lamon, p. 449. See also Political Recollections, Julian, p. 182; and Life of Colfax, Hollister, p. 175.
[4] See Seward's letters to Weed, April 29th and March 15th, 1860, Life of Thurlow Weed, vol. ii. pp. 256, 261; note in Halstead, p. 142. See Cameron's speech, May 25th, 1860, reported in Philadelphia *Press*.

senator.[1] But it became early apparent that the followers of Seward in Pennsylvania were few, and that her second choice lay between Lincoln and Bates, a vote of the delegates being 60 for Lincoln to 45 for Bates as their second choice.[2]

To win the support of the close followers of Cameron, David Davis promised that he should have a cabinet position in the event of Lincoln's election; and this, in addition to the other influences that had been used, secured nearly the whole vote of Pennsylvania.[3] Lincoln himself knew nothing of these bargains at the time,[4] and they were made against his positive direction. A careful and anxious observer of what was taking place at Chicago, he sent to his friends this word in writing, which reached them the day before the nomination: "I agree," he said, "with Seward in his 'irrepressible conflict,' but I do not endorse his 'higher-law' doctrine;" then, underscoring the words, he wrote: "Make no contracts that will bind me."[5]

Greeley, either ignorant of these bargains, or distrusting that the Pennsylvania and Indiana delegations could be brought to fulfil their part, thought, when the convention met Friday morning, that there could be no concentration of the anti-Seward forces. The Seward managers them-

---

[1] Lincoln and Seward, Welles. Welles was the chairman of the Connecticut delegation.

[2] Greeley, New York *Tribune*, May 22d. Although Pennsylvania cast but fifty-four votes, she had one hundred and eight delegates on the official roll of the convention, Halstead, p. 125; see also account of A. K. McClure, Boston *Herald*, Sept. 6th, 1891.

[3] Herndon, p. 471; Lamon, p. 449. Article of A. K. McClure, New York Sun, Dec. 13, 1891. See also Political Recollections, Julian, p. 182; and Swett's account, Life of Thurlow Weed, vol. ii. p. 292; but Swett did not know of the promises in regard to Cameron and Smith, for he wrote Drummond privately, May 27th: "No pledges have been made, no mortgages executed, but Lincoln enters the field a free man."

[4] "The responsible position assigned me comes without conditions."— Lincoln to Giddings, May 21st, 1860. Life of Giddings, Julian, p. 376.

[5] Herndon, p. 462.

selves felt so confident that they sincerely asked, and with no idea of bravado, whom the opposition would like for Vice-President.[1]

The convention met and the candidates were put in nomination without the speeches of eulogy that have since become the rule. At the mention of the name of Seward or Lincoln, the great hall resounded with applause and cheers; but the Lincoln yell far surpassed the other in vigor. Tom Hyer's men had this morning marched through the street to the music of victorious strains, and had so prolonged their march that when they came to the wigwam they found the best places occupied by sturdy Lincoln men; all of Seward's followers were not able to get into the wigwam, and much of the effect of their lusty shouts was therefore lost.

In many contemporaneous and subsequent accounts of this convention, it is set down as an important fact, contributing to the nomination of Lincoln, that on this day the Lincoln men out-shouted the supporters of Seward. One wonders if those wise and experienced delegates interpreted this manipulated noise as the voice of the people. While the shouts for "old Abe" were in a considerable degree spontaneous, due to the fact that the convention was held in his own State, art was not lacking in the production of these manifestations. The Lincoln managers, determined that the voice of Illinois should be literally heard, engaged a Chicago man whose shout, it was said, could be heard above the howling of the most violent tempest on Lake Michigan, and a Doctor Ames, a Democrat living on the Illinois river, who had similar gifts, to organize a *claque* and lead the cheering and applause in the convention hall.[2]

"As long as conventions shall be held, I believe," wrote Greeley, "no abler, wiser, more unselfish body of delegates

---

[1] Greeley, New York *Tribune*, May 22d.
[2] Life of Lincoln, Arnold, p. 167. See also letter of Leonard Swett, May 27th, 1860; also Raymond's inside history of the convention, Life of Thurlow Weed, vol. ii. p. 276.

from the various States will ever be assembled than that which met at Chicago." [1] The vigor of the young men was tempered by the caution and experience of the graybeards. Sixty of the delegates, then unknown beyond their respective districts, were afterwards sent to Congress, and many of them became governors of their States.[2] That a convention composed of such men—men who had looked behind the scenes and understood the springs of this enthusiasm—should have had its choice of a candidate dictated by the cheers and shouts of a mob, is difficult to believe.

The convention was now ready to ballot. As the calling of the roll proceeded, intense interest was manifested by leaders, by delegates, and by spectators. New England came first, and did not give the number of votes for Seward that had been anticipated, but New York's plumper of 70, announced dramatically by Evarts, almost neutralized this effect. All but $6\frac{1}{2}$ votes of Pennsylvania went to Cameron. Virginia gave surprise by casting 14 votes out of her 23 for Lincoln; and the entire Indiana delegation (26 in number), declaring for the rail-splitter of Illinois caused a great sensation. The secretary announced the result of the first ballot: Seward, $173\frac{1}{2}$; Lincoln, 102; Cameron, $50\frac{1}{2}$; Chase, 49; Bates, 48; scattering, 42; necessary to a choice, 233.

---

[1] New York *Tribune*, June 2d.
[2] See Twenty Years of Congress, Blaine, vol. i. p. 164. There were many noted men, or men who afterwards became so, in the convention. Among them were E. H. Rollins, of New Hampshire; John A. Andrew, Geo. S. Boutwell, Edw. L. Pierce, and Samuel Hooper, of Massachusetts; Senator Simmons, of Rhode Island; Gideon Welles, of Connecticut; Evarts, Preston King, and Geo. W. Curtis, of New York; Fred. T. Frelinghuysen, of New Jersey; Wilmot, Thaddeus Stevens, and Reeder, of Pennsylvania; Francis P. Blair and Montgomery Blair, of Maryland; Cartter, Corwin, Monroe, Delano, and Giddings, of Ohio; Judd, David Davis, and Browning, of Illinois; Schurz, of Wisconsin; John A. Kasson, of Iowa; Caleb B. Smith, of Indiana; Austin Blair and T. W. Ferry, of Michigan; Francis P. Blair, Jr., and B. Gratz Brown, of Missouri. Greeley and Eli Thayer sat for Oregon.

The confidence of the Seward managers was not shaken.[1] Intense excitement prevailed. "Call the roll! Call the roll!" fairly hissed through the teeth of the delegates, fiercely impatient for the second trial.[2] Vermont gave the first surprise by throwing her whole vote, which before had complimented Senator Collamer, to Lincoln; Pennsylvania gave him 48, and Ohio 14. The secretary announced the second ballot. Seward had $184\frac{1}{2}$; Lincoln, 181; and all the rest, $99\frac{1}{2}$ votes. Seward's hopes were blasted. On the third ballot he had 180, while Lincoln had $231\frac{1}{2}$, lacking but $1\frac{1}{2}$ votes of the necessary number to nominate. Before the result was declared, Cartter, of Ohio, mounted his chair, and, gaining the breathless attention of the convention, announced the change of four votes of Ohio from Chase to Lincoln. Many delegates then changed their votes to the successful candidate, and as soon as Evarts could obtain the floor he moved, in melancholy tones, to make the nomination unanimous.

A confidential letter of Greeley to Pike, written three days after the nomination, gives an inkling of the fluctuations of the contest. "Massachusetts," he wrote, "was right in Weed's hands, contrary to all reasonable expectation. . . . It was all we could do to hold Vermont by the most desperate exertions; and I at some times despaired of it. The rest of New England was pretty sound, but part of New Jersey was somehow inclined to sin against light and knowledge. If you had seen the Pennsylvania delegation, and known how much money Weed had in hand, you would not have believed we could do so well as we did. Give Curtin thanks for that.[3] Ohio looked very bad, yet turned out well, and Virginia had been regularly sold out; but the

---

[1] Greeley, New York *Tribune*, May 22d.   [2] Halstead, p. 147.

[3] "The wheels of the machine did not at any time in Pennsylvania run smooth. On nearly every ballot, Pennsylvania was not in readiness when her name was called, and her retirements for consultation became a joke."—Halstead, p. 143.

seller could not deliver. We had to rain red-hot bolts on them, however, to keep the majority from going for Seward, who got eight votes here as it was. Indiana was our right bower, and Missouri above praise. It was a fearful week, such as I hope and trust I shall never see repeated."[1]

The nomination of Lincoln was received in the wigwam with such shouts, cheers, and thunders of applause that the report of the cannon on the roof of the building, signalling the event, could at times hardly be heard inside. The excited masses in the street about the wigwam cried out with delight. Chicago was wild with joy. One hundred guns were fired from the top of the Tremont House. Processions of "Old Abe" men bearing rails were everywhere to be seen, and they celebrated their victory by deep potations of their native beverage.[2]

The sorrow and gloom of Seward's supporters were profound and sincere. Thurlow Weed shed bitter tears.[3] Men thought that talent and long service had been set aside in favor of merely an available man borne into undue prominence by the enthusiasm of the mass over a rail-splitting episode; and that the party of moral ideas had sacrificed principle for the sake of success.

Hannibal Hamlin, of Maine, was nominated for Vice-President, and the work of the convention was done.[4]

---

[1] Pike, First Blows of the Civil War, p. 519. John D. Defrees wrote Colfax: "Greeley slaughtered Seward and saved the party. He deserves the praises of all men, and gets them now. Wherever he goes he is greeted with cheers. . . . We worked hard [for Bates], but could not make it. . . . We Bates men of Indiana concluded that the only way to beat Seward was to go for Lincoln as a unit. We made the nomination." —Life of Colfax, Hollister, p. 148. On the action of New Jersey, see letter of Thomas H. Dudley, a delegate from New Jersey, *Century Magazine*, July, 1890.

[2] Halstead, p. 153.
[3] Life, vol. ii. p. 271.
[4] Besides the authorities already cited, the controversy, after the nomination, between Raymond and Weed on one side and Greeley on the

General delight prevailed in Illinois, Indiana, Ohio, and Iowa at the nominations; Pennsylvania regarded gleefully the defeat of Seward, but the first feeling among the Republicans of the other States was one of disappointment that the New York senator had not been chosen.[1]

Lowell spoke for a large number when, in the October *Atlantic Monthly*, he wrote: "We are of those who at first regretted that another candidate was not nominated at Chicago. . . . We should have been pleased with Mr. Seward's nomination for the very reason we have seen assigned for passing him by—that he represented the most advanced doctrines of his party."[2]

On hearing of the nomination, Douglas said to a knot of Republicans who gathered round him in the Capitol: "Gentlemen, you have nominated a very able and a very honest man."[3] Nevertheless, at that time no high opinion of Lincoln's ability existed outside of Illinois. But it was not long before the North came to regard the choice at Chicago as

---

other throws light on the history of the convention. Seward and his intimate New York friends thought Greeley "the chief leader" in the movement that beat him. See letter of Seward to Weed, May 24th, Life of Weed, vol. ii. p. 270. Greeley, in the *Tribune*, disclaimed the weighty influence ascribed to him. See also Recollections of a Busy Life, p. 390. The controversy had for a result the publication, on Greeley's persistent demand, of his letter, written in 1854, dissolving the firm of Seward, Weed, and Greeley. It may be found in the Life of Weed, vol. ii. p. 277, and in Greeley's Recollections of a Busy Life, p. 315. I have also used, in this account of the convention, Russel Errett's article in the *Magazine of Western History*, Aug., 1889, and the Chicago correspondence of the Cleveland *Plain Dealer*.

[1] See Washington *Constitution* and its citations from the Albany *Atlas* and *Argus*, Utica *Observer*, New York *Evening Express*, and Boston *Courier*. Franklin H. Head, then living in Wisconsin, attended the convention, and has vividly described to me his heart-sinking when it became certain Lincoln would be nominated.

[2] This article is printed in Lowell's Political Essays, p. 34.

[3] John B. Alley, Reminiscences, published by North American Publishing Co., p. 575.

the wisest that could have been made.[1] It is an indication of public sentiment that the abolitionists were grieved at the nomination of Lincoln.[2] Wendell Phillips, in a speech, said: "For every blow that Abraham Lincoln ever struck against the system of slavery, the martyr of Marshfield may claim that he has struck a hundred."[3] And later the uncompromising abolitionist called Lincoln "the slave-hound of Illinois," supporting the statement by a misrepresentation of a praiseworthy effort of his congressional career.[4]

The adjourned Democratic convention met at Baltimore, June 18th. The interim between the two meetings had afforded time for reflection, and the enthusiastic Republican convention, with the now generally cordial approval of its work, had shown the necessity of a united Democratic party. But the animosity between the Charleston seceders and the Douglas men of the Northwest had not been allayed in the slightest degree. Some of the delegates who had withdrawn at Charleston were ready to ask for admittance again to the convention, or at any rate their right to seats was advocated by the remaining anti-Douglas men. This was now the rock

---

[1] See Albany *Journal* (Weed's paper), cited by the *Tribune*, May 21st; Philadelphia *Press*, May 23d; New York *Tribune*, June 2d. The Boston *Courier* wrote, on May 18th: "Since the death of Webster we have not seen men so sober and so sad in this city." The sorrow was among Republicans, and the cause Lincoln's nomination. But A. A. Lawrence, a Bell and Everett man, wrote confidentially to J. J. Crittenden, May 25th: "The whole public sentiment which appears on the outside is in favor of 'Old Abe' and his split rails. The ratification meeting here last night was completely successful. Faneuil Hall was filled, and the streets around it."—Life of Crittenden, Coleman, vol. ii. p. 206. "The nomination of Lincoln strikes the mass of the people with great favor. He is universally regarded as a scrupulously honest man, and a genuine man of the people."—J. W. Grimes to his wife, June 4th, Life of Grimes, Salter, p. 158.

[2] Life of Garrison, vol. iii. p. 502.

[3] The *Liberator*, June 8th.

[4] Ibid., June 22d.

on which the convention split; for the Douglas faction of Alabama and Louisiana had sent delegates to Baltimore and asked for admission. After wrangling for four days in formal session by day and hurling defiance at each other by well-attended mass-meetings at night, the quarrel came to a head on the fifth day of the convention. The Douglas delegates from Louisiana and Alabama were admitted, and other action unpalatable to the minority was taken in regard to credentials. Virginia led a new secession, followed by most of the delegates from North Carolina, Tennessee, Kentucky, and Maryland; and finally the chairman, Caleb Cushing, resigned his position and joined the Southern faction.

Before the secession, New York, with her thirty-five unanimous votes, held the balance of power. Many of her delegates were eminent men of business, anxious for peace; others were adroit politicians adept at a trade and eager to hold the party together by any means. Many were the expedients devised to bring about harmony; but it was to attempt the impossible. The Southerners were exacting, the delegates from the Northwest bold and defiant. The party still remained a house divided against itself. It might have seemed that, as the contention turned on Douglas, his withdrawal would have paved the way for a reconciliation. This he well understood. On June 20th, the third day of the convention, he wrote to Richardson from Washington: "While I can never sacrifice the principle [of non-intervention] even to obtain the presidency, I will cheerfully and joyfully sacrifice myself to maintain the principle. If, therefore, you and my other friends ... shall be of the opinion that the principle can be preserved, and the unity and ascendency of the Democratic party maintained ... by withdrawing my name and uniting with some other non-intervention, Union-loving Democrat, I beseech you to pursue that course.... I conjure you to act with a single eye to the safety and welfare of the country, and without the slightest regard to my individual interest or aggrandizement."[1] As Richardson did not make this letter public, Douglas, at half-past nine in the morning of the day that the disruption occurred, sent a despatch similar in purport to Dean Richmond, the leader of the New York delegation, but this was also suppressed. Richardson afterwards explained that the action of the Southerners had put it out of his power to use Douglas's letter.

After the dissatisfied had withdrawn, David Tod, of Ohio, by request of his associate vice-presidents, took the chair. The convention proceeded to ballot, and, after the second trial, when Douglas had received all the votes but thirteen, he was by resolution declared nominated on the ground that he had received the votes of two-thirds of the delegates present. Senator Fitzpatrick, of Alabama, was nominated for Vice-President. When he afterwards declined the nomination, the national committee named Herschel V. Johnson, of Georgia, for the position.

The Baltimore seceders, joined by most of the seceders from the Charleston convention, met in another hall, adopted the Southern platform, and nominated Breckinridge, of Kentucky, for President, and Lane, of Oregon, for Vice-President.[2]

Although Congress adjourned in June, the House had done a large amount of work since its organization. It passed a bill for the admission of Kansas under the Wyandotte free constitution, which had been ratified by a large majority of the popular vote. The Senate, however, refused to take up the bill. The House repealed the slave code of New Mexico,[3] but to this the Senate did not agree. The

---

[1] Life of Douglas, Flint, p. 212.

[2] See National Political Conventions of 1860, Halstead; New York *Tribune*; Pike's First Blows of the Civil War. The Charleston seceders had adjourned to Richmond, but, on meeting there, adjourned to await the action of the Baltimore convention; and when they afterwards reassembled, they endorsed the nominations of Breckinridge and Lane.

[3] House Journal, 1st Sess. 36th Cong., Part I. pp. 220, 303; Part II. p. 815. The vote was: Yeas, 97; nays, 90.

House also passed a homestead bill. This the Senate amended, making it a less liberal measure for the landless. The House, on the principle that half a loaf is better than none, accepted the Senate's modifications; but the bill was vetoed by the President, and the necessary two-thirds vote to pass it over the veto could not be commanded in the Senate. The Morrill tariff bill, providing for a revision, and in some cases an increase, of tariff duties, went through the House, but was not acted upon by the Senate. A House committee, whose chairman was Covode, investigated the action of the administration in its attempts to carry first the Lecompton bill and then the English bill through the House of Representatives in 1858, bringing to light facts that redounded little to the credit of Buchanan and his cabinet.[1] At the North, the administration had sunk so low in public estimation, and the interest in the conventions and preparations for the presidential campaign had so engrossed public notice, that the report of the Covode committee, and the criticism by the President of its manner of procedure, did not attract the attention that their importance perhaps warranted.[2]

After the debate between Douglas and Davis, the most important event in the Senate was an oration by Sumner on the "Barbarism of Slavery." Sumner had returned from Europe just before the opening of the session. His former health and strength were restored sufficiently for him to give again systematic attention to the duties of a senator, and this was his first speech in the Senate since the one delivered four years previously, that had provoked the outrageous assault. He delivered a courageous invective against slavery, employing a line of argument now hardly necessary for Northern people, but then especially irritating to the South. He took up the question where he had left off at the close

---

[1] See p. 300.
[2] For an account of this friendly to the President, see Life of Buchanan, Curtis, vol. ii. chap. xii.

of his speech, "The Crime against Kansas;" but he apparently failed to comprehend the progress of anti-slavery sentiment, and the direction it had taken during his three and a half years of enforced absence. "We have just had a four hours' speech from Sumner on the 'Barbarism of Slavery,'" wrote Senator Grimes, an earnest Republican; "in a literary point of view it was of course excellent. As a bitter, denunciatory oration, it could hardly be exceeded in point of style and finish. But to me many parts sounded harsh, vindictive, and slightly brutal. It is all true that slavery tends to barbarism; but Mr. Sumner furnishes no remedy for the evils he complains of. His speech has done the Republicans no good. Its effect has been to exasperate the Southern members, and render it impossible for Mr. Sumner to exercise any influence here for the good of his State."[1]

The campaign of 1860 was not so animated as that of 1856, yet the problem concerning the division of the electoral votes was substantially the same. Frémont had had 114 electors; of these, and of the 4 of Minnesota, Lincoln was reasonably certain, but he needed 34 more, which must be had from some combination of the votes of the following States: Pennsylvania, which cast 27; New Jersey, 7; Indiana, 13; Illinois, 11; Oregon, 3; California, 4. While not arithmetically necessary to carry Pennsylvania, it was, as in 1856, practically so; for if the Republicans could not obtain the vote of Pennsylvania, they certainly could not hope for that of New Jersey, and one or the other was absolutely required. Had Douglas been the candidate of the united Democracy on the Cincinnati platform, the contest would have been close and exciting and the result doubtful. Douglas himself boasted that had that been the case he would have beaten Lincoln in every State of the Union except

---

[1] Grimes to his wife, June 4th, Life of Grimes, Salter, p. 127; see also editorial in New York *Tribune*, June 5th.

Vermont and Massachusetts.[1] Had the Democrats been united on Breckinridge and the Southern platform, the only conceivably different result would have been larger Lincoln majorities in the Northern States. But with the actual state of affairs, after the two nominations at Baltimore, the success of the Republicans seemed to be assured. The split in the Democratic party doomed it to certain defeat before the people; but as the contest went on, a glimmer of hope arose that while it was absolutely impossible for Douglas, Breckinridge, or Bell to obtain a majority of the electoral votes, it was within the bounds of possibility to defeat Lincoln and throw the election into the House of Representatives. Then Breckinridge might be elected, or, the House failing to make a choice, Lane would become President by virtue of having been chosen Vice-President by the Senate.[2]

This contingency created some alarm among the Republicans, whose elation had been great at the failure of the Democrats to cement at Baltimore their divided party. Pennsylvania and Indiana still held their State elections in October, and it was generally conceded that if they went Republican, nothing could prevent the election of Lincoln. Pennsylvania was the more important, and at first the more doubtful, of the two; so that, as in 1856, the contest again hinged on the State election in the Keystone State. Now, however, a new issue had been brought into the canvass. A sequence of the panic of 1857 was great depression in the iron trade. As the Democrats in Congress had voted almost unanimously against the Morrill tariff bill, which, from the Pennsylvania point of view, was expected to cure the

---

[1] Speech at Baltimore, Sept. 6th, Baltimore *Daily Exchange*.

[2] In the event of the election going to the House, the voting would have been by States, and it was conjectured that Lincoln would have 15; Breckinridge, 12; Bell, 2; and 4 were divided or doubtful.—New York *Tribune*, July 16th. Another estimate was: Lincoln, 15; Breckinridge, 11; Douglas, 2; Bell, 1; doubtful, 4—New York *Tribune*, Oct. 4th.

present trouble, Democrats in that State were lukewarm. Republicans, on the other hand, were aggressive and went to work in earnest to secure the doubtful vote, by showing the greater devotion of their party to the material interests of the State. The Chicago convention, as we have seen, recognized this sentiment by adopting a tariff plank, which, although it was called ambiguous in expression, had been satisfactory to the Pennsylvania delegation.[1] But there was no doubt about the Democratic position. Both the Douglas and the Breckinridge conventions had reaffirmed the Cincinnati platform of 1856, which declared in favor of "progressive free trade throughout the world." Andrew G. Curtin, the People's candidate for governor, a man of ability and energy, and a thorough-going protectionist, gave the key-note to the Pennsylvania campaign by pushing into prominence the tariff question. Protection to home industry, and freedom in the territories, were the watchwords; but the promise of higher duties on iron appealed more powerfully to the doubtful voters than did the plea for free soil.[2] Many speeches were made in which the sole issue discussed was the tariff, and it is safe to say that no Pennsylvania advocate of Lincoln and Curtin made a speech in his State without some mention of the question that now dominated all others in the Pennsylvania mind. The effect of this mode of conducting the canvass was so marked that by September it became apparent that, although the Democratic candidate for governor was supported by the adherents of Douglas, Breckinridge, and Bell, the chance of election lay decidedly on the side of Curtin. The fusion in 1856 had been against the Democrats; now the Lincoln

---

[1] "The *Evening Post* says the tariff plank in the Chicago platform means free trade; the *Tribune* says it means protection. . . . The tariff resolution was intended to conciliate support in Pennsylvania and New Jersey without offending free-trade Republicans in other States."—New York *World*, Oct 19th, then an independent journal inclining to Bell.

[2] In 1860 Pennsylvania produced one-half of the iron made in the whole country.

party breasted the combined opposition. Douglas himself was affected by the drift of sentiment. Although he had always been regarded as inclining to free trade, he argued in a speech made in Pennsylvania in favor of protection to the industries of that great manufacturing State.[1]

But outside of Pennsylvania and New Jersey, one hardly heard the tariff question mentioned. The theoretical difference between the contending parties was regarding slavery in the territories; but so far as the existing territory of the country was concerned, it can hardly be called a practical issue.[2] No "bleeding Kansas" gave point to Republi-

---

[1] See New York *Tribune*, Sept. 8th and 10th. "The October contest in Pennsylvania will settle the future tariff policy of the government."—Stump speech of Alex. K. McClure, Sept. 6th. The tariff plank "constitutes the essential plank in the platform" of the Lincoln and Hamlin party.—Philadelphia *North American*. In Southern Pennsylvania, "they are all tariff men and will vote solid for Curtin."—Ibid., Sept. 3d. The iron industry, said W. D. Kelley, languishes under the legislation of the free-trade Democracy.—Ibid., Sept. 4th. A club in Philadelphia was called the "Mercantile Tariff Men." A banner at a great meeting at Germantown bore the inscription, "Pennsylvania demands adequate protection to her great iron, coal, and manufacturing interests."—Ibid., Oct. 2d and 5th. At a great demonstration in Pittsburgh, "the manufacturing establishments were well represented, and the men carried mottoes relating chiefly to a protective tariff."—*National Intelligencer*, Oct. 2d. Instances like these may be multiplied. "The people of Pennsylvania, like those of New Jersey, are nearly unanimous in favor of a protective tariff. Questions concerning slavery and all other political topics hold a subordinate place in their regard to this one, ' By what action on our part shall we secure the effective Protection of Home Industry?' "—New York *Tribune*, Sept. 26th.

[2] The editor of the Memphis *Appeal*, after a trip to New Orleans, wrote a well-considered article from which I extract: "There are not enough slaves in the slave States to cultivate the States which border on the inland sea, two-thirds of the area of each of which has never yet been pressed by the foot of a slave. For centuries to come, unless other sources of supply of Southern labor are opened up, there cannot and will not be, in the possibility of things, another slave territory added to the Union. . . . If men must extend slavery, let them come out for the African slave-trade, but do not be quarrelling about the miserable twaddle of

can arguments, as had been the case in 1856. Yet the Republican canvass was a protest against the policy of Pierce and Buchanan, who had used the executive influence invariably against freedom; it was opposition to acquiring more slave territory; it was opposition to the revival in any shape of the African slave-trade, which, if accomplished, would make the territorial question as vital as ever Kansas affairs had done. The speech of Gaulden, a Georgia delegate in the Charleston convention, which had been received with demonstrations of approval, was widely published at the North, and, being regarded as the sincere avowal of one who spoke for many planters, it had produced a marked effect on Northern sentiment. "I am a Southern states-rights man," he had said; "I am an African slave-trader. I am one of those Southern men who believe that slavery is right, morally, religiously, socially, and politically. I believe that the institution of slavery has done more for this country, more for civilization, than all other interests put together. . . . I believe that this doctrine of protection to slavery in the territories is a mere theory, a mere abstraction. . . . We have no slaves to carry to these territories. We can never make another slave State with our present supply of slaves. . . . I would ask my friends of the South to come up in a proper spirit, ask our Northern friends to give us all our rights, and take off the ruthless restrictions which cut off the supply of slaves from foreign lands. . . . I tell you, fellow-Democrats, that the African slave-trader is the true Union man. . . . If any of you Northern Democrats will go home with me to my plantation in Georgia, I will show you some darkies that I bought in Maryland, some that I bought in Virginia, some in Delaware, some in Florida, some in North Carolina, and I will also show you the pure African, the noblest Roman of them all."[1]

---

slavery protection by Breckinridge, or of intervention to destroy it, on the other hand, by Lincoln."—Cited by New York *World*, Oct. 8th.

[1] New York *Tribune*, May 7th. A large part of this speech is published in Greeley's American Conflict, vol. i. p. 316.

"We can extend slavery into new territories," said Seward, at Detroit, September 4th, "and create new slave States only by reopening the African slave-trade."[1] "The same power that abrogated the Missouri Compromise in 1854," said he at Madison, September 12th, "would, if the efforts to establish slavery in Kansas had been successful, have been, after a short time, bold enough, daring enough, desperate enough, to have repealed the prohibition of the African slave-trade. And, indeed, that is yet a possibility now."[2] "I have said that this battle was fought and this victory won," declared Seward, at St. Paul, September 18th. "There is one danger remaining—one only. Slavery can never more force itself or be forced, from the stock that exists among us, into the territories of the United States. But the cupidity of trade and the ambition of those whose interests are identified with slavery are such that they may clandestinely and surreptitiously reopen, either within the forms of law or without them, the African slave-trade, and may bring in new cargoes of African slaves at one hundred dollars a head, and scatter them into the territories; and once getting possession of new domain, they may again renew their operations against the patriotism of the American people."[3] The slave States, Seward averred at New York city, November 2d, "are going to say next, as they logically must, that they should reopen the African slave-trade, and so furnish the supplies for slavery."[4]

While the divided opposition made Republican success almost certain, the lack of a common enemy, who took the same form and advocated the same principles everywhere, deprived the canvass of the vigor and excitement that prevail when a line is sharply drawn between two parties on one decided issue. In New England—excepting Connecticut—and in the Northwest, the contest lay between Lincoln

---

[1] Seward's Works, vol. iv. p. 317. [2] Ibid., p. 325.
[3] Ibid., p. 346.
[4] Ibid., p. 418; see also speech at Seneca Falls, ibid., p. 408.

and Douglas. The other candidates were barely mentioned, and as Douglas had no chance whatever of election, the contest could not be called spirited. In New York, Pennsylvania, New Jersey, and Connecticut, Breckinridge and Bell had a following;[1] but in those States there was little enthusiasm, except that drawn out by Republican meetings. In the slave States outside of Missouri, the contest lay between Breckinridge and Bell. Douglas had supporters everywhere, but it was recognized he could carry no slave State but Missouri, and his candidacy in the South resulted only as a diversion which redounded to the advantage of Bell, for the supporters of Douglas and Bell agreed in pronounced devotion to the Union; while it was practically true, which Douglas intimated at Baltimore, that, although every Breckinridge man was not a disunionist, every disunionist in America was a Breckinridge man.[2] As the canvass proceeded, Lincoln, as representing the more positive resistance to Southern domination, drew to himself Douglas Democrats at the North; while Breckinridge, as representing the logical Southern doctrine, drew from the adherents of Douglas at the South.

More political machinery was employed in the Republican canvass than in 1856. Office-seekers had been present in force at the Chicago convention, and, as the prospect of success increased, their number grew and they were on hand everywhere to do the necessary work of party organization. The Wide-awakes, in their inception merely a happy accident, were turned to good account in arousing enthusiasm. Companies and battalions of them, wearing capes and bearing torches, were a necessary feature of every Republican demonstration.[3] Lincoln's early occupation was

---

[1] Bell had a considerable following in Massachusetts.
[2] Baltimore *Daily Exchange*, Sept. 7th.
[3] For the origin of the Wide-awakes, see Nicolay and Hay, vol. ii. p. 284; see also New York *Tribune*, June 2d, and New York *Herald*, Sept. 19th. The *Herald* of that date estimated that there were over four hun-

glorified, and men bearing fence-rails might be seen in every procession. In Boston, a significant feature of a parade was a rail-splitters' battalion composed of men averaging six feet two inches in height. The Sumner Blues, a company of colored men from Portland, took part in the same procession, for it was not overlooked that the result of the election might affect the lot of the negro.[1] Lincoln meetings, large and small, addressed by men of character and ability, were a feature of the summer and autumn; in every village, town, and county, there was frequent opportunity for the inquiring voter to familiarize himself with the issue before the people. Nearly all the educational features of the campaign of 1856 were repeated; the published debates of Lincoln and Douglas were read with interest and effect; yet less reliance was placed on newspapers and campaign documents than in the previous presidential canvass.[2] The religious element, with the active personal participation of the clergy, which was one of the characteristics of 1856,

---

dred thousand drilled and uniformed Wide-awakes, and the number was constantly increasing.

[1] Boston *Evening Transcript*, Oct. 17th.

[2] "While the circulation of speeches, campaign lives, and pamphlet essays has not been remarkably large, the number of meetings and oral addresses in this canvass has been beyond precedent. We judge that the number of speeches made during the recent campaign has been quite equal to that of all that were made in the previous presidential canvasses from 1789 to 1856 inclusive."—New York *Tribune*, Nov. 8th. I will mention some of the men who spoke frequently from the stump: Seward, Chase, Senator Wade, Senator Wilson, Greeley; David D. Field, William M. Evarts, George W. Curtis, Conkling, Fenton, Charles A. Dana, C. M. Depew, and Stewart L. Woodford, of New York; Thaddeus Stevens, John Hickman, Grow, Covode, Wilmot, and Reeder, of Pennsylvania; Dayton, of New Jersey; Corwin, John Sherman, and Schenck, of Ohio; Burlingame and Charles F. Adams, of Massachusetts; Morrill and Fessenden, of Maine; Caleb B. Smith, Henry S. Lane, and Oliver P. Morton, of Indiana; Trumbull, Browning, Lovejoy, and David Davis, of Illinois; Howard, of Michigan; Senator Doolittle and Carl Schurz, of Wisconsin; Francis P. Blair, of Missouri; and Cassius M. Clay, of Kentucky.

was not now so obtrusive or pronounced;[1] but in New England and along the lines of New England influence, the hearty wishes and fervent prayers of most Protestant ministers were for Republican success. Henry Ward Beecher, and Dr. Chapin, the eminent Universalist, did not scruple to deliver political speeches from their pulpits the Sunday evening before the election. The young men and first voters, who had been studying the slavery question since 1852, took a vital interest in this campaign. They read the political literature with avidity. Filled with enthusiasm, they were glad to enroll themselves in the Wide-awake order, and make manifest their determination to do all in their power to avert the longer misrule of the Southern oligarchy. "The Republican party," said Seward at Cleveland, October 4th, "is a party chiefly of young men. Each successive year brings into its ranks an increasing proportion of the young men of this country."[2] Northern school-teachers, under the inspiration of the moral principle at stake, impressed upon eager listening boys that they were living in historic times, and that a great question, fraught with weal or woe to the country, was about to be decided. The torch-bearers of literature were on the side of Lincoln. "I vote with the Republican party," wrote Holmes to Motley; "I cannot hesitate between them and the Democrats."[3] Whittier offered the resolutions at a Republican meeting at Amesbury;[4] William Cullen Bryant was at the head of the Lincoln electoral ticket of New York, and George William Curtis spoke frequently from the stump. Few political

---

[1] See New York *Herald*, Sept. 11th. A poll of voters showed that all the clergymen of Springfield, Ill., but three, were against Lincoln. Herndon, p. 466.

[2] Seward's Works, vol. iv. p. 384. On the importance of young men, see New York *Tribune*, July 30th; for a prediction made in December, 1856, of the Republican vote in 1860, see Olmsted's Texas Journey, p. xxvi.

[3] Motley's Correspondence, vol. i. p. 341.

[4] The *Independent*, Sept. 20th.

arguments have been more cogent, or expressed in choicer phrase, than that of James Russell Lowell, published in the *Atlantic Monthly* for October. It may be said to represent the opinion of the men of thought and culture of the country. "The slave-holding interest," he wrote, "has gone on step by step, forcing concession after concession, till it needs but little to secure it forever in the political supremacy of the country. Yield to its latest demand—let it mould the evil destiny of the territories—and the thing is done past recall. The next presidential election is to say yes or no. . . . We believe this election is a turning-point in our history. . . . In point of fact . . . we have only two parties in the field : those who favor the extension of slavery, and those who oppose it." The Republican party " is not unanimous about the tariff, about State rights, about many other questions of policy. What unites the Republicans is . . . a common resolve to resist the encroachments of slavery everywhen and everywhere. . . . It is in a moral aversion to slavery as a great wrong that the chief strength of the Republican party lies." The question that needs an answer in the election is : " What policy will secure the most prosperous future to the helpless territories which our decision is to make or mar for all coming time ? What will save the country from a Senate and Supreme Court where freedom shall be forever at a disadvantage?"[1]

Dr. Francis Lieber, who for years held a chair in the University of South Carolina, and was now a professor in Columbia College, presided over a German Republican meeting in New York city. When the news reached South Carolina, the Euphradian Society of the college expelled him from honorary membership, and his bust and portrait were removed from the halls of the society.[2] " I am denounced at this moment at the South in very virulent language," wrote Lieber to his son.[3]

---

[1] See Political Essays, p. 21 *et seq.*
[2] New York *Evening Post*, Oct. 30th.   [3] Life and Letters, p. 313.

But one argument was used with any show of success by the opponents of the Republicans at the North. The sectional character of the Republican party was urged, with the averment that if Lincoln were elected, the cotton States would certainly secede from the Union. Southern speakers of ability and influence made such declarations freely, and the press teemed with threats of like tenor. The menaces were no more arrogant than those of 1856, but they seemed more grave and sincere. It may be that the Southern leaders had little idea that Lincoln could be elected, and used the threats of disunion as an electioneering cry;[1] but the less prominent speakers were terribly in earnest, and avowed themselves ready to make good their words.[2] The slaveholders whom they addressed were persuaded that Lincoln's election would mean emancipation; the poor whites were convinced that negro equality and citizenship would follow. At the South, the Wide-awakes were regarded as a semi-military organization whose determination was to see Lincoln inaugurated if elected; and soon companies of minute-men as a counter-demonstration began forming in the cotton States.[3]

In judging these events, it is impossible to divest ourselves of the knowledge of the end, yet there certainly seems in the Southern threats a seriousness that foreboded trouble, and thus to many well-informed men they appeared in 1860.

Douglas, since his nomination, had spoken in several Southern States. He knew more of the aims of the secessionists than any other Northern man, and he was sincere when he declared at Chicago: " I believe that this country is in more

---

[1] See A. H. Stephens, War between the States, vol. ii. pp. 275, 277.

[2] See Recollections of Mississippi, Reuben Davis, p. 390; Iron Furnace, pp. 15, 19.

[3] Richmond *Enquirer*, Sept. 28th and Oct. 19th; Charleston *Mercury*, Oct. 2d, 15th, 19th; New York *Evening Post*, Oct. 17th; Georgia *Chronicle*, cited by the Washington *Constitution*, Oct. 16th; Charleston *Courier*, Oct. 25th; Washington correspondence of the New York *Herald*, Oct. 30th; speech of H. W. Hilliard, New York, Sept., 1860, Politics and Pen Pictures, p. 295.

danger now than at any other moment since I have known anything of public life." ¹ The supporters of Douglas and Bell made no attempt to conceal their fears, but the cry of "wolf" was so obviously in their interest that Republicans could not be blamed for regarding it as an effort to frighten people from voting for Lincoln. And for the most part it was so looked upon. Seward said at St. Paul: "Slavery to-day is for the first time not only powerless, but without influence in the American republic. For the first time in the history of the United States, no man in a free State can be bribed to vote for slavery. . . . For the first time in the history of the republic, the slave power has not even the ability to terrify or alarm the freeman so as to make him submit, or even to compromise. It rails now with a feeble voice, instead of thundering as it did in our ears for twenty or thirty years past. With a feeble and muttering voice they cry out that they will tear the Union to pieces. . . . 'Who's afraid?' Nobody's afraid. Nobody can be bought." ² "For ten, aye for twenty, years," declared Seward at New York, four days before the election, "these threats have been renewed, in the same language and in the same form, about the first day of November every four years when it happened to come before the day of the presidential election. I do not doubt but that these Southern statesmen and politicians think they are going to dissolve the Union, but I think they are going to do no such thing." ³ Lowell spoke of "the hollowness of those fears for the safety of the Union in case of Mr. Lincoln's election," and called to mind that false alarms had been sounded before. "The old Mumbo-Jumbo," he asserted, "is occasionally paraded at the North, but, however many old women may be frightened, the pulse of the stock-market remains provokingly calm." ⁴ A certain support for this view was found in the expression of the Douglas and Bell newspapers at the South

---

¹ Oct. 5th, *National Intelligencer.*
³ Ibid., p. 420.

² Seward's Works, vol. iv. p. 344.
⁴ Political Essays, pp. 26, 41.

that deprecated any move in the direction of secession until an overt act had been committed by the coming Republican administration.[1]

There were Republicans who knew too much of the South to regard these threats as gasconade, yet who were determined to force the issue. They had not forgotten that the cry of "The Union is in danger" had elected Buchanan; and they could see no hope for the country if the Southern party were always going to be able to frighten voters from opposing the extension of slavery. Therefore, in their opinion, the North was bound to answer the threat of the South by a defiance. "We are summoned to surrender," said Carl Schurz at St. Louis. "And what price do they offer to pay us for all our sacrifices if we submit? Why, slavery can then be preserved!"[2]

Dr. Lieber, who knew by long actual contact the people of both sections, and who was linked to the South and the North by ties of family and friendship, judged the situation with remarkable insight. "As to the threats of dissolution of the Union should Mr. Lincoln be elected," he wrote to his son, "I do not reply, 'Try it, let us see;' on the contrary, I believe the threat is made in good earnest, and that it is quite possible to carry it into execution. . . . It sometimes has occurred to me that what Thucydides said of the Greeks at the time of the Peloponnesian War applies to us at present. 'The Greeks,' he said, 'did not understand each other any longer, though they spoke the same language; words received a different meaning in different parts.'"[3]

---

[1] See "Occasional" from Washington (probably J. W. Forney) to the Philadelphia *Press*, cited by New York *Evening Post*, Oct. 12th; New York *World*, Oct. 8th; extracts from Southern papers cited, and editorial comments on the same, New York *World*, Oct. 19th; also *World*, Oct. 27th.   [2] Speeches by Carl Schurz, p. 144.

[3] Lieber added, "I quote from memory."—Life and Letters, p. 314. This letter has a peculiar interest, as it was written to his son Oscar, then Southern in sympathy, who afterwards entered the Confederate army and

In truth, when Senator Hammond wrote, "Every sensible man in the country must know that the election of Mr. Lincoln will put the Union at imminent and instant hazard;"[1] when James L. Orr said that "the honor and safety of the South required its prompt secession from the Union in the event of the election of a Black Republican to the presidency;"[2] and when Alexander Stephens declared that the success of Lincoln was certain, and the result would be "undoubtedly an attempt at secession and revolution,"[3] Northern men of discretion were forced to pause and ask whether there were not as much sincerity as bravado in the threats that were heard from all parts of the South.

Efforts were not lacking to bring about a union of the opponents of the Republicans. As has been stated, the followers of Douglas and of Bell and Breckinridge supported the same ticket in Pennsylvania. In Indiana, where Bell had but little support, the Douglas and Breckinridge factions united on a candidate for governor. A partial fusion on an electoral ticket was accomplished in Pennsylvania and New Jersey; a more perfect one in New York. Jefferson Davis tried to concentrate the opposition to Lincoln on a single candidate. Bell, "profoundly impressed by the danger which threatened the country," was willing to withdraw in conjunction with Douglas and Breckinridge, provided some man more acceptable than any of the three could be put forward, and he gave Davis an authorization to open negotiations with that end in view. Breckinridge gave Davis similar authority. The matter was broached in an amicable spirit to Douglas. "He replied that the scheme proposed was impracticable, because his friends,

---

died from wounds received in battle. Two of Lieber's sons served in the Union army during the war.

[1] Letter of Aug. 5th to J. T. Broyles, published in the Charleston *Mercury*, Aug. 25th.   [2] *National Intelligencer*, Sept. 27th.

[3] Interview with a special correspondent of the New York *Herald*, Sept. 29th.

mainly Northern Democrats, if he were withdrawn, would join in the support of Lincoln rather than of any one who should supplant him; that he was in the hands of his friends, and was sure they would not accept the proposition."[1] But at no time had Douglas any hope of election. Early in the canvass he told Wilson and Burlingame that Lincoln would be elected;[2] and we may believe him sincere when in September he declared: "Believing that the Union is in danger, I will make any personal sacrifice to preserve it. If the withdrawal of my name would tend to defeat Mr. Lincoln, I would this moment withdraw it."[3] When he had this conference with Wilson and Burlingame, he told them that he was going South to urge submission to the probable verdict, and after his stumping tour in New England he wended his way southward. At Norfolk, Virginia, he had an opportunity to avow his sentiments. The head of the Breckinridge electoral ticket for Virginia asked him: "If Abraham Lincoln be elected President, will the Southern States be justified in seceding from the Union?"

"To this I answer emphatically no," said Douglas. "The election of a man to the presidency by the American people, in conformity with the Constitution of the United States, would not justify any attempt at dissolving this glorious confederacy."

Another question was put: "If they, the Southern States, secede from the Union upon the inauguration of Abraham Lincoln, before he commits an overt act against their constitutional rights, will you advise or vindicate resistance by force to their secession?" Douglas replied: "I answer emphatically that it is the duty of the President of the United States, and all others in authority under him, to enforce the laws of the United States as passed by Congress and as the

---

[1] The Rise and Fall of the Confederate Government, Jefferson Davis, vol. i. p. 52.
[2] Rise and Fall of the Slave Power, Wilson, vol. ii. p. €99; also, New York *Tribune*, Aug. 31st.   [3] New York *Tribune*, Sept. 13th.

court expound them. And I, as in duty bound by my oath of fidelity to the Constitution, would do all in my power to aid the government of the United States in maintaining the supremacy of the laws against all resistance to them, come from what quarter it might. In other words, I think the President of the United States, whoever he may be, should treat all attempts to break up the Union by resistance to its laws as Old Hickory treated the nullifiers of 1832. . . . I acknowledge the inherent and inalienable right to revolution whenever a grievance becomes too burdensome to be borne." But the election of Lincoln "is not such a grievance as would justify revolution or secession."[1] This declaration brought down upon the head of Douglas a shower of abuse from the secessionist faction at the South. The Charleston *Mercury* contemptuously called him "a regular old John Adams federalist and consolidationist."[2] Nothing daunted, however, and in spite of the remonstrance of Senator Clingman, a political friend,[3] Douglas repeated assertions similar in emphasis and vigor at other places in the South. At Baltimore he still further elaborated his position and warned his hearers of impending danger. "States that secede," he declared, "cannot screen themselves under the pretence that resistance to their acts ' would be making war upon sovereign States.' Sovereign States cannot commit treason. Individuals may. . . . I tell you, my fellow-citizens," he continued, "I believe this Union is in danger. In my opinion, there is a mature plan through the Southern States to break up the Union. I believe the election of a Black Republican is to be the signal for that attempt, and that the leaders of the scheme desire the election of Lincoln so as to have an excuse for disunion."[4]

Douglas took the unusual course for a presidential candi-

---

[1] *National Intelligencer*, Sept. 1st. The speech was made Aug. 25th.
[2] Sept. 3d.
[3] Clingman's Speeches and Writings, p. 513.
[4] Speech at Baltimore, Sept. 6th, Baltimore *Daily Exchange*.

date of visiting different parts of the country and discussing the political issues and their personal bearing. Speaking on all occasions—from the platform of the railroad car, the balcony of the hotel, at monster mass-meetings, frequently jaded from travel, many times without preparation and on the suggestion of the moment—he said much that was trivial and undignified; but he also said much that was patriotic, unselfish, and pregnant with constitutional wisdom. His love for the Union and devotion to the Constitution inspired all his utterances. The cynosure of all eyes, he taught lessons that were destined to bear important fruit. Coldly received at the South, looked upon as a renegade, he aroused great enthusiasm everywhere at the North, and his personal presence was the only feature that gave any life to the struggle against the Republicans.

Apart from the rail-splitting episode, the personality of Lincoln counted for little in the campaign. It was everywhere conceded that he was thoroughly honest, but his opponents sneered at his reputed capacity, and, outside of his own State, few regarded his nomination as other than the sacrifice of commanding ability in favor of respectable mediocrity. In popular estimation his great merit consisted in being able to carry the doubtful States. Schurz deemed it necessary to assure his constituents at Milwaukee that Lincoln was not merely an available candidate, "a second or third rate man like Polk or Pierce," but that the debate with Douglas had shown that he had a "lucid mind and honest heart."[1] The campaign went on without direction, with hardly a suggestion even, from the Republican standard-bearer.[2] Seward filled the minds of Republicans, attracting such attention and honor, and arousing such enthusiasm, that the closing months of the campaign were the most brilliant epoch of his life. It was then he reached the climax of his career. His grief and sense of humilia-

---

[1] Speeches by Schurz, p. 113.
[2] Nicolay and Hay, vol. ii. p. 287.

tion at not receiving the nomination in Chicago were poignant. "I am," he wrote, "a leader deposed by my own party, in the hour of organization for decisive battle."[1] In common with his intimate friends, he charged his defeat chiefly to Greeley. He felt towards that influential editor as much vindictiveness as was possible in a man of so amiable a nature.[2] But he did not retire to his tent. At the time of the meeting of the convention he had left the Senate and gone to his home in Auburn, where he expected to receive the news of his success surrounded by the friends and neighbors whom he loved, and who repaid his love by veneration. When the news of Lincoln's nomination came, and when his friends were quivering with disappointment, and no one in Auburn had the heart to write the conventional editorial endorsing the nomination, Seward, smiling, took pen in hand and wrote the article for the Republican evening journal. "No truer or firmer defenders of the Republican faith," he declared, "could have been found in the Union than the distinguished and esteemed citizens on whom the honors of nomination have fallen."[3] He also gave at once, over his own signature, a public and emphatic support to platform and candidates;[4] and, while then of the opinion that he would soon seek the repose of private life,[5] he came, when time had assuaged his grief, to a better conclusion, and devoted his hearty and energetic efforts to the success of the cause. "The magnanimity of Mr. Seward, since the result of the convention was known," wrote Lowell, "has been a greater ornament to him and a greater honor to his party than his election to the presidency would have been."[6]

---

[1] Letter of Seward to his wife, May 30th, Life of Seward, by Frederick W. Seward, vol. ii. p. 454.

[2] See Seward's letter to Weed, May 24th, Life of Weed, vol. ii. p. 270.

[3] Life of Seward, by Frederick W. Seward, vol. ii. p. 452.

[4] See letter of May 21st, published in the *Evening Post*, cited by the New York *Tribune*, May 25th; also Seward's Works, vol. iv. p. 79.

[5] Letter to Weed, May 24th.

[6] *Atlantic Monthly*, Oct., 1860; Lowell's Political Essays, p. 34.

Seward's friends followed the example set them. "We all feel that New York and the friends of Seward have acted nobly," wrote Swett to Weed, after the election.¹

In the early part of September, Seward began a tour of speech-making at Detroit. He went as far west as St. Paul and Lawrence, Kansas, ending with an address to his townsmen the night before election. The sincere and hearty demonstrations wherever he went were an "earnest tribute." ² The crowds that gathered to hear him felt what Schurz had put in words, that Seward was "the intellectual head of the political anti-slavery movement," and had "in the hearts of his friends a place which hardly another man in the nation could fill." ³ As the people of the sure Republican States, where he for the most part spoke, heard the words of wisdom, they could not but feel a profound regret that he was not their standard-bearer. When we consider the great moral question involved, the variety of presentation, the many-sided treatment, the fearlessness of statement, the appeal to reason and the highest feelings, the absence of any attempt to delude the people by the smallest misrepresentation, Seward's efforts in this campaign are the most remarkable stump-speeches ever delivered in this country. While he paid Lincoln well-chosen compliments, the references to the opposing candidates were courteous. The speeches are a fit type of the campaign—a campaign conducted on a great moral principle. Seward reaffirmed almost everywhere the declaration of the "irrepressible conflict," maintaining that the Republicans simply reverted to the theory and

---

¹ Life of Weed, vol. ii. p. 301.
² New York *Tribune*, Sept. 4th and 5th; New York *Evening Post*, Sept. 5th; New York *Times*, Sept. 8th; New York *Herald*, Sept. 8th and Oct. 20th; St. Louis *Democrat*, cited by *Evening Post*, Oct. 2d; New York *World*, Nov. 3d. "Listen to Mr. Seward on the prairies! Notice how free and eloquent he has been since the Chicago convention! And this change is not due to age."—Wendell Phillips, Nov. 7th.
³ Speeches of Schurz, p. 109.

practice of the fathers. He made appear at all times the political, social, and moral evil of slavery. "There is no man," he said, "who has an enlightened conscience who is indifferent on the subject of human bondage."[1] Yet he spoke with forbearance of the people of the South. "You must demonstrate the wisdom of our cause," he affirmed, "with gentleness, with patience, with loving-kindness, to your brethren of the slave States."[2] He maintained that "most men . . . are content to keep the Union with slavery if it cannot be kept otherwise."[3] At Chicago he showed what a bulwark of freedom was the great Northwest, by its prosperity and commercial importance;[4] and he prophesied that "the last Democrat is born in this nation . . . who will maintain the Democratic principles which constitute the present creed of the Democratic party."[5] The night before election he averred that the question to be decided was: "Shall freedom, justice, and humanity ultimately and in the end prevail; are these republican institutions of ours safe and permanent?" He referred to the threats of disunion, and while expressing no defiance, he declared: "Fellow-citizens, it is time, high time, that we know whether this is a constitutional government under which we live. It is high time that we know, since the Union is threatened, who are its friends and who are its enemies."[6]

At the beginning of the canvass no doubt existed on the part of the Republican managers of any of the important States but Pennsylvania and Indiana. Occasional fears were expressed about Indiana as late as August,[7] but that State soon came to be regarded as reasonably sure. By

---

[1] At Chicago, Oct. 3d, Works, vol. iv. p. 350.
[2] At Madison, Sept. 12th, ibid., p. 327.
[3] At Chicago, Oct. 3d, ibid., p. 355.
[4] Ibid., p. 360. Ibid.
[6] At Auburn, Nov. 5th, ibid., pp. 422, 429.
[7] See letter of David Davis to Thurlow Weed, Life of Weed, vol. ii. p. 299.

the latter part of August, also, owing to the vigorous and effective canvass under the leadership of Curtin and McClure, there were adequate grounds for believing that Pennsylvania would elect the People's candidate for governor in October, and choose Lincoln electors in November. Then Republican alarm began to be excited in regard to the State of New York. "Brethren in the doubtful States, trust New York; you may do it undoubtingly," said the *Tribune* in July;[1] but a different tale had to be told in September, when it announced that "the opposition are going to concentrate their efforts on New York."[2] "I think," wrote Lincoln to Thurlow Weed, "there will be the most extraordinary effort ever made to carry New York for Douglas. You and all others who write me from your State think the effort cannot succeed, and I hope you are right. Still, it will require close watching and great efforts on the other side."[3]

Without the thirty-five electoral votes of the Empire State, Lincoln could not be chosen President; and a determined effort now began to be made to carry that State against him. Negotiations were had with a view of a fusion electoral ticket; and after protracted conferences, some ending in failure, but renewed again with hope, a scheme of fusion was at last completed. Supporters of Douglas, Bell, and Breckinridge were to vote for common electors; of these, eighteen were apportioned to Douglas, ten to Bell, and seven to Breckinridge.[4] This combination had a show of success, but it had the faults of a negative programme. No intelligent opponent of Lincoln could for a moment think it possible to elect by the people any one of the other candidates,

---

[1] July 27th.   [2] Sept. 4th.
[3] Letter of Aug. 17th, Life of Weed, vol. ii. p. 297.
[4] New York *Tribune*, Sept. 25th: "New York, especially, was the arena of a struggle as intense, as vehement and energetic, as had ever been known."—Greeley's American Conflict, vol. i. p. 326. "It was only after a most determined canvass that fusion was defeated in New York."—Recollections of a Busy Life, Greeley, p. 392.

II.—32

and the movement, divested of subterfuge, was simply one to throw the election into the House of Representatives. Many men, alarmed at the condition of affairs, thought the election of Lincoln a lesser evil than to have the contest continued in Congress. In spite of the union of the opposition, the chances were all with the Republicans. "I find no reason to doubt," wrote Seward to Lincoln, after his return from the Western tour, "that this State will redeem all the promises we have made."¹ The Germans strongly supported Lincoln. Carl Schurz was making speeches everywhere in his favor.² The majority of the Fillmoreans of 1856 were also on his side.³ The elections of Maine and Vermont in September increased the encouragement of the Republicans, but as New England was considered strongly Republican, the result had little effect on the opposition.

Although great confidence was felt and expressed in the success of Curtin at the October State election,⁴ so much depended on the result in Pennsylvania that the Republicans felt a nervous anxiety until the votes had been counted. This was especially the case, since the week before election the Democrats had sent considerable money into Pennsylvania, making a last desperate effort to carry the State.⁵ But October 9th decided the contest. Curtin carried Pennsylvania by thirty-two thousand majority, and Lane in Indiana had nine thousand seven hundred and fifty-seven more votes than his competitor. The prominence given the tariff question, and the undoubted position of the supporters of Lincoln on that issue, contributed more than any other

---

¹ Life of Seward, F. W. Seward, vol. ii. p. 471.
² New York *Tribune*, June 30th, Aug. 15th, 17th, Sept. 3d, Oct. 19th.
³ New York *Tribune*, July 17th. "The names of eighty-one thousand New York men who voted for Fillmore in 1856 are inscribed on Republican poll-lists."—Letter to Baltimore *Patriot*, cited by *Tribune*, Sept. 11th. G. T. Curtis was amazed at the number of conservative men for Lincoln, *Tribune*, July 28th; also see New York *Evening Post*, Sept. 11th.
⁴ See, for example, New York *Evening Post*, Sept. 28th and Oct. 2d.
⁵ New York *World*, Oct. 10th.

one factor to the result in Pennsylvania.¹ After the October elections it was conceded, South as well as North, that nothing could prevent the election of Lincoln. "Emancipation or revolution is now upon us," said the Charleston *Mercury*.² There began a stampede of floating voters, whose desire to be on the winning side overpowered other motives. The Republican National Committee in a public address considered that the October elections settled the presidential contest, but urged unabated effort in order that a majority of the House of Representatives in the next Congress might be secured.³ From this time on the contest had the flavor rather of a congressional than a presidential canvass, except in so far as imposing Wide-awake demonstrations implied larger contrivance and greater expense than usual.

The conditions in New York were somewhat different from those existing in the other Northern States. A faint hope lingered that the fusionists might there be successful. The commercial and property interests of New York city, honestly fearing secession in the event of Republican success, bestirred themselves to use their most potent weapon in averting the threatened danger. It was reported that William B. Astor had contributed one million dollars, and wealthy merchants a second million, in aid of the fusion ticket.⁴ A systematic effort to frighten business and finan-

---

¹ "The Pennsylvania journals, without distinction of party, admit that the result of the recent election held in that State was mainly determined by politico-economical considerations growing out of the tariff policy to be pursued by the federal government."—*National Intelligencer*, Oct. 13th. The Philadelphia *American and Gazette* (Rep.) said: "Our election on Tuesday determined that the vital and absorbing question in this State is protection to American industry."—Cited by *National Intelligencer*. But see also the New York *Evening Post*, Oct. 10th.

² Oct. 18th.

³ New York *Evening Post*, Oct. 11th.

⁴ Charleston *Mercury*, cited by *National Intelligencer*, Nov. 1st; Richmond *Enquirer*, Nov. 2d.

cial interests was made with the result of causing a stock-panic in Wall Street during the last days of October. The grave charge was made that the Secretary of the Treasury, on a visit to New York city at this time, had abetted this movement by avowing repeatedly, and with no attempt at concealment, that Lincoln's election would be followed by disunion and a general derangement of the monetary concerns of the country.[1]

Three days before the election Thurlow Weed wrote Lincoln: "Since writing you last Sunday, the fusion leaders have largely increased their fund, and they are now using money lavishly. This stimulates and to some extent inspires confidence, and all the confederates are at work. Some of our friends are nervous. But I have no fear of the result in this State."[2]

Election day came and passed off quietly. In New York city, where excitement and trouble were expected—for in the decade between 1850–60 turbulent elections were not infrequent—the election was the most orderly and quiet that could be remembered. Even the newspaper reporters were forced to confess that the day was intolerably dull.[3] The Republicans were successful. Lincoln and Hamlin carried States which would give them one hundred and eighty electoral votes; Douglas would receive twelve, Breckinridge seventy-two, and Bell thirty-nine. Lincoln had carried every free State but New Jersey, whose electoral vote was divided, Lincoln receiving four, and Douglas three of her votes.[4] Of the popular vote Lincoln had 1,857,610; Doug-

---

[1] See New York *World*, Oct. 29th, 30th, 31st. The *World* asked the *Journal of Commerce*, which constituted itself the defender of Secretary Cobb, to deny these imputations, but it did not satisfactorily meet the charges. See *Journal of Commerce*, Nov. 1st; New York *Evening Post*, Oct. 29th, Nov. 2d; Boston *Evening Transcript*, Oct. 29th and 30th.

[2] Life of Weed, vol. ii. p. 300.

[3] New York *World*, Nov. 7th.

[4] This arose from the fact that a number of Douglas men would not support the whole of the fusion ticket, composed of three Douglas, two

THE ELECTION OF LINCOLN

las, 1,291,574; Breckinridge, 850,082; Bell, 646,124. Lincoln had 930,170 votes less than all his opponents combined.[1] But while all the members of the next Congress had not been elected, enough was known to make it certain that in neither the House nor the Senate would the Republicans have a majority.[2] This was understood and admitted to be the case at the South.[3]

While the electoral vote Douglas received was insignificant, his popular vote was a triumph. With the influence and patronage of the administration against him, holding the machinery of the party in most of the Northern States only by protracted struggles, fighting Breckinridge at the South and Lincoln at the North, waging a hopeless battle, and attracting hardly any votes by the prospect of success, it was a high tribute that so many turned out on election day to show their confidence and do him honor.

On election day, Longfellow wrote in his journal: "Voted early," and the day after: "Lincoln is elected; overwhelm-

---

Bell, and two Breckinridge electors, with the result that four of the Lincoln electors received more votes than the two Bell and two Breckinridge electors.

[1] Greeley's American Conflict, vol. i. p. 328, where a sufficiently exact attempt is made to apportion the fusion vote. Other interesting data are given. Lincoln received in the slave States 26,430; Douglas, 163,525. Breckinridge received in the free States 279,211; Bell, 130,151. Lincoln's majority over Douglas was 566,036. Breckinridge lacked 135,057 of a majority in the slave States

[2] The estimate of the *National Intelligencer* was—Senate: Republicans already elected, 24; to be elected, 5—total, 29. Opposition already elected, 30; to be elected, 7—total, 37; opposition majority, 8. House: Republicans already elected, 99; to be elected, 9—total, 108. Opposition already elected, 54; to be elected, 75—total, 129; opposition majority, 21. The estimate of the New York *World* was the same for the Senate, and made the opposition majority in the House 17. The representatives that were to be elected were nearly all from the Southern States, so that practically an exact estimate could be made.

[3] See speech of A. H. Stephens, Nov. 14th, 1860, The War between the States, Stephens, vol. ii. p. 282.

ing majorities in New York and Pennsylvania. This is a great victory; one can hardly overrate its importance. It is the redemption of the country. Freedom is triumphant."[1] Motley, from across the sea, wrote, when the news reached him: "Although I have felt little doubt as to the result for months past, . . . yet as I was so intensely anxious for the success of the Republican cause, I was on tenterhooks till I actually knew the result. I rejoice at last in the triumph of freedom over slavery more than I can express. Thank God it can no longer be said, after the great verdict just pronounced, that the common law of my country is slavery, and that the American flag carries slavery with it wherever it goes."[2]

The meaning of the election was that the great and powerful North declared slavery an evil, and insisted that it should not be extended; that while the institution would be sacredly respected where it existed, the conduct of the national government must revert to the policy of the fathers and confine slavery within bounds; that they hoped, if it were restricted, the time might come when the Southern people would themselves acknowledge that they were out of tune with the enlightened world and take steps gradually to abolish the system. The persistent and emphatic statement by the opposition that the Republicans were the radical party had fixed that idea in the public mind; but in truth they represented the noblest conservatism. They simply advocated a return to the policy of Washington, Jefferson, and Madison.

The North had spoken. In every man's mind rose unbidden the question, What would be the answer of the South?[3]

---

[1] Life of H. W. Longfellow, S. Longfellow, vol. ii. p. 358.
[2] Motley to his mother, Motley's Correspondence, vol. i. p. 355.
[3] Besides authorities already named, I have, in this story of the campaign, consulted Life of Buchanan, Curtis; Twenty Years of Congress, Blaine; Life of Dix; Political Recollections, Julian; Life of Bowles, Merriam; *De Bow's Review*, vol. xxix.; Life of Bryant, Godwin; Raymond and Journalism; Buchanan's Defence; Pike's First Blows of the Civil War.

INDEX TO VOLS. I AND II

ABOLITION, i. 73; Webster on, i. 152; promoted by Christianity, i. 372; obstacles to, i. 381; in Cuba, Lord Palmerston on, i. 394.
Abolitionists, work of, i. 58; and Congress, i. 67; attitude of, towards Kossuth, i. 242; increasing popularity of, i. 495; burning of the Constitution by, ii. 57; hold aloof from Republican party, ii. 98; attitude of, towards John Brown, ii. 410; Corwin on, ii. 425; desire disunion, ii. 435; distinct from Republicans, ii. 436.
Adams, Charles Francis, supports Hale in 1852, i. 264; in campaign of 1860, ii. 484 n.
Adams, Henry, on Calhoun and Jefferson, i. 380 n.
Adams, John, on Webster, i. 138 n.
Adams, John Quincy, i. 41; on Channing, i. 64 n.; on abolition, i. 69; in Congress, i. 69; character and diary of, i. 71; friendship of, with Seward, i. 162; supported by Fillmore, i. 178; on Everett, i. 291; on Jefferson Davis, i. 390; on slavery, i. 494; Seward on, ii. 147.
Agassiz, Louis, on the negro race, i. 402.
Aiken, character of, ii. 114; defeated by Banks, ii. 115; acknowledges election of Banks, ii. 116; position of, on Kansas, ii. 238.
Alcaldes in California, i. 113.
Alcott, Louisa, on John Brown, ii. 409.
Allen attacks Webster's character, i. 213–215.
Amalgamation, i. 335, 336, 341–342.
American minister rescues Kossuth, i. 231.
American Party, name of Know-nothing party, ii. 55; ii. 91; Greeley on, ii. 118.
Ames, Dr., in convention of 1860, ii. 468.
Ampère, J. J., on Fugitive Slave law, i. 208 n.; on reception to Kossuth, i. 236 n.; at dinner to Kossuth, i. 238 n.; on Douglas, i. 245, 246 n.; on Everett, i. 294 n.; on Fillmore, i. 297 n.; on slavery, i. 326; on New Orleans, i. 360 n.; on condition of slaves, i. 374 n.
Andrew, John A., on John Brown, ii. 385, 415; Chilton retained by, ii. 404; in convention of 1860, ii. 469.
Anglo-Saxon race, "the invincible," i. 93.
Anti-Nebraska convention, in Ohio, ii. 92; against slavery, ii. 93.
Anti-Nebraska elections, Douglas on, ii. 66, 67.
Anti-Nebraska party in Ohio and Indiana, ii. 60.
Anti-slavery, in the South, i. 19; Society, i. 59; in New England, i. 58–66.
Appeal of Independent Democrats, i. 441–444.
Appleton quoted by Bryant, ii. 429.
Appletons' Complete Guide of the World criticised at the South, i. 351.
Arc, Joan of, Mrs. Stowe compared to, i. 280.
Arkansas, secession of, from the Charleston convention, ii. 451.
Army appropriation bill in 1856, ii. 201.
Arnold, Benedict, Douglas compared to, i. 496.
Ashburton, Lord, and Webster, i. 140.
Ashmun, George, in Whig conven-

tion of 1852, i. 253; in convention of 1860, ii. 463.
Atchison, David R., votes on Texas boundary, i. 181; protests against admitting California, i. 182; Douglas not influenced by, i. 431, 432; Davis on, i. 432 n.; desires slavery in Kansas, i. 440; on Missouri Compromise, i. 468; mob led by, ii. 81; on Kansas, ii. 100; in Kansas struggle, ii. 101; in Wakarusa war, ii. 105; advises peace, ii. 106; Stringfellow on, ii. 106 n.; Sumner on, ii. 133; appeal of, to slave States, ii. 150; in raid on Kansas, ii. 158, 159.
Athens, South contrasted with, i. 348.
Atkinson, Edward, on John Brown, ii. 416 n.
Aurelius, Marcus, Lincoln compared to, ii. 310.
Austria, resents sympathy for Hungary, i. 205; Webster on, i. 205, 206.

BADGER, of North Carolina, reply of Wade to, i. 452, 453; on Chase, i. 462; amendment of, to Nebraska act, i. 476.
Bailey, Dr., on Seward, ii. 46; for Chase and Seward, ii. 175; Greeley and Bowles on, ii. 175 n.
Baker, Edward D., in Whig convention of 1852, i. 253; oration of, on Broderick, ii. 378, 379; at Ball's Bluff, ii. 379.
Balize, English settlement at, i. 200; W. R. King on, i. 201.
Baltimore, Democratic convention at, i. 244, ii. 473–475; Whig convention at, i. 252.
Bancroft, Frederic, acknowledgment to, i, 208 n.
Bancroft, George, honors Kossuth, i. 235, 236.
Bancroft, H. H., on debt of Texas, i. 189 n.
Banks, N. P., character of, ii. 108; supported by Greeley, ii. 109, 112, 113, 116; position on the slavery question, ii. 111; elected speaker, ii. 115; Sherman on, ii. 117; triumph of, ii. 118; Frémont's nomination desired by, ii. 177; nominated by North Americans, ii. 186; as speaker, ii. 201; speech of, in Wall Street, ii. 224.

Barksdale, of Mississippi, interrupts speech of Lovejoy, ii. 437, 438.
Barrere, of Ohio, defends Corwin, i. 298 n.
Bates, Edward, supported by Greeley and Blair, ii. 459,465; balloting for, ii. 469.
Bates, Joshua, letter of Buchanan to, ii. 210.
Baxter on slavery, i. 8.
Beecher, Henry Ward, honors Kossuth, i. 236; denounces Kansas-Nebraska bill, i. 465; political opinions of, ii. 73; pledges Sharps rifles, ii. 153; in campaign of 1856, ii. 220, 223; in campaign of 1860, ii. 485.
"Beecher's Bibles," meaning of, ii. 153.
Bell, John, in committee on Clay resolutions, i. 172; Clay's reply to, i. 175; on New Mexico, i. 180; against bill for admission of Kansas under the Lecompton Constitution, ii. 297; nominated by Constitutional Union convention, ii. 454; contest between Breckinridge and, ii. 483; proposes to withdraw from campaign of 1860, ii. 490; votes received by, in 1860, ii. 500.
Belmont, August, at The Hague, ii. 3; contribution of, in campaign of 1856, ii. 231.
Benjamin, Judah P., position of, on Cuban question, ii. 25–27; on Dred Scott decision, ii. 293.
Benton, Jessie, wife of Frémont, ii. 225 n.
Benton, Thomas H., on abolitionists, i. 67; on the Texas question, i. 78, 85, 87; on Calhoun, i. 94; not alarmed in 1850, i. 131; hears Seward, i. 166; criticises Southern address, i. 170; related to Frémont, i. 170 n.; quarrel of, with Foote, i. 169–171; votes on Texas boundary, i. 181; for California bill, i. 182; not re-elected to the Senate, i. 229; on Cushing, i. 393 n.; against Kansas-Nebraska bill, i. 426 n.; Douglas criticised by, i. 489.
Berkeley, Bishop, a slave-owner, i. 6.
Berrien, in committee on Clay resolutions, i. 172.
Bigelow, John, denounces Kansas-Nebraska bill, i. 463; letter of Bryant to, ii. 461.
Bigler, of Pennsylvania, Buchanan de-

INDEX

fended by, ii. 287; on John Brown's raid and "The Impending Crisis," ii. 427; in Charleston convention, ii. 449.
Birney, James G., i. 83.
Bissell, Governor, possible presidential candidate in 1860, ii 303.
Black Death, the, Hecker on, i. 414 n.
Black Hawk war, Davis in, i. 390.
Black, J. S., in Buchanan's cabinet, ii. 247; controversy of, with Douglas, ii. 374.
Black Republicans, ii. 117, 208, 209.
Black Warrior affair, the, ii. 16, 17, 23, 31, 35, 42.
Blair, Austin, in convention of 1860, ii. 465, 469 n.
Blair, Francis P., supports Frémont, ii. 177; Bates supported by, ii. 459; in campaign of 1860, ii. 469 n., ii. 484 n.
Blair, Francis P., Jr., in convention of 1860, ii. 469 n.
Blair, Montgomery, Chiltor retained by, ii. 404; in convention of 1860, ii. 469 n.
Blue Lodges in Missouri, ii. 79.
Bocock, of Virginia, in contest for speaker, ii. 421.
Booth, arrest of, for rescuing fugitive slave, i. 499.
Booth, Wilkes, John Brown compared to, ii. 415.
Booth, the elder, in New Orleans, i. 401.
Borland insulted in Central America, ii. 9.
Boston, Webster on, i. 263.
Boston Public Library, acknowledgment to, i. 208 n.
Botts, John Minor, rebukes Choate, i. 255; produces letter from Scott, i. 256; on Frémont, ii. 205.
Bourgogne, Marguerite de, Mme. de Soulé compared to, ii. 12.
Bourne, Edward G., Professor, acknowledgment to, i. 383 n.
Boutwell, G. S., in convention of 1860, ii. 469.
Bowles, Samuel, denounces Kansas-Nebraska bill, i. 463; reports proceedings of Know-nothings, ii. 90 n.; on Seward and Bailey, ii. 175 n.; on Frémont, ii. 181; on Douglas, ii. 306; on Seward, ii. 436.
Bradbury, James W., on the Compromise of 1850, i. 194; on Taney and Johnson, ii. 270 n.
Branch, challenges Grow, arrest of, ii. 424.
Branson, Jacob, rescue of, ii. 104.
Breckinridge, John C., on Cutting, i. 480, 481; nominated for Vice-President, ii. 172; Vice-President, in Senate, ii. 356; nomination of, ii. 475; campaign of, ii. 478; Bell and, ii. 483; in campaign of 1860, ii. 490, 497, 500, 501.
Bremer, Frederika, on negroes, i. 373.
Brett, of Cleveland library, acknowledgment to, i. 208 n.
Bright, in committee on Clay resolutions, i. 171.
British Honduras, *See* Balize.
Broderick, David C., on poor whites in South Carolina, i. 345; against Lecompton bill, ii. 297; against English bill, ii. 300; Seward and, ii. 305; agrees with Douglas, ii. 358; early life of, reply of, to Hammond, ii. 375; contest with Gwin, ii. 375, 376; remark of, to Forney, ii. 376; on Gwin, ii. 377; duel with Terry, ii. 377, 378; death of, ii. 378, 424; mourning for, ii. 379.
Brook Farm, community of, i. 360.
Brooks, Preston, related to Butler, ii. 134; Sumner assaulted by, ii. 139, 140; Sumner's attitude towards, ii. 141; Olmsted on, ii. 143 n., 147; ovation to, ii. 145; challenges Burlingame, ii. 146; resignation of, ii. 148; defended by Butler, ii. 149; influence of, on Buchanan's nomination, ii. 172; presentation to, ii. 224.
Brown, of Indiana, character of, i. 118.
Brown, of Mississippi, Walker denounced by, ii. 275; on Douglas, ii. 294; on the Constitution, ii. 356.
Brown, of Tennessee, in Buchanan's cabinet, ii. 247.
Brown, B. Gratz, in convention of 1860, ii. 469 n.
Brown, G. W., on Pottawatomie massacre, ii. 199 n.
Brown, John, partnership of, with Perkins, ii. 161 n.; character of, ii. 161, 162; in Wakarusa war, ii. 162; in Pottawatomie massacre, ii. 162, 163; reply of, to his son, ii. 164, 165; sincerity of, ii. 165; Pate captured by, ii. 166; prisoners released

506   INDEX

by, ii. 167; report of Oliver on, ii. 197; fanaticism of, ii. 216, 217; leaves Kansas, ii. 237; raid of, ii. 383-397; at Harper's Ferry, ii. 384, 394, 395; plans of, ii. 384, 385; friends of, in Massachusetts, John A. Andrew on, ii. 385-415; conference of, with Sanborn and Smith, ii. 386, 387; letter of, to Sanborn, ii. 387; ancestry of, fund raised for, ii. 388; betrayed by Forbes, ii. 388, 389; returns to Kansas, ii. 389; slaves liberated by, pursuit of, ii. 390; assisted by Smith, Stearns, and Sanborn, ii. 390, 391; rejects advice of Frederick Douglass, ii. 392; arsenal seized by, ii. 394; retreat of, to engine-house, Colonel Washington on, ii. 395; cut down by the sword, ii. 396; replies of, to Mason and Vallandigham, ii. 397, 398; Emerson on Wise and, ii. 398; Emerson and Smith on, ii. 399; influenced by history of San Domingo and Toussaint, ii. 400; indignation at South against, ii. 401; said to have applied Seward's doctrine, ii. 402; Greeley on, imprisonment of, ii. 403; rejects plea of insanity, ii. 404; receives his sentence, ii. 405; Emerson on, ii. 406, 413; compared to Sir Thomas More, ii. 406 *n.*; letters of, ii. 406, 408; execution of, ii. 408, 409; Lieber and Miss Alcott on, ii. 409; Longfellow on, ii. 409, 410; Garrison abolitionists on, ii. 410; Davis on, Douglas on, ii. 411; Lincoln and Seward on, ii. 412, 413, 415; Thoreau and Hugo on, ii. 414; compared with Socrates and Christ, ii. 414, 415; song of, ii. 416; Atkinson on, ii. 416 *n.*; Helper compared with, ii. 419; Lamar on, ii. 421; John Sherman on raid of, ii. 426; Bigler on, ii. 427; Republican convention of 1860 on invasion of, ii. 464.

Brown, Peter, ancestor of John Brown, ii. 388.

Browning in campaign of 1860, ii. 469, 484.

Brownlow, Parson, debate between Pryne and, i. 354; on immigration, i. 355.

Bryant, William Cullen, supports Pierce, i. 269; friendship of, for Lincoln, ii. 458; in campaign of 1860, ii. 485.

Bryce, "American Commonwealth" of, quoted, i. 115 *n.*; on American temperament, i. 236 *n.*

Buchanan, James, i. 202; as candidate in convention of 1852, i. 244; early life of, elected to Congress, supports President Jackson, made Secretary of State, i. 246; defeated in convention of 1852, 247, 248; defeat of, foreseen, i. 252; letter of Pickens to, i. 360 *n.*; letters of, to Pierce, on Cuba, 387, 393; appointed minister to England, offered $100,000,000 for Cuba, i. 393; letter of, on the presidency, i. 424; absence of, from House of Lords, ii. 5; costume of, ii. 6; on Marcy, ii. 7; Marcy's instructions to, ii. 11; signs Ostend manifesto, ii. 38; influenced by Soulé, ii. 40; on disagreement with Great Britain, ii. 120, 121; letter of, to Slidell, ii. 170; nomination of, ii. 171, 172; political position of, ii. 173; on Kansas-Nebraska act, on Cuba, ii. 174; letter of, on Democratic party, ii. 202, 203; to Tammany, ii. 203 *n.*; Slidell's friendship for, ii. 205; Choate declares for, ii. 206-208; letter of, to Read, ii. 209; Northern clergymen against, ii. 210; integrity of, ii. 221, 226; contest between Fillmore and, ii. 222; on the danger of disunion, ii. 227, 228; Geary on, ii. 229; supported by press of Pennsylvania, ii. 230; States carried by, ii. 235; on Kansas, ii. 237; Choate on, ii. 242; sympathies of, ii. 243; letter of, to Mason, ability of, ii. 244; cabinet of, ii. 246, 247; on rotation in office, ii. 248; pressed by office-seekers, ii 249; Seward on inaugural of, ii. 268; relations of, with Taney, ii. 269; Lincoln on, ii. 270; Walker induced to go to Kansas by, ii. 271, 272; on Kansas-Nebraska act, ii. 275, 276; on Calhoun doctrine, ii. 276; influenced by Southerners, ii. 280; letter of, to Walker, ii. 281; difference of, with Douglas, ii. 282; position of, on Lecompton scheme, ii. 283; position of, on arrest of William Walker, ii. 289, 290; letter of Stephens on, ii. 291; mes-

INDEX

sage of, on Kansas, ii. 291; Douglas hated by, ii. 322, 355 defeated in Pennsylvania, ii. 343, 344; policy of, condemned at the North, ii. 346; on Kansas, ii. 349; on Cuba, ii. 350, 351; increase of tariff recommended by, ii. 360; agreement of, with Colonization Society, ii. 367; refuses patronage to Broderick, ii. 376; Bigler a friend of, ii. 449; criticised by Covode committee, ii. 476.

Buckingham on condition of slaves, i. 334.

Buena Vista, J. Davis at, i. 390.

Buford, Colonel, company raised by, ii. 151, 152; in sacking of Lawrence, ii. 158, 159; expulsion of men of, ii. 192.

Bull, Ole, in New Orleans, i. 401.

Bulwer, Henry Lytton, concludes treaty with Clayton, i. 200, 201.

Bunker Hill, negro soldiers at, i. 13.

Burke, Webster compared with, i. 160; remark of, ii. 32.

Burlingame, Anson, on assault of Brooks, ii. 145; challenged by Brooks, ii. 146; policy of, as to Douglas, ii. 306; in campaign of 1860, ii. 484 n.; remark of Douglas to, ii. 491.

Burns, Anthony, interview of R. H. Dana, Jr., and Parker with, i. 500; sympathy for, i. 501; ii. 77; attempt of Higginson to rescue, i. 503; delivered to owner, i. 504; ransom of, i. 505 n.

Bushnell, Horace, on Douglas, i. 496.

Bushnell, S., trial of, ii. 363; defended by Spalding and Riddle, ii. 364; imprisonment of, ii. 365, 367; ovation to, ii. 366.

Butler, of South Carolina, on Fugitive Slave law, i. 188; on Sumner, ii. 132 n.; Sumner on, ii. 134, 135; Atchison defended by, character of, ii. 136; gives Wilson the lie, ii. 145; on attack of Brooks, i. 149, 150; death of, ii. 150.

CALDERON, dislikes Soulé, ii. 15; correspondence of, with Soulé, ii. 19–21, 34, 35.

Calhoun, J., of Kansas, influence of, with administration, ii. 239; pledges of, to Walker, ii. 279, 280; flight of, from Kansas, ii. 289.

Calhoun, John C., i. 41; on nullification, i. 44, 47; on the tariff, i. 45; and Clay, i. 48; and Webster, i. 50; on Texas, i. 79–85; on the Oregon question, i. 86; on the Texas question, i. 87; a closet theorist, i. 94; last term of, i. 119; last speech of, i. 127–129; on condition of South, i. 128; on fugitive slaves, i. 129; on California, i. 129; fears of, for the Union, i. 130; reply of Webster to, i. 146; compliments Webster, i. 157; hears Seward, i. 166; succeeded by Davis, i. 168, 390; views of, i. 169; difficulties attending publication of his works, i. 353; compared with Jefferson, i. 379, 380; Lieber on, Adams on, i. 380 n.; doctrine of, as to slavery, i. 460; on Missouri Compromise, i.468; Buchanan compared to, ii. 174; doctrine of, ii. 253, 260, 262, 276; Davis compared to, ii. 347; position of, on slavery, ii. 359.

California, in 1848, i. 92; slavery in, i. 94; under military rule, i. 110; routes to in 1849, i. 112; De Quincey on, i. 113; immigration to, anarchy in, i. 114; convention in, i. 115; Clay on, i. 122, 124; Calhoun on, i. 129; California, admission of, i. 135, 136, 181, 182, 184, 188, 191, 196; Seward on, i. 163; in compromise measures, i. 189.

Cameron, Simon, in Senate, ii. 283; difference of, with Green, ii. 298; army bill supported by, ii. 303; bargain of David Davis with friends of, ii. 466, 467; balloting for, ii. 469.

Campbell, James, in Pierce's cabinet, i. 388.

Campbell, Justice, in Supreme Court, ii. 250; in Dred Scott case, ii. 254.

Campbell, Lewis D., assists Burlingame, ii. 146; against Kansas-Nebraska act, i. 484, 486.

Canaan, curse of, applied to negroes, i. 332, 371, 372.

Cartter in convention of 1860, ii. 470.

Cass, Lewis, nominated for President, i. 97; in Senate, i. 108, 109; hears Seward, i. 166; in committee on Clay resolutions, i. 171; supports compromise scheme, i. 173; supports Clayton-Bulwer treaty, i.

201 ; on Kossuth, i. 237; honors Kossuth, i. 239 ; supports Kossuth, i. 242 ; early life of, governs Michigan territory, Nicholson letter of, invents doctrine of popular sovereignty, i. 244 ; paper of McLaughlin on, i. 244 $n.$; Anglophobia of, i. 245 ; Douglas contrasted with, i. 246 ; Clay on, i. 247 ; defeat of, in convention of 1852, i. 247, 248 ; Dickinson on, i. 248 ; defeat of, foreseen, i. 252 ; favors doctrine of manifest destiny, i. 295 ; on Cuban letter of Everett, i. 296 ; Corwin's reply to, i. 300 ; Douglas and, i. 424; on Missouri Compromise, i. 436 $n.$; position of, on Kansas-Nebraska bill, i. 458, 459 ; on political institutions, i. 459, 460 ; on speech of Sumner, ii. 138 ; on intentions of Pierce, ii. 192 ; position of, on Lecompton scheme, ii. 287.

Catechism for slaves, i. 332 $n.$

Catholic Church denounced by Know-nothings, ii. 90.

Catholic priests in yellow fever of 1853, i. 412.

Catholics persecuted by Know-nothings, ii. 52, 57.

Catron, Justice, in Supreme Court, ii. 250 ; in Dred Scott case, ii. 255.

Central-American question, the, ii. 120, 121.

Chambers, William, on slave-trade, i. 320–322.

Chandler, Zachariah, succeeds Cass, ii. 247 ; in Senate, ii. 283.

Chapman, of Connecticut, defends Corwin, i. 298 $n.$

Charleston, in 1860, ii. 441 ; convention in, ii. 440–452.

Chase, Salmon P., elected senator, i. 108; first appearance of, in Senate, i. 120 ; on disunion, i. 131 ; votes on Texas boundary, i. 181 ; for California bill, i. 182 ; urges Wilmot proviso, i. 192 ; opposed to Clay Compromise, i. 193 ; personal appearance of, i. 227, 449 ; works with Wade and Seward, i. 229 ; political bias of, i. 265 ; on Sumner, i. 268 ; votes for Sumner's amendment, i.. 269 ; Appeal of Independent Democrats framed by, i. 441 ; attacked by Douglas, i. 444, 445 ; defends Appeal of Independent Democrats, i. 448 ; speech of, against Kansas-Nebraska bill, i. 449–452 ; on Missouri Compromise, i. 450, 451 ; compared with Seward, i. 453 ; on Kansas-Nebraska bill, i. 460, 462 ; answered by Douglas, i. 474, 475 ; remark of, to Sumner, i. 476 ; favors formation of new party, ii. 45 ; letters of, to Grimes, ii. 59 ; prejudice against, ii. 68 ; elected governor of Ohio, ii. 93 ; position of, on Kansas, ii. 124 ; Greeley on, ii. 92 ; letter of, to Pike, ii. 92 $n.$; Parker on, ii. 175 ; position of, on slavery, ii. 177 ; withdraws from presidential contest, ii. 183 ; possible presidential candidate in 1860, ii. 303 ; letter of, to Seward, ii. 305 ; on Douglas, ii. 307 ; compared with Lincoln, ii. 327 ; as, sists Lincoln, ii. 338 ; Jefferson Davis's opinion of, ii. 348 ; speech of, on Oberlin-Wellington rescue, ii. 366, 367 ; accused of assisting John Brown, ii. 402 ; on Seward, ii. 459 ; Dana on, ii. 459 $n.$; balloting for, ii. 469 ; in campaign of 1860, ii. 484 $n.$

Chatham, Corwin compared to, i. 300 ; effect of his speeches on Frederick Douglass, i. 351.

Chilton, Brown defended by, ii. 404; Brown's case taken to Court of Appeals by, ii. 405.

Choate, Rufus, in convention of 1852, i. 253 ; personality of, i. 254; speech of, on compromise measures, 254, 255 ; his reply to Botts, his eulogy of Webster, i. 255 ; Botts influenced by, i. 256 ; his interview with Webster after convention of 1852, i. 260 ; on "Uncle Tom's Cabin," i. 280 ; on Southern literature, i. 348 $n.$; holds aloof from Republican party, ii. 97 ; declares for Buchanan, ii. 206, 207; letter of, ii. 208 ; reply of George William Curtis to, ii. 208 $n.$; on Buchanan, ii. 242, 292 ; Buchanan overrated by, ii. 244.

Cholera in 1854, ii. 58.

Christ, silence of, on slavery, i. 370 ; John Brown compared with, ii. 415.

Christianity, influence of, on abolition, i. 372, 373.

Clarendon, Lord, on Cuba, ii. 26 $n.$, 32.

INDEX

Clark, of New York, election of, ii. 63, 64.
Clark, of New Hampshire, in Senate, ii. 282.
Clark, of Missouri, John Sherman denounced by, ii. 418–420.
Clarke, James Freeman, i. 64; on slave-breeding, i. 317; anecdote told by, ii. 75.
Clay, Cassius M., in campaign of 1860, ii. 484 n.
Clay, Henry, on slavery, i 31, 303, 333; on the tariff, i. 48; defeated by Polk, i. 84; on the Texas question, i. 87; invited to Free-soilers' convention, i. 108; last appearance of, with Webster and Calhoun, i. 119; described, embraces religion, inconsistent on slavery question, i. 120; his opinion of Taylor, i. 121; Lincoln's visit to, i. 121 n.; speech of, on compromise resolutions, i. 123–125; on admission of California, i. 124; on New Mexico, i. 124, 125; on Texas, on the Fugitive Slave law, i. 125, 126, 187, 188; prophecies of, i. 127; fears of, for the Union, i. 130; on disunion, i. 137 n.; and Webster, i. 143, 149; on Seward, i. 166; views of, i. 169; elected chairman of committee of thirteen, i. 171; Greeley on, i. 173, 464 n.; remarks of, i. 175; recommends Webster for Secretary of State, i 179; on New Mexico, i. 180; on secession, i. 190, 191; on Missouri Compromise, i. 191; justification of, i. 191, 192; on ship canal from Atlantic to Pacific, i. 199; supports Clayton-Bulwer treaty, i. 201; pledge of, concerning compromise, i. 207; on execution of Fugitive Slave law, i. 208; age of, when candidate for presidency, i. 244; declares for Fillmore, i. 253; death and funeral of, i. 261; dies before decline of Whig party, i. 285; remark of, refuted, i. 334; on fugitive slaves, i. 378; vice-president of Colonization Society, i. 382 n.; efforts of, for peace, i. 428; Douglas compared to, i. 430, 431; Douglas on, i. 446; against Taney, ii. 251; referred to by Douglas, i. 322; Lincoln influenced by, ii. 327.
Clayton, John M., secretaryship of, i. 199; concludes treaty with Bulwer, i. 200; consults W. R. King as to British Honduras, i. 201; defends treaty, Cass censures, i. 202 n.; in Whig convention of 1852, i. 253; amendments of, i. 476, 490; on British influence with Spain, ii. 26; on Cuba, ii. 33 n.; on Kansas, ii. 100.
Clayton-Bulwer treaty, the, i. 199; supported by Webster, Clay, Seward, Cass, and Everett, i. 201; ambiguity of, i. 201, 202; Douglas criticises, i. 202 n.; difficulties raised by, ii. 120.
Clemens, Jeremiah, on disunion, i. 242; on Sumner, i. 268.
Cleveland, Grover, nomination and election of, i. 3.
Cleveland, Ohio, characteristics of, ii. 361.
Clingman, Thomas L., against California bill, i. 182; scheme of, concerning Cuba, ii. 23; acknowledges election of Banks, ii. 116; disapproves of Douglas, ii. 373, 492.
Cobb, Howell, elected speaker, i. 117; pledge of, concerning compromise, i. 207; advises Pierce, ii. 120, 121; in campaign of 1856, ii. 228; in Buchanan's cabinet, ii. 246, 247; influence of, in Kansas, ii. 277; Buchanan influenced by, ii. 280; panic caused by, ii. 500.
Cobden, Richard, on Cuba, ii. 31, 32.
Colfax, Schuyler, policy of, as to Douglas, ii. 306; assists Lincoln, ii. 338; letter of Greeley to, ii. 403; in the House, ii. 418; letter of Defrees to, ii. 471 n.
Collamer, Jacob, Greeley on, ii. 130; speech of, published, ii. 131; in Senate, ii. 282; on Kansas, ii. 293; complimented by Vermont, ii. 470.
Colonization Society, i. 381; Garrison on, i. 382; H. Martineau on, i. 382 n.; Buchanan and, ii. 367.
Colton, Walter, on California, ii. 111; made alcalde of Monterey, i. 113.
Columbia College welcomes Kossuth, i. 235.
"Columbian Orator," the, bought by Frederick Douglass, i. 351.
Compromise of 1850, i. 1, 122–129, 172; discussed in Senate, i. 173; Taylor opposes, i. 175; Fillmore's cabinet favors, i. 179; completion

of, i. 181–183; Mann on, i. 189 n.;
a credit to Clay and Webster, i.
191, 192; opposed by Seward,
Mann, and others, i. 193; a relief
to the North, i. 193–195; Fillmore
on, i. 207, 230; Mississippi favors,
i. 227; resolution of Foote concerning, i. 243; conventions of
1852 on, i. 249, 253; Choate favors,
i. 254, 255; Corwin's position on,
i. 300; Clay's speech on, quoted,
i. 333; Davis against, i. 388; Douglas on, i. 426, 427, 433, 446, 447;
generally accepted, i. 428; Dixon
on, i. 433; *Washington Union* on,
i. 437 n.; Toombs on, i. 461.
Compromise resolutions, of Clay, i.
122, 123; speech of Clay on, i. 123–
127; speech of Calhoun on, i. 127–
129; committee on, i. 171, 172.
Congdon, Charles T., on Douglas, i.
492; on Gardner, ii. 65, 66.
Congress on slavery, i. 23; debates
in, i. 35 n.
Congressional Library, acknowledgment to, i. 208 n.
Conkling, Roscoe, in campaign of
1860, ii. 484 n.
Conrad, Charles M., made Secretary
of War, i. 179.
Constitution of the United States,
Gladstone on, i. 16; Lowell on, i.
20; a covenant with death, i. 74;
used in campaign of 1856, ii. 220;
Lincoln on, ii. 335; convention of
1860 on, ii. 464.
Constitutional Union party, convention of, ii. 454.
Cooper, of Pennsylvania, in committee on Clay resolutions, i. 171.
Cooper Institute speech, of Lincoln,
ii. 458.
Cortes, the, vote of, on Cuban question, ii. 351.
Cortez, Scott compared to, i. 259.
Corwin, Thomas, on slavery in the
territories, i. 96; hears Seward, i.
166; made Secretary of the Treasury, i. 179; attacked by A. Johnson and Olds, defended by Barrere,
Chapman, and Stevens, i. 298 n.;
becomes attorney for Dr. Gardiner,
charges against, i. 298; character
of, i. 299; anecdote of, i. 299 n.;
speech of, on Mexican war, retort
of, to Cass, position of, on compromise of 1850, i. 300; Seward on,
i. 300 n.; on Fugitive Slave law,
i. 301; Sargent on, i. 301 n.; assists Lincoln, ii. 338; speech of, in
House, ii. 422; on abolitionists, ii.
425; in convention of 1860, ii. 469
n.; in campaign of 1860, ii. 484 n.
Costume, diplomatic, ii. 1, 2.
Cotton-gin and slavery, i. 19, 25.
"Cotton Kingdom, the," quoted, i.
303; composition of, i. 304 n.
Cousin, Victor, on Everett, i. 291.
Covode, John, in campaign of 1860,
ii. 484 n.
Covode committee, the, Cobb and,
ii. 277; report of, ii. 476.
Cox, Samuel S., on Douglas, i. 439 n.
Crackers, of Georgia, Olmsted on,
i. 344.
Crampton, withdrawal of, requested,
ii. 186; Pierce's cabinet and, ii.
187 n.; dismissal of, ii. 188.
Crawford, George W., urges Galphin
claim, i. 202, 203; receives interest
on claim, i. 203; Seward on, i. 203
n.; charges against, i. 204; Taylor's
confidence in, i. 205.
Crawford, Martin J., colloquy of,
with Stevens, ii. 420; on Seward,
ii. 422.
Creoles, of Cuba, i. 217; ii. 29.
"Crime against Kansas, the," circulation of, ii. 147.
Crimean war, recruiting for, in United States, ii. 186.
Crittenden, Col., capture and shooting of, fate of followers of, i. 219;
excitement at New Orleans over
fate of, i. 220; letters of, i. 220 n.
Crittenden, John J., Life of, quoted,
i. 134 n.; made Attorney-General,
i. 179; on Fugitive Slave law, i.
188; on General Scott, ii. 189; in
debate on Kansas, ii. 293; against
bill for admission of Kansas under
Lecompton Constitution, ii. 297;
amendment of, ii. 299; Lincoln
disappointed in, ii. 322; letter of
Scott to, ii. 428; letter of Lawrence
to, ii. 473 n.
Crystal Palace, the, of New York, i.
414–416; G. W. Curtis on, 414,
415, 416.
Cuba, proposed conquest of, i. 193,
295; expedition of Lopez to, i.
216–222; Fillmore against expedition to, i. 218; Captain-General
of, i. 220, 221; sympathy for, i.

222; speech of Everett on, i. 294; Pierce on, i. 385, ii. 17, 18; Buchanan on, i. 387, ii. 25 n., 174; offer of Buchanan for, i. 393; Soulé on, Lord Palmerston on, i. 394; Marcy desires, i. 423; ii. 10, 11, 41; supposed attempts to Africanize, ii. 25-27; Lord Clarendon on, ii. 26 n., 32; plans to attack, ii. 28-30; Cobden on, ii. 31, 32; Clayton on, ii. 33 n.; proposed purchase of, ii. 37; Ostend manifesto on, ii. 39, 40; Spanish minister on, ii. 42; Davis on, ii. 373.

Cuba bill, discussion of, ii. 351-353; withdrawal of, ii. 354.

Cuban exiles visit Kossuth, i. 235.

Curtin, Andrew G., against Seward, ii. 466; Greeley on, ii. 470; tariff question urged by, ii. 479, 480 n.; in campaign of 1860, ii. 497, 498.

Curtis, Benjamin R., on Clay Compromise, i. 195; on McLean, ii. 186 n.; in Supreme Court, ii. 250; training of, Webster's confidence in, ii. 251; in Dred Scott case, ii. 252; letter of, on Missouri Compromise question, ii. 253; on Taney, ii. 254; in Dred Scott decision, ii. 257-260; on Declaration of Independence, ii. 258, 465; on powers of Congress, ii. 259; on slavery, ii. 260; correspondence of, with Taney, ii. 262; on the authority of the Supreme Court, ii. 263.

Curtis, George Ticknor, on Webster, i. 155, 156; negro brought before, i. 209; orders arrest of Sims, i. 211; his monograph on Webster, i. 289 n; his Life of Buchanan, ii. 244; on Lincoln campaign, ii. 495 n.

Curtis, George William, on Olmsted, i. 304 n.; on journal of Fanny Kemble, i. 305 n.; on the Crystal Palace, i. 414, 415, 416; reply of, to Choate, ii. 208 n.; supports Frémont, ii. 211, 214; oration of, in campaign of 1856, ii. 212, 215; speech of, in convention of 1860, ii. 463; in campaign of 1860, ii. 484 n., 485.

Cushing, Caleb, in Pierce's cabinet, i. 388, 389; influence of, in Pierce's nomination, i. 390-391; intellect of, letter of quoted, early life of, writings of, secures treaty with China, serves in Mexican War, i.

391; scholarship of, writes for *North American Review*, for *Washington Union*, insincerity of in politics, Lowell on i. 392; desires appointment of Davis, i. 393; Benton on, i. 393 n.; on abolitionism, i. 420, 421; influence of, with Pierce, i. 482; supports Kansas-Nebraska bill, i. 483; a friend to Soulé, ii. 24; in Charleston convention, ii. 445.

Cutting, of New York, contends with Richardson, i. 480; Breckinridge on, i. 480, 481.

Cutts, James Madison, remark of Douglas to, ii. 196.

DALLAS, on dismissal of Crampton, ii. 187; Lord Palmerston on, ii. 188.

Dana, Charles A., denounces Kansas-Nebraska bill, i. 463; honors Kossuth, i. 236; letters of Greeley to, ii. 111, 112, 113, 116, 126, 130; letter of, to Pike, on McLean, ii. 180, 181; on Frémont and Seward, ii. 223; on campaign of 1856, ii. 232; on Chase and Seward, ii. 459 n.; on Seward, ii. 461; in campaign of 1860, ii. 484 n.

Dana, Richard H., interview of with Anthony Burns, i. 500; extract from Diary of, ii. 95 n.; on Choate, ii. 206; on Webster, ii. 262.

Daniel, Justice, in Supreme Court, ii. 250.

Davis, David, bargain of, with friends of Caleb Smith, ii. 466; with friends of Cameron, ii. 467; in campaign of 1860, ii. 484 n.

Davis, Henry Winter, at celebration of Lundy's Lane, i. 270.

Davis, Jefferson, letter of General Taylor to, i. 155; on speech of Webster, i. 157; states Southern claim, i. 168; demand of, i. 169; votes on Texas boundary, i. 181; protests against admission of California, i. 182; against territorial bills, i. 184; on situation in 1850, i. 189 n.; refuses command of Cuban expedition, i 217; canvass between Foote and, i. 226; defeated in gubernatorial contest, i. 227, 390; on slavery, i. 371; influenced by Calhoun, i. 380; appointed Secretary of War, i. 388; in House, i. 389, 390; military career of, intellect of, J. Q. Adams on, at Buena

Vista, in Senate, becomes leader of Southern people, i. 390; Cushing favors Pierce's appointment of, i. 393; friendship of, with Pierce, i. 421; on Kansas-Nebraska bill, i. 432 n.; assists Douglas, i. 437; trusted by Pierce, i. 438; Pierce influenced by, i. 482; favors Kansas-Nebraska act, i. 483; desires to uphold Soulé, ii. 24; friendship of, with Quitman, ii. 27; promotes cause of filibusters, ii. 28; sympathy of, with Missourians, ii. 85; on Reeder, ii. 86; favors Missouri party in Kansas, ii. 122; position of, on Kansas, ii. 240; James Buchanan compared with, ii. 245; speech of, in debate on Kansas, ii. 294, 295; Walker denounced by, ii. 275; influence of, in Kansas affairs, ii. 277; compared to Calhoun, ii. 347; Northern tour of, ii. 347, 348; speech of, at Jackson, ii. 348; discussion of, with Douglas, ii. 357, 358; position of, on slavery, ii. 359; on the slave-trade, ii. 372; on Cuba and disunion, ii. 373; on John Brown, ii. 411; resolution introduced by, ii. 430; influence of, in Charleston convention, ii. 445; arrogance of, in Senate, ii. 454 n.; speech of, ii. 455; debate between Douglas and, ii. 455, 456; tried to concentrate opposition to Lincoln on a single candidate, ii. 490.

Davis, Mrs., on negroes, i. 375.

Davis, Rev. N., i. 364, 365.

Dawes, Henry L., in Whig convention of 1852, i. 253; refuses to vote for Webster, i. 258; letter of Bowles to, ii. 175 n.

Dayton, William L., Washburne on, ii. 183 n.; nomination of, ii. 184; home of, ii. 203; in campaign of 1860, ii. 484 n.

De Bow, Professor, on condition of slaves, i. 306; on cotton culture, i. 311; on condition of South, i. 313 n.; ability of, i. 353.

De Bow's Review, on text-books, i. 351; character of, i. 353.

Declaration of Independence, the, in campaign of 1856, ii. 220; Taney on, ii. 256, 257; B. R. Curtis on, ii. 258; Lincoln on, ii. 319, 320; G. W. Curtis on, ii. 463.

De Foe, "Great Plague of," i. 409.

Delano, Columbus, in convention of 1860, ii. 469 n.

"Delta," New Orleans, gives spurious accounts of Cuban expedition, i. 220.

Democratic Convention of 1852, i. 243; platform of, i. 249.

Democratic Convention of 1856, ii. 171, 172; platform of, ii. 171.

Democratic party, strengthening of, i. 185; spoils system urged by, i. 399; supremacy of, in 1853, i. 422; Douglas on, i. 430; weakened by Kansas-Nebraska act and Ostend manifesto, ii. 44; position of, on slavery, ii. 240; broken up by Davis and his followers, ii. 359.

Democrats, the, on Texas question, i. 77; restoration of, to power, 1853, i. 385, 386.

Dennison, William, contest of, with Ranney, ii. 381; elected governor, ii. 383.

Denver, Stanton succeeded by, ii. 289; against Lecompton Constitution, ii. 292.

Depew, Chauncey M., on New York *Tribune,* ii. 72 n.; in campaign of 1860, ii. 484 n.

Dew, Prof., pro-slavery argument of, i. 316; essay of, on slavery, i. 368.

De Witt, A., signs Appeal of Independent Democrats, i. 442.

Dickinson, Daniel S., in committee on Clay resolutions, i. 171; favors Fugitive Slave law, i. 183; on slave-owners, i. 209 n.; refuses to be a candidate for nomination, on Cass, i. 248.

District of Columbia, Clay resolution respecting, i. 122; Clay on, i. 125; slave-trade in, i. 182, 183, 184, 196.

Disunion, Clemens on, i. 242; threats of, ii. 487; Seward on, Lowell on, ii. 488; Lieber on, ii. 489.

Disunionists and the Fugitive Slave law, i. 187, 188.

Dix, John A., is offered a secretaryship, i. 387; releases Pierce, i. 388; French mission offered to, political bias of, i. 395; on Pierce, i. 482.

Dixon, of Connecticut, in Senate, ii. 282.

Dixon, of Kentucky, offers amendment to Nebraska bill, on Missouri

Compromise, and compromise measures, i. 433; Douglas accepts amendment of, promises to support Douglas, i. 434; Pierce opposed to amendment of, i. 437; on Kansas-Nebraska bill, i. 441.
Dobbin, J. C., in Pierce's cabinet, i. 388.
Dodge, Sen., restrains Benton i. 171.
Donaldson, United States marshal, proclamation of, on Lawrence, ii. 157; Jones supported by, ii. 158.
Donelson, nominated by Americans, ii. 119.
Doolittle, James R., in Senate, ii.283; and Cuban bill, ii. 352 ; in campaign of 1860, ii. 484 n.
Douglas, Stephen A., supports compromise scheme, i. 173; quoted, i. 173 n.; bill of, on admission of California, i. 181; absent from Washington when Fugitive Slave law was passed, i. 183; on fugitive slaves, i. 187; address of, at Chicago, i. 197; criticises Clayton-Bulwer treaty, i. 202 n.; in convention of 1852, i. 244; early life of, created judge, elected senator, J. Q. Adams on, adaptability of foresees growth of West, i. 245 Ampère on, i. 245 n.; views of, on Cuba, Mexico, etc., Whig journal on, i. 246; lives of, i. 246 n ; defeat of, i. 247, 248, 252; favors doctrine of manifest destiny, i 295; on Cuban letter of Everett, i. 296; rivalry between Cass and, i. 424; desires support of South, i. 424, 425 ; report of, on territories, i. 425–428; on slavery in Nebraska, i. 426; on Missouri Compromise, i. 427, ii. 265; on Compromise of 1850, i. 427, 433 ; proposition of, concerning Nebraska, i. 428; ambition of, i. 429; imitates Clay, i. 430; compared with Clay, i. 431; not influenced by Atchison, Toombs, or Stephens, i. 431, 432; on Nebraska bill, i. 431 n.; discussion of, with Dixon, i. 433, 434; hesitates to set aside Missouri Compromise, i. 435; speech of, on Compromise measures, quoted, seeks aid of President, i. 436; seeks aid of Davis, i. 437; *Washington Union* on, i. 437 n.; Pierce promises support to, i. 438; Kansas-Nebraska bill of, i. 439, ii. 127; Cox on, i. 439 n.; course of, endorsed by administration, i. 441 ; false methods of, i. 443; attacks Chase, i. 444, 445; on Kansas-Nebraska bill, i. 446–448, 470–475; on Clay and Webster, i. 448; on Chase, Seward, and Sumner, i. 454, and Kansas-Nebraska bill, i. 461,462; distrust of, at South, i.468; personality of, i.471; Seward on, i. 474, ii. 284 ; answers charge of Chase and Sumner, i. 474, 475; on speech of Everett, i. 474 ; invents doctrine of popular sovereignty, i. 476, 477; on clergymen in politics, i. 479 ; supported by Richardson, i. 480; desires help of administration, i. 481; pertinacity of, i. 483; criticised by Benton, i. 489, 490; political opinions of, i. 491; intellect of, i. 492; compared with other statesmen, i. 493; civil war precipitated by, i. 494; Bushnell on, i. 496; on Know-nothings, ii. 56 ; refuted by Lincoln, address of at Chicago, ii. 61 ; reply of Lincoln to, at Springfield, ii. 62 ; assertions of, ii. 66, 67 ; compared with Seward, ii. 69 disturbed by Lincoln, ii. 70; influence of, ii. 79; warned by Lincoln, ii. 80, 81; in Virginia, ii. 88 ; on situation in Kansas, ii. 125; Kansas bill of, ii. 127; described by Mrs. Stowe, ii. 127–129; Greeley on, ii. 129, 338 n.; on Sumner, ii. 134, 138, 139; Sumner on, ii. 135,137, 138; on assault of Sumner, ii. 148, 149 ; political strength of, ii. 169, 170; votes received by, ii. 171, 172; urges nomination of Buchanan ii.172; speech of Seward to, ii. 176 n.; introduces Kansas bill, ii. 191; offers amendment to Toombs bill, ii. 192; position of, on slavery ii. 194 ; on Kansas, ii. 196 ; in campaign of 1856, ii. 230; Buchanan compared with, ii. 245; Taney compared to, ii. 261 ; on Dred Scott decision, ii. 264 ; on Missouri Compromise, ii. 265 ; urges submission to Supreme Court, ii. 271; urges Walker to go to Kansas, ii. 272 ; altercation of, with Buchanan, ii. 282; on Lecompton scheme, 283, 284 ; on Kansas, ii. 285 ; Lecompton scheme opposed by, ii. 286, 287;

514 INDEX

Wise on, ii. 290 ; on Lecompton Constitution, ii. 293; Brown on, ii. 294; removal of friends of, ii. 295; Raymond on, ii. 296; against Lecompton bill, ii. 297; against English bill, ii. 300; against Buchanan's policy, ii. 302, 303; co-operation of Seward with, ii. 305-307; Chase on, ii. 307; on Lincoln, ii. 313, 314, 340, 472, 491, 492 ; Lincoln on, ii. 316, 317, 334, 335, 336, 337; ovation to, in Chicago, ii. 317, 318 ; gift of, to University of Chicago, ii. 318; Lincoln's reply to, ii. 319, 320; debates of, with Lincoln, ii. 321-343; challenged by Lincoln, ii. 321; disliked by Buchanan, ii. 322; first debate with Lincoln, ii. 323; on the negro, ii. 324; catechises Lincoln, ii. 326; catechised by Lincoln, ii. 327; compared with Lincoln, ii. 329, 330; on disunion, ii. 331, 487. 488 ; Lincoln defeated by, ii. 339; Parker on, ii. 342; Southern tour of, ii. 354; removal of, from chairmanship, ii. 355; discussion between Davis and, ii. 357, 358; political position of, ii. 359; on the slave-trade, ii. 369, 370; article of, on Popular Sovereignty, ii. 373, 374 ; controversy of, with Black, ii. 374; Lincoln on article of, ii. 383; on John Brown, ii. 411; altercation concerning, ii. 423 ; declaration of, to Southern senators, ii. 429, 430; influence of, in Charleston convention, ii. 440, 443, 444, 445; Buchanan against nomination of, ii. 450; Yancey against, ii. 452; Stephens on, ii. 453; reply of, to Davis, ii. 455; debate between Davis and, ii. 455, 456; attitude of, towards the South, ii. 457; letter of, to Richardson, ii. 474, 475; nomination declined by, ii. 475; on the tariff, ii. 480; contest between Lincoln and, ii. 483; debates of, with Lincoln, ii. 484; on withdrawing his name, ii. 490, 491; catechised by Southerners, ii. 491, 492 ; tour of, in campaign of 1860, ii. 493; votes received by, in 1860, ii. 500, 501.

Douglass, Frederick, on condition of slaves, i. 305 ; life of, quoted, i. 310, 317, 330 ; on slavery, i, 343 ; reads Columbian Orator, i. 351 ; on Uncle Tom, i. 364 ; his early notions of geography, i. 378 ; nomination of, by abolitionists, ii. 186 n.; conference of, with John Brown, ii. 392 ; goes to Canada, ii. 401.

Dow, murder of, ii. 104, 162.

Downs, of Louisiana, in committee on Clay resolutions, i. 172.

Doyle, family of, murdered, ii. 163.

" Dred," publication of, ii. 212.

Dred Scott decision, Stephens on, ii. 255 ; Douglas on, ii. 265, 307, 318; effect of, on Democratic party, ii. 266 ; Lincoln on, ii. 267, 268, 270, 271, 316, 319 ; Seward on, ii. 268 ; Benjamin on, ii. 293; influence of, ii. 332, 334, 348.

Duane removed by Jackson, ii. 250.

Duello, the, in Southern States, i. 361, 362.

Duels, Northern sentiment opposed to, ii, 424.

Durkee, of Wisconsin, in Senate, ii. 283.

Dutch, of Pennsylvania, ii. 227.

Echo, the, capture of, ii. 367.

Edmundson, of Virginia, excitement of, in debate on Kansas-Nebraska bill, i. 486; supports Brooks, ii. 144.

Education, condition of, at South, i. 350-352.

Edwards, Jonathan, a slave-owner, i. 5.

Elgin, Lord, treaty of, with Marcy, ii. 8.

Eliot, Samuel, against Kansas-Nebraska bill, i. 466.

Elmore, Judge, hardships of, in winter, ii. 154 ; attempts to influence Buchanan, ii. 292.

Emancipation, Lyell on, i. 382.

Emerson, Ralph Waldo, on philanthropists, i. 60 ; on Webster, i, 159 ; on Fugitive Slave law, i. 207, 208 ; on Parker, i. 290 ; on climate, i. 358 n.; on African race, i. 372; on Kansas-Nebraska act, i. 498 ; supports Frémont, ii. 211 ; on Kansas, ii. 218, 219 ; on John Brown and Governor Wise, ii. 398 ; on John Brown, ii. 399, 406, 413, 415.

Emigrant-Aid Company, in Kansas, ii. 78, 79 ; Reeder on, ii. 85, 86 ; Lawrence settled by, ii. 102 n.; ii. 103 ; Pierce on, ii. 122 ; Douglas on, ii. 125, 129 ; Sumner on, ii. 126.

Emigration, Brownlow on, i. 355.

"Émile," publication of, i. 284; effect of, on the young, i. 285.
Emily, sale of quadroon girl, i. 337.
Emmet, Robert, on Seward, ii. 176 n.; on Frémont, ii. 178.
Emperor of France, intimation of, to Mason, ii. 4.
England, assists in rescue of Kossuth, i. 231; proposition of, as to Cuba, i. 294; Everett's reply to, i. 295; defiance of, in America, i. 419 n.
English Bill, passage of, ii. 299, 300; rejected in Kansas, ii. 301; Chase on, ii. 307; connection of Buchanan with, ii. 476.
English opinion of slavery, i. 7.
"Englishman in Kansas, The," ii. 200 n.
Errett, Russel, on Stevens, ii. 184 n.
Eugénie, Empress, position of, on Cuban question, ii. 32.
Evarts, William M., in Whig convention of 1852, i. 253; in convention of 1860, ii. 465, 469, 470; in campaign of 1860, ii. 484 n.
Everett, Edward, on Webster, i. 138 n.; supports Clayton-Bulwer treaty, i. 201; letter of Webster to, i. 260 n.; on death of Webster, i. 287; appointed Secretary of State, early life of, becomes a Unitarian preacher, at Göttingen, Victor Cousin on, Story on, J. Q. Adams on, King on sermon of in the capitol, i. 291; in Congress, made governor, letter of Webster to, becomes minister to England, chosen president of Harvard, i. 292; Hillard on, letters of Webster to, edits works of Webster, i. 293; deals with Cuban question, i. 294; Ampère on, i 294 n.; reply of, to England and France, in regard to Cuban question, i. 295, 296; Cass on Cuban letter of, Douglas on Cuban letter of, i. 296; *Harper's Magazine* on Cuban letter of, i. 296 n.; Marcy compared to, i. 417; speech of, against Kansas-Nebraska bill, i. 455–458; on Compromise of 1850, i. 455, 457 letter of, to Greeley, i. 456 n.; Webster interpreted by, i. 457; Douglas on, i. 474; presents protest of clergymen against Kansas-Nebraska act, i. 478; on Kansas election, ii. 83, 84; on assault of Sumner, ii. 143; supports Fillmore, ii. 206; letter of,
to Buchanan, i. 243; Buchanan overrated by, ii. 244; nominated by Constitutional Union convention, ii. 454.
Ewing, Thomas, Seward consults, i. 166 n.; at celebration of Lundy's Lane, i. 270.
Examiner, Richmond, quoted, i. 350 n.
Exiles, Marcy on protection of, i. 418.

FANEUIL HALL, assembly at, to discuss compromise measures, i. 195; assembly at, promises protection to negroes, i. 198; Mann on exclusion from, i. 212; Webster on exclusion from, i. 213.
Felton, Prof., supports Frémont, ii. 211.
Fenton, Reuben E., in campaign of 1860, ii. 484 n.
Ferry, T. W., in convention of 1860, ii. 469 n.
Fessenden, William P., in Whig convention of 1852, i. 253; question of, to Toombs, ii. 198 n.; in Senate, ii. 282; on Seward, ii. 304; in campaign of 1860, ii. 484 n.
Field, David Dudley, in campaign of 1860, ii. 484 n.
Field, Maunsell B., on authorship of Ostend manifesto, ii. 40; delivers letter to Soulé, ii. 41.
"Figures of the Past," quoted, i. 320 n.
Filibusters at work, ii. 27; connection of, with Soulé, ii. 28.
Fillmore, Millard, in House, supports J. Q. Adams, as Vice-President, in favor of Clay's compromise, Webster on, i. 178; differs from Seward, i. 178; cabinet of, i. 179; approves the Fugitive Slave law, i. 188, 189; consults Crittenden, i. 188; on compromise, i. 206, 207; on Northern views, i. 207; proclamation of, to enforce Fugitive Slave law, i. 210; concurs in proposed reduction of postage, i. 216; endeavors to prevent Cuban expedition, i. 218; recommends indemnification of Spanish consul, i. 222; sends officers and troops to Christiana, Pa., i. 223; on slavery agitation, i. 230, 231; Curtis appointed justice by, ii. 251; his candidacy for nomination, Clay declares for, i. 253; votes received by,

516 INDEX

in convention of 1852, i. 256, 257 ; Southern delegates pledged to, i. 258 ; accepts his defeat with equanimity, i. 260 ; on negro colonization, i. 296 ; character of, i. 297 ; address of Gen. Wilson on, Ampère on, made a member of Colonization Society, i. 297 *ns.*; general opinion of, i. 301 ; his execution of Fugitive Slave law, compared to Arthur, i. 302 ; nominated by Americans, ii. 119 ; on campaign of 1856, ii. 204 ; supported by Hillard, Winthrop, and Everett, ii. 206 ; supported by Ticknor, ii. 206 *n*; on Missouri Compromise repeal, ii. 215 ; integrity of, ii. 221, 226 ; in campaign of 1856, ii. 222 ; supported by Letcher, ii. 233 *n.*; letter of, to Curtis, ii. 263.

Finality, Chase on doctrine of, i. 268.

Fish, Hamilton, presents petition of clergymen, i. 477.

Fishery question, settled by Marcy, ii. 8.

Fitch, of Indiana, Douglas attacked by, ii. 287.

Fletcher, John, "Studies on Slavery" of, i. 370 *n.*

Florence, plague of, i. 409, 413 *n.*

Florida, secession of, from the Charleston convention, ii. 451.

Floyd, John B., on fugitive slaves, i. 136 ; appointed Secretary of War, ii. 246 ; ignores John Brown conspiracy, ii. 393.

Foot, of Vermont, in Senate, ii. 282.

Foote, Henry S., praises Webster, i. 157 ; defends Southern address, i. 170 ; quarrel of, with Benton, i. 169–171 ; supports compromise scheme, i. 173 ; canvass between Davis and, i. 226 ; defeats Davis, i. 227 ; on Kossuth, i. 237, 242 ; on compromise measures, i. 243 ; on Cass, ii. 287.

Forbes, John Brown betrayed by, ii. 388, 389.

Foresti, calls on Kossuth, i. 231.

Ford, Gordon L., acknowledgment to, i. 456 *n.*

Ford, Paul L., acknowledgment to, i. 456 *n.*

Forney, John W., presides over House, ii. 115 ; Buchanan quoted by, ii. 228 ; sums received by, in campaign of 1856, ii. 231 ; on campaign of 1856, ii. 233 ; remark of Buchanan to, ii. 280 ; Lecompton scheme opposed by, ii. 282 ; Wise on, ii. 290 ; on misuse of patronage, ii. 296 ; on Broderick, ii. 300 ; remarks of Douglas to, ii. 313, 314 ; remark of Broderick to, ii. 376.

Foster, of Connecticut, in Senate, ii. 282.

Fox, effect of his speeches on Frederick Douglass, i. 351.

France, proposition of, as to Cuba, i. 294 ; Everett's reply to, i. 295.

Franklin, Benjamin, diplomatic costume of, ii. 2, 11.

Frederick the Great, quoted, i. 430 ; sword of, taken by John Brown, ii. 394.

Free-soil Party, i. 97, 387, 389.

Free-soilers, i. 108 ; number of, in 31st Congress, i. 117 *n.* ; their attitude towards Clay compromise, i. 192 ; principles of, i. 264.

Free-soilism, Pierce accused of, i. 420.

Free Speech, effect of slavery on, i. 375.

Frelinghuysen, F. T., in convention of 1860, ii. 469 *n.*

Frémont, John C., elected senator, i. 116 ; related to Benton, i. 170 *n.*; nomination of, ii. 174 ; letter of, to Gov. Robinson, friends of, ii. 177 ; Dan Mace on, ii. 177, 178 ; supported by Germans, Emmet on, ii. 178 ; Pike on, ii. 178, 179 ; character of, ii. 181 ; letter of, on slavery, ii. 182 ; Washburne on, ii. 182 *n.*; Stevens on, ii. 183 ; nomination of, ii. 184, 185 ; nominated by North Americans, ii. 186 ; Toombs on, ii. 190, 204 ; political position of, ii. 202 ; birth of, ii. 203 ; Wise, Slidell, and Botts on, ii. 205 ; Choate decides against, ii. 206, 207, 208 ; Buchanan and Wise on, ii. 209 ; supported by Northern clergy, ii. 210 ; supported by literary men, ii. 211, 212 ; supported by Northern press, ii. 220 ; charges against, ii. 221, 222, 225, 226 ; Dana on, ii. 223 ; enthusiasm for, ii. 224, 225 ; distrust of, in Pennsylvania, ii. 227 ; Reeder declares for, ii. 232 ; election of, feared by Southern governors, ii.

233 ; supported by New England, ii. 235, 236 ; popularity of, ii. 303 ; campaign of, compared with that of 1860, ii. 477.
French, attempt of, to construct Panama Canal, i. 202.
French consul-general, Koszta delivered to, i. 417.
Friends, Society of, Sumner presents memorial of, i. 265.
Frothingham, O. B., on Parker's sermon on Webster, i. 289 n.
Fugitive Slave law, Seward on, i. 163, 188, 506 n. ; passed, i. 182, 183 ; exposition of, i. 185–189 ; compared with Roman law, i. 186 ; cotton States not greatly affected by, i. 186–188 ; Clay on, i. 187 ; Butler on, Crittenden on, Webster on, i. 188 ; meetings at New York, Philadelphia, Concord, approve, i. 195 ; convention at Georgia insists on, i. 196 ; meetings at Lowell, Syracuse, Springfield, Mass., and Faneuil Hall condemn, i. 196, 197 ; C. F. Adams, J. Quincy, W. Phillips, T. Parker, and common council of Chicago denounce, Douglas defends, i. 197 ; Sumner on, i. 197, 198, 208 ; denounced by the pulpit, i. 198 ; negroes at North alarmed by, promised protection against, i. 198; approved by Fillmore, i. 188, 189, 302 ; Seward Whigs on, abolitionists resist, i. 207 ; Emerson on, i. 207, 208, 498 ; Clay on execution of, Parker on, i. 208 ; Mason on execution of, i. 208, 209 ; Ampère on, i. 208, n.; Fillmore's proclamation to enforce, i. 210 ; protests of Boston citizens against, i. 212 ; in free States, i. 222, 223, 225, 226 ; denounced by G. Smith and S. May, i. 225 ; as a touchstone, i. 230 ; supported by Whig convention of 1852, i. 253 ; attitude of Scott towards, i. 256 ; N. Y. Tribune on, i. 259 ; memorial of Friends concerning, i. 265 ; proposed repeal of, i. 266 ; Sumner's oration on, i. 266–268 ; W. C. Bryant on repeal of, i. 269 ; general acquiescence in, i. 278, 279, 428 ; Mrs. Stowe's opinion of, i. 279 ; Whittier on, i. 280 ; "Uncle Tom's Cabin" directed against, i. 284 ; Corwin on, tolerated at North, i. 301 ; St. Paul quoted in support of, i. 370 ; position of Pierce on, i. 385 ; supported by clergymen, i. 479 ; becomes a dead letter, i. 490 ; revulsion of feeling as to, Lincoln's intention to enforce, i. 499 ; effect of Kansas-Nebraska act on, i. 500 ; position of Republicans on, ii. 48 ; bill of Toucey to enforce, ii. 77 ; in Kansas, ii. 99 ; disagreement of Sumner and Butler on, ii. 136 ; position of Lincoln on, ii. 326, 327 ; prominence of, ii. 360, 361 ; repeal of, demanded, ii. 366.
Fugitive Slave laws, i. 18, 24.
Fugitive slaves, in Clay compromise, i. 122 ; Clay on, i. 125, 126, 378 ; Calhoun on, i. 129 ; Floyd's proposition as to, i. 136 ; Webster on, i. 147, 152, 153, 187 ; Seward on, i. 167, 187 ; identification of, i. 185; statistics of, i. 187 n.; Douglas on, i. 187; discussed in Senate, i. 208, 209; United States marshal paid for delivering, i. 209 n.; trial of rescuers of, in Boston, i. 210 ; action of Boston common council respecting, i. 211 placard concerning hunters of, i. 211 n., 212 ; proposed appropriation for capture of, i. 266 ; letter of Washington on, i. 267; Parker on, i. 290; number of, i. 378; why so few, i. 379; in compromise of 1850, i. 427 ; rescued at Milwaukee, i. 499; sympathy with, ii. 74–77; bill in Massachusetts legislature regarding, ii. 360 ; sympathy for, at Oberlin, ii. 361.
Fuller, of Pennsylvania, political position of, ii. 110.
Fusion party in Vermont, ii. 59.
Fusionists, efforts of, in 1860, ii, 499 ; Weed on, ii. 500.
"Fuss and Feathers," sobriquet of Scott, i. 273.

GADSDEN TREATY, with Mexico, ii. 7.
Galphin Claim, urged by G. W. Crawford, i. 202; adjusted, i. 203.
Gardiner Claim, i. 298; debate on, i. 298, 301.
Gardner, elected governor of Mass., ii. 65 ; vetoes Personal Liberty bill, ii. 77.
Garrison, William Lloyd, begins abolitionist movement, establishes Lib-

erator, i. 53; apostle of abolition, i. 55; did not advocate physical resistance by slaves, indicted by North Carolina, reward offered for arrest of by Georgia, i. 57; efforts of, at the North and in Boston, i. 58; mobbed in Boston, i. 61; influence of, i. 62, 63, 65, 496, ii. 435; favored a purely moral movement, i. 74; tributes to, by Lowell and Whittier, i. 75; protests against Fugitive Slave law, i. 212; work of, did not favor political action, i. 291; remark of, to negroes, i. 323; early efforts of, i. 327; judged as infidel, i. 331; burns the Constitution, ii. 56, 57; a United States marshal on, ii. 75; on Seward, ii. 434; influence of.

Gaulden, speech of, on slavery, ii. 481.

Geary, J. W., succeeds Shannon, ii. 217, 229; despatch of, on Kansas, ii. 230; Buchanan on, ii. 237; Pierce on, ii. 238; resignation of, ii. 239.

Gênet, Kossuth compared to, i. 235.

George III. favors slavery, i. 8.

Georges, Mdlle., her impersonation of Marguerite de Bourgogne, ii. 12.

Georgia, convention in, declares they will abide by the Compromise, i. 196; contrasted with New York, i. 354; secession of, from Charleston Convention, ii. 452.

German colony, in Texas, Olmsted on, i. 358.

German deputation, Scott's reply to, i. 276.

German vote, increasing importance of, i. 273.

Germans opposed to Kansas-Nebraska act, i. 495.

Giddings, Joshua R., against slavery, failed to support Winthrop, i. 117; on Brown of Indiana, i. 118; thought cry of dissolution gasconade, i. 132; error of, respecting Webster, i. 149 *n.*; on Webster, i. 154, 158; against Texas Boundary bill, i. 189; why opposed to Clay compromise, i. 193; forms partnership with Wade, i. 228; sustains Hale, i. 264; Parker writes to, i. 289; appeal of Independent Democrats framed by, i. 441; amendment of, in convention of 1860, ii. 463; conciliation of, ii. 464.

Gilmer, of North Carolina, in contest for speaker, ii. 421.

Gladstone on the Constitution, i. 16.

Gladstone, T. H., Olmsted on, ii 199 *n.*

Glenn, speech of, in Charleston Convention, ii. 451.

Godwin, Parke, honors Kossuth, i. 236.

Gold discovered in California, i. 111.

Gorsuch, pursues two fugitive slaves, i. 222; is shot, i. 223; letter of son of, i. 224 *n.*

Gottschalk in New Orleans, i. 401.

Graham, W., made Secretary of the Navy, i. 179.

Great Britain and the Texas question, i. 81, 87; Pierce on, i. 422; in Cuban question, ii. 25.

Greeley, Horace, editorial of, i. 108. on Clay and Webster, i. 173; sustains Scott, i. 264; at celebration of Lundy's Lane, i. 270; views of, on slavery, i. 271; denounces Kansas-Nebraska bill, i. 463; on Clay, i. 464 *n.*; on Pierce and Douglas, i. 495; resolutions of anti-Nebraska convention reported by, ii. 63; on Seward, ii. 68; opinions of, ii. 71; ambition of, ii. 72; Seward on, ii. 72 *n.*; on Chase, ii. 92 *n.*; on Knownothingism, ii. 111; on election of Banks, ii. 116; assaulted by Rust, on American party, ii. 118; on Raymond, ii. 118 *n.*; on Kansas, ii. 126; on Douglas, ii. 129, 338 *n.*; on Seward and Collamer, ii. 130; on Bailey and Chase, ii. 175; supports Frémont, ii. 177; letter of, to Pike, on McLean, ii. 180; on Banks, ii. 224; letter of, in campaign of 1856, ii. 231; on campaign of 1856, ii. 232; letter of, dissolving firm of Seward, Weed & Greeley, ii. 305, 472 *n.*; favors return of Douglas to Senate, ii. 306; on contest in House, ii. 425; on Lincoln's speech at Cooper Institute, ii. 431; Bates supported by, ii. 459; in convention of 1860, ii. 465; on convention of 1860, ii. 467, 468, 470, 471; Defrees on, ii. 471 *n.*; as a stump-speaker, ii. 484 *n.*; defeat of Seward caused by, ii. 494; on New York in campaign of 1860, ii. 497 *n.*

Green, Duff, organizes Southern Literary Company, i. 351.

INDEX 519

Green, of Missouri, against Douglas, ii. 287; in debate on Kansas, ii. 293; affray between Cameron and, ii. 298; favors English bill, ii. 299.
Greytown. *See* San Juan.
Grier, Justice, tries Hanaway, i. 224; in Supreme Court, ii. 250 in Dred Scott case, ii. 255; on Missouri Compromise, ii. 257.
Grimes, James W., on slavery, elected governor of Iowa, letters of Chase to, ii. 59; on House of Representatives, ii. 424; on Lincoln, ii. 473 *n.*; on Sumner, ii. 477.
Grimke, Sarah, rebuked for slave-instruction, i. 330 *n.*
Grow, of Pennsylvania, attacked by Keitt, ii. 297; "Impending Crisis" endorsed by, ii. 419; challenged by Branch, arrest of, ii. 424.
Guadalupe Hidalgo, treaty of, ii. 7.
Guthrie, James, in Pierce's cabinet, i. 388.
Gwin, W. M., elected senator, i. 116; contest of, with Broderick, ii. 375, 376; Broderick on, ii. 377.

HALE, John P., hears Seward, i. 166; votes on Texas boundary, i. 181; for California bill, i. 182; on Wilmot proviso, i. 193; on Kossuth, i. 242; nominated by Free-soilers, supported by Wilson, Adams, and Giddings, i. 264; on Sumner, i. 268; votes for Sumner's amendment, i. 269; denounces Kansas-Nebraska bill, i. 465; on Pierce, ii. 121, 122; Greeley on, ii. 130; speech of, published, ii. 131; on Toombs bill, ii. 191; in campaign of 1856, ii. 223; in Senate, ii. 282; against Lecompton bill, ii. 297; Seward rebuked by, ii. 303, 304; discussion of amendment of, ii. 355, 356; accused of assisting John Brown, ii. 402.
Hall, Basil, on abolition, i. 356.
Hall, N., made Postmaster-General, i. 179.
Halstead, on Seward, ii. 465.
Ham argument, in defence of slavery, i. 372.
Hamilton, Alexander, on negro soldiers, i. 14; Webster's eulogy of, i. 161; article in the *Federalist* quoted, ii. 442, 443.
Hamilton, raid and massacre of, ii. 389.

Hamlin, Hannibal, letter from, i. 134; relations of, with President Taylor, i. 175; elected governor of Maine, ii. 226; in Senate, ii. 282; nomination of, ii. 471; elected Vice-President, ii. 500.
Hammond, senator of South Carolina, on panic of 1857, i. 313; on state of society at South, i. 347; in "Pro-slavery Argument," i. 367; on Lecompton Constitution, ii. 292; on the South, ii. 347; on slave-trade, ii. 367, 368; reply of Broderick to, ii. 375; on House of Representatives, ii. 424; on convention at Charleston, ii. 440; on Lincoln's election, ii. 490.
Hampton, Wade, entertains Theodore Parker and Dr. Howe, ii. 390.
Hanaway, C., Gorsuch warned by, i. 223; acquittal of, i. 224.
Hanks, John, in Illinois convention of 1860, ii. 458.
Hapsburg, House of, Webster on, i. 206; New York journal accused of favoring, i. 235.
"Hards," Democrats called, i. 389; in New York, i. 481.
Harlan, elected senator from Iowa, ii. 59; in Senate, ii. 130, 283; speech of, published, ii. 131.
Harney, General, sent to Kansas, ii. 272.
Harper, Chancellor, on slave-labor, i. 308; Pro-slavery argument of, i. 314 *n.*; on slave instruction, i. 329; on negro women, i. 333; on slavery, i. 341, 347 *n.*; in "Pro-slavery Argument," i. 367.
Harper's Ferry. *See* John Brown.
Harrison, General, political success of, i. 259; Scott compared with, i. 269; speeches of, i. 275.
Harrison campaign compared with campaign of 1856, ii. 225.
Harvard Library, acknowledgment to, i. 208 *n.*
Harvey, Sumner on, ii. 215.
Haskin, of New York, attempt to bribe, ii. 300; excitement over, in House, ii. 424.
Haven, F., letter of, to Boston *Transcript*, i. 215 *n.*
Hawthorne, at Salem, i. 103; quoted, i. 104 *n.*; his biography of Pierce, i. 250, 251; on Scott, i. 274; his intimacy with Pierce, i. 277; on J.

Y. Mason, i. 395; appointed consul at Liverpool, letter of Sumner to, character of, i. 396; dedicates to Pierce "Our Old Home," i. 396, 397; letter of on Pierce, his "Scarlet Letter," i. 397; his "Marble Faun," i. 398; Motley on, i. 398, 399; on office-seekers, i. 399.
Hayne, Webster's reply to, i. 140.
Head, F. H., on nomination of Lincoln, ii. 472 n.
Helper, "The Impending Crisis" of, ii. 418, 420, 421, 426, 428; abused in Congress, ii. 422.
Henry, Patrick, on overseers, i. 307.
Herndon, remark of Seward to, ii. 307; Life of Lincoln reviewed by the *Nation*, ii. 309 n.; remarks of, to Lincoln, ii. 315, 316.
Hickman, John, in campaign of 1856, ii. 228; in campaign of 1860, ii. 484 n.
Higginson, Thomas W., protests against Fugitive Slave law, i. 212; attempt of, to rescue Burns, i. 503; befriends John Brown, ii. 385, 390; unmolested after John Brown raid, ii. 401.
Higher-law doctrine, proclaimed by Seward in 1850, i. 163; in Oberlin-Wellington rescue, ii. 364.
Hildreth, Richard, novel of, i. 326 n.
Hillard, George S., on Everett, i. 292, 293; position of, on Fugitive Slave law, ii. 76; supports Fillmore, ii. 206.
Holmes, Oliver Wendell, on assault of Brooks, ii. 147; on the Republican party, ii. 485.
Holt, Chief-Justice, decision on slavery, i. 9.
Homestead bill, urged by Seward, ii. 352; failure of, ii. 360.
Hooper, S., in convention of 1860, ii. 469 n.
House of Representatives, the, criticises Crawford, Meredith, and Johnson, i. 204; benches introduced into, ii. 423.
House-divided-against-itself speech, the, of Lincoln, ii. 339, 374.
Houston, General, plots with Jackson, i.76; for California bill, i. 182; remark of, to Kossuth, i. 239; circulates speech of Seward, i. 453; against repeal of Missouri Compromise, i. 475.

Howard, Cordelia, her impersonation of Eva, i. 282, 283.
Howard, Mrs., acting of, i. 282.
Howard, William A., in committee on Kansas affairs, ii. 127; on Kansas, ii. 196; and Sherman, Oliver on, ii. 197; English bill opposed by, ii. 299; in campaign of 1860, ii. 484 n.
Howden, Lord, in Soulé's difficulty, ii. 13.
Howe, Dr. S. G., John Brown assisted by, ii. 385, 389; reluctance of, to assist Brown, ii. 390; goes to Canada, ii. 401.
Howell, C. N., on Cuban expedition, i. 220 n.
Hughes, Bishop, interference of, in public schools, ii. 51.
Hugo, Victor, on John Brown, ii. 414.
Hülsemann, correspondence of Webster and, i. 205; letter of, i. 221, 233; demands satisfaction for defence of Koszta, i. 417; reply of Marcy to, i. 417, 418.
Hungarian Revolution of 1848, Koszta in, i. 417.
Hungary, revolt of, i. 205, 238 n.; cause of, i. 231, 240, 241; flag of, displayed in New York, i. 232; views of Americans concerning, i. 233; Kossuth on, i. 234; sympathy in Plymouth Church for, i. 236; Webster on, Kossuth on salt mines of, i. 241.
"Hunkers," Democrats called, i. 389.
Hunt, appeal of, to Richardson, i.485.
Hunter, of Virginia, in Southern triumvirate, ii. 294; favors English bill, ii. 299.
Huszar, the, captivity of Koszta on, threatened by the *Saint Louis*, i. 417.
Hyer, Tom, at convention of 1860, ii. 468.

IMMIGRATION to California, from foreign countries, i. 114, ii. 90 n.
Indian chief, remark of, to Kossuth, i. 231.
Indians in Nebraska, i. 425, 426 n.; incursions of, in Mexico, ii. 7.
Indians, Mosquito, i. 200.
Indigo-culture under slavery, i. 5.
Ingraham, Captain, demands release of Koszta, i. 417; upheld by Mar-

INDEX 521

cy, i. 418; Congress confers medal on, i. 419.
Insurrection, servile, fears of, i. 376, 377.
Intervention, American, New York *Tribune* favors, i. 234; New York Democrats in favor of, i. 236; discussed in Senate, i. 237; Webster on, i. 238; House of Representatives on, i. 241; Kossuth fails to secure, i. 240, 242.
Irish vote, increasing importance of, i. 273.
Irishmen, Scott on, i. 273.
Iron-trade, the, depression of, ii. 478; in Pennsylvania, ii. 479 n.; Kelley on, ii. 480 n.
Irrepressible-conflict speech, the, of Seward, ii. 344–346, 402, 411, 460.
Irving, Washington, supports Frémont, ii. 211, 212; death of, ii. 411.
Isabella, Queen of Spain, in 1854, ii. 37.
Italian soldier, anecdote of, i. 408.
Italy, slavery in, Mommsen on, i. 382, 383.

JACKSON, Andrew, and Calhoun, i. 48; on a ship-canal from the Atlantic to the Pacific, i. 199; supported by Buchanan, i. 246; invents spoils system, i. 400; diplomatic costume modified by, ii. 2; Duane removed by, confidence of, in Taney, ii. 250; disliked by Marshall, ii. 250, 251; Taney appointed Chief Justice by, ii. 251; referred to by Douglas, ii. 282; decay of his party, ii. 451.
Jackson, Mich., Republican convention at, ii. 48.
Jackson, "Stonewall," cause sustained by poor whites, i. 347.
Japan, treaty with, ii. 8.
Jay, Judge, on negro burnings, i. 326 n.
Jay treaty, debate on, i. 33.
Jefferson, Thomas, on slavery, i. 10–13; ordinance of, i. 15; estate of, i. 316; on negro temperament, i. 322; position of, on slavery, i. 343, 379; South rejects philosophy of, i. 348; criticised by Hammond, i. 367; Adams, Henry, on, i. 380 n.; founder of Democratic party, i. 453; influence of, on political parties, ii. 117; decay of party of, ii. 451; policy of, ii. 502.

Jefferson's Manual consulted by Pierce, ii. 121.
Jennings, negro arrested by, ii. 362.
Jerry, befriended by Gerrit Smith, i. 224; rescued, i. 225.
Jewett, Captain, letter of Webster to, i. 297 n.
John, rescue of negro, ii. 362, 366.
Johnson, Andrew, contrasted with Fillmore, i. 302; attacks Corwin, i. 298 n.
Johnson, Herschel V., nomination of, ii. 475.
Johnson, Reverdy, connected with Galphin claim, i. 203; Seward on, i. 203 n.; charges against, i. 204; plea of, in Dred Scott case, ii. 255; Taney influenced by, ii. 269, 270.
Johnston, of Pennsylvania, nominated by North Americans, ii. 186 n.
Johnston, R. H., remarks of Stephens to, ii. 453.
Jones, Sheriff, Branson arrested by, ii. 104; message of, to Shannon, ii. 105; injuries of, ii. 155, 156; in raid on Lawrence, ii. 158, 159.
Judd, in convention of 1860, ii. 469 n.
Julian, did not vote for Brown, i. 118 n.; against Texas and New Mexico bills, i. 182; candidate for Vice-President, i. 264; on Know-nothings, ii. 56.

KANSAS, Atchison on, i. 440, ii. 100; effort to make a free State, i. 496; Emigrant-Aid Company in, ii. 78, 79; mob-law in, ii. 81, 82; Reeder on, ii. 83; interest in, at South, ii. 84, 85; Pierce on, ii. 85, 121, 238; contest over, ii. 87; Seward on, ii. 99; Clayton on, ii. 100; convention at Topeka, ii. 103; request of, for admission, ii. 107; Raymond on, ii. 119; Hale on, ii. 122; message of Pierce on, ii. 122, 123; proclamation of Pierce on, ii. 124; Collamer on, ii. 125; Douglas on, ii. 125, 285; House committee on, ii. 127, 196; Sumner on, ii. 132; preparations at South for war in, ii. 150; Northern press on, ii. 152; Bryant on, ii. 153; Mrs. Robinson on, ii. 154; struggle in, ii. 166, 167; McLean on, ii. 179; Republican convention of 1856 on, ii. 184; bill of Toombs on, ii. 189–196; protest against employment of troops in, ii. 201; G. W. Curtis

on, ii. 213; guerrilla warfare in, ii. 216, 217; story of, told by Prof. Spring, ii. 218; efforts to relieve, ii. 219, 220; Geary on, ii. 230; Buchanan on, ii. 170, 174, 237, 275, 276, 344; fraudulent returns in, ii. 278; Walker on, ii. 288; message of Buchanan on, ii. 291, 292; debate on admission of, ii. 293; Stephens on, ii. 298; English bill rejected by, ii. 301; convention of 1860 on, ii. 464.
"Kansas Crusade," quoted, ii. 160 n.
Kansas-Nebraska act, the, i. 425; Atchison on, Davis on, Butler on, i. 431 ns.; Douglas on, i. 431 n., ii. 318; Northern press on, i. 432; Dixon offers amendment to, i. 434; Sumner offers amendment to, i. 433, 434; Douglas accepts Dixon's amendment to, i. 434; Douglas consults Davis on, i. 437; introduced, i. 439; Dixon on, i. 441; Appeal of Independent Democrats on, i. 443; Northern press on, i. 444, 463; speech of Chase against, i. 449–452; speech of Wade against, i. 452; speech of Seward against, i. 453, 454; speech of Sumner against, i. 454, 455; speech of Everett against, i. 455-458; Cass on, i. 458, 459; Chase on, i. 460; urged by Douglas, i. 461, 462; denounced by Beecher and Hale, i. 465; resolutions requesting the President to veto, i. 465, 466; protests against, i. 467, 468; advocated at South, i. 469, 470; Douglas closes debate on, i. 470–475; clergy against, i. 477–480; Richardson urges, i. 480, 483, 484; supported by Pierce's cabinet, i. 482, 483; excitement over, in House, i. 485, 486; protest against, in New York City, i. 487; number of speeches on, i. 487, 488; Benton against, i. 489; consequences of, i. 490, 491; Southern opinions of, i. 496, 497; Emerson on, i. 498; Fugitive Slave law stifled by, i. 500; effect of, on Cuban question, ii. 33; Democratic party weakened by, ii. 44; formation of party opposed to, ii. 47; position of Republicans on, ii. 48; effect of, on Iowa elections, ii. 59; Lincoln on, ii. 62, 334, 335; Collamer on, ii. 125; interpretation of, in Kansas, ii. 157; referred to Supreme Court, ii. 250; influence of, ii. 266.
Kant, his enjoyment of "Nouvelle Héloïse," i. 282.
Kasson, J. A., in convention of 1860, ii. 469 n.
Keitt, Simonton threatened by, ii. 144; Grow attacked by, ii. 297, 298; on disunion, ii. 420.
Kelley, W. D., on the iron-trade, ii. 480 n.
Kellogg, of Illinois, quarrel of, with Logan, ii. 423; defends Lovejoy, ii. 438.
Kemble, Fanny, journal of, i. 305; G. W. Curtis on, i. 305 n.; quoted, i. 307 n.; on slave-labor, i. 308; extract from journal of, i. 310; on negro women, i. 311; on preaching to negroes, i. 331; on social evil at South, i. 336; on "Uncle Tom's Cabin," i. 363; on negro insurrection, i. 376.
Kentucky, secession of, from Baltimore convention, ii. 474.
Kettell, T. P., on condition of South, i. 213 n.
"Key to Uncle Tom's Cabin," i. 319, ns.
Keystone State, name for Pennsylvania, ii. 173.
Kickapoo Rangers, in Kansas, ii. 107.
King, J. A., on Seward, ii. 176 n.
King, Preston, in Senate, ii. 283; in convention of 1860, ii. 469 n.
King, Rufus, on Everett, i. 291; Seward on, ii. 147.
King, T. B., sent to California, i. 110.
King, William R., in committee on Clay resolutions, i. 172; on British Honduras, i. 201; nominated for Vice-President, i. 249.
Know-nothings, principles of, ii. 50–52; methods of, ii. 53, 54; on Roman Catholicism, ii. 54; popularity of, ii. 55; denounced by Wise, ii. 56, 88; position of, on slavery, ii. 56; attacked by Irishmen, ii. 57, 58; influence of, in Pennsylvania election, ii. 60; denounced by Douglas, ii. 61; grand council of, in New York, ii. 63, 64; strength of, ii. 64; Gardner elected by, ii. 65, 66; combated by Beecher, ii. 73; Union degree adopted by, ii. 87; division of, on slavery, ii. 89, 90; secrets of, exposed, ii. 91; con-

demned by New York Republican State convention, ii, 93; Greeley on, ii. 111; Fillmore nominated by, ii. 119; condemned by Democratic platform, ii. 171.

Kosciusko, Lopez and Crittenden compared to, i. 394.

Kossuth, Louis, leadership of, i. 205; flight of, rescue of, arrives at Statten Island, i. 231; ovation to, speech of, i. 232, on Hungarian revolution, New York press on, i. 234; compared with Washington, receives delegations, honored by Bancroft and Bryant, i. 235; toasted by Bancroft, Godwin, Beecher, and Dana, i. 236; Ampère on reception of, i. 236 n.; Foote, Cass, Sumner, and Seward on, i. 237; Webster on, received at Philadelphia, Baltimore, and Washington, met by Seward and Shields, presented to Fillmore, i. 238; Ampère on, i. 238 n.; reception of, in Senate, meets General Houston, speech of Webster at banquet to, i. 239; received in House, at the West, decline of interest in, i. 240; vote on amendment to resolution of welcome to, i. 240, 241; complaint of, at Pittsburgh, reason of interest in, i. 241; Mann on opposition to, at variance with non-intervention doctrine, expenses of suite of, i. 242; abstemious habits of, i. 243.

Koszta, Martin, protected by United States Government, i. 416, 417; defended by Ingraham, i. 417; defended by Marcy, i. 418; release of, i. 419.

Lafayette, reception to, i, 233, 263; Kossuth compared to, i. 235; reception by Senate, i. 239; Lopez and Crittenden compared to, i. 394; sword of, taken by John Brown, ii. 394.

Lamar, of Mississippi, on John Brown, ii. 421.

Lane, Henry S., against Seward, ii. 466; in campaign of 1860, ii. 484 n., ii. 498.

Lane, James H., indictment of, ii. 156; represents free-State cause, ii. 216, 219; leaves Kansas, ii. 237; in Kansas troubles, ii. 274.

Lane, Joseph, nomination of, ii. 475; campaign of, ii. 478.

Langston, Charles, speeches of, ii. 365, 366; imprisonment of, ii. 365, 367.

Law-and-order party, in Kansas, ii. 103.

Lawrence, Kansas, plan to attack, ii. 103–106, 156, 157; sacking of, ii. 158, 159.

Lawrence, Amos A., on mob in Kansas, ii. 82; letter of Robinson to, ii. 105; on Lincoln, ii. 473 n.

Lecompte, Judge, charge of, to grand jury, ii. 156; reported removal of, ii. 238.

Lecompton, convention at, ii. 278, 279.

Lecompton constitution, the, Douglas on, ii. 283, 284, 286–288, 318; recommended by Buchanan, ii. 291, 349; Elmore and Denver against, ii. 292; debate on, ii. 293; rejected by Kansas, ii. 301; speech of Seward on, ii. 305; Chase on, ii. 307; Broderick and, ii. 375; Republican convention of 1860 on, ii. 464.

Lee, of Massachusetts, refuses to vote for Webster, i. 258.

Lee, Robert E., refuses command of Cuban expedition, i. 217; and poor whites, i. 347; captures John Brown, ii. 396.

Letcher, letter of, to Crittenden, ii. 233 n.

Liberator, the, established by Garrison, i. 53; motto of, i, 55; Nat Turner insurrection not influenced by, stringent laws against circulation of at South, demand for suppression of i, 57; influence of, i. 62; criticises opposing faction of abolitionists, i. 74; Garrison in, i. 327.

Liberals, English, commend Hülseman letter, i. 206.

Liberia, negro colony at, i. 382.

Liberty, desire of negroes for, i. 377.

Lieber, Francis, on slavery, i. 94 n.; letter of, to Hillard, i. 350 n.; on Southern people, i. 359 n.; on Sumner, ii. 142 n.; on election of Buchanan, ii. 242; on John Brown, ii. 409; letter of Hammond to, ii. 424, 440; denounced at the South, ii. 486; letter of, to Oscar Lieber, ii. 489.

Lieber, Oscar, death of, ii. 489 n.

Lincoln, Abraham, i. 1; on the Mexican war, i. 92; on Seward, i. 101;

applies for office under Taylor, i. 103; visits Clay, i. 121 n.; watchword of, i. 161; reference to slave-dealers, i. 325 n.; mental discipline of, i. 492; on anti-Nebraska elections, ii. 61; reply of, to Douglas, at Springfield, ii. 62; speech of, at Peoria, Douglas disturbed by, ii. 70; on popular sovereignty, ii. 80, 81, 381; letter of, to Washburne, ii. 182; votes for Vice-President, in convention of 1856, ii. 184; reply of, to Douglas, ii. 266-268; on Declaration of Independence, ii. 267, 334; supports charge against Supreme Court, ii. 268; on Dred Scott decision, ii. 270, 271; early life of, ii. 308; character of, ii. 309; on slavery, ii. 319, 326, 331, 332, 335-337, 381, 432; in Congress, ii. 310; defeated by Trumbull, ii. 311; encounters Stanton, religious opinions of, ii. 312; opening speech of, ii. 314-317; conversation of, with Herndon, ii. 315; on Douglas, ii. 316, 317; Douglas on, ii. 313, 314, 318, 340, 472, 477; reply of, to Douglas, ii. 319, 320; debates of, with Douglas, ii. 321-343, 354, 484; at Ottawa, ii. 324-326; on the negro, ii. 325; catechised by Douglas, ii. 326; Douglas catechised by, ii. 327; compared with Douglas, ii. 329, 330; compared to Webster, ii. 332, 333; at Galesburg, ii. 333; at Alton, ii. 334; assisted by Corwin, Chase, and Colfax, ii. 338; defeated by Douglas, remark of, to Sumner, ii. 339, 340; supported by New York press, ii. 341; Longfellow and Parker on, ii. 342; Jefferson Davis's opinion of, ii. 348; Ohio speeches of, ii. 382, 383; on John Brown, ii. 412; Cooper Institute address of, ii. 430-432, 436, 458; Greeley on, ii. 431; on disunion, ii. 432; criticised by abolitionists, ii. 435; supported by Bryant, in Illinois State convention, ii. 458; struggle between Seward and, ii. 459; compared with Seward, ii. 460; letter of Bryant to, ii. 461; followers of, ii. 462, 465; positions in cabinet of, ii. 466, 467; Swett on, ii. 467 n.; letter of, to Giddings, ii. 467 n.; enthusiasm for, ii. 468; balloting for, ii. 469, 470; joy over nomination of, ii. 471; Head on, ii. 472 n.; Phillips on, ii. 473; Lawrence on, Grimes on, ii. 473 n.; against slavery, ii. 481 n.; contest between Douglas and, ii. 482, 483; clergymen against, ii. 485 n.; South on, ii. 487; Hammond and Stephens on election of, ii. 490; Douglas on election of, ii. 491, 492, 494; Schurz on, ii. 493; letter of, in campaign of 1860, ii. 497; supported by Carl Schurz, ii. 498; and Fugitive Slave law, ii. 499; the popular vote for, ii. 500; Longfellow on election of, ii. 501, 502; Motley on election of, ii. 502.

Lines, C. B., company raised by, ii. 153.

"Little Giant," Douglas called, i. 245.

Lobos Islands, Webster in affair of, i. 297.

Logan, John A., acknowledgment to, i. 493 n.; success of, in Illinois, ii. 321; quarrel of, with Kellogg, ii. 423.

London, great plague of, i. 409, 413.

Longfellow, on "Uncle Tom's Cabin," i. 280; on Sumner, ii. 142 n.; supports Frémont, ii. 211, 212; on Lincoln, ii. 342; on John Brown, ii. 409, 410; on Lincoln's election, ii. 501.

Lopez, N., expedition to Cuba of, i. 216-220; becomes tool of speculators, i. 217; embarks for Cuba, i. 218; lands near Havana, garroted, i. 219; fate of followers of, i. 219, 220; Soulé on, i. 394.

Loring, Commissioner, and Burns, i. 504; unpopularity of, i. 505 n.

Louisiana, secession of, from Charleston convention, ii. 451.

Lovejoy, Elijah P., killed at Alton, i. 72, ii. 334.

Lovejoy, Owen, a typical abolitionist, ii. 321; anti-slavery speech of, ii. 437, 438, 439; Hammond on speech of, ii. 440; in campaign of 1860, ii. 484 n.

Lowell, Free-soil meeting at, i. 196.

Lowell, James Russell, on Garrison, i. 75; on the Mexican war, i. 87, 88; remark of, on slavery, i. 152; on Mrs. Stowe, i. 279; on "Uncle Tom's Cabin," i. 280; on Olmsted, i. 304 n.; on Cushing, i. 392; on Seward, ii.

472, 494; on the Republican party, ii. 486; on disunion, ii. 488.
Lucretius, plague described by, i. 405.
Lundy's Lane, celebration of battle of, i. 270.
Lyell, Sir Charles, quoted, i. 113 *n.*; on condition of slaves, i. 334; on illegitimacy, i. 339, 340; on slavery, i. 373; on Southern hospitality, i. 374; on emancipation, i. 382.

MACAULAY, on "Uncle Tom's Cabin," i. 279; his portrait of Jeffreys, ii. 238.
McClelland, R., in Pierce's cabinet, i. 388.
McClure, A. K., on the tariff, ii 480 *n.*
McDuffie on slavery, i. 68, 366, 367.
Mace, Dan, on Frémont, ii. 177, 178.
Mackay, Charles, on slave-owners, i. 325 *n.*; on negroes, i. 373, 377.
McLaughlin, A. C., paper of, on Cass, i. 244 *n.*
McLean, Judge, letters of, on Kansas, ii. 179; Greeley and Dana on, ii. 180; supported by Lincoln ii. 182; speech of Stevens on, ii. 183; votes received by, in convention of 1856, ii. 184; objections to, ii. 185; in Supreme Court, ii. 250; in Dred Scott decision, ii. 257; Lincoln in case tried before, ii. 312; had friends in convention of 1860, ii. 459.
Madison, James, on slavery, i. 21, 41, 60; on the Union, i. 52; slaves of, i. 316; on negro women, i. 336; on race question, i. 383; policy of ii. 502.
Maine, Republican success in, in 1854, ii. 59, 60.
Mallory, of Florida, on Cuban question, ii. 352.
Mangum, of North Carolina, in committee on Clay resolutions, i. 172.
Manifest destiny, doctrine of, i. 295, 395.
Mann, Horace, on Cobb, elected to Congress, votes for Winthrop, i. 118; on Wilmot proviso, i. 122; his faith in Webster, i. 149; on Webster, i. 154, 158; against Texas and New Mexico bills, i. 182; on House of Representatives, i. 184; on compromise measures, i. 189 *n.*, 193; on exclusion from Faneuil Hall, i. 211, 212; on Kossuth, i. 242; on Congress in 1852, i. 265; on Sumner, i. 268; on the human race, i. 371 *n.*

Mansfield, Lord, his decision on slavery, i. 9, 10.
Manumission of negroes, i. 378.
Marais des Cygnes, massacre of, ii. 389.
"Marble Faun, The," i. 397; Motley on, i. 398.
Marcy, William L., candidate in convention of 1852, i. 244; bias of, in Mexican war, i. 246, 247; Mt. Marcy named for, i. 247; fails to secure nomination, i. 247, 248; in Pierce's cabinet, i. 388, 389; chief of the "Softs," opposes Free-soil movement, character of, i. 389; reply of, to Hülsemann, i. 417, 418; popularity of, justifies Ingraham, on protection of exiles, i. 418; position of, sustained i. 418, 419; Von Holst on, i. 419 *n.*; influence of, in cabinet, i. 420; ambition of, i. 423; Buchanan on, i. 423, ii. 7; position of, on Kansas-Nebraska bill, i. 481, 483; reforms diplomatic costume, ii. 1, 2; concludes reciprocity treaty with Canada, ii. 8; in affair of *Black Warrior*, ii. 28; against Cuban expedition, ii. 31; confidence of North in, ii. 33, 188; position of, on Cuban question, ii. 34, 37; reply of, to Calderon, ii. 35; letter of, to Soulé, ii. 38; on Ostend manifesto, ii. 41; and Soulé, ii. 42; Jefferson Davis compared with, ii. 240, 245; on rotation in office, ii. 248.
Marshall, Chief Justice, supplements Webster, i. 137; ability of, ii. 249; Taney supported by, ii. 250, 251; death of, ii. 251.
Marshall, Humphrey, on slavery contest, ii. 117.
Marshals, U. S., and Fugitive Slave law, i. 185, 209 *n.*
Marshfield farmers at funeral of Webster, i. 288.
Martineau, Harriet, i. 44, 54; on cotton culture, i. 312; on slaves of Madison, i, 316; on state of society at South, i. 336, 338, 374; Simms on, i. 342, 367.
Maryland, secession of, from Baltimore convention, ii 474.
Mason, James M., Calhoun's speech read by, i. 127; in committee on Clay resolutions, i. 172; votes on

Texas boundary, i. 181; protests against admission of California, i. 182; on execution of Fugitive Slave law, i. 208, 209; on disunion, ii. 205; replies of John Brown to, ii. 397, 398, 406, 414.
Mason, John Y., appointed minister to France, Hawthorne on, contempt of for abolitionists, discourtesy of to Sumner, i. 395; uniform of, at French court, ii. 4; rebuked by Marcy, ii. 5; signs Ostend manifesto, ii. 38; influenced by Soulé, ii. 40; letter of Buchanan to, ii. 244.
Massachusetts, represented in cabinets of Pierce and Polk, i. 391; hatred of, at South, ii. 84.
May, Samuel J., i. 65; befriends Jerry, i. 224; on Fugitive Slave law, i. 225; on Underground Railroad, ii. 75.
Mephistopheles, Seward called, i. 262.
Meredith, Secretary, pays interest on Galphin claim, i. 203; Seward on, i. 203 *n*.; denies knowledge of Crawford's interest, charges against, i. 204.
Mesilla Valley ceded to United States, ii. 7.
Methodist Episcopal Church, Webster on, ii. 145.
Mexican War, i. 87–93; Webster on, i. 145; Marcy's attitude in, i. 246; Scott in, i. 259; Corwin on, i. 300; how regarded at South, i. 387; Jefferson Davis in, i. 390.
Mexico, protests against slavery in Texas, i. 93; mooted conquest of, i. 193; payment to, i. 213, 214; Gardiner claim against, i. 298; treaty with, ii. 7.
Michigan Republican convention, the, ii. 49.
Millson, John Sherman denounced by, ii. 420.
Minnesota, admission of, ii. 417.
Minute-men at the South, ii. 487.
Mississippi, Union party in, i. 388; Davis defeated in, i. 390; secession of, from Charleston convention, ii. 451.
Mississippi, the, Kossuth embarks on, i. 231.
Missouri Compromise, i. 36–39, 96; Webster on, i. 98; Clay on, i. 191; Nashville convention on, i. 196; Douglas on, i. 427, 436, 446–443; moral force of, i. 428, 429; set aside by Nebraska bill, i. 432; discussed by Dixon and Douglas, i. 433, 434; Douglas hesitates to override, i. 435; repeal of, i. 436 *n*., 466; ii. 67, 68, 73, 202, 311; appeal of Independent Democrats on, i. 442, 443; Seward on, i. 454; Chase on, i. 450, 451; Calhoun on, i. 468; Atchison on, i, 468, 469; Benton on, i. 489; Lincoln on, ii. 70; Sherman on, ii. 117; Buchanan on, ii. 170; Fillmore on, ii. 215; bearing of, on Dred Scott case, ii. 252; Taney on, ii. 257; Curtis on, ii. 260, 263; Benjamin on, ii. 293.
Missouri River, the, embargo on, ii. 166.
Missourians, mob of, in Kansas, ii. 81; in Wakarusa war, ii. 105, 106.
Mommsen, on the Civil War, i. 1; on slavery, i. 382, 383.
Monroe, in convention of 1860, ii. 469 *n*.
Monroe doctrine, the, position of Pierce on, i. 385.
Monterey, gold frenzy in, i. 111.
Montez, Lola, in New Orleans, i. 401.
Montgomery, amendment of, to Lecompton bill, ii. 299.
Montijo, Countess of, criticises Mme. Soulé, ii. 12.
"Morals of Slavery," Harriet Martineau's, i. 342.
Morehead, C. S., quoted, i. 136 *n*.
Morley, John, on Arthur Young, i. 304 *n*.
Mormons, difficulties with, ii. 303.
Morrill, of Maine, in campaign of 1860, ii. 484 *n*.
Morrill tariff bill, the, ii. 476, 478.
Morris, of Illinois, on uproar in House, ii. 421.
Mortality in 1853, i. 404, 413, 415.
Morton, O. P., in campaign of 1860, ii. 484 *n*.
Mosaic law, slavery authorized by, i. 370.
Motley, John Lothrop, letter of, on Webster, i. 288 *n*.; on "Marble Faun," i. 397, 398; his "Rise of the Dutch Republic," ii. 133; on Lincoln's election, ii. 502.
Mulattoes, proportion of, in slave States, i. 340, 341; proportion of, in United States, i. 339–341.

INDEX 527

Murat, Achille, on slavery, i. 373, 374.

NASBY, Petroleum V., on Lincoln, ii. 310.
Nashville convention, i. 173, 174; dissatisfied with compromise, claims right of secession, i. 196.
Natick Cobbler, the, name applied to Henry Wilson, ii. 96.
National Era, the, "Uncle Tom" published in, i. 279.
Nativism, Scott accused of, i. 272.
Naturalization, letter of Scott on, i. 273; position of Know-nothings on, ii. 52.
Nebraska, extent of, Douglas on, i. 426–428.
Negro, the, Agassiz on, i. 402.
Negro colonization, Fillmore on, i. 296.
Negroes, civil rights of, i. 365, 366; Emerson on, i. 372; desire of, for freedom, i. 377; transported to Liberia, i. 382; Madison on i. 383; in Cuba, ii. 29; in Kansas, ii. 100; excluded from Kansas, ii.107; Taney on, ii.255,256; free,ii.258 259; Lincoln on, ii. 267, 325 ; Douglas on, ii. 324; Davis on, ii. 357; value of slaves, ii. 368, 369 ; liberated by Brown, ii. 389, 390; conduct of, in John Brown's raid, ii. 401; sale of, ii. 441.
Nelson, Justice, in Supreme Court, ii. 250; in Dred Scott case, ii. 253, 254, 257.
Neutrality, American, i. 231; Pierce enforces, ii. 31.
New England compared with South, i. 349.
New Grenada concludes treaty with Polk, i. 199.
New Mexico, in 1848, i. 92; slavery in, i. 93, 94; Clay on, i. 124; appeals to United States for protection, i. 125; Webster on, i. 149; former area of, i. 150 *n.*; declares against slavery, i. 151, 180; Clay on, John Bell on constitution of, i. 180; Taylor on, i. 190; Ranney on,ii. 382; legislature of, establishes slavery, ii. 382; Douglas on, ii. 383.
New Mexico bill, language of, applied in Nebraska bill, i. 428.
New Orleans, meeting at, i. 196; excited over Cuban expedition, i. 220; rioting in, i. 221; indemnification of Spanish subjects at, i. 222; Ampère on, i. 360 *n.*; yellow fever in, i. 400, 402–413; actors and musicians in, in 1853, i. 401; Howard Association in, i. 403, 404, 407, 412, 413; mortality in 1853 of,i.404,413; press of, on yellow fever, i. 408; soil of, i. 409, 410.
New York City, meeting at, declares for the Fugitive Slave law, i. 195; citizens of, defray expenses of slave-owners, i. 209; spoils system in, i. 399; summer-heat of 1853 in, i. 415.
New York State, contrasted with Georgia, i. 354; position of, in 1860, ii. 474, 497 *n.*; efforts of fusionists in, ii. 499.
Niagara Falls, celebration of battle of Lundy's Lane at, i. 270.
Nicaragua, proposed route through, i. 199; England captures San Juan from, pledges not to molest, i. 200; Walker in, ii. 242, 289.
Nicaragua Transit Company, settlement of, ii. 9.
Nicholson letter of Cass, i. 244.
Noah, curse of, quoted by Southern writers, i. 371, 372.
North, prosperity of, i. 193.
North American Review, edited by Everett, i. 292.
North Americans, the convention of, ii. 186.
North Carolina, secession of, from the Baltimore convention, ii. 474.
North Carolina, the, salutes Kossuth, i. 232.
Northern society compared with Southern, i. 360.
Northwest, the, growth of, i. 193, 194.
"Notes on Uncle Tom's Cabin," Stearns's, i. 315 *n.*
"Nouvelle Héloïse, La," "Uncle Tom's Cabin" compared with, i. 282, 284; effect of, on revolutionists, i. 285.
Nullification, i. 40–45; ii. 74.

OBERLIN COLLEGE, character of, ii. 361, 362.
Oberlin-Wellington rescue, the, ii. 362–367.
Office-seekers, Hawthorne on, i. 399.
Ohio, the, salutes Kossuth, i. 232.
Oglethorpe on slavery, i. 5.
Olds attacks Corwin, i. 298 *n.*

Oliphant, Laurence, on city of Washington, ii. 9 n.
Oliver, Mordecai, in committee on Kansas affairs, ii. 127; investigates Pottawatomie massacre, ii. 164; report of, ii. 197, 198.
Oliver Twist, negroes compared to, i. 305.
Olmsted, Frederick Law, on slave labor, works of, i. 303 n.; Lowell on, G. W. Curtis on, i. 304 n.; on condition of slaves, i. 305, 306, 318; on overseers, i. 308; reply of overseer to, i. 309; on cotton culture, i. 312; on slave labor, i. 314; on slave-breeding, i. 317; on slave-whipping, i. 325 n.; on slaves in Virginia, i. 327; on slave instruction, i. 330; on social evil at South, i. 337; on effect of slavery on the young, i. 343; on poor whites, i. 344; on slave-holders, i. 349; on German colony of Texas, i. 358; on "Uncle Tom's Cabin," i. 363; remark of slave-holder to, i. 369; on Charleston, i. 377; on Underground Railroad, ii. 74; on Preston Brooks, ii. 143 n.
Onesimus, Southern writers on, i. 370.
Ordinance of 1787, i. 15, 16, 31.
Oregon, admission of, ii. 417; constitution of, ii. 418.
Oregon question, the, i. 86, 95, 96.
Orr, James L., confession of Brooks to, ii. 150; in debate on Lecompton message, ii. 297; on election of Lincoln, ii. 490.
Orsini, John Brown compared to, ii. 414.
Osawatomie, sacking of, ii. 167.
Ostend Manifesto, the, substance of, ii. 38–40; Marcy on, ii. 41; antislavery and European opinions of, ii. 43; Democratic party weakened by, ii. 44; Republican convention of 1856 on, ii. 185; used against Buchanan, ii. 221; reasserted, ii. 351.
Overseers, Patrick Henry on, i. 307; brutality of, i. 308.

PACIFIC RAILROAD, the, i. 422; ii. 359.
Paine, Thomas, Lincoln influenced by, ii. 312.
Palmerston, Lord, on Webster, i. 222; on "Uncle Tom," i. 282; on abolition in Cuba, i. 394; correspondence of, ii. 120, 121; on Dallas, ii. 188.
Pampero, the, Lopez embarks in, i. 218; runs aground in Cuba, i. 219.
Panama Canal, the, Clay on, i. 199; Great Britain and, i. 200, 201.
Panic of 1857, ii. 281.
Parker, Theodore, quoted, i. 132 n.; on Webster, i. 155, 156, 158; on Fugitive Slave law, i. 197, 208; book owned by, i. 208; extract from journal of, i. 210; address of, on Sims, i. 211; doggerel from scrap-book of, i. 271 n.; sermon of, on Webster, i. 288; writes to Sumner and Giddings, character of, extract from diary of, i. 289; Curtis and Frothingham on sermon of, i. 289 n.; Emerson on, extract from diary of. held Webster responsible for Fugitive Slave law, effect of his sermon on Webster, i. 290; letter of, to Sumner, i. 291 n.; against repeal of Missouri Compromise, i. 466; influence of, in anti-slavery cause, i. 496; interview of, with Anthony Burns, i. 501; on arrest of Burns, i. 502; connection of, with Underground Railroad, ii. 75; letters of Sumner to, ii. 132, 297; on Seward and Chase, ii. 175; on Frémont, ii. 182; Lincoln influenced by, ii. 312; accused of being an infidel, i. 331; on Lincoln, ii. 342; Brown assisted by, ii. 385, 388, 389; journey of, to Cuba, ii. 390.
Parley, Peter, criticism of his writings at the South, i. 352.
Pate captured by John Brown, ii. 166.
"Pathfinder, The Brave," Frémont, ii. 225.
Patronage, Pierce's use of, i. 420.
Patti, Adelina, in New Orleans, i. 401.
Paul, St., quoted by Southern writers, i. 370.
Paulding, Walker arrested by, ii. 289.
Payne, Henry B., speech of, in Charleston convention, ii. 446, 447.
Peck, Professor, in Oberlin-Wellington rescue, ii. 365, 366.
Pennington, of New Jersey, Greeley on, ii. 112; elected speaker, ii. 426.
Pennsylvania abolition society, i. 22.
Perkins, partnership of, with John Brown, ii. 161 n.

Perkins, Warren & Co. not abolition merchants, i. 195 *n.*
Perrin, Raymond S., his "Religion of Philosophy" quoted, i. 370 *n.*; acknowledgment to, i. 383 *n.*
Perry, Commodore, treaty of, with Japan, ii. 8 *n.*
Perry, H. J., aids in settling *Black Warrior* affair, ii. 42 *n.*
Personal Liberty laws, ii. 73, 74, 76, 77.
Phelps, of Vermont, in committee on Clay resolutions, i. 171.
Philadelphia, meeting at, on Fugitive Slave law, i. 195.
Phillips, Wendell, becomes an abolitionist, i. 72; never voted, i. 74; on Fugitive Slave law, i. 197; address of, on arrest of Sims, i. 211; an exponent of abolitionism, i. 290; influence of, i. 496; on arrest of Burns, i. 502; on Kansas, ii. 167; on the Union-savers, ii. 428; on Seward, ii. 434, 495 *n.*; influence of, ii. 435; on Lincoln, ii. 473.
Pickens, F. W., on agriculture, i. 360 *n.*
Pierce, Edward L., his memoir of Sumner, i. 228 *n.*; in convention of 1860, ii. 469 *n.*
Pierce, Franklin, his address at Concord, i. 195; Clayton - Bulwer treaty, in administration of, i. 202; nomination of, i. 248; early life of, elected senator, i. 249; declines appointments, serves in Mexican war, supports compromise measures, Hawthorne's biography of, i. 250; character of, Democrats surprised by nomination of, i. 251; accepts nomination, i. 252; Van Buren declares for, i. 264; Chase refuses to support, i. 264; slanders against, i. 271; doggerel contrasting Scott and, i. 271 *n.*; charges against, inclined to side with South, i. 272; Scott's defence of, i. 274; his intimacy with Hawthorne, his tribute to Webster, his election, i. 277; inaugural of, affliction of, i. 384; criticised by Whig journals, i. 384, 385; on Cuba, on patronage, position of, on Fugitive Slave law, i. 385; popularity of, position of on slavery, i. 386; letter of Buchanan to, offers secretaryship to Dix, i. 387; appoints Davis Secretary of War,

cabinet of, i. 388; offers position to Marcy, i. 389; friendship of, with Davis, i. 390, 422; Cushing influences nomination of, i. 391; letter of Buchanan to, appoints Buchanan minister to England, i. 393; Benton on, i. 393 *n.*; desires Cuba, i. 394; Hawthorne dedicates a work to, i. 396, 397; letter of Hawthorne on, i. 397; distribution of offices by, i. 399; opens exhibition in Crystal Palace, i. 415; unpopularity of, i. 419, 420, 423; lack of firmness of, accused of Free-soilism, i. 420; Cushing on, i. 420, 421; regarded as an abolitionist, connection of with John Van Buren, i. 421; on relations with Great Britain, on reduction of tariff, on Pacific Railroad, i. 422; vanity of, i. 423; Douglas on election of, i. 430; on report of Douglas, i. 436; influenced by Davis, receives Douglas, i. 437; promises support to Douglas, confidence of in Davis, i. 438; position of his cabinet on Kansas-Nebraska bill, i. 482, 483; influenced by Davis, Cushing, and Marcy, Dix on, i. 482; criticised by London *Examiner*, ii. 6; message of, on affair of *Black Warrior*, ii. 17, 18; inaction of, in case of Soulé, ii. 24; indecision of, in Cuban question, ii. 30; warning of, to filibusters, ii. 31; criticised by Calderon, ii. 35; connection of, with Ostend manifesto, ii. 44; and Reeder, ii. 80; interviews of, with Reeder, influenced by Davis, ii. 85; desires resignation of Reeder, ii. 86; encourages Aiken, ii. 114; criticised by Hale, ii. 121, 122; message of, on Kansas, ii. 122, 123; telegram of, to Shannon, ii. 160; his view of Topeka legislature, ii. 168; political strength of, ii. 169, 170; votes received by, in Cincinnati convention, ii. 171, 172; instructed by riders, ii. 201; Buchanan on policy of, ii. 229 *n.*; on Geary, ii. 238; devotion of, to South, ii. 240, 241; Lincoln on, ii. 270 *n.*; Buchanan compared to, ii. 292; policy of, ii. 481; Schurz on, ii. 493.
Pike, James S., letter of Chase to, ii.

II.—34

530 INDEX

92 n. ; on Frémont, ii. 178, 179 ; rebuked by Greeley and Dana, ii. 180 ; on Supreme Court, ii. 255, 262 ; on Reverdy Johnson, ii. 269 n. ; letter of Wade to, ii. 302 ; letter of Dana to, ii. 459 n.; on Seward, ii. 461 ; letter of Greeley to, ii. 470, 471.
Pilgrim Fathers, Cass on, i. 460.
Pinkney, William, i. 34.
Plymouth, Mass., anti-slavery vote of, i. 71.
Plymouth Church aids Kossuth, i. 236.
Poland, Ostend manifesto on, ii. 39 ; division of, ii. 43.
Polk, Bishop, methods of, with slaves, i. 331; on "Uncle Tom's Cabin," i. 363.
Polk, James K., elected President, i. 84; on the Oregon question, i. 86; concludes treaty with New Granada, i. 199 ; and Pierce, i. 250; Buchanan in cabinet of, i. 393; objections to supporting, ii. 266 ; Schurz on, ii. 493.
Polygamy, Republican convention of 1856 on, ii. 184.
Pomeroy refuses to yield Sharpe's rifles, ii. 159.
Pompadour, allusion to, i. 284.
Poor whites, condition of, i. 344 ; oppressed by slave-holders, i. 345, 346; in war of 1861, i. 346, 347, 380 ; slave-holders imitated by, i. 362; Helper on, ii. 419.
Pope, the, "Uncle Tom's Cabin" suppressed by, i. 282; influence of, in elections, ii. 55 ; gift of, demolished by mob, ii. 57.
Popular Sovereignty, doctrine of, i. 244, 476, 477; ii. 79, 110, 264, 305–307; Lincoln on, ii. 319; Douglas on, ii. 357, 373, 374 ; Republican convention of 1860 on, ii. 464.
Postage, reduction of, i. 215, 216.
Pottawatomie massacre, the, ii. 163, 165, 391; Oliver's report on, ii. 197–199.
Potter, quarrel of, with Pryor, ii. 437–439.
Preston, Colonel, at execution of John Brown, ii. 409.
Preston, Senator, on San Jacinto victory, i. 93.
"Pro-slavery argument," the, i. 367.
Pryne, debate between Brownlow and, i. 354.

Pryor, on Helper's "Impending Crisis," ii. 421; on Seward, ii. 422 ; interrupts Lovejoy, ii. 437; challenges Potter, ii. 439.
Publishing facilities at South, i. 353.
Pugh, of Ohio, against Lecompton bill, ii. 297; favors English bill, ii. 300; agrees with Douglas, ii. 358; reply of, to Yancey, ii. 448; against Davis resolution, ii. 456.
Puritan, the, De Tocqueville on, i. 357.

QUADROON girls, life led by, i. 338, 339.
Quakers on slavery, i. 24 n.
Quincy, Edmund, becomes an abolitionist, i. 72.
Quincy, Josiah, letter of, on Fugitive Slave law, i. 197; questions Randolph, i. 320 n.

RADICALS influenced by Seward, i. 168.
Railroads, extension of, i. 416.
Randolph, John, remark of, i. 320 n.; on dread of negro insurrection, i. 376; Wise, Henry A., compared to, ii. 88.
Ranney, Rufus P., associated with Wade, i. 229 ; a great lawyer and profound jurist, ii. 380; contest of, with Dennison, ii. 381; on the territories, ii. 382.
Rantoul votes on Foote resolution, i. 243 n.
Raymond, Henry J., honors Kossuth, i. 236 ; denounces Kansas-Nebraska bill, i. 463 ; position of, on formation of new party, ii. 46; opinions of, ii. 63; envied by Greeley, ii. 72 ; address of, at Pittsburgh, ii. 118, 119 ; in campaign of 1856, ii. 223; on Lecompton Constitution, ii. 293; on Douglas, ii. 296 ; in convention of 1860, ñ. 471 n.
Rayner, efforts of, to build up Know-nothings, ii. 87.
Read, letter of Buchanan to, ii. 209.
Reciprocity treaty negotiated by Marcy, ii. 8.
Redpath, James, on Kansas, ii. 167.
Reeder, Andrew, appointed governor of Kansas, ii. 80 ; on Kansas election, ii. 83; criticised by Pierce, ii. 85; removal of, ii. 86, 99; elected

INDEX   531

delegate, ii. 102; claims seat in House, ii. 126; attempt to arrest, ii. 156; escape of, election of illegal, ii. 197; exclusion of, ii. 201; advocates free Kansas, ii. 216-219; declares for Frémont, ii. 232; political sympathies of, ii. 239; in convention of 1860, ii. 465 *n.*; in campaign of 1860, ii. 484 *n.*

Reid, of North Carolina, on Seward, ii. 194.

Religious Herald, the, slaves advertised in, i. 324.

Republican convention of 1856, ii. 118, 182-184; of 1860, ii. 456-471.

Republican party, triumph in 1860, i. 2, ii. 500; anti-slavery basis of, i. 285; formation of, i. 490, ii. 45-49; early victories of, in the States, ii. 59, 60; Seward on, ii. 95; two elements in, ii. 97, 98; expansion of, ii. 210; Seward on, Holmes on, ii. 485; Lowell on, ii. 486; conservatism of, ii. 502.

Republicans distinct from abolitionists, ii. 436.

"Resources of the South and West," De Bow's, i. 306 *n.*

Rice, Dan, in New Orleans, i. 401.

Rice culture under slavery, i. 27 *n.*

Richardson, urges Kansas-Nebraska bill, i. 480, 483, 484, 488; appealed to by Hunt, i. 485; nominated for speaker, ii. 108, 109; opinions of, ii. 110; defeated by Banks, ii. 114; reads dispatch from Douglas, ii. 172; letter of Douglas to, ii. 474, 475.

Richmond, Dean, despatch of Douglas to, ii. 475.

Riddle, A. G., his biography of Wade, i. 229 *n.*; on higher law, ii. 564.

River and Harbor bill, opposed by Douglas, ii. 61.

Rives, allusion of Buchanan to, ii. 282.

Robinson, Dr. Charles, in Kansas struggle, ii. 102; on rescue of Branson, ii. 104; on Sharpe's rifles, ii. 105; in Wakarusa war, ii. 106; elected governor of Kansas, ii. 107; on national committee, ii. 119; appeals to President Pierce, ii. 124; indictment of, ii. 156; arrest of, ii. 157; burning of house of, ii. 159; threatened with lynching, ii. 166; letter of Frémont to, ii. 177; imprisonment of, ii. 216; on campaign of 1856, ii. 233 *n.*; release of, ii. 237; followers of, ii. 277.

Robinson, Mrs., on Kansas, ii. 154, 155.

Rocky Mountains, Frémont in, ii. 225.

Roger de Coverley, imaginary plantation of, i. 374, 375.

Rogers, Thorold, on immigrants, i. 355 *n.*

Rollins, E. H., in convention of 1860, ii. 469 *n.*

Roman Catholicism, crusade of Knownothings against, ii. 50-52.

Roman Empire, slavery in, i. 370.

Rome, slavery in, i. 381.

Root, of Ohio, resolution of, i. 135 *n.*

Rotation in office, Buchanan and Marcy on, ii. 248; as conducted by Buchanan, ii. 249.

Rothschilds, the, and Mexican indemnity, i. 214.

Rousseau, effect of his "Nouvelle Héloïse," i. 282, 284, 285.

Russia, assists Austria, i. 231; interference of, i. 234, 240.

Rust, Greeley assaulted by, ii. 118.

SALT-MINES of Hungary, i. 241.

"Samaritan," the, diary of, i. 404; on purification of atmosphere, on yellow-fever symptoms, i. 405; anecdotes from, i. 406-413.

Sanborn, F. B., friend of John Brown, ii. 385; conference with Brown and Gerrit Smith, ii. 386; letter to, from Brown, ii. 387; at Revere House meeting, ii. 389; Smith, Stearns, and, aid John Brown, ii. 390; goes to Canada, ii. 401.

Sanford, disagreement of, with Mason, ii. 3, 4.

San Jacinto victory, Preston on, i. 93. Houston in, i. 239.

San Juan, captured by British, i. 200; bombardment of, ii. 9, 10.

Sardinia, representative of, befriends Kossuth, i. 231.

Schenck, in campaign of 1860, ii. 484 *n.*

Schurz, Carl, in convention of 1860, ii. 465, 469 *n.*; in campaign of 1860, ii. 484 *n.*, 498; on the South, ii. 489; on Lincoln, ii. 493.

Scott, Dred, case of, ii. 245, 251-256.

Scott, Winfield, foresees civil war, i. 131; thwarted by Marcy, i. 247;

desires nomination, i. 253; supported by Botts, i. 255 ; his opinion of Fugitive Slave law, i. 256; Southern supporters of, i. 258; character of, in Mexican war, autobiography of, i. 259; nomination of, i. 262; supported by Wade, Seward, and Greeley, i. 264; military glory of, i. 269, 270; disproves charges against Pierce, i. 271 ; charges against, i. 272; letter of, on naturalization, i. 272, 273; anecdotes of, i. 273; Hawthorne on, Van Buren on, Western tour of, i. 274 ; at Pittsburgh, at Cleveland, i. 275; at Columbus, i. 275, 276; speeches of, published by New York *Herald*, i. 276; Crittenden on, ii. 189 ; letter of, to Crittenden, ii. 428.

Secession, Webster and Clay on, i. 190, 191; of Southern States from Charleston and Baltimore conventions, ii. 452, 474 ; Douglas on, ii. 491, 492.

Senate, the United States, i. 33; in last term of Webster, Clay, and Calhoun, i. 119.

Seventh-of-March speech of Webster, i. 144–148.

Seward, William H., i. 101; influence of, over Taylor, i. 109,178; first appearance of, in Senate, i. 120; did not fear disunion in 1850, i. 131; quoted, i. 133 *n.*; on Webster, i. 138 *n.*, 139 *n.*; twice governor of New York, his speech at Cleveland in 1848, i. 162; higher-law doctrine of, i. 163, 164; compared with Webster, Clay, and Calhoun, i. 165; not the mouthpiece of President Taylor, i. 166; influenced by J. Q. Adams, i. 167; radicals follow, i. 168; opposes compromise scheme, i. 173; on death of Taylor, i. 177; votes on Texas boundary, i. 181 ; absence from Senate of, i. 184; on Fugitive Slave law, i. 187, 188 ; insists on Wilmot proviso, i. 192, 193 ; supports Clayton-Bulwer treaty, i. 201; on Galphin claim, i. 203 *n.*; works with Chase and Wade, i. 229; on Kossuth, i. 237; receives Kossuth, i. 238, 239; sympathy of, for Kossuth, i. 242 ; his influence in Whig convention of 1852, i. 258; public letter of, i. 262; influence of, i. 263; supports Scott, i. 264; on Corwin, i. 300 ; on domestic slave-trade, i. 321 *n.*; visit of, to Culpepper Courthouse, i. 328 *n.*; conversation of, with governor of Richmond, i. 342; on negroes in Virginia, i. 373; speech of, on Kansas-Nebraska bill, i. 453, 454; on Missouri Compromise, Douglas on, i. 454; on opposition to Kansas-Nebraska bill, i. 463; on Douglas, i. 474, ii. 284; desires to preserve Whig party, ii. 46; influence of, ii. 63; Greeley on, ii. 68, 130; compared with Douglas, ii. 69; on Greeley, ii. 72 *n.*; denounces fugitive-slave legislation, ii. 77; Albany speech of, ii. 93–95; on slave-holders, ii. 94, 95; on political parties, ii. 95; against Southern oligarchy, ii. 97,98; on Kansas, ii. 99; publication of speech of, ii. 131; on condition of Sumner, ii. 140 *n.*; on assault of Brooks, ii. 147 ; political strength of, ii. 174–176; T. Parker on, ii. 175 ; Bowles on, ii. 175 *n.*, 436; J. A. King on, Emmet on, to Douglas and Toucey, ii. 176 *n*; influenced by Weed, ii. 176; letter of, to Baker, ii. 176 *n.*; position of, on slavery, ii. 177 ; withdraws from presidential contest, ii. 183 ; on Toombs bill, ii. 191, Reid on, ii. 194 ; letter of, to Weed, ii. 202 *n.*; on Sumner, ii. 215; Dana on, ii. 223, 459 *n.*, 461; letter of, in campaign of 1856, ii. 227; anecdote of, ii. 236 *n.*; on Buchanan and the Supreme Court, ii. 268; Taney on, ii. 270; conference of Walker with, ii. 272, 273 ; in Senate, ii. 283; Raymond on, ii. 296; votes against Lecompton bill, ii. 297 ; English bill opposed by, ii. 299; on Stuart and Broderick, ii. 300; letter of, to his son, ii. 304 *n.*; army bill supported by, ii. 303; reply of, to Hale, ii. 304 ; letter of Chase to, ii. 305 ; embraces doctrine of popular sovereignty, ii. 305–307; Chase on, ii. 307, 459; compared with Lincoln, ii. 327 ; irrepressible-conflict speech of, at Rochester, ii. 344, 346 ; Davis's opinion of, ii. 348; Northern press on, ii. 348, 349; on Cuba bill, ii. 352; Davis on speech of, ii. 373; on the territories, ii. 382 *n.*; informed of movements of John Brown, ii. 389;

accused of assisting John Brown, ii. 402; on John Brown, ii. 412, 413; suspicions concerning, ii. 421 n.; suspected by Lamar, ii. 421; denounced by Crawford and Pryor, ii. 422; speech of, on disunion, ii. 433, 434; Garrison on, ii. 434, 435; Phillips on, ii. 434, 435, 495 n.; attitude of South towards, ii. 443; efforts to nominate, ii. 459; position of, in 1860, ii. 460, 461; Pike on, ii. 461; Bryant on, ii. 461, 462; Greeley against, supported by Weed, ii. 465; opposed by Curtin and Lane, supported by Cameron, ii. 466; Lincoln on, ii. 467; enthusiasm for, ii. 468; defeat of, ii. 469, 470; grief of Weed over defeat of, ii. 471; Lowell on, ii. 472, 494; Weed and Greeley, firm of, ii. 472 n.; on the African slave-trade, ii. 482; in campaign of 1860, ii. 484 n.; on the Republican party, ii. 485; on disunion, ii. 488; on his failure to be nominated president, ii. 493, 494; article of on nomination of Lincoln, ii. 494; Swett on, Western tour of, ii. 495; on the "irrepressible conflict," ii. 495, 496; letter of, to Lincoln, ii. 498.

Sewardism, dread of, in Georgia, i. 262.

Seymour, Horatio, nominated for governor, ii. 63.

Shadrach, case of negro named, i. 209, 210; Parker on, i. 210, 290.

Shannon, made governor of Kansas, ii. 103; in Wakarusa war, ii. 105; asks for United States troops, ii. 106; instructions of Pierce to, ii. 124; Buford's men armed by, ii. 152 n.; refuses protection to Lawrence, ii. 158; telegram of Pierce to, ii. 160; troops sent to Pottawatomie region by, proclamation of, ii. 166; succeeded by Geary, ii. 217; flight of, ii. 229; Geary compared with, ii. 237.

Sharps rifles, in Wakarusa war, ii. 105.

Sherman, General, on the discovery of gold in California, i. 111 n.; on condition of slaves, i. 310, 334; on slave-trade, i. 337

Sherman, John, acknowledgment to, i. 493 n.; on Banks, ii. 117; in committee on Kansas, ii. 127; threats against, ii. 164; on Kansas, ii. 196; quoted, ii. 228 n.; on Lecompte, ii. 238 n.; denounced by Clark, ii. 418, 420; "Impending Crisis" recommended by, ii. 419; reply of, to Clark, ii. 420; abuse of, ii. 422; General Sherman on, ii. 425; in contest for speaker, ii. 418, 421, 425, 426; in campaign of 1860, ii. 484 n.

Sherman, William, murder of, ii. 163.

Shields, receives Kossuth, i. 238, 239; sympathy of, for Kossuth, i. 242.

Silliman, Prof., supports Frémont, ii. 211; on campaign of 1856, ii. 234 n.

Simmons, of Rhode Island, in Senate, ii. 283; in convention of 1860, ii. 469 n.

Simonton, J. W., on Wade and Seward, ii. 130; threatened by Keitt, ii. 144; on Toombs bill, ii. 191; on Douglas, ii. 284, 290; letter of, on Buchanan, ii. 290.

Sims, T., case of negro named, i. 211; addresses on surrender of, i. 211–213.

Simms, William Gilmore, on slavery, i. 68; apology of, for slavery, i. 341; on Harriet Martineau's "Morals of Slavery," i. 342, 343; in "Pro-slavery Argument," i. 367, 368; works of, i. 348 n.

Sisters of Charity, in yellow fever of 1853, i. 407.

Slave labor, Olmsted on, i. 303; contrasted with white labor, i. 314.

"Slave Laws," Stroud's, i. 309.

Slave marriages, position of the Church on, i. 317, 318.

Slave-dealers, contempt for, i. 324, 325 n.

Slave-holders, tyranny of, i. 345, 346.

Slavery becomes the dominating question, i. 2; early features of, i. 3–7; Oglethorpe on, i. 5; Whitefield on, i. 5; William Penn on, i. 6; in New England, i. 6; English views of, i. 7; considered an evil, i. 6; Baxter on, i. 8; in Virginia and Maryland, i. 8; Wesley on, i. 10; Jefferson on, i. 10–13, 15; Burke on, i. 11, 12; extent of, in 18th century, i. 11; Massachusetts Supreme Court on, i. 14; Metho-

534 INDEX

dists on, i. 14; not named in the Constitution, i. 17; Madison on, i. 21–23, 40; Webster on, i. 27; Clay on, i. 31; Seward on, i. 39, ii. 194, 433; Garrison on, i. 55, 59, 62, 63; in the West Indies, i. 60; Channing on, i. 64–66, 379; Emerson on, Benton on, Simms on, McDuffie on, i. 68; in 1837, i. 72; in Mexico, i. 76; attitude of California towards, i. 116; in territories, Clay resolution respecting, i. 122; feeling in New England against, i. 132; Webster on, i. 145–148; Davis on, i. 168; Clay on, i. 303; M. C. Butler on, i. 313 n.; Brownlow on, i. 354; de Tocqueville on, i. 356, 357; declaration of German colony regarding, i. 359; influence of, on social intercourse, i. 361; Herbert Spencer on, i. 362 n.; defended by clergymen, i. 363, 364; Southern defence of, Simms on, i. 366; essays on, by Southern writers, i. 367, 368; Prof. Dew on, i. 368; scriptural arguments in support of, i. 370–372; Lincoln on, i. 381, ii. 319, 326, 331, 332, 335, 336, 432; Mommsen on, i. 382, 383; position of Pierce on, i. 386; in Nebraska, Douglas on, i. 426; in Nebraska, provision concerning, i. 427; Douglas on, i. 447, ii 327, 331, 333; Chase on, i. 449, ii. 93; Sumner on, i. 455, 490, ii. 132, 133, 135; J. Q. Adams on, i. 494; reaction in Boston as to, i. 506; Clayton on, ii. 33 n.; in Ostend manifesto, ii. 43; party opposed to, ii. 47; position of Republicans on, ii. 48; position of Know-nothings on, ii. 89; legislation in Kansas on, ii. 99; prohibited by Topeka-Kansas convention, ii. 103; Banks on, ii. 112; discussion of, in Congress, ii. 117; Raymond on, ii. 119; Republican convention of 1856 on, ii. 184; Buchanan on, ii. 246; Taney on, ii. 256, 257; Curtis on, ii. 260; Lecompton convention on, ii. 279; John Brown on, ii. 397, 398; Republican convention of 1860 on, ii. 464; Motley on, ii. 502.

"Slavery as It Is," Weld's, i. 309 n.
Slaves, whipping of, i. 309, 325; breeding of, i. 310, 311; market value of, i. 315; instruction of, i. 327–330; religious training of, i. 330–332; immorality among, 333, 335, 336.

Slave-States, climate of, i. 358.

Slave-trade, African, ii. 367–372; scheme to reopen, i. 497, ii. 241; Douglas on, ii. 369, 370; discussed in convention at Vicksburg, ii. 371; Davis on, ii. 372.

Slave-trade, Cuban, the, ii. 369.

Slave-trade, domestic, i. 315; in Virginia, i. 316; Seward on, i. 321 n.; Chambers on, i. 320–322; advertising methods of, i. 323.

Slidell, John, on neutrality, ii. 23; assault of Sumner witnessed by, ii. 148, 149; letter of Buchanan to, ii. 170; on Cuba bill, ii. 354.

Smith, Caleb B., promised cabinet position, i. 466; in campaign of 1860, ii. 484 n.

Smith, Gerrit, befriends Jerry, i. 224; denounces Fugitive Slave law, i. 225; nomination of, ii. 186 n.; subscribes money for Kansas, ii. 219; John Brown assisted by, ii. 385–387, 389, 390, 391 n.; on John Brown, ii. 391 n., ii. 399; insanity of, ii. 401.

Smith, General, Buchanan on, ii. 237.

Socialists, Kossuth's reply to, i. 235.

"Society in America," Harriet Martineau's, i. 342.

Socrates, Lincoln compared to, ii. 309; John Brown compared with, ii. 415.

"Softs," Free-soilers merged in, Marcy chief of, i. 389; in New York, i. 481.

Soulé, Mme., criticised by Duke of Alba, ii. 12.

Soulé, Nelville, duel of, with Duke of Alba, ii. 12, 13.

Soulé, Pierre, appointed minister to Spain, on Cuba, on abolition, i. 394; Spain hesitates to receive, i. 394, 395; London *Times* on, speech of to Cuban exiles, i. 395; instructions of Marcy to, ii. 10, 11, 18; costume of, at court of Madrid, ii. 11; duel of, with Turgot, ii. 13; position of, at Madrid, ii. 15; letter of, to Calderon, ii. 19; correspondence of, ii. 24, 25; and filibusters, ii. 28; letter of Calderon to, ii. 34, 35; compared with Marcy, ii. 35; trying position of, ii. 36; letter of President to, protects queen dowager of Spain,

INDEX

ii. 37; signs Ostend manifesto, ii. 38; Buchanan influenced by, ii. 40; letter of, to Marcy, ii. 41; resignation of, ii. 42.
South Carolina, convention at Charleston, in favor of secession, i. 226; Lieber on, i. 350 n.; secession of, from Charleston convention, ii. 451.
Southern Literary Company, i. 351.
Southern Oligarchy, the, i. 345, 346; represented by Calhoun and Davis, i. 380; Seward on, ii. 98 n.
Southern Pacific Railroad, the, ii. 7.
Southern people, character of, i. 359; Lieber on, i. 359 n.; how regarded in England, i. 360.
Southern prosperity, compared with Northern, i. 354.
Southern Rights convention, i. 226.
Spain, assured of friendship of United States, i. 218; followers of Lopez sent to, i. 220; Soulé appointed minister to, i. 394; hesitates to receive Soulé, i. 395; Marcy on, ii. 10, 11; queen of, ii. 14; crisis in, ii. 16; roads of, in 1854, ii. 18; revolution in, ii. 37; Ostend manifesto on, ii. 39.
Spalding, Rufus P., in Republican convention of 1856, ii. 153; Bushnell defended by, ii. 364.
Spanish army, of Cuba, i. 217.
Spanish flag, insult to, i. 221.
Spanish minister, demands redress, i. 221; note of Webster to, i. 221, 222.
Speaker, contest for, in 1855–1856, ii. 108–115.
Spencer, Herbert, on climate, i. 358 n.; on slavery, i. 362 n.
Spoils System, Pierce's rule of, i. 399, 400.
Spring, Prof., his story of Kansas, ii. 218.
Springfield, Massachusetts, meeting at, condemns Fugitive Slave law, i. 197.
St. Michael's Church, in Charleston, ii. 444.
Stanton, Edwin M., early encounter of, with Lincoln, ii. 312.
Stanton, Frederick P., sent to Kansas, ii. 272, 273; displeases free-State party, ii. 273; in Kansas election, ii. 278; removal of, ii. 288, 289.
Stanwood, Presidential Elections of, i. 249 n.

Stearns, George L., warning of, to John Brown, ii. 389; Brown assisted by, ii. 390, 391; goes to Canada, ii. 401.
Stephens, Alexander H., defends slavery, i. 118, 133; criticises President Taylor, i. 176; pledge of, concerning compromise, i. 207; supports Webster, i. 257; refuses to support Scott, i. 262; defends Corwin, i. 298 n.; Douglas not influenced by, i. 432; on factious opposition, i. 484; in debate on Kansas-Nebraska bill, i. 485; motion of, i. 488; on Kansas-Nebraska act, i. 496; on election of Banks, ii. 113; offers advice to Pierce, ii. 120, 121; on use of money in 1856, ii. 231 n.; on Dred Scott case, ii. 255; on Walker-Paulding affair, ii. 290; on fight between Keitt and Grow, ii. 298; favors English bill, ii. 299; on secession, ii. 453; on Lincoln's election, ii. 490.
Stevens, Thaddeus, against Texas and New Mexico bills, i. 182; remark of, i. 183; why opposed to Clay compromise, i. 193; pleads cause of Hanaway, i. 224; speech of, on McLean, ii. 183; reply of, to Keitt, ii. 420; in convention of 1860, ii. 469 n.; in campaign of 1860, ii. 484 n.
Still, W., on Jerry rescue, i. 224 n.; "The Underground Railroad" of, ii. 75.
Stockton, Commodore, nomination of, ii. 186 n.
Stoddard, R. H., letter of Hawthorne to, i. 399 n.
Stone, George H., acknowledgment to, i. 493 n.
Stowe, Harriet B., struggles of, i. 279; Sumner on, i. 280; admired by George Sand, i. 281 n.; at play of "Uncle Tom's Cabin," i. 282; criticised, i. 363–365; her description of Douglas, ii. 127–129; publication of her "Dred," ii. 212. See also "Uncle Tom's Cabin."
Stringfellow, on Kansas, ii. 100; in Kansas struggle, ii. 101; on Atchison, ii. 106 n.; in sacking of Lawrence, ii. 158; Stephens on, Toombs influenced by, ii. 190.
Stroud, "Slave Laws" of, i. 309.
"Studies on Slavery," i. 369.

Stuart, A., made Secretary of Interior, i. 179.
Stuart, Charles E., votes against bill for admission of Kansas, ii. 297; English bill opposed by, ii. 300; co-operation of Seward with, ii. 305; agrees with Douglas, ii. 358.
Sumner, Charles, address of, on slavery, i. 108; on Webster, i. 139; on Fugitive Slave law, i. 197, 198, 208, 266–268, 499; character of, visits Europe, i. 227; views of, on slavery, i. 228, 334 n.; elected senator, i. 228; speech of, on Kossuth, i. 237; supports Kossuth, i. 242; presents memorial of Society of Friends, i. 265; Clemens on, Hale on, Chase on, Mann on, i. 268; on "Uncle Tom's Cabin," i. 280; Parker writes to, i. 289; Mason's discourtesy to, i. 395; letter of, to Hawthorne, i. 396; signs Appeal of Independent Democrats, i. 442; Douglas on, i. 454, ii. 134, 138, 139; speech of, against Kansas-Nebraska bill, i. 454, 455; Douglas answers charge of, i. 474, 475; on Kansas-Nebraska act, i. 490; favors formation of new party, ii. 45; amendment of, ii. 77; supplemented by Wilson, ii. 96; speech of, on Kansas, ii. 131–135; letter of, to Parker, ii. 132; Butler on, ii. 132 n.; on Atchison, ii. 133; *Quarterly Review* on, ii. 133 n.; on Butler, ii. 134, 135; on Douglas, ii. 135, 137; disagreement of, with Butler, ii. 136; assaulted by Brooks, ii. 139, 140; Seward on condition of, ii. 140 n.; return of, to Senate, character of, ii. 141, 142; Everett on assault of, ii. 143; "The Crime against Kansas" of, ii. 147; witnesses of assault on, ii. 148, 149; letters of Parker to, ii. 175, 182; letter of Longfellow to, ii. 212; on young men, ii. 215; letter of, in campaign of 1856, ii. 223, 224; in Senate, ii. 282; letter of, to Parker, ii. 297; more radical than Lincoln, ii. 327; conversation of, with Lincoln, ii. 339, 340 accused of assisting John Brown, ii. 402; oration of, on slavery, ii. 476, 477; Grimes on, ii. 477.
Sumner, Colonel, sent to Soulé, ii. 34; denies request of Shannon for troops, ii. 106; legislature dispersed by, Brown coerced by, ii. 167; Buford's men expelled by, ii. 192.
Supreme Court, the, De Tocqueville on, ii. 249; members of, in 1857, ii. 250.
Swett, Leonard, on Lincoln, ii. 467 n.
Syracuse, meeting at, denounces Fugitive Slave law, i. 196.

TALLMADGE, of New York, amendment of, i. 30, 32.
Tammany in convention of 1860, ii. 440.
Taney, Chief Justice, character of, Jackson supported by, ii. 250; appointed Chief Justice, ii. 251; in Dred Scott case, ii. 252, 254; on Dred Scott decision, ii. 255–257; on Missouri Compromise, ii. 257; error of, ii. 260–262; correspondence of, with Curtis, ii. 262; Douglas on, ii. 264; reasoning of, ii. 266; resents charge of Seward, ii. 270; Lincoln on, ii. 270 n., 334; position of, on slavery, ii. 359.
Tariff question, the, in New England, i. 194; Pierce on, i. 422; Buchanan on, ii. 360; in campaign of 1860, ii. 464, 498, 499 n.; urged by Curtin, ii. 479; Douglas on, ii. 480; McClure on, ii. 480 n.
Taylor, Zachary, in Mexico, i. 87; elected President, i. 97; his character, i. 99; his cabinet, i. 100; on rotation in office, i. 102; his change of views, i. 109, 134, 135; on government of California, i. 110; on California and New Mexico, i. 119; his relations with Clay, i. 121; firmness of, towards Southern Whigs, i. 133, 134; answers Toombs, i. 133; opposes compromise scheme, i. 175; illness of, criticised by Stephens and Toombs, i. 176; death of, mourning for, Seward on, i. 177; on Texas and New Mexico, i. 190; charges against cabinet of, i. 204; European agent of, i. 205; thwarted by Marcy, i. 247; political success of, i. 259.
Tehuantepec, proposed route through, i. 199, 201.
Tell, William, Kossuth compared to, i. 237.
Temperance legislation in Maine, ii. 49; in other States, ii. 50.

Tennessee, secession of, from Baltimore convention, ii. 474.
Territorial question, the, Seward on, i. 163, 164.
Territories, slavery in, i. 93-93; report of Douglas on, i. 425-428.
Terry, duel of, with Broderick, ii. 377, 378; death of, ii. 379.
Texas, Webster opposed to annexation of, i. 77, 78, 79, ii. 33; admission of, i. 85; public debt of, Clay resolution as to, i. 122; Clay on, i. 125, 126; Webster on, i. 152; Taylor's attitude towards, i. 190; debt of, i. 189; H. H. Bancroft on debt of, i. 189 n.; Stephens on, i. 190; Everett on, i. 295; German colony of, i. 358; annexation of, i. 386, 387; secession of, from Charleston convention, ii. 451.
Texas boundary bill, discussed, i. 181; passed, i. 182; Giddings against, i. 189.
Texas question, the, i. 75; Congress on, i. 77, 81; Democrats on, i. 77; Webster on, i. 77, 86; Upshur on, i. 78; Great Britain on, i. 81; Clay on, i. 83.
Thackeray, William M., on slaves, i. 374 n.; letter of, from Richmond, i. 377 n.
Thayer, Eli, efforts of, in Kansas, sustained by Greeley, ii. 78; methods of, ii. 79; in convention of, 1860, ii. 469 n.
Thompson, of Mississippi, in Buchanan's cabinet, ii. 247; influence of, in Kansas, ii. 277.
Thoreau on John Brown, ii. 413, 414.
Thorwaldsen, group of, in Crystal Palace exhibition, i. 415.
Thucydides, plague described by, i. 405; quoted, ii. 489.
Ticknor, George, on Channing, i. 64; on gold fever, i. 113 n.; on "Uncle Tom's Cabin," i. 284; letters of B. R. Curtis to, ii. 186 n., 253; Fillmore supported by, ii. 206 n.
Tod, David, in Baltimore convention, ii. 475.
Toombs, Robert, in favor of slavery, i. 118, 133, 194; criticises President Taylor, i. 176; against California bill, i. 182; pledge of, concerning compromise, i. 207; supports Webster, i. 257; refuses to support Scott, i. 262; Douglas not influenced by, i. 431, 432; on compromise of 1850,

i. 461; advises Pierce, ii. 121; sees assault of Sumner, ii. 148; bill of, on Kansas, ii. 189, 196; lecture of, in Boston, ii. 190; character of, ii. 191; on Frémont, ii. 204; in Southern triumvirate, ii. 294; colloquy of, with Wade, ii. 295; Raymond on, ii. 296; on Cuba bill, ii. 353.
Topeka Constitution, ratification of, ii. 107; illegality of, ii. 195.
Tocqueville, de, on amalgamation, i. 335; on mulattoes, i. 339, 340; on slavery, i. 356, 357; on abolition, i. 366; on negro insurrection, i. 376; on the Supreme Court, ii. 249.
Toucey, of Connecticut, bill of, to enforce Fugitive Slave law, ii. 77; remark of Seward to, ii. 176; in Buchanan's cabinet, ii. 246, 247.
Toussaint, influence of, i. 352, ii. 401.
Townsley, in Pottawatomie massacre, ii. 163.
Tribune, New York, influence of, ii. 71, 72; anecdotes of, ii. 72 n.
Trumbull, Lyman, elected senator, ii. 62; in Senate, ii. 130, 283; on Toombs bill, ii. 191; Lincoln defeated by, ii. 311; in campaign of 1860, ii. 484 n.
Turgot, Marquis de, challenged by Pierre Soulé, wounded by Soulé, ii. 13; instructed to crush Soulé, ii. 14.
Turkey releases Kossuth, i. 231.
Turkish governor and Koszta, i. 417.
Turner, Nat, insurrection of, i. 57, 327; Douglass, Frederick, threatened with fate of, i. 330; effect of insurrection of, i. 377; admired by John Brown, ii. 162.
Tyler, President, and Texas, i. 79, 85, 87; character of, i. 79; cabinet of, i. 143; contrasted with Fillmore, i. 302; appoints Cushing minister to China, i. 391; on disunion, ii. 209.
Tyler, Samuel, remark of Taney to, ii. 270

ULLMAN, Know-nothing candidate for governor, ii. 64.
"Uncle Tom's Cabin," influence of, i. 278; publication of, Macaulay on, sale of in England, Whittier on, Longfellow on, Lowell on, Choate on, Garrison on, Sumner on, i. 280; Emerson on, i. 280 n.; reception of, in Paris, i. 281; letter in N. Y.

Tribune on, Heine and George Sand on, i. 281 *n.*; Lord Palmerston on, suppressed in Italy, dramatized, i. 282; acted in London and Paris, i. 283; G. Ticknor on, effect of, on young men, i. 284, 285; criticised, i. 324; Fanny Kemble and Olmsted on, i. 363; Frederick Douglass on, i. 364; circulation of, in South, i. 376; fidelity of, i. 377; on Underground Railroad, ii. 76; influence of, ii. 131; compared with Helper's "Impending Crisis," ii. 419.

Underground Railroad, the, routes of, ii. 74; book of William Still on, May on, ii. 75; work accomplished by, ii. 76, 77; at Oberlin, ii. 361, 362.

Union, the, fears of Webster and others for, i. 130–132; Seward on maintenance of, i. 165.

Union, La, of New Orleans, denounces Cuban expedition, i. 220; mob attacks office of, i. 221.

Union degree adopted by Knownothings, ii. 87, 88.

Union-savers, the, Phillips on, Bryant on, ii. 428.

United States Bank, war of, with Jackson, ii. 250.

Upshur on the Texas question, i. 78.

Utah, slavery not prohibited in, i. 181; Douglas on New Mexico and, i. 448.

Utah bill, i. 182; language of, applied in Nebraska bill, i. 428.

Utrecht, treaty of, and slavery, i. 7.

VALLANDIGHAM, C. L., address of, at Dayton, i. 195; reply of Brown to, ii. 397.

Van Buren, John, influence of, with Pierce, i. 421; letter of, on report of Douglas, i. 429.

Van Buren, Martin, nominated for President, i. 97; declares for Pierce, i. 264; on Scott and Pierce, i. 274.

Vanderbilt, Commodore, interested in the Nicaragua Canal, i. 199.

Vechten, Van, Philip, lieutenant under Lopez, i. 220 *n.*

Vindication, Forney's, quoted, ii. 341 *n.*

Virginia, Professor Dew on, i. 368; secession of, from the Baltimore convention, ii. 474.

Virginians, the, the nation established by, i. 379.

Volney, Lincoln influenced by, ii. 312.

WADE, Benjamin F., compared with Sumner, i. 227; early life of, forms partnership with Giddings, i. 228; works with Seward and Chase, i. 229; supports Scott, i. 264; votes for Sumner's amendment, i. 269; speech of, against Kansas-Nebraska bill, character of, i. 452; reply of, to Badger, i. 452, 453; favors formation of new party, ii. 45; on Toombs bill, ii. 192; in Senate, ii. 283; in debate on Kansas, ii. 293; reply of, to Toombs, ii. 295; against Lecompton bill, ii. 297; agreement of, with Cameron and Chandler, ii. 298; letter of, to Pike, ii. 302; reply of, to Toombs, ii. 353; nomination of, desired, ii. 459; in campaign of 1860, ii. 484 *n.*

Wade, Edward, signs Appeal of Independent Democrats, i. 442.

Wakarusa war in Kansas, ii. 105, 106.

Walker, Francis A., on class mulatto, i. 341 *n.*

Walker, Robert J., appointed governor of Kansas, ii. 271, 272; proclamation of, ii. 274; denounced by Davis and Brown, letter of Buchanan to, ii. 275; popularity of, ii. 276; in Kansas election, ii. 277, 278; reply of, to John Calhoun, ii. 280; firmness of, ii. 281; resignation of, ii. 288; favors English bill, ii. 301.

Walker, William, in Nicaragua, ii. 242; arrested by Paulding, ii. 289; Stephens on, ii. 290.

Wall Street, panic in, of October, 1860, ii. 500.

Wallace, Kossuth compared to, i. 237.

Wanderer, the, negroes landed by, ii. 368; Buchanan on, ii. 369.

Warner, Charles Dudley, on New York *Tribune*, ii. 71 *n.*

Washburn, Israel, on Douglas, ii. 306.

Washburne, E. B., letter of Lincoln to, ii. 182; on convention of 1856, ii. 182 *n.*; on McLean, ii. 183.

Washington, city of, Oliphant on, ii. 9 *n.*

Washington, Colonel Lewis, arrested

INDEX 539

by John Brown, ii. 394; on John Brown, ii. 395.

Washington, George, on negro soldiers, i. 13, 14; as a slave-owner, i. 21; Kossuth compared to, i. 237; non-intervention doctrine of, i. 242; letter of, on fugitive slave, i. 267; Sumner on precept of, i. 268; slaves of, i. 315, 316; letter of, i. 316 n.; on price of land, on slavery, i. 356; civil dress of, ii. 5; saying of, ii. 51; position of, on slavery in territories, ii. 259; policy of, ii. 502.

Washington, Mrs., escaped slave of, i. 267.

Washington Treaty, work of Webster on, i. 140, 143.

Wayland's "Moral Science" criticised at South, i. 351, 369.

Wayne, Justice in Supreme Court, ii. 250; urges Taney to write an opinion, ii. 254, 255.

Webb, James Watson, denounces Kansas-Nebraska bill, i 463; on Seward, ii. 307.

Webster, Daniel, on Ordinance of 1787, i. 16; on cotton interest, i. 26; on nullification, i. 42; and Calhoun, i. 50; on the Union and the Constitution, i. 51; on slavery, in 1837, i. 72; on the Texas question, i. 77, 87; and Lord Ashburton, i. 73; on the Oregon question, i. 86; on the Mexican war, i. 91, 145; on the Calhoun theory, i. 98; last term of, in Senate, i. 119; anxiety of, for the Union, i. 131; intellectual endowment of, i. 137; Marshall on, i. 138; Ticknor on, i. 138 140, 142; Sumner on, Hallam on, Carlyle on physique of, Quincy on, i. 139; early life of, reply of to Hayne, work of on Washington treaty, Harriet Martineau on, i 140; at Marshfield, i. 141; couplet on, i. 141 n.; ambition of, i. 142; in Tyler's cabinet, resists Clay, charges against, i. 143, 157, 158; his seventh-of-March speech, i. 144-148; on Methodist Episcopal Church, i. 145; on slavery, i. 145-147; supports Clay's compromise, i. 149; on New Mexico, i. 149, 152; Giddings on, i. 149,154,158; on Northern abolitionists, i. 152; on fugitive slaves, i. 147, 152, 153, 187; Fugitive Slave bill of, i. 153 n.; Whittier on, i. 155; testimonials to, i. 156; Calhoun on, Foote on, i. 157; Emerson on, i. 159; denies inconsistency, i. 159 n.; compared with Burke, i. 160, 161; on Hamilton, i. 161; influence of, on civil war, i. 161 n.; Seward rebuts argument of, i. 164; on Seward, i. 166 n.; views of, i. 169; in committee on Clay resolutions, i. 171; supports compromise scheme, Greeley on, i. 173; on Nashville convention, i. 174; on Fillmore, i. 178; made Secretary of State, favors compromise, i. 179, 184; supports Fugitive Slave law, i. 188; on secession, i. 190, 191; cabinet objects to paper of, i. 190 n.; justification of, i. 191, 192; supports Clayton-Bulwer treaty, i. 201; Hülsemann letter of, i. 205, 206; and Mexican debt, i. 213; vindicated by House of Representatives, i. 214; gift to, i. 214, 215; salary of, Allen's attack on, i. 215; on Spain and Cuba, i. 218; corresponds with Spanish minister, i. 221; praised by Lord Palmerston, i. 222; declines to attend banquet to Kossuth in New York, i. 236; on Kossuth, i. 238; speech of, at banquet to Kossuth in Washington, i. 239, 240; age of, when desiring presidency, i. 244; approves Whig platform of 1852, i. 253; Choate on, i. 255; votes received by, i. 256; supported by Toombs and Stephens, i. 257; attempt to nominate, i. 257, 258; defeat of, i. 260; literary project of, letter of to Everett, i. 260 n.; at Boston, tribute to Boston of, i. 263; extract from Parker's scrap-book, i. 263 n.; death of, i. 285; last words to his family, i. 286; mourning for, Everett on funeral of, i. 287; sermons on, i. 288; letter of Motley on, i. 288 n.; Parker's sermon on, i. 288, 289, 290; secures appointment for Everett, i. 292; letter of, to Everett, i. 292, 293; in affair of Lobos Islands, i. 297; letter of, to Captain Jewett, i. 297 n.; quoted, i. 365 n.; Marcy compared to, i. 417; interpreted by Everett, i. 457; Douglas on Everett's interpretation of, i. 474; influence of, ii. 74; against Taney, recommends Curtis, ii. 251;

Dana on, ii. 262; scouts Calhoun doctrine, ii. 276; Hale on, ii. 304; Lincoln inspired by, ii. 314, 327; referred to by Douglas, ii. 322; compared with Lincoln, ii. 332, 333, 342; Garrison on, ii. 434; supported by Ashmun, ii. 463.

Webster regiment, sings John Brown song, ii. 416.

Weed, Thurlow, i. 101; Memoirs of, quoted, i. 134 n.; on seventh-of-March speech, i. 166 n.; autobiography of, quoted, i. 205; denounces Kansas-Nebraska bill, i. 463; Seward influenced by, ii. 46, 68, 176 n.; influence of, ii. 63; letter of Seward to, ii. 72 n.; sympathy of, with fugitive slaves, ii. 75; supports Frémont, ii. 177, 183; on Seward, ii. 236 n.; on firm of Seward, Weed and Greeley, ii. 305; letter of Bowles to, ii. 436; project of, ii. 461, 462; in convention of 1860, ii. 465; Greeley on, ii. 470; grieved at defeat of Seward, ii. 471; letter of Swett to, ii. 495; letter of Lincoln to, ii. 497; on the fusionists, ii. 500.

Welles, Gideon, in convention of 1860, ii. 469 n.

Wentworth, John, supports Frémont, ii. 177.

Western Reserve, bar of, i. 229.

Whig Convention of 1852, i. 243, 252; platform of, i. 253; speech of Choate in, i. 254, 255; nominates Scott, i. 256.

Whig party, dissolution of, i. 185; extinction of, i. 285; principles of, ii. 47; Seward on, ii. 95.

Whigs, Northern, for and against compromise, i. 184, 207.

Whigs on slavery, i. 107, 108.

Whigs, Southern, on admission of California, i. 133; influenced by Clay, i. 135; support Clay, i. 192.

Whitefield on slavery, i. 5, 10.

Whitfield, election of, ii. 80; in House, ii. 126; Missourians commanded by, ii. 167; illegal election of, ii. 197; exclusion of, ii. 201.

Whitney's cotton-gin, i. 19, 25.

Whittier, on Garrison, i. 75; poem of, on Webster, i. 155; on "Uncle Tom's Cabin," i. 280; Frémont supported by, ii. 212; quoted, ii. 236; in campaign of 1860, ii. 485.

Wide-awakes, the, origin of, ii. 224 n.; organization of, ii. 483; how regarded at the South, ii. 487.

Wilkinson, murder of, ii. 163.

William III. and slavery, i. 7.

Willis, N. P., declares for Frémont, ii. 212.

Wilmot, David, in convention of 1860, ii. 463; in campaign of 1860, ii. 484 n.

Wilmot proviso, i. 89, 90; Mann on, i. 132; Southern feeling respecting, i. 134–136; not applied to New Mexico, i. 182; excluded from Compromise measures, i. 191; Hale on, i. 193; stifled by Kansas-Nebraska act, i. 498; Benjamin on, ii. 293; voted for by Lincoln, ii. 310.

Wilson, General, address of, on Fillmore, i. 297 n.

Wilson, Henry, quoted, i. 134 n.; against Fugitive Slave law, i. 212; on election of Sumner, i. 228 n.; supports Hale, i. 264; elected to Senate, ii. 66; and Northern Know-nothings, ii. 90; rise of, ii. 96; leaves Know-nothing party, ii. 97; speech of, on Kansas question, ii. 130; speech of, published, ii. 131; challenged by Brooks, ii. 145; on Toombs bill, ii. 191; on disunion, ii. 208; in campaign of 1856, ii. 223; visit of, to Kansas, ii. 275; in Senate, ii. 282; on Douglas and Broderick, ii. 300; policy of, as to Douglas, ii. 306; letter of, to Howe, ii. 389; in campaign of 1860, ii. 484; remark of Douglas to, ii. 491.

Winthrop, Robert C., Whig candidate for speaker, i. 117; succeeds Webster in Senate, against Fugitive Slave law, i. 182; holds aloof from Republican party, ii. 97; on Kansas, ii. 189 n.; supports Fillmore, ii. 206.

Wise, Henry A., on Know-nothings, ii. 56, 88; supports Buchanan, ii. 170, 171; on Frémont, ii. 205; on campaign of 1856, ii. 209; public letter of, ii. 290; on John Brown, ii. 398; demand of, for Gerrit Smith, ii. 401.

Wood, Dr., attends Taylor, i. 176.

Woodford, S. L., in campaign of 1860, ii. 484 n.

INDEX

Woodson, instructions of, to Colonel Sumner, ii. 167.
Wortley, Lady, on condition of slaves, i. 373.

YALE COLLEGE welcomes Kossuth, i. 235.
Yancey, William L., speech of, in Charleston convention, ii. 447, 448; against Douglas, ii. 452.
Yates, Edmund, letter of, to the women of England, i. 319 n.
Yellow fever, in New Orleans, i. 400, 402–413; compared with plague of fourteenth century, i. 413 n.; in 1858, ii. 350.

END OF VOL. II.

When Miss Dawes's Life of Sumner, Trent's Life of William Gilmore Simms, and Page's The Old South were published, the work of the printer was so far advanced that I was unable to make use of them. I am sensible that there are two sides to the question which divided the North and the South. I have tried to look fairly upon the Southern side; but as a commentary on much that I have written, and especially on Chapter IV., I am glad to commend to my readers chapter vi. of Trent's Simms and the chapters of Page's book entitled "The Old South," "Authorship in the South before the War," and "Social Life in Old Virginia before the War."

"It is not probable that we shall see a more complete or better-balanced history of our great civil war." — THE NATION.

HISTORY OF THE UNITED STATES

FROM THE COMPROMISE OF 1850
TO
THE FINAL RESTORATION OF HOME RULE IN THE SOUTH IN 1877

By JAMES FORD RHODES

Complete in seven octavo volumes, attractively bound in dark blue cloth, with gilt tops and lettering

I. 1850–1854	The first volume tells the history of the country during the four years' futile attempt to avoid conflict by the Compromise Measures of 1850, ending with the repeal of the Missouri Compromise in 1854.
II. 1854–1860	The second volume deals with the stirring events which followed this repeal, through all the Kansas and Nebraska struggles, to the triumph of the then newly organized Republican party in the election of Lincoln in 1860.
III. 1860–1862	The third volume states the immediate effect upon the country of Lincoln's election; covers the period of actual secession; the dramatic opening of the war; the sobering defeat of Bull Run; Grant's victory at Donelson; and closes with the battle of Shiloh and the surrender of New Orleans.
IV. 1862–1864	The fourth volume follows the progress of the war in vivid discussions of campaigns, battles, the patient search for the right commander, and the attitude toward this country of the British government and people.
V. 1864–1866	The fifth volume opens with the account of Sherman's march to the sea. The adoption of the Thirteenth Amendment, Lincoln's assassination, the state of society in the North and the South during the exhausting war, and the first two years of Johnson's administration are fully treated. The volume ends with an account of the political campaign of 1866.
VI. 1866–1872	The sixth volume deals with the Reconstruction Acts and their execution, the impeachment of President Johnson, the Ku Klux Klan, the Freedmen's Bureau, the ratification of the XIVth and the passage of the XVth amendments, and with foreign and financial affairs.
VII. 1872–1877	The seventh volume deals with the *Credit Mobilier* scandal, the "Salary Grab" Act, the financial panic of 1873, the continued Reconstruction, with a summing up. It closes with an account of the presidential campaign of 1876 and the disputed presidency.

Price of the set, $17.50 net *Per volume, $2.50 net*

THE MACMILLAN COMPANY
Publishers, 64–66 Fifth Avenue, New York

PRESS COMMENTS ON THE

History of the United States
By JAMES FORD RHODES

VOL. I.

By Andrew McLaughlin, in "The American Historical Review"

"Mr. Rhodes has shown unusual skill in handling redundant or conflicting testimony; and he has shown himself a historian and not a partisan. . . . He is writing a political and social history with rare judgment, accuracy, and patience, with good literary skill, and with sincerity and honesty of purpose."

From "The New York Tribune"

"A work like this, so temperate in thought, so elevated in style, so just and reasonable in exposition, so large in comprehension of causes and effects, and so tolerant and truly catholic in conclusions, could not have been written if the momentous period under consideration had not been closed. In no other recent contribution to the study of American politics is there so true a sense of historical perspective as in these volumes. The field of view is definitely outlined so that it is not obscured by haze and mist on the outer confines. Within it events, tendencies, legislation, political administrations, and the men who have been making history hand over hand, appear in their rightful relations.

VOL. II.

"The picture is perfect in proportion and in composition. It is a complete survey of a period that is finished. It is a work of great dignity of purpose, and is rich in resources of learning and political and moral philosophy. The style, while less stately and rhetorical than that of Bancroft, is direct, trenchant, often epigrammatic, and always luminous. Every page bears evidence of painstaking and laborious research. Every chapter has the impress of a cultivated, thoroughly equipped mind and of a magnanimous, tolerant nature."

From "The Athenæum," London

VOL. II.   "Mr. Rhodes not only takes great pains, but he has the art of giving pleasing literary expression to his conclusions."

From "The Spectator," London

"Mr. Rhodes's first volume deals mainly with slavery as an institution in the Southern States, and the various political compromises by which it was sought to prevent that institution from becoming the cause — or at least the excuse — for disintegration and civil war. In the second we seem to drift helplessly toward the conflict. . . . We have indicated that one of Mr. Rhodes's chief excellences as a literary artist is his power of characterization. This is admirably illustrated by his sketches of Charles Sumner and John Brown. . . . These volumes are something more and better than a gallery of political portraits. But the portraits will, from their being so well executed, remain longer in the memory than anything else."

From "The Saturday Review," London

VOL. III.   "Mr. Rhodes is not merely impartial and laborious, but he is determined that his research and the judicial character of his work shall be patent on the face of his writing. He almost always tells us, if not directly, at least by implication, the process by which he arrives at his conclusions, and the nature of the conflicting views between which he strikes a balance. His impartiality, too, is really judicial, and never results from missing or underrating the greatness of the issues wherewith he is dealing. . . . It is one of the most readable works on the subject which it has been our fortune to meet."

From "The Daily Chronicle," London

"Although Mr. Rhodes is long, he is never dull. He can tell a story; he can expound a series of connected arguments with great skill; he can pierce to the heart of his subject and reveal the essential purpose of the political

VOL. III. struggle of the period. He has his convictions, which are strong and sound; but he is never, so far as we have observed, other than scrupulously fair all round."

From " The Edinburgh Review," Scotland

" Mr. Rhodes's work is full, intelligible, and, on the whole, impartial. . . . We read his work with increasing respect as we proceed. We acknowledge the thoroughness with which he has investigated a great historical episode, and the impartiality with which he has approached a subject which stirred his fellow-countrymen to the very depths of their souls."

From " The Nation," New York

VOL. IV. "We find ourselves following with unflagging interest his strong synthesis of current facts, actions, and opinions, which make vivid the actual life of the time. We breathe the atmosphere of the period itself, and share the doubts, the fears, and the deep solicitude of the actors in it. . . . The historian so well preserves his own balance of judicial calmness, and his full knowledge of all the facts which should temper and modify our judgment is so well at his command, that we easily yield to his interpretation of events even against our own predilections. Our consciousness of this effect upon ourselves goes far to make us believe that here we have something very near to what time will prove to be the accepted story of the nation's great struggle for self-preservation. . . . The definite clearness of judgment and the right-minded fairness of criticism shown in each chapter support our earlier judgment that the whole book will be a trustworthy guide and a friendly companion in our study of the time, as indispensable to those whose canons of political judgments may differ from the author's as to those who fully accord with him."

From " The Yale Review "

" For the conception and execution of the task in this spirit, Mr. Rhodes is exceptionally well qualified."

By W. A. Dunning, in "The American Historical Review"

Vol. IV.

"Mr. Rhodes has now attained that agreeable position in which a new volume of his history is distinctly an 'event.' The position has its responsibilities; but the present volume offers abundant evidence that the author is quite capable of sustaining them. In guiding us through the central heat of the Civil War, he never loses the clearness of head and the calmness of spirit with which he brought us up to the conflagration."

By Frederick Bancroft, in "Harper's Weekly"

"No writer of United States history has ever made such thorough use of all the materials and shown such industry and good judgment, together with much literary skill. . . . He sees with extraordinary clearness the leading characteristics of great men. His descriptions of the heroes, like Lincoln, Grant, Sherman, Sheridan, Lee, and Jackson, are realistic and impressive. . . . He shows us the real Abraham Lincoln as no one else has ever done. . . . It greatly enhances the permanent value of this great work, which is sure to remain a standard."

From "The New York Tribune"

Vol. V.

"Mr. Rhodes is painstaking in research, showing a full acquaintance with the sources of accurate knowledge. He has capacity for weighing evidence and grasping the essential truth of contemporary impressions or reports of eye-witnesses, while guarding against insufficient inductions, balancing them with less vivid official records. He has charm and lucidity of style and a rare gift for quotation, not the trick of essayists who make a pastiche of other people's clever sayings, but the faculty of seizing the word or phrase from letter, speech, or debate which reflects the actual movement of events and makes his reader the participant in a living scene. Above all he is inflexibly judicious, without causes to plead, friends to eulogize, or enemies to condemn, but with one sole aim, the truth."

From " The Speaker," London

" Masses of records, pamphlets, newspapers, private letters, have been ransacked in order to correct the false traditions which register contemporary misconceptions and hallucinations during times of turmoil and passion. The havoc wrought by war among the non-combatants has never been described with more convincing fidelity than in the painstaking account given by Dr. Rhodes of the condition of the South during 1863 and 1864, and his rendering of events during the presidency of Andrew Johnson is a singularly careful attempt to assist the judgment of citizens in understanding the most tangled bit of modern American history."

By Wm. Roscoe Thayer, in " The Atlantic Monthly "

" In selecting and presenting evidence, he is conspicuously fair ; and his plain style reassures those who fear that brilliance means untrustworthiness."

By Walter L. Fleming, in " The Political Science Quarterly "

" In summing up, it may be said that the history of Mr. Rhodes, while as fair and judicial as any American can now make it, is distinctly from the Northern standpoint ; that there is the intent, usually successful, to meet the other side with fairness, though a sympathetic treatment of both sides is naturally impossible at present. . . . As a whole the book is far superior in liberality to anything that has yet been written."

" The New York Sun "

" The volume contains 626 pages, not one of them dull or unworthy the critical attention of the student of history. The author's grasp of detail is sure, his sense of proportion seldom, if ever, at fault ; his judgment of the reader's interest in a subject admirable ; and his impartiality can never be doubted. His style is adequate, never lacking in vigor, precision, and color. No one need hesitate to hail Mr. Rhodes as one of the great American historians."

"The New York Times"

Vol. V. "Since Mr. James Ford Rhodes began to publish his now famous 'History of the United States from the Compromise of 1850,' twelve years have elapsed, years filled with events in the art and science of history writing; yet nothing has lessened the interest of scholars and the general public in this important work. From time to time new instalments have been quietly, unostentatiously given to the reading world, until now the fifth volume is before us. It was a great undertaking — an account of our momentous Civil War and its consequences on American destiny. The first volume set a hitherto unattained standard of judgment, of criticism, of fairness to all parties concerned. Not a single chapter nor a single paragraph of the four succeeding ones has fallen short of the high promise of the first."

"The Brooklyn Eagle"

Vol. VI. "Throughout the sixth volume, which covers the first administration of Grant, and his reëlection in 1872, our historian never loses sight of the prominent place which the Reconstruction policy holds in the history of the period. . . . The judicious and fair-minded way in which the whole subject is handled by Mr. Rhodes commands the admiration and strengthens the confidence of the reader as to the historical value and soundness of his conclusions."

"The South Atlantic Quarterly"

Vol. VII. "The seventh volume deals in the same vivid fashion with the Credit Mobilier and Sanborn Contract scandals, the panic of 1873 and the consequent financial legislation, culminating in the resumption act of 1875 and the inflation act which was vetoed by Grant. The narrative continues with accounts of the campaign and the election of 1874, with the success of the Democratic party and the struggle of the South for good government. . . . No better account has ever been written in a general way of the struggle then going on in the South."

GENERAL COMMENT

From "The Herald," Boston, Mass.
"The work is thoroughly admirable in point of style—clear, concise, and really fascinating in its narrative. A more thoroughly readable book has seldom been written in any department of literature. . . . We commend these volumes to those in search of a war history, as much the most readable and interesting, as well as the most genuinely instructive, of anything on the subject that has yet appeared. It will afford a revival of memories to the older class of readers, and a value in instruction to the younger, difficult to be overestimated."

By Charles Dudley Warner, in "Harper's Magazine"
"Written with a freshness of style which will appeal even to those who are not interested in its subject. Its vivid biographical sketches portray the men of whom they treat. It shows no little research, and no small amount of literary skill; it is, above all, honest and impartial."

From "The English Historical Review"
"Without a touch of rhetoric he brings out in full force the moral and economical evils of slavery as it existed in the South, its baneful effect on domestic life, on class relations, on industry. But he never fails to distinguish with singular fairness between the evil of a system and the moral responsibility of these individuals on whom the maintenance of a system has almost of necessity devolved."

From "The Nation," New York
"There is the same abundant and almost exhaustive collation of material, the same simplicity and directness of method, the same good judgment in the selection of topics for full treatment or for sketchy notice, the same calmness of temper and absence of passionate partisanship. He may fairly be said to be a pupil of the Gardiner school and to have made the great English historian a model in subordinating the literary element to the judicial, and in compelling his readers to accept his guidance as that of a trustworthy pilot through the mazes of conflicting evidence and the struggles of opposing principles."

From "The Plain Dealer," Cleveland
"In truth, Mr. Rhodes's 'History of the United States' has the fascination of a novel, while it has been accepted on both sides of the Atlantic as standing in the very front rank of histories of the period for its accuracy and sound judgment, as well as its pellucid style."

From "The Daily News," London

"His history, the work of an acute thinker and an earnest and liberal-minded politician, will doubtless take rank as a standard authority on the period with which it deals."

By Wm. G. Brown, in "The American Historical Review"

"It is not unreasonable, I think, to claim for the work of this American historian an importance not quite equalled by the work of any of his contemporaries who are writing history in the same tongue. The judgment of competent critics is . . . fairly unanimous, and the essence of their consensus is, that Mr. Rhodes tells the truth."

By John T. Morse, in "The Quarterly Review"

"Mr. Rhodes's 'History of the United States' is marked by a tone of such judicial fairness towards both men and measures that it finds no superior since the days of Thucydides."

ON THE PUBLICATION OF VOLUMES VI AND VII

From "The Congregationalist"

"The difficulty of maintaining a judicial tone in recounting and passing judgment upon the events and motives of such recent history Mr. Rhodes has well surmounted. His tone is grave and he is studious of truth. He has worked through the abundant sources with an explorer's enthusiasm and a scholar's caution."

From "The Outlook"

"The distinguishing characteristics of this work are noteworthy fairness, sound scholarship, and a high degree of narrative skill. Looking at it a little more in detail, perhaps the most striking features are the ease displayed in controlling the management of the vast material utilized and the emphasis placed on dramatis personæ. For all his leisureliness, it cannot be said — unless in the discussion of the attitude taken by England during the war — that Mr. Rhodes indulges in undue disquisition or elaboration."

From "The Brooklyn Eagle"

"He tells the story so well that the reader never wearies, while the narrative is so essentially dramatic in the very nature and quality of the facts which make up the story, that its interest never flags for a moment. Mr. Rhodes's work will stand as one of the great additions to American historical literature. He was fortunate in his choice of a subject, he has been singularly able and successful in the way in which he has handled his theme."

From "The London Times"

"Mr. Rhodes possesses the dramatic instinct in no inconsiderable degree, with the faculty to seize on the essential points of interest in a narrative, and so to set his scene and group his characters that the persons live for us and the incidents stand out clear cut and full of movement. In telling the story of a nation composed of a number of federated States, the historian is necessarily confronted with one inherent difficulty, in that the events in those several States by no means always follow the same course, and it often occurs that the threads of the same narrative have to be traced separately in each. In doing this there is constant danger of losing grip of the unity of the narrative as a whole, and of overloading it with detail. With this difficulty Mr. Rhodes wrestles with more than usual success."

From "The Dial"

"Giving up a promising business career and devoting oneself to the writing of history is an occurrence not common in this so-called commercial age. Such in brief has been the life of Dr. James Ford Rhodes, who has devoted nineteen years of the best part of his life to a period of our history but little more extended in time. The loss of the business world has been one of immense gain to the world of historical literature. The word 'literature' is used designedly here. Possibly Dr. Rhodes's works may not stand a rigid application of all the tests invented by the schoolmen to determine what is literature, but they certainly carry the stamp of verisimilitude and have the force necessary to lure the reader on and invite him to return."

From "The World To-Day"

"The history is one of the distinctly great achievements of the historical scholarship of this generation. It is one upon which American scholarship may well challenge comparison with the best that Europe has recently produced."

From "The New York Evening Post"

"Of Mr. Rhodes's success in his published volumes there can be only one opinion. He has written a history of an eventful, even critical period, that will long remain a standard; and he has to a remarkable degree met the principal requirements of modern historical methods. Great industry in compiling his authorities, marked capacity for weighing them, clear arrangement and a balanced judgment of men and events — such qualities have resulted in a series of notable volumes, in a dispassionate tone. Never attempting the florid or eloquent, he never falls to the dull or turgid."

Thomas Bailey Aldrich, in " Life "
" Mr. Rhodes deals with a momentous period — the years spanned by the Compromise of 1850 and the rehabilitation of the South in 1877. An attentive reading of his work, now completed by the issue of the seventh volume, is a liberal education. Even those of us who were actors and observers in 1860–1865 can learn much from these seven volumes; those of us who were born after the close of the war can learn everything. There is a kind of greatness in the lucid simplicity with which Mr. Rhodes has handled his vast and complicated material. His impartiality, insight, and authentic knowledge of the events and characters presented on the broad stage of his narrative give his work an incomparable and lasting value. The writer brought to his task too high a mood for mere partisanship. Here are pages to stir alike the Northern and the Southern pulse. I was about to say that his history is as absorbing as a play; but I would like to see a play that is half so absorbing."

From " The South Atlantic Quarterly "
" In his first five volumes Mr. Rhodes set a high standard for himself, viewing his work from whatever standpoint one might. His work has become noted for its completeness, accuracy, and impartiality; the latter, too, in treating of a period in relation to which impartiality has been only a rare exception. His treatment has always been thoroughly scientific, and at the same time, the result has been thoroughly readable, a result, by the way, that has not always been attained by the scientific historical writer of latter days. The last two volumes do not depart from the high standard set by the preceding ones, exacting as that is. They are calm, judicious, and, at the same time, sympathetic in their treatment of those vexed and stormy years from 1866–1877."

From " The New York Sun "
" By deliberate choice Mr. Rhodes is a pupil not of the school of Macaulay and Froude, but of the school of Stubbs and Gardiner. Gibbon is the only English historian who has succeeded in combining extreme accuracy with extreme attractiveness. With the author of the work before us attractiveness was only a secondary object; yet his pages are neither dull nor dry. Not satisfied with the immense labor expended by him in exploring and winnowing a vast mass of material, he has striven earnestly and successfully to present his conclusions in a simple, lucid, and engaging way. That is why his book is sure to be widely read while his right to a high place among authorities will be undisputed."